DATE DUE

HANDBOOK
TO LIFE
IN RENAISSANCE
EUROPE

HANDBOOK
TO LIFE
IN RENAISSANCE
EUROPE

SANDRA SIDER

Facts On File, Inc.

Handbook to Life in Renaissance Europe

Facts On File, Inc.
132 West 31st Street
New York NY 10001

Library of Congress Cataloging-in-Publication Data

Sider, Sandra.
    Handbook to life in Renaissance Europe / Sandra Sider.
        p. cm.
    Includes bibliographical references and index.
    ISBN 0-8160-5618-8
    1. Renaissance—Handbooks, manuals, etc. I. Title.
    CB361.S498 2005
    940.2′1—dc222004020088

Facts On File books are available at special discounts when purchased in bulk quantities for businesses, associations, institutions, or sales promotions. Please call our Special Sales Department in New York at (212) 967-8800 or (800) 322-8755.

You can find Facts On File on the World Wide Web at http://www.factsonfile.com

Text design by Cathy Rincon
Cover design by Semadar Megged
Maps by Jeremy Eagle

Printed in the United States of America

VB Hermitage 10 9 8 7 6 5 4 3 2

This book is printed on acid-free paper.

This book is dedicated to my husband

CONTENTS

LIST OF ILLUSTRATIONS _____

LIST OF MAPS

ACKNOWLEDGMENTS

Colin Eisler; Paul Grendler; Albert Rabil, Jr.; and Henry Rasof read my initial outline for the book and made several wise suggestions, for which I am extremely grateful. Additional thanks are due Paul Grendler for his superb work as editor of the *Encyclopedia of the Renaissance* and Gordon Campbell for *The Oxford Dictionary of the Renaissance*, two important resources for the present book. Abby Sider, my daughter, graciously did the research for the List of Museums. I would also like to thank my excellent editor at Facts On File, Claudia Schaab, as well as the copy editor, Susan Thornton.

INTRODUCTION: ORIGINS OF THE RENAISSANCE

The period covered by the Renaissance varies, depending on the geographic region or subject under discussion. The Renaissance began in northern Italy in the latter 14th century, culminating in England in the early 17th century. Consequently the present book spans two centuries, c. 1400–c. 1600, emphasizing the pervasive influence of Italian sources on the development of the Renaissance in other parts of southern Europe as well as in the north.

Although the ideal of the Renaissance individual was exaggerated to the extreme by 19th-century critics and historians, there was certainly a greater awareness of an individual's potential by the 16th century. Emphasis on the dignity of man (though not of woman) distinguished the Renaissance from the relatively humbler attitudes of the Middle Ages. In the love poetry of Petrarch and the great human scheme of Dante's *Commedia*, individual thought and action were prevalent. Depictions of the human form became a touchstone of Renaissance art, from Giotto's lifelike frescoes to the altarpieces of the van Eyck brothers and Michelangelo's heroic statue of David. In science and medicine, from cosmography to anatomy, the macrocosm and microcosm of the human condition inspired remarkable strides in research and discovery. The Earth itself was explored, as intrepid adventurers pushed past the southern tip of Africa to claim parts of the Orient, and into the North American continent, searching for gold and converts to Christianity. Magellan's circumnavigation of the globe both defined and extended the Earth, situating Europeans within a vast world of possibilities.

The word *renaissance* means "rebirth," and the most obvious example of this phenomenon was the rediscovery of Europe's classical Roman past. Although important texts of ancient Greek authors, such as Homer and Plato, first became known in Western Europe during the Renaissance, very little was understood about the culture of ancient Greece. Roman history, law, literature, and art dominated the classical rebirth of Renaissance Europe. Greek texts and works translated from Arabic and Greek contributed to advances in science, medicine, and technology.

Although the Renaissance commenced in northern Italy, classicizing elements rapidly became assimilated in other regions. By the early 1500s, these influences had resulted in imitations and variations in the Late Gothic culture of France, Spain, Germany, the Netherlands, Austria, Hungary, and Poland. The latter 1500s experienced the Renaissance as a new syncretic mode of thought and activity. With the aim of treating the major origins and influences of the Renaissance in a comprehensive manner, the present book focuses on western Europe, occasionally mentioning eastern Europe and European colonies in the East and West. Scandinavia is beyond our scope because Renaissance style did not flourish there until the 17th century, and it was tempered by influences of the early baroque.

The geographic concept of "Europe" strengthened during the early Renaissance, originating in the continent's identification as Christendom. With Muslims in north Africa and southern Spain, and Greek Orthodox Slavs and Turks as well as Muslims to the east, Europe was unified in its spiritual focus against these perceived common threats. The medieval Crusades had reiterated Europe's multilateral cooperation against "infidels." In addition, Europe's religious fervor had been heightened by fervent and desperate responses to the biomedical devastation of the 14th century. Between 1347 and 1350, approximately 20 million deaths resulted from what was called the pestilence, known as the Black Death several centuries later because of the plague's hideous black buboes, and possibly from anthrax (only recently discovered). Western Europe lost one-third of its population. While 25 percent of the aristocracy may have died, the peasantry suffered the loss of some 40 percent of its people. Peasants did not have the luxury of escaping from crowded living conditions into the relative safety of country houses. Several smaller epidemics further reduced the population during the second half of the 14th century.

With grain and grapes rotting in the fields, herds untended, and foot soldiers rapidly dwindling in supply, the peasants who survived found themselves in a new, much better bargaining position. Landlords were forced to raise the standard of living for peasants throughout Europe, making it possible for many of them to buy their freedom and become yeomen. Peasants freed from the land were able to seek a potentially better life elsewhere. One far-reaching result of the plague may have been the gradual influx of more individuals into towns and cities. This class of workers contributed to the rise of the wealthy merchant families who would provide much of the funding for Renaissance patronage.

Epidemics of the 14th century caused the deaths of numerous churchmen and monks, partly because any large group of people living together was susceptible to contagion. To keep the monasteries functioning, many younger, untrained men were allowed to enter. Although some university graduates were available, many of the new ecclesiasts were not ready for holy orders, personally or professionally. Abuses of the system were sharply criticized as greedy churchmen attempted to take advantage of the chaotic administration of church property. Another meaning of rebirth for the Renaissance was the Catholic Church's movement to investigate corruption within, with the goal of reforming and returning to the purer religion of early Christianity. By the 16th century, proposed reforms were deemed insufficient and Protestants broke away to create their own Reformation.

Renaissance philosophy was involved in efforts to understand the pristine theology of the early church. The Christian Platonism of Marsilio Ficino (1433–99) and his circle of learned friends in Florence explained the ideas of Plato in Christian contexts. This new philosophy, called Neoplatonism, led to esoteric symbolism and other forms of hidden meaning in literature, art, architecture, and music. Neoplatonism is one important example of the new philosophical strains in Renaissance thought. Although directly affecting only small groups of scholars, these movements functioned as an undercurrent in the cultural innovations of the 15th and 16th century.

Renaissance classical scholarship was enhanced, if not made possible, by Greek teachers and scholars who had arrived in Italy from the East. Numerous individuals emigrated from Constantinople during the late 14th and early 15th centuries, many of them to Venice. Then a major wave of Greeks escaped to Italy immediately before and after the fall of Constantinople to the Turks in 1453. Scholars in general studied and corrected ancient texts, including the Bible. This process of textual criticism inevitably led to a questioning of authority, from Roman rhetoricians to church fathers.

New attitudes, ideas, and images from 15th-century Italy were disseminated across Western Europe by the printing press. Some scholars have argued that the advance of printing caused the Renaissance, whereas others have stated that the Renaissance caused the spread of printing. The process was more of a reciprocal arrangement, of Renaissance innovations and printers promoting each other. The works of Italian artists, for example, became known in the north through printed engravings, and the engravings, in turn, encouraged Flemish, Dutch, and German artists to try their hand at painting and printmaking.

Although the Renaissance in general is often conceptualized by rebirth, as we have seen, the idea of renewal also expresses the cultural basis of life in Renaissance Europe. Europe had several new beginnings, affecting every aspect of life described in this book, and they usually were connected. The Protestant Reformation instituted new attitudes toward marriage that affected the daily life of thousands of converts; the so-called advancement of fired projectiles in military encounters led to new European empires in Asia and the Americas; secular music with the innovation of words to match the music developed into opera, which in turn influenced dramatic writing of the early 17th century; and, in medicine, new knowledge of the human body not only made life in the Renaissance more tolerable but also made survival more likely. These are only a few examples of the spirit of change experienced by Europeans during the 15th and 16th centuries.

Political Boundaries

The political map of continental Europe was quite different during the Renaissance from what it is today, and different in the 16th century from what it had been during the previous century. In 1400 the kingdom of France possessed less than half the area it had by 1600, Spain was divided into several kingdoms, Germany was peppered with independent principalities and townships, and Italy had more than a dozen city-states and republics, with the peninsula split across its central region by the Papal States, and Aragon possessing the kingdom of Naples after 1443. At the beginning of the 15th century, the Netherlands and Flanders (roughly present-day Belgium plus Zeeland) had been consolidated into one realm under the control of the dukes of Burgundy, and by 1519 the Holy Roman Empire extended from Vienna to Madrid. Except for skirmishes along their common border, England and Scotland had the same boundaries in the Renaissance that they have today.

In the Italian Peninsula, the papacy ruled the Papal States, territories stretching from Rome to the Adriatic Sea, and the pope also claimed Bologna. The Republic of Venice, which included an extensive area of the mainland near Venice during part of the Renaissance, controlled the northeastern Italian Peninsula. The Republic of Genoa dominated the northwestern coast, and the Republics of Florence and of Siena ruled most of Tuscany. Other major city-states and principalities were the duchies of Milan, of Ferrara, and of Savoy, as well as the marquisate of Mantua and the smaller duchy of Modena.

The Holy Roman Empire encompassed lands owned or claimed by the Habsburgs. Germany formed the core of the empire during the 15th century, and several regions later broke away as a result of the Protestant Reformation. The territories ruled by the Holy Roman Emperor and king of Spain Charles V (1500–1558) were Spain, the kingdom of Naples, and the Holy Roman Empire, including a huge swath of territory in eastern Europe extending from the Tyrol to the borders of Hungary and from Bohemia (today part of the Czech Republic) to the Venetian republic.

The geographic area of early 15th-century France was much smaller than the country ruled by Francis I (1494–1547) at the end of his reign. The rich province of Burgundy became part of eastern France in 1477, the very large province of Brittany (the peninsula comprising most of northwestern France) in 1532, and the eastern region of Bresse in 1536. France also ruled Navarre (on the border with Spain) during the Renaissance. France's northeastern border, including Alsace and Lorraine, was disputed during much of the Renaissance. The port city of Calais was ruled by the English until the mid-16th century.

The Iberian Peninsula still had an enclave of Muslims ruling the kingdom of Granada in the south of present-day Spain. They were conquered by the Spanish in 1492. Except for Navarre to the northeast and the kingdom of Aragon along the Mediterranean coast, the remainder of Spain belonged to Castile and León. Portugal, which had its modern borders during the Renaissance, was ruled by Spain from 1580 to 1640. Spanish forces also controlled much of the Netherlands during the second half of the 16th century, as well as the entire southern half of Italy and the islands of Sicily and Sardinia.

During the 15th century, the Netherlands ("Low Countries") had become part of the Burgundian duchy, which included Holland, Belgium, Luxembourg, and several areas in northeastern France. Through marriage this territory, called the Circle of Burgundy in the early 16th century, was absorbed into the Holy Roman Empire. Charles V officially claimed the Netherlandish provinces as part of the empire in 1548. The Protestant Reformation and its resultant hostilities led to the Dutch Revolt in the latter 16th century, with a truce in 1609 and ultimately the independence of the United Provinces by the mid-17th century.

Renaissance Poland was a tremendous territory, joining the Baltic states with present-day Belarus and Ukraine. By the early 15th century, Poland was linked dynastically with Lithuania. The grand dukes of Lithuania were also kings of Poland during much of the Renaissance.

How to Use This Book

The topical organization of the present book includes 12 aspects of the Renaissance, allowing each chapter to function as a lens on that slice of life. In general, information is presented from south to north, reflecting the predominance of Italy in the development of the Renaissance. The chapters by necessity present rather compact descriptions and explanations of each topic; for greater depth of study the reader might consult the list of recommended readings at the end of each chapter, which note the specific area treated in each reference unless the book or article comprehensively covers the section for which it is listed. The bibliography gives the full citation for each item in the readings, with general reference works on the Renaissance (not listed in the readings) at the beginning. Chapter 1, organized chiefly by geographic regions, concerns history, government, and society. Italy and the Holy Roman Empire are discussed first, followed by other areas of continental Europe and then England and Scotland. Chapter 2 pertains to religion, opening with sections on the Catholic Church and papacy, followed by the Protestant Reformation and brief sections on Judaism and Islam. Chapter 3, on art and visual culture, is organized by genres: painting, tapestries, sculpture, prints, and decorative art. Chapter 4 focuses on architecture and urban planning in Italy and France, beginning with a section on the rise of

the architect with the major works of each architect mentioned. The next two sections analyze the influence of Rome and ecclesiastical buildings; secular buildings are organized by fortresses and castles, villas, and Italian patronage in general. Finally, several important buildings outside Italy and France are described. Chapter 5, which concerns literature and language, opens with a discussion of humanism, philology, and publishing. Literary theory is followed by sections on the four genres of poetry, prose, drama, and oratory along with rhetoric. The final section pertains to library collections. Chapter 6 on music begins with sections on sacred and secular music, then continues with working conditions and patronage. The two final sections discuss musical instruments and the publication of musical material.

Chapter 7 on warfare has six sections, beginning with major wars, armor, and traditional weaponry. The fourth section discusses soldiering and battle conditions, and military medicine and fortifications end the chapter. Chapter 8, which concerns commerce, first describes banking and accounting. The remainder of the chapter is organized by areas of commercial production: mining; textiles; agriculture; wine, beer, and spirits; crafts; publishing; and slavery. Chapter 9 on exploration and travel opens with geography and cartography, followed by a discussion of travel and travelers. The final section on exploration takes the reader from Africa to Asia, and then to the Americas. Chapter 10 on science and medicine opens with the cosmic topics of astronomy and astrology, then focuses on chemistry, mathematics, and optics. The final two sections, on botany and drugs and on anatomy and medicine, include information about medical treatment. Chapter 11, which concerns education, begins with teaching in Latin in humanistic schools and at the universities. The three other sections treat education in the vernacular languages, apprenticeship, and the education of girls and women (in Latin as well as in the vernacular). Chapter 12 discusses several areas of daily life, beginning with time and the calendar. The analysis of family life includes information on marriage, children, and housing, and the section on ceremonies focuses on various aspects of public life in the community. The section on clothing and costume describes the apparel of different classes of society, and the next section, on food and cooking, also discusses the discrepancies among social classes. The final section concerns disease, illness, and death. Important individuals appear in several chapters, with their contribution to that particular subject emphasized.

Except for chapter 12 on daily life, each chapter has brief notes about major figures, along with their dates, preceding the list of readings. The extensive index should be consulted to locate all instances of specific individuals and subjects. Readers should also use the glossary, which describes approximately 185 terms, including numerous non-English words.

My goal in writing this book was to encourage students to become interested in this fascinating and provocative epoch of world history. I hope that they might use this text as a springboard to meaningful research of their own.

Note on Names, Orthography, and Bibliography

Because the main audience for this book are anglophone students, many names have been given in their anglicized form, and spelling and accents have been modernized. For the same reason, all entries in the bibliography are works in English, including translations of several originally published in other languages. Within this limitation, many of the most recent useful books have been included. Concerning proper names, surnames are used in the text except in a few instances of rather famous individuals, such as Leonardo da Vinci, who are universally known by their first name.

1

HISTORY, GOVERNMENT, AND SOCIETY

European government and society changed more during the two centuries of the Renaissance than in the previous 500 years. The feudal society of the Middle Ages chiefly consisted of the nobility and peasants living on large estates and monks residing in monasteries. The majority of medieval cities had a relatively small population, consisting of nobility, clergy, and townspeople, from merchants to poor laborers. From the Middle Ages through the Renaissance, there was little possibility of changing one's position in society. Even during the Renaissance, members of the clergy were locked into different social classes, ranging from wealthy landholding bishops to priests with poor rural parishes.

By the late 14th century the Italian city-states had begun to prosper from an increased level of trade with the East; that prosperity led to the development of banks and monetary commerce. Although isolated parts of Italy, especially in the south and far north, had a feudal society during much of the Renaissance, guilds and merchants influenced the course of political events in the city-states and republics. Wealth began to concentrate in the cities dominating their respective regions, and a new social class of bankers and wealthy merchants arose. The great banking families opened branches in other countries, notably in cities such as Brussels and Seville at the nexus of trading routes. Consequently, cities with rapidly expanding commercial opportunities attracted residents.

While the vast majority of people continued to live in rural areas, as they had for centuries, free peasants who relocated to cities during the 15th century provided labor for construction, factories, transportation, and other areas important for urban development. On the one hand, urban society was becoming more complex, with more causes for social unrest. On the other hand, individuals in cities had the potential for advancement through business, education, or religious training. The present book focuses predominantly on life in cities because most of the movements and events that we identify as the European Renaissance, especially in literature, music, and art, occurred in urban contexts. The rulers of nation-states gathered together members of their court in and near the great cities of Europe, and the important political leaders resided in urban locations. Cities had become major centers of politi-cal and economic power by the 16th century. During the Italian Wars of the late 15th and 16th centuries, forces from northern Europe invaded Naples, Rome, and the northern Italian city-states. Consequently cities in northern Europe also became centers of Renaissance culture as Italian artists, engineers, humanists, scientists, musicians, and others fled the economic destruction of their homeland and made their way north. Society in general became more refined, with Italianate tastes dominating fashion, cuisine, and other aspects of daily life.

The political structure of Renaissance Europe consisted of city-states in the Italian Peninsula, principalities in Germanic areas, and nation-states in most other parts of the continent. Several countries, especially Spain, France, and England, developed into unified national states with organized governmental systems between 1400 and 1600. This unification enabled the rulers of such states to gain prestige and power far exceeding those of the dukedoms and regional kingdoms of the late Middle Ages. The role of the monarch was changing, and this development would lead to the rise of absolutism in the 17th century. Many of the noble families, such as those in France, appeared to support the monarch while maintaining foreign allies with the hope of seizing the throne by force or by marriage. Monarchs began to gain a wider base of political support by forging new alliances with members of the middle class. In addition, the Great Schism and later the Protestant Reformation reduced the influence of the pope, while the fragmentation of the empire weakened that of the Holy Roman Emperor. Thus the political framework of modern Europe slowly took shape, with the bureaucracy of national and regional administrative offices giving rise to a new professional class, the civil servant. The governments of Portugal, England, Spain, France, and the Netherlands had important colonies beyond the borders of Europe. A complicated network of administrative offices was required to keep track of settlers, land grants, mercantile affairs, shipping, lawsuits, and jurisdictional disputes with the Catholic Church. These colonies also provided new opportunities for young men in all levels of society. Many of the Spanish conquistadores, for example, were farmers' sons from the far western part of Spain.

Map 1. Europe, c. 1460

As governments became more complex, they required administrators, secretaries, and notaries to manage the financial, legislative, and judicial aspects of running the country. Many governments in Renaissance Europe had some type of representative body, each functioning in different ways from the others. Whereas some actually had the power to enact laws, others only advised the secular ruler. England had Parliament to approve laws, whereas the Estates General of France functioned as a judicial body. The Cortes in Aragon and Castile were the representative bodies of Spain, and diets served various regions in Germany. Although these bodies had existed in some form before the 15th century, their political philosophy was affected to some degree during the Renaissance by new humanistic ideals of representative government. These ideals originated in Italy, where the history of the Renaissance begins.

ITALY

A politically unified Italy as we know it did not exist until the 19th century. During the Renaissance, the Italian Peninsula was fragmented into city-states, principalities, dukedoms, republics, and the Papal States ruled by the pope, with Naples, Sicily, and

Sardinia under Spanish or French control for most of this period. Venice was famous for having the oldest form of republican government, and Florence followed closely behind. Both Siena and Lucca had a republican government, and Genoa was ruled by an oligarchy of powerful merchants rather than by a single individual. Even in autocratic Milan, firmly ruled by the Visconti and then the Sforza dukes, the Ambrosian Republic (1447–50) lasted almost three years when the last Visconti died. In no instance, however, did any sort of representation in government extend beyond the cities and towns themselves; workers in the surrounding countryside were treated as subjects with no rights at all. To those at the bottom level of society, it made no difference whether the local government was a voting republic or a hereditary principality.

Guilds had been an important political force during the late Middle Ages, and in several towns, such as Bologna, guild members revolted against papal administrators to establish republican rule. They were the strongest element of the rising middle class. Guilds provided microcosms of self-government, with their constitutions and elected officers and councils. Renaissance Italy, with its strong history of communal government during the Middle Ages, enjoyed much more self-government than did the rest of western Europe. The *Politics* of Aristotle was analyzed by early Italian humanists, who distinguished between autocratic rule and political rule, in which government was limited by the people's law. Knowledge of the ancient sources on political philosophy, rhetoric, and oratory greatly expanded during the 15th century. These subjects contributed to the humanistic character of Renaissance republicanism.

During the 16th century, the Italian Wars changed the political structure of several parts of the peninsula. In 1494, the French king, Charles VIII (1470–98), invaded Italy; he entered Naples in the spring of 1495. Through the house of Anjou, he claimed Naples as part of his inheritance. His ultimate political goal was to use the port of Naples as a strategic point from which to capture Constantinople and become emperor of Byzantium. (He failed to accomplish this endeavor.) Charles VIII's chief opponent in the Italian campaigns was the Holy Roman Emperor, Maximilian I (1459–1519), who refused to accept French claims on the duchy of Milan. Except for three years between 1508 and 1511, when he allied himself with France against Venice, Maximilian continued the Habsburg-Valois battle on Italian soil for as long as he was able to fight. Although lacking the support of the German princes in his Italian campaigns, the emperor nevertheless attempted to capture territory on the Venetian mainland, which bordered Habsburg lands. He also claimed Milan as an imperial duchy.

When Francis I became king of France in 1515, one of his goals was to maintain French administrative control of Milan and Genoa, important buffer zones between France and Habsburg dominions. In the ensuing military campaigns, Imperial forces under Charles V seized Milan in 1521, and the French lost Genoa. Because Charles V was also king of Spain, the previous balance of power with the French in northern Italy, the Spanish in the south, and Italians in central Italy was upset by these losses. French forces, however, did not have a chance to regain lost territory because both the pope and the king of England sent troops to assist the Imperial army. In 1524 the French invaded Italy again, seizing Milan, but were decisively defeated at the Battle of Pavia, and Francis I was sent to Spain as a hostage. In the Treaty of Madrid (1526), Francis relinquished his claims in Italy, but he repudiated the agreement as soon as he was released. In the subsequent conflict, the city of Rome was sacked in 1527 by the troops of Charles V. In 1528 the city of Naples suffered during a siege by the French, led by the Genoan admiral Andrea Doria (1466–1560). Doria, however, decided that Francis I had betrayed him, and he returned to Genoa to create a republican state protected by the Spanish Crown. When the duke of Milan died in 1535 without naming an heir, Charles V took charge of the city by appointing an imperial governor. Thus the emperor and the kings of France continued to encroach upon Italian territory, with city-states occasionally playing these foreign rulers against each other. In 1552, for example, the citizens of Siena asked France to protect them from the Imperial troops that they had driven out of the city. The Italian Wars finally ended when Henry II of France and Philip II of Spain signed the Treaty of Cateau-Cambrésis in 1559.

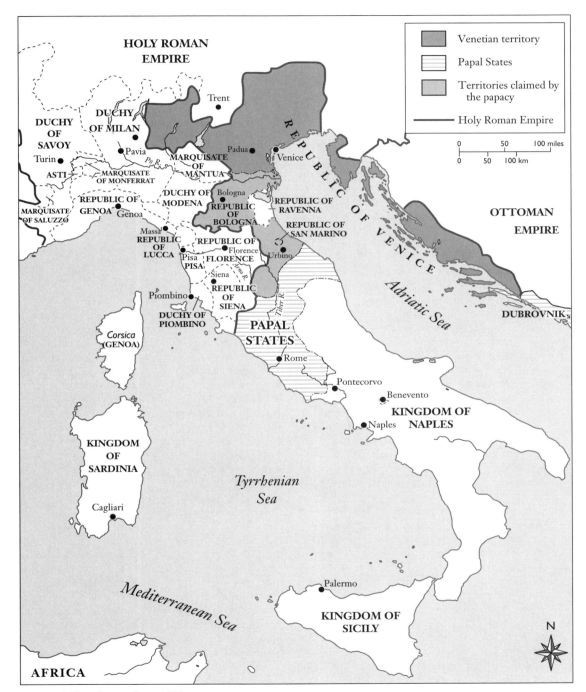

Map 2. Italian Peninsula, c. 1500

Northern Italy

VENICE

Venice's largest governing body was the Great Council, whose membership had been closed in 1297 and opened only once, in 1381, to allow several more members. This body drawn from the aristocracy elected the doge, who ruled for his lifetime but could not pass on the position to an heir. Venice was unlike other Italian republics in that membership in the Great Council was lifelong and hereditary, making the council a relatively closed, rigid society. As we shall see later, elsewhere in Italy short terms of office were considered an important element of successful republican government. The Great Council, totaling more than 2,500 adult males during the Renaissance, also elected members of the Senate, the main legislative body. This smaller, inner body of some 200 men advised the doge and determined which business would be raised before the Great Council. Within the Senate was a core of advisers, the Council of Ten. The doge and his six councilors, the three heads of the court of criminal appeal, and 16 ministers composed the Collegio. This Collegio, along with the Council of Ten and three attorneys general, determined which business would pass before the Senate. These 39 men were the oligarchy ruling Venice, and they often rotated from one position to another. The structure of government in Venetian maritime dominions, such as the island of Crete, mirrored that of Venice itself. The Great Council of Venice elected the governor of Crete, a member of the Venetian nobility. Crete, in turn, had its own Great Council, which comprised resident Venetians and lesser officials elected by that body.

During the 15th century, Venice had expanded its territory to include parts of the mainland, or *terraferma*. As in the maritime possessions, the Venetian government interfered as little as possible. A governor, the podesta, was appointed for each major city, along with a captain. These were the two Venetians who took their instructions from the Senate, or from the Council of Ten in urgent matters. Local councils were left to deal with details such as sanitation, medical care, water supplies, and transportation, following their own statutes. Venice left well enough alone as long as commerce flourished, peace was preserved, and taxes were collected. The island republic, with almost no land, needed the grain and wine from its dominions.

In Venice, as in other "republics," rights of the working class, whose members were viewed as servants for those having the responsibility of government, were not recognized. The humanistic ideals of virtue and service applied only to the nobility and to well-educated males. This sort of upper-class attitude led to revolts and temporary republicanism in other cities, but not in Venice. As for the clergy, the Senate of Venice claimed jurisdiction over them, opposing what Venice considered to be papal interference. The conflict over Venice's rights versus those of the papacy accelerated toward the end of the 16th century, and the republic was placed under papal interdiction in 1606–07. (This was not the first time that Venice experienced interdiction.)

FLORENCE

Although the ruling class in Florence was not as rigidly closed as that in Venice, Florence nevertheless had an oligarchic republic in spite of the proclaimed openness of its election laws. Although Florence did have representative institutions during the 15th century, the Medici family became powerful enough by the 1430s to dominate the government. The history of the Florentine republic is intertwined with the history of the Medici. When open votes were being cast by city leaders during the 1480s, for example, Lorenzo de' Medici (1449–92) was known to have walked threateningly around the room, noting how each man voted. In the city of Florence the highest executive body was the Signoria, in which several elected men equally represented the four main quarters of the city. As in many other cities in northern Italy with this quarter system, population density was not a factor; all "fourths" had the same number of representatives. Each fourth in turn was divided into four, creating the *gonfaloni* (sixteenths) that constituted the foundation of the city's administrative organization. The most powerful positions in Florentine republican government were held by members of the Signoria and by the heads of the various councils. Several deliberative bodies also advised the Signoria.

Whereas Lorenzo de' Medici virtually ruled Florence as a prince, his son, Piero II de' Medici

(1471–1503), did not command the same respect. When the French invaded northern Italy and Piero subsequently fled, the people of Florence revolted. Rather than rebelling with weapons and violence, they ridiculed Piero for his cowardice, shouting from windows and ignominiously pushing his family members along the streets and out of the city. Townspeople sacked the Medici palace and plundered the houses of the Medici bank's officers. An oligarchy of important families quickly assumed the reins of government, publicly hanging the unpopular Medici government official who had been in charge of the public debt. Thus the Medici hold over the Florentine republic was broken for several years. One important result was that noble families who had been exiled by the Medici began to return to Florence, expecting to gain their social and political positions and to have their confiscated property returned. The constitution and administrative structure were inadequate for the civic unrest of 1495, and reforms were obviously necessary. Into this situation stepped Girolamo Savonarola (1452–98), a Dominican friar and famous preacher who had predicted the apocalyptic fall of the Medici. (See chapter 2 for information pertaining to religion and chapter 12 for his influence on daily life.)

Supported by thousands of his adherents, including many members of the middle class, Savonarola began to direct a movement for drafting a new constitution, His initial goal was to create a more representative, democratic government. The model followed was that of Venice, the most stable republic in Italy, with a Great Council replacing the medieval councils. This council elected members of the new Senate (the Eighty), just as in Venice. The chief executive branch still consisted of the Signoria, the *gonfaloniere* of justice, and eight priors. Each held office for only two months. Thus the legislative system of Venice was combined with the old executive system of Florence, with the significant difference that in Florence the more cumbersome Great Council, with its advisory bodies, determined policy. It was impossible for the government of Florence to act quickly, especially without an authority figure such as the doge. The first laws passed were influenced by Savonarola, a strict moralist who opposed gambling, blasphemy, and other vices.

In addition to his efforts on behalf of Florence, Savonarola had antagonized the pope by creating a new, nonsanctioned congregation of monks. He was excommunicated in 1497, and the following year Florentine leaders agreed with the pope that Savonarola should be arrested. He had become too powerful within Florentine politics, and he was hanged and his body burned.

Because of external threats and the inherent weakness of the new Florentine republic in dealing with them, the Medici were welcomed back in 1512. With the national militia and the Great Council abolished, oligarchic rule once again became the accepted form of government. Although the Medici were expelled between 1527 and 1530 (the "Last Republic"), the family was restored to power by the Habsburg emperor, Charles V, and Cosimo I (1519–74) became

1.1 Portrait of Cosimo I de' Medici. Workshop of Bronzino. (The Metropolitan Museum of Art, Rogers Fund, 1908 [08.262])

the first grand duke of Tuscany. During the 16th century, political stability increasingly depended upon aristocratic rule.

MILAN

Milan and its territory were ruled by authoritarian ducal lords (*signori*), namely, the Visconti, between 1287 and 1447, then the Sforza between 1450 and 1515, 1521 and 1525, and 1529 to 1535. They were advised by several councils with appointed members, the most important being the Secret Council and the Council of Justice. Milan was briefly occupied by the French and by imperial forces, becoming part of the Holy Roman Empire in 1535 and then in 1546 a dependency of Spain. Here we shall discuss a short-lived but historically interesting phenomenon, the Ambrosian Republic of 1447–50. The last Visconti duke made no preparations for a successor or for an interim form of government. After his death, overnight the leading citizens of Milan proclaimed the republic of Saint Ambrose (patron saint of the city). This action revealed not only the resentment of all classes against seignorial government, but also the undercurrent of popular political tendencies reminiscent of medieval communal government. While generals in the ducal military force argued among themselves about the succession, the republic was born. The population of the city gathered near the cathedral with shouts of "Liberty!" in true revolutionary fashion.

Commoners, however, had nothing to do with formulating the new constitution, which was finalized in secret by an oligarchy consisting of a group of noblemen and lawyers with political experience, who had consulted prominent bankers and heads of the major guilds. As a first step, this group appointed a council of 24 captains, the chief governing body, with six-month terms of office. Parish elders were then given the task of selecting members of the Council of Nine Hundred, with equal representation of each district of the city. Fiscal problems, including massive debts left by the Visconti, haunted the city. The captains ordered that tax documents be destroyed (thus causing irreparable loss to Milan's archives) and attempted to create a public fund in which citizens could invest, to no avail. Moreover, Milan was losing income from sub-ject cities in the territory that were rebelling against the authority of the Ambrosian Republic and attempting to establish their own republic or turning to other powerful cities for support. During the winter of 1449, accusations of treachery led to the execution of dozens of men. Several months later, on the day before elections, the people revolted against the captains, storming the palace, murdering one of them, and sacking the homes of the others. In the midst of this chaos, the troops of Francesco I Sforza (1401–66) were blocking deliveries of food to the city, whose inhabitants slowly began to starve. The Ambrosian Republic lasted for 30 months, finally subdued because members of the nobility, wealthier merchants, and former ducal advisers defected to the camp of the mercenary captain Francesco I Sforza. As the husband of Bianca, the sole offspring of the last Visconti duke, Francesco had been promised the dukedom and thus was a logical choice for those who abandoned the republic.

Southern Italy

Southern Italy is defined here as the southern section of the Italian Peninsula (below the Papal States) and the relatively large islands of Sicily and Sardinia. Sardinia's political history is fairly simple during this period as it was ruled by Aragon and then by Spain. The chief governing body was the Sardinian Cortes, with a viceroy assigned to the island in 1487. With the Cortes convening only at 10-year intervals, the government was administered by feudal lords. Between 1432 and 1600 Sicily, as was Sardinia, was nominally ruled by Aragon and then Spain. The Sicilian viceregal government was installed early, in 1432, because the island was seen as an important stepping stone to the kingdom of Naples. Alfonso V of Aragon (Alfonso I, king of Naples, 1396–1458) jointly ruled both Sicily and Naples between 1443 and 1458, but the Angevin dynasty (from Anjou in France) claimed Sicily when he died in 1458, and the island was in dispute for much of the 16th century. Naples itself had been ruled by the Angevins from 1266 until 1442, often in conflict with the powerful Neapolitan barons and other members of the nobility. The French ruled Naples briefly between 1495

1.2 Portrait of Alfonso V. Neapolitan School, 15th century. (Kunsthistorisches Museum, Vienna, Austria/ Bridgeman Art Library)

and 1502, when the kingdom fell under Spanish administration that lasted until 1707.

HOLY ROMAN EMPIRE

Seven electors held the power to elect the German king, who until 1508 would then travel to Rome to be crowned Holy Roman Emperor. The seven electors were the king of Bohemia, the count palatine of the Rhine, the duke of Saxony, the margrave of Brandenburg, and the archbishops of Mainz, Cologne, and Trier. The Holy Roman Empire began to be called Holy by its subjects in the 12th century, when the emperor and the pope were fighting for control of northern Italy. After 1273, with the acces-

sion of Rudolf of Habsburg to the Imperial throne, the Holy Roman Empire no longer included any part of Italy. It then consisted of present-day Germany, eastern France, the Netherlands, Switzerland, Austria, Poland, and areas of the modern Czech Republic. By the time that Charles V abdicated in 1556, the new emperor, Ferdinand I (1503–64), was only the titular head of a federation of German principalities. (See page 15 on Germany.) During the Renaissance, the empire gained and lost territory in Italy, Hungary, Bohemia, and the Netherlands.

Imperial military power was at its height during the 12th century. By the 15th century, the emperor's power was waning. Major campaigns required allies, and emperors were often allied with the popes. The emperor's relationship with the popes between 1400 and 1600 usually consisted of mutual support in both military and religious matters, concerns that often overlapped. Emperors joined the holy leagues with the pope and other allies to combat the French in Italy as well as the Ottoman Turks. Imperial troops combated Protestantism in the north in several campaigns, with the pope's blessing and financial support. Although not actually crowned by the pope, the Holy Roman Emperors of the Renaissance had his recognition and approval.

The last emperor who was crowned in Rome was Frederick III (1415–93), chosen by the electors in 1440. (Charles V, the last emperor crowned by a pope, received his crown in Bologna because Rome was in ruins from the 1527 sack.) By marrying his children with the children of powerful rulers across Europe, Frederick guaranteed that his Habsburg line would be part of Europe's political future. Beginning with Frederick III, the Habsburg dynasty dominated the Imperial elections. The fact that the Spanish king, Charles I, was a Habsburg was distinctly to his advantage when the French king, Francis I, competed with him for the Imperial crown in 1519.

In the 1480s, the archbishop of Mainz, one of the seven electors, attempted to create a centralized imperial administration in Germany. This movement succeeded only partially because regional rulers were unwilling to relinquish control over their territories, and the emperor balked at what would have been a loss in status. The seven hereditary electors were especially autonomous, as their families were granted special privileges. Nevertheless, as a result of the Diet of 1495, an official Public Peace (Landfriede) assured law and order and an Imperial Court of Chancery (Reichskammergericht) was established. This tribunal, responsible not to the emperor but to the Diet, held jurisdiction throughout the empire. It was not, however, an executive body and the administration of justice was often difficult. Finally, in 1500, the Council of Regency (Reichsregiment) of 21 members was set up to deal with executive aspects of Imperial administration. The other administrative body, established by the emperor himself, was the Aulic Council (Reichshofrat), which functioned as a high court of justice.

By the early 16th century, the empire included Germany, Austria, Hungary, Bohemia, parts of Italy, and the Burgundian Netherlands. Although this list may sound impressive, in matter of fact the empire was more a concept than an actuality. The "king of the Romans," as the king of Germany (the emperor) was called, did not even rule Germany because so much authority was vested in local princes and dukes. It was virtually impossible for him to raise any revenue from his own country, unlike the sovereigns of France, Spain, and England—the "new" monarchies of Europe. One important reason why the Habsburgs were welcomed as dynastic emperors is that each of them had personal territories in his own realm that produced appreciable income. The German king did, however, have political influence, whereas the influence of the princes was local, or at best regional.

FRANCE

When Francis I (1494–1547) took the throne of France in 1515, he asked the political theorist Claude Seyssel (c. 1450–1520) to write a work describing the French monarchy. His *La grande monarchie de France* (The great monarchy of France, 1519) explained how royal power had been tempered by Christian standards, custom, and local regulations. The French kings were, in fact, named "Most Christian" at their coronation, a title taken seriously during the Renaissance. The "custom"

referred to by Seyssel was customary law, which prevailed in the north of France, with regional parliaments adjudicating disputes. In the south of France, Roman law was stronger, often modified to conform to the local needs of municipal government. French kings during the 15th century recognized that this fragmentation of legislative and judicial policy hindered the administration of government at the national level. With ducal kingdoms competing against the Crown, centralization was quite difficult. Although the Valois king Charles VII (1403–61) began a project to record and organize local customary laws throughout France, not until 1510 was the first compilation published, during the reign of Louis XII (1462–1515). This early 16th-century monarch was able to begin uniting France as a centralized monarchy. Because of his focus on Italian military campaigns, however, the continuation of this endeavor fell to Francis I.

Francis I

Reigning for more than three decades, Francis I consolidated an extensive territory of some 15 million inhabitants, including its independent-minded nobility. Considering France as a European power, he wanted a modern model of government different from the feudal system described by Seyssel. Guillaume Budé's (1467–1540) *Institution du prince* (Office of the prince, 1518), influenced by Niccolò Machiavelli's (1469–1527) famous book on the Renaissance prince, interpreted the king as the embodiment of God on Earth, to be obeyed in all matters. While recognizing the necessity for a council of advisers as well as for respect for the law and the church, Francis I often attempted to rule as if he had absolute power. Early in his rule, one purpose of this behavior was to expose corrupt officials, especially those with access to the treasury who had been robbing the Crown of revenue from taxes. Most importantly, Francis I firmly believed that only the king could make political decisions affecting the entire state, such as making treaties. After a confrontation with the Parlement of Paris during which the president informed him that the people gave Parlement its power, Francis issued an edict limiting Parlement to its judicial role, forbidding its members to become involved with national politics. Unlike the monarchs of England (see pages 17–18), the French king was not required to have royal edicts approved by a legislative body.

Renaissance France did not have, or pretend to have, representative government. The Estates General—a national assembly of the three classes of French citizenry, the clergy, the nobility, and the commoners—was blatantly ignored. Even though the King's Council numbered into the hundreds, these appointed advisers were scattered throughout the country and never met as a single group. Administrative affairs were carried on by several smaller councils, none of which convened with any other, and often with overlapping jurisdiction. The wheels of government turned very slowly in France. Partly because the system was so cumbersome and communication so slow, Francis I had a small core of a

dozen advisers at court, namely, his close relatives and favorites. The structure of this group foreshadowed the secretaries of state of late 16th-century France. For regional administration, the king himself selected governors. In 1515 France had 11 provinces, each with a governor entitled royal councillor representing the king in all matters. The governors were also expected to support the interests of wealthy and important individuals within their respective provinces, selling governmental posts and other lucrative positions. France's political system during the Renaissance provided income for the nobility and wealthy bourgeoisie, while taxing the middle and lower classes on necessities such as salt.

SPAIN AND PORTUGAL

Unlike most other parts of western Europe, Iberia, the areas that today we refer to as Spain and Portugal, struggled during the Middle Ages to defend itself against eastern invaders who had settled in its territory. For centuries, governmental policies focused on driving out the Muslims, with society very much divided between "us" and "them." Iberia was a society of warriors, churchmen, and workers; of chivalric values that prevailed into the early 16th century. At the beginning of the Renaissance, the peninsula was divided into the large central region of Castile, Aragon to the east, Portugal to the west, and tiny Navarre (claimed by France) in the north, with an enclave of Muslims still occupying Granada in southern Castile. In 1492 the Muslims, and then the Jews, were expelled from Spanish domains. Each kingdom of Iberia was governed by a Corte (an aristocratic legislative body), whose members passed legislation and approved financial measures. The Cortes of Aragon were by far the most powerful, infused with the independent Catalan spirit. Each monarchy also had various advisory councils. Local governors or viceroys administered the law, and some of these individuals became quite influential. After Charles, king of Spain, was elected as Holy Roman Emperor in 1519, royal councils increased in number and in power because of the king's prolonged absences from the country. Responsibilities

1.3 Portrait of Francis I. Workshop of Joos van Cleve. (The Metropolitan Museum of Art, The Friedsam Collection, Bequest of Michael Friedsam, 1931 [32.100.120])

of the Spanish monarchy extended into Portugal as of 1580, when the Portuguese king died without an heir and the king of Spain became also the king of Portugal.

Both Spain and Portugal developed relatively sophisticated administrative offices to supervise colonial territories. Portugal managed lucrative mining operations and the slave trade in Africa, as well as its empire extending from several ports in the Middle East to India and China. Spices, textiles, and other commodities from these overseas possessions necessitated governmental bureaucracy to handle taxes and mercantile rights. Spain's burgeoning empire was to the west, in the so-called New World of the Americas. The House of the Indies in Seville was the clearinghouse for gold, silver, agricultural products, and other goods, and slaves transported across the Atlantic. Hundreds of inspectors, tax collectors, and secretaries were required in both Portugal and Spain to administer foreign territories and appoint viceroys and other colonial officials. These offices provided opportunities for social advancement for commoners with the appropriate training.

Spain

ISABELLA I AND FERDINAND V

Spain, which did not exist as such during the Renaissance period, consisted of the kingdom of Castile (which included León) and the kingdom of Aragon. The latter included the kingdom of Naples and the Two Sicilies (Sicily and Sardinia). In the south of Spain, the Moorish kingdom of Granada was ruled by Muslim leaders, who paid tribute to Castile. Although Granada was famous for its culture and architecture, the Muslims were not a strong military force by the 15th century. Castilian monarchs wanted to drive the Muslims completely out of Spain, to give Castile the entire sweep of the peninsula from north to south. In Castile, however, aristocrats who had profited from the seizure of Muslim estates and who benefited from Muslim tribute payments were reluctant to disturb the status quo. They enjoyed special privileges, being exempt from taxation and entitled to trial in special

courts that were presided over by their fellow aristocrats. Nevertheless, the Muslim rule in what Castile considered its rightful territory was a constant presence in the mind of 15th-century Castilians, who valued the heroic ideal of the soldier-citizen in service to the king. They needed only a determined monarch who could convince them that the main purpose of their government should be to reclaim Granada for Castile. As it turned out, that monarch was a woman, Isabella I (1451–1504).

Although the Castilian Corte exerted local authority, it was not as powerful as the Corte of Aragon. In Castile the monarch was not required to hold regular meetings of the Cortes and could pass laws without their permission or participation. In Aragon, however, the three main regions were governed by three different Cortes. Each new law had to be approved by all three Cortes, and these groups were summoned on a regular basis. In 1469 the future king of Aragon, Ferdinand V (1452–1516, later Ferdinand II of Castile and León) and Isabella I, future queen of Castile and León, were married. After a civil war was waged to determine whether Isabella would be heir to the throne, she and Ferdinand began to rule in 1479. Ferdinand subsequently spent most of his life in Castile, supporting the constitutional rights of the Cortes. In 1494 he approved the creation of the Council of Aragon, a powerful supervisory body based in Castile. Because both Ferdinand and Isabella believed that the monarch should be directly involved in government, their court was itinerant, traveling around the realm. They redistributed power among various levels of society, appointing royal officials from members of the middle class. Many of these officials administered new institutions and social systems to care for the poor. Isabella, a staunch Catholic, argued for greater governmental control of church income and for the right to make church appointments. By achieving these goals, Ferdinand and Isabella enlarged their base of power. In addition, they had papal permission to institute a tax on members of the clergy, called the *cruzada*, for the avowed purpose of financing their crusade against the Muslims. After the final stage of the Reconquest was completed, however, the royal coffers continued to be subsidized with income from this tax. Isabella turned her attention to the Jews after the Muslims were conquered in 1492, giving Jewish residents four months to leave the country. At least 120,000 did so, taking their wealth and skills with them, a tremendous loss to society and commerce.

In 1492, Isabella selected Jiménez de Cisneros (1436–1517), an austere Franciscan friar, as her confessor. She trusted completely in his judgment, following his advice in affairs of state. Because religion was so embroiled in politics during this time, Cisneros became an important statesman and took charge of relations between Castilian authorities and Muslims in the kingdom of Granada. Those who refused to convert to Catholicism via mass baptism in order to be loyal subjects of the Crown were exiled. After the death of Philip I, Cisneros ruled Castile as regent between 1506 and 1507, when Ferdinand returned from Aragon and made Cisneros inquisitor general. Because the bishop had been such a politically powerful figure, with numerous officials answering to him, Cisneros was able to unleash the Spanish Inquisition, first established by Ferdinand and Isabella in 1478, with unparalleled results (see chapter 2, on religion).

CHARLES I (CHARLES V)

When Philip I (1478–1506), king of Castile, died in 1506, his son and heir to the throne, the future Charles I (1500–58), was only six years old. Charles was the grandson of Holy Roman Emperor Maximilian I (1459–1519) and of Isabella and Ferdinand. Because Ferdinand had returned to Aragon, a Regency Council headed by Bishop Cisneros was established. Charles I assumed rule of the Netherlands, the Spanish dominion where he spent his boyhood, in 1515. He was crowned king of Castile and León the following year after Ferdinand died. At the time the young king could not speak Spanish and was alienated from his Iberian subjects. He had great difficulty extracting money from the Cortes, and revolts erupted in both Castile and Aragon while Charles was in Germany competing in the election for Holy Roman Emperor, which he won in 1519. (He was subsequently referred to as Charles V.) In Valencia

1.4 Portrait of Charles V. Netherlandish painter, c. 1520. (The Metropolitan Museum of Art, The Friedsam Collection, Bequest of Michael Friedsam, 1931 [32.100.46])

(southern Aragon), for example, the rebels, refusing to recognize the monarchy, intended to create a republican form of government. In 1521 royal troops defeated them; Charles ordered the execution of the rebel leaders but pardoned everyone else. This policy for dealing with dissention won many followers for the king, who was learning to deal diplomatically with social unrest. During most of his reign, Charles had to travel between Spain and the Netherlands, dealing, for example, with financial problems in the south and the increasing hostility of Protestants in the north. Years of his life were consumed by traveling back and forth. Because the king could not always be present, royal councils administered governmental business. The councils consisted of men trained in the university system as lawyers and of members of the lesser nobility, and the Council of the Indies was incredibly powerful by midcentury. This council was in charge of Spain's dominions in the New World, appointing viceroys, overseeing commercial interests, and settling disputes.

PHILIP II

In 1555 Charles abdicated in favor of his son, Philip II (1527–98), leaving Spain virtually bankrupt from the vast sums spent on wars against France and the Turks. The burden of taxation fell on the common people, who were reduced to miserable conditions. Philip declared in 1557 that all payments from the monarchy to banks had to be suspended, taking the country through a phase of financial adjustment. Philip II took charge with a vengeance, gathering as much power as possible and centralizing it within Spain. As of 1559 he ruled from his palace complex of El Escorial near Madrid, the first time in nearly a century that Spanish court society was focused in one location. In 1563 Philip established the Supreme Council of Italy, making all Spanish dominions (which included the duchy of Milan) directly answerable to his central government. After 1580, he was also king of Portugal and sent a Spanish viceroy to Lisbon. Portugal lost autonomy in several legal, judicial, and financial matters.

Portugal

During the 15th and most of the 16th century, Portugal's rulers were the house of Avis, founded in 1385. As was Spain's, Portugal's monarchy was tempered by representational bodies, the Cortes, who included commoners. John I (1357–1433), an illegitimate son of the king, was elected to the monarchy by the Cortes after the heir to the throne died. The Cortes thus asserted their power over the king of Spain, who claimed Portugal. During the reign of John I, his respect for chivalric ideals was reflected in society at large. Because his grandson, Afonso V (1432–81), was only five years old when he inherited the crown, his mother and uncle ruled as regents. Afonso later had aggressive territorial ambitions, leaving the government in the hands of the Cortes while he ventured out on several futile campaigns. Manuel I (1469–1521), king of Portugal, using income from overseas colonies, provided numerous jobs and built up the economy with his ecclesiastical architectural commissions. Social programs benefited from the influx of funds. On the negative side, he expelled the Jews from Portuguese domains, losing a significant percentage of skilled workers as well as wealthy taxpayers. Other individuals were also leaving Portugal, but as colonists to overseas possessions. Not only did these adventurers help fill the coffers of the royal treasury, but they also left jobs that could be filled by others, thus keeping society fluid and peaceful. Unlike Spain, Portugal experienced relatively little

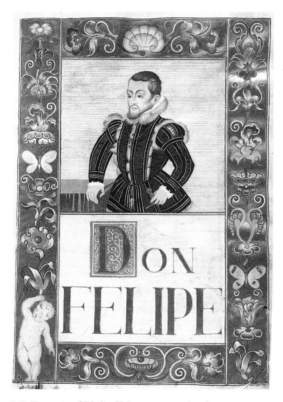

1.5 Portrait of Philip II in a manuscript document, Granada, 1572. (Photograph courtesy of Sotheby's, Inc., © 2003)

civic unrest during this period. King Sebastian I (1554–78) had no interest in governmental business, which he delegated to his advisers and councils. When Sebastian was killed in battle in 1578, the situation was ripe for internal turmoil and conflict. Between 1580 and 1640, Portugal was ruled by the Spanish Crown.

GERMANY

Germany was the core of the Holy Roman Empire, whose seven electors voted to select the emperor (see pages 20–21 for a list of their offices). These men also composed a permanent electoral body who formulated the conditions of rule for prospective emperors. Along with other rulers in Germany, the electors continually strove to assert their authority over that of the emperor. In effect, they maintained feudal power systems well into the Renaissance era. Emperor Charles V, also king of Spain, was drawn into conflict in Italy and elsewhere during the 1520s. With his attention diverted to these military campaigns, several German princes seized the opportunity to convert to Protestantism and to oppose Imperial power.

In Germany the Protestant Reformation and the powerful guild organizations contributed to the rise of popular governmental reform. Many German princes and dukes converted to the new religion to remain as head of state with a minimum of internal strife. Encompassing more than three hundred principalities and cities that had separate secular or ecclesiastical rulers and no centralized control, Germany was particularly vulnerable to a reform movement such as Protestantism. Except for the emperor, there was no centralized power that could move swiftly to stifle protest, and the emperor often had responsibilities in other parts of the continent. Although towns answered to their territorial ruler, a few cities became independent enough to answer only to the emperor. Imperial knights, members of the nobility, also answered only to the emperor. The fate of Germany was historically linked with that of the Holy Roman Empire because the emperor was chosen by German electors and also served as the king of Germany. Maximilian I (1459–1519) helped modernize the legal system by establishing the Aulic Council (Reichshofrat) and the Imperial Court of Chancery (Reichskammergericht), whose jurisdiction sometimes overlapped. The Aulic Council judged cases pertaining to criminal charges involving Imperial subjects and issues concerning succession in the fiefdoms, and the Court of Chancery heard most other lawsuits. Maximilian began to centralize the governing of his Imperial dominions, including Austria, but Germany remained a disparate group of principalities and imperial cities. In spite of the various reform movements, most of Germany was governed by feudal law; the Hohenzollern family in Brandenburg and the Wittelsbach family in the Palatinate were particularly powerful.

The weakness of each principality chiefly lay in the relatively small size of each territory, as many cities had no control of the population beyond their city walls. Living conditions of the peasant class deteriorated during the 15th century, with rising prices and princes' demands for increasing sums in taxes and tribute. Local leaders had no interest in national politics, only in their own aggrandizement.

THE NETHERLANDS

The provinces of the Netherlands included semiautonomous cities (similar to Italian city-states), provinces under the Holy Roman Empire (notably Holland), and provinces claimed by France. Several of these city-states were wealthy through international trade, which provided economic opportunity and social advancement for members of the middle class. During much of the 15th century, part of the Netherlandish territory was ruled by the dukes of Burgundy. In the northern provinces, the governors selected magistrates for the town council from among the most prosperous citizens. In the south, however, urban constitutions created by the powerful guilds of dyers and weavers allowed for representative government, giving a voice to commoners. Even the most autocratic ducal rulers had to negotiate with representatives of the towns in order to collect the income that the merchant class could provide. One method of gaining partial control of a region was to control the bishop, and the dukes of Burgundy occasionally installed one of their sons in that office, for example, in Utrecht. Episcopal government in Netherlandish towns, while tempered by town councils, remained strong through the early 16th century with support from members of the aristocracy. One reason for this was that the names of members of the nobility friendly to the clergy were sometimes entered on rolls listing local tradesmen, giving the aristocracy a voice in town government. Nevertheless, the dukes of Burgundy often convened the Estates General of the Netherlands, whose members—some elected and some appointed—represented the various provinces. As of 1477, the Estates General had the power to convene meetings, approve royal marriages, levy taxes, and declare war. Government was authorized at the grassroots level; delegates returned home to canvass local councils before any major proposal could be ratified. Thus the townspeople of the Netherlands held a significant amount of power. The only centralized secular government was that in the Burgundian domain.

Holy Roman Emperor Charles V, born and raised in the Netherlands, spoke the Flemish language and initially had the cooperation of the Estates General. When the town of Ghent revolted, however, in 1540, he dealt harshly with the rebels and the town lost its privileges. The relationship between the Netherlands and Imperial authority increasingly deteriorated during the following decade. When the Netherlands became part of the inheritance of the Spanish king, Philip II, he alienated the Estates General by demanding higher taxes to finance his military campaigns. During the latter 1560s, the Spanish king attempted to force absolutist rule on his Dutch subjects by sending in Spanish troops. In response, William I of Orange (1533–84), governor of the United Provinces, convened the Estates of the provinces of Zeeland and Holland to form a provisional independent government. Although Netherlandish provinces in the south reaffirmed their loyalty to Spain, the seven northern provinces founded a republic that lasted more than two centuries. The heads of state of this new government were members of the house of Orange.

POLAND AND HUNGARY

Located at the eastern edge of Europe, both Poland and Hungary consisted of large masses of continuous territory, quite different from other European monarchies ruling scattered regions separated by foreign possessions. Both countries had abundant supplies of grain and other basic necessities, and they needed very little from outside their own borders. With a nobility that ruled self-sufficiently in their respective fiefdoms, and with a powerful Diet assembled from these individuals, neither Poland nor Hungary felt the need for a strong centralized government or an ongoing foreign policy.

Poland

Poland occupies a special place in Renaissance political history, as religious freedom was incorporated into the principles of government in 1573. Protestants, Muslims, Jews, and other groups coexisted in the same cities during the 16th century as they had during the 15th, with no expulsions or official persecutions. Commoners in general experienced a greater atmosphere of personal freedom than in other parts of eastern Europe. The Polish Diet had two houses, the Senate (upper house) consisting of appointed members, and the Chamber of Deputies (lower house) consisting of elected representatives. This governmental body functioned both judicially and legislatively, and new laws were approved only by the Diet. Because actions of the king himself could be reviewed before the Diet, Renaissance Poland was a parliamentary monarchy. Significantly, electors from the Diet chose Poland's kings.

After 1569, the principality of Lithuania was formally unified with Poland, creating a territory three times the size of present-day France. The Diet was extremely powerful during the 16th century, when the provincial diets were virtually autonomous. Although the king could appoint administrative officials, he was not permitted to remove them from office. This policy encouraged an independent attitude among those in charge of local administration, making centralization of the government impossible. When Poland doubled its land area in 1569, government at the national level faltered. The consolidation that might have made Poland a powerful presence in European politics never occurred.

Hungary

Until 1526, Hungary's Diet had only one house, which consisted of the entire nobility of the country rather than delegates. The Magyar nobility included ennobled representatives of corporations in several of the towns, all of whom were required to attend meetings of the Diet. This rather large group convened annually, but there was no real leadership at the national level. On the other hand, the Diet attempted to balance power among the executive, judicial, and legislative councils, and the gentry had an equal voice with members of the old nobility in the Privy Council. Although Hungary was a monarchy, the king's powers were limited by the Diet, and there was no attempt to formulate foreign policy for the country as a whole. For much of the Renaissance, Hungary was under the rule of foreign houses. The most noteworthy Hungarian king was Matthias Corvinus (1443–90), who was elected in 1458. The emperor's brother, Ferdinand (who would become Emperor Ferdinand I), was elected in 1526; however, the Turks captured Buda in 1541 and much of Hungary fell under Turkish domination. By 1568, Hungary was partitioned, its western and northern sections under Austrian rule and central and eastern sections under Turkish domination.

ENGLAND AND SCOTLAND

Ireland and Wales were nominally ruled by England during the 15th century; Wales was formally incorporated into England in 1537 by the Union of Wales and England Act. Ireland was under English sovereignty by 1540. The rule of English law was established in Wales by an act of 1542. The Irish and Welsh had the same legal rights and responsibilities as the English, and Wales had representatives in Parliament. Although Ireland had its own parliament, it could not convene without the permission of the ruling monarch of England. The earls of Kildare had control of much of Ireland and ruled in the king's or queen's name. Ireland experienced several violent rebellions during the 16th century; most of them concerned the imposition of the Church of England as official religion. The house of Stuart ruled Scotland, but their reign was opposed in the early 15th century. The king was assassinated when Scottish lords asserted their autonomy and civil war disrupted the country for several years. Another 15th-century king was imprisoned while his son seized the throne. Although Scottish soldiers clashed with English in several battles near the northern border of England, Scotland did not extend its territory. The political history of Scotland during the Renaissance was influenced not only by English opposition, but also by the regional focus of Scottish lords and the increasingly powerful commoners, notably the Protestant faction.

England

England's Parliament had (and has) two houses, the House of Lords and the House of Commons. Although the latter body was intended to represent townspeople, during the 16th century the towns delegated more knights than commoners to represent them. Until the reign of Henry VIII (r. 1509–47) Parliament had met sporadically, usually less than once a year. Beginning in 1529, Parliament sat for five years to work through the details of royal reforms, especially the closing of monasteries and the impounding of monastic property. In 1534, Henry VIII denied papal authority in England and assumed the role of head of the Church of England, or Anglican Church (see chapter 2, religion). Parliament also had long sessions during the reign of Elizabeth I (r. 1558–1603) to finalize details concerning the independence of the Church of England. Not until the Stuart dynasty of the 17th century did England have an absolute monarch who refused to convene Parliament, and he was executed in 1649.

HENRY VIII

England was at peace when Henry VIII (1491–1547) was crowned in 1509. Henry claimed the crown of France, especially the provinces of Normandy, Guyenne, Gascony, and Anjou. Although English forces attacked France three times during his reign, Henry kept only the cities of Calais, Tournai, and Boulogne, and the French king, Francis I, paid him a hefty pension as satisfaction for his claim. The port city of Calais was actually enfranchised as part of England in 1536 (lost in 1558), but the other two cities remained under the French Crown. The district outside Calais known as the Pale is important in European political history because that was the location of the Field of the Cloth of Gold. For three weeks in June 1520, Francis I and Henry VIII, with their full retinues and court advisers, met in an extravagant diplomatic display that lasted for three weeks. Francis attempted in vain to persuade the English king not to join forces with Holy Roman Emperor Charles V, knowing that such an alliance would threaten France from all sides except the western coast.

Henry VIII's international prestige was enhanced by this meeting, and his power in England backed by Imperial support. His major political initiatives during the latter 1520s involved his efforts to obtain papal dispensation for a divorce from his first wife, Catherine of Aragon (1485–1536). Because she had not produced a male heir, Henry wished to remarry. To break with the Catholic Church over this issue, Henry acted as "king in Parliament," a prerogative whereby the acts of this legislative and judicial body are sanctioned by the Crown as well as by the people. Besides calling the entire Parliament nine times during his reign, Henry met repeatedly with the Great Council (the king and the House of Lords, his close peers).

The king also created 40 new constituencies for the House of Commons. Parliament granted funds for extraordinary purposes, such as defense, and Henry VIII needed money from these new constituencies. Cardinal Thomas Wolsey (c. 1474–1530), the king's chaplain and lord chancellor, proposed a new basis for taxation. Unlike most countries in western Europe, England did not exempt the nobility from taxes. Wolsey proposed that royal commissioners should assess the estimated value of property, and that taxes should be based on that amount. Parliament, however, voted on the frequency of taxation. Thus Parliament, as this example demonstrates, somewhat balanced royal power with a modified form of popular government.

Elizabeth I was the daughter of Henry VIII and his second wife, Anne Boleyn (1507–36). During her long reign as queen, she formalized the Church of England as the official church of the realm, and she blended politics and religion by forcing Protestantism on the Irish. Parliament generally supported Elizabeth, who recognized the importance of its cooperation in domestic government.

Scotland

Although some statesmen advocated having a common monarch for Scotland and England as the only way of ending the debilitating conflict between them, that goal was not accomplished until the death of Elizabeth I in 1603. During the Renaissance, Scotland was an independent country with its own parliament, ruled locally by some of the fiercest knights in western Europe. James IV, along with many of Scotland's knights, died in the 1512 Battle of Flodden fighting the English. His son, James V (1512–42), had a long minority, during which commerce flourished and the merchant class began to gain political leverage in Scotland. Protestantism vied with Catholicism as the state religion. As the new religion began to influence political decisions, many Scots leaned toward England. Hostile to Henry VIII of England, James V promoted members of the Catholic party, and his French wife, Mary of Lorraine (Marie of Guise, 1515–60), raised their, daughter, Mary (1542–87), as a Catholic. Because Mary, queen of Scots, was only an infant when she inherited the throne, her mother ruled as regent. England, which repeatedly attempted diplomatic negotiations to control Scotland, succeeded only when Elizabeth I agreed to have her cousin, Mary, executed. Mary's son James VI (1566–1625) became king of both England and Scotland, but the countries were not united as a single kingdom until 1707.

MAJOR RULERS AND THEIR DATES OF OFFICE

(All dates are the dates of reign)

Italy

VENICE

Francesco Foscari, doge of Venice	1423–1457
Pietro Mocenigo, doge of Venice	1474–1476
Giovanni Mocenigo, doge of Venice	1478–1485
Agostino Barbarigo, doge of Venice	1486–1501
Leonardo Loredan, doge of Venice	1501–1521
Andrea Gritti, doge of Venice	1523–1538
Francesco Donato, doge of Venice	1545–1553

FLORENCE

Cosimo de' Medici the Elder, ruler of Florence	1434–1464
Piero I de' Medici, ruler of Florence	1464–1469
Lorenzo de' Medici, ruler of Florence	1469–1492
Giulio de' Medici, ruler of Florence	1519–1523
Alessandro de' Medici, duke of Florence	1531–1537
Cosimo I de' Medici, grand duke of Tuscany (ruler of Florence, 1537–1560s)	1569–1574

MILAN

Gian Galeazzo Visconti, duke of Milan (lord of Milan, 1378–1395)	1395–1402
Giovanni Maria Visconti, duke of Milan	1402–1412
Filippo Maria Visconti, duke of Milan	1412–1447
Francesco I Sforza, duke of Milan	1450–1466
Galeazzo Maria Sforza, duke of Milan	1466–1476
Ludovico Sforza, duke of Milan (ruler of Milan, 1480–1494)	1494–1499

FERRARA

Niccolò III d'Este, marquis of Ferrara	1393–1441
Léonello I d'Este, marquis of Ferrara	1441–1450
Borso d'Este, marquis of Ferrara	1450–1471
Ercole I d'Este, duke of Ferrara	1471–1505
Alfonso I d'Este, duke of Ferrara	1505–1534
Ercole II d'Este, duke of Ferrara	1534–1559
Alfonso II d'Este, duke of Ferrara	1559–1597

MANTUA

Gianfrancesco Gonzaga, marquis of Mantua	1407–1444
Ludovico II Gonzaga, marquis of Mantua	1444–1478
Gianfrancesco II Gonzaga, marquis of Mantua	1484–1519
Federigo II Gonzaga, marquis of Mantua (duke of Mantua, 1530–1540)	1519–1540

PARMA

Ottavio Farnese, duke of Parma and Piacenza	1547–1549, 1550–1586
Alessandro Farnese, duke of Parma and Piacenza	1586–1592

RIMINI

Sigismondo Malatesta, lord of Rimini	c.1433–1468

URBINO

Federigo II da Montefeltro, duke of Urbino	1474–1482
Guidobaldo I da Montefeltro, duke of Urbino	1482–1508
Francesco Maria I delle Rovere, duke of Urbino	1508–1516, 1521–1538
Guidobaldo II delle Rovere, duke of Urbino	1538–1574

NAPLES

House of Anjou

Ladislas I, king of Naples	1400–1414
Joanna II, queen of Naples	1414–1435
René I of Anjou, king of Naples	1435–1442

House of Aragon (under Spain)

Alfonso I, king of Naples (Alfonso V of Aragon)	1443–1458
Ferrante I, king of Naples	1458–1494

Holy Roman Empire

HOUSE OF LUXEMBOURG

Sigismund I, Holy Roman Emperor	1410–1437

HOUSE OF HABSBURG

Frederick III, Holy Roman Emperor	1440–1493
Maximilian I, Holy Roman Emperor	1493–1519
Charles V, Holy Roman Emperor	1519–1556
Ferdinand I, Holy Roman Emperor	1556–1564
Maximilian II, Holy Roman Emperor	1564–1576
Rudolf II, Holy Roman Emperor	1576–1612

France

FRANCE

House of Valois

Charles VII, king of France	1422–1461
Louis XI, king of France	1461–1483
Charles VIII, king of France	1483–1498

Orléans dynasty

Louis XII, king of France (king of Naples, 1501–1503)	1498–1515

Angoulême dynasty

Francis I, king of France	1515–1547
Henry II, king of France	1547–1559
Charles IX, king of France	1560–1574
Henry III, king of France	1574–1589

House of Bourbon

Henry IV, king of France	1589–1610

BURGUNDY (CLAIMED BY FRANCE)

House of Valois

Philip the Bold, duke of Burgundy	1363–1404
John the Fearless, duke of Burgundy	1404–1419
Philip the Good, duke of Burgundy	1419–1467
Charles the Bold, duke of Burgundy	1467–1477

Spain and Portugal

SPAIN

Castile and León

John II, king of Castile and León [in Spain]	1406–1454
Henry IV, king of Castile and León	1454–1474
Isabella I, queen of Castile and León [in Spain]	1474–1504

Aragon

Alfonso V, king of Aragon [in Spain] (Alfonso I of Naples)	1416–1458
John II, king of Aragon [in Spain]	1458–1479
Ferdinand V, king of Aragon [in Spain] (Ferdinand II of Castile and León, 1474–1516)	1479–1516

House of Habsburg

Charles I, king of Castile and Aragon [Spain](Emperor Charles V)	1516–1556
Philip II, king of Castile and Aragon [Spain](king of Portugal as of 1580)	1556–1598

PORTUGAL

House of Avis

John I, king of Portugal	1385–1433
Duarte I, king of Portugal	1433–1438
Afonso V, king of Portugal	1438–1481
John II, king of Portugal	1481–1495
Manuel I, king of Portugal	1495–1521
John III, king of Portugal	1521–1557
Sebastian I, king of Portugal	1557–1578

Germany

KINGS OF GERMANY

House of Wittelsbach

Ruprecht of the Palatinate, king of Germany	1400–1410

House of Luxembourg

Sigismund I, king of Bohemia (also emperor)	1410–1437

House of Habsburg

Albrecht II, king of the Romans	1438–1439
Frederick IV, king of the Romans (also emperor, as Frederick III 1440–1493)	1440–1486
Maximilian I, king of the Romans (also emperor, 1493–1519)	1486–1519
Charles V, king of the Romans (also emperor, 1519–1556)	1519–1558
Ferdinand I, king of the Romans (also emperor, 1556–1564)	1558–1562
Maximilian II, king of the Romans (also emperor, 1564–1576)	1562–1575
Rudolf II, king of the Romans (also emperor, 1576–1612)	1575–1612

BRANDENBURG

House of Hohenzollern

Frederick II, elector of Brandenburg	1440–1470
Albrecht III Achilles, elector of Brandenburg (intermittently)	1470–1486
Johann Cicero, elector of Brandenburg	1486–1499
Joachim I, elector of Brandenburg	1499–1535
Johann Georg, elector of Brandenburg	1571–1598

HESSE

Philip, landgrave of Hesse	1509–1567
Wilhelm IV, landgrave of Hesse	1567–1592

PALATINATE

House of Wittelsbach

Ludwig III, elector of the Palatinate	1410–1436
Ludwig IV, elector of the Palatinate	1436–1449
Friedrich I, elector of the Palatinate (as regent, 1449–1452)	1452–1476
Philipp the Upright, elector of the Palatinate	1476–1508
Ludwig V, elector of the Palatinate	1508–1544
Friedrich II, elector of the Palatinate	1544–1556
Otto Heinrich, elector of the Palatinate	1556–1559

Simmern dynasty

Friedrich III, elector of the Palatinate	1559–1576
Ludwig VI, elector of the Palatinate	1576–1583
Friedrich IV, elector of the Palatinate	1583–1610

SAXONY

House of Wettin

Albrecht the Bold, duke of Saxony	1464–1500
Johann Friedrich I, elector of Saxony	1532–1547
Maurice, duke of Saxony (elector of Saxony, 1547–1553)	1541–1553

The Netherlands

HOUSE OF VALOIS

Philip the Bold, duke of Burgundy	1363–1404
John the Fearless, duke of Burgundy	1404–1419
Philip the Good, duke of Burgundy	1419–1467
Charles the Bold, duke of Burgundy	1467–1477

HOUSE OF HABSBURG

Philip the Handsome (son of Mary of Burgundy and Emperor Maximilian I)	1482–1506
Margaret of Austria, regent of the Netherlands (in the name of Charles V)	1507–1530

HOUSE OF ORANGE-NASSAU

William I, Stadtholder of the United Provinces	1572–1584
Maurice, Stadtholder of the United Provinces	1585–1625

Poland and Hungary

POLAND

House of Lithuania

Casimir IV, king of Poland	1446–1492
Sigismund I, king of Poland (ruled with his son Sigismund II as of 1530)	1506–1548

Sigismund II, king of Poland (ruled with his father, Sigismund I, 1530–1548)	1530–1572

House of Transylvania

Stefan Batóry, king of Poland	1575–1586

House of Sweden

Sigismund III, king of Poland	1587–1632

HUNGARY

Matthias I Corvinus, king of Hungary	1458–1490

England and Scotland

ENGLAND

House of Lancaster

Henry V, king of England	1413–1422
Henry VI, king of England	1422–1461 and 1470–1471

House of York

Edward IV, king of England	1461–1470 and 1471–1483
Richard III, king of England	1483–1485

House of Tudor

Henry VII, king of England	1485–1509
Henry VIII, king of England	1509–1547
Edward VI	1547–1553
Mary Tudor, queen of England	1553–1558
Elizabeth I, queen of England	1558–1603

House of Stuart

James I, king of England (James VI of Scotland)	1603–1625

SCOTLAND

House of Stuart

James IV, king of Scotland	1488–1513
James V, king of Scotland	1512–1542
Mary, queen of Scots	1542–1587
James VI, king of Scotland (James I of England)	1567–1625

MAJOR FIGURES

Albrecht III Achilles, elector of Brandenburg (1414–1486), was the son of Friedrich I of Hohenzollern. In 1473 Albrecht III issued a famous edict by which primogeniture would determine inheritance. The eldest son would rule the mark of Brandenburg and the other sons would share the Hohenzollern domains in Franconia.

Alexander VI, pope *(Rodrigo de Borja y Doms)* (1431–1503), born in Valencia (Spain), studied law in Bologna. His main interest in both Italian and foreign affairs was in marrying his children into powerful families, to promote political and territorial objectives. In the 1494 Treaty of Tordesillas, Alexander VI affected the foreign policies of both Spain and Portugal by setting the demarcation line of their New World claims in present-day Brazil. He gave his support to the University of Rome, restored the Castel Sant' Angelo, built the Torre Borgia in the present-day Vatican, and commissioned Pinturicchio for the paintings.

Alfonso V, king of Aragon *(Alfonso I, king of Naples)* (1396–1458), spent the final 15 years of his life in the capital city of Naples, ruling with a firm but pious hand. A patron of learning and of the arts, Alfonso most famously commissioned the sculpted triumphal arch that functioned as an entrance to his castle overlooking the Bay of Naples. It still can be seen today. In addition to patronizing the University of Naples, he founded a university in Catania and a Greek school in Messina.

Bloody Mary See MARY TUDOR, QUEEN OF ENGLAND.

Charles V, Holy Roman Emperor *(Charles I, king of Spain)* (1500–1558), inherited the largest European empire since Charlemagne's. He was hindered in his efforts at holding together the Empire by its geographic extent, the hostility of his Spanish subjects, and his failure to settle conflicts with Protestant leaders in Germany and the Netherlands.

Charles VII, king of France (1403–1461), became regent in 1418 because his mentally ill father was proclaimed unfit to rule. With the help of Joan of Arc, he was crowned in 1419, but he later failed to rescue her from the English. Distrustful of the aristocracy, Charles gathered around him a group of bourgeois advisers. When members of the noble class rebelled, the king was able to suppress them because of the loyalty of his lesser subjects.

Charles VIII, king of France (1470–1498), has the dubious distinction of having refused to call an assembly of the Estates General (the chief governing body) during his reign. (This type of autocratic behavior by the French monarchy continued until 1560.) Charles married Anne of Brittany in 1491, aligning that duchy under the aegis of France. His invasion of Italy in 1494, to reclaim his Neapolitan title, initiated the Italian Wars.

Charles IX, king of France (1550–1574), was a weak monarch who permitted his mother, Catherine de' Medici, to intervene in decisions directly affecting the welfare of his subjects. Himself a poet, Charles patronized the writers belonging to the Pléiade, and he supported the Academy in Paris.

Charles the Bold, duke of Burgundy (1433–1477), aspired to be crowned king of Burgundy, to be the equal of the king of France. As the husband of Margaret of York, he was supported by Edward IV of England, her brother. Charles was defeated in his effort to become king of Burgundy, and his autocratic power was limited. Had Charles the Bold become a king, the network of alliances between the court and Burgundian nobility would have shifted, with unpredictable results.

Clement VII, pope (*Giulio de' Medici*) (1478–1534), is best remembered for his patronage of literature and the arts, especially his commissioning of Michelangelo for frescoes in the Sistine Chapel. In Rome when the city was sacked in 1527, Clement was imprisoned. One of the results was the overthrow of the Medici by a republican government in Florence.

Contarini, Gasparo (1483–1542), a nobleman born in Venice who served the republic as a diplomat and wrote *De magistratibus et republica Venetorum* (*On the Magistrates and the Republic of the Venetians*, 1543). In that work he cited several reasons why the Venetian republic lasted 12 centuries and why it was superior to that of Rome. He later became a reforming cardinal.

Elizabeth I, queen of England (1533–1603), is known for the stability of her reign, notably her part in unifying English society after the chaos of her sister, Mary's, attempt at rule. Her long reign gave Elizabeth the opportunity to unify the Protestant church in England, especially with the Thirty-nine Articles, and she was famous for her patronage of poets and musicians. She was also an effective diplomat in her dealings with Philip II, and her encouragement of "sea dogs" such as Drake expanded England's command of maritime initiatives.

d'Este, Alfonso I, duke of Ferrara (1486–1534), was opposed by members of his own family, who fomented rebellion with the support of sympathetic patricians. Although he suppressed this group, Alfonso feuded with the pope, putting his dukedom in jeopardy. Alfonso studied military weaponry and was well informed about artillery. As head of the papal troops, he defeated the Venetian fleet, and in 1512 he helped the French win the Battle of Ravenna. He also patronized the arts at his court in Ferrara, commissioning paintings by Titian and Giovanni Bellini.

Ferdinand I, Holy Roman Emperor (1503–1564), was the younger brother of Charles V. In the 1521 Partition of Worms, he was given control of the Habsburg territories in Austria and Germany, and he later became king of Hungary. He allied himself with the Utraquists in Bohemia by granting them the religious sacrament of Communion, but he opposed the Lutherans in Germany. His administrative systems lasted until 1918; of them the Privy Council, Treasury, and Council of War were especially important.

Ferdinand V, king [consort] of Spain [Castile and León] (*Ferdinand II, king of Aragon*) (1452–1516), was guided in his rule by the three Cortes of Aragon, one for each major geographic region. As governing bodies that convened regularly, they approved any new laws. In 1469 he married Isabella of Castile; the union that eventually unified Iberia itself. Ferdinand supported Isabella in implementing the Inquisition in Spanish territory, in expelling the Jews from Spain, and in financing the voyages of Christopher Columbus.

Ferrante I, king of Naples (1423–1494), was authoritarian in his government of Naples and Sicily. When members of the nobility revolted in Naples, Ferrante promised them amnesty but later had them murdered. Alerted to the dynastic threats of the king of France, Ferrante attempted to create an alliance with the pope and the duke of Milan. He failed, however, and Naples was left vulnerable after his death in January 1494.

Francis I, king of France (1494–1547), created a royal council that attended to various needs of the government. Although he contributed to the centralization of the legal system, Francis never called an assembly of the Estates General during his reign. He supported many artists and humanistic scholars; his chateau of Fontainebleau was notable for paintings and sculpture by several Italian artists. Francis wanted to become Holy Roman Emperor, but the election went to Charles V. The enmity of these two rulers led to military encounters over several decades, during which Henry VIII vacillated between the two.

Gianfrancesco II Gonzaga, marquis of Mantua (1466–1519), was away from his court for long periods. During the marquis's absences, his wife, Isabella d'Este (1474–1539), became an important figure in court culture and politics. They both patronized art and music, including the building of the Palazzo San Sebastiano. Gianfrancesco served as a military leader for Venice, France, Florence, and the pope.

Gonzaga, Ludovico II, marquis of Mantua (1412–1478), received a humanist education and ruled as a virtuous and honorable lord of the city. During the early years of his rule, Ludovico was involved in the conflicts between Venice and Milan, leading troops for each side. After the 1454 Peace of Lodi, he was able to turn his attention to patronizing humanistic scholars such as Francesco Filelfo and

artists such as Mantegna. He also commissioned Alberti to design the Church of Sant' Andrea in Mantua.

Henry VII, king of England (1457–1509), founded the Tudor dynasty. A nephew of Henry VI, he married Elizabeth of York and thus united the houses of York and Lancaster. Directly involved in affairs of government, he was chiefly responsible for the sound financial condition of England at the close of his reign.

Henry VIII, king of England (1491–1547), used his position as monarch to create the Church of England after he feuded with the pope about his divorce of Catherine of Aragon. His closing of the monasteries, many of which administered to the poor, led to criticism and social unrest. Although royal seizure of monastic property greatly added to the treasury, Henry's military engagements against France and Scotland depleted the kingdom's resources.

Henry III, king of France (1551–1589), was manipulated by members of the Catholic faction to repress the Huguenots. Although he agreed to peace in 1576, the religious wars continued. He fought bravely, leading the royal army in several victories. Henry was assassinated during the siege of Paris. (For a brief period before his brother's death in 1574, he had been the king of Poland.)

Henry IV, king of France (1553–1610), was a firm ruler who instituted strict financial reforms throughout the country, strengthening royal power. As Henry of Navarre, he was raised as a Protestant. After becoming king, he supported limited toleration of Protestantism.

Isabella I, queen of Spain [Castile and León] (1451–1504) married Ferdinand II of Aragon in 1469 and consolidated non-Moorish Spain. The Corte of Castile did not have the power of those in Aragon, and Isabella based her administration on several advisers, including her confessor. A staunch supporter of Catholicism, Isabella reconquered Granada and drove the Jews from the Spanish mainland. She sent Chistopher Columbus on his voyages of exploration, not only for treasure but also for the spreading of the Catholic religion.

Julius II, pope *(Giuliano della Rovere)* (1443–1513), was known for his successful mediation of foreign affairs, beginning with negotiating the Burgundian inheritance between Louis XII, king of France, and the emperor Maximilian I. Julius was also a great patron of the arts; he commissioned Michelangelo to sculpt his tomb and paint the ceiling of the Sistine Chapel and Bramante to design a new basilica for Saint Peter's. He also created the first bishoprics in the New World.

Leo X, pope *(Giovanni de' Medici)* (1475–1521), was the second son of Lorenzo de' Medici. To finance his lavish patronage of art and learning and the campaign against the Turks, he levied a tax on benefices. His later sale of indulgences contributed to the rebellion of Martin Luther against clerical corruption, and in 1521 the pope excommunicated him. Leo had the bad fortune to be pope during the Italian Wars. In the 1516 Concordat of Bologna, he signed over Piacenza and Parma to the French, but he managed to retain Florence for his family, the Medici. In Rome, he refounded the university and established a printing press for Greek books. Leo's art patronage included works by Raphael and Sansovino.

Louis XI, king of France (1423–1483), was the first monarch to unify France under a centralized administration. He succeeded in extending French territory to the Pyrenees and prevented an English invasion in the north by paying off Edward IV. Though his various taxes, including a tax on salt, were unpopular, they helped stabilize the economy. Louis convened the Estates General only once and often ignored the recommendations of the Parlement of Paris.

Louis XII, king of France (1462–1515), paid little attention to French domestic affairs, focusing instead on the Italian Wars, which drained his treasury. Although the invasion of Italy gained France few tangible benefits during Louis's reign, French Renaissance culture benefited enormously from exposure to the Italian Renaissance of the late 15th and early 16th centuries.

Louise of Savoy, duchess of Angoulême (1476–1531), was the mother of Francis I. She ruled France in his name whenever he was absent for any length of time, and she herself was responsible for governing the duchies presented to her by Francis. She was one of the most powerful regents of the Renaissance.

Margaret of Austria, duchess of Savoy (1480–1530), was regent of the Netherlands from her widowhood in 1507 until her death. She had the opportunity as a young woman to observe the workings of government in France (she was betrothed to Charles VIII at the age of two and raised at the French court) and of Savoy (she was married to the duke for three years). Margaret was a patron of artists, especially composers, who set her poems to music.

Margaret, duchess of Parma (1522–1586), was regent of the Netherlands from 1559 until her resignation in 1567, which resulted from severe opposition to her implementation of the Inquisition by order of Philip II. At times she had only nominal authority, as the Spanish king pursued his own interests in her domain. The result of his stringent policies was the Revolt of the Netherlands.

Mary, queen of Scots *(Mary Stuart)* (1542–1587), was queen of Scotland and briefly of France (the latter through her marriage to Francis II, who died in 1560). Most of her reign was consumed with efforts to gather enough Catholic support to take the English throne from Elizabeth I, whose legitimacy was not recognized by many of her Catholic subjects. A Protestant uprising in Scotland forced Mary to flee to England, where she was arrested. She was executed by order of Elizabeth I in 1587.

Mary Tudor, queen of England *(Mary I or Bloody Mary)* (1516–1558), ruled from 1553 to 1558. Daughter of Catherine of Aragon, she was raised in the Catholic faith. Her main goal in governing England was to destroy the Church of England and restore Catholicism as the official religion of the country. The resulting Protestant rebellions, however, made England more than ready to accept Elizabeth I as queen when Mary died.

Matthias Corvinus (1443–1490) was elected king of Hungary in 1458. He left domestic government chiefly in the hands of advisers while he sought to expand his powers into Bohemia and push imperial troops out of Vienna. He had humanistic courts in both Buda and Vienna. Educated as a humanist, Matthias was personally involved with building his substantial library collection and patronizing the arts.

Maurice, count of Nassau (1567–1625), was governor of the United Provinces and, as of 1618, prince of Orange. He acted as chief executive, but government was administered by the Estates General, which during his reign was increasingly influenced by members of the middle class. An expert military commander, Maurice reorganized his army on classical models of small battalions, with special units of artillery. Between 1588 and 1598, his troops drove the Spaniards out of the northern provinces.

Maximilian I, Holy Roman Emperor (1459–1519), was embroiled in conflict for much of his reign with the independent German princes and with the Estates General of the Netherlands. In the 1495 Diet of Worms, he agreed to the creation of a legal council and an advisory council but managed to prevent the establishment of an executive council. Maximilian's problems in the north caused him to lose face in Italy, and his dream of a centralized Imperial administrative system was not realized. Maximilian had a scintillating court, which patronized musicians and artists such as Dürer.

Medici, Catherine de', queen of France (1519–1589), was a powerful figure during the reign of her sons, ruling as regent for part of that time. Orphaned at a young age, she was under the protection of Clement VII, a Medici pope. He and Francis II arranged her marriage to the dauphin, Henry. After Henry's death in 1559, Catherine reigned as regent for many years. Although she initially made several major concessions to the Huguenots, later she schemed against them and was partly responsible for the Saint Batholomew's Massacre of 1572. As a result, the Protestant masses turned against her and Catherine's authority at court was usurped by members of the Guise family.

Medici, Cosimo I de', duke of Florence and grand duke of Tuscany (1519–1574), was a son of the famous condottiere Giovanni de' Medici. He was elected by the Council of Forty-eight to the dukedom in 1537. His election was opposed by a group of nobles whom he subsequently defeated, and he ruthlessly quelled any further opposition by execution.

Medici, Lorenzo de' (1449–1492) inherited the Florentine commercial empire of the Medici bank. Lorenzo manipulated the governing bodies of the republic and virtually ruled as a prince for more than two decades. He was called "Il Magnifico" (the magnificent), signifying that he functioned as the head of state even though he was not actually a prince. A poet himself, Lorenzo supported numerous artists and writers, including Botticelli, Ghirlandaio, Leonardo, Pico della Mirandola, and Poliziano.

Montefeltro, Federigo II da, duke of Urbino (1422–1482), ruled Urbino and its environs as a warlord, assisted by his band of condottieri. During his reign, several architectural and artistic projects enhanced the beauty of Renaissance Urbino. Among these were an entire room in his palace decorated with trompe l'oeil intarsia work and a similar room in the palace at Gubbio (today installed in the Metropolitan Museum of Art, New York).

Moro, Il   See SFORZA, LODOVICO.

Philip II, king of Spain (also of Naples and Portugal, and duke of Milan) (1527–1598), was known as a pious, serious man and a stern ruler. Although the Aragonese nobility rebelled against his reign in 1591, Philip quelled their independent spirit, as he had that of his morisco subjects in Granada in 1570. He was also instrumental in the spread of the Spanish Inquisition and directly responsible for the Revolt of the Netherlands. His most impressive commission was El Escorial near Madrid, a palace complex that included a monastery.

Philip of Hesse (1504–1567), a German landgrave, was coleader of the Schmalkaldic League. He understood the powerful potential of the Protestant Reformation in European politics, and became a Lutheran early in his reign. Philip was hailed by Protestants throughout Germany when his troops defeated Imperial forces in 1534. His initial goal was to conquer the Habsburg emperor, but he was forced to sign a short-lived treaty with Charles V in 1541. Once again fighting for the Protestant cause a short time later, he was captured and imprisoned. After his release in 1552, he spent the remainder of his life as a Protestant champion.

Philip the Good, duke of Burgundy (1396–1467), maintained the chivalric ideals of his father, in an aristocratic court surrounded by his knights, members of the nobility. His court was a major center of Flemish music and art, including the works of the painter Jan van Eyck. Philip also founded the chivalric Order of the Golden Fleece.

Rudolf II, Holy Roman Emperor (1552–1612), needed funding to suppress rebellion in the Netherlands and to wage war against the Turks. Thus his various provinces gained important concessions, for both Protestants and Catholics, in return for their financial support. Organizing his court in Prague in 1573, Rudolf became a patron of the arts and sciences, collecting works of art and scientific specimens from across Europe. Both Brahe and Kepler were at his court; the latter's *Rudolphine Tables* of 1627 were named after the emperor.

Sebastian I, king of Portugal (1554–1578), ruled for only 10 years until he was killed in battle. Focusing on mysticism and military crusades, Sebastian left the administration of government to others, including Jesuits, who had entered positions of power in Portugal. Refusing to marry, he set the stage for the Spanish to take over the throne of Portugal after his death. Sebastian was killed in north Africa during his second crusade against the Moors.

Sforza, Francesco I, duke of Milan (1401–1466), ruled as the first Sforza duke of Milan. Initially, however, he had to confront the Ambrosian Republic (see the section, Italy). His court attracted renowned humanistic scholars, and he permitted his daughter, Ippolita, to become proficient in Latin. Francesco's building projects included a canal that allowed Milan to reach the Adda River and the Ospedale Maggiore (today part of the University of Milan).

Sforza, Lodovico, duke of Milan (1452–1508), had complete power over the government of the duchy of Milan, but he often left the administration of government in the hands of advisers because of his personal focus on military endeavors. He was very much involved in the Italian Wars because Milan was a desirable duchy. In 1500 Lodovico lost Milan to the French; he spent the rest of his life in prison. Until 1499, however, his patronage was lavish, extending to music, science, art, and architecture. His most famous commission was for the Church of Santa Maria della Grazie, for which Bramante built the dome and Leonardo painted *The Last Supper* (which remains there today).

Sigismund I, king of Poland (1467–1548), spent most of his reign in military campaigns. Although supported by the aristocracy, he was opposed by members of the lesser nobility serving in the Diet of Poland. In Poland he had to fight the Teutonic Knights, whose order he suppressed in 1521. He also battled the troops of Ivan IV on the eastern front.

READING

Becker 1988: social structure; Brown 1997, 41–47: republican politics; Griffiths 1968: representative government; Hale 1971: society and the individual; Koenigsberger 1971: dissenters; Richardson 2002: Henry VIII, Francis I, and Charles V.

Italy

Brucker 1977: Florence; Finlay 1980: Venice; Fubini 2000: diplomacy in the city-states; Gilbert 1965: Florence; King 1986: Venice; Lubkin 1994: Milan; Martines 1988: city-states; Muir 1981: Venice; Rubenstein 1997: Florence.

Holy Roman Empire

Doyle 2000: Mary of Hungary and patronage; Knecht 1999: French opposition; Mulgan 1998: monarchies; Weber 1995: theories of absolutism.

France

Baumgartner 1995: 16th-century politics; Bohanan 2001: nobility; Bosher 2000: New World colonies; Kelley 1981: society and ideology; Le Roy Ladurie 1994: society and the state; Stephenson 2004: Marguerite de Navarre and patronage.

Spain and Portugal

Corteguera 2002: Barcelona; Elliott 2002: Spain and the empire; Gschwend 1998: Portugal (viceroy, 1583–1593); Hillgarth 2003: political history; Mulgan 1998: monarchies; Perrone 2001: clerical opposition; Von Barghahn 1985: symbols of monarchy.

Germany

Barraclough 1984: Germany as a nation; Carsten 1959, parliaments; Eyck 1998: Christianity and politics; Wiesner 1998: gender issues in politics.

The Netherlands

Darby 2001: Dutch revolt; Davids 1995: Dutch Republic; Gelderen 1992: Dutch revolt; Tilmans 2002: republicanism; Verlinden 1981: government and economic policy.

Poland and Hungary

Balázs 1989: Magyars and the Hungarian nation; Friedrich 2000: Polish independent government.

England and Scotland

Burns 1996: Scotland (kingship); Donaldson 1983: Mary Stuart's politics; Edington 1994: Scotland; Etty 2002: border disputes; Fleming 1998: English regionalism; Goodare 1999: Scotland (society); Mason 1998: politics in Reformation Scotland; Morgan-Russell 2002: More's *Utopia*; Ormrod 1996: political ramifications of the Black Death; Rae 1966: Scotland's frontier.

2

RELIGION

Religion during the Renaissance was characterized by various reforming tendencies, from the Catholic Inquisition on one end of the doctrinal spectrum to the discipline of Calvinism on the other. The root of this conflict can be traced to the Middle Ages, with the split of Christianity in 1054 into the Catholic Church and the Eastern Orthodox Church. (This was the first Great Schism.) The Western church gradually became semisecularized, dealing with land ownership and military campaigns. During the 12th century, the papacy was in conflict with the Holy Roman Emperor, not over spiritual matters but over territory in Italy. Churchmen became wealthy landlords, and many of them took mistresses and lived in luxurious surroundings. Pope Gregory VII undertook to reform the church during this period, enforcing the rule of celibacy for priests. In the 13th century, Pope Innocent III increased the power of the papacy by reducing that of the emperor. With Imperial might diminished, however, national governments began to rise to power. The king of France refused to send any gold to Rome, and the papacy was bankrupted and then moved to Avignon in 1305. Between 1378 and 1417 (the second Great Schism), antipopes were elected to rival the pope established in Avignon. Martin V, elected by the Council of Constance, effectively healed the rift in the church, though two rival popes had very small groups of supporters for several years thereafter. As of 1417, the papacy was once again based in Rome. One way that the church raised money for numerous projects, such as building programs in Rome during the 15th and early 16th centuries, was the selling of indulgences. These were papers that released a sinner from temporal penalties once he or she had been forgiven. The opposition to indulgences would become the rallying point for Martin Luther (1483–1546) and his supporters in the early stages of the Protestant Reformation in Germany. Inquisitional tribunals that had merely responded to papal assignments during the Middle Ages were given extraordinary powers during this period, ferreting out heretics of all kinds, including suspicious humanists, Protestants, and converted Jews who had secretly recanted.

The seriousness with which religion was regarded in Renaissance Europe was among the causes of the Protestant Reformation and of reform movements within the Catholic Church itself. All aspects of life were affected by religion during the 15th and 16th century, when religious motifs and symbolism dominated visual art. By the mid-16th century, even modest homes displayed devotional imagery, in prints or small wooden statues. Much of Renaissance architecture concentrated on constructing or renovating religious buildings. The church, synagogue, or mosque served as the center of a community, and spiritual considerations often took precedence over earthly affairs.

THE PAPACY

The Renaissance papacy had a difficult beginning, in that the office had been split between Rome and Avignon between 1378 and 1417, as antipopes competed with the pope in Rome. This Great Schism was resolved by the Council of Constance, which installed Martin V as the new pope. Although two antipopes also demanded recognition, the Western Church followed Martin V as their leader.

The word *papacy* derives from *papa*, Italian for "father," and the pope functioned as the spiritual father of the Western Church. As was the Catholic Church in general, 15th-century popes were concerned about abuses within the papacy. Pope Pius II (1405–64), for example, denounced corruption during the 1458 meeting of the college of cardinals that elected him as pope: "The richer and more influential members of the college summoned the rest and sought to gain the papacy for themselves or their friends. They begged, promised, threatened, and some, shamelessly casting aside all decency, pleaded their own causes and claimed the papacy as their right" (Ross and McLaughlin 1968, p. 631). Pius II was well aware that the papacy offered wealth and prestige. The pope ruled the Papal States, consisting of Romagna, Umbria, the Marches, Campagna, Marittima, Rome, and the Patrimony of Saint Peter, with Ferrara as his vassal. (Some of these regions were claimed by others at various times.) These were productive agricultural regions that also manufactured textiles and paper, with a salt mine in Cervia and an alum mine in Tolfa. Income from the Papal States was managed by the Roman Curia, supervised by the college of cardinals and the pope himself. The popes of the Renaissance represented many types of men, from libertines who had numerous illegitimate children to saintly scholars who promoted the study of theology. The most memorable Renaissance popes are discussed in the sections that follow.

Martin V

Martin V (Oddo Colonna, 1368–1431) was elected in 1417 by a conclave of cardinals and representatives at the Council of Constance. He called for regular conciliar meetings, as agreed when he became pope, although he would have preferred not to recognize the councils' authority. He used his position to commission the restoration of several important buildings, including churches, in Rome. Remarkably, Martin V seemed to be compassionate toward Jews, tolerating if not respecting their religious law. On the negative side, he enabled his relatives to assume extensive control of land in the Papal States.

Nicholas V

Nicholas V (Tommaso Parentucelli, 1397–1455) became pope in 1447, at a time when the papacy was faced with serious diplomatic and financial problems. An educated and cultivated scholar, he strove to maintain harmony among disparate rulers with his considerable skills in diplomacy. He was also a shrewd manager, using the Jubilee of 1450 as an opportunity to raise income for the Holy See. Part of that money was applied to works commissioned from artists and architects hired by Nicholas to beautify Rome, the capital of Christendom. His greatest cultural achievement was collecting some 1,200 classical manuscripts, many of which contained patristic texts that he ordered translated. These manuscripts became the foundation collection of the Vatican Library.

Pius II

Pius II (Enea Silvio Piccolomini, 1405–64), elected in 1458, introduced his love for humanistic learning to the papacy. His Latin poems, histories, and geographical works were praised during his lifetime, and his autobiography gives an intimate view of the papal office during the mid-15th century. Constantinople had fallen to the Turks five years before Pius became pope, and his unrealized lifelong desire was to organize a crusade to reclaim the city. Obsessed with that goal, Pius failed to consider French demands concerning Naples, setting the stage for increased French hostility toward the papacy as well as toward the king of Naples.

Sixtus IV

Sixtus IV (Francesco della Rovere, 1414–84) assumed the papal tiara in 1471. He appointed six of his nephews as cardinals and found positions in the Curia for other members of his family. Nepotism at this exaggerated level would soon become the norm for Renaissance popes and was one of the abuses of authority discussed in church councils. Both France and Spain were able to impose their will on Sixtus, who could not claim ecclesiastical authority in the former and who agreed to the Inquisition in the latter. He also became caught up in various Italian conspiracies that resulted in revolts in several cities, including Rome. As a humanist, however, he encouraged study of the classics, and he refounded the Vatican Library. He also improved the city of Rome by widening and paving the streets.

Innocent VIII

Innocent VIII (Giovanni Battista Cibò, 1432–92) was elected in 1484. He has the distinction of being remembered as one of the worst popes of the Renaissance. Innocent's main goal as pope was to provide income to his illegitimate children, which he accomplished by auctioning positions in the Curia. He made the colossal diplomatic blunder of excommunicating the king of Naples and giving his kingdom to Charles VIII of France, an act that led to the destructive Italian Wars a few years later (see chapter 7, on warfare). Finally, Innocent's only religious concern seems to have been his hatred of alleged heretics. He established the Inquisition in Germany and ordered that witches be burned.

Alexander VI

Alexander VI (Rodrigo de Borja y Doms or Borgia in Italian, 1432–1503) became pope in 1492. He loved two things, money and women, bribing his way into the papacy so that he could provide for his illegitimate children. He also provided lucrative posts to the male relatives of his mistresses. Unlike the ineffectual Innocent VIII, Alexander personally participated in international diplomacy, but usually for personal gain. Although he had supported the French king's claims to the kingdom of Naples, the pope changed sides when one of his sons married the granddaughter of the king of Naples. When the king died in 1494, the pope crowned Alfonso II (1449–96). This decision prompted Charles VIII to invade Italy, with the ultimate result that Alexander sided with the French in 1498. The papal abuse of authority was targeted by Savonarola as one of the evils that the "knife of God" would destroy, but the preacher himself was cut down by the pope, who had him hanged and his body burned.

Julius II

Julius II (Giuliano della Rovere, 1443–1513), a nephew of Sixtus IV, was elected in 1503. Initially he opposed Alexander VI, called for his resignation, and was forced to flee to France. Later he decided to recognize the authority of the papacy in spite of his dislike for the man acting as pope and served as a papal diplomat. As did Alexander, Julius bought the papacy through bribery, but he later eschewed the nepotism of his predecessor and literally became a warrior for the Catholic Church. In full battle armor, he fought in several campaigns to regain sections of the Papal States that had been seized by others, including France and the Republic of Venice. (See chapter 7, on warfare, for information about Julius and the Holy League.) Julius II was also a patron of the arts, commissioning Michelangelo to sculpt his tomb and paint the ceiling of the Sistine Chapel, and Donato Bramante (c. 1443/44–1514) to design a new basilica for Saint Peter's.

Leo X

Leo X (Giovanni de' Medici, 1475–1521), second son of Lorenzo de' Medici (1449–92), became pope in 1513. Trained as a humanistic scholar and destined as a child for the church, Leo was also influential in the Medici government of Florence. Although Julius II had signed a decree forbidding simony in church politics, Leo installed his relatives in important positions. The Italian Wars drained the papal treasury, so Leo instigated a tax on benefices to fund his proposed campaign against the Turks. To pay for the rebuilding of Saint Peter's, he renewed the sale of indulgences permitted by Julius II. This decision instigated the Protestant Reformation. In 1521 he excommunicated Martin Luther, misjudging the potential power of Luther and his supporters.

2.1 Portrait of Pope Leo X (seated). Raphael, 1518. (Galleria degli Uffizi, Florence, Italy/Bridgeman Art Library)

Clement VII

Clement VII (Giulio de' Medici, 1478–1534), raised by his uncle, Lorenzo de' Medici, became pope in 1523. His uncle's patronage of the arts and learning influenced Clement, who commissioned works by artists such as Raphael and Michelangelo, including frescoes for the Sistine Chapel. His papacy was hindered by his adversarial relationship with the emperor Charles V, settled only after Clement conceded a portion of the Papal States to the Holy Roman Empire. This enmity had contributed to the 1527 sack of Rome by Imperial troops and the destruction of numerous monuments and works of art. Seeking an ally in the king of France, Clement married his grandniece, Catherine de' Medici (1519–89), to a son of Francis I (1494–1547). She would become queen of France and then the powerful queen mother, persecuting Huguenots and other alleged heretics. Clement, however, was powerless to confront Protestants in the north.

Paul III

Paul III (Alessandro Farnese, 1468–1549) was elected in 1534. He attracted the attention of important men in Rome through his sister, who was a mistress of Alexander VI. Paul fathered four children by his own mistress and abandoned her to become a priest in 1519. He made sure that his sons and grandsons benefited from his papacy, granting them part of the Papal States and other property belonging to the church. Ironically, he subsequently campaigned against this sort of corruption and became known as one of the reforming popes of the 16th century. Paul III realized that the church could best survive the Protestant Reformation by changing within. He formed a commission to make recommendations for improvement, and the resulting report formed the basis of discussions at the Council of Trent.

Paul IV

Paul IV (Giam Pietro Carafa, 1476–1559), a member of a powerful Neapolitan family, became pope in 1555. He was an ascetic man who as a youth loved humanistic scholarship and correspondence with learned friends. In 1524 he cofounded a new religious order known as the Theatines, becoming militantly reformist and rejecting humanism. Although he ruled for only four years, Paul accomplished significant reforms in the Curia and in church policy. An important reform concerned the benefices of monasteries, which no longer could be awarded to members of the secular clergy. Because of his prominence as a reformer, Paul became closely identified with the Catholic Church, so that devout Catholics began to think of themselves as papal supporters. (Enemies of the Church pejoratively referred to them as papists.) The people of Rome, however, hated Paul III, whose zealous condemnation of public immorality was quite unpopular. Upon his death, the population rioted, smashing the office of the Inquisition and releasing the prisoners sequestered there.

Pius IV

Pius IV (Giovanni Angelo de' Medici, 1499–1565) became pope on Christmas day in 1559. He was able to limit the jurisdiction of the Inquisition, and he reissued the Index of Prohibited Books with a more temperate listing in 1564. Pius IV also reconvened the Council of Trent, dormant since 1552. His bull of 1564 published the council's decrees, and he encouraged Catholics throughout Europe to implement them.

Pius V

Pius V (Antonio Ghislieri, 1504–72) was elected in 1566. A Dominican, he began his career as a lecturer in theology and philosophy at the University of Padua. Then he was appointed as an Inquisition official in 1551, and supporting the Inquisition became an important goal of his papacy. He excommunicated Queen Elizabeth and sent financial aid to France to battle the Huguenots. Pius V was also responsible for the holy league that defeated Turkish forces at the 1571 Battle of Lepanto.

Gregory XIII

Gregory XIII (Ugo Buoncompagni, 1502–85), elected in 1572, devoted his career to the strict implementation of Counter-Reformation policies formulated by the Council of Trent. In his campaign to improve the education of members of the clergy and missionaries, he founded several colleges. Many of these missionaries were trained to return to their Protestant countries to reclaim those areas for Catholicism. He attempted to expand Catholic dominion in eastern Europe, and he succeeded in drawing Poland away from the Eastern Church to reconcile it with the Church of Rome. With all of the attention he paid to reform, however, this pope neglected the Papal States, and bandits were harassing several regions during the final years of his papacy. Gregory XIII is best known for his reforms of the calendar; the Gregorian calendar is the one we use today. (See chapter 12, Daily Life, for information about the calendar reforms.)

Sixtus V

Sixtus V (Felice Peretti, 1525–90) became pope in 1585. During his tenure as pope, Sixtus executed bandits in the Papal States as well as members of the nobility harboring them. He was also a famous proselytizer, supporting missionary activity from China to South America. Sixtus sold ecclesiastical offices and imposed new taxes, raising money to improve public works in the Papal States and to renovate the city of Rome. These improvements included construction of a new aqueduct and completion of Saint Peter's Basilica.

CATHOLIC CHURCH

With the pope as its spiritual leader, the single greatest activity of the Catholic Church during the Renaissance was ecclesiastical reform from within, directed by the Holy See (not called the Vatican until the 20th century). The Protestant Reformation developed in response to the perceived inadequacies of this movement. In a sermon preached in Florence in 1495, the Dominican friar Girolamo Savonarola (1452–1498) warned, "The sword of the Lord comes soon and swiftly over the earth. Believe me that the knife of God will come and soon" (Elmer 2000, p. 286). This sort of extremist rhetoric protested the corruption that plagued ecclesiastical government and wealthy monasteries. Five major church councils were convened during the Renaissance, each dealing with reform. The punishment of heretics, the Inquisition, and the Index of Forbidden Books were intended to help purify the church and its congregations. Missionaries were sent to foreign lands to spread the message of the "one true Church," and the Counter-Reformation reinforced the new discipline and order of Catholicism.

Clergy

The most important members of the clergy, or clerics, were bishops and priests, who had felt called by the Holy Spirit to remain celibate and serve God. Their supreme head on Earth was the pope. Within Catholic Church hierarchy, bishops had full jurisdiction in their diocese. They possessed the right to allow priests to preach and administer the sacraments (see pages 38–39). The sacraments were the linchpin that assured the religious authority of Catholicism because only priests were permitted to administer them. The ordination of priests, also one of the sacraments, set them above the laity and condoned a class system that was attacked by the Protestant Reformation. Bishops and priests were the secular clergy, meaning that they lived in the outside world. The regular clergy ("regulars"), in addition to the vows of ordination, took vows of poverty and obedience. These men lived by certain rules (Latin *regulae*) of their religious order (see pages 35–37), in chapter houses or in communities. Regulars known as canons usually were affiliated with a church or cathedral. Members of the clergy were privileged individuals, exempt from military obligations. In addition, they did not pay normal taxes and were subject only to ecclesiastical justice. (A special tax was levied on clerical benefices to support Crusades against the Turks.) They could not be tried in civil courts, regardless of the alleged offense.

Priests led the worship service in Catholic churches. Unlike medieval structures, with screens

altarpiece placed behind and above it. After the Counter-Reformation mandated Crucifixions and images of patron saints for Catholic religious buildings, paintings and statuary filled the chapels of Catholic churches. Worship services offered both visual and aural stimulation to heighten one's sense of awe and reverence.

Orders and Other Religious Groups

The reform movements in the religious orders of the 15th century had several precedents, notably those of the 14th century. During the Middle Ages, monasteries had served as centers of intellectual as well as devotional life, where scholarly scriptoria preserved ancient, ecclesiastical, liturgical, and scriptural texts. With the rise of universities, monasteries became more isolated from society and thus lost some of their prestige and purpose. Many of their abbots were not monastic men but rather were powerful secular clergy such as bishops who were mainly interested in profiting from their position. In addition, the pandemic of 1347–50, which killed numerous monks and nuns, weakened the administrative structure of the orders. With abuses increasing, the orders themselves began taking steps toward reform during the latter 14th century.

The earliest important religious order for men was the Benedictines, founded during the Middle Ages. Not long afterward, the more austere Cistercian order split away from the Benedictines. The Cistercians were known for their very plain churches and monochromatic illustrated manuscripts. The most populous mendicant orders, who vowed to live in poverty, were the Dominicans, Franciscans, Augustinians, and Carmelites. Some of the canons regular among the Augustinians were influenced by the teachings of Gerhard Groote (1340–1384), founder of the Brethren of the Common Life. This lay order followed the precepts of *devotio moderna* (modern devotion), emphasizing meditation and personal prayer. The Carmelites focused on the Bible and teachings of the church fathers. Dominicans were the great preaching order, or *Ordo Predicatorum*, denoted by *O.P.* after the name of members. Franciscans were

2.2 *Full-page miniature of the Resurrection in a manuscript life of Saint Margaret of Antioch, one of the saints whose voices inspired Joan of Arc. France, 15th century. Convent libraries often included biographies of female saints.* (Photograph courtesy of Sotheby's, Inc., © 2003)

segregating the altar and main part of the sanctuary from the rest of the church, post-Tridentine Renaissance churches usually had a more open plan, welcoming all Catholics in good standing to the altar to receive Communion. Nothing more than an altar railing separated the holiest part of the sanctuary from the congregation in most churches constructed during this time, and the screens were removed from many medieval sanctuaries. Light from a cupola often illuminated the altar and the painted or carved

the Order of Friars Minor, or *Ordo Fratrum Minorum*, which was divided in 1517 into the Friars Minor and Conventual Franciscans. An even stricter form of Franciscan observance was followed by the Minims and by the Capuchins, the latter wearing the famous pointed hood, the *capuche*. The Society of Jesus, or Jesuits, was established in 1534, with Ignatius Loyola (1491–1556) and Francis Xavier (1506–52) among the founding members. They modeled themselves on the biblical disciples, spreading the word of Jesus, and the initial goal of the society was proselytization through foreign missions. By the close of the 16th century, more than 8,500 men had joined the Society of Jesus, teaching in schools, colleges, and overseas missions.

Until the Council of Trent, nuns were not required to live in cloistered communities. During much of the Renaissance, spiritual women were involved in charitable works such as ministering to the sick and to orphans, and especially to the poor. Although some orders pressured their female members to live secluded in convents, most nuns were not required to do so, and many were not required to take vows. The sheltering of holy women, denying them the opportunity to participate in society, occurred in the mid-16th century. In northern Europe, the simple piety of the *devotio moderna* movement appealed to some women, who became Sisters of the Common Life, living together in secular congregations. Eventually many of them took religious vows and entered convents. As were many of the monasteries in northern Europe, most of these convents were destroyed during the Protestant Reformation. The Beguines, established in the 13th century, were an association of philanthropic and evangelical women who took vows of chastity but otherwise lived communally, without formal ties to a religious order. In addition to teaching children, they took care of sick people and did the washing of the dead. The Beguines were self-supporting and became famous for their handicrafts. They can be viewed as spiritual predecessors of the Sisters of the Common Life, who maintained the long tradition of ascetic women.

Two of the important associations for spiritual women created during the 16th century were the Company of Saint Ursula and the Discalced (shoeless) Carmelites. Teresa of Ávila founded the Discalced branch of the Carmelites. The nuns in her reformed order wore coarse wool habits and sandals instead of shoes and practiced strict vegetarianism at a time when meat was the chief food of most people. (Those who could not afford to purchase meat often poached it from private estates or lands owned by the church.) Saint Teresa's nuns experienced mystical, ecstatic religious revelation, as opposed to less dramatic forms of prayer and meditation. Founded in 1535, the Ursulines were avowed virgins who initially lived in their own home, devoted to taking care of sick women and teaching girls of poverty-stricken families. In the 1570s the Ursulines were taken under the rule of the Augustinian order, in which they maintained their tradition of teaching. Ursulines also served as missionaries, founding a mission in Canada during the 17th century.

2.3 Church of Santa Croce, Florence, founded by the Franciscan order. (Courtesy of Sandra Sider)

CONFRATERNITIES

Also known as guilds, confraternities were religious organizations for the laity. Members followed strict rules of propriety and piety, with each confraternity dedicated to specific good works. These groups patronized hospitals, funded welfare for the poor, cared for orphans and widows, helped those imprisoned for debt, and even ministered to prisoners condemned to death. Members also cared for the souls of their deceased colleagues, paying for masses and prayers, and contributed to funds for unemployed or sick members. Confraternities are especially famous for their commissioning of works of art. Some confraternities maintained autonomy from local religious authorities; in northern Europe and England, however, they often supported the local parish, paying for repairs and church music. Religious plays usually were funded by confraternities, whose members participated as actors. An estimated 10 to 20 percent of individuals not among the poor classes belonged to confraternities during the Renaissance, making these groups important contributors to social programs and to the religious life of the community. The mendicant orders sponsored numerous confraternities, whose members undertook a novitiate process similar to that experienced by monks and nuns. Their civic character and spiritual values were investigated before their membership was official. In general, confraternities were suppressed in areas where Protestants gained control.

Foreign Missions

The missions discussed below were associated with the Catholic Church. In principle, neither Lutherans nor Calvinists supported missionary activity, although Jean Calvin (1509–64) did allow several members of his church to participate in the first mission to Brazil. (Not until the 18th century did Protestant missionary activity flourish outside Europe.) Although Catholic missions were active as early as the 14th century, the Counter-Reformation was a catalyst that prompted the church and its various orders to carry Catholicism to the far corners of the Earth. The Counter-Reformation (see page 44) included foreign missions among its primary goals. From the early Renaissance, missionary teaching was embroiled in issues concerning slavery and colonialism. As Christianity was introduced to Africa, Brazil, and Asia by the Portuguese; to the Americas and Philippines by the Spanish; and to Canada by the French, expansionists used these contacts to further their own goals of economic and territorial domination. Jesuit missionaries, for example, were associated with Portuguese traders and merchants in Mozambique. The Portuguese converted numerous Africans along the west coast to Christianity, including the Congolese king, whose son maintained profitable diplomatic relations with Portugal. During the early 16th century, Africans were sent to Portugal to train as priests and returned as missionaries to their own people. As the slave trade accelerated, however, the mission in the Congo gradually became inactive. Jesuit missionaries were especially successful, partly because of their excellent training and willingness to learn native languages. In South America and Mexico, Franciscans were eager to communicate in the native languages so that they could become more effective teachers. The first steps in any new mission were to build a church and convent; a school or college soon followed, and a hospital as well. Missionaries founded the first six universities in the Americas. Resistance to Spanish missionary activity in the Americas was futile because of the military power of Spanish troops. Native Americans who refused to convert and cooperate as slaves were massacred. Although fair-minded missionaries such as Bartholomé de Las Casas (1474–1566) respected the Indians as human beings (unlike many of his contemporaries), they never expressed any respect for their religion and believed that Christianity was necessary to the salvation of the soul of indigenous people.

In 1500 Portuguese ships carried missionaries to India, where they found a large community of Christians claiming to date from the days of the apostles. Although these Christians welcomed the Portuguese, there was little missionary activity until the Jesuits arrived. Francis Xavier encouraged his colleagues to learn Indian customs as well as languages and adapt themselves to Indian life. He became one of the most renowned missionaries of the Renaissance as he converted thousands in India and Japan, providing an

2.4 Saint Francis Xavier and his missionary entourage, painted on a folding screen. Japanese School, 16th century.
(Musée Guimet, Paris, France/Bridgeman Art Library)

example to other Jesuits. Matteo Ricci (1552–1610) used Xavier's methods in China, mingling his Christian message with Confucianism and allowing converts to continue ancestor worship. With this approach, he diverted potential resistance to his teaching.

Sacraments

The devotional life of Catholicism was (and is) based on the seven sacraments: the Eucharist, bap-

tism, confirmation, marriage, penance, extreme unction, and ordination (for the clergy). The Eucharist (from the Greek word for "thanksgiving"), also called Holy Communion, was part of the liturgy celebrated during mass. Worshipers consumed wine and bread, which were believed to be miraculously transformed into the blood and body of Christ. Although Lutherans believed in a variation of this doctrine, the Calvinists and Zwinglians (see pages 43–44) did not. Because most theological disputes of the Protestant Reformation involved the Eucharist, this sacrament is discussed in greater detail later. Penance, the confidential and sincere confessing of sins to a priest, followed by absolution, was the other sacrament repeated throughout one's life. Friday was set aside as a general day of penance, when Catholics were forbidden to consume meat. Penance was a private sacrament whereas the Eucharist and its Mass were public, observed in the church by the entire congregation as each person received the host (holy wafer). (For more information about the Catholic liturgy, see chapter 6, on music.)

EUCHARIST

Originating in the Last Supper of Christ with his disciples, the Eucharist was discussed in detail by the medieval theologian Thomas Aquinas. He explained how the mundane properties of wine and bread could be changed into the "substance" of Christ, a process known as transubstantiation. Most Lutherans believed in consubstantiation, meaning that the substance of Christ was present with the substance of wine and bread. They did not believe in an actual change in the properties of the wine and bread. This latter interpretation, promoted by Martin Luther (1483–1546), was one of the fundamental disagreements between Catholic and Protestant doctrine. In addition, by the Renaissance, Catholic congregations usually consumed only the wafer while the wine was reserved for the priest administering the Eucharist. In prints as well as paintings, the Last Supper was a popular image, appearing in missals and even as the frontispiece to Christian commentaries on classical texts. One early 16th-century woodcut depicted the Last Supper inserted below an image of the Crucifixion.

In the Catholic Church, where images were sacrosanct, the public nature of the Eucharist gave rise to elaborate monstrances (from *monstrare*, Latin "to show"), where the host wafer was displayed and venerated. These vessels could be quite large, gold or silver, ornamented with engraving, precious stones, and rock crystal. Often they were in the shape of a tabernacle, presenting the host in its own churchlike structure. During the annual feast of Corpus Christi (body of Christ), processions of the faithful paraded through the streets, carrying the monstrance with its host. The spiritual power of the Eucharist and its mass was often called upon to protect a congregation from plague, drought, and other threats, and masses were celebrated for the dead to ease their way through purgatory.

2.5 Gilt silver monstrance for presenting the Eucharistic host. Cristóbal Becerril, c. 1585. (Courtesy of The Hispanic Society of America, R3019)

Heresies

The word *heresy* derives from a Greek word meaning "choice." In the epistles of Paul, the word is used to refer to a cause of divisiveness and friction within the church. The opposite of heresy is orthodoxy, or the following of the rules of church doctrine. Three main types of heresies have been persecuted by the Catholic Church: The first is a heretical syncretism of Christianity and another religion, belief, or practice, such as Jewish law or witchcraft; the second is related to doctrine, involving repudiation of or unacceptable emphasis on one or more theological issues; the third concerns movements such as Protestantism whose goal is to reform the church itself. Persecution of heretics did not begin in the Renaissance, but was condoned by the emperor Constantine during the fourth century, and heretics were executed as early as 385. Thousands of people were killed in southern France during the Albigensian Crusade of the 13th century. The church thus attempted to enforce unity and the supremacy of the papacy. During the 16th century, Protestants also condoned the persecution of heretical individuals, such as Michael Servetus (1511–53), whose execution in Geneva was not contested by Jean Calvin (1509–64).

PERSECUTION OF WITCHES

Although the medieval Inquisition investigated allegations of witchcraft, not until 1398 was it given any jurisdiction over suspected witches. In the latter 15th century, two German inquisitors, the Dominicans Jakob Sprenger and Heinrich Institoris, persuaded Pope Innocent VIII (1432–92) to give them direct jurisdiction over witchcraft trials in Germany. His papal bull to this effect was published with the inquisitors' book on witchcraft, *Malleus Maleficarum* (Hammer of evils, 1486). Translated into seven languages and surpassed in popularity only by the Bible, *Malleus Maleficarum* gave major momentum to the hysteria about witchcraft that was to sweep across Europe in the next decades. The majority of individuals killed for supposedly practicing witchcraft were not executed by order of the Inquisition; many civil authorities, especially in rural areas, were responsible for these actions. The papal bull of 1484 simply gave free rein to all witch hunters in northern Germany, an area specifically mentioned in the pope's text. In the 15th century several thousand people, most of them elderly women but also men and children, were tortured and killed. Many of these women were midwives and healers, who worked their "magic" by using medicinal herbs and practical medical techniques passed on by their mother or another older woman. An estimated 50,000 to 100,000 people, the vast majority female, were killed as witches, including those in Massachusetts in 1692. (So-called sodomites [homosexuals] were persecuted with the same degree of severity as witches.) The Catholic Church did not repeal its statutes concerning witchcraft until 1736.

ANTI-SEMITISM

Persecution of Jews began in Roman times, when baptism was forced on them as early as the seventh century. The Fourth Lateran Council decreed in 1215 that Jews were required to wear clothing distinguishing them from Christians. England drove out its Jewish population in 1290, and Jews were expelled from France at the beginning and end of the 14th century. Many people in Germany blamed the plagues of that century on resident Jews, and several cities forbade them to continue to live within the city walls. Other cities forced Jews to live in ghettos. By the 16th century, many cities, such as Vienna, Rome, and Prague, had ghettoized the Jewish population.

Although Protestants as well as Catholics attacked Jews for their cultural practices and religious beliefs, the Catholic phobia of the Jewish religion was more deep-seated and became a major impetus for the Spanish Crown to grant extraordinary powers to the Spanish Inquisition (see page 41). Various libels had been perpetuated against the Jews during the Middle Ages and early Renaissance, the most insidious of them the blood libel and the host libel. The blood libel consisted of the myth of Jews' stealing and killing Christian infants and young boys to drain their blood for ritual use, including the baking of unleavened bread for Passover. An entire Jewish community in Trent was massacred in 1475 after a Jew was accused of murdering a Christian boy. The host libel involved a Christian's being persuaded to steal the host during mass so that a Jew could vilify the host and thus torture Christ. Both of these libels were connected to the accusation that the Jews were responsible for the Crucifixion of Christ. Moreover, the very Jews whose money helped to salvage numerous Christian businesses were considered unclean because of their expertise in monetary management. After the expulsion of Jews from Spain in 1492 and from Portugal three years later, the massive influx of Jewish families into other parts of western Europe led to strained relations among Jews and Christians. Partly because of the Inquisition's treatment of Jews, in bigoted minds the spiritual "contamination" of the Jewish religion developed into an accusation of actual physical infection. Thus the Renaissance witnessed anti-Semitism not only in the form of verbal harassment of Jews but also in the proliferation of Jewish ghettos in many of the major cities.

Inquisition and Index of Prohibited Books

INQUISITION

The word *Inquisition* derives from the Latin for "inquiry," *inquisitio*. The Catholic Church already had an inquisitional process during the Middle Ages. In western Europe, four separate but related inquisitions were in operation between the last quarter of the 15th century and the early 19th century. (The fourth Inquisition, in Latin America, did not officially end until 1834; people accused of practicing witchcraft were burned there during the early 19th century.) Inquisitional investigations flourished in Catholic countries, but with less success in areas such as Switzerland, with its Calvinist partition, and Bohemia, with its strong component of Waldensians and other sects. Although Germany was known for its inquisitional tribunals during the early 16th century, these hearings later began to lose effectiveness in the principalities as the Protestant Reformation increased its adherents. In France, the Inquisition was forbidden to operate. Henry II (1519–59), however, had his own organization for persecuting heretics; wishing to rid France of the Protestant

threat, he established a special tribunal for that purpose.

Founded in 1478 by order of the Spanish monarchy under Isabella I and Ferdinand II (see pages 12–13), the Spanish Inquisition was charged with investigating conversos, converted Jews and Muslims. The latter were called Moriscos (Moorish people) and the former Marranos (pigs). Wholesale persecution of Jews in Castile and Aragon had begun nearly a century earlier, culminating in thousands of Jews' being murdered and many more being forced to convert to Christianity. These Jewish Christians and their descendants gradually became assimilated into Spanish society, assuming prestigious positions in finance, banking, and other commercial endeavors. By the mid-15th century, hostility toward the conversos was openly expressed in Castile, where many individuals were accused of observing crypto-Jewish rituals. By the 16th century, new Christians were forbidden to teach in universities, join military or religious orders, and serve in municipal offices. Jews were ridiculed in art and literature, and anti-Semitic satire was especially virulent. The concept of "blood purity," *limpieza de sangre*, dominated Inquisition tribunals in Spain, Portugal, and the Spanish Netherlands. Cardinal Cisneros, appointed grand inquisitor in 1507, had been responsible for mass conversions in Granada at the turn of the century. He was a driving force for the Inquisition, especially during the final decade of his life. Founded in 1536, the Portuguese Inquisition was especially violent toward conversos. The country's population had been increased approximately 10 percent by Jews expelled from Spanish dominions during the latter 15th century. Those not expelled in 1497 were forced to convert, and many still practiced Judaism secretly. Because numerous conversos immigrated to Goa, that city in India had an office of the Portuguese Inquisition. For the same reason, Spain authorized tribunals in Lima, Mexico City, and Cartagena.

The Roman Inquisition was founded in 1544, specifically in reaction to the Protestant Reformation. This Inquisition achieved its main goal of preventing the spread of Protestantism in the Italian Peninsula. Whereas other inquisitions were instigated by secular powers, the Holy Office of the Inquisition in Rome was established by the pope.

Thus the work of its tribunals superseded that of any other court, including ecclesiastical courts. Nevertheless, in independent city-states and republics, secular authorities monitored Inquisition activities and severe punishment or extradition to Rome usually required their permission. In Venice, for example, lay assessors sat in on Inquisition hearings. Observers usually were not, however, permitted to have access to pertinent documents in most areas. The accusation and trial of an alleged heretic were always administered by Inquisition officials. If the accused refused to recant and the trial proceeded to the stage of sentencing, the individual was then handed over to secular authorities, who carried out the punishment.

The procedure for an Inquisition investigation usually began with the accused's being under suspicion of Judaism, Islam, Protestantism, witchcraft, or extreme mysticism. Teresa of Ávila (1515–82), one of the most renowned mystics of the Renaissance, happened to be a member of a family of conversos, a background that contributed to accusations against her. Teresa, who was canonized in 1622, was called before the Spanish Inquisition by members of the Carmelite order. Teresa had broken away from this order to establish the Discalced Carmelites ("unshod" and wearing sandals instead of shoes). Thus she is an example of a devout and well-known Catholic woman who nevertheless was charged and imprisoned for writing an independent spiritual text; only her powerful friends prevented severe punishment. Countless others were not so fortunate. The most famous victim of the Inquisition was probably the scientist Galileo Galilei (1564–1642), placed under house arrest for the final nine years of his life. Numerous others had their writings banned and destroyed. Those victims burned at the stake included Giordano Bruno (1548–1600), Étienne Dolet (1509–46), and William Tyndale (c. 1494–1536).

In addition to the suspects mentioned, priests who took advantage of their authority to obtain sexual favors were also investigated, and sometimes even punished. Accusers for any Inquisition-related offense could remain anonymous, and they often received a percentage of the suspect's property if it was confiscated. In Spain, Portugal, India, and Latin America, there was no appeal of an Inquisition tribunal's decision. In the Roman Inquisition,

however, an appeal could be made to the Supreme Congregation.

Archival research completed during the 1990s has revealed that the sensationalist history of the Inquisition should be somewhat revised. Although several thousands of individuals indeed were put to death, many more thousands were given light sentences. First offenders had the mercy of the court, often required only to pay a small fine. Those imprisoned often were released on parole after serving only part of their term. Repeat offenders, however, found themselves in deep trouble, and those who refused to recant could be burned at the stake. Those who recanted at the last minute were beheaded or strangled before the fire was lit. These public burnings of human beings, so hideous to us today, were attended by huge crowds who felt compelled to witness such "edicts of faith," or *autos-da-fé* in Spanish.

INDEX OF PROHIBITED BOOKS

Censorship of books occurred at the beginning of the Christian era. From that time until the 15th century, however, *"books"* were handwritten books, which simply did not reach many people. With the advent of the age of printing in conjunction with the Protestant Reformation a few decades later, Catholic officials as well as secular rulers, such as Charles V (1500–1558), began publishing edicts prohibiting hundreds of books. Some of the lists published by the Spanish Inquisition contained some 2,000 names and titles. If the author was known, everything that person had written could be censored; the noted humanist Desiderius Erasmus (c. 1466–1536) provides a good example of a writer who was listed by name in the edicts. Otherwise a specific work was listed by its title. By the 1520s, Inquisition officials were policing libraries and bookstores, sometimes with the full cooperation of civil authorities in most cities. Punishment for possessing a prohibited book was harsh: Those found guilty were excommunicated and occasionally executed, and their property was confiscated. The theology faculty at the University of Paris issued the first printed list of banned books in 1544.

As the Reformation gained converts, the papacy became sufficiently alarmed to establish a commission to compile an Index of Prohibited Books. This list was published in 1559, and its severity modified by the revised version of 1564. The Council of Trent authorized the papacy to issue this Tridentine Index, based on that of 1559. Ten rules in the index influenced all further decisions concerning prohibited books, including the provision that some books could be distributed after objectionable passages were expurgated. Today we have numerous examples of seemingly innocuous books from the Renaissance, such as dictionaries, that have struck-through passages because they contained "suspect" information. For a long time, any mentions of sexual parts of the body, of astrology, and of other taboo topics were blacked out by Inquisition inspectors. The Catholic Church's Index of Prohibited Books was not officially withdrawn until 1966. Much research concerning the effects of the index on Renaissance readers remains to be done. Instead of preventing individuals from reading banned items, the lists may have whetted the curiosity of more than a few people, making them eager to see those very books.

Church Councils

Issues and problems of the Catholic Church were discussed at councils, which were lengthy meetings of international significance attended by ecclesiasts such as abbots and bishops. Their decisions were supposed to be binding, even on the pope. Because the councils were of such long duration, attendees usually were from the moneyed classes or were subsidized by wealthy individuals or institutions. Representatives to the councils sometimes had to leave for months at a time to attend to business elsewhere, a circumstance that often shifted the power structure for those remaining. During the 15th century, the Councils of Constance, Basel, and Florence were the most important. During the 16th century, the Council of Lateran V and the Council of Trent were especially noteworthy.

COUNCIL OF CONSTANCE (1414–1418)

The Council of Constance opened with three popes claiming the papal throne, its main purpose to heal the Great Schism in the Catholic Church. After all

three popes were deposed, the council elected Pope Martin V (1368–1431) in 1417. Its other goals were to stamp out heresy and to begin certain reforms, for example, in the Franciscan order. The actions against heresy included the desecration of the corpse of the English reformer John Wycliffe (c. 1328–84) and the trial and burning at the stake of Bohemian dissenter Jan Hus (c. 1372–1415).

COUNCIL OF BASEL (1431–1449, WITH SEVERAL BREAKS)

Besides being the longest church council of the Renaissance, the Council of Basel is remembered for asserting its authority over the papacy. Not long after the council opened, the pope ordered it closed to protect his supremacy, but in vain. With the support of the emperor, the Republic of Venice, and other secular powers, those who attended reaffirmed the council's right to determine ecclesiastical policy. This attitude was part of the conciliar movement of the Renaissance by which church councils became the supreme authority in church matters. An important aspect of this movement was that councils would meet regularly, regardless of whether the pope agreed. Because of the pope's hostility, the Council of Basel went so far as to elect an antipope, but he abdicated when the council closed in 1449. Those who attended the council voted that those council members who had elected the antipope were to be excommunicated for heresy.

COUNCIL OF FLORENCE (COUNCIL OF FERRARA-FLORENCE, 1438–1445)

Opening in Ferrara, the Council of Florence moved to Florence in 1439, then to Rome in 1442. Convened for the purpose of attempting to unite the Byzantine Church with the Roman Church, this council originally had been part of the Council of Basel. The delegates from Greece, however, requested a location closer to their homeland. The eastern emperor John VIII Palaeologus (1390–1448) was in attendance with his retinue. He was inclined to agree with the council's decisions because he desperately needed military aid against the Turks. Disputed points of doctrine were settled fairly easily, but the issue of papal authority over the Byzantine

Church eventually caused the synod in Byzantium to reject the decree of unification. The Council of Florence established the principle of papal supremacy not only over the Byzantine Church, but also over any future councils.

COUNCIL OF LATERAN V (1512–1517)

Held in the Lateran Basilica in Rome, the Fifth Lateran Council (as it is also called) was convened by Pope Julius II to countermand the ineffective but schismatic Council of Pisa. The latter council (1511–12), instigated by the king of France, Louis XII (1462–1515), and initially supported by Holy Roman Emperor Maximilian I (1459–1519), attempted to depose Julius II. Julius died in 1513, and his successor, Leo X (Giovanni de' Medici, 1475–1521), vowed to continue the Fifth Lateran Council and set aside any decisions made by the Council of Pisa. An average of approximately 110 prelates attended this council, which was obviously considered an important undertaking in the eyes of the Catholic Church. Besides confirming articles of faith, such as the soul's individuality, this council created a commission for ecclesiastical reform and launched the plans for a crusade against the Turks. This crusade may have served to unify Christian Europe more than any other accomplishment of the council.

While this council was in process, Leo issued the sale of an indulgence in 1516 that would become a crucial focus for Luther's protests. The Council of Latern V closed, however, in March 1517, seven months before Luther posted his Ninety-five Theses on the Wittenberg church door. This council could not have foreseen that Protestantism would develop into a major confrontation that should have been addressed by its members.

COUNCIL OF TRENT (1545–1563, WITH SEVERAL LONG BREAKS)

The Council of Trent (Trento, Italy) was the first major Counter-Reformation council of the 16th century. Its focus was on countering the threat of Protestantism and reforming the church from within. The council opened in the hope that the Lutherans, Calvinists, and Zwinglians might be drawn back into the Catholic Church, but issues such as transubstantiation of the Eucharist (see pages 38–39) made this goal unattainable. Reconciliation would no longer be possible. Plans for internal reform of the Catholic Church were more successful, with revisions of the Vulgate Bible, catechism, breviary, and missal accomplished before the end of the century. The Congregation of the Index, for the Index of Prohibited Books, was also established. Pope Pius IV (1499–1565) spent the last few years of his pontificate directing the Council of Trent, publishing its doctrinal decisions in a bull of 1564.

Counter-Reformation

The Council of Trent gave its imprimatur to Counter-Reformation policies, including a new era of censorship. Carlo Borromeo (1538–84), one of the most famous reforming cardinals of the 16th century, greatly influenced the decisions of the council because the pope heeded his advice. Borromeo not only "purified" church music, but also had most of the ornamentation removed from the cathedral of Milan, where he was bishop. Church leaders referred to these policies as reforms; the term *Counter-Reformation* was not used for this movement until the 18th century. In addition to opposing Protestantism and virtually eliminating it in the Italian Peninsula, the Counter-Reformation attempted to curb abuses in ecclesiastical administration by imposing stricter discipline on the orders and on priests. The papacy became a stronger force within the church, and Catholics began to think of themselves as papists (see pages 30–34). The Council of Trent also affirmed traditional devotional practices, such as the veneration of saints and Catholic mysticism. As a result, many artists benefited from commissions to sculpt or paint devotional images, and architects were hired to erect new chapels.

The Counter-Reformation had a deleterious effect on some Renaissance art, the most famous example of which is censorship in the Sistine Chapel. Michelangelo and his assistants painted the ceiling of the Sistine Chapel during the early 16th century; then three decades later he painted the fresco of *The Last Judgment* on the wall behind the altar and completed it in 1541. The latter work caused quite a scandal, partly because of the censorious nature of the Counter-Reformation. The accusations included charges of heresy and immodesty, most based on several male figures whose genitalia were visible. Initially, in 1564, the fresco was going to be destroyed. Then the decision was made to overpaint the offensive parts, but even this step did not satisfy everyone at the Vatican. Finally, modest apparel (similar to bathing suits) was painted over the lower torsos of the figures and the fresco as a whole was saved.

Bible

Humanistic scholarship of the 15th and 16th centuries made major improvements in the textual accuracy of the Christian Bible. (For a discussion of Reformation Bibles and Hebrew Bibles, see pages 52–54.) Even though the lists of prohibited books included some new editions of the New Testament and of the entire Bible, the Catholic Church welcomed new scholarship correcting errors in the Vulgate Bible. The first book printed in the Renaissance was the Vulgate, in 1456, called the Gutenberg Bible after its printer, Johannes Gutenberg (c. 1394/99–1468). Thought to have been written by Saint Jerome in the late fourth or early fifth century, the Latin translation known as the Vulgate (in the vulgar, or common, Latin tongue) was the standard version used by the church. Advances in Greek and Hebrew philology during the Renaissance contributed to a better knowledge of the biblical text. In addition, manuscripts not previously studied by European scholars became available. Greek biblical manuscripts taken to Basel from Constantinople in the early 15th century, for example, were consulted by Desiderius Erasmus (c. 1466–1536) and others who worked on the New Testament. The French scholar Jacques Lefèvre d'Étaples drew upon his humanistic training to apply comparative methods of textual analysis to the Pauline Epistles and to the Old and New Testaments. He also published a gospel commentary and a French translation of the Bible that was later used by Calvin. In his attempt to reconcile and harmonize variant texts, Lefèvre d'Étaples provided a model derived from pious Christianity. Erasmus based his biblical scholarship on the theological writings of church fathers, tempered by the French scholar's respect for the text.

Several scholars and churchmen collaborated on the first major multilingual printed Bible, the

2.6 Leaf from a Gutenberg Bible. Mainz, c. 1454–55. (Photograph courtesy of Sotheby's, Inc., © 2003)

Complutensian Polyglot Bible (the title taken from the university in Spain where they worked). With numerous manuscripts gathered by Cardinal Francisco Jiménez de Cisneros (1436–1517) as its source, this massive six-volume publication of 1522 featured the Latin Vulgate of the Old Testament alongside the texts in Hebrew and the Septuagint (Old Testament in Greek and Aramaic). The New Testament had both the Vulgate text and the original Greek. The other famous multilingual Bible of the Renaissance was the eight-volume 1572 production by Christophe Plantin (c. 1520–89) in Antwerp, with texts in Hebrew (new fonts cut for this), Greek, Chaldaic, and the Latin Vulgate. The standard edition of the Vulgate itself was accomplished by Robert Estienne (1503–59) in 1538–40. His Greek New Testament of 1544–51 was the first printed Bible that arranged chapters in numbered verses.

Religious Literature, Dramatic Presentations, and Preaching

During the Renaissance, most nonclassical literature had a religious component, either overt or allegorical. This section discusses overtly Catholic literature, including devotional treatises, books of prayer, religious drama, and preaching. Devotional literature was based in a firm medieval tradition of such works, with the addition of the *ars moriendi* (art of dying) treatises in response to the apocalyptic disasters of plague and war during the 14th and early 15th centuries. Many of these publications were illustrated with gruesome woodcuts, and the skeletons of the Dance of Death were a popular image in prints. In general, the 15th-century books of devotion concentrated on personal meditation and spirituality, and 16th-century examples added activities involving charitable acts. Devotional literature had something for everyone, from the urban merchant who could temporarily escape the bustle of the city by reading (or by listening to someone read) the meditations of a desert hermit, to the cloistered nun who experienced mystical ecstasy through a text such as Teresa of Ávila's *Castillo interior* (Inner castle, 1588). The two most popular devotional figures were Christ and the Virgin, and the Passion (the torment and death of Jesus) dominated many treatises encouraging the imitation of Christ. For Catholics, the Sacred Heart and the Five Wounds were especially powerful. Numerous woodcut examples of these images were produced, and most Catholic homes, however modest, displayed them in a woodcut or small painting. Marian devotion (dedication to the Virgin Mary) often focused on the Immaculate Conception, which refers not to the conception of Christ by Mary but to the conception of Mary by her mother, Ann through divine intervention. This close connection between the Virgin and her mother resulted in depictions of Ann and her young daughter, many of which show the child holding a book and evidently learning to read. The veneration of Ann, especially in northern Europe, helped to encourage literacy among women.

Books of prayers were meant for individual devotion as opposed to liturgical works and vocal prayers shared by a congregation. By far the most popular type for Catholics were the books of hours, produced during the Renaissance in both manuscript and printed formats. Ranging from luxurious productions copied by hand and illuminated on large sheets of vellum to tiny "girdle books" attached to one's belt, books of hours were used several times each day. Each of the eight canonical Hours of the Virgin was associated with a particular image from her life, usually beginning with the Annunciation for matins (early morning) and ending with the Coronation (late evening). These images were visual reminders of the importance of the Virgin to devout Catholics.

Religious drama was performed both inside and outside the church setting. Civic religious plays were popular throughout Europe, often patronized by wealthy sponsors such as confraternities as well as individuals. Beginning as early as the mid-14th century, religious drama treated the Passion, the miracles of the saints, and the battle between virtue and vice or Satan's struggle to control the soul. Passion plays, also called mystery plays, involved the participation of the entire town and usually lasted several days. These multimedia events, performed outdoors, could focus on an event in the life of Christ or a saint or summarize the entire spiritual life of humankind. They were elaborate, expensive undertakings, with decorative allegorical costumes and musical accompaniment. The most ornate religious dramas were performed during Holy Week (Easter week) and on a patron saint's day. Morality plays depicting the struggle between vice and virtue became increasingly popular during the 16th century, when church authorities began to prohibit Passion plays and miracle plays. A new category of religious drama developed during the 16th century as humanistic writers created Latin drama concerning the saints and biblical figures. Especially in Jesuit and Benedictine grammar schools these plays were performed into the 18th century.

Renaissance preachers had several resources to aid them as they prepared their sermons. Both Catholics and Protestants used homiletic collections, such as commonplace books concerning the vices and virtues, books of exemplary lives, and the *Golden Legend* of Jacobus de Voragine, as well as preaching manuals. The manuals benefited from humanistic works on classical eloquence, as preaching was considered the sacred form of eloquent speech. Humanists also edited collections of homilies and sermons from church fathers, making some available for the first time and improving others. Renaissance preaching also took advantage of corrected biblical texts in their exposition of the Scriptures. The church councils addressed the problem of corrupted preaching, especially the Fifth Lateran Council, which threatened excommunication of rabble-rousers who preached apocalyptic messages. Bishops were charged with responsibility for preachers in their diocese and were instructed to monitor their public activities. Preaching experienced a revival during the 16th century, when some bishops themselves became famous as preachers.

PROTESTANT REFORMATION

Educated as a boy by Brethren of the Common Life, Martin Luther attended the University of Erfurt and was ordained a priest in 1507. At the University of Wittenberg, he became professor of biblical studies. As an Augustinian, he was put in charge of several monasteries of his order. When Luther posted his Theses on the Wittenberg church in 1517 to protest the sale of indulgences, his purpose was to reform abuses as a member of the Catholic community. But the text of his Theses was being discussed across Europe, and Luther himself defended it against the noted theologian Johann Eck (1486–1543) in the Leipzig Disputation of 1519. The pope was compelled to excommunicate Luther the following year. After speaking out at the 1521 Diet of Worms, Luther was condemned to death, but he escaped to Wartburg castle with the aid of the elector of Saxony. During his 10 months there, Luther translated the New Testament into German, probably his greatest achievement of the Protestant Reformation. Twelve years later his translation of the entire Bible into German appeared in print. In 1524 Luther renounced his association with the Augustinian order and married a former nun.

For the remainder of his life, Luther focused on taking his message of reformation to the people at large. He translated the liturgy into German, so that the entire congregation chanted with the priest, and he wrote hymns and possibly music for a few of them. Luther was the first to compose catechism booklets illustrated with woodcuts that children could study by themselves; instead of listening to a lecture by a priest reading from the catechism, a child could sit alone and study the text while being instructed by simple woodcut images that reinforced the message. Luther had a huge following during his last two decades. Protestant hymns influenced German poets, many of whom wrote lyrics specifically for religious uses. Although Luther believed that special individuals should be appointed to perform certain religious ceremonies, he taught that church hierarchy was not necessary for salvation. Instead, salvation could be found in the communion of a devout congregation. Men and women worshiped together, in a church without the extravagant devotional imagery prevalent in many Catholic sanctuaries (see page 53 for information on iconoclasm).

German princes who supported Martin Luther submitted a decree to the 1529 Diet of Speyer that began with the word *Protestatio* to protest the banning of Lutheranism in their provinces. Thus the reform movement publicly begun by Martin Luther

2.7 *Martin Luther at the Wittenberg church door in 1517. Woodcut, German School, 16th century.* (Private Collection/Bridgeman Art Library)

GENES. VI, & VII.

Aduersus imminens diluuium arca excitatur.

*Nunciat effusis perdendum fluctibus orbem
Numen, vt humanum mergeret imbre genus:
Ingentemq́ iubet fieri compagibus arcam,
Qua Noëlus seruet seq́ suamq́ domum.*

*2.8 Noah's ark in an illustrated book of Genesis.
Woodcut designed by Bernard Salomon. Lyon, 1558.
Such illustrated biblical stories were very popular with
adults, and even children who could not read Latin
might learn from the pictures.* (Photograph courtesy of
Sotheby's, Inc., © 2003)

in 1517 became known as Protestantism. Although heretical individuals had previously broken away from the Catholic Church, their followers either were annihilated, decided to recant, or went underground. Violent fighting occurred again in France during the 16th century during the Wars of Religion (see pages 50–51). Nevertheless Luther, along with Jean Calvin (1509–64) and Huldrych Zwingli (1484–1531), successfully led spiritual revolutions throughout northern Europe.

The Protestant Reformation succeeded for several reasons where earlier attempts at breaking away from the Catholic Church had failed. The Great Schism in the Catholic Church, which ended only in 1417, destroyed the historic unity of its government. Simultaneously, the Black Death destroyed entire communities and led to unqualified individuals

being appointed as local religious leaders. Both of these events led to abuses of clerical power that were vehemently criticized by reformers of the 15th century. The 16th-century reformers were driven by their hatred of clerical corruption and inspired by the biblical studies of humanistic scholars. Many of Luther's enemies, including the inquisitors and their assistants, had also been the enemies of certain humanists in the previous century. Finally, in Germany, where the Protestant Reformation first succeeded, local princes and others created their own autonomy from the Holy Roman Emperor by supporting Martin Luther, the new popular force in Germany. Luther had made the strategic decision not to support the German peasants in their uprising of 1524, enhancing his stature in the eyes of the German princes.

Spread of the Reformation

BOHEMIA

Religious reform in Bohemia was rooted in incipient nationalism at the beginning of the 15th century. Jan Hus (c. 1372–1415), executed at the Council of Constance, had advocated a classless society and communal ownership of property. He also spoke out against clerical immorality in his sermons and translated a prohibited work by Wycliffe into Czech. After the Hussite Wars (discussed later), a reform group known as the Bohemian Brethren, or Unity of the Brothers, spread in Bohemia. They believed in communal living and were located in rural areas. During the 1530s, the Brethren became interested in Lutheran theology, especially his doctrine of the Eucharist. Persecuted by the emperor, many of them fled to Poland and formed alliances with the Calvinists there. (Poland welcomed religious exiles of all persuasion.) Those who remained in Czech lands established the head of their church in Moravia and were the spiritual ancestors of present-day Moravians. They followed a strict Calvinist version of Reformed Protestantism.

Hussite Wars
The rebellion in central Europe known as the Hussite Wars began when local parishes in Bohemia

drove away their Catholic priests to protest the murder of Jan Hus. As the protest movement grew, Hussites became bolder in their actions. In 1419 a group of angry Hussites marched through the streets of Prague to the town hall, where they threw the magistrates out of the windows. This famous Defenestration of Prague accelerated the conflict, as King Sigismund led a crusade against the Bohemian rebels after Pope Martin V declared war in 1420. In spite of repeated invasions by Imperial troops, the Hussites held firm. Their representatives were invited to the Council of Basel in 1433, but the opposing groups could not agree to a peace treaty. In 1436 the conflict was settled by the Compacta of Prague, which also recognized the Czech national church and Sigismund as king of Bohemia.

GERMANY

Philipp Melanchthon (1497–1560), a leading theologian of the Lutheran Reformation, assumed Luther's position of leadership while the latter was held in the Wartburg (see pages 46–48). Melanchthon had defended those who preached in the German vernacular, a practice forbidden by the church. During the 1530 Diet of Augsburg, Melanchthon wrote and Luther approved the Augsburg Confession. This historic document set forth the new confession of faith, which included a list of ecclesiastical abuses that the Lutherans demanded be corrected. It also set forth Luther's conviction that faith, not good works, merited divine grace. This doctrine was known as justification by faith alone. Luther also argued that priests, monks, and nuns be allowed to marry. A revised version of the Augsburg Confession was published in 1531; as a result the doctrinal points of Lutheranism could be easily disseminated. The printing press, in fact, was a major agent in the spread of Protestantism. Anticlerical prints and images on printed broadsides proliferated from Reformation presses. Members of the clergy were sometimes shown as deformed or involved in obscene acts. These publications served as an important tool of propaganda, especially among people who could not read. In popular German poetry such as the *Fastnachtspiele*, the satire often extended beyond the clergy to ridicule the pope.

SWITZERLAND

Reformed Protestantism spread in French-speaking Switzerland through the leadership of Jean Calvin (1509–64). Trained at French universities in humanities and civil law, Calvin was destined for a career in the church. After the Augsburg Confession, however, he became attracted to Lutheran doctrine and fell into disfavor. Calvin fled from Paris to Basel, where in 1536 he first published his *Institutio religionis christianae* (Institute of the Christian religion). Invited to Geneva to help spread the Reformation, he ran into difficulties with the Zwinglians (discussed later). This group, based in Bern, disagreed with some of the stricter aspects of Calvin's proposed church discipline, and he moved to Strasbourg. There, Calvin preached and wrote for three years, translating his

2.9 Portrait of Jean Calvin in his study. Engraving in his Works, *1671. (Note that books in the Renaissance were typically shelved with their spine to the wall).* (Photograph courtesy of Sotheby's, © 2003)

Institutes into French. Finally he settled in Geneva, where he established a dogmatic government that functioned as a watchdog of public morality.

Huldrych Zwingli (1484–1531) helped spread Reformed Protestantism in German-speaking Switzerland. In 1518 Zwingli moved to Zurich, appointed as a priest in the Old Minster, and the following year he preached the first Reformation sermons in the Swiss Confederation. Zwingli began publishing Protestant tracts, denouncing the authority of bishops and the pope. Zwingli's break with the church was initially based on the issue of the celibacy of priests. In a public disputation of 1523, he persuaded the Zurich council to adopt his theses and announce its independence from Catholic authority. In a debate with an advocate of the pope, Zwingli had successfully defended 67 theses detailing his beliefs. In 1531, Swiss cantons loyal to Catholicism attacked Zurich and Zwingli was killed during the battle.

THE NETHERLANDS

The Netherlands had a diversity of religions, including a large community of converted Jews in Amsterdam. Anabaptists (whose name means "rebaptized"), considered heretical by Luther, had several sects in the Netherlands. Believing that infant baptism was insufficient, they required that adults be baptized. As pacifists, they refused to take oaths of allegiance or to serve in the military. Thousands of Anabaptists were executed for their aberrant doctrinal stance and unorthodox behavior. Menno Simons (1496–1561) was a leader of Dutch Anabaptists. Renouncing practices such as polygamy and public nudity, for which Anabaptists had become infamous, Simons called for his followers to live meekly, away from the world. Adherents to Anabaptism outside the Netherlands, such as members of the Swiss Brethren, joined the Mennonites to escape persecution.

The two major Reformation groups in the Netherlands were Lutherans and Calvinists, and the latter became the dominant force. Dutch Calvinists seemingly took the fiercely moralistic overtones of Calvin's doctrine and transformed it into an aggressively militaristic crusade against Catholic troops sent by the king of Spain. In the Netherlands, Calvinism helped propel the United Provinces to independence in the 17th century.

ENGLAND

Henry VIII, king of England (1491–1547), was responsible for establishing a modified form of Protestantism in England. Because his wife, Catherine of Aragon (1485–1536), was unable to produce an heir, the king wanted to marry Anne Boleyn (1507–36). When the pope refused to grant him a divorce or annulment, Henry denied all papal authority in England, and he assumed the role of head of the Church of England (Anglican Church) in 1534. In doctrine, the Church of England followed a compromise between Protestantism and Catholicism, its rituals explained in the Book of Common Prayer (1549–59, see pages 52–53). After Henry broke away from the church, the statesman Thomas Cromwell (c. 1485–1540) became his secretary as well as vicar-general of the Church of England. Cromwell engineered the dissolution of English monasteries between 1536 and 1540, when most of the property was seized and distributed to members of the nobility. This redistribution of property worth millions of dollars, more than any other factor, assured the success of the Reformation in England. Cromwell also had Miles Coverdale's (1488–1568) English translation of the Bible published in 1535, and he commissioned work for the Great Bible of 1539.

During the reign of Mary I (1516–58, ruled 1553–58), Protestants were persecuted in England. The daughter of a Spanish princess and married to the king of Spain, Mary had been raised in a strict Catholic household. Her chief goals as queen were to exterminate Protestant rebels and to restore England to the Catholic fold. After her death, Elizabeth I (1533–1603) established herself as head of the Church of England and reinstated Protestantism. During the first decade of her reign, a group of reformers voiced the complaint that the Church of England was not strict enough in its doctrine and standards of behavior. They became known as Puritans for the purity of their morality and beliefs.

SCOTLAND

Calvinism prevailed in Scotland, opening the way for Scotland to become politically united with England in the early 17th century. Mary, queen of Scots (1542–87), a devout Catholic, was never accepted by her subjects because of the rising tide of Calvinist faith. The reformer who did more than anyone else to establish Protestantism in Scotland was John Knox (c. 1513–72). Fleeing to Europe after Mary I became queen, he met with Calvin in Geneva. Although Knox was banned from England by Elizabeth because of his rather unflattering book *First Blast of the Trumpet against the Monstrous Regiment of Women* (1558), his influence in Scotland was pervasive. He helped write the Scottish Book of Common Order.

FRANCE

French Protestants, known as Huguenots, practiced Calvinism. Their first synod was established in Paris in 1559. During the reign of Francis I (1494–1547), he at first was tolerant of religious reformers, partly because of his sister, Marguerite of Navarre (1492–1549), who had evangelical tendencies and sheltered dissidents at her court. But in 1534 the Affaire des Placards caused the king to respond with ruthless persecutions. Broadsides (*placards*) denouncing the mass had been posted all over Paris, including the door of the royal bedchamber. This event demonstrated the radical nature of French Protestantism, which until then had not been fully understood. Ten years later, Francis permitted the slaughter of Waldenses in Provence who had formally renounced the Catholic Church. These violent actions toward reformers in France set the stage for the Wars of Religion (discussed in the following section).

Wars of Religion in France

The kings of France were closely connected to the papacy and the Catholic Church; their oath of coronation included a vow to eradicate heretics and support the faith. One of the king's titles, in fact, was "Most Christian King." To understand the forces that led to the eight devastating Wars of Religion in France between 1562 and 1598, one must look at the personal relationships among several families. The stage was set for violence in 1559, after the death of Henry II, who had been planning to persecute heretics, notably the Huguenots. His son, Francis II (1544–60), was only 15 when he became king. Francis's wife was Mary, queen of Scots (1542–87), who happened to be the niece of the two Guise brothers, Charles of Guise, cardinal of Lorraine (1525–74),

and Francis of Lorraine, duke of Guise (1519–63). The latter was a militant Catholic who dominated court politics during the two years of Francis's reign, causing a group of Protestants to plot to kidnap the young king in 1560. Their plot was exposed, and hundreds were hanged in retribution, many of their bodies swinging for days from the window ledges of the palace in Amboise for all to see. This massacre galvanized Huguenot members of the nobility as well as those in the middle and lower classes.

When Francis II died, his brother, a boy of 10, was crowned as Charles IX (1550–74). Their mother, Catherine de' Medici (1519–89), acted as regent, even after Charles was of age. She was the real power behind the throne until 1588. Initially Catherine de' Medici attempted to establish a compromise between Protestants and Catholics, allowing Protestants the freedom to preach openly. This moderate path led only to heightened hostility among powerful Catholics, who used the printing press to propagandize against the Huguenots. War was the result; Catholic troops mowed down Protestants as they gathered to worship outside city walls, as required by the government. Huguenots once again plotted to kidnap the king, and he panicked, ordering that the Huguenot leaders in Paris be assassinated. His order was applied in the broadest sense, and some 2,000 people were killed in Paris on August 24, 1572, the infamous Saint Bartholomew's Day massacre. France was in religious turmoil for much of the next quarter-century. Charles IX was succeeded in 1574 by his brother, Henry III (1551–80), who failed to produce a male heir. The nearest heir was Henry of Navarre (1553–1610), an arch-Protestant who had fought alongside Gaspard of Coligny (1519–72), commander in chief of the Huguenots. When Henry III was assassinated in 1589, Henry of Navarre, Catherine's son-in-law, claimed the throne as Henry IV. He converted to Catholicism, uttering the famous words "Paris is well worth a mass."

Theological Elements of the Movements

Hussites were adherents of Utraquism (so named from the Latin *sub utraque specie*, of both kinds) because they demanded to take wine from the chalice as well as the wafer of the host during the Eucharist. In this doctrine, they did not view themselves as breaking away from Catholicism. On the contrary, Hussites thought that having the eucharistic wine aligned them with the traditions of the early church in its purer form. The Council of Basel, in fact, allowed them the wine, but this decision was not ratified by the pope. Lutherans differed from Calvinists and Zwinglians in the belief that during the Eucharist the wine and bread were transformed into the blood and body of Christ (in a variation of Catholic doctrine). Calvinists and Zwinglians did not believe that the wine and bread were actually transformed. The Zwinglians split with Luther on their interpretation of the Eucharist, which Zwingli said was merely commemorative (a doctrine called sacramentarianism at the time). Calvinism was a severe form of Protestantism that demanded church attendance, forbade most worldly pleasures, and emphasized the doctrine of predestination. Anabaptists, who included several sects, required adults to be baptized, even those who had been baptized as infants. Each sect had specific doctrinal rules. The Swiss Brethren, for example, had no association with secular government, believed in the Zwinglian form of the Eucharist, permitted only adherents who had been rebaptized to partake of it, and abstained from all secular pleasures. Anglican theology was the closest to Catholicism of any Protestant sect, and the Church of England was considered a middle road between the two main ideologies. The Book of Common Prayer was carefully worded in its doctrine so as not to subvert the Eucharist or other sacraments. What was subverted was the supremacy of the pope as head of the church, a political change rather than a religious revolution.

Church Hierarchy

The pope or any other central authority was superfluous in Lutheran doctrine because ministers were to be elected by their congregation or by local Lutheran secular leaders. Zwingli followed this model, with an additional emphasis of the pastor as a shepherd caring for his flock. He also envisioned

more of a separation between the minister, who was divinely inspired, and the congregation, who received his message. By the end of the 16th century, however, a Lutheran hierarchy, consisting of ministers and their superintendents, both answering to an administrative body, was established. Calvinism had several offices for the clergy: The minister, or pastor, taught the Scripture; the deacon was responsible for administering to the poor; and the presbyter, or elder of the church, worked with the pastor when members of the congregation needed to be disciplined. Calvin based his organization of these offices on examples from the New Testament. Unlike Protestant sects on the Continent, the congregation of the Anglican Church did not elect its priests. The English monarch appointed bishops, and bishops appointed all members of the clergy without consulting the congregation or secular officials. The monarch was the head of the church but was not a priest and could not consecrate bishops.

Early Lutheran churches were plainer than Catholic churches, but they included an altar for the Eucharist. The altar often was a table with a cloth placed over it, with a paten and chalice for the Communion service. Instead of an elaborately painted altarpiece, many Lutheran churches had a simple carved crucifix. Holy Communion was truly a communal experience, as every member of the congregation was permitted to partake of both the bread and the wine. Participants were also encouraged to join in the singing of hymns.

Protestant Bible

Part of the break with the Catholic Church involved use of the Scripture. Protestants believed in the Bible as the only divine authority, and in the right of individuals to read the text (or at least hear it read) in their native language. Religion became more private, with personal Bible study recommended as part of one's spiritual life. As noted, Luther's translation of the complete Bible into German was published in 1534, but sections had been published since 1522. Various authors translated Luther's High German into Low German, thereby spreading the text to many more readers. Between 1541 and 1550, the first Bibles in Swedish and Danish were published, but a Bible for Dutch Protestants did not appear until 1637.

At the beginning of the 16th century, printing a Bible translated into English was not permitted in England. William Tyndale (c. 1494–1536) moved to Antwerp and translated the Bible into English and was burned at the stake for his efforts. The English Bible by Miles Coverdale (1488–1568), printed on the Continent in 1535, was sold in England. Subsequently, church authorities in England asked him to create a new edition, which became known as the Great Bible (1539). Several humanistic scholars who had fled from England during the reign of Mary I (1516–58) moved to Geneva, where they produced the Geneva Bible (1553–58). This English translation was the accepted version for the remainder of the Renaissance. The Bishops' Bible of 1568, lavishly illustrated with woodcuts, went through several editions. Finally, the King James Bible of 1611 became the standard English translation for nearly four centuries. Most of the text was based on that of Tyndale.

Religious Literature and Book of Common Prayer

Biblical exegesis spurred the Reformation. Because Protestant doctrine and daily practice were based in the Bible, interpreting it correctly was crucial. Understanding of the Old Testament was thought to be necessary for a more thorough knowledge of Christ, and leaders such as Luther (Psalms) and Calvin (Song of Songs) published exegetical works concerning books of the Bible. Luther was especially prolific in publishing Reformation works in general. Of approximately 500 Reformation texts published in German in 1523, for example, more than four hundred were by Luther. Both Geneva and Lyon (in southeastern France) became strongholds of Protestant printing. Verse translations of the Psalms became popular among Protestant poets, and famous men and women of the Bible inspired playwrights. Satirical treatments of the pope and other Catholic figures were effective tools of the Reformation. Some of these were dramatic texts that ridiculed church authorities in public performances. Finally, by the latter 16th century, Reformation histories had begun to appear, notably John Knox's *History of the Reformation of Religion in Scotland* in 1587 (incomplete edition).

The Book of Common Prayer first was published in 1549, with a revised version in 1552. Thomas Cranmer, archbishop of Canterbury (1489–1556), helped formulate the text with the assistance of a commission appointed by the king. (The text was not finalized until 1662.) The first version followed Lutheran doctrine, but in wording that recalled the Catholic mass. This wording was changed in the 1552 edition. The priest could celebrate Holy Communion only with the congregation, and the group as a whole would partake of both the wine and the wafer. Prayers for the dead were included in 1549; these were expurgated for the subsequent edition, along with any mention of purgatory or of an altar, which was referred to as a table. Finally, by 1552, the Eucharist would be only a commemoration; that change aligned the Anglican Church with the Reformed Protestantism of the Continent.

Iconoclasm

Although ephemeral printed images and texts served the purposes of the Reformation, Luther and his supporters spoke out against ornate imagery in churches. In a letter of 1522, for example, he wrote, "I condemn images . . . so that trust will not be put in them, as has happened so far and still happens. They would fall of their own accord if an instructed people knew that they were nothing in God's eyes" (Elmer 2000, p. 341). Protestant iconoclasm resulted in altars being removed or their ornamentation cut or broken away. Luther envisioned a pure communion between God and the congregation, with the altar transformed into a simple table laid with a cloth, as if for a meal. Zwinglianism was as strict as Calvinism in its iconoclasm, so all works of art were removed from churches in Zurich and the mass was suppressed. There was no place in Protestant churches of the Renaissance for gilt statues, stained glass, and other types of decoration found in Catholic churches.

This iconoclastic attitude caused the wholesale destruction of innumerable works of art, especially in northern Europe and England. Because of Protestantism, England and the Netherlands lost much of their Gothic and early Renaissance religious art. The

Lollards, John Wycliffe's followers, were avid icono-clasts. The enthusiasm with which Catholic works of art and architecture were destroyed in England after 1534 may have sprung from Lollard sympathizers.

JUDAISM

This section discusses the Jewish religion in its relationship to Catholicism, the dominant religion of western Europe during the period covered by the present book. (See page 40 for information on the background of this conflict.) The rich cultural traditions of European Judaism, not treated here, would provide fertile ground for further study. For the Catholic Church, the forced conversion of many thousands of Spanish and Portuguese Jews introduced the problem of sincerity of faith, and this issue helped catapult Spain into the Inquisition, with papal approval. Another problem for the church was the demand of Franciscan preachers that Jews be forbidden to practice usury, or lending money for interest. (The usual interest was 20 percent, which outraged Renaissance borrowers. That happens to be the approximate interest rate charged today by many credit card companies.) The pope had to proceed with caution concerning Jewish bankers because the papal treasury could not afford to support a bankrupt community. Partly for this reason, Roman Jews enjoyed somewhat better treatment than their colleagues elsewhere in the Papal States. Not until the 1580s were Jews in Rome forced to attend Catholic sermons. Finally, the decision to move Jews into ghettos was made during the Renaissance, unintentionally herding Jewish families together for future anti-Semitic attacks. The main purpose for ghettos at his time was to remove Jews from Christian society so that they would not "pollute" Catholics, and some Jewish communities preferred to be isolated: The ghettos gave them a sense of security.

Bible

Jews very much revered the sacred text. Some of the most extraordinary manuscripts of the Renais-

2.10 First leaf of the book of Joshua from an illuminated Hebrew Bible. Decorated in southern Castile or Andalusia, 15th century. (Courtesy of The Hispanic Society of America, MS. B241)

sance are illuminated Hebrew Bibles, meaning, of course, the Old Testament and its associated books, on vellum or heavy paper. Some of the ornamentation in these manuscripts was executed by Christian artists. Often the initial page of each book of the Old Testament opens with a panel featuring the first word highlighted in gold, with geometric shapes in different colors filled with patterns in gold and with a decorative border featuring peacocks and other birds, butterflies, and flowers. Unlike Catholic Bibles, most Hebrew Bibles avoided the use of human figures. The remainder of the pages usually contain only the Hebrew script, in stately rows of carefully scripted ink. Even after Hebrew Bibles were printed during the 16th century, beautiful copies in manuscript continued to be produced. The most sacred part of the

Bible was (and is) the Torah, or Pentateuch, the first five books of the Old Testament, written on parchment or leather in the format of a large, impressive scroll (see the following section).

Synagogue

Each congregation had its synagogue, with the rabbi as its head. Unlike Catholicism, Judaism did not (and does not) have a hierarchy of leaders. Each rabbi had autonomy within his synagogue, advised by a small group of highly respected men within the congregation. Traditionally, Renaissance synagogues were relatively small structures intended to serve the local community. The dislocation and diaspora of many thousands of Jews during the late 15th and early 16th centuries caused their local rites—Spanish, German, Italian, and others—to be introduced into the communities to which they immigrated. (Neither England nor France had a Jewish community, because they had driven them out during the Middle Ages.) Each rite usually had its own synagogue, with services on Saturday, the Jewish sabbath. Christians observed the sabbath on Sunday. As Catholic churches had an altar for the host, synagogues had a platform where the Torah was read aloud as well as an ark in which the Torah was stored. Some synagogues had both the ark and platform at the same end of the building; others had the ark at one end and the platform at the other. A decorative lamp or lantern hung in front of the ark. Although both men and women attended services, the sexes were segregated. Men sat on the ground floor near the Torah, with women above them in the balcony.

2.11 *Entrance hall of the Regensburg Synagogue. Etching by Albrecht Altdorfer, 1519. According to the caption, dated February 21, the artist documented this historic synagogue on the day before it was demolished, February 22.* (The Metropolitan Museum of Art, Harris Brisbane Dick Fund, 1926 [26.72.68])

The Torah scroll was the most precious object in a synagogue, followed by the ark. In most synagogues the decorations of the Torah, the crowns, finials, and so on, were solid silver. There was also a silver rod for pointing out sections of the Torah to be read because the holy text was never to be touched by human hands. Elaborately embroidered covers for the Torah and ark were made by Jewish women, who gave them to the synagogue. For Christians, both Catholic and Protestant, the Bible never became such a talismanic object. Certain taboos applied to the Bible, such as never placing a Bible on the floor, but Catholic priests handled them during church services, and Protestants had their own copies, which were read each day.

Sermons

Jewish sermons were usually delivered in the vernacular languages, although the preparatory notes were often written in Hebrew. Judging by the evidence of published sermons, we can assume that those preached in synagogues remained fairly conservative, using the medieval method of homiletic exposition.

Christian preachers observed the same tradition. Even the humanistic scholar Isaac Abravanel (1437–1508), whose philosophical commentaries on the Bible interested Christian scholars, followed the conservative mode in his sermons. During Abravanel's lifetime, however, young Jewish men began to be educated in classical rhetoric in the curriculum of their Hebrew schools. The ancient Roman authors Quintilian and Cicero were influential by the early 16th century, and mythological analogies, for example, entered the texts of sermons by Judah Moscato (c. 1530–c. 1593), a rabbi in Mantua. His eclectic style of preaching combined comments from the Talmud (collection of Jewish tradition), mystical writers, Aristotle, and Jewish philosophers. Jewish preachers were intellectuals, trained in rabbinical disputation.

Religious Practices

In different parts of Europe, the details of specific religious practices could differ considerably. But in most Jewish communities, three of the most important practices, all of which distinctly set Jews apart from Christians, were usually observed. These were circumcision of male infants, the ritual bath of women after menstruation, and family celebration of the eve of sabbath on Friday. Even in communities where dancing was banned, the prohibition was rescinded for the nights immediately preceding the circumcision ceremony. The birth of a male child was a cause of rejoicing in Jewish as well as Christian homes; the birth of a female child was not celebrated. In fact, the father of a newborn daughter was sometimes sent notes of condolence by his friends. For Christians, sending an actual note of condolence would have been considered inappropriate. The ritual bath for Jewish women certainly distinguished them from Christians as it required complete immersion. Bathing of this sort was not often practiced during the Renaissance (see chapter 12, Daily Life).

Cabala

Cabala (also spelled kabbalah or cabbala), a principal component of Jewish theosophy, consisted of interpreting the Old Testament through mystical, esoteric methods, often using ciphers and acronyms. The greatest mystery involved decoding meanings in the tetragrammaton, the four letters of the divine name. Major schools of cabala were located in Spain (until 1492), Italy, and Israel (notably the school at Safed). Christians also studied the Cabala, using it to formulate christological interpretations of the Old Testament. The philosopher Pico della Mirandola (1469–1533) learned about the Cabala, probably after seeing a manuscript of the *Zohar*, a famous mystical text. In 1486 he wrote a Cabalistic doctrinal work, *Conclusiones cabalisticae* (Cabalistic conclusions), and the theologian Johannes Reuchlin (1455–1522) published his *De arte cabalistica* (On the Cabalistic art) in 1517. These writers blended cabala with Neoplatonism in a syncretic mode of interpretation. One of the most influential Christian Cabalists was Guillaume Postel (1510–81), an extraordinary French scholar who specialized in oriental texts. Postel was imprisoned by the Inquisition because of his grand idea for world peace, that all sects should unite in a universal religion. His tolerance of Judaism and Islam was viewed as particularly subversive.

ISLAM

This section discusses Muslims in Spain, the only area of western Europe where Islam was practiced on a significant scale. Although Islam dominated much of the Iberian Peninsula for several centuries after the Arab conquest in the eight century, by the early 15th century only the kingdom of Granada remained under Muslim control. Until the Turkish capture of Constantinople in 1435, Spaniards tolerated the Muslim presence. The Ottoman Muslims, however, threatened the stability of the entire Mediterranean, as well as the borders of eastern Europe. The fall of Constantinople caused Muslims everywhere, including Spain and North Africa, to be viewed with suspicion and hatred. They had become the dreaded "infidels," even those who had been residing peacefully in Spain for several generations and whose contributions to western culture were well known. The medieval Crusades against the Turks had never been forgotten.

Mosques

As in Judaism, in Islam there was no (and is no) religious hierarchy. Each mosque has a designated imam (holy man), with spiritual teachers who assist him in enlightening the Muslims under his care. The idea for the mosque originated in the Prophet Muhammad's dwelling, dated 622, in Medina. Its design of a hall of columns surrounded by a courtyard became the usual arrangement for a mosque. Because Muslims turned toward Mecca when praying (and still do so), in a mosque the wall facing Mecca was indicated by a mihrab, a highly decorative niche or other distinctive element. In Spain this ornamentation often consisted of lusterware tiles. In front of the mihrab, a screen allowed the sultan and other high officials to pray in privacy. There was also a screened area behind which women could pray; they were not permitted to be among the male worshipers. The sermon was given from a pulpit above a flight of stairs, as in many Christian churches. Each mosque had at least one minaret, a tower from which the call for prayer could be heard. Although Muslims usually attended the mosque once each week, the call for prayer sounded five times each day. Muslims were expected to stop their activities, face toward Mecca, and kneel for prayer, bowing their face to the Earth. Neither Jews nor Christians practiced such a regular, public form of worship. The courtyard of the mosque contained fountains or wells because Muslims were required to perform ritual washing of their face, hands, and feet before entering the mosque. (The bathing traditions of Islam would have seemed excessive to any of their European contemporaries.) Mosques had gloriously ornate surface decoration, in tiles, marble, or carved wood. There were not, however, any representations of forms in nature because they were forbidden by the religion.

Spain's most important mosques were those in Granada and Córdoba. The monumental mosque of Córdoba was erected during the Middle Ages, in a city that included 700 mosques by the 10th century. The Muslim city of Córdoba was probably the greatest cultural resource of the time, containing some 70

2.12 *Prayer carpet. Turkey, late 16th century. The central section depicts a mihrab (prayer niche) like those in mosques.* (The Metropolitan Museum of Art, The James F. Ballard Collection, Gift of James F. Ballard, 1922 [22.100.51])

libraries with staffs of scribes, artists, and scholars. When Christian forces conquered Córdoba in the late Middle Ages, the exterior of the great mosque was allowed to remain standing. It was so massive that the Christian cathedral could be constructed within its center. When Granada was reconquered in 1492, however, most of the mosques were destroyed.

Muslim Philosophy

The sacred book of Islam is the Qur'an (or Koran), believed to be revelations from Allah (the divine being) given to Muhammad. The other basic text of

Islam is the Hadith, a collection of sayings from Muhammad and other holy men consulted as a source of religious authority. Islam was not a proselytizing religion, therefore, Muslims in Spain could live peaceably with the Jews and Christians whom they conquered during the Middle Ages. The famous philosophical schools of Toledo, Córdoba, and Granada welcomed (male) students of all faiths, in a prototypical globalization of knowledge. The open-minded attitudes of scholars in the Muslim world of Spain originated in Islam's exploration of humans' relationship to the One, the supreme being. During the late medieval period and early Renaissance, human intellect became valued as a powerful instrument for seeking eternal truths. This is the legacy of the Islamic religion to Renaissance science, mathematics, medicine, and philosophy.

Major Figures

(For information on the popes, see pages 30–34.)

Abrabanel, Isaac (1437–1508), Jewish scholar who served at the Portuguese and Spanish courts and settled in Venice in 1503. His biblical commentaries were studied by Christian scholars.

Agrippa von Nettesheim (1486–1535), noted philosopher and scholar of the Cabala, wrote a popular treatise on magic, *De occulta philosophia* (On occult philosophy, 1510).

Amerbach, Johannes (c. 1445–1513), Swiss humanist, founded an important printing house in Basel in 1484. His editions of patristic writers, especially Saint Augustine, set new standards for Renaissance publishing.

Anchieta, José de (1534–1597) founded a Jesuit mission school in the area where São Paulo, Brazil, is now located. He spoke out against Native American slavery.

Aquaviva, Claudio (1543–1615), superior general of the Jesuit order for 34 years, was largely responsible for more than doubling membership and expansion of the Jesuits into Asian and American colonies.

Arias Montano, Benito (1527–1598) is most famous as editor of the Polyglot Bible. He also taught oriental languages at the Escorial, where he was librarian.

Arminius, Jacobus (1560–1609) worked to revise the statements of creed for the (Calvinist) Dutch Reformed Church. He was embroiled in theological controversy, accused of Pelagianism because he did not believe in predestination.

Arndt, Johann (1555–1621) was a Lutheran mystic who emphasized the union between the true believer and Christ.

Báñez, Domingo (1528–1604), a Spanish Dominican and scholar of the works of Thomas Aquinas, was the spiritual adviser of Teresa de Ávila.

Baro, Peter (1535–1599) was a French theologian who converted to Calvinism. He fled to England and taught divinity at Cambridge.

Bellarmino, Roberto, cardinal (1542–1621), lectured on theology at the Jesuit College in Rome. He was influential in the revision of the Vulgate Bible.

Benedict XIII, antipope at Avignon (*Pedro da Luna*), (c. 1328–1423), refused to be deposed. Because Spain, Portugal, Scotland, and Sicily recognized him as pope, he caused the Great Schism to be prolonged for many years.

Bessarion, Basil, cardinal (1403–1472), was a Greek scholar who favored reuniting the Roman and Byzantine churches. After his conversion to Catholicism, he was made a cardinal. Bessarion continued to study Greek and Latin manuscripts throughout his life and left his substantial collection to the republic of Venice.

Bèze, Théodore de (1519–1605), theologian and historian, was a Protestant who fled to Switzerland. He taught in Geneva and published several Calvinist works. His Latin translation of the New Testament was published in 1556.

Borja, Francisco de (1510–1572) gave up a dukedom in southern Spain to join the Society of Jesus (Jesuits). He gave enormous prestige to the society, as the great-grandson of both King Ferdinand V and Pope Alexander VI. Borja served as the second general of the Jesuits.

Borromeo, Carlo, cardinal (1538–1584), was canonized in 1610. He helped reform church music and presided over part of the Council of Trent. As bishop of Milan he enforced the strict Tridentine decrees, removing some of the ornamentation from Milan Cathedral. Borromeo also reformed the religious orders and persecuted witches and other heretics.

Bruno, Giordano (1584–1600) was burned at the stake in Rome after his pantheistic theology and heterodoxy were condemned by an Inquisition tribunal.

Bucer, Martin (1491–1551), Protestant reformer, participated in several conferences before settling in England to teach divinity at Cambridge. Queen Mary I ordered his tomb desecrated and his body burned, but Elizabeth I later restored the tomb.

Bullinger, Heinrich (1504–1575) was a Protestant polemicist who argued with Luther over the doctrine of the Eucharist, among other topics. His sermons were published in German, Latin, and English.

Cajetan, San (*Gaetano Thiene*), (1480–1547) founded the Order of Theatines, with the goal of promoting apostolic purity.

Cajetan, Tommaso, cardinal (1469–1534) was a renowned scholar of the works of Thomas Aquinas. He served as general of the Dominican order and papal legate. Cajetan fell out of favor because of his leniency toward Lutheranism.

Calvin, Jean (1509–1564), founder of Calvinism, spent most of his adult life in Geneva. After an initial controversy with the Zwinglians, he was made head of the city government. The Latin version of his *Institutes* (1559) became a standard text of the Reformation.

Campion, Edmund (1540–1581) was an English Jesuit, ordained in Rome in 1578. After teaching in Prague, he helped lead the Jesuit mission to England. There Campion was captured by Protestant authorities, tortured, and executed.

Cano, Melchior (1509–1560), Spanish Dominican, supported Philip II in his conflict with the papacy concerning ecclesiastical revenues. He was a professor of theology at the University of Salamanca.

Carranza, Bartolomé de (1503–1576) was an eminent Spanish Dominican whose career vacillated between royal and Imperial representation to long-term imprisonment by the Inquisition. He advocated several clerical reforms and wrote a controversial treatise on the catechism.

Cassander, Georg (1513–1556), Catholic theologian, was spurned by both Catholics and Protestants for his attempts to reconcile their doctrinal stances.

Catherine de' Medici (1519–1589) was queen mother and then regent of France as of 1560. She initially supported toleration of French Protestants but by 1572 encouraged their persecution. She was the power behind the throne until 1588.

Charles of Guise, cardinal of Lorraine (1525–1574), was the brother of the duke of Guise. He vehemently opposed the Reformation, particularly the Calvinists.

Chemnitz, Martin (1522–1586), Protestant theologian, was a student of Melanchthon. He became an important Lutheran polemicist, defending Luther's doctrine of the Eucharist and criticizing the Council of Trent.

Cisneros, Francisco Jiménez de, cardinal (1436–1517), became the confessor of Queen Isabella I. Reluctantly accepting his appointment as a bishop, he continued to live in modest conditions. He was also grand Inquisitor general for Castile and Léon (Spain).

Coligny, Gaspard of (1519–1572) was commander in chief of the French Huguenot army. He was killed during the Saint Bartholomew's Day massacre.

Coverdale, Miles (1488–1568) translated the entire Bible into English, drawing upon William Tyndale's translation of the New Testament.

Cranmer, Thomas, archbishop of Canterbury (1489–1556), revised the liturgy for the Church of England under Henry VIII and contributed to the first two Books of Common Prayer. He was burned at the stake during the reign of Mary I.

Cromwell, Thomas (c. 1485–1540) was secretary to Henry VIII. He instigated the dissolution and looting of monasteries in England.

Des Périers, Bonaventure (c. 1500–1544) assisted with the first translation of the Bible into French. He was a member of the court of Marguerite de Navarre.

Dolet, Étienne (1509–1546) was a French humanist whose affinity for the skepticism of classical authors led to his denial of the immortality of the soul. He was burned at the stake, condemned by Sorbonne theologians.

Eck, Johann (1486–1543) was a Catholic theologian who vehemently opposed Luther. He dedicated his life to crushing Protestantism, traveling back and forth between Rome and Germany.

Edward VI, king of England (1537–1553), was only nine years old when he succeeded to the throne. His ministers continued to strengthen the Church of England and published the first Book of Common Prayer.

Elizabeth I, queen of England (1533–1603), reigned from 1558 until 1603. Although several Catholic dissenters were executed during her reign, she tolerated Catholics who posed no threat to her authority.

Erasmus, Desiderius (c. 1466–1536), Augustinian priest and renowned humanist, carried on numerous arguments with Luther, for instance, on the freedom of the human will. He also edited the New Testament in Greek.

Erastus, Thomas (1524–1583) was a Zwinglian theologian after whom Erastianism is named. This creed affirmed the superiority of the state over the church in ecclesiastical affairs.

Fisher, John, cardinal (1469–1535), became chancellor of Cambridge University. He vehemently opposed Henry VIII's demand for a divorce and was executed for refusing to recognize the authority of the Church of England.

Flacius Illyricus (1520–1575) was a Protestant theologian who became an adherent of Lutheranism and a friend of Luther's. He was famous for his scholarly biblical exegesis.

Fonseca, Pedro da (1528–1599), Portuguese Jesuit, was chancellor of the University of Evora and later worked for the church in Rome.

Foxe, John (1516–1587) wrote an influential book on Protestant martyrs in England, *Acts and Monuments of Matters Happening in the Church* (1554). During the reign of Mary I, he lived in exile, returning to England after Elizabeth I became queen.

Francis of Lorraine, duke of Guise (1519–1563) and brother of the cardinal of Lorraine, fought in the Italian Wars and the Wars of Religion on the Catholic side. Troops under his leadership killed a group of Huguenots in 1562, instigating the Wars of Religion. The duke died of a gunshot wound the following year.

Gutenberg, Johannes (c. 1394/99–1468) successfully printed the first book with the new technology of movable type. That book was the Vulgate Bible, known as the Gutenberg Bible.

Henry IV, king of France (1553–1610), was raised in a Protestant household. Forced to renounce his faith in 1572, he recanted after escaping from house arrest and joined the Huguenot rebels. However, in 1593, he converted to Catholicism after becoming king.

Henry VIII, king of England (1491–1547), broke with the Catholic Church when the pope refused to grant him a divorce. He founded the Church of England, confiscated Catholic property, and closed the monasteries.

Hooker, Richard (c. 1554–1600) was an English divine whose multivolume work *Of the Laws of Ecclesiastical Polity* became the foundation stone of Anglicanism.

Hus, Jan (c. 1372–1415), born in Bohemia, studied theology at the University of Prague. His preaching was censured for criticism of the clergy; then Hus fell into greater disfavor as a result of papal politics. In 1411 Hus was excommunicated, forbidden to have any contact with members of the church, and exiled from Prague. With a safe-conduct pass from the emperor, he journeyed to the Council of Constance to appeal his excommunication, but he was burned at the stake by order of the pope. His followers responded to this outrage with the Hussite Wars.

John VIII Palaeologus, emperor of Byzantium (1390–1448), sought to unite the Eastern and Western churches. He was present for the Council of Florence and agreed to the decree of 1439 reconciling the two churches. The agreement was rejected in Byzantium.

Junius, Franciscus (1545–1602), Protestant theologian, spent many years translating the Old Testament into Latin. He was a professor of theology and Hebrew, who concluded his career at the University of Leiden.

Knox, John (c. 1513–1572) was a Scottish Protestant who worked on the second *Book of Common Prayer.* Knox is infamous for his attack on female rulers, *First Blast of the Trumpet against the Monstrous Regiment of Women* (1558), for which he was banned from England by Elizabeth I even though he served the Church of England.

Latimer, Hugh (c. 1485–1555), royal chaplain for Henry VIII, was a Protestant reformer. When he refused to recant under Mary I, she had him burned at the stake.

Laínez, Diego (1512–1565), second Jesuit general, defended papal authority at the Council of Trent. He also promoted Jesuit missionary activity.

Lefèvre d'Étaples, Jacques (c. 1460–1536), French humanistic scholar, studied and corrected biblical texts. Although this work brought him under suspicion of the Sorbonne, he was protected by the king and his sister, Marguerite of Navarre.

L'Hôpital, Michel de (1505–1573), chancellor of France, supported religious toleration and attempted to prioritize the interests of the state over those of religion. He eventually was forced to resign his office because of opposition from the church.

Loyola, Saint Ignatius (1491–1556), a Spaniard, founded the Society of Jesus (Jesuits). The society was recognized by Pope Paul III in 1540. Saint Ignatius's *Spiritual Exercises* (1548), originally published in Spanish, was the first book issued by the society.

Luther, Martin (1483–1546) disapproved of clerical and papal corruption. His initial criticisms were intended to reform the Catholic Church from within, but he soon advanced from criticism to formulate new doctrines. Luther began the Protestant Reformation and translated the Bible into German.

Maier, Georg (1502–1574) was taught at the University of Wittenberg by Melanchthon and Luther. A Lutheran theologian, Maier lectured that good works were necessary for salvation, in addition to the justification by faith preached by Luther.

Mary I, queen of England (*Mary Tudor*) (1516–1558), was known as "Bloody Mary." She relentlessly persecuted Protestants. Married to Philip II of Spain, Mary did not produce an heir, thus allowing Elizabeth to become queen.

Mary, queen of Scots (*Mary Stuart*) (1452–1587), was married to Francis II, heir to the throne of France, but he died not long after their wedding. Fleeing from Protestant forces in Scotland, she was imprisoned and ultimately executed by her cousin, Elizabeth I.

Melanchthon, Philipp (1497–1560), Protestant reformer, sought to reconcile Lutheranism, Calvinism, and Zwinglianism. At heart Melanchthon was a humanistic scholar with a synergistic view of religion, which alienated him from many Protestants.

Molina, Luis de (1535–1600) was a Spanish Jesuit who spent most of his career teaching in Portugal. Molinism, named after him, involves the theology of grace.

More, Sir Thomas (1478–1535) become lord chancellor of England in 1529. He opposed Henry VIII's divorce, however, and was executed.

Motilinía, Toribio de (c. 1490–1569) was a Spanish missionary in Mexico. His work on the Aztecs is an important early source concerning their religious practices.

Müntzer, Thomas (c. 1489–1525), a German student of theology and a Catholic priest, became a religious visionary. He was rejected by Luther for his extreme beliefs. Müntzer led an army during the Peasants' Revolt in Thuringia and was subsequently captured and executed.

Nicholas of Cusa (1401–1464), born in the German town of Kues (hence his name), wrote numerous Latin treatises, including religious and philosophical works. His best known treatise is *De docta ignorantia* (On learned ignorance, c. 1440), which concerns human understanding of God.

Oecolampadius, Johannes (1482–1531), a German Protestant, encouraged participation in church government. Along with Zwingli, he persuaded the canton of Bern to adopt Protestantism.

Osiander, Andreas (1496/98–1552) was a Protestant reformer who argued with Luther about justification by faith.

Pfefferkorn, Johannes (1469–1524) was a Jew who converted to Catholicism and attempted to persuade Maximilian I to destroy all Jewish writings. The Hebrew scholar Reuchlin persuaded him otherwise.

Philip II, king of Spain (1527–1598), also controlled the Netherlands as part of his Burgundian inheritance. He attempted to quell the 1567 Revolt of the Netherlands by dispatching Spanish troops.

This action only fueled the Protestants' desire for independence, in conflicts that lasted until a truce of 1609.

Pole, Reginald, cardinal (1500–1558) and archbishop of Canterbury, turned against Henry VIII in support of the papacy. His family was persecuted because he propagandized against the English Crown. When Mary I became queen, Pope Paul III sent Pole as legate to England.

Reuchlin, Johannes (1455–1522), humanist and Hebrew scholar, persuaded Emperor Maximilian I not to order the wholesale destruction of Jewish books and manuscripts.

Ricci, Matteo (1552–1610) was a Jesuit missionary in China. His work became controversial because he permitted converts to practice ancestor worship.

Servetus, Michael (1511–1553), a Unitarian theologian opposing Trinitarianism, was denounced by Calvin. He was burned at the stake in Switzerland by order of the city council of the Calvinist stronghold of Geneva.

Sigismund, king of Hungary and Bohemia (1368–1437), was crowned as Holy Roman Emperor in 1433. For 17 years he had to battle the Hussites in Bohemia before his kingship was firmly established there.

Simons, Menno (1496–1561), who had been a Catholic priest, joined the Anabaptists and became a minister. Greatly influenced by the writings of Luther, he preached that people should lead a life of service and advocated peace. The Mennonites named themselves after him.

Stumpf, Johannes (1500–1578) was a Swiss Protestant theologian, many of whose Catholic parishioners converted with him.

Teresa of Ávila (1515–1582), Spanish mystic, founded a reformed house of the Carmelite order, known as Discalced (shoeless) Carmelites, who lived in strict poverty. Members of the regular order denounced her to the Inquisition, and she was forced to write to defend herself. In 1970 Saint Teresa became the first woman honored as a doctor of the church.

Thiene, Gaetano See CAJETAN, SAN.

Thomas à Kempis (c. 1380–1471), devotional writer, was probably the author of the immensely popular *Imitatio Christi* (Imitation of Christ).

Tyndale, William (c. 1494–1536) translated the Bible into English. He was executed in the Netherlands for heresy.

Wolsey, Thomas, cardinal (c. 1474–1530), served as chaplain for both Henry VII and Henry VIII. As lord chancellor he was given the task of negotiating the king's divorce, then charged with treason when he failed. Wolsey died before he could respond.

Xavier, Francis (1506–1552), Spanish Jesuit, was a disciple of Ignatius de Loyola. He spent most of his career as a missionary to the Far East, establishing missions in Goa and elsewhere, introducing Catholicism to thousands. He is buried in Goa but had the posthumous honor of having his right arm detached and taken to the Gesù church in Rome.

Wycliffe, John (c. 1328–1384), an Oxford man, was tolerated by the government when he criticized corrupt members of the clergy and taught that the Bible is the supreme source of doctrinal information. He attacked the Eucharist, however, as a source of superstitious behavior and was ordered to leave his position at Oxford in 1382. The Lollards, his followers, originally were members of the aristocracy, but Wycliffe's fall from grace caused the movement to die out among the upper class. It was submerged among members of the middle and lower classes and may still have been smoldering in the early 16th century.

Zwingli, Huldrych (1484–1531) was an important theologian in the Swiss Reformation. He broke with Rome over the issue of marriage for priests and subsequently broke with Luther over his interpretation of the Eucharist. Zwinglianism, the creed named after Zwingli, promoted the practice of the Eucharist as only a commemorative ritual.

READING

The Papacy

D' Amico, *Renaissance Humanism*, 1991: papal Rome; Grendler 1999: Bologna; Hallman 1985: cardinals and reform; McGinness 1995: Counter-Reformation; O'Malley 1979: reform in Rome; Partner 1972: the Papal States; Partner 1990: papal service; Prodi 1987: papal monarchy; Signorotto 2002: politics in Rome.

Catholic Church

Alden 1996: Jesuit missions; Black 1989: confraternities; Crowder 1977: heresies in the 15th century; DeMolen 1994: religious orders; Donnelly 1999: confraternities; Hay 1977: Italy in the 15th century; Housley 2001: holy wars; Kloczowski 2000: Poland; Oakley 1979: early Renaissance; Peters 1988: Inquisition; Racaut 2002: French Counter-Reformation; Raitt 1987: spirituality; Tedeschi 1991: Inquisition; Weinstein 1970: Florence.

Protestant Reformation

Bainton 1956: mostly Germany; Belloc 1992: impressionistic description of Reformation individuals; Bergsma 1999: Netherlands; Diefendorf 1991: Paris in the 16th century; Holt 1995: wars of religion in France; Oberman 1994: effects of the Reformation; Pelikan 1996: the Bible; Stadtwald 1996: antipapalism in Germany; Unghváry 1989: Hungary; Waite 2000: drama and propaganda.

Judaism

Bonfil 1990: rabbis; Frojmovic 2002: Jewish–Christian relations; Gitlitz 1996: crypto-Jews; Langmuir 1990: anti-Semitism; Meyers 2001: *conversos;* Mulsow 2004: converts to Judaism; Oberman 1994: anti-Semitism; Reinharz 1982: Jewish intellectual history; Roth 1984: (general study); Ruderman 1981: Jewish culture; Ruderman 1992: Italy.

Islam

Armour 2002: conflicts; Beckingham 1983: travelers; Blanks 1997: Islam as the "other"; Burnett 1999: Italy; Cardini 2001: general study; Fuller 2001: English converts to Islam; Mastnak 2002: Islam and Western politics; Miller 2000: Luther on Islam.

3

ART AND
VISUAL CULTURE

Until the 20th century, *Renaissance art* chiefly meant painting, sculpture, and architecture, including the illuminated painting in manuscripts. Scholarly writing in art history focused mostly on Italian artists working in these media, influenced by Giorgio Vasari's (1511–1574) *Delle vite' de' più pittori, scultori, ed architettori* (Lives of the most excellent painters, sculptors, and architects, 1550). The 18th- and early 19th-century art markets were driven by the connoisseurship of scholars and collectors, and the artists described by Vasari dominated the market. Although his *Lives* remains an extraordinary insight into the artistic life of the Renaissance, Vasari's bias toward Florentine artists sometimes caused him to disparage the work of those working in other areas, such as Siena and Venice, and, of course, no northern European artists are included in the first edition of his book. Today we have a much fuller picture of the period and can better appreciate the visual idiosyncrasies of Renaissance art from various regions of Europe. In addition, we now see that northern European art played a significant role in the development of certain media, notably wood carving, oil painting, printmaking, and metalwork. Several exhibitions and publications of the 19th and early 20th centuries informed scholars and collectors about Netherlandish art of the Renaissance, and today we have a more balanced view of the artistic productions of northern and southern Europe during the 15th and 16th centuries. Scholarship of the latter 20th century explored the relationships between the Renaissance art of western Europe and that of other cultures, such as the hybrid forms that developed in the Iberian Peninsula under Islamic influence.

Students of the Renaissance now look at the entire panoply of visual culture in which artists of the time lived and worked. We still admire, of course, the masterpieces of painting, sculpture, and architecture that have defined Renaissance art for four centuries. That admiration, however, is both enriched and tempered by the knowledge that many of the same artists producing these works also drew designs for other media such as prints, medals, embroidery, and tapestries and sculpted small works such as mirrors, jewelry, and decorative details for furniture. Looking at art from the Renaissance point of view, we should

understand that tapestries, especially those from Flanders and Italy, were often valued more highly than paintings. These portable forms of textile wall art could be transported from one residence to another, whereas frescoes remained on the wall where they were painted and large sculptures remained on their pedestals.

Except for the visual art in public buildings and churches, the majority of the population did not see the masterpieces of Renaissance art. Many of the major commissions were for private residences of the pope, monarch, or local official and for their private gardens or for private organizations such as guilds. Town and city dwellers viewed artistic works during festivities and funerals, for which artists were commissioned to design and paint wooden triumphal arches, decorations for pageants, banners, coats of arms, and other works. Many people living in rural areas during the 15th century spent their entire life worshiping in a medieval church, oblivious to art of the Renaissance. By the 16th century, however, prints and illustrated books were making their way into even the smallest towns. This explosion of imagery affected the social and cultural stability of western Europe, causing people to question assumptions about political hierarchies, social stratification, and religion.

The new visual culture contributed significantly to the Protestant Reformation, which relied on prints and illustrated books to spread its propaganda, especially among the lower classes.

Realizing the power of religious imagery, Protestant leaders advocated iconoclasm, causing the wholesale destruction of Catholic crucifixes, stained glass, paintings, carvings, sculpture, prayer books, and choir books. Some areas of Protestant northern Europe escaped this onslaught; England was not so fortunate. In the reigns of Henry VIII (1491–1547) and Edward VI (1537–53), England lost almost all important Catholic art, most of it Gothic and some recently imported from the continent. Several English artists, influenced by Flemish painters, were working in their native country during the late 15th and early 16th centuries. Most of their religious art was destroyed. The Reformation in England discouraged both painting and sculpture, except for the production of alabaster statuary and the painting of portraits, especially in miniature. Italy, of course, did not suffer this deprivation, and the story of Renaissance art begins there.

PAINTING

To appreciate the differences between early Renaissance painting, which largely means northern Italian art, and the medieval (or Gothic) painting that it eventually superseded, we must realize that medieval paintings had a relatively flat picture plane with stiff, two-dimensional figures. Although individual objects could be rendered realistically, the overall picture usually resembled the iconic style of Byzantine paintings. Often there was no background to the composition, only a gilt surface occasionally decorated with punched or incised patterns. Giotto di Bondone's (1267–1337) frescoes of the *Lives of the Virgin and Christ* painted between 1305 and 1308 for the Arena Chapel in Padua, with their well-proportioned figures and various lifelike gestures, are among the earliest representations of the new art form. Giotto, in fact, was designated by Vasari in his *Lives* as the founder of Renaissance painting, on the basis of the assumption that Giotto

3.1 *Apparatus for translating three-dimensional objects into two-dimensional drawings. Woodcut by Albrecht Dürer, published 1525.* (Private Collection/Bridgeman Art Library)

had painted the frescoes in the upper church of San Francesco in Assisi. Although most scholars now believe that another artist executed those works, Vasari's assessment of Giotto's significance was not inappropriate. Frescoes, or mural paintings, were the first medium in which Renaissance artists excelled, followed closely by paintings on wood panels and illuminated manuscripts. The single greatest achievement of painting during the Renaissance was the understanding of perspective, which was used by artists in both southern and northern Europe by the mid-15th century. The other major achievement was a new understanding of how to render form and mass, or a "sculptural" feeling for figures in two-dimensional space.

Leon Battista Alberti's treatise on painting, *De pictura* (1435), included the first published description of one-point perspective, or linear perspective. Alberti referred to the "centric point" (vanishing point) to describe the method used to create the illusion of depth on a two-dimensional surface. He and the architect Filippo Brunelleschi (1377–1446) may have been working on this concept together in Florence. Because linear perspective can be used to situate human and mythological figures properly within pictorial space, it was one of the most important advances in Renaissance art. Alberti emphasized that the story (*istoria*) or narrative of a painting was its main purpose, and that story was expressed through figures. He assumed that artists knew anatomy, which was crucial for the composition: "Before dressing a man, we must first draw him nude, then we enfold him in draperies. So in painting the nude we place first his bones and muscles which we then cover with flesh so that it is not difficult to understand where each muscle is beneath" (Alberti 1966, p. 73). A new sense of precision entered artistic vocabulary with Alberti's text, as compositions were based on measurements and accurate proportions in figures and buildings. Alberti encouraged painters to introduce a sense of movement by using the *contrapposto* pose found in ancient statues, in which one foot is placed slightly forward, balanced by a turn of the head or an extended arm. This particular pose became important not only for Renaissance painting, but also for sculpture. By the 1520s in Italy, many artists were creating works featuring twisted and exaggerated figures, with

3.2 Linear perspective illustrated in a woodcut of the interior of a building. Hieronymus Rodler, Perspectiva, *Frankfurt, 1546.* (Photograph courtesy of Sotheby's Inc., © 2003)

plaster as it dried. Details could be added in *secco* (dry work) after the plaster dried, and the color blue usually had to be added after the plaster dried because that pigment did not dissolve properly in water. Most Renaissance frescoes were created in Italy, though usually not in Venice, because humid conditions caused the surface to deteriorate. The most famous fresco of the Renaissance is Michelangelo's (1475–1564) Sistine Chapel ceiling in Rome. Giotto's Arena (Scrovegni) Chapel in Padua is among the earliest (see previous discussion). Although most fresco painters, as were artists in general, were men, some religious frescoes in convents were painted by nuns.

Fresco painting during the early Renaissance was a demanding medium that required an excellent visual memory and a sure, quick hand. The painter sketched the design on a plaster base, deciding which section would be painted on a particular day because the pigments had to be applied before the plaster dried. Then a thin, smooth coat of plaster was applied over that section, covering the sketch that was now in the artist's memory so that the actual painting could commence. By the mid-15th century, fresco painters had learned to sketch their designs in full scale on pieces of paper, then transfer the sketch to sections of the final layer of plaster by pricking along the sketched lines or pressing lightly with a stylus. Some artists also used pieces of cloth pressed onto the damp plaster to prevent it from drying out until that section could be painted. Because the pigments in fresco (except some blues) were physically bonded into the plaster, their colors remained fresh and vibrant, and the images were strengthened visually by becoming part of the structure of the wall or ceiling. These paintings were not restrained or defined by frames: Angels could appear to fly around the ceiling and people could seem to be walking along the walls. Unlike most panel paintings and paintings on canvas, frescoes were not covered over with varnish or other protective material. Whereas most Renaissance paintings in other media are now darkened or discolored by the very material intended to protect them, many frescoes have retained their original brilliance or can be cleaned to reveal it. Frescoes give a good idea of the bright colors that must have appeared in other painted media of the time.

dramatic lighting or texture highlighting these figures in the style known as Mannerism that influenced other Renaissance art of the latter 16th century. By the turn of the century, Mannerism had evolved into the grand exuberance of baroque.

Painting on Walls

Mural painting, or wall painting, was usually done in the form of fresco for images that were meant to be permanent, with powdered pigments dissolved in water. The fresco technique, from the Italian word for "fresh," involved painting onto freshly applied plaster so that the paint hardened into the

Because mural painting could be executed in a monumental scale, figures could be life-sized and narrative could easily be incorporated into the imagery. In Florence, as in other important cities, monastic orders often commissioned mural paintings to preserve and celebrate the history of their institution, creating a sort of group memory. The cloisters of monasteries were perfect locations for such murals because the monks or nuns and their visitors habitually strolled around this area, the open center permitted sunlight to illuminate the paintings, and the roofed loggia protected the murals from inclement weather. During the Middle Ages, cloister decoration was chosen by and pertained to wealthy families, patrons of the order, who had the right to be buried within the cloister. By 1420 in Florence, however, such paintings, which contributed to the public perception and communal memory of the orders, began to be designed by them. The narrative scope of fresco cycles also told stories such as the lives of the Virgin and Christ or the life of the patron saint of a wealthy individual donor or guild. Taddeo Gaddi (fl. 1325, d. 1366), Giotto's assistant for some 24 years, painted the fresco cycle *The Life of the Virgin* (1332–38) in the Baroncelli Chapel of Santa Croce in Florence, as well as other frescoes in the church. In *Lives of the Most Excellent Painters, Sculptors, and Architects* Giorgio Vasari, however, assigned these works to Giotto. It is important to understand that Renaissance readers viewed their own art history through Vasari's eyes.

EXAMPLES OF 15TH-CENTURY FRESCOES

The first Renaissance painting depicting an equestrian statue was executed in fresco (1436), by Paolo Uccello (c. 1397–1475), for the Florence cathedral. Modeled after ancient Roman sculpture, the painting celebrated John de Hawkwood, an English mercenary (*condottiere*) who had fought for Florence. The painting, which observes the rules of linear perspective, is nearly 30 feet in height. Vasari praised the geometric proportions of the horse and the painting in general: "Paolo drew in perspective a large sarcophagus, as if the body were inside, and above it he placed the image of the man in his commander's armour astride a horse. This work was and is still considered to be a most beautiful painting" (Vasari 1998, p. 80). The equestrian statue and its

representation in painting and prints would become a favorite topos for rulers in Renaissance art.

Masaccio's (1401–c. 1428) fresco cycle in the Brancacci Chapel of Santa Maria del Carmine in Florence was painted near the end of his short life, for a private patron. It is still extant, although somewhat damaged by an 18th-century fire and subsequently repaired. Fresco was the perfect medium for this artist's innovative use of the luminous qualities of light, with figures modeled after classical examples. Vasari elevated Masaccio to a position of honor among 15th-century artists, and Renaissance artists in Florence studied his compositions in the Brancacci Chapel. Vasari praised his realism: "Masaccio constantly tried to create the most lifelike figures with a fine animation and a similarity to the real. His outlines and his painting were done in such a modern style, and so different were they from those of other painters, that his works can surely stand comparison with any kind of modern design or colouring" (Vasari 1998, p. 103). When Vasari wrote "modern," he meant the new style influenced by classical models, as opposed to the older Gothic style, which he called "German." Thus, as in other aspects of Renaissance culture, ancient classical models became the "modern" prototypes.

Piero della Francesca (1415–1492) painted the fresco cycle *Legend of the True Cross* in the choir of the Church of San Francesco, Arezzo, between circa 1455 and 1460. Beautifully preserved today, this work became justifiably famous during the Renaissance through Vasari's adulation: "But over and above every other consideration of Piero's talent and technique is his depiction of Night, where he shows an angel in flight, foreshortened with its head foremost on the plane . . . and, with his depiction of the darkness, Piero makes us realize how important it is to imitate real things and to draw them out, deriving them from reality itself" (Vasari 1998, pp. 165–166). This striving toward naturalism would become the single most important goal for painters of the latter 15th century, and its fulfillment would be achieved by Flemish artists. Numerous other 15th-century Italian artists worked in fresco, including several, such as Andrea Mantegna (1430/31–1506), Domenico Ghirlandaio (1448/49–1494), and Sandro Botticelli (1445–1510), who also were in demand for their panel paintings.

EXAMPLES OF 16TH-CENTURY FRESCOES

The Vatican's Sistine Chapel, originally commissioned by Pope Sixtus IV (1414–84), has been a focal point of papal history since it was built. Each new pope is elected by the conclave of cardinals in this room. Between 1481 and 1483, frescoes were painted on the walls by several artists, including Botticelli, Ghirlandaio, and Perugino (c. 1440–1523). In the early 16th century, Michelangelo and his assistants painted the ceiling under the patronage of Pope Julius II (1443–1513); three decades later he painted the fresco *The Last Judgment* on the wall behind the altar. The latter work caused quite a scandal, partly because of the dour nature of Counter-Reformation adherents (see page 44 in chapter 2, on religion). The Sistine Chapel ceiling is a triumph of trompe l'oeil illusionistic architecture and interactive figures in various scale. During the 20th century, the paintings received a controversial cleaning that revealed the bright colors that one expects to see in Renaissance frescoes. (Several experts believe that the colors are too bright.) Recent scholarship has revealed that the iconographic program of the ceiling evidently was planned by the humanistic theologian Egidio da Viterbo (1469–1532), working with Michelangelo. Jewish cabalistic mysticism was used as the source of the symbolism, in the belief that the kingdom of heaven on Earth could be projected through the union of numerology, mystical symbols, and Christian imagery. Although only Vatican officials and humanistic elite at the time would have known about this use of the cabala in a Christian context, Michelangelo assuredly knew, especially since he would have been introduced to the doctrines of Christian Neoplatonism and cabala at the Medici court when he was younger. Vasari, however, knew nothing about the Jewish aspect of this sacred fresco cycle.

Long before Vasari suggested that mid-16th-century artists should use the Sistine Chapel ceiling as their model, Raphael (1483–1520) did so. Commissioned by the pope to decorate the Vatican apartments (the Stanze) in fresco, Raphael looked at Michelangelo's work in the chapel and changed the focus of his own imagery. In his painting *Liberation of Saint Peter from Prison* (1511–14), for example, he emphasized the dramatic effect as Michelangelo might have. This fresco challenged Raphael's ingenuity as it had to be designed for a lunette into which the top of a window intrudes. Millard Meiss in *The Great Age of Fresco*, 1970, explained how the artist drew attention away from the window by creating four sources of light within a rather dark painting (dark for a fresco, that is). Raphael was recognized for the "sweet style" of his painting, which can easily be seen in his classicizing frescoes celebrating the sea nymph Galatea (1513) in the Villa Farnesina, Rome.

Correggio (1494–1534) executed the cupola of San Giovanni Evangelista in Parma. Painted between circa 1518 and 1522, the top of the cupola

3.3 Portrait of Michelangelo. Giorgio Vasari, Le vite de' piu eccellenti pittori . . ., *Florence, 1588.*
(Photograph courtesy of Sotheby's Inc., © 2003)

(which has no lantern and thus no light from above) is approximately 100 feet from the floor of the church. The subject he painted is usually referred to as *The Vision of Saint John*, with Saint John observing Christ's ascending into heaven, surrounded by his apostles. The renowned Venetian painter Titian (c. 1489–1576) praised Correggio for his fresco painting in the dome of Parma cathedral, which is an *Assumption of the Virgin* (1526) similar to the ascension in San Giovanni Evangelista. In the latter painting, Correggio created "light" from the cupola by causing Christ to appear to float up into an endless, glowing heaven of gold and white.

Veronese (1528–88) was a masterful illusionistic painter, as exemplified by his frescoes in several private villas, notably the Villa Barbaro in Maser (the Veneto) built by Andrea Palladio (1508–80). Because it is part of the wall itself, fresco easily lends itself to depictions of fictive three-dimensional architecture. In the Villa Barbaro, Veronese's visual wit created a false balustrade with a "rural scene" visible in the distance, a woman holding a violin that seems to project beyond the surface, a little girl seeming to open a door and look into the room, and similar amusing *trompe l'oeil* imagery. By the early 1560s, when the villa was painted by Veronese, painters were appreciated for their wit as much as for their skill.

In Castile (present-day Spain), Juan de Borgoña (fl. from 1495, d. 1535) designed several frescoes for the cathedral of Toledo, including "windows" that opened into gardens filled with flowers, fruit trees, and birds. He himself painted three large battle scenes in 1514 celebrating his patron, Francisco Jiménez de Cisneros (c. 1436–1517), who had led a campaign against Muslims in Morocco in 1509. Originally from Burgundy (as his name implies), Borgoña apparently spent three years studying painting in Rome. His frescoes demonstrate that he understood linear perspective and the classical modeling of human figures. On the vault above his battle scene of Oran, Borgoña painted a *trompe l'oeil* coffered ceiling in perfect Italian style.

The royal hunting lodge of Fontainebleau has one of the most ornate examples of a frescoed Renaissance interior, in the Salle de Bal (ballroom), full of mythological allegories. Commissioned by King Henry II (1519–1559), it was painted by Francesco Primaticcio (1504/5–70) and Niccolò dell'Abbate (c. 1512–1571) between 1551 and 1556. Originally working with Il Rosso (1494–1540) on the frescoes and stuccoed wall decoration for the lodge, Primaticcio became director of the project in what is now called the School of Fontainebleau. There were several assistants and student artists in the workshop, from both northern and southern Europe. Under the guidance of their Italian master, these artists produced a syncretic effusion of color, realism, and sensuality. Primaticcio's greatest achievement in fresco at Fontainebleau, the Gallery of Ulysses, was destroyed during renovations by King Louis XV. Although highly valued by Renaissance artists, the imagery in the gallery did not conform to later tastes.

Painting on Wooden Panels

Wooden panels were a portable, relatively inexpensive medium for Renaissance painters. After the surface was prepared with a ground of white gesso, panels could be executed in either water-based tempera or paint prepared with oil. The surface could also be prepared with a cloth stretched over it, then gessoed. In his early 15th-century treatise *Il Libro dell' Arte* (The craftsman's handbook), the painter Cennino Cennini (c. 1370–c. 1440) gave detailed instructions for preparing panels and then drawing and painting on them. This very practical treatise includes recipes and tips for the artist, for example: "When the gesso has all been scraped down, and comes out like ivory, the first thing for you to do is to draw your . . . panel with those willow coals which I taught you to make before. But the charcoal wants to be tied to a little cane or stick, so that it comes some distance from the figures; for it is a great help to you in composing" (Cennini 1954, p. 75).

Panel painting involved an artistic process different from the technique of fresco painting. Even for multiple panels in a large altarpiece, panel painting usually covered a much smaller area than fresco painting, and the artist could proceed at a more leisurely pace because there was no concern about plaster's drying out. Cennini made the point that panel painters could pause in their work and consider the composition before picking up the brush and continuing to paint. Because panels could be painted in the artist's studio and then transported to a purchaser, patrons and other clients often visited the studio instead of the artist's visiting the building in which a fresco would be executed. Clients could thus have the opportunity to buy from the artist's stock of paintings in addition to commissioning specific works. Unlike fresco painting, which presented no problems of installation, panel paintings had to be mounted or otherwise fixed for display. Artists sometimes sent instructions for installation along with their paintings. Albrecht Dürer (1471–1528), for example, sent this note in 1509: "If the picture is set up, let it be made to hang forward two or three finger breadths, for then it will be well visible, on account of the glare" (Holt 1981, p. 335). Although panel painting includes several genres, we shall concentrate on altarpieces and portraits, two important types for the Renaissance. Mythological scenes, such as Botticelli's *Primavera* (Uffizi Museum, Florence), and historical scenes were also popular. We should note that many single-panel paintings from the Renaissance with Christian themes might originally have been part of an altarpiece. As a result of the Protestant Reformation, French Revolution, and other disruptive and destructive activities, numerous altarpieces were disassembled or destroyed. Today we have examples of historic altarpieces whose central panel and wings are in different countries, or even different hemispheres.

ALTARPIECES

Altarpieces are the crowning glory of Christian churches. They are painted or carved representations of the Crucifixion or other Christian subjects, placed on, behind, or above an altar in a church or chapel. Various words are used for an altarpiece, *retablum* (behind the altar) in Latin. *Retable* and *reredos* (from French, behind the altar) are used in English; the latter usually denotes a large screen carved in wood or stone and only rarely painted. Many Renaissance altarpieces were constructed of three wooden panels hinged together (a triptych), and some had four or more hinged panels (polyptychs). Use of two panels (diptychs) is rather rare in churches, but diptychs evidently were used for private devotional purposes. Although installed near an altar, altarpieces are not part of the official liturgical ensemble. Usually their iconography celebrates the saint associated with each church, and Counter-Reformation policy supported this aspect of Christian art. In southern Europe, especially Italy, altarpieces of the early Renaissance usually consisted of one large panel, or a central panel with two stationary wings. In northern Europe, hinged, movable panels were preferred, and by the latter 15th century this fashion had become popular in Italy. Hinged panels gave artists the opportunity to paint scenes on the exteriors of the wings. When such an altarpiece is closed, these scenes are the only visible component unless the altarpiece has a predella, a relatively narrow strip of paintings along the horizontal base of the structure. In this section we shall describe examples of painted altarpieces; carved altarpieces are discussed later (see Sculpture, pages 81–82).

Examples of 15th-Century Painted Altarpieces

The van Eyck brothers, Hubert (c. 1385/90–1426) and Jan (1385?–1440/41), probably created the monumental Ghent Altarpiece (1432?, Altarpiece of the Lamb, Cathedral of Saint Bavo in Ghent). Jan completed the painting after Hubert's death. In fact, given the vastly differing scale of figures between the top and bottom sections, Jan van Eyck may have assembled this famous altarpiece from several paintings left in his brother's studio when he died (see Snyder 1985, p. 93). The largest extant altarpiece of the Renaissance era, it was considered wondrous and miraculous. Recent scholarship has proposed that the Ghent Altarpiece, commissioned for the Church of Saint John in Ghent (now called Saint Bavo), was not simply displayed in wooden framing, but rather installed within an elaborate framework that may have resembled a cathedral. Such a display would have made the Ghent Altarpiece even more magnificent.

The Portinari Altarpiece (Uffizi Museum, Florence) by the Flemish artist Hugo van der Goes was one of the most influential altarpieces of the 15th century. Probably commissioned in Bruges between 1474 and 1475, it measures approximately 101 by 121.5 inches (253 by 304 centimeters). Only the Ghent Altarpiece is larger among Renaissance works in this genre. The subject of the Portinari Altarpiece is the Adoration of the newborn Christ child. In 15th-century Florentine altarpieces, the subject of

3.4 Altarpiece (retable) of the Apotheosis of the Virgin. Altarpieces usually featured the Virgin or Christ in the center, with saints and donors on the sides and at the bottom. Spanish artist, late 15th century. (Courtesy of The Hispanic Society of America, A13)

the Adoration usually focused on the magi, not the shepherds, as in van der Goes's composition. In both iconography and monumental proportions the Portinari commission stood out from contemporary altarpieces, and in an astounding way since the shepherds are highlighted so realistically. This altarpiece is an important example of the sacred art being commissioned by Italian merchants; the donor portraits are discussed later. The Flemish realism of van der Goes and his contemporaries made a tremendous impact on European painters of the second half of the 15th century.

In France circa 1498, the Master of Moulins (name unknown, fl. c. 1480–1500) painted a triptych altarpiece now in Moulins Cathedral. Its subject is the Madonna of the Immaculate Conception, with an Annunciation scene in *grisaille* (monochromatic gray) on the two exterior wings. The donor portraits are mentioned later. (The doctrine of the Immaculate Conception proclaims that the Virgin herself was conceived without sin, her mother Ann being in a state of divine grace.) This altarpiece is noteworthy for its amazingly luminous color. The seated Virgin has her feet on a crescent Moon (symbol of the Immaculate Conception), with concentric circles in pale and bright colors tunneling into a golden, Sun-like orb behind her. She thus becomes a Madonna of the Sun, a popular northern Renaissance image.

Examples of 16th-Century Painted Altarpieces

The Isenheim Altarpiece (1515, Musée d'Unterlinden, Colmar) was painted by the German artist Matthias Grünewald (c. 1470–1528) for a monastic hospital at Isenheim. With its images of healing saints and grossly diseased individuals, the altarpiece offered what the Renaissance believed was the best possibility of recovery, namely, prayer and devotional meditation. For severely ill people, because there was little hope of recovery, the altarpiece was a reassurance of life after death through Christian salvation. Unlike the other painted altarpieces described in this chapter, the Isenheim Altarpiece was a complicated movable structure with three sets of hinged wings. The wings provided several levels of revelation as the altarpiece was gradually opened; the final interior presentation was a carved wooden shrine, gilded and polychromed, by Nikolaus Hagenaur (fl. 1493–before 1538). Saint Anthony Abbot, patron saint of the monastery, is celebrated in the shrine.

Piero di Cosimo's (1461/62–1521) Immaculate Conception altarpiece painting for San Francesco in Fiesole was probably executed shortly after 1510. In typical Italian style, it is painted on a single panel. Piero di Cosimo evidently was not known for his altarpieces, but for secular mythological paintings. This altarpiece is famous today for its extraordinary composition, in which Saints Jerome and Francis, kneeling on a stone slab and each holding an inscription, presumably are discussing the Immaculate Conception. This painting originally would have been placed behind the altar, and the stone slab seems to project back into the picture plane from the bottom edge of the painting and to be comparable to a back section of the altar. The saints to the left and right of the slab are in three-quarter view (heads to thighs), with their feet "standing" below the actual picture. They seem to be standing within the church itself. For Renaissance worshipers, in a shadowy space illuminated only by candles, the devotional effect of this interactive painting must have been powerful.

The Altarpiece of the Holy Kinship (or Saint Ann Altarpiece, 1507–09) by the Antwerp painter Quentin Metsys (1466–1530) was commissioned by the Confraternity of Saint Ann in Louvain for their Church of Saint Peter. During the early 16th century, Antwerp was experiencing an economic upsurge as the city became a major port via the river Scheldt. Both art and commerce flourished, generating many significant artistic commissions. This altarpiece by Metsys, executed with typically Flemish attention to detail, has the soft colors of contemporary Venetian paintings and the type of setting found in many Italian compositions. Ann, the mother of the Virgin, is placed on a porch with Mary, the infant Jesus, and two female relatives. Behind them are Ann's male relatives, standing in a classicizing loggia with a landscape opening into the far distance. Such fantasy landscapes would soon become a popular component of Mannerist painting in northern Europe. In the confraternity's church, this infinite landscape may have lifted the worshipers' inner vision beyond the limits of the earthly building.

PORTRAITURE

Today we usually think of portraiture as reproducing an exact photographic likeness, recording how a person looks at a particular stage in life. Renaissance portraiture was somewhat more complicated, as might be expected of an age that did not yet have the medium of photography. Until Flemish realism began to dominate European portraiture, the quality of being lifelike, or naturalistic, was the major goal of a successful portrait, even if the painting did not look exactly like the sitter. Precise physical representations were not necessarily the goal of portraiture, and artists sometimes treated the sitter as a type; the result, for example, would be a regal or spiritual visage that did not conform to outward reality. For women, beauty and "virtue" were important attributes, leading to subtle manipulations of facial characteristics, especially in portraits sent to prospective suitors. Representations of age, particularly for women of power, were a problem for most artists. In this instance, painters could be ordered to copy a portrait made when the sitter was younger instead of painting an aging subject. Finally, one genre of portraiture did approach photographic precision, namely, the masks made of a living or recently deceased subject. Death masks were often used to create the facial aspects of tomb sculpture.

The media in which the Renaissance produced portraits included drawing, painting, prints, illuminated manuscripts, statues, and medallions. Painted portraits are treated in this section; other media except drawings are discussed later. The focus here is on portraits painted on panels, with passing mention of frescoed portraiture. In general, Italian painters during the early Renaissance depicted their subjects in a profile pose, probably influenced by the profiles of Roman emperors on coins and medallions. Although the profile portrait may lend imperial grandeur to the subject, it seems distant and unconnected with the viewer. Flemish and Franco-Flemish painters used the more intimate and descriptive three-quarter view for the head, and this pose prevailed throughout western Europe by the mid-16th century. The northern portrait tradition influenced southern artists in other ways: Entire compositions often were copied with a different individual depicted in the portrait. The most prestigious type of painted portrait was the representation of donors and their families in altarpieces, ambitious projects that could take several years. Other important types included royal portraits, bridal or dowry portraits, and marriage portraits.

Portraits were created in a variety of circumstances, ranging from painting a subject who sat for the artist to attempting a painted portrait from a sketch sent by another artist to painting a portrait purely from memory. New portraits of ancestors or famous individuals for whom no portrait was extant sometimes were desired, in which case the painter would have had to rely on representing the subject as a specific type, following a written description of the person, or using someone (perhaps a descendant) as a model. There was, of course, no professional lighting mechanism. Portraits painted by sunlight streaming in through a window could result in a harsh treatment, and portraits painted by candlelight or lamplight could be too somber and dark. Artists learned to compensate for such problems, using linen curtains to diffuse sunlight as well as mirrors and light-colored walls to boost the illumination of candlelight. Finally, once the sitter was satisfied with a portrait, the artist often had to provide painted copies. Many art students and apprentices learned their technique by copying portraits, as the master usually completed only the face and hands, if those. The market for portraits in western Europe was amazingly strong, especially during the 16th century, when collectors paid handsomely for well-executed portraits, even of unknown sitters. Portrait miniatures (discussed at the end of this section) were particularly desirable. During the Renaissance, the aesthetics of portraiture had its beginnings.

Donor Portraits in Painted Altarpieces
Unlike the Ghent Altarpiece, with its donors on the exterior wings, the Portinari Altarpiece incorporates the Portinari family into both interior side panels with the members kneeling and praying to the Virgin. Although the donors and their children are part of the interior scenery, they are nevertheless distanced from the Virgin by their discrete panels. The left wing depicts Tommaso Portinari, head of the Medici bank in Bruges until 1477, with his elder son, Antonio, and younger son, Pigello, accompanied by their patron saints, Saint Anthony Abbot and Saint Thomas. In the right wing, Mary Magdalene is standing behind the daughter, Margherita, while Saint Margaret is behind her mother, Maria. The nearly life-sized scale of the Portinari portraits kept the family perpetually present behind the altar of their family church, Saint Egidio, with the children shown at about the same size as the angels in the foreground. Naturally, this altarpiece was commissioned as sacred art that might ease the Portinaris' path into heaven. It was also, however, an obvious status symbol for Tommaso Portinari, who was bitterly competing commercially and financially with his Florentine rival, the banker Angelo Tani, also a patron of the arts. The rising merchant class across western Europe commissioned elaborate altarpieces

as an indication of social rank as well as of their allegiance to the church.

In the circa 1498 altarpiece by the Master of Moulins (discussed earlier), the donors' portraits along with that of their daughter are painted on the two interior wings. As it was for the Portinari Altarpiece, the impetus for this work was competitive, but in a more congenial vein. The duke of Bourbon, John II (d. 1488), commissioned an altar and stained-glass window celebrating the Madonna of the Immaculate Conception for the Collegiate Church of Moulins. After John II's death, his brother, Pierre II, who succeeded him as duke, commissioned the altarpiece for the chapel of the church. The duke's patron saint is Saint Peter, depicted behind him wearing the golden, jeweled papal tiara and luxurious robes, greatly enhancing the duke's own status. Pierre II and his family are very lifelike, even to the extent that his little girl looks sickly and his wife looks exhausted, indicating the high value placed on naturalistic portraiture in northern Europe. Even the angels appear to be individual children, each with a distinctive physiognomy.

Patrons sometimes were depicted within the main, central panel of an altarpiece instead of in the wings, as in Hans Memling's (c. 1430–1494) *Donne Triptych*, in which the donors are virtually at the Virgin's knees with their clothing touching the edges of her rug. Such compositions may have had talismanic qualities, actually giving the donors an illusion of attachment to the Virgin's purity and to her power of intercession for their sins. The Portuguese painter Nuno Gonçalves (fl. 1450–71) was a court painter for Afonso V (1432–81) influenced by the new Flemish style, possibly because of a diplomatic visit that Jan van Eyck made to Lisbon in 1428. The central panel of Gonçalves's Saint Vincent Polyptych (c. 1465, now in the National Museum, Lisbon) is filled with lifelike figures with seemingly individualistic features, as if he had been painting a portrait of each person. These are thought to be representations of members of the royal family, his patrons.

Painted Portraits of Royalty and Other Notables

Owning a portrait of a powerful individual conferred status during the Renaissance, and powerful individuals who displayed their own portrait enhanced their commanding presence. Members of royal and ducal families had their portrait painted not only for their immediate family, but also for presentation as diplomat gifts. Papal portraits had the greatest status among Catholics, and Raphael was one of the greatest portrayers of Renaissance popes. In 1511 or 1512 he painted a portrait of Julius II (1443–1513) that looked almost alive (National Gallery, London). Vasari remarked that viewers were actually frightened by its realistic appearance. In England, except for portrait miniaturists (see later discussion), the portrait painters were Flemish or German; the most famous was Hans Holbein the Younger (1497/98–1543). He made several portraits of Henry VIII (1491–1547) and members of the court. His famous portrait of the king grimly staring forward, costumed in jeweled velvet finery and massively filling the picture, was as forbidding to Renaissance people as it is to viewers today (National Gallery, Rome). The Dutch artist Anthonis Mor (c. 1516/20–76/77) was painter to the Spanish court in the Netherlands. His stern yet lifelike depictions of the Habsburgs and Spanish nobility, including Philip II's (1527–98) wife, Mary Tudor (1516–58), placed Mor in the vanguard of portraitists. A female artist, Sofonisba Anguissola (1532–1625), gained international fame with her work in court portraiture. While painting in Madrid, Anguissola also gave art lessons to the queen, Elisabeth of Valois, herself a talented portraitist.

Painted Bridal or Dowry Portraits and Marriage Portraits

Especially in 15th-century Italy, husbands commissioned portraits of their new bride to show off not only her beauty, but also the wealth of jewels either owned by the bride as a dowry or presented to her by the husband as a wedding gift. These portraits exclusively depicted young women, their ideal age about 16 years old. We can tell that they are married because their hair is bound up; unmarried women had freely flowing hair. Besides being symbolically associated with womanly virtues such as chastity (meaning faithfulness for a married woman) and fertility, the jewels depicted in these portraits reinforced the social status of the husband. For artists painting the portraits, the ornate hairstyles intertwined with pearls, rubies, and other strings of gems, combined with the lovely youth of the subjects, presented an excellent opportunity to create some of the most beautiful portraits of Renaissance women. Noteworthy artists who executed such bridal portraits included Pisanello (c. 1395–1455/56), Fra Filippo Lippi (c. 1406–69), and Antonio del Pollaiuolo (c. 1432–98). Marriage portraits commemorating the wedding depicted the married couple and were popular in both northern and southern Europe. Among the best known examples is *Arnolfini Wedding Portrait* (1434, National Gallery, London) by Jan van Eyck, portraying Giovanni Arnolfini and his wife. The couple, holding hands, are standing in a bedroom with a brass chandelier and sumptuous orange bedcoverings. Their portraits are full length, showing the luxury of their fur-trimmed garments. Most other Renaissance marriage portraits are less than full-length portraits, often with a plain background.

Some Other Types of Painted Portraits

All the types of portraits described popularized the genre among the wealthy middle class, prompting commissions from husbands, parents, and others who wished to immortalize their family members in painted portraits. Today the most famous individual portrait of the Renaissance is *Mona Lisa* (Louvre Museum, Paris), executed by Leonardo da Vinci (1452–1519) in the early 16th century. Leonardo, whose extant portraits are only of women (unusual for the time), may have become somewhat obsessed about what probably began as simply a commission for the sitter's husband. The painting quickly became famous in the 16th century, partly because of Vasari's published description: "The mouth, with its opening joining the red lips to the flesh of the face, seemed to be real flesh rather than paint. Anyone who looked very attentively at the hollow of her throat would see her pulse beating . . . And in this portrait by Leonardo, there is a smile so pleasing that it seems more divine than human, and it was considered a wondrous thing that it was as lively as the smile of the living original" (Vasari 1998, p. 294).

In his book *Utopia* (1516), Sir Thomas More (1478–1535) recommended that portraits of noteworthy individuals be displayed in the marketplace so that their descendants might be reminded of their virtue and emulate them. In this case, the viewer would be receiving the impetus toward noble thoughts and deeds via the portrait. Another type of

Renaissance portrait had a different goal, as the artist painted an individual as a saint or mythological deity and thus imbued the sitter with qualities of the particular saint or deity. Agnolo Bronzino (1503–72), for example, painted a portrait of the great admiral Andrea Doria (1466–1560) as Neptune, god of the sea. Portraits were introduced into the narrative compositions of mural painting, such as the frescoes painted by Raphael in the Vatican apartments. For his portraits of historic popes, the artist used the likenesses of Renaissance popes, his patrons. Sometimes the artists inserted portraits of themselves into such group scenes, usually gazing toward the viewer. One popular type of portraiture was the genealogical tree, with individual heads inserted in circles or other shapes. Although ancestors usually had idealized portraits, the heads of Renaissance contemporaries could be realistic. Portrait miniatures are treated in the following section.

3.5 Head of the Virgin. Drawing by Leonardo da Vinci, late 15th or early 16th century. (The Metropolitan Museum of Art, Harris Brisbane Dick Fund, 1951 [51.90])

Painting on Vellum and Parchment

Vellum and parchment were the preferred media for painting portrait miniatures. (Illuminated manuscripts on vellum and parchment are discussed in chapter 5.) The court painter Hans Holbein also created miniature portraits, including a self-portrait head and shoulders in watercolor, on vellum less than two inches in diameter (The Wallace Collection, London). Several female artists excelled in miniatures, but individual attribution is impossible to determine. The best known English Renaissance painter of portrait miniatures was Nicholas Hilliard (c. 1547–1619), who produced miniatures of the royal family. In addition to the usual bust portraits in miniature, Hilliard painted full-length examples, some less than six inches in height. Although we have no extant miniatures of living subjects earlier than the 1520s, inventories from the 15th century document portraits in miniature, some on ivory instead of vellum. Much more personal than portraits in fresco or painted on panels, the miniatures were keepsakes, often gifts intended for loved ones. Some of them were inserted in brooches or lockets and worn as sentimental jewelry by the recipients.

TAPESTRIES

In the latter 14th century, important tapestry workshops were established in the duchy of Burgundy, which included Flanders, and northern France. The driving forces behind this productivity were four brothers: Charles V, king of France, and the dukes of Burgundy, Berry, and Anjou. Their commissions supported numerous tapestry weavers, especially in Arras, Tournai, and Brussels. By the 16th century, Brussels had become one of the most important tapestry centers of Europe, along with other cities in Flanders such as Bruges, Ghent, and Lille. In addition to producing tapestries, some of these workshops trained foreigners in the craft. The English weavers who managed the famous Sheldon workshops established in England in the 1560s were taught in Flanders. Italy had tapestry workshops established under the auspices of various city-states, those of Florence, Milan, and Ferrara the most significant. Many tapestry commissions required months, if not years, of labor. These luxurious wall decorations, also serving as insulation from cold and damp, often were created in a series of a dozen or more pieces. Single tapestries in the series sometimes were as high as 15 feet and as long as 30 feet. Entire galleries of royal residences had tapestries in series covering the walls, providing visual entertainment, warmth, and prestige.

Artists designed the tapestries by drawing sketches for the patron; secular imagery, especially that involving classical mythology, was almost as popular as sacred imagery. Once the sketches were approved, the designs were converted into full-scale cartoons. Weaving the tapestry was a painstaking process because the weaver had to keep checking the cartoon being copied. There are isolated examples of tapestries commissioned to reproduce wall paintings, the most notable of which is the series created circa 1540 that copied the frescoes in the Gallery of Francis I at Fontainebleau (Kunsthistorisches Museum, Vienna). Many tapestry designs, of course, reflected the styles of famous painters, some of whom themselves created the designs. Because tapestries were portable, they were carried from one residence to another, and they also were used for ceremonial purposes. Tapestries commissioned by Pope Leo X (1475–1521) and designed by Raphael (woven in Brussels, 1515–19) covered the walls of the Sistine Chapel on special occasions. Italian Renaissance art, particularly individualized figural forms and linear perspective, had a significant impact on 16th-century Flemish tapestry design. Because tapestries were woven from luxurious fabrics, including finely spun wool, silk, and sometimes gold or silver thread, and because the process was quite time-consuming, tapestries were among the most costly and desirable art objects of the Renaissance. King Henry VIII owned more than 2,000 of them. (See Ceremonies, pages 299–302 in chapter 12, for more information on tapestries.)

3.6 The Last Supper. *Tapestry designed by Bernaert van Orley, probably woven in Flanders by Pieter de Pannemaker, before 1530.* (The Metropolitan Museum of Art, Robert Lehman Collection, 1975 [1975.1.1915])

Flemish Tapestries

Pictorial designs in tapestry became the preferred mode for Renaissance tastes, with early examples influenced by the religious work of artists such as Rogier van der Weyden (c. 1400–64), whose studio was in Brussels. Narrative designs were very popular, especially since tapestries provided an expansive surface on which the story could be displayed. Hunting scenes, highly sought after, often contained symbolic imagery within a gorgeous surface filled with colorful costumes. During most of the 15th century, Flemish narrative tapestries were crowded with numerous people and animals as Gothic taste prevailed in the north. Italian Renaissance artists, such as Raphael and Bronzino, began to create cartoons, and they designed tapestries with life-sized figures in their own pictorial space, often placed within proper linear perspective. Italian prints of the 16th century provided a plethora of sources for Flemish tapestry designers, particularly in the graphics of Marcantonio Raimondi (c. 1470/82–c. 1527/34), who reproduced well-known Renaissance paintings in Rome in detailed graphic images (see Prints, page 85). The Flemish artist Bernaert van Orley (c. 1492–1542) was the best representative of the new "Roman style" in northern tapestry production, influenced by Raphael's cartoons executed as papal commissions. Orley worked for the Habsburgs, particularly Margaret of Austria (1480–1530), regent of the Netherlands, and her heir, Mary of Hungary (1505–1558), sister of Emperor Charles V (1500–1556). He designed both sacred and secular tapestries, including *Maximilian's Hunts* (Louvre Museum, Paris) celebrating Margaret of Austria's father, Emperor Maximilian I (1459–1519). Because of the political instability of the Spanish Netherlands during the 1560s and later in the 16th century, many Flemish weavers moved their workshops into German territory, and a few emigrated to England or France.

Italian Tapestries

Because tapestry workshops in Italy were created under the patronage of specific individuals and funded directly by them, the weavers often had to close the shop or emigrate when the dynasty of the city-state died out or was conquered. In general, this workshop system was smaller and less independent than the large factory workshops of northern Europe. The market was local, whereas an international clientele patronized workshops in Flanders. Three of the more productive Italian workshops were those in Milan, Ferrara, and Florence.

Francesco Sforza (1401–66), duke of Milan, founded that city's tapestry workshop in 1450. About the same time, Leonello d'Este (1407–50), lord of Ferrara, established a workshop in Ferrara shortly before his death that was still productive during the 16th century. The Flemish weaver Nicolas Karcher (fl. 1517, d. 1562) and his brother, Jan, worked in the shop. One of the more famous series of tapestries produced by them depicted the mythological themes of the Latin poet Ovid. After working in Mantua for the Gonzaga court, Karcher relocated to Florence and set up a tapestry workshop in 1546 under the patronage of Cosimo I de' Medici (1519–74). His tapestry series in 20 pieces, the *History of Joseph* (1546–52, Palazzo Vecchio, Florence), included designs by Jacopo da Pontormo (1494–57) and his student, Agnolo Bronzino.

SCULPTURE

Renaissance sculpture was the medium most obviously influenced by ancient forms, as Italian artists created sculpture in a truly classical style. Because the polychrome color was lost from ancient statues and buildings, Italian artists thought that the ancients did not color their sculpture, and thus their classicizing sculpture usually remained uncolored. During the 15th century, many northern sculptors, as well as southern sculptors living outside Italy, continued the medieval practice of coloring their work. As in painting, the renewal of sculpture began in northern Italy, where artists combined the realism of Flemish style with an understanding of human anatomy and of the movement of the human figure in volumetric space. Using classical statues as their inspiration, Italian 15th-century sculptors created "the beginning of good modern style" (thus Vasari 1998, p. 92, describes the work of Ghiberti). The Florentine goldsmith and sculptor Lorenzo Ghiberti (1378–1455) owned a collection of antique sculpture, including bronze statuary. He achieved artistic immortality in 1401, when he won a much-publicized competition to create bronze-paneled doors for the baptistry in Florence, the first major sculpture commission of the Italian Renaissance.

These contests, which continued throughout the Renaissance, were necessary because a patron undertaking a major sculptural project was committing to a significant investment in time and materials. The cost of transporting stone from the quarry, for example, could be prohibitive. Unlike a painting or tapestry, which could be commissioned on the strength of sketches, the three-dimensional quality of sculpture, as of architecture, usually required that artists submit models and budgets. Models were required for major commissions. Not surprisingly, the public nature of such competitions not only enhanced the fame of the winner, but also helped to raise the status of sculptors in general.

Sculpture in Wood

German, Netherlandish, and English wood-carvers were renowned for their expertise, particularly in altarpieces that consisted of numerous sacred figures within intricately filigreed structures. The flexibility and relatively light weight of wood permitted wood-carvers to produce enormous altarpieces with elaborate compositions. Viet Stoss (c. 1438–1533) was a German sculptor who moved to Poland in 1477 for the purpose of creating a wooden altarpiece for the Church of Our Lady (Cracow), commissioned by the community of German merchants in the city. With double-folding wings, it is one of the most ambitious carved wooden altarpieces of the 15th century. It was fully painted in polychrome, probably by another artist. Sculptors often worked in collaboration with a painter when a piece was to be polychromed. Stoss seemed to have bypassed Renaissance style completely, joining the vertical Gothic style to the turbulent expressionism of the baroque. His treatment of drapery exemplifies the exuberant movement of this huge altarpiece as a whole. It is important to realize that many artists of the 15th and 16th centuries, especially those in northern Europe, retained Gothic elements in their work through the end of what we call the Renaissance period.

Tilman Riemenschneider (c. 1460–1531), a master of both wood and stone, created two elaborate triptych altarpieces in limewood that remain in their original locations: the Altarpiece of the Holy Blood in the Jakobskirche (Rothenburg), and the Altarpiece of the Assumption of Mary in the Herrgottskirche (Creglingen). Limewood has a very fine grain, which allows minute details to be carved much more easily

3.7 Swabian (German) limewood sculpture of the Virgin and Child. Devotional statues of the Christ child and his mother were popular throughout Europe. Circle of Hans Multscher, third quarter of the 15th century. (Photograph courtesy of Sotheby's, Inc., © 2003)

than in less receptive wood. These two altarpieces attest to Riemenschneider's originality, especially his flowing treatment of drapery as it harmoniously follows the movement of the three-dimensional figures. Both altarpieces have Renaissance spatial characteristics, with figures in the central section situated inside a chapel having small "windows" in the back, allowing light to play against the backs of the carvings and flicker across the sides of their faces—an effect that can make them seem almost lifelike. These altarpieces, as is much of Riemenschneider's work, were uncolored so that the fine texture of the wood can be appreciated. The more sacred of the two altarpieces is that of the Holy Blood (1501–05) in the Jakobskirche, with its relic of the blood of Christ and depiction of the Last Supper. The figures are rather large; the contract called for figures four feet in height. Most wood-carvers made smaller wooden sculptures for stock, and people purchased devotional statues such as crucifixes and Madonnas at fairs and sales stands. Although some of these carvings were made for mass consumption and thus are rather crude, they permitted even the lower classes to have a devotional object in their private home. The Protestant Reformation caused many of these pieces to be burned, along with more important art such as wooden altarpieces and shrines.

Sculpture in Stone

For sculpture in stone, marble was highly valued because most types of marble are very durable and can be beautifully smoothed and polished, as in ancient Roman statuary. Other stone favored by Renaissance sculptors included limestone and sandstone. Relief sculpture was often executed in a combination of marble and limestone. In some instances, artists created Renaissance stone sculpture from pieces of ancient Roman buildings or actual Roman sculpture, such as in the Medici tombs by Michelangelo. The dense Cararra marble found near Pisa was considered the best marble in Italy. Michelangelo personally traveled to the Carrara quarry in 1495 to select the large block of marble from which he would sculpt the *Pietà* for Saint Peter's Basilica. Although most stone sculptors were men, one female sculptor was praised by Vasari, Properzia de' Rossi

(c. 1490–1530). She worked in her native Bologna, creating church sculpture and portrait busts. In his chapter on this artist, Vasari made a very interesting remark about women in general: "It is extraordinary that in all the skills and pursuits in which women in any period whatever have with some preparation become involved, they have always succeeded most admirably and have become more than famous, as countless examples could easily demonstrate" (Vasari 1998, p. 338).

Tomb sculpture provided commissions for many sculptors working in stone during the 15th and 16th centuries. Unlike in the Middle Ages, when tombs were usually decorated years and even decades after the individual had died, many Renaissance patrons had their own tomb sculpture completed while they still were very much alive. In Gothic tomb sculpture, effigies, as if asleep, were often carved on a stone slab or sarcophagus installed on the floor of a church, with heraldic insignia to identify them and faces of portrait quality. There might also be a statue of the person as he or she looked when alive. In Italy, tomb sculpture was usually installed above the floor in a wall niche, with stone molding or curtains framing the niche. Tombs of royalty and other important people often included statues as "mourners," including allegorical figures and ancestors. Michelangelo's tomb sculpture for the Medici, created between 1521 and 1534 (Church of San Lorenzo, Florence), was famous among his contemporaries. Lorenzo de' Medici is seen not as in death, but as a pensive, armored male figure seated in a niche above the sarcophagus. Two magnificent nude allegorical figures, one male and one female, partially recline on the classical sarcophagus. Vasari said of the Medici tomb sculpture that "these statues are carved with the most beautifully formed poses and skillfully executed muscles and would be sufficient, if the art of sculpture were lost, to return it to its original splendour" (Vasari 1998, p. 456).

Renaissance sculpture based on classical models was spread to other parts of Europe by Italian sculpture that was imported, Italian artists who worked outside Italy, and foreign artists who were trained in workshops in Italy. Several Spanish sculptors, for example, studied in Naples, which was part of the Spanish kingdom. Members of the Mendoza family preferred Italianate art, and Pedro González de

Mendoza (1428–95), who in 1473 became a cardinal, patronized Renaissance humanists and the new classicism. His tomb in the cathedral of Toledo, evidently by an Italian sculptor, includes a magnificent triumphal arch in Roman style. Funerary monuments in France began to have classicizing elements by the latter 15th century, and in the early 16th century several important tombs by Italian artists combined the medieval-style recumbent effigy with a classical-style sarcophagus. Receptacles for the heart of the deceased were sometimes commissioned separately from the tomb sculpture proper. The French artist Pierre Bontemps (c. 1512–c. 1570) created the classical urn for the heart of Francis I (Saint Denis, near Paris). Both the urn and its rectangular pedestal have Renaissance strapwork cartouches, oval on the urn and round on the pedestal, with allegorical figures representing the arts and sciences.

Secular sculpture in stone included garden statuary, such as fountains, allegorical and equestrian figures, portraits (especially bust portraits), and classical shapes such as urns and obelisks. Gardens sometimes had bust portraits mounted on high pedestals or columns so that those strolling through the garden would see the faces eye to eye. Garden sculpture included both ancient and modern pieces. Several important Italian villas, such as the Villa Farnese, had a "secret garden" or "garden of love." These featured monstrous, erotic, or amusing statues and inscriptions, installed to surprise or delight visitors. Several villas had a *nymphaeum*, a wading pool or small swimming pool like those found in private houses in ancient Rome. With mosaic floors in glass and ceramic tile, the *nymphaea* (plural form) often included statues of water nymphs.

Sculpture in Bronze

Renaissance bronze sculpture was not carved as wood and stone were but instead cast in a mold via the lost-wax process. In this process, a wax model was closely coated with a substance that could withstand high temperatures, then heated until the wax melted. The result was a mold into which molten bronze was poured. After the bronze cooled, the coating was removed. Bronze, an alloy of copper and tin, was superior to brass, an alloy of copper and zinc. Artists were able to apply finishes, such as gilt, to bronze statues and decorative objects, and the natural patina of bronze was appreciated by Renaissance collectors. Ghiberti (see page 80) was the first great bronze sculptor of the Renaissance, closely followed by another Florentine artist, Donatello (1386–1466), whose bronze statue of David was the first life-sized, free-standing nude in Renaissance style (1430–32, Bargello, Florence). Although Donatello carved biblical figures in stone in a formalized manner, as if they were ancient Romans, his David, in a relaxed *contrapposto* pose, could not be more realistic. Donatello executed commissions in both Florence and Rome, including sculptural work for Saint Peter's Basilica.

Funerary monuments in bronze were highly prized during the Renaissance. The Vischer foundry in Nuremberg was active from the latter 15th century until 1549, and two of the director's sons were influenced by a visit to Italy. This firm was known for its bronze tomb monuments, which were exported to Poland, Hungary, and elsewhere. The Italian sculptor Leone Leoni (c. 1509–90), who settled in Milan, produced bronze portraits for the Habsburgs and members of the Spanish royal family. (King Philip II was also duke of Milan at the time.) Leone's son, Pompeo Leoni (c. 1533–1608), created the famous funerary group of gilded bronze portraits composing the royal family's tomb sculpture at the Escorial (1597–1600).

Leone Leoni also made small round portrait medals in bronze, of such famous contemporaries as Michelangelo, Titian, and Andrea Doria. With his expertise in engraving coins for the mints of several city-states, Leoni could work with ease in such small scale. Pisanello, in 1439, cast the first known Renaissance portrait medal, of the Holy Roman Emperor. Early in the 15th century, collecting antique Roman medals and coins, as well as medieval reproductions of such pieces, had become popular among the aristocracy. Because the heads of Roman emperors and their contemporaries were almost always in profile, Renaissance portrait medals also depicted heads in profile. Given the individualized appearance of many Renaissance medals, we assume that they portrayed the head with some degree of accuracy. There are several examples of portraits sketched from life for people who also have portrait medals extant, and in most instances the likenesses are quite similar. In addition to providing visual information about the appearance

3.8 *Portrait of Iolanta Ludovica, wife of Philibert II of Savoy. Silver coin, late 15th or early 16th century.* (Hermitage, Saint Petersburg, Russia/Bridgeman Art Library)

molded, thrown, and sculpted ceramic sculpture could be included in permanent architectural installations. Because the color was baked into the clay during the firing process and not just applied as paint, it was very durable, especially in the relatively mild climate of northern Italy. With this technical improvement, the artistic status of ceramic artists was enhanced. The white Madonna and Child, in relief against a blue background in a circular wreath, became della Robbia's signature image and thus became a standard component of many Renaissance buildings. The French artist Bernard Palissy (c. 1510–89) created a new type of white enamel for his glazes that improved the durability of his ceramics. A noted naturalist, Palissy molded realistic snakes, fish, and other creatures for his garden projects as well as for his pottery. Catherine de' Medici commissioned him to create a ceramic grotto for the Tuileries Gardens in Paris (c. 1573). Because terra-cotta was such an inexpensive material, artisans made stock pieces to sell at fairs and in shops, especially devotional imagery. Inexpensive, small

of such luminaries as popes, monarchs, and *condottieri*, Renaissance portrait medals help to document buildings that are no longer standing or that have been altered. Alberti's façade for the Tempio Malatestiano in Rimini, for example, is preserved on a coin honoring Sigismundo Malatesta, who commissioned the project (see chapter 4, on architecture).

Because bronze was an excellent material for artillery, numerous Renaissance bronzes were melted down in subsequent centuries by military leaders desperate to obtain munitions. The imagery of some of these lost works of art has been documented in drawings, engravings, and verbal descriptions by artists and collectors.

Sculpture in Clay

Luca della Robbia (1400–1482) was the first major ceramic sculptor of the Renaissance. Terra-cotta, a material abundantly supplied by the Earth, has been an artistic medium in Italy since the beginning of recorded history. Della Robbia discovered how to glaze terra-cotta to make it waterproof, so that

3.9 *Painted enamel plaque of the Crucifixion. Limoges, France, second half of the 16th century.* (Photograph courtesy of Sotheby's Inc., © 2003)

low reliefs in clay, many depicting the Madonna and Christ child, for example, were a popular export commodity from both Utrecht and Cologne.

PRINTS

The earliest European prints were woodcut reliefs, and the earliest extant examples are playing cards and devotional images. Block books of the 15th century were produced as prints, with each page of the images and text carved on a single block of wood. Because during the latter 14th century, paper mills in northern Europe were well established, printers of the early Renaissance had a ready supply of paper. By the mid-15th century, intaglio engraving on metal had become feasible. Several of the best printmakers were trained as goldsmiths, a craft that requires the same close attention to detail as does printmaking. The present section discusses a few of the artists who were important printmakers during the Renaissance. (See chapter 2, Religion, for more information on religious prints; chapter 4, Architecture and Urban Planning, for views; chapter 5, Literature and Language, for information on illustrated books; and chapter 9, Exploration and Travel, for information on printed maps and exotic imagery.)

Martin Schongauer (1435/50–91), though known as a painter during his lifetime, is now remembered for his prints. The style of this northern artist is Gothic, in that much of his religious imagery consists of swirling crowds of figures. He refined the technique of engraving, however, with clarity of line and delicacy of expression. Another significant contribution were his engravings of ornaments, some of which were surely used by artisans in creating the decorative arts described later. With the advent of such prints, artists no longer needed to draw their own pattern books as a source for ornamental designs. Schongauer's work had a tremendous influence on the young Albrecht Dürer, who traveled to Colmar, then part of Germany, to study with Schongauer but arrived after he had died. Dürer became famous through the international marketing of his prints, beginning with the 15 large woodcut prints in his *Apocalypse* series issued in 1498. His style in this series combined the Gothic idiom with harmonious appropriation of pictorial space. Dürer's nude Adam in his print *Adam and Eve* represents a bold step forward in northern figural form, virtually transforming Adam into a Roman deity. His many prints provided a lively business for the artist, as well as a medium of exchange with other artists, such as Lucas van Leyden and Raphael.

Although only a few engravings by the Gonzaga court painter Andrea Mantegna (1430/31–1506) are extant, they show his mastery of classical forms, especially the bacchanals. These prints also demonstrate his ability to create emotional power through figural expression in the monochromatic medium of prints. Raphael collaborated with Marcantonio Raimondi to publish his compositions as prints, an arrangement that greatly benefited the engraver. Raimondi established a workshop for reproducing artworks in print format, setting strict standards for his pupils. He helped to make printmaking a profession that functioned within the workshop system. Raimondi's prints distributed the designs of Renaissance painters worldwide, giving artisans new models to follow. Titian used both woodcuts and engravings to make his compositions available to a broader market, simultaneously advertising his paintings. Scholars think that Titian himself may have drawn directly onto the wood block rather than trusting someone else to transfer his drawing to the block for cutting. Given the tonality of Titian's paintings, the greater sensitivity of intaglio engraving was more suited to his style, and by the mid-16th century he was issuing his images from engravings.

DECORATIVE ART

Decorative art consists of secular objects valued for the visual pleasure of their appearance, as much as for any intrinsic value of their materials. Although a great altarpiece may be beautiful, it is not decorative because the art was meant to serve a higher purpose. In a similar manner, propagandistic and political art is not decorative because its main value lies in its subversive power. Renaissance aristocracy and the wealthy merchant class desired material comfort and the status of having fine objects in their homes. Artists and artisans responded to this market with tableware in gold and silver, delicately hand painted ceramics, ornate glass vessels, carved and painted furniture, and expert needlework.

Gold and Silver

Benvenuto Cellini's (1500–1571) gold saltcellar with mythological imagery created for Francis I is probably the most famous piece of Renaissance decorative art made of metal. Given the expense of precious metals, especially gold and silver, only the upper class could afford such objects. Royal families, however, commissioned entire table services of gold and silver. For the commercial market, cups and goblets were made of silver; northern artists ornamented these objects with enameling or incised patterns. English silversmiths, most of whose production was for the local market, made some unusual tableware, such as saltcellars in the shape of animals. Tableware was made of solid silver, much less costly than gold. Because gold was prohibitively expensive, it was often used in an alloy with copper, brass, or another cheaper metal. The color was still bright, if a little brassy. Gold was also made into a paste and rubbed onto another metal with a higher melting point. When fired, the gold would then fuse with the base metal, producing a "golden" object. Donatello used this process, as did other goldsmiths in the 15th century.

Ceramics

The Italian majolica so valued by the Renaissance had its European beginnings in southern Spain, near Valencia (in Catalonia), and its origins in the Islamic world. The name *majolica* derived from the name of the Spanish island Majorca. Arab ceramists had discovered a method that used coated tin oxide in the glazing process that resulted in a brilliant surface. Because glass was such a luxury, ceramics and pottery resembling glass were in demand. Ceramic workshops in Italy did not know how to make lusterware during the 15th century, but in the early 16th

century, the Deruta factory in Umbria (central Italy) discovered a profitable method of producing it by double-firing the vessel. With the 15th-century expansion of trade with the East, ceramic factories such as that in Deruta had access to a greater spectrum of colors as new pigments were imported. With its new lusterware technique, Deruta exported more pottery during the 16th century than in any other century until the 1900s. This factory, one of the few for which a detailed history has been published, exemplifies the extraordinary market for Italian ceramics during the second half of the Renaissance. During this period, the painted motifs of Deruta combined the factory's signature fish-scale design with classical imagery taken from prints, heraldry, and foliate designs.

Ceramic tiles were produced in both Italy and Spain; there was minimal local production in Portugal by the end of the 16th century. Lusterware tiles, the most expensive, were used sparingly in wall decoration and almost never for floors. Until the early 16th century, Spanish tiles were ornamented only with the geometric shapes preferred by Arab artisans who worked in the tile factories. The designs were painted on or created by raised and stamped shapes. Francisco Niculoso ("El Pisano," d. 1529), an Italian potter, introduced the decorative motifs of Italian Renaissance ceramics to Seville near the turn of the century. His main contribution to Iberian ceramics was the Italian concept of using many tiles to compose a single large picture. His altarpiece made in 1504 for a chapel in the Alcázar, Seville, is such a scene, framed by grotesques.

Glass

Venetian glass, including beads, was the most prestigious glass in western Europe. The glass mosaics of Venice were internationally famous. In the latter 13th century, glassmakers in Venice were united in a guild protecting their industrial secrets. Also since that time, the glassmakers have been located on their own island of Murano, where the factories continue to operate today. There were other glassmaking centers in Europe by the late 15th century, some of them founded by emigrant artisans from Murano.

3.10 Lusterware plate with the arms of Aragon and Sicily. Manises, Spain, c. 1500. (Courtesy of The Hispanic Society of America, E651)

The factory at Saint Germain-en-Laye near Paris, for example, executed commissions for the French royal family. With various advances in the applied sciences, several media in the decorative arts achieved new standards of excellence. For glass, the discovery of clear, pure *cristallo* gave Venice an edge in the market. Renaissance tastes preferred ornamented glass, such as the enameled and gilded pieces favored by Catherine de' Medici (1519–89), queen of France, who influenced aristocratic tastes at court. Glass was also painted from the back, such as glass platters stenciled on the bottom with a design that was then painted by hand. Although the painting could be sealed with a clear substance, it could not be heated and was thus rather fragile. In this technique, portraits, heraldic motifs, and classical imagery could be painted on commemorative vessels, such as large cups celebrating a marriage. Imagery from famous Renaissance paintings was occasionally copied and painted onto glass. Clear or monochromatic glass could be textured with ribbing or another simple pattern, and the rim gilded or enameled. The decorative glass described here was largely a product for the upper class; a poor family might have nothing more than a commemorative cup or bowl, if that.

Furniture

During this period, wood-carvers undertook many different types of commissions, from altarpieces to storage chests. They often had large workshops that were run by family members or by an artist acting as overseer. Wooden furniture was a good market because every middle-class household needed the basics: beds, chests, cabinets, tables, chairs. Oak and walnut were the preferred woods. Because members of the aristocracy regularly moved from one residence to another as the seasons changed, most furniture was made in sections so that it could be taken apart and easily transported in wagons. Upholstered furniture had not yet been invented; people spread carpets or pieces of carpets over tables, beds, and chairs, along with cushions, thus brightening the house and providing some padding. Chests and cabinets often were painted with figural scenes or were carved. For wealthy households, furniture might have gilt details. Intarsia, with small pieces of different-colored wood inlaid, was a durable form of flat decoration that could be used on the top of a table or other flat surface. Some intarsia artists took this technique to extremes, executing commissions to create entire *trompe l'oeil* rooms in which every wall contained objects "painted" in wood. Florentine furniture makers also used tortoiseshell, ivory, and mother-of-pearl for inlaid designs.

3.11 Intarsia paneling in the study of the duke of Urbino. Designed by Baccio Pontelli, latter 15th century (before 1492). (Palazzo Ducale, Urbino, Italy/Bridgeman Art Library)

Needlework

Besides the lace used for trim and small curtains, the most pervasive forms of needlework for interior decoration were needlework carpets (thread hooked through coarse mesh) and embroidery. Steel needles were available by the early 16th century, greatly facilitating the fine stitchery of Renaissance embroiderers. Although women made embroidery for their household use, much commercial embroidery was produced by members of guilds. The most lavish household embroidery was that for ornamental bedcovers and bed hangings, and canopy beds had elaborate panels that sometimes combined embroidery with quilting. Many painters, including Raphael and Pollaiuolo, made embroidery designs, or cartoons. Although most examples of this craft consist of colored yarn or thread on a neutral background, cutwork embroidery done in linen was a popular white-on-white technique for tablecloths.

3.12 Liturgical garment with metallic embroidery on black velvet. Spain, 16th century. (Courtesy of The Hispanic Society of America, H3920)

MAJOR ARTISTS

Abbate, Niccolò dell' (c. 1512–1571) began his career painting wall decorations and portraits in Bologna; then in 1552 he moved to France to assist in the paintings for Fontainebleau. His mythological landscapes inspired French artists of the 17th century.

Aertsen, Pieter (c. 1507/8–1575) mainly painted large works, most of still life (especially of meat), in Amsterdam and Antwerp. None of his painted altarpieces has survived intact.

Agostino di Duccio (1418–c. 1481) was a Florentine sculptor who also worked in Rimini on the Tempio Malatestiano (Church of San Francesco). His work in low-relief sculpture has a unique style; there is no record of his training.

Alari-Buonacolsi, Pier Jacopo di Antonio   See ANTICO.

Alberti, Leon Battista (1404–1472), a painter, architect, musician, writer, and man of many other talents, wrote the first Renaissance treatise concerning the theory of painting, *De pictura*, in 1435, and translated it into Italian the following year. Although his paintings and engravings are no longer extant, several monuments testify to his expertise in architecture.

Allegri, Antonio   See CORREGGIO.

Altdorfer, Albrecht (c. 1480–1538), German painter and architect, spent most of his life in his native Regensburg. Altdorfer's specialty was landscape painting, in which he was influenced by both northern and southern artists.

Andrea del Sarto (1486–1530) was a Florentine painter trained in the studio of Piero di Cosimo. He is best known for religious mural paintings in grisaille, located in monasteries in Florence.

Angelico, Fra *(Fra Giovanni da Fiesole)* (1395/1400–1455) was a devout member of the Dominican order who worked in Florence most of his life. Because he painted only religious subjects, he was called "Brother Angelic," or Fra Angelico. His paintings use perspective in simple yet naturalistic compositions.

Anguissola, Sofonisba (1532–1625) is famous as the first internationally known female painter in western Europe. Trained by Bernardino Campi, she worked in Madrid and Sicily. Anguissola produced approximately 50 paintings, most of them portraits.

Antico *(Pier Jacopo di Antonio Alari-Buonacolsi)* (c. 1460–1528) was an Italian sculptor who worked mainly in gold, bronze, and other medals. His name *Antico* derived from his affinity with antique Roman style in "re-creating" statuettes of ancient statues extant only in fragments.

Arcimboldo, Giuseppe (c. 1530–1593) learned painting in his family's studio in Milan, especially while assisting with the art for Milan Cathedral. His work included designs for tapestries and stained glass. In 1562 Arcimboldo began working for the imperial court, in Vienna and Prague.

Baldovinetti, Alessio (c. 1425–1499) was a painter in Florence who also worked in stained glass and mosaics.

Baldung Grien, Hans (c. 1484–1545) had the name Grien (or Green) added while working in Dürer's workshop. His painted altarpieces are best known for their supernatural subjects and bright colors.

Barbarelli, Giorgio   See GIORGIONE.

Barbari, Jacopo de' (c. 1440–1516), born in Venice, was known as Jakob Walch in northern Europe, where he worked for much of his career. An engraver and painter, de' Barbari became the court painter for Maximilian I, and then for Margaret of Austria in Brussels.

Bartolommeo, Fra *(Baccio della Porta)* (1472–1517) was a Florentine Dominican who became director of the San Marco workshop. His painting style was influenced by the two years he spent in Rome.

Bellini, Gentile (c. 1429–1507), son of Jacopo Bellini, was best known for his paintings of religious processions. He also spent three years working at the court of the sultan in Constantinople.

Bellini, Giovanni *(Giambellino)* (c. 1431/36–1516) was the younger son of Jacopo Bellini. His sister, Nicolosia, married Mantegna, and Giambellino's early work was influenced by that of Mantegna. His later paintings feature innovative uses of light and texture that became important for later artists, such as Giorgione.

Bellini, Jacopo (c. 1400–1470), father of Gentile and Giovanni Bellini, was born in Venice and stud-

ied under Gentile da Fabriano. His Venetian workshop handled some of the city's most significant commissions.

Bening, Sanders *(Benig)* (d. 1519), Flemish manuscript illuminator and father of Simon Bening, worked in Bruges and Ghent. *The Hours of Mary of Burgundy* (National Library, Vienna) has been attributed to him.

Bening, Simon *(Benig)* (c. 1483–1561) was Sanders Bening's son and also a Flemish illuminator. *The Grimiani Breviary* (Pierpont Morgan Library, New York) was among his greatest accomplishments.

Berruguete, Alonso (1488–1561) was the son of the Spanish painter Pedro Berruguete. He worked with his father and also spent time in Italy studying classical models. Berruguete became a master of Mannerism, especially in his painted altarpieces featuring low-relief sculpture heavily ornamented with gilt.

Berruguete, Pedro (c. 1450–1504), father of Alonso Berruguete, was Spanish court painter to Ferdinand and Isabella. He may also have worked in the Ducal Library of Urbino.

Betto, Bernardino di   See PINTURICCHIO.

Bontemps, Pierre (c. 1512–c. 1570) assisted Primaticcio with the decorative sculpture at Fontainebleau. This French sculptor executed the heart receptacle for Francis I and worked on his tomb sculpture (all now in Saint Denis, near Paris) from designs by Philibert Delorme (see chapter 4, Architecture and Urban Planning).

Borgoña, Juan de (fl. from 1495, d. 1535), Spanish painter, worked mainly in and near Toledo. His major works are the frescoes in the cathedral of Toledo.

Bos, Cornelis (c. 1510–c. 1566), Dutch engraver, probably studied in Rome. Much of his work reproduces Italian paintings of the time.

Bosch, Hieronymus *(Jeroen Bosch)* (c. 1450–1518) was a Dutch painter best known for the surrealistic imagery in his religious subjects, especially depictions of sinners and their punishments.

Botticelli, Sandro (*Alessandro Filipepi*) (1445–1510), who apprenticed in Florence under Andrea del Verrocchio, assisted in the painting of the Sistine Chapel during the 1480s. In addition to religious works, Botticelli painted mythological scenes.

Boulogne, Jean   See GIAMBOLOGNA.

Bouts, Dieric (c. 1400–1475), Dutch painter, worked in Louvain most of his career. He is known for the landscapes and bright color in his religious art. Both his sons became artists.

Bronzino, Agnolo (*Agnolo Tori di Cosimo di Moriano*) (1503–1572), Florentine poet and painter, trained under Jacopo da Pontormo. He is best known for portraits of court figures.

Brueghel the Elder, Pieter (*"Peasant Brueghel,"*) (c. 1520–1569), a Flemish painter, specialized in representations of peasants in rural landscapes and villages. His two sons, Pieter and Jan, were also painters.

Caliari, Paolo   See VERONESE.

Campi, Bernardino (1522–c. 1591), painter in Cremona, is not to be confused with the goldsmith of the same name who died in 1573. Campi is now famous as the teacher of Sofonisba Anguissola. He worked mainly on church frescoes.

Campin, Robert (c. 1375/79–1444), Flemish artist now assumed to be the Master of Flémalle. He painted individual portraits as well as altarpieces.

Caravaggio (*Michelangelo Merisi da Caravaggio*) (1573–1610) spent much of his career in Rome, specializing in realistic representations of religious subjects. During his later life, Caravaggio was in exile, painting in Naples, Sicily, and Malta. His style had become baroque by the close of his career.

Carucci, Jacopo   See JACOPO DA PONTORMO.

Cellini, Benvenuto (1500–1571), born in Florence, was a sculptor in marble and goldsmith who worked first in Rome, then Fontainebleau, and finally Florence. His autobiography includes lively accounts of

Cellini's contemporaries. Cellini's golden saltcellar with mythological figures completed for Francis I is a masterpiece of the art (today located in the Art History Museum, Vienna).

Cennini, Cennino (c. 1370–c. 1440), trained in Florence by Taddeo Gaddi's son, Agnolo, wrote the first technical treatise of the Renaissance on painting. None of his own paintings has survived.

Christus, Petrus (c. 1420–1472/73), Flemish painter, was influenced by the work of Jan van Eyck and Rogier van der Weyden. Christus was one of the earliest northern painters to use linear perspective.

Clouet, François (c. 1516–1572), son of Jean Clouet, was a painter of genre scenes and portraits.

Clouet, Jean (c. 1485–1540/41) began his painting career in Burgundy and then became court painter for Francis I.

Clovio, Giulio (*Julije Klovic*) (1498–1578) was a Croatian illuminator and painter who worked in Venice, in Rome, and at the Imperial court. The manuscript *Farnese Hours* (Pierpont Morgan Library, New York) is among his masterpieces.

Correggio (*Antonio Allegri*) (1494–1534), a painter who worked chiefly in Parma, was influenced by Mantegna. His subjects were mythological as well as religious.

Cranach the Elder, Lucas (1472–1553), German painter and engraver, worked for the electors of Saxony and executed portraits of Maximilian I and the future Charles V. A friend of Martin Luther, Cranach often dealt with Reformation themes in his paintings. All three of his sons became artists.

Crivelli, Carlo (1430/35–c. 1495), born in Venice, spent his career in remote Ascoli Piseno in central Italy. His heavily ornamented religious paintings feature numerous decorative motifs.

David, Gérard (c. 1460–1523), Dutch painter, worked in Bruges and Antwerp. He specialized in scenes from the domestic life of Christ, popular subjects copied by many of his contemporaries.

Della Robbia, Andrea (1435–1525), nephew of Luca Della Robbia, was a ceramic artist and sculptor. He executed the blue and white roundels for Brunelleschi's famous Ospedale degli Innocenti in Florence. All five of his sons worked in the Della Robbia ceramic studio.

Della Robbia, Luca (1399/1400–1482), uncle of Andrea Della Robbia, was the first major Renaissance artist to use ceramics for sculpture. He invented a method for glazing terra-cotta to render it waterproof, and his creation of the blue-and-white *Madonna and Child* in a circular wreath became a standard for Renaissance ornamentation.

Donatello (*Donatello de Betto di Bardi*) (1386–1466), Florentine sculptor, spent part of his career completing commissions for Cosimo de' Medici. He also worked in Rome, in Saint Peter's Basilica. Donatello is noted for his bronze statue of David, the first life-sized, freestanding nude statue of the Renaissance (1430–35, now in the Bargello in Florence).

Dürer, Albrecht (1471–1528) was a painter and engraver, working in both wood blocks and copper plates. Born in Nuremberg, he was influenced by southern artists during his travels in Italy. His work included commissions for Maximilian I, and he wrote about human proportions, perspective, geometry, and fortifications.

Eyck, Hubert van (c. 1370–1426) was probably the brother of Jan van Eyck. Although none of his paintings is extant, he evidently produced the design for the Ghent Altarpiece.

Eyck, Jan van (1385?–1440/41) was probably the brother of Hubert van Eyck, who taught him how to paint and whose designs Jan evidently completed in the Ghent Altarpiece. He was court painter for the duke of Burgundy, creating religious works and portraits, and one of the first major European artists to work in oil-based paint.

Filipepi, Alessandro   See BOTTICELLI, SANDRO.

Flémalle, Master of   See CAMPIN, ROBERT.

Fontana, Lavinia (1552–1614), daughter of Prospero Fontana, was the second Renaissance woman to become famous for her paintings. She worked in portraiture as well as historical scenes.

Fontana, Prospero (1512–1597), born in Bologna, was best known for his portraits. Fontana's most gifted student was his daughter, Lavinia. He assisted in the decoration of buildings in Rome and Florence, and at Fontainebleau.

Fouquet, Jean (*Foucquet*) (c. 1415/20–c. 1481) was a French illuminator and painter, influenced by his several years of living in Rome. He was a portrait painter at the French court for much of his career.

Gaddi, Taddeo (fl. 1325, d. 1366) was Giotto's assistant for more than two decades; he also worked in Pisa and Pistoia. Some of his paintings were executed for the Church of Santa Croce in Florence, where they can be seen today.

Geertgen tot Sint Jans (fl. 1475–1495), a Dutch painter, worked for the religious order of the Brotherhood of Saint John in Haarlem.

Gentile da Fabriano (c. 1370–1427) began his career as a painter in Venice, where Jacopo Bellini was among his pupils. Gentile worked in both frescoes and panel painting. The altarpieces are regarded as his masterpieces, especially *The Adoration of the Magi* of 1423 (Uffizi Museum, Florence).

Ghiberti, Lorenzo (1378–1455), born in Florence, was one of the most renowned sculptors of the early Renaissance. He executed bronze panels for the doors of the baptistry in Florence.

Ghirlandaio, Domenico (1448/49–1494) was a talented Florentine portraitist who incorporated representations of his contemporaries in some of his altarpieces. Michelangelo was one of his pupils.

Giambellino   See BELLINI, GIOVANNI.

Giambologna (*Jean Boulogne*) (1529–1608), Flemish sculptor famous for his fountains. He worked mostly in Florence, and his work was compared favorably with that of Michelangelo.

Giannuzzi, Giuliano See ROMANO GIULIO.

Giorgione (*Giorgio da Castelfranco or Giorgio Barbarelli*) (c. 1477–1511) was born in Venice. He is most famous for situating his figures in evocative landscapes. After Giorgione died of plague, many of his paintings were completed by Titian.

Giotto di Bondone (1267–1337), born near Florence, is thought to have studied with the medieval painter Cimabue (d. c. 1302). Giotto's lively compositions are among the earliest indications of Renaissance art, especially his frescoes *Lives of the Virgin and Christ* in the Arena Chapel, Padua.

Giovanni Battista di Jacopo See FIORENTINO, ROSSO.

Giulio Romano (*Giulio Pippi or Giuliano Gianuzzi*) (c. 1499–1546) was born in Rome and studied under Raphael. He worked as both an architect and a painter, mainly in Rome and for the court of Mantua.

Goes, Hugo van der (c. 1440–1482), a Flemish painter who began his career in Bruges designing festivity and funeral art. Later he lived in the Rode Kloster in Brussels as a lay member, executing commissions in the monastery. His most famous work is the *Portinari Altarpiece* (Uffizi Museum, Florence).

Gonçalves, Nuno (fl. 1450–1471) was a Portuguese painter in service to Afonso V whose work featured lifelike realism.

Greco, El (*Doménikos Theotokópoulos*) (c. 1541–1614), born on the Greek island of Crete, worked first in Venice and then in Rome. He relocated to Toledo in 1577 and spent the remainder of his life in Spain. Known as a Mannerist artist, El Greco painted elongated figures in intensely dramatic light.

Grien, Hans Baldung See BALDUNG, HANS.

Grünewald, Matthias (*Mathias Gothart Niethart*) (c. 1470–1528) worked as an engineer and painter

for two archbishops of Mainz. His expressive religious imagery was realized to its fullest extent in the *Isenheim Altarpiece* (1515, today in Colmar).

Heemskerk, Maerten Van (1498–1574) was a Dutch painter who worked in Italy during the 1530s. His later work was strongly influenced by that of Michelangelo.

Hilliard, Nicholas (c. 1547–1619), English painter of miniature portraits, was also a goldsmith. His most famous miniatures are portraits of the royal family.

Hoefnagel, Joris (1542–1600), born in Antwerp, was most famous for his drawings and paintings of towns and cities, many of which were published as engravings during his lifetime in *Civitates orbis terrarum* (Cities of the world, 1572–1618).

Holbein, the Younger, Hans (1497/98–1543) trained in the Augsburg studio of his father, Hans Holbein the Elder. In Basel he converted to Protestantism; subsequently he painted only a few religious pictures. Holbein worked for Thomas Cromwell as well as for the English court, especially in portraiture.

Jacopo della Quercia (c. 1374–1438), born in Siena, was a sculptor of religious art. He worked on the Siena baptistry and executed panels for tombs, portals, and other parts of churches in Tuscany.

Jones, Inigo (1573–1652), architect and designer of theatrical sets, was influenced by Palladio's buildings during trips to Italy. His own designs helped popularize Palladian architecture in England.

Juan de Flandes (c. 1465–c. 1519) was a Flemish painter in service to Isabella, executing religious art in several Spanish cities.

Julije Klovic See CLOVIO, GIULIO.

Lafréry, Antonio (1512–1577), an engraver from Burgundy, spent much of his career in Rome, creating views of the city. Many of his contemporaries viewed Rome through Lafréry's eyes.

Laurana, Francesco (c. 1430–c. 1502) was a Dalmatian sculptor who worked in Naples at the court of Alphonso V, and in France for René of Anjou, king of Naples.

Leonardo da Vinci (1452–1519), engineer, architect, painter, and sculptor, painted the famous *Mona Lisa* (today in the Louvre Museum, Paris). He spent much of his career in Milan, working for Ludovico Sforza, and his fresco of the Last Supper is in a church there. His notebooks include sketches of a submarine, helicopter, and automobile.

Leoni, Leone (c. 1509–1590), goldsmith and sculptor in bronze, worked for the papacy and the Imperial court before settling in Milan. He engraved coins and medals, many with portraits of contemporary rulers, in addition to making portrait sculpture. His son, Pompeo, learned bronze casting in his foundry.

Leoni, Pompeo (c. 1533–1608), son of Leone Leoni, worked mostly in Spain as a sculptor. He created the gilded bronze tomb sculpture for the high altar of the Escorial and returned to Milan to cast the statues.

Limbourg brothers (dates not known) Hennequin, Herman, and Pol, were French illuminators who worked at the ducal courts. Their book of hours decorated for the duke of Berry, *Très riches heures* (Condé Museum, Chantilly), is the most famous illuminated manuscript of 15th-century Europe.

Lippi, Fra Filippo (c. 1406–1469) was born in Florence. He painted religious art and was especially known for his delicately graceful Madonnas. His use of perspective indicated knowledge of contemporary Flemish painting.

Lomazzo, Giovanni Paolo (1538–c. 1590) was a Milanese painter and poet. After he became blind at 33, Lomazzo dictated two theoretical treatises that became milestones of art history: *Idea del tempio della pittura* (Idea of the temple of painting, 1590) and *Trattato dell'arte della pittura* (Treatise on the art of painting, 1584).

Lombardo, Pietro (c. 1435–1515) spent most of his career in Venice, creating marble sculpture with classicizing elements. His son Tullio was also a sculptor in Venice.

Lombardo, Tullio (c. 1455–1532) worked in a more purely classical style of sculpture than did his father, Pietro.

Lorenzetti, Ambrogio (fl. c. 1317–1348) was a Sienese painter who also worked in Florence. His *Good and Bad Government* fresco in the Palazzo Pubblico (Siena) is considered the earliest major depiction of landscape by an Italian artist. Lorenzetti's brother, Pietro, was also a painter.

Lorenzo, Piero di   See COSIMO, PIERO DI.

Luciani, Sebastiano   See PIOMBO, SEBASTIANO DEL.

Malouel, Jean (*or Maelwael*) (c. 1365–1415), Flemish painter, worked in Paris before moving to the court of Burgundy. He served both Philip the Bold and John the Fearless as court painter.

Mander, Karel van (1548–1606) was a Flemish poet and painter. For much of his career he was in Haarlem, where he cofounded an art academy. His handbook for artists, *Het schilderboeck* (The painter's book), was published in 1604.

Mantegna, Andrea (1430/31–1506) trained in the studio of Francesco Squarcione in Padua. He became court painter to the Gonzagas in Mantua, where his illusionistic art and skill in handling foreshortening earned an international reputation.

Marmion, Simon (c. 1425–1489), Franco-Flemish painter, was known for his wide spectrum of colors and densely populated surfaces.

Masaccio (*Tommaso di Giovanni di Simone Guidi*) (1401–c. 1428) began his painting career in Florence and then settled in Rome in 1428. His use of perspective and classically modeled figures were praised by Vasari. Most of Masaccio's paintings did not survive; his most famous work is the fresco cycle in the Brancacci Chapel, Florence.

Maso di Bartolomeo (1406–1456) was a sculptor in bronze who also collaborated on architectural projects with Donatello and Michelozzo.

Mazzola, Francesco See PARMIGIANINO.

Memling, Hans (*or Memlinc*) (c. 1430–1494) first worked under the supervision of Rogier van der Weyden, then moved to Bruges c. 1467. He was in demand as a portrait painter and achieved international fame during his lifetime.

Metsys, Quentin (*Matsys or Massys*) (1466–1530) was a Flemish painter who lived in Antwerp. He executed altarpieces and portraits in which the influence of Italian works is apparent.

Michelangelo Buonarroti (1475–1564), one of the most famous artists of the Renaissance, was an architect and poet as well as a sculptor and painter. After apprenticing with Domenico Ghirlandaio, Michelangelo studied at the court school of Lorenzo de' Medici. The *David* in marble is his best-known sculpture and the ceiling of the Sistine Chapel his best-known painting.

Mor van Dashorst, Anthonis (*Antonio Moro*) (c. 1512/1525–1575) was a Dutch painter who traveled extensively and executed portraits of the members of several ruling families.

Morales, Luis de (c. 1520–1586) was a Spanish painter who lived in the remote western region of Extremadura. He mainly painted devotional subjects.

Moriano, Agnolo Tori di Cosimo di See BRONZINO.

Moulins, Master of (*name unknown*) (fl. c. 1480–1500) was a French painter with a sculptural style so distinctive that several works have been attributed to him, including portraits and an altarpiece in Moulins Cathedral.

Negroli, Filippo (fl. 1531–1551) was a member of a family of weapon and armor makers in Milan. His embossed parade armor for the emperor Charles V is his most famous extant work.

Niethart, Mathias Gothart See GRÜNEWALD, MATTHIAS.

Orley, Bernaert van (c. 1492–1542) was an artist in Brussels who worked chiefly for Margaret of Austria and Mary of Hungary. Besides painting religious subjects and portraits, he designed tapestries and stained glass.

Palissy, Bernard (1510–1589), French potter, was also a ceramic artist, trained as a glass painter. He invented a new type of white enamel for his glazes that improved the surface ornamentation. Catherine de' Medici commissioned him to create a ceramic grotto for the Tuileries Gardens in Paris (c. 1573).

Paolo di Dono See UCCELLO, PAOLO.

Parmigianino (*Francesco Mazzola*) (1503–1540), etcher and painter, was born in Parma (hence his name). His Mannerist paintings of figures are known for the elongation of their hands and neck. In etching, Parmigianino evidently executed the first woodcuts in chiaroscuro.

Pasti, Matteo de' (c. 1420–1467), born in Verona, was a medalist, architect, and illuminator, whose portrait medals are among his few extant small works. Pasti completed sculpture for the interior of the Tempio Malatestiano in Rimini.

Pellegrini, Pellegrino See TIBALDI.

Perugino (*Pietro di Cristoforo*) (c. 1440–1523), born near Perugia, learned oil painting in Florence. He was chosen to direct the group of artists painting frescoes in the Sistine Chapel.

Piero della Francesca (1415–1492) painted frescoes and altarpieces, notably the fresco cycle *Legend of the True Cross* (c. 1455–1460) in the Church of San Francesco, Arezzo. He understood perspective and wrote several treatises on the relation of mathematics and geometry to painting. His manuscript treatise *De prospectiva pingendi* (On perspective in painting) was written in Italian (though its title is Latin).

Piero di Cosimo *(Piero di Lorenzo)* (1461/62–1521) trained in Florence and was influenced by the work of Leonardo. He is best known for mythological subjects, portraits, and the *Immaculate Conception* altarpiece painting for San Francesco in Fiesole (c. 1510?). Andrea del Sarto was among Piero's pupils.

Pinturicchio *(Bernardino di Betto)* (c. 1452–1513), born in Perugia, was a student of Perugino's and assisted him in painting frescoes in the Sistine Chapel. His main works are fresco cycles in the Vatican and in the cathedral of Siena.

Pippi, Giulio   See GIULIO ROMANO.

Pisanello *(Antonio Pisano)* (c. 1395–1455/56) grew up in Verona, then worked with Gentile da Fabriano on frescoes in Venice and finished some of his colleague's frescoes in Rome. Pisanello is best known for his portrait medals and painted portraits.

Pisano, Andrea (c. 1270–1348/49) was a sculptor who worked in Florence, notably on bronze doors for the baptistry. He also carved reliefs for the campanile.

Pisano, Antonio   See PISANELLO.

Pollaiuolo, Antonio (c. 1432–1498) and his brother, Piero, worked together in their Florentine studio. Piero basically painted, while Antonio worked as a painter, goldsmith, sculptor, and designer of embroidery for vestments. He created bronze sculptures for the tombs of two popes.

Pontormo, Jacopo da *(Jacopo Carucci)* (1494–1557) trained under Andrea del Sarto and spent his entire career in Florence, painting altarpieces and frescoes. His work is Manneristic, with distorted poses and elongated figures.

Porta, Baccio della   See FRA BARTOLOMMEO.

Primaticcio, Francesco (1504/5–1570), born in Bologna, worked mainly at Fontainebleau, painting mythological scenes and assisting as architect.

Pucelle, Jean (c. 1300–c. 1355) was a French illuminator who directed an important studio in Paris. His work was influenced by Italian art.

Quercia, Jacopo della   See JACOPO DELLA QUERCIA.

Raimondi, Marcantonio (c. 1470/82–c. 1527/34) was a Bolognese engraver who worked in Venice and then settled in Rome, where he reproduced many famous paintings of the time in his prints.

Raphael *(Raffaello Sanzio or Raffaello da Urbino)* (1483–1520) was best known as a painter. After studying under Pietro Perugino, Raphael moved to Florence and gained a reputation for his Madonnas. For Pope Julius II he painted monumental frescoes in the Vatican Palace (the Stanze, rooms), including *School of Athens*, depicting ancient philosophers.

Riemenschneider, Tilman (c. 1460–1531) was a versatile sculptor working in stone, marble, and wood, including altarpieces carved in wood. His marble tomb in Bamberg Cathedral for Emperor Henry II and Empress Kunigunde is his masterpiece in that medium.

Robusti, Jacopo   See TINTORETTO.

Rossi, Properzia de' (c. 1490–1530), the first woman recognized as a sculptor in Renaissance Italy, executed a marble panel and two angels for San Petronio in her native Bologna. She also made portrait busts and copper engravings.

Rosso Fiorentino *(Giovanni Battista di Jacopo)* (1494–1540), a painter born in Florence, is best known for his collaboration with Primaticcio in what has come to be called the School of Fontainebleau.

Sánchez Coello, Alonso (c. 1531–1588), born in Spain of Portuguese parents, followed Antonio Moro as court painter to Philip II. He specialized in portraiture.

Sassetta *(Stefano di Giovanni)* (c. 1400–1450) was a Sienese painter who mainly painted altarpieces.

Schongauer, Martin (1435/50–1491), painter and engraver, spent most of his life in his native Colmar (then part of Germany). He was best known for religious engravings.

Sebastiano del Piombo (*Sebastiano Luciani*) (1485/86–1547) first studied to be a musician in Venice, then turned to painting, studying with both Giovanni Bellini and Giorgione. He spent most of his life in Rome and became known for portraiture.

Simone Guidi, Tommaso di Giovanni di See MASACCIO.

Simone Martini (c. 1284–1344), born in Siena, painted altarpieces for several Italian cities. The *Annunciation Altarpiece* of 1333 (now in the Uffizi Museum, Florence) executed for the Siena Cathedral was the earliest known Italian altarpiece with a narrative subject.

Sluter, Claus (c. 1360–1406) was a sculptor from Haarlem who served at the Burgundian court. He worked on the famous Chartreuse de Champmol near Dijon, planned as the ducal mausoleum.

Squarcione, Francesco (c. 1395–1468), born in Padua, became a painter after working for several decades as a tailor. Although he trained several artists in his workshop, including Mantegna, no unassisted work by Squarcione himself survives.

Stefano di Giovanni See SASSETTA.

Stoss, Viet (c. 1438–1533) was a German sculptor who was in Kraków (Poland) from 1477 to 1489 carving the wooden altarpiece for the Church of Our Lady, considered his masterpiece. After 1489 he was in Nuremberg producing pieces for the city's churches.

Tibaldi (*Pellegrino Pellegrini*) (1527–1596), architect, painter, and sculptor, completed several commissions for Cardinal Carlo Borromeo and served as architect for Milan Cathedral. His final creations were the frescoes painted for Philip II at the Escorial.

Tintoretto (*Jacopo Robusti*) (1519–1594) worked chiefly as a painter in Venice, completing numerous commissions from the doge. His most famous series of paintings are the biblical scenes executed for the Scuola di San Rocco. Tintoretto's son, Domenico, was also a painter.

Titian (*Tiziano Vecellio*) (c. 1489–1576), who trained in Venice under Giovanni Bellini, was a prolific painter who created altarpieces, portraits, and mythological scenes. He was best known among his contemporaries as a colorist. Philip II of Spain was his patron for much of the 1550s.

Theotokópoulos, Doménikos See GRECO, EL.

Uccello, Paolo (*Paolo di Dono*) (c. 1397–1475) was a painter and mosaicist trained by Ghiberti. Several paintings were executed by him for the cathedral in Florence. Uccello understood perspective, using it in *The Hunt in the Forest* (c. 1460, now in the Ashmolean Museum, Oxford).

Vasari, Giorgio (1511–1574), architect and painter, studied under both Michelangelo and Andrea del Sarto. His most renowned architectural project was the Uffizi in Florence. Vasari's *Delle vite de' più eccellenti pittori, scultori, ed architettori* (Lives of the most excellent painters, sculptors, and architects, 1550) is an invaluable biographical record of Renaissance artists.

Vecellio, Tiziano See TITIAN.

Veneziano, Domenico (fl. c. 1438–1461) evidently spent most of his career as a painter in Florence, where he was known for using oil in his fresco cycle of the life of the Virgin (now lost) in the Church of Sant' Egidio. Panels from his *Saint Lucy Altarpiece* are extant but scattered.

Veronese, Paolo (*Paolo Caliari*) (1528–1588), born in Verona, established his workshop in Venice, where he had several major commissions. He also did decorative painting for villas, notably the Villa Barbaro designed by Palladio. Assisted during his final years by his brother and two sons, Veronese completed work for an international clientele.

Vischer the Elder, Peter (c. 1460–1529) was the head of an important bronze foundry in Nuremberg. His three sons learned bronze sculpture there and managed the business after their father's death. Two of the sons traveled to Italy and introduced classical motifs into the sculpture produced in Nuremberg.

Vivarini, Antonio (c. 1415–1476/84) painted altarpieces and other works in Venice, with his brother-in-law Giovanni d'Alemagna. Antonio's brother Bartolomeo and son Alvise were also painters.

Vries, Adriaan de (c. 1560–1626) was a Dutch sculptor who studied in Florence under Giambologna. He worked in Rome and Prague, specializing in fountains.

Walch, Jakob   See BARBARI, JACOPO DE'.

Weyden, Rogier van der (*Roger de la Pasture*) (c. 1399–1464) studied under Robert Campin and set up his own studio in Brussels circa 1435. His religious paintings influenced the following generation, such as Hans Memling, one of his students.

Witz, Konrad (c. 1400/10–1445/47) was a German painter who worked primarily in Switzerland, creating altarpieces.

Wolgemut, Michael (1434–1519), famous as the teacher of Albrecht Dürer, ran an important studio in his native Nuremberg. Wolgemut painted altarpieces and engraved in wood.

Zuccaro, Federico (c. 1540–1609), Taddeo Zuccaro's younger brother, took over his studio after Taddeo's death and worked on his brother's commissions. After painting portraits at the English court, he traveled to Spain and executed several altarpieces for the Escorial. Zuccaro returned to Rome and founded the Accademia di San Luca (for artists). His treatise *L'idea de' pittori, scultori ed architetti* (The idea of painters, sculptors, and architects) was published in 1607.

Zuccaro, Taddeo (1529–1566) was a painter who had a studio in Rome large enough to allow him to create monumental canvases of historical subjects. Because history painting was his specialty, Zuccaro was given several important commissions for designing decorative sets of majolica, including a table service depicting the life of Julius Caesar as a gift for Philip II of Spain.

READING

Painting

Babelon 1968: fresco (Fontainebleau); Barolsky 1998: naturalism; Blunt 1991: France; Brown 1991: fresco (Toledo); Campbell 1990: portraiture; Franklin 2001: fresco, portraiture; Holt 1981; Hood 1995: fresco; Kempers 1992: patronage; Lübbeke 1991: Germany; Meiss 1970: fresco; Rodrigues 2000: Italian influences in Portugal; Sagerman 2002: Sistine Chapel ceiling; Snyder 1985: panel painting, portraiture in northern Europe.

Tapestries

Campbell 2002: many illustrations of tapetries; Domínguez Ortiz 1991: Spanish royal collection; Hunter 1912: (general history); Snyder 1985: tapestries in northern Europe.

Sculpture

Blunt 1991: France; Böker 1999: emblematic influences; Chapuis 1999: Riemenschneider; Decker 1969: Italy; Goldschneider 1952: portrait medals; Martín González 1991: Spain; Mulcahy 1994: sculpture (Escorial); Snyder 1985: sculpture in northern Europe; Welch 2000: Italy.

Prints

Johnson 1999: social context; Landau 1994: (general survey); Stock 1998: printmaking in Antwerp; Woodward 1996: maps as prints; Zigrosser 1939: (general survey).

Decorative Art

Amico 1996: Palissy; Baskins 1998: *cassone* painting; Jourdain 1924: England; Kavaler 2000: Netherlands; Raggio 1996: Gubbio studiolo; Welch 2000: Italy; Wells-Cole 1997: England.

4

ARCHITECTURE AND URBAN PLANNING

The classical forms and decorative ornaments of Renaissance architecture originated in Italy and rapidly spread into France; these two regions were the chief representatives of the new style during the 15th and 16th centuries. This chapter mainly discusses Italy and France; architecture in other regions is described later (see Beyond Italy and France, pages 117–120). Renaissance architecture is distinguished by a proliferation of designs influenced by Roman models, and by the rise to importance of the architect as a single individual in charge of the complete building project. Even when several architects collaborated on a major project during the Renaissance, the building usually was the vision of one person. Great buildings of the Middle Ages, especially the cathedrals, entailed long-term projects usually lasting at least from 75 to 100 years. These buildings were created by group efforts, usually with no single genius guiding the endeavor. Often the design of medieval cathedrals was changed during construction as political or financial conditions demanded, and as the project lengthened in time and outlived its initial builders. Although the accomplishments of medieval building programs are impressive, they are very different from the unified vision of Renaissance architectural endeavors. The most important building program of the 15th century was the renovation of Florence. During the 16th century, Rome became a focus of urban renewal through papal patronage. The first part of this chapter charts the general development of the architect and Renaissance architecture, and the second part discusses specific examples of various types of buildings.

This chapter also touches on the 16th-century stylistic shift from purely classical Renaissance style to the Mannerism (whimsical or witty capriciousness) that prevailed into the latter 16th century. Because chapter 3 includes information on sculpture in architectural and garden settings, the present chapter focuses on architecture in general and not on details of sculptural decoration. Chapter 7, Warfare, discusses fortifications and military engineering. Harbors and canals are treated in chapter 9 in the section, Travel.

RISE OF THE ARCHITECT

The idea of an architect as the individual who both designed a building and saw it through all stages of construction did not begin to crystallize until the 16th century. During the 15th century, the title *architect* could pertain to several individuals, such as the designer of a building or the person in charge of paying for the work. Occasionally designers of buildings left the on-site supervision to a colleague working on building materials, sculpture, or another aspect of the construction. Architects supervising projects from a distance included Leon Battista Alberti (1404–72), who wrote *De re aedificatoria* (On the art of building in ten books, c. 1450), the first architectural treatise of the Renaissance. By the early 16th century, architects were working closely with patrons, usually supervising on-site development of their projects. They sometimes, however, were working from drawings provided by others, especially the court artist. As we shall see, the court artist or sculptor often became the architect. This section explains the development of the architect as a Renaissance phenomenon.

Northern Italy

BRUNELLESCHI

Filippo Brunelleschi's (1377–1446) participation in the construction of the Florence cathedral was an important step in the rise of the Renaissance architect. The cathedral of Florence, begun in 1296, had advanced by 1420 to the stage at which a dome was needed to cover the huge octagon space at its eastern end. The dome was consecrated in 1436. In collaboration with several colleagues, Brunelleschi designed a complex octagonal dome requiring no central support because the stress was contained within the double-walled dome itself. Inside the inner and outer walls a circular structure of bricks evenly distributed the weight. Brunelleschi also constructed special hoisting mechanisms that were used to manipulate sections of the dome into position—these, too, were marvels of engineering for the mid-15th century. Although the dome could have been modeled on the ancient Pantheon of Rome, which Brunelleschi may have studied, his accomplishment was praised as revolutionary. No one with eyes who lived in Florence or visited the city could help but notice this imposing feature of the cityscape, and the view into the cupola from the floor of the cathedral was (and is) an uplifting experience. In Alberti's preface to his treatise *Della pittura* (On painting, 1435/36) he praises Brunelleschi ("Pippo"): "Who could ever be hard or envious enough to fail to praise Pippo the architect on seeing here such a large structure, rising above the skies, ample to cover with its shadow all the Tuscan people, and constructed without the aid of centering or great quantity of wood? Since this work seems impossible of execution in our own time, if I judge rightly, it was probably unthought of among the Ancients" (Alberti 1966, p. 40).

Although the cathedral's dome was impressive, it was not a model easily emulated because of its technical complexity and massive scale. Brunelleschi designed another building whose dome did provide a model followed by other architects—the Sacrestia Vecchia (old sacristy) in the Medici parish church of San Lorenzo. Designed in perfectly concentric shapes, the sacristy consists of a hemispherical dome constructed on a cube. Pendentives (bridges from corner to corner) support the circular base of the dome. The geometric details of this harmonious design are highlighted in dark stone against the light stucco background, an effective technique that was copied by other builders. Brunelleschi's construction of the Ospedale degli Innocenti (hospital or home for orphans) in Florence, begun circa 1419, provided an elegant prototype of a monumental building that influenced other architects during the 15th century. The arcaded portico with its rounded columns, Corinthian-style foliage in the capitals atop the columns, and classical symmetry of design provided an excellent example of the new

all'antica (antique) style that would define early Renaissance architecture.

MICHELOZZO

Michelozzo di Bartolommeo (or Michelozzi Michelozzo, 1396–1472)—usually called Michelozzo—worked mainly in Florence. As a gifted sculptor, he was given commissions by members of the Medici family. Brunelleschi was the first to make the transition in his career from sculptor to architect, at a time when the "architect" was only beginning to be recognized as a distinct professional. A generation later Michelozzo could make that same transition with ease. Brunelleschi's influence was so pervasive that we are only recently learning that some of the buildings attributed to him during past centuries may have been designed by others. The Pazzi Chapel at the Church of Santa Croce in Florence, probably designed by Michelozzo, is one example. Michelozzo was prominent during his lifetime for several noteworthy buildings, such as the Palazzo Medici in Florence. Begun circa 1445, the palace was commissioned as the Florentine residence of Cosimo de' Medici the Elder (1389–1464, not to be confused with Cosimo I de' Medici, born in 1519). The building project was ambitious, and no fewer than 20 houses were demolished to make way for the palace. The three-story exterior wall was heavily rusticated, with the stones randomly chiseled to give them the appearance of strength and age. Erected on a large corner where two busy streets converge, this prestigious palace advertising Michelozzo's genius was the first of several palaces built by Florence's new ruling class. Containing more than 40 rooms, the building had a garden, a loggia, and a courtyard with a colonnade modeled on Brunelleschi's Ospedale degli Innocenti. The ornately classical cornice below the edge of the roof helped define the Palazzo Medici as a true Renaissance structure featuring elements of Roman republican style. This building designed by Michelozzo influenced architects commissioned to build other private residences in the city. Michelozzo also introduced Renaissance architecture to Lombardy (north of Tuscany). He designed the

Portinari Chapel in the Church of Sant' Eustorgio in Milan circa 1462.

ALBERTI

Leon Battista Alberti was known during his lifetime as a prodigiously gifted Renaissance personality. In his preface to Alberti's treatise on architecture first published in 1485/86, the humanist scholar and poet Angelo Polizano (1454–94) wrote: "He was able to grasp every principle of ancient architecture and renew it by example. . . . He had moreover the highest reputation as both painter and sculptor, and . . . he achieved a greater mastery in all these different arts than only a few can manage in any single one" (Alberti 1997, p. [1]). In addition to his architectural treatise, Alberti wrote other books, including a treatise on painting discussed in chapter 3. He enhanced his status as an artist in several fields by these writings, especially the presentation of beautifully crafted manuscripts to important patrons such as Pope Nicholas V (1397–1455). Rather than a handbook of rules, Alberti's treatise is an inspirational humanistic text meant to celebrate great architecture and great architects (not forgetting himself), and to encourage creative solutions for buildings and renovations initiated in Alberti's own time.

Alberti's first and last major commissions exemplify his rise to prominence as an architect. They are the Tempio Malatestiano circa 1450 in Rimini (a new façade for the medieval Church of San Francesco) and the Church of Sant' Andrea in Mantua begun in 1470. Alberti's humanistic design for San Francesco hailed a new age for architecture, and the parts of Sant' Andrea that were finished had an important influence on other Renaissance churches. Although neither structure was completed according to Alberti's plan, and both have passed through renovation and reconstruction, the evidence that remains is a remarkable witness to Alberti's creativity and to the ingenuity of his builders. The Tempio's very name, from the Latin *templum*, associates the structure with classical antiquity. The façade of the entrance alludes to an actual Roman triumphal arch in Rimini, the Arch of Augustus. Commissioned by the lord of Rimini, Sigismondo Malatesta, the Tempio was a tribute to him and his mistress, Isotta degli Atti, meant to unite them for eternity though they were

not then united in the eyes of the church. This Tempio would be their joint tomb; Alberti believed that sepulchres were an effective means of preserving a name for posterity. The building's harmonious, balanced façade and antique-style ornamentation proved to be a monument not only to his patron, but also to Alberti's genius as an architect—even though he was not present at the building site. Letters extant from Alberti give instructions to the sculptor Matteo de' Pasti (c. 1420–67) for building the Tempio. Pasti was working on the site, supervising workers, while Alberti was in Rome directing the project. There is even an extant letter (now in the Pierpont Morgan Library, New York) in which Alberti drew an ornamental detail for the roof, but evidently he did not journey to Rimini, far away on the Adriatic coast, to inspect the Tempio's progress. Pasti followed Alberti's modular design, which created precisely proportioned surfaces derived from ratios in painting and mathematics.

The Church of Sant' Andrea was commissioned by Lodovico Gonzaga (1412–78), marquis of Mantua, a soldier and humanist who as a young man studied with none other than Vittorino da Feltre (1378–46) in his famous Casa Giocosa (discussed in chapter 11, Education). Lodovico fought for both Venice and Milan and married Barbara of Brandenburg, niece of the emperor Sigismund. After the Peace of Lodi settled Italian conflicts in 1454, Lodovico was able to rule peacefully for more than two decades, during which his patronage extended to numerous artists and humanists. He also became one of Alberti's major patrons. When Alberti wrote to Lodovico in 1470 about his proposal for Sant' Andrea, the architect had been involved with Gonzaga projects for nearly a decade (however, his precise degree of involvement is debated by scholars). Sant' Andrea's plan had to be worthy of a church whose main relic was supposedly the actual blood of Christ, and it had to be large enough to contain safely the vast crowds who thronged to the church whenever the relic was displayed. The Sant' Andrea commission presented Alberti with the opportunity to design an entire church at the culmination of his career as an architect. The building was his crowning achievement, the largest structure built from his designs. The design of Sant' Andrea's interior was based on Rome's ancient Basilica of Maxentius with its gigantic nave and wide openings into lateral spaces. The width of the façade of Sant' Andrea equals its height: perfectly proportioned according to Alberti's theoretical system of ratios and definitively recognizable as his design.

SERLIO

Although one château and one doorway are the only remainders of Sebastian Serlio's (1475–c. 1554) buildings, his illustrated books on architecture were enormously influential in the rise of the architect. Trained as a painter by his father in Bologna, Serlio began his architectural career in Rome. In 1527 he fled to Venice after Rome was sacked; he worked in the northern republic until 1541 when he moved to France by invitation of the king to work on Fontainebleau (see page 13). His *Archittetura* (Archi-

tecture) was published in several books between 1537 and 1547. Because of Serlio's years in Rome, the treatise used architectural examples from such noteworthy sources as Raphael (1483–1520) and Bramante, disseminating their classicizing style throughout western Europe. During the Renaissance, Serlio's books were translated into French, Spanish, Dutch, and English. His work was the first published Renaissance documentation of the five "orders" of architecture—including the system by which columns and their capitals, and so on, were designed, as described in his fourth book. Although Renaissance editions of Vitruvius as well as Alberti's treatise discussed the orders, Serlio was the first to publish detailed illustrations. The five orders of columns (somewhat simplifed) are Tuscan (the plain Italic style), Doric (the plain ancient style), Ionic (an inverted scroll at each

4.1 *Part of the 16th-century cloister of the Monastery of San Giovanni Evangelista in Parma, Italy. The rondel ornamentation is typical of the Renaissance, and the arches have the proportions of classical style.* (Photograph by the author, 2003)

end of the capital), Corinthian (ornamental acanthus leaves), and Composite (a combination, usually of Ionic and Corinthian). Each order was thought to have its own unique character. Here Serlio describes the Tuscan order: "the greatest and rusticke order of Building, that is, the Thuscan, being the playnest, rudest, and strongest, and of least grace and seemeliness" (Holt 1982, p. 45). Architects were taught that each order of architecture was appropriate for specific types of buildings, and that columns on a façade should be arranged with plain capitals for the first floor, Ionic for the second, and Corinthian or Composite for the third. Architects who followed this classical model demonstrated that they were well educated and working within classical precedents.

PALLADIO

Andrea Palladio (1508–80), more than any other architect of the 16th century, adhered to the classical rules of building as stipulated by the Roman architect and engineer Vitruvius (fl. 46–30 B.C.E.). Palladio worked in Venice and the Veneto. His buildings had coherence and dignity, often centrally designed and with porticoes like those of ancient temples. These porticoes usually have several columns surmounted by a decorative flat entablature (comparable to a tabletop) across their capitals that supports a decorative frieze and triangular pediment, with small statues (*acroteria*) at the point of the pediment and at each end. Such buildings were re-creations of classical designs, down to the smallest details. Palladio owed his rise to fame as an architect to the patronage of Gian Giorgio Trissino (1478–1550), a poet and dramatist (whose work is discussed in chapter 5, Literature and Language). Trissino befriended Palladio, who grew up in the poet's hometown of Vicenza in northern Italy, working as a stonemason and architect. Having served in Rome as a papal diplomat, Trissino subsequently enjoyed the support of the Vatican. In 1545 he took his friend to Rome, where Palladio studied ruins of ancient buildings. With this firsthand knowledge, Palladio won an important competition in Vicenza in 1547 to renovate a palazzo that came to be known as the Basilica Palladiana. His career as an architect flourished after that accomplishment; several of Palladio's other projects are described in the following.

Rome

BRAMANTE

Donato Bramante (c. 1443–1514) began his career as a painter in Urbino and continued it in Milan circa 1479 as an architect under the patronage of its rulers, the Sforza family. Twenty years later, when the French occupied Milan, Bramante escaped to Rome. There his status as an architect was enhanced in 1503 when Pope Julius II (1443–1513) selected him to renovate and rebuild the Holy See (Vatican, seat of the popes). The first building he designed in Rome, the cloister of Santa Maria della Pace, derived from antique Roman models such as the Theater of Marcellus. Although Bramante died before he could realize his Greek cross plan for Saint Peter's Basilica, the grand sweep of his Cortile del Belvedere at the Vatican provided an archetypal terraced courtyard that used antique forms. The performance space included a system of hydraulics for flooding the enclosure so that mock naval battles could be staged, similar to those in ancient times. No less an authority than Serlio praised Bramante for reviving the art of architecture, meaning his Renaissance interpretation of classical models.

RAPHAEL

Raphael (1483–1520) is best known as a painter (see chapter 3, Art and Visual Culture). Partly because of his skill as a draftsman, he was selected as architect of Saint Peter's Basilica in 1514. Raphael's completed buildings include the Villa Madama in 1518 (see page 111-112) and the Chigi Chapel in the Church of Santa Maria del Popolo circa 1516.

MICHELANGELO

Michelangelo Buonarroti (1475–1564) is a special case because his fame as a painter and sculptor was widespread before he began working as an architect at the age of 40 (see chapter 3). His expertise as a sculptor made him a likely candidate for designing building façades, and indeed Pope Leo X (Giovanni de' Medici, 1475–1521) commissioned Michelangelo to create a new façade for the family's parish church of San Lorenzo in Florence. Although this project was never realized, Michelangelo did complete the New Sacristy, which balanced Brunelleschi's Old Sacristy and gave the church symmetrical chapels. With this project, Michelangelo increased his standing as an architect by placing himself on the same level as Brunelleschi's earlier genius. Toward the end of his career, Michelangelo was commissioned by Pope Paul III (1468–1549) to complete Saint Peter's Basilica. The gigantic hemispherical dome was completed after his death, but with a pointed top not part of his original design.

VIGNOLA

Giacomo da Vignola (1507–73) moved to Rome in 1530 after studying architecture in Bologna; there he became architect to Pope Julius III (1487–1555). Vignola caught the attention of everyone involved in the arts in Rome when he designed an oval dome, the first in Europe, for the Tempietto (little temple) di San Andrea constructed for the pope. Vignola's status in the profession was assured by his plans for Il Gesù, the Jesuit church begun in 1568. The façade was designed by Giacomo della Porta (c. 1490–1577) after Vignola died. Vignola's extravagantly spacious interior (a nave approximately 60 feet wide) and elegant forms were emphasized by light streaming in from innovative windows cut through the clerestory. Because the Gesù church was copied by Jesuit communities around the world, Vignola's fame was international. He published in 1562 *Regole delle cinque ordini d'architettura* (Rules of the five orders of architecture), closely focusing on one of the most significant topics treated by Serlio. This publication established Vignola as an authority in the field of Renaissance architecture.

VASARI

Giorgio Vasari (1511–74) is best known for his *Vite de' più eccelenti architetti, pittori e scultori* (Lives of the most excellent architects, painters and sculptors), first published in 1550 and greatly expanded in 1568. He was also a renowned painter and an architect of some importance, especially for his design for the Uffizi Palace. This building, in classicizing style, was constructed to house the administrative offices of Grand Duke Cosimo I de' Medici (*uffizi* means

4.2 The Tempietto (little temple), 1502, was designed by Donato Bramante. It originally was to have been framed by a much grander setting. This monument in classical Roman style was constructed on the site where St. Peter was believed to have been martyred. (Courtesy of Sandra Sider)

"offices" in Italian). Vasari believed that the written word provided the best possible record for posterity of great works, and time has proven him correct in many instances.

France

DELORME

Philibert Delorme (1514–70), the son of a stonemason, spent several years in Rome during the mid-1530s. This was an exciting time for Renaissance architecture because of the rebuilding and urban renewal that followed the 1527 sack of the city.

Delorme's subsequent architectural projects were influenced by the buildings he studied in Rome; that influence gave him new status as an architect in his homeland. His publications, especially *L'Architecture* of 1567, as well as his designs were important for French architecture during the second half of the 16th century. Unfortunately, most of his buildings have been destroyed, including the Tuileries in Paris commissioned by Queen Catherine de' Medici (1519–89) near the end of his career.

DUCERCEAU

Jacques Androuet Ducerceau the Elder (c. 1515–85) was the patriarch of a family of architects, engravers, and engineers. His son, Baptiste (c. 1545–90), responsible for construction of the Louvre, also erected Pont Neuf (the oldest bridge still standing in the city of Paris). In 1539 Jacques Ducerceau published the first French architectural handbook, *Livre d'architecture*. His most important work for later architects was *Les plus excellents bâtiments de France* (The most excellent buildings of France, 1576 and 1579), which documented not only the buildings but also their gardens. The exuberant ornamentation of Jacques Ducerceau's style, evident in his architectural engravings, helped introduce the Mannerist mode to France. Mannerism, consisting of very stylized details in surface ornamentation and design, became the dominant artistic style of latter-16th-century France.

INFLUENCE OF ROME

The city of Rome influenced Renaissance architecture in two ways: The ruins and history of ancient Rome inspired architectural designs and motifs, and the building projects of 16th-century Rome provided a contemporary model of urban renewal. Venice, for example, was favorably compared to ancient Rome, especially the Ducal Palace. The sack of Rome by Imperial troops in 1527, which destroyed much of the city, generated rebuilding and renovation in the remainder of the 16th century.

Ruins of Rome: 15th Century

We have seen that most of the architects who rose to prominence during the 15th and 16th centuries included allusions to ancient Rome if not to actual Roman ruins in some of their most famous buildings. At the beginning of the 15th century, Rome essentially was a large medieval town, with sheep pastured in its meadows and the hills virtually abandoned. Parts of a few of the ancient buildings and of the city wall were visible, but even those were being destroyed as residents took stones to build and repair their own structures, or to crush and burn into lime. Although Rome had been part of the Papal States for centuries, between 1309 and the election of Nicholas V in 1447 the instability of the papacy prevented any serious attention from being paid to the city itself. From 1309 until 1377 the popes resided in Avignon (a period known as the Great Schism or Babylonian Captivity; see chapter 2, Religion), and for another seven decades a series of rival popes caused the schism to continue in Italy. During the latter 14th century, Petrarch surveyed the city and praised it in his poetry (see chapter 5, Literature and Language), but his identification of ruins was filled with errors. Nevertheless, his descriptions of the city inspired antiquarians and architects to begin serious study of the ruins of Rome. They were supported in this effort by the popes and the Holy Roman Emperors, many of whom viewed themselves as equal to the emperors of ancient Rome, especially Augustus Caesar.

When Nicholas V became pope, Rome was in a lamentable state, sacked and partially destroyed in 1413 by troops serving under the king of Naples. Italy was fractured into several competing city-states, notably Milan and Bologna, against the Holy See. Using the Jubilee year of 1450 to promote Rome as the center of Christianity, Nicholas V helped to unify the Italian states and stabilize the Papal States. This relatively peaceful era in Italian affairs drew much-needed income into Rome during the mid-15th century as thousands of pilgrims were able to travel safely to and from the Holy See. During Nicolas V's papacy, the cultural legacy of Rome began to thrive, guided by humanists such as Poggio Bracciolini (1380–1459). Trained in Florence, Poggio (as he is usually called) moved to Rome in 1403 and worked in the service of eight popes. His scholarly focus involved discovering the manuscripts and editing the texts of Latin classics. Poggio's travels in Europe with the papal entourage gave him the perfect opportunity to explore the great monastic libraries, such as Saint Gallen, and he often took the manuscripts he found back to the papal library. Among these Latin texts were descriptions of Rome as well as inscriptions, and Poggio traveled around the city in his spare time inspecting and describing the ruins in his attempt to understand the texts. Most importantly, Poggio deplored the despoliation of ancient Rome and emphasized the need to preserve the ruins that remained.

The Roman Academy was founded by the humanist Pomponio Leto (1425–98), who succeeded the great historian Lorenzo Valla (1407–57) in the Latin chair at the Gymnasium Romanum. Along with the Accademia Platonica (Platonic Academy) in Florence and Accademia Pontana (Academy of Pontano) in Naples, the Roman Academy was among the first in a long tradition of learned societies in Italy. The Academy in Rome was significant for the study of classical architecture because Leto was fascinated by the ancient city—its monuments as well as its literature. He and his colleagues wandered over Rome and down into the catacombs, documenting inscriptions and other antiquities. Leto lectured on the monuments of ancient Rome at the university, informing numerous students about his interpretations of ancient sites as well as referring to the work of the ancient antiquarian Varro. Leto was more systematic in his archaeological studies than previous scholars, helping his contemporaries understand the purpose of ancient buildings, their relationships within a site, and other information useful to architects modeling their designs on classical buildings. Finally, he taught his students to study ancient structures in the context of ancient texts (and vice versa), a bold interdisciplinary approach that introduced historical validity to architectural planning of the early Renaissance. Another forerunner of Roman archaeology was the papal secretary Flavio Biondo (1392–1463), who wrote meticulously about the topography of Rome. He supplemented classical sources by field study of actual ruins; his *Roma instaurata* (Rome restored) was consulted as a reference source by artists and architects for more than a century.

Pope Sixtus IV (1414–84), elected in 1471, founded a museum on the Capitoline hill in 1474. By then the craze for collecting antiquities was helping to preserve individual statues, inscriptions, and architectural ornaments, though at the same time causing these works to be dislocated from their original locations and thus obscuring the historical record. Although some collectors made notes of where their pieces had been found, others were more interested in impressing visitors with their treasures. Sixtus IV vastly improved the city's infrastructure by commissioning a building program that included the much-needed advancement of widening and paving the streets. Even though parts of ruins were destroyed or relocated during the construction, that work uncovered more of the medieval and ancient city, which the next generation could then study. Except in isolated examples, such as the papal town of Pienza, urban planning as such did not progress outside Rome during the 15th and 16th centuries. In Rome the popes used their authority to sweep aside ruins, domestic dwellings, and small institutional buildings to modernize both the city and the Holy See. In other cities, however, the private vision of patrons such as the Medici, Rucellai, and Sforza usually prevailed; magnificent private residences were constructed without much thought about modernizing the city as a whole or even specific neighborhoods. The main public squares of Renaissance cities, however, were notable exceptions as efforts were made to frame these spaces with complementary buildings. Venice is the best example of this aspect of urban planning (see Libraries and Museums, page 117).

We should note that Roman antiquities were not the only treasures available to architects in Renaissance Rome. The Roman emperors had transported several massive obelisks from Egypt to Rome, and the obelisk near Saint Peter's was still standing during the Renaissance. Sixtus V (1525–90), who did not place any value on preserving Rome's ancient legacy, wanted to transfer this obelisk from the side of Saint Peter's into the main piazza (where it stands today). Architects in Rome had long discussions concerning the hydraulic engineering that would be required for such a feat, which led to improved knowledge of hydraulics. But not even Michelangelo would undertake the project, which was finally accomplished by Domenico Fontana (1543–1607).

Restoring Rome: 16th Century

Pope Leo X commissioned Raphael to draw sketches to document the ruins of Rome, suggesting how they

might be preserved. Raphael was also appointed custodian of classical antiquities, a position that gave him ample opportunity to study antique buildings and fragments for his own architectural designs. With papal support, Rome was flourishing as a center of architecture and art in the 1520s. The Italian Wars (see chapter 7, Warfare), however, reached the gates of Rome in 1527. The papacy had been in league with France, Venice, and the duke of Milan against the emperor Charles V, whose German and Spanish troops of some 30,000 soldiers overran Rome in May 1527, sacking the city and destroying monuments for several months. The occupation by foreign troops lasted nine

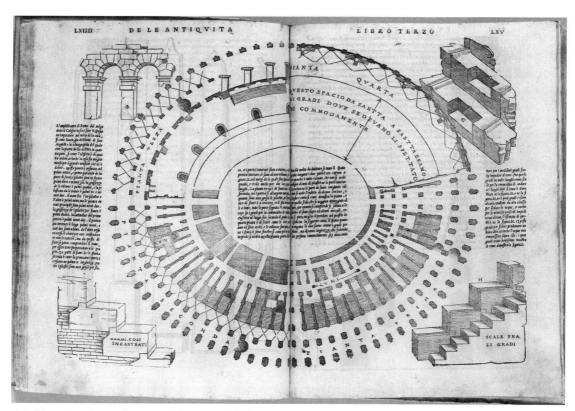

4.3 *Plan, elevation, and section of the ruins of the Roman Colosseum. Woodcut by Sebastiano Serlio, in his* Il terzo libro nel qual si figurano, e descrivono la antiqua di Roma *(Third book in which are illustrated and described the antiquities of Rome, 1540, the book on which many other Renaissance books illustrating architecture were modeled).* (Photograph courtesy of Sotheby's Inc., © 2003)

months and Rome was devastated, physically and financially. As we have seen, this attack caused noted architects to flee from Rome to other areas. They took their classical training and affinity for the antique to cities that otherwise might not have had access to their expertise. Rome, however, did not recover from the events of 1527–28 for several decades.

Many of the artists who were in Rome to learn about classical styles and building techniques made drawings of the ruins they were studying. This documentation gives us a fairly clear idea of the major monuments as the Renaissance saw them. The French painter Etienne Dupérac (c. 1525–1604), for example, journeyed to Rome in 1550. His drawings executed during the next three decades provided a valuable historic record, especially the engravings published in 1575, *Vestigi dell'antichità di Roma* (Remains of the antiquity of Rome). Another tool for architects and city planners were the maps of Rome, including maps and views of the ancient monuments, published during the 16th century. Although such maps were being drawn during the 15th century, for example, by Alberti, topographic printing of the 16th century gave architects across Europe greater access to this visual information. These maps also helped to promote interest in preserving the vestiges of the ancient city among antiquarians and scholars.

Architectural Inscriptions

Epigraphy, or the study of inscriptions, delighted Renaissance humanists. They spent many hours in their academies debating interpretations of Latin inscriptions and pondering where fragmentary inscriptions might once have been located in ancient Rome. The visual interest of inscribed characters, especially on an otherwise blank wall or entablature, appealed to Renaissance architects and artists. Moreover, such monumental inscriptions in Latin enhanced the grandeur of buildings on which they appeared, recalling the monuments of ancient Rome. The Venetian Church of San Francesco della Vigna (discussed later) is a perfect example of "antique" inscriptions in Renaissance architecture.

ECCLESIASTICAL BUILDINGS

The dome of the cathedral of Florence is the quintessential Renaissance ecclesiastical structure of the 15th century. Brunelleschi's achievement was recognized in perpetuity by his burial within the cathedral, with an epitaph lauding him as "Filippo the Architect." Renaissance architects functioned within a hierarchical mode of esteem for public buildings, in which municipal buildings were valued least, palaces more, and churches most highly. The greatest honor was to design and construct an ecclesiastical building, above all a cathedral or basilica. Saint Peter's Basilica at the heart of the Holy See was the grandest religious building of the 16th century. Not completed until 1614, it had been planned as early as the mid-15th century by Pope Nicholas V. Architects who designed or modified the basilica included Bramante and the artists Raphael and Michelangelo. When he was on his deathbed, Nicholas V said that the churches he commissioned were for the general public, who should be awestruck by their magnificence.

Italy

Santa Maria Novella (Florence) was founded as a Dominican church in the mid-13th century. The façade was never completed above the main floor; the vaulted (curved) central roof and sloping roofs of the side aisles projected above the façade. Santa Maria Novella was the parish church of the Rucellai family, who commissioned Alberti to create a façade for the upper level. Renaissance architects were often asked to complete or restore medieval buildings. Using his modular system of proportions, Alberti designed a façade that complemented the original design in shape and color, using green and white marble in striped patterns (c. 1458–70). The upper level was finished with a classicizing pediment above the frieze with its inscription, and with a gable on each side topped by a long, sloping scroll. The latter feature became a popular component of Renaissance façades designed in antique style.

4.4 Coffered ceiling in the porch of the Pazzi Chapel, 15th century, Florence, Italy. (Courtesy of Sandra Sider)

The Pazzi Chapel (Florence), probably by Michelozzo, functioned as a chapter house for meetings of members of the Franciscan order at the Church of Santa Croce. Commissioned by Andrea de'Pazzi, a wealthy Florentine and enemy of the Medicis, the building was his family burial chapel. Opening onto a courtyard, the Pazzi Chapel is a rectangular domed structure featuring a porticoed entrance and porch with triple-vaulted ceilings. The central ceiling of the porch is lavishly decorated in polychromed tiles, and both of the lateral barrel-vaulted ceilings are handsomely coffered in squares of Renaissance floral and geometric motifs. The interior coffered ceilings, in barrel-vaulted bays on each side, echo the design of the porch. With cream-colored stuccoed walls, darker geometric detailing, and glazed terra-cotta rondel reliefs of the apostles in blue and white, the interior of the Pazzi Chapel is a scintillating example of 15th-century architectural design. Michelozzo added an innovative touch in four large polychromed rondels of the Evangelists installed in pendentives supporting the dome. The curved ornamentation and structure

of the chapel, including arches inscribed around the walls and rondels on the doors, unify the space, making it both vibrant and serene. The Pazzi Chapel is a jewel of Renaissance architecture.

Bramante's 1502 Tempietto for the Church of San Pietro in Montorio (Rome) was a revolutionary structure. Loosely based on Roman models such as the Pantheon, the round Tempietto is only 15 feet in diameter. Nonetheless, with its lofty dome and deep niches, it is a powerful memorial to the martyr Saint Peter. The effect of the Tempietto is iconic, in that it was meant to be experienced as a three-dimensional image from the outside, more than as a structure that one entered.

Andrea Palladio, who published *Le antichità di Roma* (The antiquity of Rome) in 1554, designed three churches for the Republic of Venice between 1562 and 1577. They all have classical porticoes like those on ancient temples, a Renaissance style that was seen as essentially Palladian. One of these churches, San Francesco della Vigna, is remarkable for its use of inscriptions. Palladio designed the façade in 1564, for a church built 30 years earlier from Sansovino's plans. (The committee approving Sansovino's design included Serlio, then living in the Veneto.) The grand bronze lettering on the façade, combined with the statuary, comprises an emblematic text indicating that the church was modeled on the "temple" of the human body. Relating structures and texts to the human body was a basic tenet of Renaissance humanism.

France

The classicizing style of 15th-century Italy entered France through the south; the first ecclesiastical example was the Chapel of Saint-Lazare constructed 1475–81 in the cathedral of Marseille. The chapel, commissioned by René of Anjou, king of Naples, features on its façade Renaissance shell niches along the top and antique-style carved reliefs, the composite capitals surmounted by an entablature. The architect was Francesco Laurana (c. 1430–c. 1502), who had worked at several humanistic courts, especially that of Alphonse V of Aragon in Naples. In France, the antique style came to be called *la mode italienne* (Italian style) as French nobility returned home from the Italian Wars and imported Italian architects and workers to construct and renovate their châteaux.

For monumental architecture such as churches, the Gothic style prevailed in France until the mid-16th century. Nevertheless, with the dissemination of Serlio's practical handbook of architecture in the 1530s, antique elements of Roman Renaissance architecture (the High Renaissance) began to influence French patrons and architects, engendering an affinity for classical style. The exterior of the choir built for the Church of Saint-Pierre in Caen (northern France) in 1528–35 demonstrates an early stage in France of the massive volume of Roman style. Ornate, crusted surfaces and pierced openwork in the stone have been replaced by clean, flat surfaces and relatively simple, classicizing contours.

Philibert Delorme's Chapel of Anet built in 1549–52 for the château of the same name (discussed later) was the first circular church in France. As we have seen, Delorme had studied ancient architecture in Rome. For the chapel he put his theoretical knowledge to practical use and created a structure with coffered dome (the first hemispherical dome in France), fluted Corinthian pilasters (rectangular flattened columns barely projecting from the wall), and canted corners with the cornice tilted outward. All these elements of antique style were united by Delorme to produce a fine example of French classicism.

FROM FORTRESSES AND CASTLES TO RENAISSANCE PALACES

Many medieval fortresses or castles were actually small fortified towns (the word *castle* is derived from the Latin word *castrum*, fort). Seen from the outside, they impressed viewers by their sheer mass, having high, thick walls of stone or sometimes brick, a single gated entrance usually with a drawbridge over a moat, and only a few small, narrow windows. Often the castle had a forecourt and second gate past the drawbridge so visitors could be closely inspected in the forecourt before being permitted to enter the castle grounds. Usually square or rectangular in shape, the earliest European fortresses were based on ancient Roman foundations. During the Middle Ages, fortified secondary and even tertiary walls of defense extended the protective sphere of the castle past the primary structure. These walls developed into the fortified city walls of many medieval towns and cities as houses, shops, schools, and other structures were built into and between the walls. Parts of the old city walls and gates are still visible across Western Europe. They are preserved almost in their entirety in historic towns such as Siena in central Italy and Dinan in northwestern France. During the Renaissance, architects had the challenge of converting sections of delapidated, war-torn, or burned city centers into more open, spacious urban environments. Private and royal palaces, with stepped approaches and symmetrical façades featuring columns or pilasters, larger windows, and fine ornamentation, created a new architectural aesthetic in Renaissance cities. The rising merchant class helped to pay for numerous private palaces while royal coffers funded the construction of many others.

Italy

The Palazzo Rucellai (Florence) of circa 1460 deviates from contemporary Florentine palaces, such as the Palazzo Medici discussed earlier, in that its façade is truly in elegant Renaissance style. Unlike the other palaces with deeply rusticated façades, the Palazzo Rucellai, possibly designed by Bernardo Rosellino (c. 1407–1464), has the stones smoothed over to create a more stately appearance. In addition, there are three tiers (stories) of pilasters framing the doors and all the windows, one pilaster above the other. The result is an imposing edifice of pleasingly symmetrical proportions.

Rome's Villa Madama was a palatial residence, constructed in the 1520s by Antonio da Sangallo the Younger (1483–46) following Raphael's design. Named after Margaret of Austria ("Madama"), who married Allesandro de' Medici in 1536 and was presented with the palace, it originally was built for Cardinal Giulio de' Medici (1478–1534). Giulio was a patron of the arts as well as an antiquarian; in 1523 he was elected to the papacy as Clement VII. The Villa Madama was designed to his antique tastes, with a central dome never before used in a Renaissance residence. Although only the garden loggia remains today; its frescoed vaulted ceiling and lofty piers (squared columnar supports) recall the grandeur of Emperor Nero's ancient Golden House, on which the decoration of the palace apparently was based.

Sangallo was working as an architect for Pope Paul III (Alessandro Farnese, 1468–1549) in the early 1540s when he was commissioned to undertake remodeling of the Palazzo Farnese in Rome. (This building should not be confused with the Villa Farnese described later). After Michelangelo began supervising the renovation, he emphasized the sculptural quality of the building by adding weight and monumentality to the structure with a massive Florentine-style cornice that extends from the roofline out over the façade. Sangallo's antique inspiration for the courtyard was expressed by large masonry piers resembling those in Roman ruins such as the Colosseum. The Palazzo Farnese stands in Rome today, dominating an expansive piazza evidently planned concurrently to complement the palazzo—an example of effective urban planning in Renaissance Rome. (Today the building houses the French embassy.)

France

In France the word *hôtel* was used for a palatial urban residence, whereas a palace outside the city was called a château (both singular and plural pronounced "sha-toe" with emphasis on the second syllable). These lavish structures gave Renaissance architects an opportunity to experiment with different styles and display their virtuosity. The best examples of châteaux were commissioned by the royal family and their immediate circle. Because many of the royal archives were destroyed during the French Revolution, we unfortunately do not have information about the architects commissioned to create most of the buildings.

The Louvre in Paris (now the French national museum) was begun as a renovation of a 13th-century medieval fortress, commissioned by King Francis I

(1494–1547). The castle keep, with its dungeon in the cellar, was demolished to open up a courtyard. Although only a small portion of the Louvre as conceived by its architect Pierre Lescot (1510/15–78) was constructed before the close of the 16th century, his Italianate square courtyard greatly influenced other French Renaissance architecture. Lescot's façade on the west wing overlooking the square court was completed in 1546. Created in collaboration with the sculptor Jean Goujon (c. 1510–c. 65), the façade is a masterpiece of classical style, with fluted columns and

4.5 Château of Langeais, France, constructed during the latter 15th century. Although the entrance was designed as a medieval fortress, this façade facing the garden is in a transitional early Renaissance style. Note the rows of mullioned windows. (Courtesy of Sandra Sider)

niches for statuary between the columns. In addition, the spaces between windows on the shorter third story are filled with sculpture in relief, like that found on ancient pediments. The result is a lively yet harmonious whole.

In 1528 Francis I commissioned the French architect Gilles de Breton (c. 1500–c. 1552) to begin renovations of the small medieval fortress of Fontainebleau, situated in a forest approximately 40 miles southeast of Paris. We also know that Serlio was working at Fontainebleau, called there by the king to work on the renovations. The Gallery of Francis I, whose Italianate interior decoration is discussed in chapter 3, was a model of Renaissance style. Fontainebleau was famous at the time for its gardens, including a grotto like those that were popular in Italy. One of the earliest garden grottoes in France, it still exists today.

Renovations at the French royal residence of Blois, in the Loire Valley, commenced in 1514. The Italianate wing added by Francis I has Bramantesque elements of rectangular windows with mullions, flanked by pilasters. The building features a unique external spiral staircase dominating the courtyard. Shaped as a hexagon, part of it ingeniously inside the building and the rest outside, the staircase is capped by a handsome classical balustrade. Defined by the staircase, the façade has the presence of a monumental Roman structure, even in the context of medieval elements in other parts of the château's roofline and façade.

Chambord, also in the Loire Valley close to Blois, was renovated for the king from 1519. This splendidly grandiose edifice, a converted hunting lodge, was not completed until 1550. The main, central building is designed with a Greek cross floor plan and four circular structures at each corner. Because such a balanced floor plan was already popular in Italian villas and palazzos, scholars have proposed that the architect was Italian. The most striking feature of Chambord is its double spiral staircase at the center, leading up to the top of the third story. Italianate in its perfect symmetry, the staircase permits those using it to see each other but not to cross over from one staircase to another.

Anet, approximately 50 miles west of Paris, was constructed between 1546 and 1552. This creation was the château of Diane de Poitiers (1499–1566), a gift from her lover, Henry II, king of France (1519–59). The architect was Philibert Delorme, whose grand scheme unified the château and gardens in a single design. Although such planning was usual for Italian architects, Anet was the first example in France of this Italianate scheme. Only sections of the structure are known to us today, but Delorme's application of the architectural orders, triumphal arch, and heavy classical moldings indicate that the original château was an archetype of French classicism.

VILLAS

The Italian terms *villa* and *palazzo* (palace) can be confusing. Although *villa* usually designates a country house and *palazzo* a large house in the city, readers find occasional references to villas in the city and palazzos in the country. Here we shall discuss villas constructed as retreats in the country (suburban villas that qualify as palaces are discussed in Palaces, pages 111–113). Palladio designed the most perfectly classical villas and palaces of the Renaissance.

The Country House

By the close of the 15th century, a spectacular view had become an important component of villa design, almost as important as the house itself. Alberti wrote circa 1450 that the villa should have "a view of some city, town, stretch of coast, or plain, or it should have within sight the peaks of some notable hills or mountains, delightful gardens, and attractive haunts for fishing and hunting" (Alberti 1997, p. 145, book 5.16). Villas might also overlook part of the estate's farmland, for rural activities were very much part of villa life. Cosimo de' Medici the Elder, in his villa at Careggi (near Florence), was reported to have pruned his vineyards and read patristic manuscripts in the same morning.

The tales in Giovanni Boccaccio's (1313–75) *Decameron* are narrated by aristocratic Florentines in a country villa, enjoying the leisure of a house and garden away from the noise, dirt, and intermittent plague of the city. The pleasant diversion of the storytellers' literary pursuit typifies the relaxed sort of activity enjoyed by the owners and guests in Renaissance villas. The ancient Roman idea of the villa was that of a *locus amoenus* (pleasant place), with sunny gardens, pungent groves, and soothing fountains or streams—a concept that certainly appealed to Renaissance aristocracy. To make good use of the gardens, the villa design was often the opposite of that for houses in town, which usually had an open central courtyard and massive walls facing the street. In the villa, at least one side could be a roofed loggia facing the gardens, with the central space used as a room. The warm, dry climate of Rome and north central Italy permitted this type of partially open design.

Nevertheless, the 14th-century style of fortified villas having the defensive aspects of castles (castellated) persisted when the individual commissioning a villa suspected that bandits, mercenaries, or the danger of political rivals could be a threat. Not only did such a design provide actual defense, but also it incorporated elements historically associated with strength and power, especially small windows, thick walls, and towers. Although we think of castles as essentially medieval forms and villas as a Renaissance phenomenon, during the 15th century many villas had castellated features. As we have learned in other chapters of this book, the Middle Ages and Renaissance overlapped in numerous ways. In no area was this overlapping more obvious than in architecture, with literal juxtaposition of medieval and Renaissance forms. The Medici Villa at Careggi is a good example of such a hybrid building. In 1457 the architect Michelozzo (1396–1472) converted the medieval manor house into a villa, adding a double loggia opening onto a garden and leaving most of the fortified exterior.

Palladian Villas

Palladio, schooled in humanism, was also trained as a stonemason. The Villa Rotonda in Vicenza, begun by Palladio in 1567, is one of his most ambitious villas. It was designed after the Pantheon in Rome, with a rounded dome in the center and with four porticoes, one on each side. Palladio studied not only Renaissance buildings built in Rome by his contemporaries, but also ancient monuments and ruins. His villas are in the Veneto, the area ruled by the Republic of Venice, especially near the town of Vicenza. Several of the town's wealthy residents commissioned Palladio to design country retreats in the classical style, with colonnaded porticoes and symmetrical proportions. These villas, meant to recreate the villas of classical Rome, gave birth to a new style called Palladianism.

Other Villas

The Palazzo Te, located on the island of Te near Mantua, was commissioned by the Gonzaga family (the ducal rulers of Mantua). Designed by the artist Giulio Romano (c. 1499–1546), the villa complex was built between 1527 and 1534 as a rustic retreat for dining and entertaining. As in many other Renaissance building projects, the architect had to contend with a preexisting medieval structure. Here, the architect integrated medieval, classical, and capricious forms in surprising Mannerist combinations. Giulio Romano also played with the classical forms themselves. For example, every now and then a sculpted decoration on the architrave (the horizontal beam running along the base of the entablature above the columns) is set partly below the beam. The façade is thus destabilized in a distinctly unclassical fashion. The educated guests at the Gonzaga villa would have appreciated such Mannerism as an architectural joke.

Giacomo da Vignola was commissioned by Cardinal Alessandro Farnese (1520–89) to design a luxurious villa at Caprarola, outside Rome. Because of its grand scale and extensive gardens, this villa is sometimes referred to as the Palazzo Farnese, which confuses it with the palazzo in the city of Rome built for an earlier Cardinal Farnese (see page 112). Completed in 1583, the Villa Farnese has four stories plus a basement. Vignola's design, based on an earlier pentagonal foundation, ingeniously united the house with the gardens by connecting them via bridges. In addition, the terraced gardens gracefully lead up to the villa by a series of wide staircases shaped like horseshoes.

Gardens

Many villa gardens in Italy were intended to replicate the ancient Roman garden, with cypress, myrtle, pomegranates, fig trees, boxwoods, and pungent or sweet herbs and flowers such as lavender, rosemary, narcissus, and violets. Although no ancient gardens survived as such into the Renaissance, patrons and architects could read about Roman gardens in classical texts. (Today our visual knowledge of Roman gardens has greatly benefited from the frescoes discovered at Pompei in the 18th century.) Cicero mentioned the serenity of his garden near the river by his country house, and Ovid claimed that he was inspired while working in his garden. Ancient writers wrote in detail about several aspects of gardening. Topiary, for example, was described by Pliny the Elder as popular in ancient villa gardens. This garden art was revived in Italy during the 15th century to create ornamental shapes such as ships and animals. In French and English Renaissance gardens these shaped bushes and shrubs often were geometrical rather than representational. Serlio in his 1537 treatise on architecture included a section pertaining to garden design that featured illustrations of geometrical plantings.

Water played an important role in the plantings designed for Italian villa gardens. Suburban villas near aqueducts could have water piped into the property, permitting the inclusion of several fountains and lush, exotic greenery. More remote villas did not always have predictable sources of continuous water. Their gardens required larger trees and ground cover that would be able to sustain several seasons of drought. Even in remote areas, however, Italian villa gardens usually included at least one fountain with antique-style statuary. Some of this statuary functioned as automata, moving as water flowed through them. French gardens used less water than those in Italy, partly because villa and palace gardens in France were designed on relatively flat terrain; there were fewer areas that allowed water to flow from one level to another. Whereas Italian gardens favored cascades, if not torrents, of water when it was available, gardens in France were more restrained in the use of water. Another difference in French villa gardens of the early Renaissance was the creation of *parterres* (discrete areas with their

own design), often with a separate gazebo or small pavilion, that usually could be viewed from the villa. Several important Italian villas, such as the Villa Farnese, had a "secret garden," "wild garden," or "garden of love." Their decoration is mentioned in chapter 3 Sculpture, (see page 83).

Patronage in Italian Civic Architecture

As we have seen, the Medici in Florence and the popes in Rome were outstanding patrons of Renaissance architecture, commissioning many of the buildings and renovations that remain today as witnesses to the genius of Brunelleschi, Michelozzo, Alberti, Bramante, and their colleagues. Papal influence in civic architecture extended far beyond Rome. The first permanent building for the University of Bologna, for example, was commissioned in 1562 by order of Pope Pius IV (today the Palazzo dell'Archiginnasio, which houses the municipal library); Pope Pius II, born in a remote village known as Corsignano, renamed Corsignano as Pienza, after himself. The entire village was redesigned with symmetrical roads and buildings, the central piazza featuring a cathedral, palace, and town hall. Such displays of wealth and magnificence, especially in northern Italy, prompted other individuals and institutions to commission buildings that would perpetuate their own name and status. Schools, guild halls, town halls, libraries, theaters, and other buildings, especially hospitals and their adjacent churches, benefited from this competitive impetus. The religious groups known as confraternities, often funded by lay associates, built hospitals for lepers, the poor, and other disadvantaged people.

Hospitals

The hospital of Santa Maria Nuova in Florence, founded by the Portinari family in the 13th century, was expanded in 1334 when a cruciform ward was completed. This new model for a hospital, with an altar at the center and four wings radiating out from it, was emulated during the 15th and 16th centuries—as far away as England and Spain. Previously, most hospitals, being rather small, were simply one or two large open rooms. In Italy, the cruciform design for hospitals became the foundation for modernizing hospital architecture. When Pope Sixtus IV commissioned the rebuilding of the Pammatone hospital in Genoa circa 1475, the plan was in the shape of a cross. Filarete (Antonio Averlino, c. 1400–1469) was a Florentine architect and sculptor who began his career in Rome as a sculptor. He designed the Ospedale Maggiore (great hospital) in Milan, begun in 1457, commissioned by Francesco Sforza, duke of Milan. This was to be the most ambitious hospital project of the 15th century, planned as two cruciform units united in the center by a chapel. Although Filarete's original plan was not achieved as he had envisioned it, such as leaving the lower-level colonnade open to fresh air, the building was a monument to the Sforza patronage. It was by far the largest hospital begun during the Renaissance, with a front façade measuring approximately 1,000 feet.

Banks and Exchanges

Banks as such did not exist in western Europe before the latter 14th century. Even into the 15th century, merchant bankers carried out monetary transactions in their private palazzos. The first significant banks in Italy were commissioned in cities outside the home base of the bankers patronizing their construction, partly to impress other merchants. Michelozzo probably designed the Medici bank in Milan circa 1455–60, recorded in a drawing by Filarete in his treatise on architecture. The two-story edifice was ornately decorated with sculpted leafy swags and masks in the antique style. This bank was also the residence of Pigallo Portinari, head of the Medici bank in Milan. Not until the late 16th century did public, secular banks (as we know them today) come into existence.

Town Halls

European town halls originated with the meeting rooms in an enclosed second-story space above an open market arcade. By the mid-13th century, the arcade area sometimes was enclosed, creating an additional space for meetings and council offices on the ground floor. The medieval Bargello in Florence was the first major example of this new style. Renaissance town halls usually followed the medieval mode, with a meeting space one story above an arcade. Although Filarete designed a commercial square in the early 1460s with a central town hall flanked by two mercantile piazzas, the plan never came to fruition. The Uffizi in Florence fulfilled several civic functions. Vasari had designed the Medici complex for offices in general, and during the latter 16th century the Uffizi housed the offices of guilds as well as of prominent city officials. Palladio's 1547 design for the town of Vicenza involved the renovation of the Palazzo della Ragione, in which the city council held its meetings. As we have learned, this building was called the Basilica by Palladio himself because of its stylistic affinities with Roman civic buildings. Palladio redesigned the two-story loggia to create bays of equal width, with perfect Renaissance symmetry.

Theaters

Until the Renaissance, theatrical presentations usually were open-air events, as performers often strolled from one location to another. Religious drama was also performed within churches and other institutions. With the revival of classical drama, involving relatively stationary players orating before an audience, the desire for theaters in the classical mode arose. The best example of such a theater from the Renaissance is the Teatro Olimpico in Vicenza (near Venice), Palladio's final commission, which he began in 1580 as a replication of a classical theater. It was built for the Accademia degli Olimpici for entertaining their members. One of the distinguishing features of this structure, which still stands, is that the permanent background scenery was designed as actual buildings, in linear perspective. Looking through the arches of the front stage scenery, the audience can see the façades of buildings receding into the distance. These views in perspective were designed by Vincenzo Scamozzi (1522–1616), who was trained by Palladio, succeeded him, and completed the Teatro Olimpico in 1584. Following classical models, this antique-style space features a colonnade topped by statuary curving along the back of the seating area.

Libraries and Museums

Clement VII, a Medici pope, commissioned Michelangelo to build a library for the cloister of San Lorenzo to house the manuscript collection of the Medici. Work began in 1524 on the Biblioteca Laurenziana; the structure was completed in 1559 by others, including Vasari, as Michelangelo sent models of the building and written information from Rome. Whereas the reading room was designed in the linear Florentine idiom of the 15th century, with dark geometric forms against a light background, the stairway at the entrance is a marvel of sculptural brilliance. Constructed within a small yet high space, the stairway has three sections. The angular side stairways are invigorated by a monumental central section consisting of curving steps scrolling into volutes on each end. This entranceway portends the dynamic sculptural qualities of baroque architecture.

Jacopo Sansovino became city architect for Venice in 1529, after escaping the sack of Rome. In 1536 the city commissioned him to create an important building that would stand across the Piazzetta (little piazza) of San Marco from the medieval Palazzo Ducale (palace of the doges, or leaders, of Venice). This was a daunting task as the Palazzo Ducale is a magnificent, imposing structure with Oriental overtones. Sansovino had to design a complementary Renaissance building that would command, with the Palazzo, the main approach of visitors approaching the city by water. In 1537 the doge decided that the new building would contain the collection of manuscripts stored in the Palazzo, making them available for scholars to study. The library was known as the Libreria del Sansovino (now called the Loggetta and housing the Museum of Archaeology; the Biblioteca Marciana long ago moved to an adjoining space). Sansovino drew upon his vocabulary of antique Roman forms to create a double loggia of two stories, topped by an opulent balustrade with statuary

to balance the roofline details of the Palazzo Ducale. The arched bays with a column applied to each supporting pier give the structure a weighty, sculptural feeling that balances the airy, open façade of the Palazzo. In addition, both the lower and upper friezes are opulently sculpted in rondels and leafy swags, appropriate for the richly ornamented surfaces of Venetian architecture.

During the Renaissance, most museums (from the word Muses) were spaces for storing and exhibiting antiquities. Thus a museum often was called an *antiquariam*, and many were owned by individuals. In addition to displaying antique sculpture in gardens or loggia, such as at the Villa Madama, collectors commissioned architects to design special galleries. Scamozzi, for example, built a gallery at Sabbioneta (near Mantua) between 1583 and 1590 for Vincenzo Gonzaga. Nearly 300 feet long, the long, narrow room was open to sunlight on one wall with niches for exhibiting sculpture on the other. A few years earlier, the Medici Villa in Rome was expanded to include a sculpture gallery. Other villas featured portrait galleries of paintings or busts of contemporary individuals, but we have very little information about their design.

BEYOND ITALY AND FRANCE

During the 15th and 16th centuries, the Gothic style remained popular outside Italy, including in all of France, and some regions missed the Renaissance entirely. Italianate Renaissance style usually was confined to ornamental details of façades, such as the swags and scrolls on the palace of Margaret of Austria in Mechelen rebuilt circa 1517. Nevertheless, especially in centers of trade and at courts influenced by Italian art and architecture, some remarkable Renaissance structures were erected. Several of the best examples outside France and Italy are described in the following. Not all of these buildings, however, are in the classical mode that usually defines Renaissance architecture.

Ecclesiastical Buildings

Use of Renaissance architecture in the antique style in ecclesiastical buildings had very few supporters outside Italy and France, and indeed not many in France. The great cathedrals had already been established by the early 15th century, and renovations or extensions were accomplished in Gothic style or a regional variation of the same. An example of such a regional variation is the Manueline style named after Manuel I (1495–1521), king of Portugal, the most distinctive architectural style to develop in Portugal during the Renaissance. Manueline architecture was based on the Spanish Renaissance style known as Plateresque, characterized by an effusion of opulent Gothic, Moorish, and Italian surface ornamentation unrelated to the structural elements of a building. Manueline architecture transformed structures by aggressively incorporating ornamental forms. Windows, for example, are framed by masses of sculpted ropes and coral, and cosmographic armillary spheres seem to support cornices. Much of the imagery is maritime, celebrating Portuguese exploration and overseas colonies. The Convento do Cristo (convent of Christ) at Tovar in Portugal, designed by Diogo de Arruda (c. 1470–1531), was built between 1510 and 1514. The west façade is a marvel of Manueline style, featuring sails, ropes, seaweed, and other maritime imagery.

Palaces

In 1526 Emperor Charles V visited Granada and decided to build a Renaissance palace within the complex of the Alhambra (a Moorish castle). Pedro de Machuca (d. 1550), awarded the commission for the project, had worked in Italy for several years as a painter and had relocated to Granada circa 1520 to paint altarpieces. His experiences with Renaissance antique forms and the architectural models of Raphael and Bramante influenced the simple, Italianate structure of the palace. Although work continued sporadically from 1526 until 1568, the place was never completed. The stately forms that remain, such as the round courtyard with its curving colonnade, testify to the power of the Italian Renaissance on Machuca's artistic imagination.

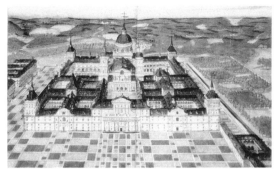

4.6 Bird's-eye view of the Monastery of El Escorial, Spain. Engraving in Braun and Hogenberg's Civitates orbis terrarum *(Cities of the world, c. 1572).* (Private Collection/The Stapleton Collection/Bridgeman Art Library)

Since the emperor must have approved the design, then he, too, was attracted to the majestic style of classical Rome.

The Escorial, the royal residence in the countryside outside Madrid commissioned by Philip II (1527–98), was constructed between 1563 and 1582 by Juan de Herrera (1530–97) and Juan Bautista de Toledo (d. 1567). The palace is part of a gigantic walled complex that included a church and a monastery. Toledo died during the early stages of the project, and his assistant, Herrera, completed his plan with a few modifications. Toledo had lived for a while in Rome, assisting Michelangelo at Saint Peter's Basilica and learning about the classical forms that would influence his designs in Spain. At the Escorial site Toledo lived to see the completion of his Patio de los Evangelistas (patio of the Evangelists), modeled on the Palazzo Farnese in Rome (discussed previously). The Escorial is ordered (using the five orders) and symmetrical, and, with the façades virtually unadorned, follows the ascetic tendencies of the king and his court. (The interior decoration is discussed in chapter 3.)

Robert Smythson (c. 1535–1614) was an architect known for his English country houses. Wollaton Hall in Nottinghamshire was built by him between 1580 and 1588 for Sir Francis Willoughby (c. 1546–96). Centrally planned, the house may have been inspired by a design by Serlio with ornamentation taken from other 16th-century treatises. Renaissance architecture did not flower in England until the early 17th century, with the designs of Inigo Jones (1573–1652). He visited Italy and later became the "Palladio" of England. Although his work is beyond the chronological scope of this book, we should note that Jones designed the Queen's House in Greenwich as a villa in Italian Renaissance style, as well as the first classicizing church in England, Queen's Chapel in Saint James Palace, between 1623 and 1625.

Civic Architecture

The Renaissance town hall in Antwerp (Belgium), designed by Cornelis Floris de Vriendt the Younger (c. 1513/14–75), was constructed between 1561 and 1565. Obviously influenced by the work of Bramante, Floris created a magnificent four-storied edifice, with symmetrical wings featuring cross-mullioned windows flanked by pilasters. The central part of the building has arcuated windows with balustrades, the height of this section lifted to five stories, creating a tower crowned by an aedicule (pedimented temple-like form). Supporting the building from the ground floor is an arcade of thick, rusticated piers. The Antwerp town hall is justifiably famous as the most classically Renaissance civic building of northern Europe.

As we have seen, the symmetrical cruciform plan of Santa Maria Nuova in Florence had an impressive effect on Renaissance hospital designs. The first such hospital in Spain was the Hospital Real (royal hospital) in Santiago de Compostela, the pilgrimage destination in northwest Spain. The architect was Enrique Egas (fl. c. 1480–1534), who also worked on the cathedral of Toledo. His family originated in Brussels and emigrated to Toledo in the 15th century; they produced several architects. Egas constructed the hospital in Santiago de Compostela between 1501 and 1511, making it the first modern hospital in the Iberian Peninsula. Its ornamentation is in the flat, pure Florentine style. He went on to build other hospitals in Toledo and Granada.

London's Swan Theatre was constructed circa 1595, designed for both sports and dramatical performances. Unlike most other theaters in London, it was evidently commissioned by an entrepreneur rather than by the director of a company of performers. The unroofed wooden structure was circular, with a foundation of bricks. Its wooden pillars on the stage, painted in the antique style to resemble marble, featured ornately carved capitals and monumental bases. Inigo Jones (who did not plan the Swan) designed a Palladian-style theater, Cockpit-in-Court, consisting of an octagon within a square. It was built in 1629.

The Royal Exchange in London was completed in 1566 in response to the city's increasing importance as a trading center. Sir Thomas Gresham (1519–79), Queen Elizabeth I's (1533–1603) financial adviser in Antwerp for some 20 years, raised the money to build the Royal Exchange. The original building, in elegant Florentine fashion, comprised a large central courtyard surrounded by a loggia at ground level with two stories above it. Interestingly, after the complex burned in the Great Fire of 1666, it was restored almost to the original plan. The one anomaly, a glaring fault that clashes with the Renaissance design, is an inept triumphal archway at the entrance topped by an out-of-scale tower. Such later additions detracted from the Renaissance purity of several of the buildings discussed earlier.

Gardens

In England, the first noteworthy Renaissance garden was created at the end of the 15th century for the royal palace at Richmond. In the fashion that would become popular in England during the 16th century, this garden had galleries and covered walkways. Palace gardens of the 16th century, such as that of Hampton Court, featured elements of both French and Italian design. Usually at least one area was strictly geometrical, divided into quarters with a knot garden in each segment. Knot gardens, originating in France, consisted of interlacing strips of plants that created a sort of carpet design. Mounts and mazes were also popular, especially in the rather large gardens of aristocratic houses. In Poland, Italian garden design predominated, with terraces being the major feature of several Renaissance gardens. As in Italy, Polish aristocrats favored gardens extending from both sides of the domicile, so that a pleasant garden view could be enjoyed from several places inside the house. Renaissance-style gardens did not become popular in Germany until the latter 16th century, after gardening books in Italian and French had been translated into German. The gardens of Germany featured Italianate elements, such as grottoes, and French structures, such as pavilions. Important German gardens were found in Munich and Heidelberg, and in several Austrian cities. Because of Arabic traditions, both Portugal and Spain had Renaissance gardens with fountains and large, reflective pools of water. Usually laid out in geometric arrangements, these gardens had cool arcades alongside the pools, with most of the surfaces decorated with colorful tiles. The best surviving example is the garden of the Alcázar in Seville.

Major Architects

Alberti, Leon Battista (1404–1472), a painter, musician, writer, and man of many other talents, wrote the first treatise on Renaissance architecture, *De re aedificatoria* (On the art of building in ten books). His buildings were based on humanistic ideals of perfect proportion. Important projects attributed to him are the upper façade of Santa Maria Novella in Florence, the Church of San Andrea in Milan, and the Tempio Malatestiano in Rimini.

Bramante, Donato (c. 1443–1514) was born in Urbino and may have been influenced by artists at that ducal court. He began his career as a painter and later worked as an architect for the duke of Milan, for whom he remodeled several important churches. Bramante designed the Belvedere Court of the Vatican, as well as a Greek cross plan for Saint Peter's Basilica.

Brunelleschi, Filippo (1377–1446), engineer and architect, was originally trained as a goldsmith. All of Brunelleschi's commissions were in Florence, including the Ospedale degli Innocenti, the nave and choir of the Church of Santo Spirito, the Old Sacristy of San Lorenzo, and, his most famous accomplishment, the dome of the cathedral of Florence.

Delorme, Philibert (1514–1570), the son of a stonemason, visited Rome and returned to France filled with classical ideas for architectural commissions. His most complete building was the château of Anet outside Paris, featuring the first circular church in France.

Ducerceau the Elder, Jacques Androuet (c. 1515–1585) wrote *Livre d'architecture* (Book of architecture, 1539), the first such handbook published in France. Best known as an engraver, in his books he documents buildings and decoration of the time, much of which is now lost to us.

Filarete (*Antonio Averlino*) (c. 1400–1469), famous as a sculptor and goldsmith, created the bronze doors of Old Saint Peter's in Rome (now the west door of the Basilica). His major architectural legacy is the Ospedale Maggiore in Milan, begun in 1456.

Floris de Vriendt the Younger, Cornelis (c. 1513/14–1575), usually referred to as Cornelis Floris, was one of a family of painters and architects. Floris designed the splendid 16th-century town hall of Antwerp. He was also famous for publishing engravings of Italian ornamental material.

Fontana, Domenico (1543–1607) was commissioned by Sixtus V to modernize the city of Rome. His engineering family placed the Egyptian obelisk now outside Saint Peter's, and Fontana was the architect for what is known as the Vatican Library, completed in 1590. He was among the architects working on completing the dome for Saint Peter's Basilica.

Herrera, Juan de (1530–1597), trained as a mathematician, collected a library of scientific material. In 1563 he began working on the Escorial under the guidance of Juan Bautista de Toledo and supervised the project after Toledo died. His other major contributions included the Exchange in Seville and the cathedral of Vallodolid.

Lescot, Pierre (1510/15–1578) was a French architect working in and near Paris. His masterpieces were the Italianate courtyard of the Louvre, surviving today, and the Fontaine des Innocents (1547–49), which has been reconstructed.

Michelangelo Buonarroti (1475–1564), one of the most famous artists of the Renaissance, also worked as an architect, creating a new sense of sculptural form in his projects. He designed the New Sacristy for San Lorenzo as well as the Biblioteca Laurenziana in Florence. In 1546 he commenced work on Saint Peter's but had not quite completed the dome at his death 18 years later.

Michelozzo di Bartolommeo (or *Michelozzi Michelozzo*) (1396–1472) first worked as a sculptor in Florence. The Medici commissioned him to renovate their villa at Careggi, and in 1444 he designed the Palazzo Medici, providing the model for other Florentine palazzos. His major works include the Convent of San Marco in Florence, notably the elegant library, and probably the Pazzi Chapel.

Palladio, Andrea (*Andrea di Pietro della Gondola*) (1508–1580) took the Roman classical style to the Veneto, creating classicizing villas with porticoes and pediments. His most famous villa is La Rotonda in Vicenza, completed by Scamozzi. Palladio was influenced by Raphael and Bramante in the designs for his façades.

Peruzzi, Baldassare (1481–1536) moved from Siena to Rome in 1503 and assisted in the building of Saint Peter's for much of his career. He also designed villas, such as the Villa Farnesina in Rome, commissioned for Agostino Chigi (1465–1520), a powerful banker from Siena.

Raphael (*Raffaello Sanzio*) (1483–1520) was best known as a painter. He became architect of Saint Peter's in 1514 and a few years later designed the Villa Madama. Much of his work in architecture involved painting frescoes to decorate their walls.

Rossellino, Bernardo (c. 1407–1464) began his career as a sculptor, then during the 1450s he worked in Rome as a papal engineer. Upon returning to Florence, he was in charge of building the Palazzo Rucellai and designed the lantern atop the cathedral's dome. Rossellino was the architect selected by Pius II to remodel Pienza as a Renaissance town.

Sangallo the Younger, Antonio da (1483–1546) was trained as an architect by his uncles. In 1516 he succeeded one of them as architect of Saint Peter's and worked at that post for three decades. Sangallo designed the Palazzo Farnese in Rome as well as laying the foundations for the Villa Farnese at Caprarola.

Sansovino, Jacopo Tatti (1486–1570) spent most of his career working for the city of Venice, notably the Libreria del Sansovino (or Libreria Vecchia), praised by none other than Palladio. He also designed or renovated several churches and palazzos, including the Church of San Francisco della Vigna, for which Palladio created the façade.

Scamozzi, Vincenzo (1522–1616), Palladio's pupil, completed several of his buildings. He also wrote two treatises relating to architecture, *Discorsi sopra le antichità di Roma* (Discourses on the antiquity of Rome, 1582) and *L'idea dell'architettura universale* (The idea of universal architecture, 1615).

Serlio, Sebastiano (1475–c. 1554) first studied architecture in the studio of Peruzzi, learning about ancient Roman buildings. His books on architecture were very influential, especially since they included woodcut illustrations. Serlio was the first to publish an explanation of the architectural orders.

Toledo, Juan Bautista de (d. 1567) designed the Escorial. After having worked for the Spanish viceroy in Naples, he returned to Spain in 1559 to become royal architect. His most important ecclesiastical commission was the façade of the church of the Convento de Descalzas Reales in Madrid.

Vasari, Giorgio (1511–1574) was a multitalented artist as well as a writer. His most important building project was the Uffizi complex in Florence, and he collaborated on the design for the Villa Giulia. Vasari's biographies of his contemporaries, first published in

1550 and expanded in 1568, constitute a precious record of their life and work.

Vignola, Giacomo da (1507–1573) was both an architect and a garden designer. In 1530 he became architect to Julius III and designed several churches in Rome, including the famous Gesù. His 1562 publication on the orders was considered a masterful treatment of the subject.

Vredeman de Vries, Jan (1527–c. 1606) worked in northern Europe. He was chiefly a landscape architect, who included galleries and other structures in his garden designs. Vredeman de Vries published pattern books of perspective drawings, gardens, and decorative material, and his own work included the Renaissance royal gardens in Prague.

READING

Rise of the Architect

Heydenreich 1996: Italy; Payne 1999: architectural treatises; Trachtenberg 2002: (general study).

The Influence of Rome

P. F. Brown 1995: Venice; Claridge 1998: Rome; Giedion 1967: (part of a general study on influences); Grafton 1993: Rome and Renaissance culture; McDonald 2002: the Pantheon; Serlio 1982: (facsimile of his Renaissance treatise).

Ecclesiastical Buildings

Ackerman 1971: Michelangelo; Heydenreich 1996: Italy; Sparrow 1969: inscriptions; Trachtenberg 2002 (general study); Wittkower 1971: humanistic influences; Serlio 1982: (facsimile of his Renaissance treatise).

From Fortresses and Castles to Renaissance Palaces

Blunt 1991: France; Heydenreich 1996: Italy; Trachtenberg 2002: (general study).

Villas

Alberti 1997: (translation of his Renaissance treatise on building); Lillie 1995: humanism; Trachtenberg 2002: (general study).

Patronage in Italian Civic Architecture

Ackerman 1971: Michelangelo; Heydenreich 1996: Italy; Howard 1997: techniques and materials; Martines 1988: city-states; Pevsner 1976: (general history); Trachtenberg 2002: (general study).

Beyond Italy and France

Pevsner 1976: (general history); Trachtenberg 2002: (general study).

5

LITERATURE
AND LANGUAGE

During the Middle Ages, a work of literature was often read aloud or recited because the vast majority of people could not read or write, and books in manuscript were comparatively expensive. Although collective reading continued throughout the Renaissance, it usually was in the context of a court, salon, or coffeehouse, in which the reading became a social activity. By the 16th century, private reading for pleasure and study (which often may have been "sounded out" rather than done in silence) was normal for the educated class. In general, literacy rates for young males increased significantly across western Europe between 1400 and 1600; young women also learned to read in scattered areas (see chapter 11, on education). With the spread of printed books, literature became easily attainable, even for members of the middle class. Illustrated books, with woodcuts or engravings, helped to popularize histories, biographies, novels, plays, and several types of poetry. During the 16th century, libraries of printed books began to be appreciated as much as the famous manuscript libraries had been in the 15th century, and several collections functioned as public libraries for the upper classes.

Classical texts and Renaissance works in Neo-Latin (rarely in Neo-Greek) were marketed at the book fairs alongside tales of medieval romance, popular ballads, reports from explorers, medicinal treatises, prayer books, emblem books, and many other forms of literature that proliferated during the late 15th and 16th centuries. Although the Renaissance began with Latin as the universal European tongue, and although several renowned humanists advocated Latin as the preferred literary language, literature in the vernacular flourished. Meanwhile, Renaissance Latin had an impact on the vernacular, notably in poetry. The present chapter discusses the genres of poetry, prose, drama, and oratory, including nonfiction prose, considering "literature" in its broadest sense. Although it is impossible to explore the work of every author in this 200-year period, the highlights of each genre are treated in the chapter. In addition, a list of major authors identifies many of the noteworthy writers. Several important works concerning religion, art, architecture, music, warfare, travel, and science are treated in the chapters on those topics. Bibles and biblical literature are discussed in chapter 2.

HUMANISM, PHILOLOGY, AND PUBLISHING

Writers and editors of Renaissance literature naturally were concerned with the accuracy and appropriateness of their texts. In the early Renaissance, the main preoccupations with textual accuracy pertained to the writings of classical Greek and Roman authors, as well as to biblical and patristic texts. By the late 16th century, such philological awareness included not only classical works and literature created during the 15th century, but also new writing as authors consulted lexicons, dictionaries, grammars, and other tools produced by humanists to enhance the written word. Renaissance translators often justified their linguistic methods in prefaces that emphasized the power of rhetoric in literary language and the power of language itself. Words and language as concepts were included among the literary images in several major works, for example, in the novels of François Rabelais (1483–c. 1553). Renaissance humanism was the principal impetus for the new textual focus, especially for works written in Latin, the universal language of educated people. As the printing press made texts available to a much broader audience than had been possible in the manuscript market of the early 15th century, literature in the vernacular languages became increasingly popular. Learned individuals debated the validity of writing in the vernacular language (the Italian spoken in Tuscany was the first example) instead of in the classical Latin of Cicero and his contemporaries. Similar controversies in several regions of Europe resulted in the eventual literary ascendancy of English over the Celtic (Gaelic) of Scotland, French over the Celtic (Breton) of Brittany, and so on, as the various national literatures began to coalesce into their modern forms. Other

5.1 *Scene of the assassination of Julius Caesar, from the first illustrated edition of the works of the classical Roman poet Horace. The woodcut illustrated an ode to Caesar by Horace. Published in Germany in 1498, this book was also the first edition of Horace issued by a printer in Germany (actually Strasbourg, a German city at that time).*
(Photograph courtesy of Sotheby's, Inc., © 2003)

debates concerned the appropriateness of classical Latin itself as a literary language.

Latin as a Literary Language

A work of prose by the French royal librarian Guillaume Budé (1467–1540) presents a good example of the impact of classical Latin rhetoric on Renaissance humanistic writing, in both its content and its form. His *De philologia* (On philology, 1532) pretended to be a dialogue of table talk between the king and the author, but in Latin rather than French. In lofty language and sonorous phrases, Budé convinced the king of the power of eloquence, using Homer as one of his models. He compared humanistic Renaissance writers to the demigod Hercules, stating that they deserve honor for their country as well as for themselves. At the same time, by using rhetorical figures of speech such as those taught from the classical *Rhetorica ad Herrenium* (*Rhetoric for Herennius*, ascribed to Cicero during the Renaissance), and by displaying his facility in literary Latin, Budé assured his own status as a man of letters. Numerous learned writers during the 15th and 16th centuries truly believed that only Latin would prevail as a literary language. Other writers, some of whom were unskilled in Latin, continued to use the vernacular. Many noted authors, such as Rabelais and Ludovico Ariosto (1474–1533), were equally comfortable writing in either Latin or their native tongue. Latin verse and orations in Latin were showcases for writers displaying their dexterity in the language of Cicero and Catullus. One of the most popular Latin poets was the Dutch writer Johannes Secundus (1511–36), who composed odes, elegies, and epigrams in Latin and received recognition from the Holy Roman Emperor. His love poems *Basia* (Kisses) were translated into several languages.

For the Renaissance, the question was, Which Latin should be used? Lorenzo Valla (1407–57) promoted a conservative yet flexible approach to Latin usage in the preface to his grammar, *Elegantiarum linguae latinae libri sex* (Six books on the glories of the Latin language, written in 1440, published 1471). Adhering to Latin as the only appropriate language for the liberal arts, Valla explained that scholars were relearning the classical language, whose rules were partly lost with the fall of the Roman Empire. The ongoing debate between Scholastics and humanists focused on three points. Renaissance Scholastics, especially theologians, resisted change, feared that pagan classical texts could corrupt Christian readers, and opposed sophisticated literary language. They preferred simple language to express pious thoughts. A dialogue by Desiderius Erasmus (c. 1466–1536), for example, represented the critics of humanism describing Horace, Virgil, and Ovid as monstrous figures. This controversy was exacerbated by the circumstance that humanists were competing with Scholastics for teaching positions in the major universities. Moreover, contemporary writers influenced by the language and style of pagan texts threatened the status quo. Although this debate was similar in some ways to the ancient contrasts between philosophy and rhetoric, the Christian component of the arguments against humanistic rhetoric introduced an element of extremism into the dialectic, especially during the Reformation.

From our modern point of view, both sides of the argument had their merits, and the compromises in Latin usage suggested by Valla prevailed during the 16th century. As the dogmatic extremism of Reformation theologians, such as relegating classical authors to the depths of hell, failed to impress learned individuals of the 16th century, the strict Ciceronianism of the 15th century alienated many contemporary writers. Radical humanists of the 15th century sought to purge Latin of any modern words, with rather silly effects in their Neo-Latin literature; for example, *nun* became *Vestal Virgin* and *violin* became *lyre*. Largely because the Jesuit colleges favored a moderate form of Ciceronian Latin, in which reasonable neologisms could be inserted, that strain of Neo-Latin proliferated in European intellectual circles. From Italy Neo-Latin literature spread to northern and eastern Europe, Britain, and finally Scandinavia and Denmark. The main advantage of Latin literature was that it could be read by the educated classes throughout Europe. In addition, it placed the writer within a prestigious tradition of classical authors. Neo-Latin literature was a driving force in European culture until the 17th century, when writers in the vernacular were confidently achieving the same effects in their neoclassical compositions.

Latin versus the Vernacular

Francesco Petrarch (1304–74), the first poet of the Italian Renaissance, wrote most of his works in Latin. It would have been impossible for Petrarch to believe that posterity would revere him not for his Latin epic poetry, which is largely forgotten, but rather for his love poetry celebrating Laura and written in Tuscan, his native tongue. During his lifetime, Italy was filled with numerous dialects (as it still is), Tuscan but one of them. The primacy of Tuscan developed long after Petrarch's death. Although the great medieval poet Dante wrote his masterpiece in Tuscan, no other Italian poet before Petrarch was famous for using the vernacular. Latin reigned supreme during the 15th century as it had for more than a dozen centuries, the language of the Catholic Church and of the courts.

Valla considered Latin as the civilizing force of the Western world: "For this language introduced . . . all peoples to all the arts which are called liberal; it taught the best laws, prepared the way for all wisdom; and finally, made it possible for them no longer to be called barbarians" (Ross and McLaughlin 1968, p. 131). In describing the effect of Latin on the vernacular languages of people conquered by Rome, Valla wrote (in Latin, of course): "They recognized . . . that the Latin language had both strengthened and adorned their own, as the later discovery of wine did not drive out the use of water, or silk expel wool and linen, or gold the other metals, but added to these other blessings" (Ross and McLaughlin 1968, p. 132). Valla and his learned contemporaries believed that Latin was preferable to the vernacular, the "gold" versus the base metals of everyday vernacular speech. Many humanists did not accept the linguistic richness of native tongues or understand that after Latin had indeed "strengthened and adorned" the vernacular languages of Europe, they would surpass Latin itself. If literature had been restricted to the circle of the upper class, Latin might have prevailed indefinitely. As it was, Latin dominated the universities, science, law, and the church until the 19th century. For literature, however, the printing press took the works of Renaissance writers not only to the middle class, many of whom knew only rudimentary Latin, but also to people in remote areas where only the priest truly understood Latin. Largely because of the proliferation of inexpensive printed books, literature in the vernacular increased in popularity over the course of the 16th century. Even for deluxe printings of Latin works in the early 16th century destined for only a few aristocratic patrons, texts in the vernacular were sometimes printed beside the main Latin text. The dedication or preface could also be in the vernacular, making the book a more personal statement from the editor or author to the book's intended audience.

The Printed Book

Until the 1450s, the only method for obtaining a copy of a written work, short of copying it oneself, was to purchase or commission one in manuscript. While scribal workshops in monastic settings provided many of the religious texts, scribes at universities and at the major courts made copies of secular texts as well as of certain religious works. During the early years of printing, books were made chiefly for the religious and academic markets (Bibles, grammars, canon law books, patristic texts, etc.). Under the influence of humanistic studies, more attention was paid to philological standards, especially for texts and translations of the Greek and Latin church fathers and classical authors. Printing in Europe began in Germany but dispersed to Italy and France after warfare between two archbishops resulted in the Sack of Mainz in 1462. Most aristocratic collectors at first preferred manuscripts, especially those elaborately decorated with gold highlights and painted illustrations, on luxurious vellum or parchment. By the mid-1470s, however, printers were leaving spaces in their text blocks for ornamental initials to be added by hand, as well as generous margins so that at least the first page and sectional divisions of a book might have decoration added later, according to the taste of the purchaser. By the late 1470s, several printers were adding woodcut initial letters, marginal decorations, and illustrations such as maps or scientific diagrams, and a few printers were experimenting with metal cuts for illustrations. Although some 15th-century collectors were averse to acquiring printed books, the new technology was praised, especially for the durability of its ink. Here is a somewhat biased panegyric of 1466 by a writer who worked in an early print shop: "Why go to the trouble of borrowing the book [i.e., in manuscript] and paying the price for that, when the same price would . . . give you a copy to keep? This true copy cannot be transcribed into a false likeness: from one constant setting of type a thousand good copies can be produced. Again, the test of corrosive wax and acid water proves that this ink is not fugitive. No foul stream can wash away a letter, so durable is the paper" (Barker 1999, p. 198).

The German printers Sweynheim and Pannartz established a printing house near Rome in 1465 and later moved into Rome itself. Their press issued 10 first editions of Latin classical texts, using not the spiky Gothic letters of medieval hands, but rather the rounded cursive letters favored by Italian humanists. This type style, still called roman today, perpetuated the classical style in book design and became the norm by the end of the 16th century. We probably can assume that roman letters were easier to read, and that this is one reason why they were eventually preferred to the Gothic font. By the close of the 15th century, books were being printed in runs of 1,000 and more; as a result the price of many individual titles was decreasing. Publishers in Venice were especially prolific, issuing some 4,000 editions before 1500. Other major centers of production included Lyon, Paris, Cologne, Augsburg, Nuremburg, and Basel. The early efforts at illustrating printed books blossomed into a new industry in these and other publishing centers. The market for many books issued in the vernacular languages was expanded by illustrations that made the texts more enjoyable and more accessible to the general reading public.

LITERARY THEORY

Among the ancient texts that evolved between 1400 and 1600, Aristotle's *Poetics* was the most crucial for the development of literary theory and literary criticism. Aristotle was important to Renaissance writers because he was the first ancient author known to have formulated poetic terminology and standards. He both quantified and qualified literary genres, and his rules for tragedy were especially interesting to Renaissance authors and critics. Translations and editions of the *Poetics* provided the first serious literary theory of the Renaissance, as prefaces and commentaries explained Aristotle's ideas. Other literary theory was discussed in treatises supporting either Latin or the vernacular as appropriate vehicles for literary language. The *Ars poetica* (Art of poetry) of the classical Roman writer Horace provided a rhetorical basis for literature that appealed to many Renaissance authors. Finally, beyond the debate of whether Latin or the vernacular was preferable, literary theorists argued over whether authors should follow the dictates of classical treatises or the actual practices of popular Renaissance authors such as Ludovico Ariosto and Torquato Tasso (1544–95).

Aristotle's *Poetics*

Medieval texts of Aristotle's *Poetics* would hardly have been recognized by Aristotle himself. They stemmed from corrupt and incomplete manuscripts, and from misinterpretations of Aristotle by Averroës, an Islamic philosopher of the 12th century. Translated into Latin, the *Poetics* as interpreted by Averroes was first printed in 1481, presenting the Renaissance with a theory of poetics based on logic and rhetoric, and twice removed from the original Greek. The additions by Averroes, although philosophically interesting from a medieval point of view, were distinctly unhelpful to anyone attempting to craft a work of literature. Fifteenth-century critics attempted to distinguish the basic text of Aristotle from the additions of Averroes, and a good Latin translation was available by the end of the 15th century. Nevertheless, Aristotle was viewed in the context of Horace, and the concept of plot was considered within a rhetorical framework of persuasion. The humanistic scholar Pietro Vettori (1499–1585), who held chairs of both Latin and Greek in Florence, specialized in commentaries on the works of Aristotle. In 1560 he published *Commentarii in primum librum Aristotelis de arte poetarum* (Commentary on the first book of Aristotle concerning the art of poetry), which finally categorized the parts of tragedy properly. During the remainder of the 16th century, several vernacular translations of the *Poetics* with commentary promoted the ascendancy of plot over character and the importance of representation of action. Lodovico Castelvetro's (1506–71) *Poetica d'Aristotele vulgarizzata et sposta* (Poetics of Aristotle translated and explained, 1570) included a commentary on the dramatic unities. Alessandro Piccolomini's (1508–78) Italian translation was published in 1572, and his *Annotationi nel libro della Poetica d'Aristotele* (Annotations on the book of Aristotle about the art of poetry) in 1575. The latter text promoted the author's interest in vernacular Italian literature. These and other Italian treatises concerning the *Poetics*, including several of the works discussed in the following sections, influenced literary theory throughout western Europe.

Renaissance Treatises

In France, three members of the original Pléiade group of poets (see the section, Poetry) wrote important literary treatises: Peletier, du Bellay, and Ronsard. Jacques Peletier's (1517–82) preface to his 1541 translation of Horace's *Ars poetica* (Art of poetry) encouraged French authors to write in French rather than in Greek or Latin. His preface was a call to arms for writers, who were charged with making their native literary language more illustrious. His own *Art poétique* (Art of poetry) published in 1555 reinforced his earlier message while expounding on the divine nature of poetry, the role of imitation in literature, and the various poetic subgenres. Joachim du Bellay (1522–60) wrote *La Défence et illustration de la langue française* (Defense and illumination of the French language, 1549), which became the most famous poetic treatise of the French Renaissance. Written in an intense, almost inflammatory style, du Bellay's text assured contemporary writers that the French language was capable of exalted poetic expression. His treatise promoted vernacular literature in general, explaining that French authors should familiarize themselves not only with the classics, but also with noteworthy literature written in the languages of modern Europe. Pierre de Ronsard (1524–85), leader of the Pléiade, published his *Abregé de l'art poétique françois* (Handbook of the art of French poetry) in 1565. This handbook offered practical advice for young poets, including an appreciation of the classical languages. Julius Caesar Scaliger (1484–1558), an Italian scholar residing in France, wrote the lengthy treatise *Poetices libri septem* (Seven books of poetics, 1561) emphasizing strict decorum in literary productions. His Aristotelian ideas had a tremendous impact on French dramatic works of the 17th century.

Two subgenres that presented special problems for Renaissance theorists were romance and tragicomedy, partly because classical literature did not encompass them and thus they had no rules. Some writers rejected tragicomedy outright as a mongrel form. Sir Philip Sidney (1554–86) in his *Apologie of Poetry* (c. 1583) suggested that poetry was an effective medium for teaching virtue and that tragicomedy subverted this goal: "All their plays [by his contemporaries] be neither right tragedies nor right comedies; mingling clowns and kings . . . with neither decency nor discretion" (Preminger 1965, p. 693). Giovanni Battista Guarini (1538–1612), who wrote the immensely popular pastoral drama *Il paster fido* (The faithful shepherd, 1590), was well aware that he was violating literary protocol and antagonizing strict theorists with this tragicomedy. Hesitant to say that he wrote simply to entertain his readers, Guarini suggested that the noble nature of some of the shepherds should redeem the work in the eyes of his critics.

Italian theorists argued especially about the structure and style of epic poetry, particularly within the context of the works of Ariosto and Tasso. Giambattista Cinthio Giraldi (Il Cinthio, 1504–73) attempted to include chivalric romance as a heroic mode, comparable to epic, and Torquato Tasso in his *Discorsi del poema epico* (Discourses on the epic poem, 1594) wrote that epic should concern Christian knighthood. This controversy was discussed among English poets, who were struggling during the 16th century to write epic poems in response to nationalistic fervor in their own country. Although the king's (or queen's) English might be acceptable for conversation at court, whether it was appropriate for a national epic was debatable. Edmund Spenser's (c. 1552–99) *The Faerie Queene* (1590, 1596), with its use of rustic language and chivalric romance, outraged Sidney and caused the dramatist Ben Jonson (1572–1637) to exclaim that Spenser "writ no language." The fluidity of the vernacular as manipulated by writers such as Spenser and Shakespeare, however, guaranteed the vitality of English as a literary language.

POETRY

Poetry was studied within the subjects of both rhetoric and grammar during the Middle Ages, and this connection continued into the Renaissance. In the towns of Flanders and Holland, for example, the "chamber of rhetoric" was the official term for salons where vernacular writers gathered to read each other's work and discuss art in general. In

France, poets of the early Renaissance were called *rhétoriqueurs*, meaning those who use elaborate rhetorical devices in their work. The Renaissance definition of *poetry* was quite general, encompassing imaginative writing in general, and treatises on "poetics" covered creative writing in its various representations. The present section discusses only nondramatic literature written in verse, unrhymed as well as rhymed. Contemporary treatises on Latin prosody influenced the work of numerous poets, and the quantitative measures of classical poetry imposed artificial rules on the accented rhythms of European vernacular languages. The resulting verses were often stilted and awkward. Nevertheless, discussions of Latin prosody heightened writers' awareness of the rhythmic effects of poetic meter in their own language. In addition, certain types of medieval vernacular poetry were refined and expanded during the Renaissance. By the 16th century, several subgenres of poetry, such as pastoral and satire, were illustrated with woodcuts. Many of the numerous editions of *Das Narrenschiff* (Ship of fools, 1491; see later discussion), for example, reprinted the original woodcut images, enhancing the book's appeal. Major poetic subgenres discussed in the following sections include the epic, lyric, pastoral, and emblem.

Epic Poetry

Renaissance poets knew the ancient epics of both Homer and Virgil, but the latter's *Aeneid* appealed to them more than the *Iliad* and the *Odyssey*. First, *Aeneid* could be read in its Latin original whereas Homer's Greek was impossible for most writers. More important, Virgil's epic celebrated the destiny of the ancestors of Italy and glorified the city of Rome, enhancing the *Aeneid* for early Italian humanists. As Homer wrote about great heroes, Virgil wrote about the history of a great people. The nationalistic tendencies of western Europe caused poets to look to Virgil as their model. Virgil also was considered a proto-Christian writer, as interpreted by allegorists during the Middle Ages, and Dante had selected Virgil as his guide through the underworld of the *Divine Comedy*. Homer, nonetheless, was revered because he was the first to

create poetry in the hallowed epic mode. Angelo Poliziano (1454–94), a renowned Hellenist and poet in Latin as well as Italian, not only translated Homer into Latin hexameters (the meter of the *Aeneid*), but also presented his inaugural lecture on Homer's work. One poet who did emulate Homer in an epic poem was Gian Giorgio Trissino (1478–1550) in his *Italia liberata* (Italy liberated) of 1547, written in blank verse. Writers often referred to Homer when discussing epic and structured their own works to be more like the *Aeneid*. Poets even attempted to structure their career to emulate that of Virgil, creating pastoral eclogues during their youth and later attempting to write an epic. Only a few managed to succeed, partly because epic is a daunting form. Sustaining story and meter for the length required by epic poetry was found to be a Herculean task. Pierre Ronsard (1524–85), leader of the Pléiade group of poets in France, managed to write only the first four books of *La Franciade* (1572), though he had planned an epic of 20 books.

Os Lusíadas (The Luciads or The sons of Lusus, 1572) by Luis de Camões (between 1517 and 1524–80) is the great national epic of the Portuguese Renaissance, and one of the most successful epic poems of European literature. Written in 10 cantos and modeled on the *Aeneid*, *Os Lusíadas* relates the history of Portugal through the narration of the explorer Vasco da Gama (c. 1460–1524) as he sails to India in 1497–98. Classical deities are involved in the voyage, as Venus supports the enterprise while Bacchus attempts to sabotage it. The poetry is rich and lush, full of sea imagery and of the wonders of the East. Camões's personal history enhanced the reception of his epic in Portugal. Imprisoned because of a brawl in Lisbon, he was sent to India in 1553 as a soldier and eventually served eight viceroys and spent time in Macao (China) as well. He wrote *Os Lusíadas* in India, narrowly survived a shipwreck, and salvaged his manuscript. Had the Spaniards not taken control of Portugal in 1580, *Os Lusíadas* might have been translated into English before 1655 and thus could have influenced Spenser in his own epic poem, *The Faerie Queene* (discussed previously). Although Camões's epic was famous throughout Portugal during the late Renaissance, it was not well known in the rest of Europe.

Other Renaissance authors created a new type of long narrative poem, based on chivalric romance. By far the most popular work in this mode was *Orlando furioso* (Mad Orlando, 1516, 1521, 1532) of Ariosto, written in octave stanzas. The poem was not only an epic in its conception, but also a parody, responding to Matteo Boiardo's (1441–94) unfinished romance *Orlando innamorato* (Orlando in love, 1495). Although the tone of *Orlando furioso* switches between romance and epic, many of Ariosto's contemporaries who commented on the work praised its epic qualities. Set in the historic time of Charlemagne, the poem was used as a vehicle to comment on contemporary issues, such as military alliances and war machinery. By 1600 more than 100 editions had appeared, placing *Orlando furioso* among the top-selling books of the Renaissance. As some critics argued that the poem was actually better than the epics of classical antiquity, Ariosto's poem achieved its own status as a classic. Editions published during the latter 16th century even included commentary, historical notes, and other sorts of additions that usually accompanied texts of ancient Greek and Latin authors.

Lyric Poetry

SONNET

Petrarchism, which included Neoplatonic attitudes toward love, inspired lyric poets for more than two centuries after Petrarch's death in 1374. Petrarch's sonnets were especially important, for their innovative structure as much as for their visual imagery describing the lady's beauty and strong moral qualities. During the 15th century, Petrarchism was pushed to extremes, with strained rhetorical devices, forced rhyme, and excessive praise of one's love. In his *Prose della volgar lingua* (Essay on the vulgar tongue) of 1525, Pietro Bembo (1470–1547) formulated new standards for Renaissance Italian, recommending Petrarch as the best model for lyric poetry. Bembo, however, suggested that contemporary poets should personalize their own experience within the general outline of Petrarchan verse, to avoid platitudes and stereotypes. The sonnet format, with its

interlaced rhyme, could be easily assimilated to any of the Romance languages with their naturally occurring rhymes, especially in noun forms. Outstanding composers of sonnets in the Romance languages included Ronsard in French, Luis de Camões in Portuguese, Juan Boscán (c. 1490–1542) in Spanish, and Vittoria Colonna (1492–1547) in Italian. Although other European languages presented more difficulty for poets writing sonnets, several authors succeeded famously in English, such as Thomas Wyatt (1503–42) and William Shakespeare in his sonnets about a "dark lady" (1564–1616). During the 16th century, the sonnet became a popular poetic form in Poland, the Netherlands, Germany,

5.2 Portrait of Louise Labé, an influential writer of French sonnets during the 16th century. Engraved by Dubouchet, 1555. (Private Collection/Roger-Viollet, Paris/Bridgeman Art Library)

Denmark, Sweden, and Russia. Although sonnets were written in Latin, the loftiest subgenre for Latin was the ode.

ODE

The ode is a ceremonious form of poetry, written in a serious, often intense tone. The more personal odes of Horace were reflective and philosophical, concerning life in general, whereas those of the classical Greek poet Pindar were written for specific public occasions, such as an athletic victory. Because it was a serious verse form containing exalted language, the ode was recognized as an easy target for parody and lampooning. Pindaric odes, requiring complicated metrics, were difficult for Renaissance poets to achieve. The Pléiade poets in France, under the guidance of Ronsard, were the first to publish odes closely related to the flowing, swirling structure of those by Pindar (first printed in 1513). In his youth, Ronsard had studied and emulated the more accessible Latin odes of Horace. He also read the Latin odes of Italian poets who attempted to copy Pindar's style. Ronsard referred to Horace and Pindar as the two diverse harpists that influenced his own compositions. He understood music, and Pindar's original odes were performed within a musical context (which unfortunately is lost to us). When Ronsard died, his contemporaries lamented that Pindar had died with him. That, however, was not the case, as his odes had been studied by poets in other countries, such as Bernardo Tasso (c. 1493–1569), who helped to maintain the Pindaric tradition in western Europe.

OTHER FORMS OF LYRIC POETRY

Sonnets and odes were only two forms of lyric poetry among many, including metrical forms deriving from the Middle Ages. Some poets created their own verse forms, such as the "skeltonics" of John Skelton (c. 1460–1529), also known as "tumbling" verse. Perhaps derived from Anglo-Saxon poetry, skeltonics typically feature short lines and rhyme that never crosses in the verses, as the same rhyme often continues for several lines. Although Dutch lyric poetry in the vernacular did not flourish until the 17th century, during the Renaissance Dutch occasional verse was revivified by metrics taken from folk songs. The greatest Renaissance poet of Poland, Jan Kochanowski (1530–84), published two books of occasional verse set to music as well as epigrams (*Fraski*, or *Trifles*, 1584) modeled after those of the Greek writer Anacreon. Poets in both Portugal and Spain were affected by the publication in 1516 of the *Cancioneiro geral* (Universal book of poems), a collection of poems by approximately 200 Spanish and Portuguese poets, mostly of the 15th and early 16th centuries. These works included specifically Iberian verse forms such as the *cantiga*. Much of the lyric poetry in Germany was written for hymns and other religious purposes, the work of Martin Luther being the best example.

Satiric verse, which can be quasi-dramatic if conceived in dialogue form, can also play outside the rules of poetic genre. Indeed, the rules and genres themselves were sometimes the target of Renaissance poetic satire and parody, such as pastoral poetry written in a purposefully vapid manner. As did classical satirists, Renaissance authors usually portrayed the speaker as a well-meaning, honest person whose sole intent was to inform society of a grievous wrong, or of a grievously wrong individual, using rhetorical modes. Sebastian Brant (1458–1521) wrote chiefly satirical works. His *Das Narrenschiff* (Ship of fools, 1491), published in several editions and translations during the author's lifetime, appealed to Protestants because he criticized abuses of the Catholic Church. As might be expected, uncensored satire was recognized by Renaissance political authorities as dangerous to the state and perhaps even to them. In Elizabethan England the printing of satires was prohibited, and those of noted writers such as John Marston (1576–1634) were publicly burned. Satires also lampooned entire classes of people, depicting the lower classes as well as the aristocracy, especially courtiers, as subjects of scorn; Skelton's *The Bowge of Court* is a good example of the latter. Satirists also made fun of the seriousness of religion, government, business, and other potentially boring and corrupt aspects of society. The *Grand Testament* of François Villon (c. 1431–after 1463), for example, satirized the process of writing one's last will and testament.

Pastoral Poetry

The *Idylls* of the classical Greek poet Theocritus and the *Eclogues* of Virgil were the chief models for Renaissance pastoral poetry. Written from a courtly point of view, the pastoral form treated the life of shepherds in an appropriate rural setting. By extension, pastoral sometimes included other rural subjects, such as fishermen, or characters such as a knight who might accidentally enter the pastoral realm. Because Aristotle had not presented pastoral as one of his canonical genres, Renaissance literary theorists debated the validity of writing pastoral as a serious creative pursuit. One of the criticisms of pastoral poetry, and indeed of the pastoral in general, was its artificiality. Theocritus had been raised in the countryside of Sicily and could genuinely long for the simplicity of that life, or appear to be longing for it, while writing his *Idylls* at the court in Alexandria. Virgil's *Eclogues* refined the sentiments of Theocritus from the viewpoint of an urbane Roman, and most Renaissance poets acquired their knowledge of Theocritus through a polished Virgilian lens. Pastoral poetry was spawned by Renaissance humanists who translated Theocritus into Latin and wrote their own versions of eclogues. Dante, Petrarch, and Giovanni Boccaccio (1313–75) all wrote eclogues and sometimes added elegiac laments to their verse. The best-known and most influential eclogue of Renaissance England was Spenser's *Shepheardes Calender* of 1579. He enhanced the realism of his characters by having them speak in simple, rustic language. Eclogues were easily parodied, and court figures were ridiculed in thinly veiled satire posing as pastoral poetry—even more so in pastoral drama (see later discussion).

Emblems

Produced chiefly for didactic purposes, an emblem consists of a motto, picture (woodcut or engraving), and explanatory verse or stanza of poetry, often on the same page. Although a short prose passage could substitute for the verse, most emblems had the commentary in poetic form. In both subject matter and purpose, emblems were related to proverbs, epigrams, and fables. Although the terms *device* and *emblem* were sometimes interchangeably, a device in the Renaissance was a personal symbol and an emblem had more universal symbolic qualities. The first published emblem book was the Latin *Emblemata* (1531) of Andrea Alciati (1492–1550), which became immensely popular in its many editions and Renaissance vernacular translations. Original emblem books by Renaissance authors began to appear in the 1530s, and by the early 17th century almost every vernacular of western Europe had its emblem books. Authors of emblem books in Spanish specialized in spiritual and devotional subjects, Dutch authors were partial to emblems about love (both human and divine), and the earliest English emblem books per se concerned religion. Emblems were popular among various classes of readers, as their witty combinations of text and image inspired poets such as Spenser, painters such as Raphael, and anonymous decorative artists such as needleworkers.

PROSE

During the course of the Renaissance, prose literature was important because it not only developed along with the national vernacular, but also helped to set new standards of grammar, vocabulary, orthography, and style. Unlike poetry, and even unlike many forms of dramatic writing, prose literature sometimes was written in the style of the spoken word. An excellent example of this phenomenon would be the autobiography in French of Michel de Montaigne (1533–92) published between 1580 and 1595. Renaissance historical writers demonstrated how writers in the 15th and 16th centuries found themselves at a cultural crossroads, looking back toward the Middle Ages and forward to the golden age of the present or future. One aspect of this golden age in literature was the development of the novel, even while that subgenre incorporated elements of medieval chivalric romance. Satirical prose writers used all the formats of literary narrative to structure their works, in which the humor ranged from descriptions of bodily functions to humanistic wordplay. Major prose subgenres discussed in the following sections are history, the novel, and satire.

History

History, in the Renaissance, meant something entirely different than it had in previous epochs. For better or worse, Renaissance humanists conceived of themselves as existing in a pivotal historical position, in a golden age quite superior to the "gothic" spirit of the immediate past. What had happened in the past was viewed as different not only in kind, but also in degree. Periodization of history began in the Renaissance; 15th-century Italian historians believed that the Roman empire ended with the transfer of its capital to Constantinople. Because their focus was on Rome and Roman civilization, they refused to accept most medieval culture as valid representations of civilized society—even though medieval chivalric romances were among the most popular forms of literature read during this time. Renaissance writers considered themselves qualified to interpret history rather than simply to report it, year by year, as had been done in medieval chronicles. As in other forms of literature, their models were classical authors; Livy was an important initial source, and Tacitus appreciated later in the 15th century. As humanistic writers studied the texts of ancient history, they learned to question secondary sources, and to recognize unreliable evidence, and they began to understand patterns of behavior and motivation. While nationalist fervor colored the historical interpretations of some Renaissance writers, others concentrated on the lessons that scholarly historical writing could teach all educated readers.

The first Renaissance history was, of course, written in Latin. Leonardo Bruni (1370–1444) contributed the earliest example, *Historia florentini populi* (History of the Florentine people, not published until 1610), of which many copies circulated in manuscript. He set high standards for this subgenre of writing, in both style and comprehension of historical evidence. Most 15th-century historical writing was accomplished in Ciceronian Latin prose, stately and sophisticated. History written in the vernacular, however, often retained medieval characteristics, such as archaisms and episodic form. One of the best

gothic "historical" works written during the Renaissance was *Les illustrations de Gaule et singularités de Troie* (The glories of Gaul and distinctions of Troy, 1510–13) by Jean Lemaire de Belges (c. 1473–1525), which was part legend and part historical fact. By the mid-16th century, entire historical works were being written on near-contemporary subjects, such as Paolo Giovio's (1483–1552) *Historiarum sui temporis libri* (History of his time, 1550–52), mainly concerning the wars that were devastating Italy. Various Italian writers attempted to analyze and understand the causes and consequences of the Italian Wars, including the sack of Rome in 1527. Niccolò Machiavelli (1469–1527), best known for his pragmatic advice to rulers in *Il Principe* (The prince), also wrote the important *Istorie fiorentine* (History of Florence, 1525, in Italian). This work praised the republic of Florence and rationalized its current problems as stemming from mismanagement by the Medicis. Francesco Guicciardini (1483–1540) wrote his famous *Storia d'Italia* (History of Italy, published posthumously in 1561) using the archives of Florence as his chief source of information.

Philippe de Commynes (c. 1446–c. 1511), Flemish historian, produced annals of the French monarchy published as *Mémoires* (1524). Translated into several languages, this text contributed to European knowledge of early Renaissance France. In France, humanistic history was best represented by Jacques Auguste De Thou (1553–1617), whose *Historia sui temporis* (History of his time, 1604, part 1) discussed the wars of religion from a scholarly and relatively unbiased point of view. In Spain, the unification of Aragon and Castile in the latter 15th century under Ferdinand V (1452–1516) and Isabella I (1451–1504) awakened interest in Spanish historiography. Nevertheless, it was 1592 before a complete history of Spain was published, by the Spanish philosopher and jurist Juan de Mariana (1536–1623/24), *Historiae de rebus Hispaniae* (History of the affairs of Spain). Originally published in Latin, this comprehensive work was quickly translated into Spanish. Historical writing in Germany, the Netherlands, England, and Scotland was strongly affected by the Reformation. In both England and Germany, history was written to justify the "restoration" of religious order by Protestant rulers. Mention should be made of Jewish historiography, especially that written after the Jews were expelled from the Iberian Peninsula in 1492. This event, combined with the new research methods of Renaissance humanism, prompted considerations of persecution from a truly historical perspective. Jewish scholars also attempted to reconcile historical contradictions in rabbinical texts.

BIOGRAPHY AND AUTOBIOGRAPHY

Biography and autobiography are specific subgenres within history, and the powerful rulers who patronized Renaissance writers were pleased when scholars included their patron's genealogy and biography in historical analyses. Oddly, the word *biography* was not known during the Renaissance, though the histories of individual lives were presented as examples of good or bad character. Biographical works of rulers sometimes were illustrated with "portraits" of the subjects, many of which were idealized representations rather than lifelike portraits of the actual person. Classical writers, particularly the Greek authors Xenophon and Plutarch, provided the models for writing about individual lives. Biography—fabricated as well as real—was interwoven with history. Autobiography was sometimes written by an unreliable narrator, for example, in the exaggerated accounts of the artist Benvenuto Cellini (1500–1571). His autobiography, not published until 1728, contains many outrageous situations in which Cellini is always superior and always proved right. Although immensely entertaining and historically useful for details about art processes and court life, such quasi-fictional autobiography is more like a novel than the historical documentation of a person's life. Michel de Montaigne wrote the most famous autobiography of the Renaissance: Published between 1580 and 1595, the clear, firm prose of his *Essais* (Essays) supported religious tolerance and philosophical neostoicism. The quality of his French prose probably helped raise standards of prose composition during the latter 16th century. Within the work Montaigne discussed other types of writing, such as letters, which he wrote himself rather than dictating to a secretary: "I never copy them over, and have accustomed my eminent correspondents who know me to put up with my erasures, my words written one over the other. . . . Those I work

hardest over turn out the worst" (Montaigne 1999, pp. 146–147).

Collections of autobiographical letters, considered as quasi-literary forms during the Renaissance, are important to scholars today for their documentation of everyday life as well as of the decorum usually required in polite society. Pietro Aretino (1492–1556), for example, left numerous insights about living in Venice: "Carriages in their places! Litters for those who like them! The deuce with horseback riding! . . . But the little gondolas rest you, they lull you to sleep, they soothe your spirit, limbs, and body" (Aretino 1967, p. 320). For women's history, letters document an important subculture of Renaissance life. Many women who otherwise were not known to have written anything at all have left an abundance of letters. A few of these collections were published during the Renaissance, notably Vittoria Franco's (1546–91) *Lettere famiglia a diversi* (Friendly letters to diverse men, 1580). These letters gave advice to various powerful and famous men troubled by love affairs. Within the subgenre of letter writing, fictional letters were enjoyed for their erudition and wit. A good example is the book *Epístolas familiares* (Friendly letters, 1539–42) of the Spanish writer Fray Antonio de Guevara (c. 1480–1545), a Franciscan who served the royal court as a writer and preacher. His most famous work was *Reloj de príncipes y libro aureo de Marco Aurelio* (Mirror of princes and golden book of Marcus Aurelius, 1529), containing ideals for the Christian ruler. This book was in epistolary format, purporting to be letters written by the Roman emperor Marcus Aurelius. With collections of fictional epistles, "historical" writing approached the novel or novella, a major subgenre of prose that originated during the Renaissance.

Novel

Novels and novellas are prose fiction, but for many Renaissance readers the boundaries of fact and fiction may have been more fluid than they are today. Chivalric and picaresque novels (discussed later) provided not only literary escapism, but also examples of how to behave (or not, as the case might be). During a period when knights in armor still mounted their steeds and engaged in tournaments, it

5.3 Scene from a novella painted on the panel of an Italian cassone (storage chest). By Liberale da Verona (Liberale di Jacomo), Italy, latter 15th century or before 1527/29. (The Metropolitan Museum of Art, Gwynne Andrews Fund, 1986 [1986.147])

was very easy to believe that the ladies and their champions in chivalric novels actually existed. As for the rogues who went from one antic to another in picaresque novels, there were more than enough thieves, knaves, and tricksters in the cities of Europe for such characters to be literally believable. Then, in 1531 or 1532, *Pantagruel*, the first volume of Rabelais's novel in French relating the exploits of Gargantua and his son, Pantagruel, appeared. Related in the reading public's mind to satirical works such as the long poem *Narrenschiff* (Ship of fools, 1491) of Sebastian Brant (1458–1521, see pre-

vious discussion), Rabelais's work was much more than satire. It was a great, sprawling, imaginative invention—picaresque, chivalric, obscene, humanistic, and evangelistic. As the protégé of Marguerite de Navarre (1492–1549), sister of the king, and as a close friend of Cardinal Jean du Bellay, Rabelais was in a position to write freely. His tales of battling giants and fantastical scenery composed the first real novel, in our modern sense of the term. Marguerite de Navarre herself published a series of novellas in 1559, *Heptameron*, famous for candid discussions among its narrators of relations between the sexes.

One of the greatest novels of world literature was published in the waning years of the Spanish Golden Age: *Don Quixote* (*Don Quijote* in modern Spanish) of Miguel de Cervantes Saavedra (1547–1616), issued in two parts, in 1605 and 1615. Even before Cervantes could finish writing the second part, part one had been reprinted four times in Spanish (in three countries) and translated into English and French. The first part is basically an ingenious comic farce and the second part somewhat more serious yet still with comic elements. The protagonist is the idealistic, aristocratic Don Quijote de La Mancha, who is perfectly balanced by his fool of a squire, Sancho Panza. Inspired by reading medieval chivalric romance, Don Quijote ventures out on a quest, only to tilt at windmills. Cervantes's story, with its entertaining secondary narratives and colorful characters, including some spicy females, appealed to readers at every level of society. Rabelais invented the novel; Cervantes catapulted the form into the modern age.

Some Renaissance novels blended the chivalric and picaresque modes, for example, Joanot Martorell's *Tirant lo Blanc* (Tirant the white, 1490, written in Catalan). While still in the medieval mode of prose fiction, such works often introduced original approaches to the narrative format. Martorell must have startled readers by shifting from educated to lower-class dialogue within the same scene. In Germany, prose fiction in the vernacular was largely based on folk literature, such as the Volksbuch subgenre, which presented prose versions of medieval romances. When written in continuous form, the Volksbücher (plural) had the formal appearance of novels. By far the most popular of these books during the 16th century was the anonymous *Till Eulenspiegel* (the title is the name of the comic peasant who connects the stories). The roguish hero, who played jokes on the wealthy, resembled the *pícaro* (rogue) of Spanish picaresque novels.

PICARESQUE NOVEL

Spanish writers began composing novels with a *pícaro* as the protagonist because they were bored by the saccharine nature of pastoral romances being published. Although not precisely parodies of individual pastoral novels, picaresque novels parodied the subgenre in general. The first important novel of the picaresque was the anonymous *Lazarillo de Tormes* (the title is the rogue's name, 1554), translated into French in 1560 and influential on writers in several countries during the second half of the 16th century. (We should note that the term *pícaro* was not associated with these novels until the late 16th century.) In *Lazarillo*, the "hero," actually a servant, relates his grotesque treatment at the hands of masters who evidently respect their peers but not their servants. Because Lazarillo was a rogue, however, the reader was faced with the interesting task of deciding whether to believe his first-person narrative. Several of the roguish protagonists in picaresque novels were female (*pícaras*). The most popular among these novels was *La tragicomedia de Calisto y Melibea* (*La Celestina*, 1499) by Fernando de Rojas (c. 1465–1541). Prostitution of the *pícaras* managed by the lusty old lady Celestina drives the narrative of the novel, revealing misogynist elements of the society in which the story takes place. With novels such as *La Celestina*, Renaissance writers were as far as possible from the chivalric ideal. At the end of the 16th century, Mateo Alemán (1547–1614) published *Guzmán de Alfarache* (The rogue, or The life of Guzmán de Alfarache, 1599, part 1; 1604, part 2), one of the best picaresque novels of the age. The author used a galley slave, Guzmán, as his protagonist, with the narrative technique of having a reformed rogue present the outrageous story of his life. This book was so popular that it was even translated into Latin (1623), rather unusual for picaresque novels.

CHIVALRIC OR COURTLY ROMANCE

Chivalric romance originated with medieval poems and tales about the court of Charlemagne and of King Arthur with the knights of his Round Table. (The word *chivalric* derives from the French word for horse because knights rode on horseback.) These stories encouraged refined behavior, proper etiquette, military prowess, Christian belief, and feudal loyalty. Although society was changing during the Renaissance, military leaders still supported these ideals, and new chivalric orders were created. The most noteworthy was the Order of the Golden Fleece, founded by the duke

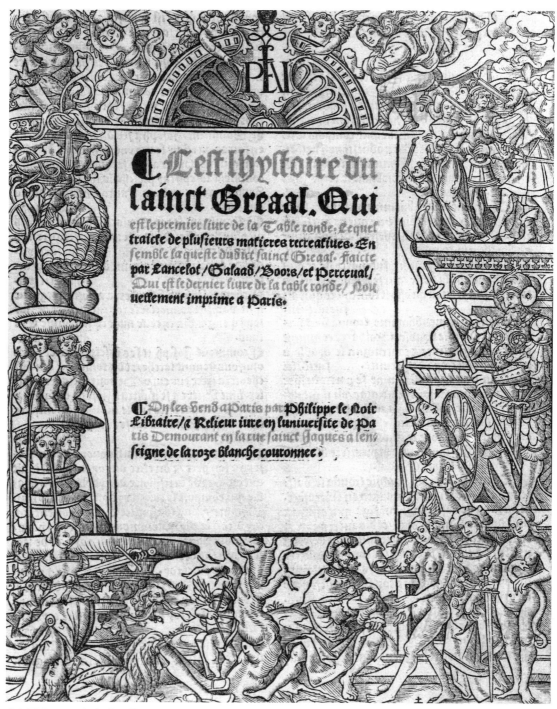

5.4 Title page of a book in French about King Arthur's search for the Holy Grail. Woodcut border by Geofroy Tory, in Cest lhystoire du sainct greaal *(This is the history of the Holy Grail, 1523).* (Photograph courtesy of Sotheby's Inc., © 2003)

of Burgundy in 1431. Members of this order included the Holy Roman Emperors. The concept of knighthood was expanded so that members of the new wealthy class could buy their way into a brotherhood or order. In tournaments, coronations, and similar public events, those belonging to a chivalric order paraded in processions wearing the regalia of their respective order.

One of the most popular chivalric romances was Diego de San Pedro's (c. 1437–c. 1498) Spanish novel *La cárcel de amor* (The prison of love, 1492). During the 16th century alone, it went through 20 translations, influencing countless writers. *Amadís de Gaula* (Amadis of Gaul, 1515), first printed in the Spanish version, had many copies in manuscript during the 15th century. Perhaps first written in Galician or Portuguese, this chivalric romance based on the story of Sir Lancelot originated in French medieval tales. It influenced several Renaissance writers in this subgenre. Among Spanish readers, chivalric romances were by far the best-selling books of the 16th century, and King Charles V was virtually addicted to them. In Portugal, chivalric novels based on Spanish models appeared throughout the 16th century. They perpetuated the medieval ideals of gallant knightly behavior and loyalty to the throne. Renewed interest in the Crusades was also part of the chivalric mode, as contemporary Turkish threats against southern Europe reawakened hostility toward forces in the East.

PASTORAL ROMANCE

Pastoral romance, which often mixed songs and poems with prose narrative, had the same rural setting as pastoral poetry (see earlier discussion). Jacopo Sannazaro (1458–1530), who lived at the court of Naples, wrote *L'Arcadia* (Arcadia, 1504), the first important pastoral romance of the Renaissance. The *Diana* (c. 1559) of Jorge de Montemayor (1519–61), a Portuguese who wrote in Spanish, was based on Sannazaro's work. Translated into Spanish in 1547, *L'Arcadia* spawned an entire generation of pastoral imitators. That work, *Diana*, and their translations were seminal influences for the pastoral subgenre during the Renaissance. The scenic "Arcadia" of writers such as Sir

Philip Sidney and Lope Félix de Vega Carpio (1562–1635) was modeled on that of Sannazaro and Montemayor. One of the main themes in pastoral was the open, authentic nature of simple, rural characters versus that of the urban sophisticates who must survive at court and in the turmoil and temptations of the city. This conflict of personality types provided fascinating material for Renaissance dramatists (discussed later).

Satire and Humor

When studying satire and humor of the Renaissance, indeed from any other society besides our own, we often have difficulty determining what other cultures might regard as humorous. In general, Renaissance humor was much earthier than ours. Toilet humor, even scatological jokes, evidently was enjoyed by all classes of readers. Rampant scatology and similar satirical references that to our eyes might seem grotesque were quite funny and witty in the Renaissance. Comedic writing, especially collections of joke books, short stories, and longer prose satires, was among the most popular of all literary forms of prose published during the 16th century. Whereas satiric poetry and drama often made their points through short, witty phrases, or episodic scenes, satiric prose could sustain a lengthy narrative scene or dialogue. Topics could be anything under the sun. Johann Fischart (1546–90), who translated Rabelais rather freely into German, wrote satire with a Protestant moralistic slant. His topics included a misogynist battle between fleas and women and a humorous tale about gout. Medical conditions and doctors were often the object of satire, as were lawyers. Although some satirical writers wrote in a rather hateful tone, the most popular prose satire was in a lighter comedic vein. Satirical short stories were especially popular in Italy and France, and English writers excelled in shorter anecdotes with a punch line. Sir Thomas More's novella *Utopia* (1516) is a satiric category unto itself. Profoundly humanistic, the enlightened island of Utopia is a representative democracy with compassion for the poor and a respect for learning. The more he praises this ideal community, the more the author satirizes contrary conditions in the real world.

DRAMA

Dramatic literature clearly demonstrated the parallel development of humanistic works in the vernacular and traditionally medieval forms that continued to be used in the Renaissance with slight modifications. There was occasional overlapping, for example, in biblical subjects familiar from medieval plays used in 16th-century tragedies. In tragedy, the ancient models were Seneca, Sophocles, and Euripides. In comedy, Plautus and Terence served as classical examples. Although every national vernacular in Europe had its playwrights during the 16th century, many of the plays were quite derivative because the point of writing a classical tragedy or erudite comedy was to emulate the work of ancient authors. Court theater predominated in Italy and France. Except for the street performances by the commedia dell'arte, plays were mainly written for the aristocracy. Most German drama, however, was written to appeal to the Protestant masses, with much of the content blatantly religious. There was no set format for dramatic speech, and playwrights wrote in prose as well as in several types of verse. European theater was evolving during this period. In addition to plays performed in piazzas, inn yards, great halls, and roving wagons, new dramatic works began to be performed in permanent theaters during the second half of the 16th century. These new structures, with resident companies of actors, helped to legitimize playwriting and acting as serious professions.

Fortunately, we have some knowledge about earlier Renaissance performances and stage setting from contemporary reports, especially in personal letters. In 1513, for example, Baldassare Castiglione (1478–1529), author of *Il cortegiano* (The courtier, 1528), wrote about the stage scenery of a comedy that premiered at the court of Urbino. The play was *La calandria* by Bernardo Dovizi, Cardinal Bibbiena, which became one of the most acclaimed comedies of the early 16th century. According to Castiglione's report, it took four months to construct the following scenery: a wall with two towers; a rampart; tapestries of the Trojan War hung above the tiers of seats; wires extending from the cornices holding 13 gigantic carved letters, each with torches to light the

stage; building fronts in relief "in scenic perspective"; an elaborately decorated octagonal temple; a triumphal arch with an equestrian statue; and even more. Renaissance theatrical performances had intermissions in which short skits were performed, often with music and dancing. Castiglione also described the *intermezzi* of the Urbino play, one of which was a chariot of the goddess Juno: "This car was drawn by two peacocks so beautiful and lifelike that I could not believe my eyes, and yet I had seen them before, and had myself given directions how they were to be made" (Ross and McLaughlin 1968, pp. 461–465). Although many stage-settings were by no means so elaborate, the scenery for *La calandria* is representative of that of the plays commissioned by the powerful Renaissance courts.

Major dramatic subgenres discussed in the following include tragedy, comedy, and the masque. The commedia dell'arte, which usually performed comedies, is treated in a separate section. Religious drama, another important subgenre, is discussed in chapter 2, and theatrical architecture is discussed in chapter 4.

Tragedy

Initially ancient tragedy was revived as a purely literary form, and many Renaissance tragedies were written in verse. Until the 15th century, most classical tragedies were known only in selections or fragments. Virtually nothing was understood about staging, and indeed it is unclear whether the early humanists knew that classical tragedies were performed in public by different players. Partly because of this confusion, original Renaissance tragedies were written as dialogues in narrative form, with an emphasis on plot rather than stage action. Trissino's *Sofonisba* of 1515, the first vernacular tragedy, was not performed until 1562. Other 16th-century tragedies had a long lapse between publication and first production. Giambattista Cinthio Giraldi (1504–73), a major Renaissance playwright, staged the first Italian tragedy in 1541, his *Orbecche*. The chief classical models were the plays of Seneca the Younger and of the ancient Greeks. Aristotle's *Poetics* (see earlier discussion) was not influential until the late 16th century. Seneca's dramatic presentation of

5.5 Illustrated page from the plays of the classical Roman dramatist Terence. Published in Strasbourg, 1496. (Photograph courtesy of Sotheby's, Inc., © 2003)

bloody horror, ghosts, witches, and other shocking elements was easily assimilated by 16th-century playwrights. One of the best tragedies following the Senecan model was *Les Juives* (The Jewish women, 1583), on a biblical topic, by Robert Garnier (1535–90). As writers became more experienced in handling tragic situations, violence was often internalized by the characters in a more psychologically oriented treatment by the author.

Besides the works of Trissino, other notable drama writing in the tragic mode included Luigi Alamanni's (1495–1556) *Antigone* (1566), adapted from Sophocles; Pietro Aretino's *Orazia* (1546); and Torquato Tasso's *Re Torrismondo* (King Torrismondo, 1587). For Germany, the prolific Hans Sachs (1494–1576) warrants mention here. Best known for his songs, Sachs was a cobbler without any humanistic education. Yet he wrote 58 German tragedies, a major contribution to Protestant drama. (The comedies by Sachs are mentioned later.) German vernacular drama of the 16th century was heavily influenced by humanism. Biblical themes, for example, were structured like classical plays. Swiss authors writing in German created dramatic plots with more action than most writers in Germany, who usually favored dialogue over action. In Spain, Cervantes attempted to create a national theater on the Aristotelian model, with clear delineation between tragedy and comedy. His patriotic tragedy *Numancia*, written in the classical mode, was about a town in Spain destroyed by the Romans in the second century B.C.E. Spanish writers, however, preferred to ignore the restrictions imposed by Aristotle. The dramatist Lope Félix de Vega Carpio (1562–1635), who wrote more than 300 plays, ignored the ancients and established new, relatively simple rules in Spain without any formal distinction between tragedy and comedy. All plays of every sort were called *comedias*, and many of them had great success. French humanists in the circle of Francis I studied classical models closely and produced neoclassical tragedies during the second half of the 16th century. They were familiar with the structure and tone of tragedy through the Latin plays written by George Buchanan (1506–82) in the 1540s while he was teaching in France. Théodore de Bèze (1519–1605) published the first French tragedy, *Abraham se sacrifiant* (Abraham sacrificing himself)

in 1550, based on a biblical subject, and Jacques Grévin (1538–70) the first French historical tragedy, *César*, in 1561. There were also adaptations of plays by the Greek tragedians Sophocles and Euripides. Writers in both France and Italy made translations of newly discovered ancient tragedies, including *Oedipus Rex* and *Electra* by Sophocles and *Iphigenia in Tauris* and *Hecuba* by Euripides. The publication of these new translations heightened excitement among contemporary writers and prompted new dramatic works. In general, following ancient examples, Renaissance tragedy focused on the tension between a powerful state and the rights of an individual.

Dramatic tragedy in Renaissance England culminated with the masterpieces of William Shakespeare (1564–1616), whose predecessors had introduced the subgenre into vernacular English. From the beginning, the audience for tragedy was somewhat different in England than in the Catholic countries. As were part of Germany and the Netherlands, England was Protestant territory by the time that Thomas Norton (1532–84) and Thomas Sackville (1536–1608) staged the first English tragedy, *Gorboduc*, circa 1561, with Queen Elizabeth (1533–1603) attending the performance. In Protestant countries, the lower classes, often barely literate, were an important sector of the viewing public of dramatic performances. They paid less for their standing-room tickets than those who had seats but nevertheless paid something. In England, playwrights were aware that their productions either had to compete with other lower-class entertainment, such as bear baiting, or to provide the same level of diversion for those who frequented such events. Whereas tragedians in Italy and France wrote for the aristocracy, English playwrights did not have that luxury. At the end of England's Renaissance, masques would be written for court audiences (see later discussion). During the latter 16th century, tragedies had to be written in broad strokes, to appeal to the masses. Tragedies usually incorporated moralistic homilies and domestic doom, as in the anonymous *Arden of Faversham* (1589–92) and *A Warning for Fair Women* (1598–99). Anonymous history plays were also popular, notably *The Famous Victories of Henry V* (1583–88). Part of Shakespeare's genius was his ability to transform earlier plays and stories into more complicated yet interesting plots with unforgettable characters. He created Prince Hal, for example, from the cardboard figure of Henry V and heightened the tension in Falstaff's persona. Three of his major tragedies, *Hamlet, Othello,* and *King Lear,* were written between 1601 and 1605, at the very end of Elizabeth's reign and the beginning of that of James VI (1566–1625, James I of England as of 1603).

Comedy

Because tragedy was a noble form of great seriousness that appealed mainly to the educated classes, in Europe as a whole it was not as popular as comedy. Though the lower classes might not catch the nuance of every comedic speech, they could appreciate the buffoonery and slapstick humor prevalent in most productions. Renaissance comedy began with works in Latin written by Italian humanists, based largely on the classical comedies of Plautus. In these presentations, the story concluded decorously though most of the characters were ridiculed during the course of the play. In England the braggart soldier of Plautus was immortalized in *Ralph Roister Doister* (printed 1566, performed earlier) by Nicholas Udall (c. 1505–56). Italian comedies modeled on those of Plautus were favorites of the Este court at Ferrara, and Isabella d'Este (1474–1539) patronized the earliest vernacular comedies by Ludovico Ariosto: *La cassaria* (The casket play, 1508) and *I suppositi* (The pretenders, 1509). The Latin comedy of Terence also became influential, especially after his *Andria* was edited by Poliziano and translated by Machiavelli. The focus of Renaissance erudite comedy usually was a family situation, with wife pitted against husband or children against parents, and various "advisers" who served only to complicate matters and enrich the plot. This restricted story line facilitated the classical unities of time and place, as the dramatic events took place in a single location within the time span of a single day. This structural unity prevailed in erudite comedy, in which the action occurred in five acts.

The farce was a loose form of low comedic drama in medieval France, extremely popular with the common people. When Rabelais was a medical student, he may have performed in student farces, which continued throughout the Renaissance. Marguerite de Navarre wrote a farce, and there were guilds in Paris that performed farces during the 16th century. Related to the farce were the *sotties* (fools' plays) written in French for carnival, or Shrovetide, performances. In Germany, the carnival plays were called Fastnachtspiele, and the latter 15th century saw some excellent examples. During the days just prior to the fasting of Lent, Catholics were permitted to ridicule church authorities and, in general, behave outrageously. The master of these German carnival plays was Hans Sachs. He wrote more than 100 of them, full of untrustworthy priests, spying neighbors, and other characters depicted with humor and wit. Although Sachs concluded his comedies with a moral lesson, they were not antipapal, unlike the Fastnachtspiele discussed in chapter 2.

Renaissance comedies could have vastly different types of "comedic" endings. Whereas Shakespeare's concluded in a congenial tone, other plays purporting to be comedies had more serious endings. In Ben Jonson's (1572–1637) *Volpone* of 1606, for example, one character was whipped and sent to the galleys and Volpone himself was taken away to be chained in prison. Tragicomedy, a hybrid form criticized by several literary theorists, often concluded in an unsuspected or (according to critics) inappropriate manner. Tragicomedies were, however, popular among moralistic writers who wished to demonstrate wisdom or redemption through suffering. Ultimately tragicomedy was accepted in the guise of pastoral drama, with the action somewhat removed from daily life. One of the best examples was *Il pastor fido* (The faithful shepherd, 1589) of Giovanni Battista Guarini (1538–1612), copied by playwrights throughout the continent.

Masques

Although masques originated in Italy, they reached the height of their form in England, especially during the early years of the reign of James VI. His remarkable queen, Anne of Denmark (1574–1619), was patroness of the masques commissioned for their court. As the daughter of Frederick II, king of Denmark (1534–88), she gave Scotland permanent claim to the Orkney and Shetland Islands with her marriage to James in 1589. Ignored in her efforts to become involved in politics, Anne enthusiastically participated in court festivities, wearing in turn the jewels and some 6,000 dresses she inherited from Queen Elizabeth. Well loved for making the court so gay, Anne herself acted in the masques, playing everything from a nymph to a black woman, the latter in Ben Jonson's (1572–1637) *Masque of Blackness* (1605), written at her request. Masques were able to have amateur performers because they consisted mostly of disguise, poetry, dance, and music. There was very little plot, except perhaps a simple pastoral story. Jonson introduced an "antimasque," often with grotesque or savage characters, supposedly as a negative foil to the positive society depicted in the masque proper. His actual purpose, however, may have been to enliven an increasingly stilted performance. Because it required more dramatic skill, the antimasque usually included professional performers. Unlike the parsimonious court of Elizabeth, the Jacobean court spared no expense on these scintillating spectacles. The architect Inigo Jones (1573–1652) designed many of their ingenious stage settings.

Commedia dell'Arte

Commedia dell'arte is a later term for the troupes of itinerant Italian performers during the 16th and 17th century who improvised much of their material. Women as well as men were members of these companies. They were documented as traveling to Germany, France, Spain, England, and Poland. The actors played stock parts; a commedia dell'arte company required young lovers, maids (one usually quite old), a daffy scholar named Graziano, a pompous aristocrat named Pantalone, numerous clowns (the *zanni*), and additional characters as the story might require, depending on whether the drama was tragedy (usually tragicomedy) or comedy. The comedy they performed was often quite similar to the French farce. Actors often doubled in the roles, and the clowns played everything from gypsies to satyrs. Except for the lovers and maids, the commedia dell'arte players wore masks or other types of facial modifications. Costumes could be extravagantly colorful, such as those worn by Pulcinella and Arlecchino (Harlequin). Staging was minimal, often consisting of trestle tables set up in a piazza and the second story of a dwelling used for any balcony scenes. The commedia dell'arte actors were multitalented, singing, dancing, and playing instruments in most performances. The actors were also quite witty, improvising on the texts of plays published by their contemporaries. In some instances, these improvisations were incorporated in revised editions of the plays. Two of the more famous troupes were the Gelosi and Accesi, both of whom performed for royal audiences.

ORATORY AND RHETORIC

Oratory, or public speaking, is a form of literature that is performed by a single individual. Although Renaissance speakers wanted each audience to feel that every speech was directed specifically to them, and although a good orator could convince an audience that a speech was extemporaneous, Renaissance orations usually were well-crafted pieces of writing. On the assumption that they were following the dictates of Cicero, 15th-century orators emphasized stylistic aspects of public speaking rather than the logical development of their argument. After Cicero's mature works on oratory were discovered by humanistic scholars, it became clear that a good oration has to be based on reasonable arguments and that style is the ornament that propels the listener to accept the speaker's logic.

Classical Rhetorical Treatises

In his *Rhetoric*, Aristotle wrote that a speech had to have only two parts, delineation of the case at hand and proof of one's argument. This rather matter-of-fact approach to oratory did not appeal to Renaissance speakers, who preferred to follow what they thought were the dictates of Cicero in the pseudo-Ciceronian *Rhetorica ad Herennium* (Rhetoric) and in Cicero's own *De inventione* (On invention). The declamatory oratory of the Renaissance gave writers the opportunity to display publicly their classical erudition and wit. In addition to Aristotle's arrangement of argument and proof (or disproof), the Latin treatises had lengthy sections on memory, style, and delivery, with speeches divided into low, middle, and high style. Early Renaissance oratory emphasized the stylistic aspects of public speaking and delivery that affected the emotions. During the 15th century, humanistic scholars discovered major treatises by Cicero concerning oratory, such as *De oratore* and *Brutus*, along with the complete text of Quintilian's *Institutio oratoria*. These works presented a fuller picture of ancient oratorical practices, especially the necessity for logical arguments.

Humanistic Rhetoric and Oratory

Rudolphus Agricola (1444–85), a Dutch humanist, wrote poems, orations, and classical translations and commentaries. His *De inventione dialectica* (On the invention of logic) was important for the development of Renaissance rhetoric. Those who studied Agricola's work realized that for purposes of persuasion, logical arguments in proper arrangement were just as important as style and manner of speaking. Petrus Ramus (Pierre de la Ramée, 1515–72) wrote in Latin on Aristotle's use of logic in rhetorical argument and in 1555 published his *Dialectique* (Dialectic) concerning logical deduction, a significant contribution to Renaissance rhetoric. As the first published work in French concerning a major philosophical subject, the *Dialectique* had a tremendous impact on writers, especially since it was written in the vernacular.

Humanistic orations often used the rhetorical trope of comparison to praise or castigate the subject at hand, especially comparison of the ancient and the modern world. An oration delivered in the Sistine Chapel in 1508, for example, with Pope Julius II (1443–1513) in the audience, favorably compared Rome under his papacy with ancient Greece: "You, now, Julius II, Supreme Pontiff, have founded a new Athens when you summon up that prostrated world of letters as if raising it from the dead, and you command . . . that Athens, her stadiums, her theaters,

her Athenaeum, be restored" (Rowland 2000, p. 157). The purpose of this eloquence was to contrast the culture of Rome with the "barbaric" nature of the Turks, whose "ancient evil" would be erased by the "sponge" of learning and "circumcised" at its roots. This cutting reference finally led the oration to the actual occasion of the speech, namely, the Feast of the Circumcision. Such stylistic circumlocutions exemplify humanistic oratory of the 15th and early 16th centuries.

During the 16th century, writers argued about whether it was proper to present official orations in the vernacular and, if it was, what type of vocabulary should be utilized. In 1553, Thomas Wilson's *Arte of Rhetorique*, for example, advocated plain speaking and avoidance of "inkhorn" words. He opposed the neologisms being invented from Latin and sometimes Greek by his learned contemporaries. In the interest of English nationalism, even a few classical scholars participated in the Inkhorn Controversy, supporting Wilson's point of view. In the end, however, new words coined from Latin and Greek made their way into public speaking, thus entering the vernacular vocabularies of western Europe.

Sermons

Even more than humanistic oratory, sermons were meant to direct the emotions of listeners. Sixteenth-century sermons that have been published preserve the words of the great preachers of the Renaissance, but not the oratorical fervor with which they were delivered. Egidio da Viterbo (1469–1532), cardinal and humanist, was such a preacher. A member of the Augustinians, he became their prior general. Contemporary accounts of his preaching provide an indication of his rhetorical prowess: "Who else among the multitudes seems so uniquely born to persuade, to win over the minds of the Italians, whose speech is so seasoned with the salt of literary elegance, so that all the sap of content is present in the supreme harmony of his words, and it flows so gently and rhythmically with the pitch and variety of his voice that one seems to hear sounds like that of a plucked lute?" (Rowland 2000, p. 145). As did other members of the itinerant Catholic preaching orders, he preached effectively to mixed audiences, with various rhetorical devices directed to different classes of listeners. Protestant preachers, many of whom were trained as priests or humanists, also used the tools of classical rhetoric to persuade their audiences. Homilies (inspirational sayings) related to biblical verses gave both Catholic and Protestant preachers the opportunity to construct persuasive arguments in understandable, down-to-earth vocabulary.

LIBRARY COLLECTIONS

Renaissance library collections—their formation, use, and dispersal—reflected the vagaries of Renaissance cultural history. From the great manuscript collection of the dukes of Milan (taken as war spoils to France) to ancient Greek texts in the French royal library printed from freshly designed type, libraries preserved literary masterpieces important to Renaissance readers. These included not only new writing, but also newly edited texts of classical literature that influenced Renaissance authors. The earliest Renaissance libraries of any significance for literature were those of humanistic scholars, beginning with the collection of Francesco Petrarch. Cardinal Bessarion's (1403–72) collection contained more than 1,000 volumes, most of them Greek manuscripts. Another major humanistic library was that of Giovanni Pico della Mirandola (1463–94), which included manuscripts of contemporary literature. Court libraries were symbols of prestige and patronage during the 15th century, for example, those of Naples, Urbino, Mantua, Ferrara, and Milan. In Germany, the outstanding ducal libraries were those in Munich and Wolfenbüttel. The Imperial library in Vienna, rich in Burgundian illuminated manuscripts acquired as dowry, was only beginning to become accessible to readers by the latter 16th century. University and other institutional libraries, often available only to students and faculty, began to open their doors to the educated public toward the close of the 16th century. The Bodleian Library at Oxford, for example, was accessible as of 1602. Private libraries, as one might imagine, tended to focus on the professional interests of the owners. The subjects usually collected were law, medicine, natural history, and technical treatises, rather than literature per se.

Humanistic and Court Libraries

From inventories, notes written in the margins of various texts, and contemporary reports such as letters, we have information about the contents of several humanistic libraries that no longer exist as discrete collections. The earliest was that of Petrarch, whose library of Latin works included texts of Cicero and Seneca, historical books, and poetry. Although not able to read Greek, Petrarch was given a copy of Homer's *Iliad* as a gift, which he treasured. At a time when many people had only a few books (in manuscript, of course) stored in an armoire or stacked on a shelf, two of Petrarch's residences had a separate room used as a study or library. The collector Niccolò Niccoli (1363–1437), who advised the Medici rulers of Florence on sources of classical manuscripts, had a renowned library and owned some 800 manuscripts that were eventually bequeathed to the Biblioteca Laurenziana in Florence. By the early 1400s, humanists and their agents were traveling in the East and to remote monasteries in Europe, purchasing and "borrowing" Greek manuscripts of classical authors.

Libraries served as important cultural centers in ancient Rome, and Renaissance monarchs, dukes, and other figures of authority were well aware of the ancient precedent for their own magnificent libraries. The papal library in the Holy See had the most impressive collection of any court library of the Renaissance (see later discussion). It is important to note that many of the court collections were accessible for readers and thus functioned as public libraries for the upper classes. From some of them books could even be borrowed, including manuscripts taken out for copies to be made. Renaissance court libraries served as models for princely collectors for more than two centuries. A few these collections are described in the following section.

Examples of Court Libraries

VATICAN LIBRARY

Today's Vatican library, or Biblioteca Apostolica, was first developed under the guidance of Pope Nicholas V (1397–1455), a humanistic scholar partial to ancient Greek writers. During his early career as Tommaso Parentucelli, he had served Cosimo de' Medici (1389–1464) as librarian in the Monastery of San Marco in Florence, a collection that functioned as a public library from which items could be borrowed. He developed a systematic arrangement for the collection that was used in other Italian court libraries. During his brief papacy from 1447 to 1455, Nicholas V basically founded a new papal library. Organizing the Curia as a sort of academy, he welcomed Byzantine and Italian editors and translators, and he commissioned Lorenzo Valla to translate the Greek historians into Latin. The classical and patristic texts produced by the intellectual creativity at the papal library were those used by several printers and publishers during the latter 15th century. Borrowers of these manuscripts, including some of the expertly illuminated examples on vellum or parchment, included priests, scholars, and copyists. Subsequent popes added to the library's literary wealth and continued to allow access to the collection.

FRENCH ROYAL LIBRARY

King Charles V (d. 1380) accumulated one of the greatest collections of manuscripts of any monarch in Europe. He also commissioned French translations of works in Latin. Writers such as Christine de Pisan were welcome to use his libraries, and the king himself spent time there reading his books. During their reign Charles VI (d. 1422) and Queen Isabeau permitted many items to be borrowed that were never returned. In 1424, most of the manuscripts in the royal library were shipped to England by the duke of Bedford, English regent of France. When Charles VIII (1470–98) invaded Italy in 1491, he in turn seized most of the humanistic library of Alfonso, king of Naples. These manuscripts included the texts of ancient Greek tragedies unknown to scholars in France. More Italian literary booty entered the French royal collection after Louis XII invaded Milan and took part of the Visconti-Sforza library back to France. When Francis I (1494–1547) ascended to the French throne in 1515, the royal library with all these manuscript treasures was located in the Château of Blois. Guillaume Budé (1468–1540), the first royal librarian, persuaded the king to move it to the court at Fontainebleau. During Francis I's long reign, from 1515 until 1547, the royal library served not only scholars and writers, but also designers working to create new fonts and a new Renaissance style for books in Greek, Latin, and the vernacular.

AUSTRIAN IMPERIAL LIBRARY

The Austrian National Library in Vienna, or Hofbibliothek, was organized by the Dutch humanist Hugo Blotius, beginning in 1575. Emperor Maximilian II (1527–76) owned more than 7,000 volumes that had been gathered together by the Holy Roman Emperors since the late 14th century. Unlike many other monarchs of the time, the emperor did not encourage outsiders to use these books and manuscripts. Blotius was determined to modernize the library and make it accessible for readers under specific rules, but apparently he did not succeed. Manuscripts were removed by the emperor Rudolf II (1552–1612) to his court in Prague, never to be seen again in Vienna, and Blotius himself allowed individuals to borrow books that were never returned. Undaunted, he continued to permit readers to use the collection, stating, "A library that keeps its doors closed is like a candle inside a barrel, which burns but gives no light" (Staikos 2000, p. 440). He made numerous efforts to improve the collection, especially an attempt to acquire one copy of each book published under the Imperial franchise. The deposition in official libraries of books granted special publishing licenses, which commenced in the Renaissance, continues today.

MAJOR WRITERS

Abrabanel, Judah ben Isaac See LEONE HEBREO.

Acciaiuoli, Donato (1429–1478) was a Florentine scholar who translated Plutarch's *Lives* into Latin and wrote biographies of classical figures.

Agricola, Rudolphus (1444–1485), a Dutch scholar, studied in Italy and later published poems, orations, and classical translations and commentaries. His *De inventione dialectica* (On the invention of logic) contributed to Renaissance rhetoric.

Alamanni, Luigi (1495–1556), Florentine humanist, wrote satire, poetry, and drama. His much-admired *La coltivazione* (Cultivation, 1546) in blank verse imitated the *Georgics* of Virgil.

Alciati, Andrea (1492–1550), a native of Milan, taught law in Avignon, Bourges, and northern Italy. In addition to writing humanistic legal treatises, Alciati popularized emblem books and published the first, *Emblemata* (1531), which had numerous editions and translations.

Alemán, Mateo (1547–c. 1614), born in Seville, spent several years in Mexico. He wrote *Guzmán de Alfarache* (1599, part 1), one of the greatest picaresque novels of the Renaissance.

Ambrogini, Angelo See POLIZIANO.

Amyot, Jacques (1513–1593) was a French humanist best known for his translations of classical Greek authors. His most important work was *Les vies des hommes illustres grecs ou romains* (The lives of illustrious Greek or Roman men, 1559), translated from Plutarch. Not only did this work influence literary prose in France, but its English translation also provided Shakespeare with the historical information for his Roman plays.

Aragona, Tullia d' (c. 1510–1556), courtesan and poet, was famous for her epistolary sonnets and a Neoplatonic work, *Dialogo della infinità di amore* (Dialogue on the infinity of love, 1547).

Aretino, Pietro (1492–1556), a versatile Italian writer who lived in Rome and later in Venice, published plays, satires, and sexy sonnets. His letters reflect the life and times of an irreverent Renaissance spirit.

Ariosto, Ludovico (1474–1533), dramatist, satirist, and poet, served the Este court. His plays (mostly comedies) were performed in Ferrara in a theater that he helped to design. Ariosto's masterpiece is *Orlando furioso* (Mad Orlando, 1516, part 1).

Ascham, Roger (1515–1568), who wrote *The Scholemaster, or Plain and Perfect Way of Teaching Children the Latin Tongue* (1570), was Latin secretary for Mary I (Mary Tudor, 1516–58) and served as a writer for both Elizabeth I and Edward VI. He also wrote a handbook on archery, *Toxophilus* (1545), a model of the dialogue format.

Baïf, Jean-Antoine de (1532–1589), born in Venice of a French father and Venetian mother, became an illustrious poet. A member of the Pléiade, he cofounded the Académie de Poésie et de Musique in 1570.

Barclay, Alexander (c. 1476–1552) was an English translator and poet, whose writings include satirical elements. His *Eclogues* (c. 1513) were the first poems in English to use the eclogue form.

Barzizza, Gasparino (c. 1360–1431) founded an institute for classical Latin in Padua in the early 15th century. Between 1407 and 1421 he taught students in Padua who boarded in his home. His letters in Latin became stylistic models for other humanists.

Beaumont, Francis (1584–1616), English dramatist, collaborated with John Fletcher on dozens of romantic plays and comedies.

Bellay, Joachim du (1522–1560), one of the Pléiade, he published in 1549 the earliest French Petrarchan sonnet. Works included Latin verse and satire. He also wrote an important theoretical treatise, *La Défence et illustration de la langue française*, also in 1549.

Bembo, Pietro (1470–1547), born in Venice, wrote poetry and literary theory. He was involved in the language debate of the early 16th century, suggesting that the 14th-century Tuscan of Boccaccio and Petrarch should provide the model for literary Italian of the 16th century.

Bijns, Anna (1493–1575), born in Antwerp, published three important collections of poems that set a new standard for Dutch literature in the vernacular. She included criticism of Martin Luther in two of these publications (1538 and 1567).

Biondo, Flavio (1392–1463) pioneered the study of archaeology. One of his historical publications, *De verbis Romanae locutionis* (On Roman speech, 1435), closely tied Italian to the Latin language.

Boccaccio, Giovanni (1313–1375) was born in northern Italy and educated in Naples. His *Decameron*, a famous collection of novellas, was the first significant model of Italian (Tuscan) writing in prose. Boccaccio's poetry provided sources for Chaucer (considered a writer of medieval English, whereas Boccaccio's work is proto-Renaissance).

Boccalini, Traiano (1556–1613), Italian satirist who lambasted Italian society in general and Spaniards in Italy in particular.

Boiardo, Matteo Maria (1441–1494) served the court of Ferrara. He wrote comedies, sonnets, and the unfinished romance *Orlando innamorato* (Orlando in love, 1495).

Boscán, Juan (*Joan Boscà i d'Almogaver in Catalan*) (c. 1490–1542), born in Barcelona, wrote in Castilian Spanish. His poems in *octava rima* (*octava real* in Spanish) helped to bring about the dominance of Castilian as the main poetic language of Iberia.

Bracciolini, Poggio (1380–1459) served in the papal scriptorium for many years. He returned to Florence and became chancellor in 1453. Poggio advocated the use of Latin as a living language, adapted to current conditions, versus the strictly Ciceronian style of Lorenzo Valla (1407–57), with whom he had a famous feud over the Latin language. For Valla, Latin was frozen in its classical usage; for Poggio, new words and new uses of classical words were possible.

Brant, Sebastian (1458–1521), German poet, wrote chiefly satirical works. His *Das Narrenschiff* (Ship of fools, 1491) was published in several editions and translations during Brant's lifetime.

Bruni, Leonardo (1370–1444) returned to Florence in 1415 after working for the papal secretariat. He became chancellor of Florence in 1427 and championed humanistic studies from this position of power. Bruni translated several ancient Greek authors into Latin and wrote an important history of the Florentine people modeled on classical historiography.

Buchanan, George (1506–1582), Scottish humanist, taught at universities in France and Portugal. He was a Neo-Latin poet and philosopher. Influential as the tutor of the future James VI, king of England, Buchanan opposed tyranny in any form.

Budé, Guillaume (1467–1540), humanistic jurist, was King Louis XII's (1482–1515) ambassador to Pope Leo X (1475–1521), and later Francis I's librarian at Fontainebleau. He was a renowned classical philologist, publishing on Roman law, weights and measures, and Greek.

Camden, William (1551–1623) was an English historian who wrote a survey of British antiquities as well as annals of the reign of Queen Elizabeth I.

Camões, Luiz Vaz de (c. 1517 and 1524–1580), born in Lisbon, was one of the most important poets of the Portuguese Renaissance. Also a soldier, he spent nearly two decades in India and other Portuguese colonies in Asia. His great epic *Os Lusíadas* (The Lusiads, 1572) celebrates Portuguese exploration.

Caro, Annibale (1507–1566) served members of the Farnese family. A poet, dramatist, and satirist, Caro translated the *Aeneid* into Italian blank verse (not published until 1581).

Casaubon, Isaac (1559–1614) was a French Huguenot and Greek scholar who published editions of several ancient authors.

Castanheda, Fernão Lopes de (d. 1559), who spent 10 years in India and the Moluccas ("Spice Islands"), wrote *História do descobrimento e conquista da India pelos Portugueses* (History of the discovery and conquest of India by the Portuguese, published after his death). In their various translations, extracts from this multivolume work were the basis of European knowledge of this phase of Portuguese history.

Castelvetro, Lodovico (1506–1571), who was involved in the language debate, also wrote literary theory. His work on Aristotle's *Poetics* included an important commentary on the dramatic unities.

Castiglione, Baldassare (1478–1529) wrote poetry but is best remembered for his dialogue *Il cortegiano* (The courtier, 1528), set at the court of Urbino.

Castillejo, Cristóbal de (c. 1491–1550) was a Spanish poet who favored simple Castilian verse forms over the Italianate style of Boscán and others. He was a trenchant satirist of courtly life.

Castro y Bellvís, Guillén de (1569–1631) wrote many plays, including dramatic adaptations from the work of Cervantes. He was a founding member of a literary academy in Valencia.

Celtis, Konrad (1459–1508) was a German writer of history and Latin poetry. In 1487 he was crowned as the first Imperial poet laureate, an honor awarded for excellence in composing Latin poetry.

Cervantes Saavedra, Miguel de (1547–1616), arguably the greatest writer of the Golden Age in Spain, wrote plays, poems, and several novels. His most famous work is *Don Quijote* (1605, part 1).

Christine de Pisan (c. 1364–c. 1430) was born in Venice, the daughter of an astrologer. Because her father was appointed as royal astrologer for Charles V, king of France, Christine was raised at the French court. She became a poet, championing the cause of women in prehumanistic France and advocating equal educational opportunities for young women.

Cinthio, Il   See GIRALDI, GIAMBATTISTA CINTHIO.

Colonna, Francesco (1433–1527), an Italian Dominican, wrote an allegorical romance resonating with Neoplatonic philosophy, *Hypnerotomachia Polifili* (Polifil's dream of love's strife, 1499). The language of the text mixes Italian and Latin, and the first edition was handsomely illustrated by woodcuts. The book has been a collector's prize since its first publication.

Colonna, Vittoria (1490–1547) was one of the most important women poets of Renaissance Italy. Her sonnets range from emotionally intense to philosophically detached.

Commynes, Philippe de (c. 1446–c. 1511), Flemish historian, wrote annals of the French monarchy published as *Mémoires* (1524). Translated into several languages, they contributed to European knowledge of early Renaissance France.

Coornhert, Dirck Volckertszoon (1522–1590) translated several classical and Italian works, including tales from Boccaccio, into Dutch. He was also a poet, playwright, and engraver.

Cueva, Juan de la (1543–1610), born in Seville, spent several years in Mexico. He wrote poetry and plays, especially satire and historical drama.

Dante Alighieri (1265–1321), Florentine patriot, served as a model for Italian poets. His most famous work was the *Divina commedia* (Divine comedy) written in the Tuscan dialect.

Des Autels, Guillaume (1529–1581), French poet and a member of the Pléiade. He also wrote about current events and orthography.

Desportes, Philippe (1546–1606), born in Chartres, became enmeshed in the French wars of religion. He wrote Petrarchan verse and a poetic translation of Psalms.

De Thou, Jacques Auguste (1553–1617) was a French historian. His *Historia sui temporis* (History of his time, 1604–20) concerned French history from 1545 to 1584, including the wars of religion.

Dolce, Lodovico (1508–1568), was an Italian dramatist who wrote tragedies based on biblical and classical subjects.

Donne, John (c. 1572–1631), a Protestant poet known for his religious verses and "metaphysical" poems. Also a preacher, he was dean of Saint Paul's in London.

Drayton, Michael (1563–1631), a versatile English poet, wrote sonnets, eclogues, and other forms of verse.

Du Bartas, Guillaume de Saluste (1544–1590) wrote French biblical epics and Calvinist poetry. A diplomat and soldier who fought for Henry of Navarre, he died in battle.

Du Bellay, Joachim   *See* BELLAY, JOACHIM DU.

Elyot, Sir Thomas (c. 1490–1546) wrote the *Book Named the Governor* (1531) explaining how humanistic education benefits the state. Sir Thomas translated several treatises concerning statecraft and served the English Crown as a diplomat.

Erasmus, Desiderius (c. 1466–1536) was born in Rotterdam of humble origins. Trained as a humanist, Erasmus advocated reform within the Catholic Church. His philological work included editing texts for publishers such as Aldus Manutius.

Ercilla y Zúñiga, Alonso de (1533–1594), born in Madrid, was both a poet and a soldier. During the 1550s, while fighting in Arauco (Chile) and Peru, he wrote his epic poem *La Araucana* (1569, part 1), describing the conflict.

Estienne, Henri (1528–1598), French Greek scholar and printer, edited several classical Greek authors. His work on Greek epigrams was very influential on members of the Pléiade.

Everaerts, Jan Nicolaeszoon   *See* SECUNDUS, JOHANNES.

Ferreira, António (1528–1569) was a Portuguese dramatist and poet, writing in Portuguese in the classical style of the Latin poet Horace.

Ficino, Marsilio (1433–1499) lectured and wrote under the patronage of Cosimo de' Medici. Neoplatonism in Renaissance Florence was championed by Ficino. His Latin translations of and commentaries on Plato and other Greek authors set standards of excellence for Renaissance humanism.

Fischart, Johann (1546–1590), German satirical writer, is most famous for his ingenious translation of Rabelais's novels (1575).

Fletcher, John (1579–1625), English dramatist, collaborated with Francis Beaumont on dozens of romantic plays and comedies.

Florio, John (c. 1553–1626) was an Italian whose family moved to England because of religious persecution. He is best known for his English translation of the *Essais* of Montaigne.

Fonte, Moderata (1555–1592), a Venetian noblewoman, wrote dramatic verse for musical productions and religious poetry.

Franco, Veronica (1546–1591), the daughter of a Venetian procuress, became a courtesan and poet. She habituated literary salons, publishing her own work as well as editing collections of poems by her contemporaries. Franco is known for her candid attitude toward sexuality in her poems and letters.

Garcilaso de la Vega (c. 1501–1536), born in Toledo, was a poet in military service to the emperor Charles V. His travels included a journey to Naples, where he met several Italian poets and was influenced by Italian verse forms. His eclogues and love poems are among the finest of the Spanish Renaissance.

Garcilaso de la Vega, el Inca (1539–1616) was the son of a Spanish father and an Inca princess in Cuzco (Peru). His histories of Peru and Florida were important additions to European knowledge of Spanish possessions in the New World.

Garnier, Robert (c. 1545–1590) wrote poems and plays in French, notably tragedies based on classical models.

Gascoigne, George (1525–1577), an English soldier-poet, also wrote plays and a novella.

Giovio, Paolo (1483–1552) served the Medicis, including Pope Clement VII. His writings included biography, history, and a book on imprese. Giovio also collected antiquities, portraits, and other works.

Giraldi, Giambattista Cinthio (Il Cinthio, 1504–1573) wrote literary theory, plays, and novellas. From 1542 to 1559 he was at the court of Ferrara.

Góis, Damião de (1502–1574) served the Portuguese court as a diplomat. His historical publications include accounts of the reigns of the Renaissance kings of Portugal.

Góngora y Argote, Luis de (1561–1627), born in Córdoba, was a poet known for complex language and imagery, called *culteranismo* in Spanish. This Manneristic style in early 17th-century poetry became known as Gongorism.

Górnicki, Lukasz (1527–1603), Polish essayist, was educated in Italy. His most important work was *Dworzanin polski* (1566), an imitation of Castiglione's *Courtier.*

Gringore, Pierre (c. 1475–1538), French dramatist and poet, was also an actor. He wrote a mystery play as well as comedies.

Guarini, Giovanni Battista (1538–1612), born in Ferrara, was a poet and playwright at the Este court. His pastoral drama *Il paster fido* (The faithful shep-

herd, 1590) was influential across Europe, with several translations.

Guevara, Fray Antonio de (c. 1480–1545) was a Spanish Franciscan who served the royal court as a writer and preacher. His most famous work was the *Reloj de principes y libro aureo de Marco Aurelio* (Mirror of princes and golden book of Marcus Aurelius, 1529), containing ideals for the Christian ruler.

Guicciardini, Francesco (1483–1540), born in Florence, wrote the famous *Storia d'Italia* (History of Italy, published posthumously in 1561), covering four decades of Italian history from 1494 to 1534. This work was rapidly translated into the major European languages.

Harington, Sir John (1561–1612), English poet, translated Ariosto and wrote epigrams and satires. He was infamous at the English court for publishing the satirical *Metamorphosis of Ajax* (1596), which explained the need for flush toilets in England.

Harvey, Gabriel (c. 1545–1630) was a literary critic who wrote about classical poetry and rhetoric.

Herrera, Fernando de (1534–1597), born in Seville, was chiefly a poet. His best known works were three odes celebrating contemporary heroes. Herrera also wrote a biography of Sir Thomas More.

Heywood, John (c. 1497–c. 1580) wrote plays and satirical poems. He also sang and played the virginal at the English court.

Holinshed, Raphael (d. 1580) compiled the first comprehensive history of Britain written in English, *Chronicles of England, Scotland, and Ireland* (1577).

Houwaert, Jean Baptista (1533–1599) was a member of the Brussels Chamber of Rhetoric and in service to the ducal court in Brabant. He published several plays on mythological subjects.

Hurtado de Mendoza, Diego (1503–1575) was a poet, historian, translator, soldier, and diplomat. His participation in suppressing the Moorish rebellion in Granada resulted in his most significant historical publication, *La guerra de Granada* (The Granada war, 1610).

Hutten, Ulrich von (1488–1523), German humanist, wrote several satires in the dialogue form, in Latin and German translation. These works contributed to the popularity of the dialogue as a Renaissance literary form.

Jodelle, Étienne (1532–1573) was a poet, playwright, and member of the Pléiade. His *Cléopâtre captive* (Captive Cleopatra, c. 1552) was one of the earliest tragedies written in French.

Jonson, Ben (1572–1637), poet, actor, and dramatist, was a friend and rival of Shakespeare's. The principal playwright at the court of James I, he wrote masques that were staged by Inigo Jones.

Kochanowski, Jan (1530–1584), Polish poet and dramatist, was distinguished in his use of Polish rather than Latin for writing poetry. He served at the court of King Sigismund II.

Kyd, Thomas (1558–1594) wrote many plays that were published anonymously. *The Spanish Tragedy* (c. 1589), a drama of revenge, is his most famous work.

Labé, Louise (1524–1566) influential poet known for elegies and love sonnets. She encouraged women to focus on culture rather than jewels and fashion.

Landino, Cristoforo (1424–1504), Italian philologist and poet, wrote commentaries on classical authors associating their works with Christian doctrine and Neoplatonism.

Lebrija, Antonio (*also Antonio Nebrija*) (1442–1522) studied at the Universities of Salamanca and Bologna. Most of his career was spent teaching the classics at the University of Alcalá de Henares, where he became Spain's most illustrious humanistic scholar. In addition, Lebrija wrote the first grammar of Castilian Spanish (1492).

Lemaire de Belges, Jean (c. 1473–1525), born in Hainaut, mainly wrote poetry. His outstanding prose work is *Les illustrations de Gaule et singularités de Troie*

(The glories of Gaul and distinctions of Troy, 1510–13) about the legendary origins of France.

Leone Hebreo (*Judah ben Isaac Abrabanel*) (c. 1460–c. 1521) was son of the Jewish scholar Isaac Abrabanel. A Portuguese philosopher influenced by Neoplatonism after he fled to Naples, Leone Hebreo is known for his *Dialoghi d'amore* (Dialogues on love, 1535), which concerned mystical Neoplatonic doctrine.

Lipsius, Justus (1547–1606), born near Brussels, was the chief Renaissance supporter of Christian Stoicism and conciliation in political affairs. He also published editions of the classical authors Seneca and Tacitus.

Lope de Vega Carpio, Félix (1562–1635), a prolific Spanish poet and playwright, he has more than 300 plays extant. These dramatic works were inspired by medieval tales as well as by classical sources.

Lopes, Fernão (c. 1380–1460) was commissioned by the Portuguese Crown to write chronicles of past dynasties. His historical texts were models of Portuguese prose for the early Renaissance.

López de Gómora, Francisco (1511–1566), secretary to Hernán Cortés, was a historian whose account of Spanish activities in Mexico, *Historia de las India y conquista de México* (History of the Indies and conquest of Mexico), was published in 1552.

Luis de Léon, Fray (c. 1527–1591), Spanish Augustinian, was a poet and translator who wrote classical-style odes in Spanish based on the Horatian model, which were published until 1631. During his lifetime, he was known as a teacher and biblical scholar.

Lyly, John (c. 1554–1606) is famous for writing *Euphues: The Anatomy of Wit* (1578), a prose romance that spawned the term *euphuism* (see Glossary). He was also a playwright.

Machiavelli, Niccolò (1469–1527), political theorist and playwright, is most famous for *Il principe* (The prince, 1513). He also wrote comedies, satires, poems, and commentaries on classical authors.

Malherbe, François de (1555–1628), born in Normandy, was court poet to Henry IV. His clear, classical style, as opposed to the rhetorical ornamentation of earlier poets, was welcomed by 17th-century critics.

Manrique, Gómez (c. 1412–c. 1490), soldier-poet and dramatist, wrote some of the earliest plays of Renaissance Spain. He was the uncle of Jorge Manrique.

Manrique, Jorge (1440–1479), soldier-poet, is known for lyric poems and a famous elegy on the death of his father, *Coplas por la muerte de su padre* (published posthumously in 1494). He was the nephew of Gómez Manrique.

March, Ausiàs (1397–1459) was a Catalan poet whose work was influenced by that of Dante and Petrarch.

Marlowe, Christopher (1564–1593) wrote poems and plays; the latter works influenced those of Shakespeare. Marlowe's long poem *Hero and Leander* (1598) in blank verse is one of his best known works.

Marguerite de Navarre (*also Marguerite d'Angoulême*) (1492–1549), queen of Navarre, was the sister of Francis I. A patron of learning and the arts, she wrote religious poetry as well as the stories of her *Heptameron* (1558) exploring relations between the sexes and women's place in society.

Mariana, Juan de (1536–1623/24), Spanish historian and philosopher trained as a Jesuit, wrote *Historiae de rebus Hispaniae* (History of the affairs of Spain, 1582). In 1605 he expanded the text to include the reigns of the three most recent kings.

Marot, Clément (1496–1544), Protestant poet and translator, worked under the patronage of Marguerite de Navarre. He spent part of his life exiled from France, writing bitter satire as well as love poems and sonnets.

Marston, John (1576–1634), playwright and satirist, whose most famous work was *The Malcontent* of 1604, a tragicomedy that satirized corruption at court.

Mary Herbert, countess of Pembroke (1561–1621), Philip Sidney's sister, was a poet in her own right. After her brother's death, she completed his translation of Psalms.

Mena, Juan de (1411–1456), poet and translator, is best known for *Las trescientas* (The three hundred [stanzas], completed in 1444). The long poem represents the earliest Spanish effort to incorporate classical references in contemporary poetry.

de Mendoza, Íñigo López, marquis of Santillana (1398–1458), poet and literary theorist, was also an eminent statesman. His sonnets are the first known Spanish poems in that format.

Montaigne, Michel Eyquem de (1533–1592) was the most famous essayist of the French Renaissance. Published between 1580 and 1595, the clear, firm prose of his *Essais* supported religious tolerance and philosophical neostoicism.

Montemayor, Jorge de (1519–1561) was a Portuguese poet and translator who wrote in Spanish. His best known work is the pastoral romance *Diana* (c. 1559).

Morales, Ambrosio de (1513–1591) wrote *Crónica general de España* (Chronicle of Spain, 1574–77), using historical documents in a modern analytical approach rather than repeating the romantic stories of medieval chroniclers.

More, Sir Thomas (1478–1535), English statesman, is most famous for his satiric novella *Utopia* (1516), which introduced a new word and new concept of life's possibilities into English. Although he served Henry VIII faithfully, More's defense of papal supremacy led to his execution.

Murner, Thomas (1475–1537), a German Franciscan, was the most vitriolic satirist of his generation. His chief target was Martin Luther. Murner also translated classical works, notably the *Aeneid*, into German. He was crowned Imperial poet laureate in 1505.

Nashe, Thomas (1567–1601), English satirical writer, criticized contemporary society. He also collaborated with Christopher Marlowe on an early dramatic work.

Noot, Jan Baptist van der (1539–1595), Flemish poet, modeled his Dutch poems on those of the Pléiade.

Peletier Du Mans, Jacques (1517–1582), translator and poet, was also a mathematician. A member of the Pléiade, Peletier Du Mans wrote a poetic manifesto, *Art poétique* (1555) after translating the *Ars poetica* (Art of poetry) of Horace.

Pérez de Guzmán, Fernán (c. 1378–c. 1460) was a Spanish poet best known for his chronicles of contemporary illustrious men.

Petrarch, Francesco (*Petrarca* in Italian*)* (1304–1374) provided the first significant model of Italian (Tuscan) writing in poetic form. He also wrote works in Latin, including allegorical dialogues. In 1341 Petrarch was crowned poet laureate in Rome for his Latin verse.

Piccolomini, Aeneas Silvius See PIUS II.

Piccolomini, Alessandro (1508–1578), born in Siena, was a philosopher, poet, and dramatist. He translated Aristotle's *Poetics* into Italian (1572) and published his commentary of the text in 1575.

Pico della Mirandola, Giovanni (1463–1494) was a humanist and controversial philosopher. His published works included a lengthy diatribe against astrologers.

Pirckheimer, Willibald (1470–1530), German humanist and translator of classical Greek works into Latin, also was the author of a famous humorous essay on gout, *Apologia seu podagrae laus* (Defense or praise of gout, 1510).

Pius II (*Aeneas Silvius Piccolomini*) (1405–1464), pope from 1458 to 1464, was trained as a humanist.

He was a renowned Latinist, who wrote a famous autobiography, biographies of his contemporaries, history, novellas, poems, and other works.

Poliziano (*Angelo Ambrogini*) (1454–1494) spent most of his life under Medici patronage in Florence. A brilliant humanist and philologist, Poliziano was equally at ease writing poetry in Greek, Latin, and Italian. His most famous poem is the unfinished *Stanze per la giostra del Magnifico Giuliano* (Stanzas for the joust of the magnificent Giuliano [de' Medici], 1478).

Pontano, Giovanni (between 1426 and 1429–1503) was a humanist serving at the court of Naples. A versatile Neo-Latin writer, he composed poems, essays, history, and dialogues. The Neapolitan Academy was later named Accademia Pontaniana in his honor.

Rabelais, François (1483–c. 1553), humanist and physician, mainly wrote satirical works. His novels of the tales of Gargantua and Pantagruel contain some of the most original and idiosyncratic prose writings of the French Renaissance.

Ramus, Petrus (*Pierre de la Ramée, 1515–1572*) wrote in Latin about Aristotle's use of logic and in 1555 published his *Dialectique* (Dialectic) concerning logical deduction, a significant work in Renaissance rhetoric. This was the first published work in French exclusively concerning a philosophical subject.

Rojas, Fernando de (c. 1465–1541), born in Toledo of a converted Jewish family, is chiefly known as the author of *Celestina* (1499), a Renaissance best-seller. The protagonist of the play is the procuress Celestina, an old woman who has surprising resources.

Ronsard, Pierre de (1524–1585), leader of the Pléiade, was one of the most important French poets of the Renaissance. His odes in classical style and Petrarchan sonnets were immensely popular. In 1565 Ronsard published his handbook of poetic composition, *Abrégé de l'art poétique françois*, which encouraged poets to write in the vernacular.

Sá de Miranda, Francisco da (c. 1481–1558), a Portuguese poet who also wrote in Castilian Spanish, traveled in Italy, and introduced Italian verse forms, such as the sonnet, to Portugal. He was also a playwright.

Sachs, Hans (1494–1576), born in Nuremberg, was a shoemaker-poet who wrote in several genres, including dramatic works. He is best known for songs performed by the Meistersinger school in Nuremberg.

Saint-Gelais, Mellin de (1487–1558) was one of the first French poets to compose sonnets. He also translated contemporary Italian literature and wrote several dramatic works.

Salutati, Coluccio (1331–1406) served as chancellor of Florence for three decades, attracting humanistic scholars such as Manuel Chrysoloras to the city. Salutati wrote poetry and works of moral philosophy based on classical sources, as well as letters in classical style.

Sambucus, Johannes (*János Zsámboki*) (1531–1584), Hungarian humanist and physician, served at the Habsburg court in Vienna. He wrote on several subjects, including emblems; his popular emblem book *Emblemata* was published in 1564.

Sannazaro, Jacopo (1458–1530) spent most of his career under the patronage of the Neapolitan court. He wrote poetry in both Latin and Italian; his most influential work was the pastoral romance *L'Arcadia* (1504).

San Pedro, Diego de (c. 1437–c. 1498), a Spanish government official, wrote *La cárcel de amor* (The prison of love, 1492), a novel of courtly romance that became very popular.

Sebillet, Thomas (1512–1589) wrote an important work of literary theory, *L'Art poétique français* (1548), in which he suggested that both medieval and classical models can be useful.

Scève, Maurice (c. 1510–1564) wrote French love poems and pastoral verse. His most famous work is the sonnet cycle *Délie, objet de plus haute vertu* (Delia, object of the highest virtue, 1544), illustrated with emblematic woodcuts.

Secundus, Johannes (*Jan Nicolaeszoon Everaerts*) (1511–1536), Dutch writer, composed odes, elegies, and epigrams in Latin. His love poems entitled *Basia* (Kisses) were translated into several languages.

Shakespeare, William (1564–1616) was the most famous dramatist of the Renaissance, if not of all time. Also a poet, he wrote some of the best love sonnets of the era.

Sidney, Sir Philip (1554–1586) wrote sonnets, a prose romance, and *Apologie of Poetry* (c. 1583), which suggests that poetry is an effective medium for teaching virtue.

Skelton, John (c. 1460–1529), English poet, wrote in a running verse form that came to be called "skeltonics." A court poet under Henry VII and tutor to Prince Henry, Skelton wrote works celebrating the Crown as well as satirical works such as *The Tunning of Elynour Rummyng* (c. 1521).

Spenser, Edmund (c. 1552–1599) was one of the most illustrious poets of Queen Elizabeth I's reign. *The Faerie Queene* (1590, 1596) celebrated her monarchy.

Sponde, Jean de (1557–1595), French humanist and poet, wrote sonnets and an essay on Psalms.

Stampa, Gaspara (1523–1554), Italian poet, wrote verse inspired by that of Petrarch. She was a member of the Accademia of Pellegrini in Venice.

Surrey (*Henry Howard, Earl of Surrey*) (1516–1547), English poet, was an early practitioner of the sonnet form. He also wrote a blank-verse translation of part of the *Aeneid*.

Tasso, Bernardo (c. 1493–1569), father of Torquato Tasso, was a poet who modeled his work on that of Horace.

Tasso, Torquato (1544–1595), son of Bernardo Tasso, was a poet and playwright. For many years he was at the Este court in Ferrara, where he wrote his epic poem *Gerusalemme liberata* (Jerusalem liberated, 1581) about the First Crusade.

Terracina, Laura (1519–c. 1577), who lived in Naples, published poetry and *Discorso sopra il principio di tutti i canti d'Orlando furioso* (Discourse on the first cantos of *Orlando furioso*, 1549).

Thyard, Pontus de (1521–1605), a member of the Pléiade, published essays and three volumes of sonnets.

Trissino, Gian Giorgio (1478–1550), a poet and playwright based chiefly at the papal court, was involved in the question of language during the early 16th century. His own work included odes, sonnets, and the tragedy *Sofonisba* (1515), which were based on Greek models instead of that of Seneca. His *Italia liberata* (Italy liberated) of 1547, modeled on Homer, was in blank verse.

Valdés, Alfonso de (c. 1490–1532), brother of Juan de Valdés, served at the court of Holy Roman Emperor Charles V. His satirical writings defended the policies of the emperor.

Valdés, Juan de (c. 1490–1541), brother of Alfonso de Valdés, was a humanist who spent most of his career in Naples. He was known for his defense of Spanish as a literary language.

Valla, Lorenzo (1407–1457), one of the most illustrious Italian humanists, celebrated Latin as the proper language for eloquent discourse. He was a pivotal figure in the language controversy of the early Renaissance.

Vergil, Polydore (c. 1470–c. 1555), an Italian who lived in England, was a historian. His best known work is *Anglicae historiae libri XXVI* (History of England, 1534–55).

Villena, Enrique de (1384–1434) translated Dante's *Divine Comedy* and the entire *Aeneid* into Spanish. He was also a cook and wrote a treatise about use of knives.

Villon, François (c. 1431–after 1463) regarded as a notorious poet, Villon disappeared from the historical record when he was banished from Paris in 1463. His best work was in satiric verse, such as the *Grand Testament* (Last Will and Testament, 1461),

in which the bequests make fun of such serious documents.

Visscher, Pieter Roemer (1547–1620), born in Amsterdam, wrote Dutch poetry in the classical mode. More important, the humanistic tone of his household produced two famous 17th-century poets, his daughters, Anna and Maria.

Wyatt, Sir Thomas (1503–1542) was an important innovator of the sonnet as an English poetic form.

Zsámboki, János   See SAMBUCUS JOHANNES.

Zurita, Jerónimo de (1512–1580), Spanish historian, was the official chronicler for Aragon. His historical writing was based on archival research rather than chivalric tales.

READING

Elsky 1989: England; Hampton 2001: France; Herman 1999: cross-cultural influences; Kinney 2000: England; Lewis 1954: England, nondramatic literature; Whinnom 1994: Spain.

Humanism, Philology, and Publishing

Barker 1999: printing; Birnbaum 1985: humanism in Hungary and Croatia; Hankins 1993: papacy; Lewis 1954: England; Nichols 1979: Neo-Latin; Rowland 2000: Rome in the 16th century; Rummel 1998: humanism and Scholasticism; Trapp 1983: manuscripts; Winn 1983: presentation manuscripts (patronage).

Literary Theory

Baldwin 1959: classicism; Holyoake 1973: France; Preminger 1965: (terminology); Quint 1983: originality; Schmitt 1983: Aristotle; Weinberg 1961: Italy.

Poetry

Baldwin 1959: classicism; Binns 1999: England; Navarrete 2000: Italian influences; Preminger 1965: (terminology); Silver 1981: France; Sullivan 2001: Germany; Willett 2004: (translations of three Renaissance prefaces to French poetic works); Wright 2001: metrics.

Prose

Aretino 1967: (translation of his Renaissance letters); Cox 1992: the dialogue; Ferguson 1986: gender issues; Fowler 1997: consideration of the New World; Hannay 1985: Tudor women; Montaigne 1999: (translation of his Renaissance autobiography); Rhodes 1997: England; Shepherd 1985: women pamphleteers.

Drama

Adams 2001: Spain; D'Amico 1991: England (images of the Moor); Foster 2004: tragicomedy; McKendrick 1992: Spain; Robinson 2002: England (history plays); Ruiter 2003: Shakespeare (images of fasting and festivity); Taunton 2001: England (war imagery).

Oratory and Rhetoric

Le Sylvain 1596: (translation of a Renaissance handbook); Mack 1994: (general study).

Library Collections

Grafton 1993, 3–46: Vatican Library; Staikos 2000: (survey of great libraries).

6

MUSIC

Medieval music, in both its sacred and secular manifestations, continued to be composed as well as performed in western Europe well into the 15th century. Although literature and art now thought of as "Renaissance" had commenced by the early 1400s, Renaissance music was still in its early stages of development. Certain progressive aspects began in England, while on the continent Franco-Flemish composers were praised during the 15th century for their innovative style. As many of these northerners moved south into Italy, Spain, Portugal, and Provence, composing and playing at the major courts as well as working for the pope, the center of Renaissance music shifted to Italy. By the 16th century, Italy had become the musical power of western Europe. The most important shift in music between the Middle Ages and Renaissance, the increasing use of instrumentation, was due to technical advances in instrument production and the proliferation of printed music and books about musical theory. In Renaissance singing, the voice was generally used to emphasize the text, following the sense of the words and thus moving the soul of the listener. Whereas medieval music had been a rarefied abstraction of musical relationships, Renaissance music attempted to project the meaning of the text.

SACRED MUSIC

Motets and settings for the mass, often in large-scale polyphony, dominated sacred music for Catholic services during the 15th and 16th centuries, with melodies derived from both secular songs and sacred plainsong. The foundation of all sacred music during this period, as in medieval music, was the church choir. Consisting solely of men, church choirs provided the "heavenly" voices intended to uplift the congregation. The chief differences between Catholic and Protestant music were that hymns and chorales in the latter often were written in vernacular languages instead of Latin and that congregations joined in the singing. Lutheran music popularized the chorale, sung in unison by the entire congregation. Strict Calvinist churches prohibited the use of musical instruments.

Catholic Services

Unlike most other innovative aspects of Renaissance culture, changes in music originated in northern Europe and influenced composers writing for courts, churches, and civic institutions in the Italian and Iberian Peninsulas. Franco-Flemish polyphony sung in Latin, which resounded in the cathedrals of Europe during the 15th century, introduced new structural elements into liturgical compositions for the mass as several voices sang the various parts. Sections of the mass, such as the Gloria and Credo, and the Sanctus and Agnus Dei, became musically or liturgically (textually) related as pairs. These pairs might each open with the same melody or have the same plainsong tenor (the basic melodic line). A sin-

6.1 Musical instrument maker's workshop. Engraving by Jost Amman, c. 1570. The artisan is depicted playing a lute. (Private Collection/Giraudon/Bridgeman Art Library)

gle *cantus firmus* (fixed song) sung in unison often supported the composition. Some of these innovations originated with English composers, notably Lional Power (d. 1445), John Dunstable (c. 1390–1453), and their contemporaries. Dunstable's music, largely based on the harmonic intervals of thirds, was described as a sweet new style. Power was best known for linking cycles in the mass through related chants, and he trained chapel choirs for the duke of Clarence and Christ Church, Canterbury.

Composers in western Europe had ample opportunity to hear each other's church music, such as during the Council of Constance (1414–18, see chapter 2, on religion). The various church councils of the 15th and 16th centuries drew together bishops, cardinals, and other officials, who usually arrived with their own composers, musicians, and singers. The Holy See and Rome naturally were important locations for sacred music, and papal appointments as chaplains or choirmasters were considered plums among composers. Until about 1550, non-Italian composers such as Adriaan Willaert (c. 1490–1562) dominated sacred music in Italy. Then, in 1562, the Council of Trent appointed Cardinal Carlo Borromeo to head a commission charged with "purifying" sacred music of secular influences such as madrigals (see Secular Music, page 162). Giovanni Pierluigi da Palestrina (1525/26–94) became the most influential composer of the new reformed style of sacred music.

Protestant Services

LUTHERANISM

Sacred music for Protestant churches in Germany during the second half of the 16th century was quite similar to that for Catholic usage, especially in the performance of motets. These vocal compositions set in harmony were very popular with both groups. There were, however, alterations in the contents of Protestant sacred music. Texts in honor of the Virgin Mary were changed to emphasize Christ, and motets in honor of the various saints were omitted from Protestant services. Most importantly, many Latin texts were translated into German even when Latin remained in the liturgy

in the larger cities and in universities. Many composers wrote sacred music for both Catholic and Protestant use. Ludwig Senfl (c. 1486–1542/43), who worked chiefly for Emperor Maximilian I, also composed motets for Duke Albrecht of Prussia, who embraced Lutheranism, and two motets for Martin Luther. A Latin composition by Senfl on unity and brotherhood was performed when the Augsburg Diet convened in 1530 (see chapter 2, on religion), in the futile hope that religious factions might be reconciled.

Martin Luther (1483–1546), a lutenist and singer of some repute, wrote both the words and music for his hymns. The composer Johann Walther (1496–1570) collaborated with Luther to make plainsong that would be appropriate for words in German. Unlike music for the Catholic mass, in which the organ became increasingly prominent, Luther's church music relied on the human voice. Through Lutheran music, the a capella (voices only) chorale grew in popularity, with entire congregations' joining in to sing the hymns. For Luther, words and music, as well as the manner of singing, derived from one's native language. In addition, Luther demanded that practical musical training be included in pastoral education.

CALVINISM

Although Jean Calvin (1509–64) evidently had no formal musical training, he gathered from his humanistic education that music has the potential to affect behavior. Calvinist church music became as strictly severe as the religion itself. No musical instruments were permitted, the music was monophonic because polyphony was thought to detract from the text, and the text had to be in the vernacular. In 1542 the so-called First Genevan Psalter made monophonic settings of the Psalms widely available to Calvinist congregations. The relationship between music and text was even more basic than in Lutheran music, as the melody followed syllables of the words. Subsequent publications of the Calvinist Psalter became popular in Germany and the Netherlands and eventually were used by Lutherans as well. Polyphonic versions of the Psalter were used in private, domestic worship, usually as chorales in four voices.

Secular Music

During the 15th century, the French genres of *ballades* and *chansons* dominated secular music. By the early 16th century, French rondeaux and Italian madrigals were becoming popular, often with their melodic lines taken from well-known sacred music. Besides jocular pieces and music lamenting lost love, secular music during the 16th century included lyrical works supposedly based on the principles of ancient Greek tonal music, influenced by the research and writings of Renaissance humanists. Madrigals were the most popular genre of European secular music during the second half of the 16th century.

Major Genres

BALLAD

Although *ballad* has been used as a translation for the French word *ballade*, the ballad was a different type of musical piece. Originally similar to the *ballade* in its form and function as music for folk dancing, by the 14th century the ballad had become almost exclusively a narrative folk song performed solo. These were (and are) songs for storytelling, each stanza expressing a stage in the narrative. Their poetic meter is most often iambic or trochaic, and the verse patterns are closely intertwined with the melodies.

BALLADE

The *ballade* was a French medieval poetic form set to music, usually with the scheme AAB, and very popular during the 15th century to accompany dancing. This musical form consisted of three stanzas, all with the same refrain. Although *ballades* were written to celebrate patrons or commemorate historic events, their most common use by far was for love songs.

CHANSON

Chanson, French for "song," referred to several types of vocal music and could include virtually any secu-lar composition. Examples are drinking songs and sophisticated songs performed at court. While the fixed forms of *ballade*, rondeau, and *virelai* gradually died out, the more inventive *chanson* became increasingly popular during the 16th century. The Parisian *chanson*, which developed during the 1530s and 1540s, gave a new elegance and simplicity to the structure of the *chanson*. With no fixed rhyme scheme, the Parisian *chanson* of the 16th century allowed for musical repetitions with greater freedom of expression.

MADRIGAL

The vocal polyphony of madrigals became very much appreciated during the 16th century, beginning in the Italian Peninsula and spreading all the way to England. Many of the early madrigals featured poems in the style of Petrarch set to music in a stately cadence (see chapter 5, Literature and Language). Later in the century madrigals were written with more chromatic and dramatic expressiveness. The later madrigals allowed both composers and performers to lengthen a phrase, lighten the texture, or vary the song in some other way to delight or respond to the audience. Almost any genre of poetry was fair game—erotic, pastoral, epic, philosophical, and others. Madrigals were a favorite genre of Elizabeth I's (1533–1603), popularized in England by Thomas Morley (1557/58–1602), a student of William Byrd's. Although most composers of madrigals were men, several women were famous during their lifetime for writing madrigals and other secular music; they usually were also talented singers who wrote much of their own music. Four madrigals by Maddalena Casulana (c. 1540–c. 90) included in an anthology published in 1566 were the first pieces of music by a woman to appear in print. By the 1580s, virtuoso female singers of madrigals were welcomed at many of the Italian courts.

MOTET

Motet was a very general musical term during the Middle Ages, and the motet developed into an important genre for polyphonic compositions during the Renaissance. In structure, the medieval motet usually featured a tenor voice sustaining the rhythmic base while higher voices sung the words at a somewhat faster speed. By the 15th century, motets of several types featured structures of various degrees of complexity, with three or more sections of tenor voices and with instruments paired with voices.

RONDEAU

The rondeau was a song with a refrain, from the idea of *ronde* (round) as the refrain came back around at the end of each verse. Rondeaux were the dominant fixed form of song in western Europe during the 15th century, and their circular structure reflected the dances for which they were originally intended. The refrain was the focus of the song, using the complete melodic line even though its text was often quite short.

VILLANCICO

The *villancico* (from the word for peasant) was Spanish popular verse set to music. Madrigals influenced polyphonic additions during the 16th century. Although *villancicos* used traditional melodies, their poetic structure was quite flexible. Their content became more spiritual toward the end of the 16th century under the influence of the Counter-Reformation. (Today a *villancico* is simply a song for Christmas.)

VIRELAI

The *virelai* was a French medieval poetic form set to music, usually ABBAA, popular during the 15th century. It may have originated from Arabic songs transmitted by Provençal troubadours during the 12th century. With *virer* (to twist) as its root word, the *virelai* was closely related to dance. This genre can be distinguished from the *ballade* by its refrain of several lines, placed in the first section of the music.

Humanism and Music

The musical treatises by Johannes de Tinctoris (c. 1435–1511), referring to numerous classical author-ities such as Aristotle, Plato, and Plutarch, were highly valued as sources of both theory and practice. Humanist composers believed that the purpose of music was to appeal to the listener, with the words clearly carried by the voice, following a passage in book 3 of Plato's *Republic*. Tinctoris was in service to Ferrante I, king of Naples (1423–94), as tutor to his daughter, Beatrice. Educated by the famous humanist Lorenzo Valla (1407–57), Ferrante I respected the humanistic educational system and patronized the work of Tinctoris. Although his treatise on the origin of music is lost, Tinctoris's dozen extant works include the earliest printed dictionary of musical terminology. Among other diplomatic tasks, he was charged by Ferrante I with persuading singers in service to the French court to leave King Charles VIII (1470–98) and move to the court in Naples.

During the 15th century, the itinerant French royal court traveled with its retinue of singers and musicians, residing in castles along the Loire River. By 1500 the court was established in and near Paris. Shortly after Francis I (1494–1547) was crowned in 1515, humanistic studies began to flourish under the leadership of Guillaume Budé (1467–1540), a brilliant scholar of ancient Greek. Francis I's sister, Marguerite de Navarre (1492–1549), supported the Protestant poet Clément Marot (1496–1544, see Chapter 5, Literature and Language), whose folklife verses set to music defined the *chanson* for his generation. The king, on the other hand, encouraged humanistic efforts to revivify ancient Greek songs, or odes. A group of seven poets known as the Pléiade wrote poetry in "classical" meter (see chapter 5). The name Pléiade derived from a group of seven classical Greek poets, living during the Hellenistic era, who had called themselves the Pléiade after the constellation with seven stars. An example of the Renaissance classical meter was Pierre Ronsard's (1524–85) book *Amours* (Loves), published in 1552, produced as *chansons* in collaboration with several musicians. Unlike the simple *chansons* of Marot and his contemporaries, the new humanistic *chanson* was strictly measured to follow the text. In 1571 the Academy of Poetry and Music was founded in Paris, for the purpose of promoting the "new" forms and upholding their new standards. Orlando di Lassus (1530/32–94) was among the composers influenced by this measured style.

By the mid-16th century, Italian humanists who had studied the available treatises of ancient Greek music made an effort to revive this genre or to restore it through their own compositions. New poems written in classical Greek meter were meant to be set to music in the ancient mode. Vincenzo Galilei (late 1520s–91), father of the scientist Galileo Galilei and of the lutenist (lute player) Michelangelo Galilei, wrote a treatise entitled *Dialogo della musica antica et della moderna* (Dialogue on ancient and modern music), published in 1581. He and his colleagues in Florence, including the singer Giulio Caccini (c. 1545–1618) and the composer Jacopo Peri (1561–1633), formed a group called the Camerata who met in the home of Count Giovanni de' Bardi. One of the purposes of Galilei's *Dialogue* was to criticize the erroneous assumptions about ancient music of his contemporaries, notably his teacher, Gioseffo Zarlino (1517–90), a noted musical theorist. Zarlino, chapel master of Saint Mark's in Venice, published *Le istitutioni harmoniche* (Harmonic principles) in 1558. Although his system of harmonic yet imperfect consonances was a major contribution to the development of Renaissance music written for voice, Zarlino had misunderstood many of his ancient sources, as pointed out by Galilei.

Zarlino had used the modal system of the Swiss humanist Heinrich Glarean (1488–1563) without acknowledging his source. Glarean studied at the University of Cologne and achieved recognition from Emperor Maximilian I in 1512 when he sang one of his pieces for an assembly in Cologne. Befriended by Erasmus, Glarean taught music and the classical languages in Basel and later in Freiburg. After studying manuscript sources in ancient Greek and Latin, in 1547 Glarean published his influential book *Dodecachordon* (Twelve chord [system]). This work's chief value is the discovery that the Greek Ionian mode was equivalent to the major scale (prevalent in most music during his time) and that the Aeolian mode was equivalent to the natural minor. Glarean's explanation of ancient modal music facilitated the work of composers who were attempting to link their work with the "newest" ancient sources.

WORKING CONDITIONS AND PATRONAGE

Unlike most other forms of art patronage (paintings, sculpture, architecture, costume), for which the patron paid for a commodity and then no longer required the presence of the artists, music required both singers and musicians to interpret and perform many of the pieces commissioned. These individuals were part of the courtly retinue and became a status symbol of the respective court, with dukes, kings, emperors, and popes competing for the services of the most renowned composers, musicians, and singers.

Patronage

Every Imperial, royal, and major ducal court in western Europe patronized composers of sacred music; service for the Vatican was particularly sought after, because the papal choir was one of the best in western Europe. During the 15th century, the Burgundian ducal court (controlling much of northern France and the Netherlands) was one of the most important patrons of music in all of Europe. Among the Habsburg monarchs, Emperor Maximilian I (1459–1519) was the first to become internationally known during the Renaissance for patronage of music. Through his first wife, Mary of Burgundy (1457–82), Maximilian I was exposed to music from the Netherlands, and through his second wife, Bianca Maria Sforza, he learned about Italian music. Musicians and composers at the court cities of Vienna and Innsbruck included Ludwig Senfl, famous for his polyphonic motets, and Jacob Obrecht (c. 1450–1505). The imperial Kapelle (chapel choir and orchestra) featured trumpets, lutes, trombones, drums, shawms, crumhorns, fifes, and, of course, singers. In addition to instruments, choirs had books of music, usually shared among the choir members.

Emperor Charles V (1500–1558) became king of Spain in 1516, moving his court from Brussels to Spain, but he often journeyed to other court centers with an extensive entourage. Charles V's Flemish choir followed him on his various travels throughout Europe. His choir directors included Corneille Canis [de Hondt] (d. 1561), known for contrapuntal techniques. Nicolas Gombert (c. 1490–c. 1566), probably the most famous student of the renowned composer Josquin Desprez (c. 1440–1521), was a master of the Imperial choirboys for more than a decade. The fame and prestige of this choir, especially since it could be experienced firsthand in the cathedrals of several cities, helped to publicize the skill of Flemish singers during much of the 16th century. When Charles V abdicated the Spanish throne in favor of his son, Philip II (1527–98), he bequeathed his Flemish choir to the new king. Charles V was known by his contemporaries for his musical erudition and appreciation of fine music, and numerous pieces were dedicated to him, such as songs by Desprez.

Court patrons supported the work of many composers, commissioning pieces for specific occasions. The aunt of Emperor Charles V, Margaret of Austria (1480–1530), especially favored the music of Josquin Desprez. Margaret herself was a talented keyboard player. As regent of the Netherlands from 1506 to 1515 and again from 1519 until 1530, she established a lively, cultured court at Mechelen (in present-day Belgium). Some of Margaret's own poetry was set to music by composers at her court. Composers who flourished at Mechelen included the organist Henry Bredemers and the singer/composer Pierre de La Rue. In the early years of Margaret's reign, the future emperor Charles V and his sister, the future Mary of Hungary (1505–58), were educated in music and the other arts under the direction of their aunt. Bredemers was their tutor in music. In 1531 Mary assumed the regency of the Netherlands after Margaret's death and continued to be a patron of court musicians and composers.

The Mechelen court was part of the Spanish Habsburg empire, which controlled the Netherlands, Sicily, Naples, Spain, and Spanish colonies in the Americas. In 1521 the entire Habsburg empire was divided into Spanish and Austrian houses. In the latter, Emperor Ferdinand I (1503–64) championed music in Vienna and other court cities; the imperial Kapelle had expanded to 83 performers by the time that Maximilian II (1527–76) became emperor in

6.2 Three angels singing from a shared choir book, the usual procedure for church choirs. Detail from a painting by Botticelli of the Madonna and Child with Saint John the Baptist, latter 15th century. (Villa Borghese, Rome, Italy/Bridgeman Art Library)

1564. His Kapellmeisters Jacobus Vaet (d. 1567) and Philippe de Monte (d. 1603), with Maximilian's encouragement, directed numerous secular musical events, such as carnivals and tournaments. During the latter 16th century, Italian musicians became very popular in the court cities of Vienna, Innsbruck, and Graz, opening the way for Italian opera to thrive in the Austrian Habsburg empire during the 17th century.

Courtly patrons in the Italian Peninsula included the Medici family in Florence, the Gonzaga dynasty in Mantua, the Este in Ferrara, the Sforza in Milan, the doges of Venice, and the kings of Naples. Galeazzo Maria Sforza (1444–76), the second Sforza duke of Milan, learned to sing at the age of eight. As an adult, the duke was said to enjoy musical performances more than any other pastime. In the process of building his chapel and hiring northern singers and musicians, he antagonized many of his contemporaries, such as Duchess Yolanda of Savoy, by luring away their best performers. The duke paid Josquin Desprez the respectable sum of 160 ducats annually (at a time when one ducat would purchase 10 chickens), although one should note that other musicians and singers were given nonmonetary rewards such as horses, beyond their regular salaries. He also supported the election of Pope Sixtus IV (1414–84), an important patron of music, who built the Sistine Chapel and founded the Sistine choir.

Singing and Performance

Members of the nobility, especially young women, learned to sing and play musical instruments. Mary, queen of Scots (1542–87), for example, was a talented lutenist. Several composers were famous as singers; Ockeghem was known for his deep bass tones. During the late 15th century, sacred music often featured the bass voice, especially in harmony with the contrapuntal line. Itinerant poet-singers maintained the troubadour or Minnesinger tradition of the Middle Ages. These very popular composers, usually men, sang their own music. By the mid-16th century, handbooks were focusing on musical ornamentation, notably for musicians playing the flute and other instruments in the higher tonal ranges. Because the human voice also functions in this range, the same principles of ornamentation could be applied to singing. Even though the handbooks originally pertained to sacred music such as motets, the art of ornamentation also appeared in madrigals and other genres of secular music.

Isabella d'Este, marchioness of Mantua (1474–1539), was an accomplished player of the lute and keyboard as well as a gifted singer. She also had an impressive collection of musical instruments. But in her time, music was largely written for male voices. Later in the 16th century, the soprano voice became a new standard for composers. Vocal parts for soprano were written up to high G. The popularity of ornamentation and the increased range of vocal parts eventually led to extreme virtuosity between about 1575 and 1600. This mannerist development, while dismaying composers who could hardly recognize their own works, contributed to the musical language of early opera. The first opera was presented in Florence in 1598; its music and libretto have not survived. Jacopo Peri's drama *Euridice* was set to music and first performed in 1600. Another result of the desire of audiences and congregations to experience virtuosity in the higher octaves was the castration (removal of the testicles) of boys, to prevent their voices from changing. Because women were not permitted to sing in Catholic choirs, *castrati* sang the soprano parts. (In fact, they did so in Europe until the early 20th century.)

Working Conditions and Social Status

Working conditions for musicians and singers varied, of course, depending on their social standing and on uncontrollable factors such as climate. For choirboys—the largest class of singers by far—their lives revolved around their position as performers of sacred music. They lived together, in housing provided by the cathedral, college, or other institution in which they sang, but their choir master often had to provide other necessities. A document from Tudor England dated 1564 granted one Richard Farrant, master of choristers in Queen's Chapel, his own housing, an organist, and a clerk, with an annual salary of approximately 81 pounds. In turn, for the choirboys Farrant had to "provide them not only clothes and diet but also bedding, and to leave them as well clothed as he finds them" (Scott *Tudor Age*, pp. 103–104). In addition, if a boy was unable to perform, the master of choristers had to find a replacement within one month or be fined by the church. The social status of choir boys was much lower than that of professional solo singers; the former literally singing for their supper while the latter enjoyed the company of nobility and payment for performances. In general, during the Renaissance professional singers were treated better and had a higher social status than did musicians.

Certain instruments were ranked as loftier than others; the loud wind instruments were thought of as being so lowly that women were prohibited to play them in public until the latter 16th century. In addition to producing brash sounds, wind instruments when played required grotesque facial expressions that would have been considered inappropriate for women. In 1514 Castiglione praised courtiers who accompanied their singing on the lute but disparaged accompaniment by wind instruments for producing too unpleasant a sound. Musicians who played wind instruments could not rise to the status of singers, partly because they were not able to accompany themselves singing on instruments that required their breath to be played.

Many municipalities and courts had special bands of wind players, called *piferri* in Italian. One can hear the sound of puffing in the name itself; the word means "shepherd's pipes." During the early 15th century, many *piferri* consisted solely of shawm players (see Wind Instruments, pages 168–169). Then, around 1450, a trombone was added for greater tonal range. These wind bands, being more musical than the military trumpet bands, were more versatile and played at diplomatic functions, local ceremonies such as weddings, and other festive occasions. Most importantly, they provided music for dancing. Wind bands at court, along with all musicians and singers in that environment, usually enjoyed higher social status than municipal bands. Because the various courts competed for the best performers, musicians' salaries were at the level of artists, court physicians, and other professionals. The wind ensembles also played sacred music; the Holy See had both a wind band and a trumpet band.

Beginning in 1580, the Este family in Ferrara patronized the first ensemble of professional female singers—Anna Guarini, Livia d'Arco, Tarquinia Molza, and Laura Peverara. Molza also composed music, chiefly for the harp, viol, and lute. As the fame of this group spread to other Italian city-states, female singers' performing secular music in public became socially acceptable. Although women still were not permitted to sing in Catholic church choirs, the door had been opened for respectable women to perform in public during the late Renaissance. Nevertheless, scholars have questioned whether these women actually benefited from their

rather significant salaries, which probably went directly to their father, uncles, or husband. Whereas noteworthy male composers and performers often were rewarded with luxurious rooms in the palace or country houses, their female counterparts evidently received only a salary, dowry, or tips.

MUSICAL INSTRUMENTS

The spread of Renaissance instrumental polyphony would not have been possible without innovations in instrument production. "Families" of woodwind, brass, and stringed instruments were invented to complement the human voice, in the bass to soprano range. This tonal grouping facilitated the music of instrumental ensembles and enhanced instrumental accompaniment for the human voice. Many medieval instruments, especially the brasses, were improved by scientific advancements in metallurgy and other technical processes. In addition, new instruments such as the harpsichord and violin were invented during this period.

Percussion Instruments

Many of the same types of percussion instruments used during the Middle Ages continued to be popular during the Renaissance. Modern speculations about how percussion instruments were played during the Renaissance are based mostly on visual material and textual comments. From what we can determine through these means, percussion instruments maintained the beat of music for dancing and singing and usually did not add ornamentation or flourishes. For military musical purposes, drums were used to maintain the rhythm of marching, much as they are today. Besides their place in music, drums were sometimes played vigorously before battle. (During the 14th century, Saracen military drummers were famous for the terrifying sounds they produced.)

The side drum and the kettledrum were created during the Renaissance; both became popular during the 16th century. Unlike the medieval tabor drum played with only one stick, the side drum was played with two. This innovation allowed much more flexibility in the style of drumming, and the roll and drag entered the repertoire of military music. The kettledrum, constructed from copper or brass with an average diameter of approximately two feet, could be as shallow as one foot. German instrument makers used two hoops for the drumhead, with the skin first draped over a wooden hoop and a metal hoop then fastened over the rim. Tensioning screws around the rim gave musicians more control over the timbre of their instruments, permitting the kettledrum to produce harmonic sounds for the bass parts of the music. For ceremonial music, kettledrums introduced a majestic presence not heard previously at court. In 1542 King Henry VIII of England (1491–1547) ordered not only kettledrums from Vienna, but also men who knew how to play them well.

Other popular percussion instruments in Renaissance Europe included the tambourine, triangle, cymbals, and castanets, all of which are played today in slightly altered forms. The xylophone and chime bells were valued for both their percussive and melodic qualities. The tuned chime bells did not have clappers; they were struck with small hammers to produce clear, sharp sounds. Shaped as upside-down cups, the bells were made in various sizes, the

6.3 Cortege of drummers and soldiers at the royal entry of Henry II, king of France, into Rouen in 1550. Painted on vellum, c. 1550. Military music was an important aspect of royal patronage. (Bibliothèque Municipale, Rouen, France/Giraudon/Bridgeman Art Library)

largest accompanying church choirs. Smaller sets helped students learn to sing the scale.

Wind Instruments

Renaissance wind instruments consisted of brass instruments, organs, and woodwinds. In *Il Cortegiano* (The courtier, 1528), Baldassare Castiglione (1478–1529) praised keyboard instruments for their sweet harmony, and by the mid-16th century organs produced the most sonorous harmony of all. Especially in Germany, the ponderous church organ of the Middle Ages yielded its importance to more refined instruments with stops and reed pipes for better resonance and control. Arnolt Schlick's (c. 1460–c. 1521) book *Spiegel der Orgelmacher und Organisten* (Mirror of organ makers and organ players, 1511) included building instructions as well as a handbook for both fingering and pedaling.

The three main brass instruments of the Renaissance were the cornet, trumpet, and sackbut (trombone), in various lengths and degrees of complexity. Particularly for trumpets and sackbuts, because of their curved shapes, advances in metallurgy during the Renaissance contributed to their development. New casting techniques and alloys permitted instrument makers to produce brass instruments with much better tonal qualities. The German city of Nuremberg was the leading center for this manufacture. Brass instruments were very important for ceremonial events; for example, 17 trumpets and six sackbuts were played during the coronation of Queen Elizabeth I (1533–1603) in 1558.

Woodwind instruments proliferated during the 15th and 16th centuries. They were quite popular in northern courts, such as those of Emperor Maximilian I and King Henry VIII. Venice, however, was the main center of production, where woodwinds were made in graduated matched sets to guarantee that their sounds would be complementary. The chief woodwind instruments were the shawm, crumhorn, bagpipe, recorder, and flute. Recorders are the woodwind that everyone today associates with early music, and indeed they were played virtually everywhere in both sacred and secular settings. In Spain, for example, the cathedral of Seville owned several recorders, said to give variety to the music, and in 1549 a box of large recorders was received by the new cathedral in Guatemala. Flutes were usually produced in three sizes, tuned to A, D, and G. Flutes played in ensembles became popular in France; Elizabeth I's ambassador to the French court included flute players among his musicians. Renaissance texts about flutes sometimes confused them with recorders, but this error did not pertain to the transverse flute held against the side of the face (what we think of today as a flute). The bagpipe, basically a solo instrument, was played in unison with other bagpipes during military ceremonies and campaigns. Henry VIII's inventory of property listed five bagpipes with ivory pipes, probably used for military occasions. Bagpipes began to be closely associated with Scotland and Ireland during the 16th century, and with simple folk music. The crumhorn ("curved horn"), shaped in a simple J curve, was the earliest woodwind instrument with a reed cap. Made of boxwood, the curved shape was ornamental and served no practical purpose. Crumhorns were especially popular for dances and madrigals, such as the six-part madrigal played during the Medici wedding celebration of 1539. The shawm had a broad cane reed that enabled musicians to produce piercing notes. Because of their loud, bright sounds, shawms were a favorite instrument for outdoor performances. (Today they are still used in parts of Spain for traditional dances and outdoor bands.)

Stringed Instruments

Except for harps, Renaissance stringed instruments had frets and were played by being strummed, bowed, or plucked. We probably think of the lute as the quintessential Renaissance stringed instrument, and both listeners and theorists in the Renaissance would have agreed. Of Moorish origin, the lute has the shape of a pear sliced vertically, with the rounded back creating a lush resonance of sound. Strings were constructed as they had been during the Middle Ages, of either metal or sheep gut. The metal used was brass or steel. Not until the 17th century were strings produced with a central core spun around by brass, which improved the tone on the lower notes. Although the lute could be played with either a plectrum (for plucking) or the fingers, by the mid-15th century strumming or plucking with the fingers was preferred. The lute was considered the ideal musical instrument, with the musician's fingers in close control of the strings creating the purest possible sound, as witnessed by a 16th-century listener, who described a lutenist's playing "with such ravishing skill that, little by little, making the strings languish under his fingers in a sublime way, he transported all those who were listening with so pleasurable a melancholy that . . . it was as if the listeners were ecstatically carried away by some divine frenzy" (Smith 2003, p. 135).

Because of the unsatisfactory lower tones produced on the lute, the slightly larger theorbo and the much larger chitarrone were created during the mid-16th century to accompany the lute. A portrait of Mary Herbert, countess of Pembroke (d. 1622), in Penshurst Place depicts her holding an upright chitarrone almost as tall as she is. The cittern, slightly smaller than the lute, was a medieval instrument usually played solo. Musicians during the Renaissance continued to play it by plucking in the medieval style. Other members of the lute family included the smaller mandora, popular for dance music, and the colascione.

The vihuela and guitar were quite similar, both having frets consisting of gut strings tied around the fingerboard. The guitar was used more for popular and folk music; the vihuela was a favorite instrument of aristocratic society in both Spain and southern Italy. By the close of the 16th century, the guitar had eclipsed the vihuela and was being played throughout Europe. The bowed instruments of the Renaissance included the viol and violin, the former with six strings and the latter four. Partly because the vihuela was very similar to the tenor viol in tuning and shape, the viol is thought to have its origins in Spain during the second half of the 15th century. The violin did not attain its fullest form until the second half of the 16th century. Whereas the violin was (and is) played under the chin or on the shoulder, musicians playing members of the viol family are seated, with the instrument held on the ground or between the legs. The violin was used almost exclusively by professional musicians during the Renaissance, especially for dance music and in the intervals between acts of dramatic performances.

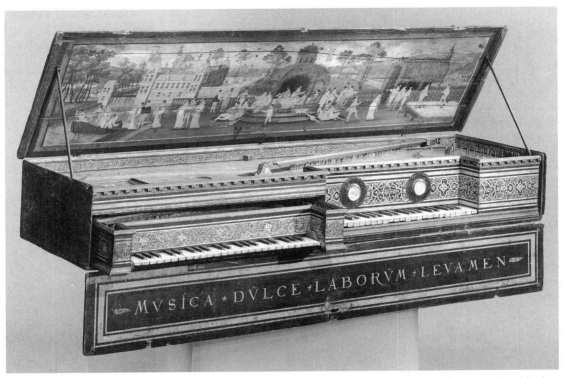

6.4 *Double virginal with pictorial lid. By Hans Ruckers the Elder, 1581.* (The Metropolitan Museum of Art, gift of B. H. Homan, 1929 [29.90])

The harpsichord, perfected during the 15th century, is played by keys that trigger the plucking of strings, unlike the modern piano, in which strings are hammered. Elizabeth I's favorite instrument was a virginal, a member of the harpsichord family. Italy was a major center of harpsichord production during the early 16th century; the earliest extant example is dated 1521 (today in the Victoria and Albert Museum). By the end of the century, Antwerp, notably the shop of Hans Ruckers and his sons, had become known for its harpsichords. Harpsichord cases were elegant pieces of furniture, often lined with velvet, with exteriors of inlaid wood or painted ornamentation including mottoes about music in various languages. They most definitely were instruments for the courtly patron.

PUBLICATION OF MUSICAL MATERIAL

Until the early 16th century, "publishing" musical material usually entailed producing copies in manuscript. These included liturgical manuscripts, often large enough for a small choir to read the music from a single volume. Much secular music circulated in manuscript copies, even during the 16th century after books of printed music were fairly widespread. Until the early 16th century, music was printed from wood blocks, and plainsong printing had achieved technical excellence. However, music with measured signs (usually written within four lines) presented more complications, which were solved in Venice by 1501, and the Venetian method quickly spread to other parts of Europe. Pierre Attaingnant in Paris was the first to print a book of Renaissance music in one impression.

Manuscripts

Examples of liturgical music in multivolume sets that can be viewed today, such as at the cathedral of Toledo, are close to three feet high. Usually produced and bound in monastic shops, such manuscripts were truly a labor of love. Some of the most beautiful manuscripts created during the 15th century are liturgical works hand copied on vellum, with luminous initial letters as large as eight inches square, depicting saints and biblical figures. King David, who played a harp, was a popular image for manuscript psalters. Unlike mass-produced printed music created for a large market, manuscripts could be executed for quite specific audiences. Each Catholic diocese and monastic community localized both the text and music, making it very difficult for printers to provide standard editions of liturgical works. Moreover, the size needed for choir books made printing prohibitively expensive. As late as the 18th century, liturgical music for use of the choir was still being produced in manuscript. These manuscripts in deluxe, illuminated copies were valued as gifts in presentation copies. For example, a manuscript choir book decorated with Margaret of Austria's coat of arms may have been given by her as a gift to Pope Leo X (1475–1521).

For secular music, singers often had manuscript copies of the specific part that each was performing. Called part books, these also appeared in printed versions. In fact, by 1600 most printed music was being produced in this form and not in the scores that we usually think of today. Well into the 17th century, scribes were employed to copy musical texts, especially for operatic performances.

Printed Books

During the 15th century, printers experimented with several methods for printing music with wood blocks, and by about 1473 success had been achieved, as evidenced by a single surviving gradual (part of the liturgy). As printers began to market musical works during the latter 15th century, the diversity of local religious usage, for example, in the Offices, necessitated books in which the Latin text was issued without music with space left for the local text to be inserted by hand. There were also books of sacred music in which only the music appeared, allowing a vernacular text to be inserted if desired. In this stage of early printing, the musical notes were created by wood blocks, in a separate impression from the text. When staves were added, three impressions were required. Ottaviano Petrucci in Venice originated a method for printing music in movable type rather than with wood blocks, reducing the passes through the press. Finally, in 1527/28,

6.5 Three musicians with books of music. By the Master of the Half Figures, between 1500 and 1533. (Hermitage, Saint Petersburg, Russia/Bridgeman Art Library)

the first music book executed in one impression was produced by Pierre Attaingnant in Paris: *Chansons nouvelles en musique a quatre parties* (New songs in music for four parts). His achievement helped to make books of music more easily affordable.

With the spread of printed books during the first half of the 16th century, Protestant churches were able to supply their congregations with personal copies of hymnals and other devotional works. Instead of a trained choir gathering around one gigantic manuscript choir book or sharing a few smaller handwritten books of music, sacred music could be performed by individual worshipers participating personally in the church service. This was only one way in which the art of printing helped to popularize the Protestant religion in Renaissance Europe.

In addition to books discussed previously, the titles described in the following sections are among the printed works that were especially important in the history of Renaissance music. In 1536 Luis de Milán (c. 1500–c. 1561), a Spanish composer living in Valencia, published his *Libro de música de vihuela de mano intitulado El maestro* (Book of music for the vihuela entitled The master). This publication, which includes dance music, was significant because of its indications of tempo. The *Trattado de glosas* (Treatise of glosses) by Diego Ortiz (c. 1510–c. 70) included instructions for ornamentation. Director of the chapel orchestra and choir for the Spanish viceroys in Naples, he wrote this didactic manual about stringed instruments played with a bow. As we have learned, the tonal values of this music permitted the information about ornamentation to be transferred to voice training.

The *Dialogue on Ancient and Modern Music* by Vincenzo Galilei is a good example of how printed information helped to disseminate ideas that otherwise might have remained within a small circle of specialists. Many of the ideas in Galilei's treatise were based on his collaboration with the humanist Girolamo Mei (d. 1594), who had extensively studied ancient Greek musical modes but never published the part of his studies that concerned contemporary music. Most important among these ideas was Mei's criticism of polyphony, which he found musically disordered and inferior for projecting textual meanings. He supported, however, the

cantus firmus (fixed song), which he further developed with an emphasis on textual content of the song. Through Galilei's book, Mei's advocacy of monodic music (sung in a single melodic line) helped bring about an innovation in Western music that contributed to the birth of opera.

MAJOR COMPOSERS

Binchois, Gilles (c. 1400–1460), along with Dufay and Dunstable, was one of the three most significant composers of his time. In the late 1420s Binchois became a member of the court chapel of the duke of Burgundy, where he served as both composer and singer for three decades. His work defined and dignified Burgundian court music, and many of his melodic (tenor) lines were used in the music of other 15th-century composers. Because this court valued tradition, Binchois was not inspired to introduce innovations in his compositions. He was, nevertheless, a master of the rondeau, the dominant form of secular song during the 15th century. Some of Binchois's songs were known in England, not surprisingly, given the cultural interchange between the English and Burgundian courts.

Byrd, William (1543–1623) All the notable Renaissance composers wrote for Catholic Church services; most of them also composed and played secular music. The versatile English composer William Byrd was organist and choirmaster at Lincoln Cathedral from 1563 to 1570. During these years, he learned to experiment with various genres and forms to create his own individual style blending old and new. Byrd may have invented the particularly English form known as the verse anthem: Some of his metrical settings for the Psalms feature stanzas ending with a simple chorus. Between 1570 and 1580, the composer worked for the Chapel Royal (London), where his genius was recognized by influential members of the nobility and royal family, including Queen Elizabeth I. Byrd wrote the music for a piece celebrating English victory over the Spanish Armada, its words written by the queen (entitled "Look and bow down"). In Protestant

England, Byrd did not have appreciable success with most of his published work because of its Catholic overtones. In 1588, however, his *Psalmes, Sonets, and Songs*, published to persuade "every one to learne to singe," became quite popular. Known as *Byrd's Lullabys*, they included sacred music.

Desprez, Josquin (c. 1440–1521), of French origin, was documented as a singer at the cathedral in Milan between 1459 and 1472. During the 1480s and 1490s, he was in Rome as a member of the papal choir. By the turn of the century, Desprez was unofficially working for Louis XII of France, for whom he wrote a motet and songs while recruiting Flemish singers for the court of Ferrara. From 1503 to 1504 he was not only director of the chapel at Ferrara, but also a virtuoso singer commanding the highest salary ever paid to a singer at that court. Desprez ended his career as a singer-composer in northern France at the cathedral of Notre Dame in Condé-sur-l'Escaut. Praised by the writers Castiglione and Rabelais, Desprez was also a favorite composer of Martin Luther's. Desprez is considered the most outstanding composer of his time, on the basis of an impressive 60-year career. His motets have an exceptional expressive range, and the music he wrote for masses usually is closely tied to the words, within ingeniously inventive structures.

Dufay, Guillaume (c. 1400–1474) was one of the most famous French composers of his time. He composed music in Bologna, was papal chaplain in Rome, and worked at the courts of Burgundy and Savoy. His most famous work of music during his lifetime was probably the motet he wrote for the dedication in 1436 of the dome of the Florence Cathedral. Finally, he became director of the chapel in Chambéry for Amadeus, duke of Savoy, writing music in several forms, including motets, masses, and secular ballads. Dufay wrote music for the marriage of the duke's son in 1434, an international event attended by the duke of Burgundy and his entourage.

Dunstable, John (c. 1390–1453) was the most prominent English composer of the early 15th century; 70 works are credited to him, many of which can be found in Continental manuscripts. Between 1422 and 1435 he was in France as a musician in service to John, duke of Bedford, possibly enhancing his reputation outside England. Dunstable's music includes cycles for the mass, motets, and several typically English carols. His compositions were recognizable by their clear harmonies.

Gombert, Nicolas (c. 1490–c. 1566) composed densely textured music, frequently with overlapping phrases and few rests for the voices, preferring five or six voices rather than four. He wrote motets and masses for several important court events, such as the birth of Philip II in 1527 and the coronation of Charles V in Bologna in 1530. More than 60 motets are attributed to Gombert, the texts usually from Scripture, especially Psalms. One of his most famous motets is *Musae Jovis* (Muses of Jove), written in tribute to his teacher Josquin Desprez and utilizing a melodic line from Desprez as the *cantus firmus*. Gombert also left more than 70 *chansons*, most with verses lamenting unhappy love. His concentrated style influenced an entire generation of composers, partially because of the widespread dissemination of his work through collections published in 1539 and 1552.

Lassus, Orlando di (1530/32–1594)   The music of Orlando di Lassus, one of the most admired Franco-Flemish composers of the 16th century, was extraordinarily expressive and inventive. Much of his liturgical work is characterized by precise vocal scoring and chordal harmony. As a boy, Lassus entered the household of Ferrante Gonzaga, a member of the Mantuan dynasty whose court was based in Palermo (Sicily). During his young adulthood, Lassus resided in Naples and Rome; he became choirmaster at Saint John Lateran in 1553 (two years before Palestrina's arrival). In 1556 he accepted an invitation from Duke Albrecht V of Bavaria to join the court in Munich as a tenor in the chapel choir. Lassus remained in Munich as a singer, composer, and musician. His prestige was so great by the time he died that two sons successively inherited his position. Orlando di Lassus wrote at least 60 masses and 101 settings for the *Magnificat*, many of which he adapted from secular music, such as a madrigal by Palestrina. His music for the *Magnificat* circulated widely in manuscripts and printed books. He also wrote a great many motets, including settings for specific ceremonial events honoring the Habsburgs and other court luminaries. These works often alluded to classical texts or included Renaissance humanistic poetry for the words.

Ockeghem, Johannes (c. 1420–1497)   Although the Franco-Flemish master Johannes Ockeghem completed a relatively small number of masses, he was highly esteemed by his contemporaries. Interestingly, two of his unfinished masses were based on melodies from his own secular songs (*chansons*), with polyphonic voices transferred to different parts for the masses. Ockeghem's motets, usually for the Virgin, feature vocal coloration and other forms of ornamentation. His career included two years in Moulins writing music for Charles I, duke of Bourbon, and then many years of service at the French court for kings Charles VII and Louis XI. During the years Ockeghem worked in France, no other composer equaled his creative use of musical sources. Johannes Tinctoris, in his *Liber de arte contrapuncti* (Book on the art of counterpoint), praised the sweetness of Ockeghem's music.

Palestrina, Giovanni Pierluigi da (1525/26–1594) began his career as a choirboy in the church of Santa Maria Maggiore in Rome. In the 1540s Palestrina was playing the organ and teaching music at the cathedral of Palestrina. He returned to Rome in 1551 and a few years later was appointed choirmaster of Saint John Lateran. Palestrina gained a thorough knowledge of techniques and styles as applied to motets and masses. Although in later life he apologized for composing frolicsome madrigals, during his career he wrote some 140 pieces in this genre. The final phase of his career was 23 years as choirmaster for the famous Cappella Giulia at Saint Peter's in Rome. Palestrina's work as a composer of sacred music was prodigious, and 43 of the 104 masses and 177 motets were published during his lifetime. He was one of the greatest composers of sacred music for the Counter-Reformation.

Power, Lionel (d. 1445), along with Dunstable, pioneered the unified mass cycle and was a leader in English music during the first half of the 15th century. Forty works of sacred music are definitely attributed to Power. His compositions in the early-15th-century Old Hall Manuscript, which contains works by several individuals, feature sonorous tones and syncopated rhythms. Power is best known for his innovative rhythmic passages, with asymmetric sequences expressed in modern notation through fluctuating bar lengths. He was also a teacher of music, as master of the choir of the Lady Chapel at Canterbury, where he was in charge of training the choir boys.

Victoria, Tomás Luis de (1548–1611) was the most revered Spanish composer of the 16th century. He wrote sacred music exclusively, using only the Latin texts. Born in Ávila, Victoria was a choirboy in the cathedral and experienced the spiritual ambiance of the town in which Saint Teresa was establishing her rigorous convent life guided by her Discalced ("shoeless") Carmelites of the Reform. From his Jesuit school in Ávila, Victoria was sent to the Jesuit Collegio Germanico in Rome, probably circa 1565. Four years later Victoria was a singer and organist at the Aragonese church in Rome, and in 1572 he published his first collection of motets. By that time he had become choirmaster of the Collegio Germanico, communicating with his German students in Latin. Victoria dedicated his 1583 book of masses to King Philip II and requested to be transferred back to his Spanish homeland. Victoria spent the final three decades of his career in Madrid, as chaplain, choirmaster, and organist. He served the dowager empress Maria, widow of Maximilian II (and daughter of Charles V), at her Franciscan convent, Monasterio de las Descalzas Reales, which had been endowed by her sister, Juana, queen of Portugal. The small chapel in the convent was very beautiful, attracting wealthy merchants and members of the court. This audience helped popularize Victoria's masses and motets. During his lifetime, Victoria was able to publish almost all of the music that he had written (an unusual feat for a Renaissance composer).

Willaert, Adriaan (c. 1490–1562), Flemish composer and singer, began his adult career in the service of the Este court in Ferrara. The well-connected Cardinal Ippolito I d'Este, in whose account books Willaert is listed, probably provided excellent social and political opportunities through which the composer's music became widely known. In 1527 Willaert was appointed as chapel master of Saint Mark's in Venice, where he worked until 1560.

Known for his versatility, Willaert composed Latin masses, motets, hymns, and psalms, as well as Italian madrigals and French *chansons*.

READING

Knighton 2003: listing of important manuscripts and their locations in index, genres in glossary.

Sacred Music

H. Brown 1999: (general study); Burgess 2000: England; Fernandez Collado 2001: Spain (choir books); Haggh 2001: performance, musical culture; Harper 2000: liturgy; McIver 2002: art and music; Nelson 2000: Spain; Oettinger 2001: German Reformation; Pointer 2002: colonial Mexico.

Secular Music

H. Brown 1999: (general study); Bryce 2001: Florence (women performers); Haar 2003: humanism; Henze 2001: love songs; Peters 2000: southern France.

Working Conditions and Patronage

H. Brown 1999: (general study); Macy 2003: women; Mateer 2000: court patronage.

Musical Instruments

Leach 1973: (general survey); McGrattan 2001: wind instruments; Montagu 1976: cultural contexts; Munrow 1980: instruments and their uses; Paganelli 1988: (general study); Polk 2001: Brussels (instrumental music); Smith 2003: plucked instruments.

Publication of Musical Material

Fallows 2003: polyphony; Haines 2004: manuscripts; Noone 2003: manuscripts.

7

WARFARE

Although the Hundred Years' War between England and France ended in 1453 and the Peace of Lodi in 1454 concluded fighting in the Italian city-states, Europe was never free of warfare during the 15th century. England's civil conflict, the Wars of the Roses, lasted from 1452 until 1487, and France was fighting to gain control of both Brittany and Burgundy during this time. Unified under Ferdinand I (1503–64) and Isabella the Catholic (1451–1504), Spain waged a successful campaign against the last Muslim stronghold on the peninsula in 1492. The balance of power of these monarchies was shifted toward Spain in the early 16th century, when its king became Holy Roman Emperor Charles V (1500–1558). His position was strengthened by revenues pouring in from Spanish conquests in the New World.

The regional governing powers in both Italy and Germany were weakened during the late 15th and 16th centuries, the former by invasions of foreign troops and the latter by religious strife. Wars of religion in France essentially became civil war between 1560 and 1598, as Catholics fought Huguenots. Finally, Spanish mismanagement of the Netherlands resulted in several bloody revolts between 1567and 1609. Forces of western Europe occasionally joined against a common foe. In 1571, for example, the joint navies of the emperor, the pope, and Venice defeated the Turks at the Battle of Lepanto. Although ostensibly organized to halt the spread of the "infidel religion," the campaign also sought to dominate trade routes. Economic factors were significant in every major conflict except a few of the religious wars.

Colonial warfare, ostensibly waged to spread Christianity to indigenous people, also had economic motivations as Europeans gained new territory. Even though precious metals in many of these new possessions were less ubiquitous than had been assumed, other riches from the land, such as lumber and spices, validated the expense of military conquest. Warfare in European colonies included the Portuguese in Africa and Asia, the Dutch in Brazil, and the Spanish in Mexico and South America. Although colonial warfare affected western Europe, it is beyond the scope of the present book.

Advances in technology and architecture, especially in metallurgy, the European manufacture of gunpowder, and fortification design, led to changes in battle tactics, armor, and weaponry. French small artillery proved to be a decisive factor in the Hundred Years' War, effectively moving the fighting into the open field. More soldiers were needed because casualties increased, and more mercenaries were hired as the 16th century progressed. By 1550, fortifications were being renovated with the addition of bastion defensive positions, again making it possible to withstand siege warfare waged with artillery. Military medicine progressed somewhat, in that amputations were performed with a greater degree of accuracy as anatomical knowledge advanced. Nevertheless wounds continued to threaten the lives of soldiers because the nature of infection was not understood.

MAJOR WARS

Wars were usually undertaken to gain additional territory or to reclaim lost territory, with rights of inheritance and claims through marriage or treaty given as the reasons for fighting when negotiations failed to produce a settlement of conflicting claims. The potential threat of loss of territory, for example, France's fear that the Holy Roman Empire's possessions would block its access to the rest of Europe via land routes, also prompted military response. Indeed the frontiers of most monarchies were susceptible to attack, regardless of whether the rulers were officially at war. Even in the relatively brief respites between declared campaigns of war, bands of renegade soldiers took advantage of the instability along international borders to plunder towns and estates. During much of the 15th century, conflict was localized. The Italian city-states fought each other as well as foreign threats on Italian soil, the rulers of Spain suppressed their Muslim neighbors, soldiers of the Swiss Confederation successfully asserted independence against the Imperial army, and forces within England struggled over the accession to the throne. France's struggle to put Brittany and Burgundy under control of the Crown set the stage for French hostilities against the Holy Roman Empire, which had possession of Burgundian domains, in the following century.

In the 16th century, the rulers of France, England, and the Holy Roman Empire (who during

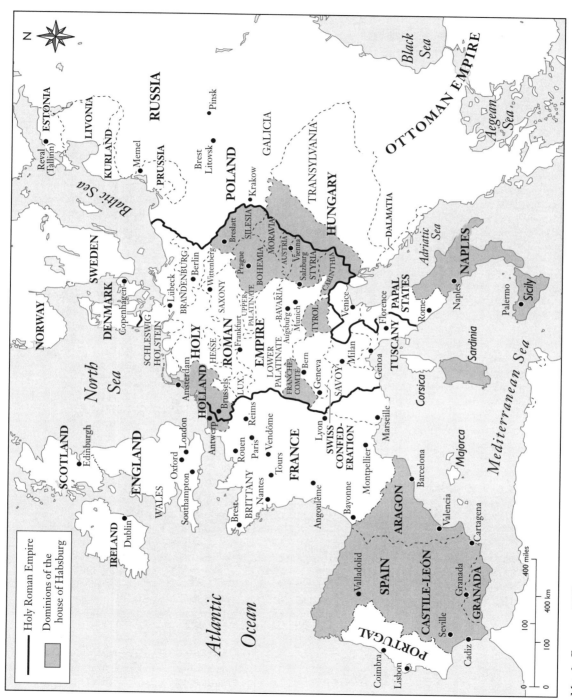

Map 3. *Europe, c. 1519*

part of the 16th century included the king of Spain) dominated warfare in international military campaigns. Their battles were staged in both northern and southern Europe, where personal animosity and competitive egos contributed to their determination to win. During most of their long reigns, Francis I, king of France (1494–1547); Henry VIII, king of England (1491–1547); and Charles V were at war with each other, in sometimes shifting allegiances. Subsidiary hostilities involved conflict between England and France, and between France's royal house of Valois and Charles V's house of Habsburg. At various times, the pope or his allies supported one or more of these three monarchs, particularly in their common cause against Turkish forces. The doge of Venice repeatedly allied his troops with anyone opposing the Turks, because Venice was vulnerable to attacks from its neighbors to the east. By the 1560s, religious turmoil led to the wars of religion in France (see chapter 2) and to fragmented regions across northern Europe. Several monarchs, notably Elizabeth I, queen of England (1533–1603), took advantage of prevailing conditions to billet their own troops in the Netherlands and other areas. Nominally sent for the purpose of assisting Dutch Protestants against the Spanish, these troops also gave England control of two important Dutch ports. As in today's world, countries not technically "at war" still could maintain a hostile presence outside their own borders.

The major wars discussed in the sections that follow present a summary of military conflicts between 1400 and 1600, which often were embroiled with marriage contracts, commercial negotiations, and arguments concerning colonial territory, when the fighting sometimes took place in the colonies themselves.

Hundred Years' War

Technically, the Hundred Years' War between England and France lasted from 1337 to 1453, with intermittent periods of peace. Its premise was England's claim via marriage to the French throne, with hostilities encouraged by the ducal leaders of Burgundy and Brittany in France. During the conflict England lost Gascony and Normandy but kept control of the port city of Calais until 1558. This war ended with the Treaty of Tours, but other Anglo-French conflicts during the Renaissance were rooted in simmering hostilities engendered by the Hundred Years' War, exacerbated by religious differences after the 1530s.

Wars of the Roses

The Wars of the Roses during the 15th century, civil wars over the succession to the English throne, were fought between the house of Lancaster and the house of York. Both families had a rose as their heraldic device. From the outset, the Lancastrians were less popular because they had been responsible for the huge drain of men and other resources lost in the Hundred Years War. Fighting was notoriously brutal because hundreds of angry soldiers returned from France and enlisted haphazardly on either side, simply to have the opportunity to fight and plunder. Begun in 1455, the Wars of the Roses ended with the Battle of Bosworth in 1485, after which Henry VII (1457–1509) was crowned as king and the house of Lancaster was defeated. A member of the house of Tudor, he was a nephew of the house of York and married Elizabeth of York.

The Final "Reconquest" in Spain

The Reconquest of Spain (Reconquista in Spanish) commenced in the 13th century when Spanish Christians captured the city of Córdoba from the Muslims. By the late 13th century, only the region of Granada remained under Muslim control. Isabella and Ferdinand rallied their troops in 1491 and took Granada in January 1492. This victory, which marked the last stage of the Reconquest, was celebrated throughout Europe as a triumph over the "infidel."

Swiss Wars

The Swiss Confederation, consisting of German-speaking cantons united for military defense, became known during the 15th century for the organization and expertise of their fighting men. They defeated the Burgundian army in several encounters between 1456 and 1477. In the major Swiss War, against Emperor Maximilian I (1459–1519), the Confederation was victorious over Imperial troops in 1499. Thus the Confederation gained its independence and Swiss mercenaries became the most sought-after soldiers in western Europe.

Italian Wars

During the Italian Wars the Austrian Habsburg dynasty and the French Valois dynasty fought for supremacy in Italy. The wars lasted from 1494 until their official end in the 1559 Peace of Cateau-Cambrésis (discussed later). Whereas localized wars in Italy were ubiquitous in the major northern cities during the 15th century, the Italian Wars were characterized by international involvement of foreign powers. The papacy initially supported its traditional ally, the Holy Roman Emperor, Charles V, but later, alarmed by the increasing power of the Habsburgs in Italy, formed a league with the French King, Francis I. Several Italian rulers of city-states also participated in this conflict, sometimes preferring probable temporary foreign domination to control by neighboring cities. France relinquished all claims in Italy in 1559. (See the discussions of the major battles, many of which pertain to the Italian Wars.)

Austro-Turkish Wars

The Turkish army assaulted Austria twice during the 16th century, advancing as far as Vienna in 1529 and 1532 but failing to take the city. The most famous siege of Vienna took place in 1529, when the 20,000 soldiers in the city were outnumbered by Turkish forces 10 to one. Ironically the sultan was foiled by the huge number of troops because his source of supply was too far away to support such a large encampment. The siege was lifted by a combination of brilliant defensive fighting within the city and the threat that Imperial forces would be sent to aid the Austrians.

Schmalkaldic War

Lasting only two years, 1546–47, the Schmalkaldic War was fought between Imperial troops of Charles V and German Protestant princes who had formed the Schmalkaldic League in 1531. Charles V won a decisive victory at the Battle of Mühlberg, supported by Maurice of Saxony (1521–53) and his army.

Anglo-Scottish Conflicts

Anglo-Scottish skirmishes concerning their common frontier accelerated into an international conflict during the 1560s and 1570s, with the influence of Mary, queen of Scots (1542–87), supported by the French. The daughter of a member of the house of Guise, Mary was raised in a household where the French language and French sympathies prevailed. Descended from Henry VII, Mary claimed to be heir to the throne of England, and as a Catholic she had the backing of the king of France. Her marriage in 1558 to Francis II (1544–60), heir to the French Crown, enhanced her appeal to the French but alienated her from Protestant groups in Scotland as well as from Protestant England. When Mary's own subjects rose up against her in 1567, she sought asylum in England, where Elizabeth placed her under house arrest. Mary's ongoing plotting with the French against England finally resulted in her execution.

Revolt of the Netherlands

In 1555 Philip II, king of Spain (1527–98), became the duke of Burgundy, which controlled the Netherlands at the time. Desiring to live in Spain, he appointed his half sister, Margaret of Parma (1522–86), as regent. Philip also assigned Jesuits to the Netherlands to fight Protestantism and establish the Inquisition. Beginning in 1567, the provinces rebelled and Philip's response was relentless. Led by William of Orange (1533–84), the Protestant forces took Holland and Zeeland. In 1576, however, marauding Spanish troops attacked the city of Antwerp in what has been called the "Spanish fury," murdering thousands and destroying entire neighborhoods. The fighting became very fierce during the 1580s, as England and France entered the war to assist the United Provinces. For France, this action was a continuation of the Habsburg–Valois hostilities discussed earlier. Although a truce declared in 1609 gave the Dutch colonial rights in the West Indies, a treaty was never completed. These hostilities led to the Thirty Years War, the most violent in Europe's history until the 20th century.

Turkish War

The Turkish War was fought between Hungary and the Ottoman Turks, between 1593 and 1606. Austrian forces aided the Hungarians, with the aim of ending Turkish prospects of further European expansion. The Ottomans won several battles and raised the siege of Buda in 1602, but coalition forces captured Pest. The war was settled by treaty in 1606, whereby Turkey officially recognized the Holy Roman Empire.

ARMOR AND TRADITIONAL WEAPONRY

As weapons became more lethal during the 15th century, especially as firearms began to be used in warfare, body armor and armor for horses were modified to provide better protection. Increased protection meant decreased mobility, however, and full body armor consisting of tempered steel plates was not thick enough to withstand short-range gunfire. In Western society, the Renaissance was the only period during which plated armor covering the entire body was used in warfare. By the 17th century, firearms had become so powerful and efficient at short distances that defensive measures necessitated good marksmanship, which required the ability to maneuver quickly and adroitly. Thus Renaissance body armor, which somewhat restricted movement, became obsolete.

Tournament armor, unlike field armor, was heavy and thick to prevent mortal injury. Parade armor, purely ceremonial, was extravagantly decorated by a variety of metalworking techniques.

Armor

FIELD ARMOR

Medieval body armor consisted of chain mail, a strong mesh of small iron rings. Although this type of armor allowed great flexibility, that very attribute was its weakness. There was no rigid resistance against the points of arrows and spears and against bludgeoning from missiles such as stones and rocks. Chain mail was later supplemented with plates of solid bone, leather hardened by boiling, and steel. By the 14th century, soldiers were protected by plates of metal attached to a heavy fabric vest, with separate plates shielding the arms and legs and a metal helmet for the head. The development of tempered steel crossbows and efficient firearms, however, necessitated additional protection. Between 1400 and 1600, as advances in technology improved offensive capabilities, defensive tactics and weapons also were improved, and military budgets rose at astronomical rates. The most skillful armor makers during the early Renaissance were in Milan, and by 1420 they had created a full suit of plate armor. Moderate flexibility was achieved by overlapping or interlocking the plates, which were connected by leather straps or rivets. Even for a relatively large combatant, a suit of field armor rarely weighed more than 60 pounds; unwieldy, heavy armor would have been disastrous in warfare. The steel in 15th-century armor was extremely hard, designed to deflect arrows and blows from pikes, swords, maces, and other weapons. Steel of this hardness, however, could split or shatter if fired upon by guns. A soldier with slivers of steel embedded in his flesh was much more susceptible to infection than a soldier wounded by a simple musket ball. Although armor makers attempted to produce steel that was more pliant and could bend slightly instead of shattering, they were not very successful. In the end the only effective method for making armor resistant to firearms was to make it thicker, and soldiers could not fight when wearing full body armor thick enough to resist fired projectiles. The answer was to focus on vital parts of the body, including the head and torso, and heavy breastplates and plates for the back replaced full armor by the end of the 16th century. Armor for horses during the Middle Ages consisted of chain mail extending over the tops of the legs and a helmet of chain mail. Cavalry horses during the Renaissance also had armor, including a helmet covering most of the head. While horse helmets often were made of thick leather, the body armor of horses consisted of curved or interlocking metal plates, with raised bosses for deflecting arrows and other projectiles. The legs, however, were left uncovered for speed and mobility.

TOURNAMENT AND PARADE ARMOR

Tournament armor during the Middle Ages was the same used as field armor. During this period tournaments (or jousts) served as training and conditioning for actual warfare. Men were sometimes killed during tournament competition, which could be brutal. By the 15th century, public tournaments resembled sporting events, and specific armor was used for each type of competition. Because tournament armor was worn only a short time for a specific purpose, it was thicker and heavier to provide maximal protection for the participant. This armor sometimes required a winch to lift a knight onto the horse, and anyone wearing such armor often could not stand up in it after falling to the ground. Firearms were not used during Renaissance tournaments; the usual weapons were lances for horseback contests and swords and axes for fighting on foot.

Parade armor, which evolved during the early 16th century, was not worn in any type of battle, including tournaments. All Renaissance armor was decorated, even if only with a narrow band incised around the edges; however, parade armor was magnificently ornamented, for both knights and horses. Artists such as Holbein and Dürer made designs for etching on armor. The three techniques for armor decoration were etching, embossing, and damascening, in conjunction with gilding and bluing. Inlays often consisted of gold and silver. Parade

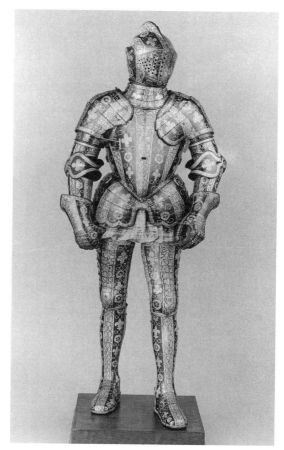

7.1 *Armor of George Clifford, third earl of Cumberland, c. 1580–85. Made in the royal workshops, Greenwich, England.* (The Metropolitan Museum of Art, Munsey Fund, 1932 [32.130.6])

armor was a symbol of status and power, and ancient Roman motifs were used in the ornamental imagery. Classical figures were displayed alongside biblical quotations and saints, with heraldic designs proclaiming the wearer's identity and rank. Parade shields gave artists an especially cohesive surface for creating elaborate designs; the inner surface of these shields was sometimes lined with fabric and painted with hunting scenes or other appropriate motifs.

Traditional Weaponry

HANDHELD WEAPONRY

Medieval handheld weapons, improved by advances in metallurgy, continued to be used by soldiers during the first half of the Renaissance. The chief types of traditional weaponry were those with sharp edges, those with sharp points on a staff, and those that shot projectiles such as arrows, supplemented by projectiles hurled from a sling. Sharp-edged weapons for warfare included daggers and swords. The heavy medieval sword, wielded with two hands for cutting, metamorphosed into a lighter, narrower weapon that could be used to stab into the body where pieces of plate armor were joined. Cavalry most often used the lance, a steel-tipped staff 10 to 12 feet in length. Held by a seasoned knight charging at full tilt on an experienced horse, the lance was a formidable weapon. Foot soldiers used the halberd or pike, on a staff approximately six feet long. Swiss pikemen, who often stood their ground against a cavalry charge, were the most respected foot soldiers of the era. Archers used the crossbow or longbow; the English were renowned for their superiority in the latter. The longbow had one advantage over the crossbow in that its rate of fire was at least twice as fast. Loading the crossbow and winding the tension lost crucial seconds in the midst of battle.

ARTILLERY

During siege warfare, very large slings and catapults were used to bombard walls with stones in attempts to create a breach through which troops could attack. One of the most powerful of these was the trebuchet, originally operated by teams of men pulling on a rope to create the tension that, when released, would hurl projectiles. During the 12th century, counterweights replaced human force. Winches pulled the counterweight down, and a trigger released the heavy projectile with some degree of accuracy. By the 15th century, accuracy had been improved by the use of round projectiles, including iron spheres. Aggressive bombardment by a trebuchet against a medieval wall was bound to cause significant damage. One disadvantage of this sort of mechanical siege machine, however, was that sol-diers operating it were somewhat vulnerable to defensive firepower. Open space was required so that no one would be injured when the trigger was released.

Fired Projectiles

Gunpowder originated in China, and probably reached western Europe in the 13th century. Firearms as well as larger artillery were being used in western Europe by the 14th century, and the price of gunpowder dropped significantly after it could be manufactured in Europe. This decreased cost was one reason that larger artillery guns became feasible near the turn of the 14th century. By 1409, the duke of Burgundy had a cannon that could shoot stones weighing up to 900 pounds. One of the famous artillery pieces of the 15th century was the iron "Mons Meg" made in Flanders, with a bore diameter of nearly 20 inches (on display today in Edinburgh). The amount of gunpowder required to fire such a cannon was prodigious, meaning that a single piece of artillery could normally use more than 100 pounds of powder during a siege. By the mid-15th century, military commanders had devised a system of utilizing smaller firearms to provide covering fire while gunpowder was repacked in the firing chamber by the artillery crew. Firearms were used in conjunction with artillery as well as with more traditional weapons and were especially effective in siege warfare. The Hussites, for example, devised a weapon known as the Wagonburg in which a group of soldiers firing arquebuses fought alongside archers with crossbows. Gunpowder led to new battle tactics, different types of armor, and finally, lethal warfare such as the world had never witnessed. In 1620 the philosopher Francis Bacon claimed that gunpowder was one of the major agents of change in Western society. Between 1400 and 1600 the manufacturing of firearms and their use in warfare altered not only technological processes but also the political face of Europe.

FIREARMS

There were no standards for ammunition or for the caliber of guns. Certain general statements can, however, be made concerning several aspects of firearms. Gun barrels gradually became longer, the size of the charge increased, the highest-quality firearms were made of cast bronze, and forged iron was used for smaller, cheaper weapons. Cast-iron technology was only beginning in Europe during the Renaissance. Obviously, a firearm cast in one piece was safer and more reliable than one forged in several parts. New field tactics developed to maximize the power and noise of firearms, even though the trajectory of their projectiles was somewhat unpredictable. The "Swiss Square" battle formation, for example, was a mass of soldiers with long pikes grouped in a solid square, with groups of soldiers on two sides armed with arquebuses. Until ballistics improved considerably during the 17th century, soldiers with firearms usually were complemented by soldiers equipped with traditional handheld weapons. In Renaissance warfare, except in very close-range firing, soldiers did not take aim at a specific individual. They simply fired toward the enemy, hoping to hit someone. More often than not, their shots went awry.

ARTILLERY

Artillery discharged with gunpowder was a much more effective weapon than small firearms during this period. In the Bohemian civil wars during the early 1420s known as the Hussite Wars, small cannons played an important role in the decisive victory of rebel forces. Fear of Hussite advance spurred Germany to focus on the manufacture of firearms and to incorporate artillery in military planning. French artillery became famous across Europe when it ended the final phase of the Hundred Years War, and Span-ish cannons drove the Muslims out of Granada in 1492. To military strategists at the beginning of the 16th century, artillery was clearly the key to future conquests. Warfare changed considerably during the 16th century, especially field warfare fought in the open, and cavalry gradually ceased to be an important component of warfare. The Italian Wars, fought between 1494 and 1559, were a testing ground for new weaponry and new battle tactics, especially among Spanish troops who had benefited from their experience in Granada. Although breech-loading cannons were used in Italy, the majority of the artillery pieces were muzzle loading. Soldiers had special tools for cleaning and loading the cannon, and for tamping the charge into the breech. There were also daggers marked on the blade with a scale for weighing shot. Gunners used a quadrant to sight the target in order to know how high to elevate the barrel.

SOLDIERING

Mercenaries dominated the armies of Renaissance Europe, sometimes changing sides when the price was right or refusing to fight if they had not been paid. By the 16th century, these companies were supplemented by standing professional armies along with militia. During the 15th century, cavalry mercenaries such as the condottieri of Italy were important elements of fighting in the open field. With the technological advancement of fired projectiles, skilled infantrymen became more strategically useful.

Although women did not fight as soldiers, they were ordered to the barricades and bulwarks in times of siege warfare. Tremendous amounts of dirt had to be moved to construct bulwarks, which often had to be erected on short notice. Women of all ranks and ages, from 12 to 50, shoveled dirt and carted it in wheelbarrows. Occasionally they were recognized and rewarded for their participation in defensive warfare. In 1472, for example, the sumptuary laws were relaxed in Beauvais (France) for the women who had helped prevent the duke of Burgundy from seizing control.

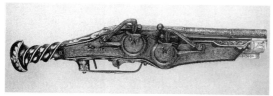

7.2 *Double-barreled wheel lock pistol of Charles V, c. 1540–45. Made by Peter Peck, Munich, Germany.* (The Metropolitan Museum of Art, gift of William H. Riggs, 1913 [14.25.1425])

7.3 Battle scene depicting pikemen and cavalrymen. Woodcut in Sebastian Franck, Germaniae Chronicon *(Chronicle of Germany, 1538).* (Photograph courtesy of Sotheby's, Inc., © 2003)

The Army

MERCENARIES

Mercenaries are soldiers who fight because they are paid for their services, and usually they are employed by countries to which they have no allegiance. During the Renaissance the majority of fighting soldiers were mercenaries. The total number of mercenary troops in Europe in the 16th century has been averaged at 500,000. When we mention "the troops fighting for Metz in 1490," for example, those soldiers included Albanians, French, Italians, Flemish, Germans, and Spaniards. During France's aggressive actions in Italy during the late 15th and early 16th centuries, Swiss pikemen were a mainstay of the French infantry. As did the Swiss companies and the German Landsknechte, most small companies of mercenaries during the Renaissance consisted of soldiers recruited as a group from one geographic area. Typically these regions, such as Gascony, Swabia, and Scotland, were plagued with a high rate of unemployment and depressed economy. Because language barriers could be a problem, it was strategically important that the most cohesive groups of fighting men be able to communicate effortlessly among themselves. By 1500 these companies might have more than 100 men. Heavily armed cavalrymen and pikemen dominated the market for mercenaries in the 15th century, and infantry soldiers experienced in use of artillery and small firearms gradually replaced most of the cavalry between 1500 and 1600. The most famous mercenaries on horseback during the 15th century were the condottieri of Italy (discussed later).

Regular pay was only one of the benefits of fighting as a mercenary. Taking prisoners for ransom was a lucrative business in Renaissance warfare. Mercenaries also looted the baggage trains of enemy forces and seized booty in conquered cities. Occasionally they were out of control, as in the 1527 sack of Rome and the 1576 sack of Antwerp. In these events, mercenaries stole priceless treasures from the sacristies of churches and cathedrals and destroyed property. They were also infamous for cruelty and sexual excesses. The life of a mercenary probably appealed to some men who had maverick, asocial personalities. Nevertheless, mercenaries had their own codes of honor and sometimes refused to fight, or only pretended to fight, when opposed by fellow countrymen.

CONDOTTIERI

Italian condottieri were leaders of (mainly) cavalry-men working under a *condotta*, a contract in which they promised to supply a certain number of soldiers for a finite period. Condottieri and their companies were the most efficient and respected fighters of 15th-century Italy. Most condottieri companies originated in city-states other than those for which they were fighting, with the result that they might find themselves fighting in their home state against home forces. Apparently this system was acceptable to those who followed the profession of soldier. Many Italian mercenaries fighting for condottieri were from Umbria, Romagna, or the Marche, remote or economically depressed regions. Although one condottieri was the son of a butcher and another the son of a baker, normally such leaders did not advance through the ranks. Most condottieri were of noble birth, and several of the most noteworthy were lord of their city-state, such as the Estes and Gonzagas. Although almost all condottieri were Italian, or at least half-Italian, a few illustrious foreigners led Italian mercenary companies. The most famous was the Englishman Sir John de Hawkwood (c. 1320–94).

STANDING ARMIES AND MILITIA

As warfare became a predictable aspect of life by the mid-15th century, commanders in chief began to think about how they could be best prepared for the next conflict. France was the first country to establish a standing permanent army: Charles VII (1403–61) ordered that permanent companies of cavalry be organized, and Louis XI (1482–1515) established a permanent infantry. Naturally as soon as one major European power had a standing army, others had to follow. Italy, especially Milan, Venice, and Naples, soon had standing armies as well. One serious problem was that permanent armies existed to fight. During peacetime these soldiers often marauded through towns and villages on their chargers, wreaking havoc and terrifying the populace. In addition, they were usually accompanied by prostitutes and other unsavory characters. Of another caliber completely were the impressive numbers of permanent guards who protected the immediate vicinity of rulers across Europe. Queen Isabella, for example, had 1,100 infantry and 130 knights, and Francis I had 720 soldiers assigned to his household. These soldiers, much more than just bodyguards, often marched to war with their leader and instructed new recruits.

Although militia were organized during the 16th century, their members had very little training or opportunity to practice with their weapons, which were handheld. The strategy of military commanders during this period depended on maneuvering fairly large groups of soldiers as single units, such as pikemen alongside gunners. Small towns in Europe usually did not have groups of men who all fought with the same weapon. The following report describes the battle readiness of a typical English village: "The said armour and ammunition . . . is kept in one several place of every town, appointed by the consent of the whole parish, where it is always ready to be had and worn within an hour's warning. . . . Certes there is almost no village so poor in England (be it never so small) that hath not sufficient . . . readiness to set forth three or four soldiers, as one archer, one gunner, and a billman [man with a bill-hook] at the least" (Scott 1976, p. 244, from William Harrison's 1587 *Description of England*). These soldiers often set out without any idea of how to follow instructions for deploying their weapons during actual warfare. The situation became even worse toward the end of the 16th century, when firearms used in battle were not always the same firearms used in hunting, so that militiamen had to fight not only in unfamiliar formations, but with unfamiliar weapons. There were, of course, exceptions to these conditions, such as militia near court centers who were occasionally drilled by the princely guards.

COMMUNICATIONS AND SUPPLY LINES

An army could advance no faster than its supplies, and heavy artillery slowed the daily pace of baggage wagons pulled by horses. Depending on the weather and terrain, an army transporting artillery could move forward no more than three to nine miles per day. Ammunition had to be hauled for firearms because soldiers no longer could use local stones for siege attacks. Even though wheat or other grain was sometimes acquired from local suppliers, each army usually traveled with its own flour mills and portable ovens, necessitated by the great quantity of bread required for provisioning troops. Moreover, as plate armor became heavier, soldiers no longer wore it on long marches unless the enemy was nearby. Armor, too, had to be transported in the baggage trains, adding to the weight and slowing the march. The numbers of individuals who had to be supplied with food were staggering, an average of one noncombatant for each soldier, doubling the mouths to be fed. Every member of the nobility had several attendants, and some of them even took their "wife," although that practice was discouraged if not forbidden. When the French king Henry II (1519–59) joined the Lutheran princes to oppose Charles V, he estimated that his 50,000 troops would be accompanied by almost as many noncombatants.

During battle, communication could be impeded by the international composition of the troops. One advantage of hiring mercenaries was that at least each company's own members could communicate easily. Certain basic commands were effected by hand signals and signal flags; fighting usually ended at nightfall. When those engaged in battle needed reconnaissance information, a runner was sent. Military runners also carried communications between front-line commanders and the commander in chief. For such communications carried over an appreciable distance, a rider was used. The practical limits of communication with military headquarters by horseback riders became evident as the Turks advanced across eastern Europe. Turkish efforts in the siege of Vienna were futile because Vienna was too far from Constantinople to allow effective transmission of battle plans.

COMMAND STRUCTURE

During the Renaissance the main purpose of a military command structure was to impose discipline and cohesion on a disparate group of individuals. Developing out of feudal warfare in which a knight was the smallest fighting unit, the earliest command structure in the 15th century employed a horseman in armor in charge of a small combat group. This fighting unit, called a lance, was first organized in France. It consisted of a knight, his squire and page, a few mounted archers, and a servant. For battle the lances were organized into "conroys" of fewer than 100 men, in groups based on geographic origin or language. The convoys fought alongside mercenary bands with comparable numbers of men and alongside groups of Swiss pikemen.

As warfare became more professionalized during the 15th century and the discipline of Swiss pikemen became the standard to be emulated, the concept of a military regiment evolved within the Landsknechte. Mustering, in which recruits were read their terms of service and swore to follow their officers, was required. Each company (of approximately 400 men) was overseen by a colonel, and each platoon of 40 men elected its own leader. Other appointed officers mediated disputes among platoon leaders and imposed disciplinary measures. This regimental system was adopted by military commanders in other areas, who recognized the value of the esprit de corps fostered within the platoon. The commander in chief was, of course, the king or duke, whose general commanded the colonels in charge of each company. When the monarch was present at a battle, he usually commanded a special reserve group who would charge into the conflict if the general faltered.

BATTLE TACTICS

Organizing a battle in the field was a matter of selecting groups of fighters appropriate for the specific conditions and type of enemy to be engaged. Mountainous terrain, for example, required more infantrymen and archers than horsemen in heavy armor. Whatever the configuration of soldiers, having more troops than the enemy was crucial because sheer numbers often won the day. Military commanders usually arranged their troops in a main battle line, with a vanguard, rearguard, and two flanks. The battle line could have several shapes, depending on the terrain and available men; favorite arrangements were a dense, solid square of pikemen or a thick crescent of infantrymen. Archers or gunners often filled the ranks of the flanking troops. Battle tactics during this period involved "shock" tactics of hitting the enemy first and hitting him hard with pikemen, armored horsemen, or artillery. Surprise encounters, however, were sometimes effective, and the best surprise were massive desertions by the enemy's own soldiers. One tactic used as a last resort, but surprisingly successful when used, was for a large group of soldiers to pretend to flee. An enemy who broke ranks to chase them became vulnerable to attack from flanking troops who could be hiding in a forest or behind a hill.

The Navy

During the late 15th and even more so during the 16th century, the experience of sailors during naval warfare changed considerably. Before the invention of naval artillery, sailors and officers usually won battles in the open sea only by close hand-to-hand combat. The main alternative was ramming a vessel broadside, a very risky maneuver. Before the invention of gunpowder, medieval war machines could be used to sling or catapult projectiles against the decks of enemy ships during naval encounters near shore. On the open sea, smaller war machines could be used from the attacking vessel. If burning pitch was hurled, it could burn the sailors as well as set part of the ship on fire. In the days of sailing vessels, a ship was disabled if the rigging and sails were severely damaged. Catapulted rocks could jeopardize a ship, but the damage to individual enemy sailors was limited. On the open water, an attacking ship had to row or sail close enough to an enemy ship to toss grappling hooks against the rails, then haul the ship alongside to board it for combat. With the pitching and tossing of ships in the open sea, arrows were usually less effective than on land. Sailors often had to fight aboard the enemy ship, with daggers, swords, clubs, and other medieval types of weaponry. One group of attackers was often assigned to search the captain's cabin and the bridge for maps and sailing charts. When an attack was imminent, some captains tossed their maps into the sea rather than risk their being seized and used by the enemy. The Portuguese, for example, were famous for destroying their sailing charts in the face of an attack.

Naval artillery consisted of large carriage-mounted cannons. Although cannons had been used in naval warfare as early as the 14th century, they required heavy, awkward mounts on the main deck of a ship. This location made smaller ships top heavy and exposed both the artillery and sailors operating it during bombardment. Not until the early 16th century did military engineers devise a better method for installing naval artillery. Gun decks were added, closer to the waterline for better stability, along with gun ports through which the weapons could be discharged. The main disadvantage was that if a ship with cannons close to the waterline was damaged and began to sink, water could pour in through the gun ports and the weight of the weaponry could drag the ship underwater. This happened to the English vessel *Mary Rose* in 1545 while engaged in battle with the French near the coast of Portsmouth. Most naval artillery during the Renaissance was made of iron and fired stones or pieces of iron. Bronze cannons were significantly lighter, but also much more expensive to produce. (Some ancient bronze statues were melted down during this period to provide the raw material for casting cannons and other weapons.) The weight and deployment of this type of artillery ultimately led to the popularity of the full-rigged, relatively large galleon as a battleship.

European superiority in naval artillery won the 1571 Battle of Lepanto for the Christian coalition united against the Turks, the greatest military triumph of the Renaissance. The victory was celebrated in songs, poems, paintings, and tapestries. This encounter is also famous in military history as the last major battle involving ships propelled by oars. The ships of the Holy League met the Turkish fleet near the Gulf of Corinth, and more than 500 vessels participated in the conflict. Including slaves, conflicts, and press-ganged men as oarsmen for the galleys, along with sailors, there were at least 140,000 individuals involved in the battle. The Christian captains ordered their officers to fire at point-blank range, killing some 20,000 Turkish sailors by cannon impact, fire, or drowning. The damage inflicted on a ship's personnel by repeated artillery fire could be horrific, for example, during the 1596 English attack on the Spanish port of Cádiz when ships were burning: "The spectacle was very lamentable on their side; for many drowned themselves; many, half-burnt, leapt into the water; very many hanging by the ropes' end by the ship's side, under the water even to the lips; many swimming with grievous wounds, strucken under the water, and put out of their pain. And withal so huge a fire, and such tearing of the ordnance in the great *Philip*, and the rest, when the fire came to them, as if any man had a desire to see Hell itself, it was there most lively figured" (Scott 1976, p. 259, letter written by Sir Walter Raleigh). The English sunk almost all the enemy ships in the harbor.

MILITARY MEDICINE

Advances in anatomical knowledge during the 16th century allowed more efficient surgical procedures, and more successful amputations were a direct result in military medicine. Broken bones could also be repaired after a fashion if the break was clean and the bones were not crushed. In treating open wounds, such as slashes from a sword, surgeons began to understand more fully the locations of major blood vessels and how to tie them off to prevent hemorrhaging. The French surgeon Ambroise Paré (1510–90) was a pioneer in Renaissance military medicine. Although he did not comprehend the nature of microbes, he experimented with various field dressings to fight infection, and he attempted to make the treatment of soldiers a more humane process. The brutal nature of fighting, however, exacerbated by the increasing popularity of firearms during the 16th century, challenged the scientific knowledge of medical specialists during this era.

Infection

Soldiers often died of infected wounds; stabs and gunshot wounds were especially difficult to treat because often they were punctures deep into the flesh. When Ambroise Paré first began working as a field surgeon, the common treatment for a gunshot wound was to pour boiling oil into the hole and cauterize it. Having run out of the proper oil on one occasion, Paré acci-

dentally discovered a better, more humane dressing for this type of wound: "At last I wanted oil and was constrained instead thereof to apply a digestive of yolks of eggs, oil of roses, and turpentine . . . [The next morning] I found those to whom I had applied my digestive medicine, to feel little pain, and their wounds without inflammation or tumor . . . The others, to whom was used the said burning oil, I found feverish, with great pain and tumor about the edges of their wounds. And then I resolved with myself never so cruelly to burn poor men wounded with gunshot" (Ross and McLaughlin 1968, p. 561). Later in his career Paré bribed an Italian surgeon to reveal the secret of an amazingly successful field dressing; it consisted of turpentine, oil of lilies, and crushed earthworms boiled up with newborn puppies. Although such procedures may seem barbaric in today's world of modern medicine, we must realize that gunshot wounds were relatively new problems in battlefield medicine. Gangrene was the result of badly infected wounds, and amputation was usually the only remedy.

Field Conditions

Wealthy officers and commanders took their doctors with them on military campaigns, and bands of mercenary soldiers paid for their own barber-surgeons. For the common soldier, however, the ratio of men to doctors was probably about 150 to one. Although this ratio might be acceptable in a peaceful village, it was inadequate during warfare. Triage approaches to treatment could leave a soldier with "only" a gunshot wound lying in a filthy field for hours, until infection was unpreventable. On the whole, soldiers shot by guns died more often than those wounded by pikes and similar weapons, but the latter weapons often caused more bleeding and obvious trauma, which had to be treated. Other traumatic conditions in Renaissance warfare were frostbite and freezing—the former causing disfigurement if fingers and toes or a nose and ears had to be amputated, and the latter causing death. Numerous soldiers froze to death while sleeping in the fields around Metz, for example, during the siege of 1552. Unlike in medieval warfare, when armies in the north of Europe usually went home during the winter, Renaissance campaigns became year-round events, especially in siege warfare.

Also, during an era when microbes were not properly understood, in any large group of people gathered closely together as soldiers are during warfare, epidemic diseases were rampant. Dysentery, sweating fevers, and typhoid were particularly virulent during some campaigns, killing more soldiers than did battle.

Aftermath of Warfare

An aspect of military medicine unrelated to warfare itself was the return home of large numbers of sick and mutilated veterans, who discovered that they had no pension and no recognition of any value. Moreover, no medical treatment was provided for those who needed additional care, such as surgery correcting a badly set bone or cleaning of the stump of a botched amputation. In an age that had no industrialized machinery with its concomitant accidents, men in such wounded condition were rarely seen in public on a daily basis. The psychological damage must have been severe, especially for those who no longer were able to support their family and were forced to become beggars. One notable exception to this situation was the attention paid to injured and fallen condottieri in the republic of Venice. To encourage greater loyalty, Venice offered medical care to the injured, military pensions, state funerals, and occasionally monuments honoring the memory of great soldiers.

FORTIFICATIONS

At the beginning of the Renaissance, fortifications had to be completely reconsidered as a result of developments in artillery. During the Middle Ages, well-stocked fortresses with a source of potable water stood a fairly good chance of resisting siege warfare. Such assaults usually began in the spring or early summer, and hostile troops returned home at the onset of cold weather if success did not appear imminent. Because repeated artillery bombardment of medieval structures often yielded rapid results, warfare continued year-round by the latter 15th century. Even though winter might be approaching,

military commanders persisted in barrages of artillery as long as supplies were available for their troops, certain that they could break the siege in a few more days or weeks. A new type of defensive fortification was needed, and it was designed in Italy.

Early Renaissance

Medieval fortified structures consisted of high walls and towers with slot windows, constructed of brick or stone. These buildings were designed to withstand a long siege by hostile forces. The only ways to capture

7.4 *Wooden siege tower with soldier preparing to ascend. Woodcut in a German edition of* Vegetius, Rei militaris instituta *(Military handbook, 1529).* (Photograph courtesy of Sotheby's, Inc., © 2003)

such a fortification were (1) to roll a wooden siege tower against the wall and climb over, but such towers were quite flammable and could be threatened by fiery objects catapulted over the wall; (2) to batter down part of the wall, under an assault of arrows, hot pitch, and other weapons hailing down from above; and (3) to tunnel under the foundation, a process that could take a very long time. Conventional towers and high walls were no match for artillery bombardment, which could be accomplished from a distance with no threat to the invading army. In addition, the walls and towers of medieval fortifications were not equipped for the placement and utilization of heavy defensive artillery. During the 15th century, European towns began to construct low, thick walls against their main defensive walls, permitting pieces of artillery to be rolled along the top and positioned as needed. The outer walls were often sloped outwardly or slightly rounded to deflect projectiles at unpredictable angles back toward the enemy. Bulwarks, usually U-shaped formations of earth, timber, and stone, were built to protect the main gate and to provide defensive artillery posts. In both central and northern Europe, many towns constructed gun towers whose sole purpose was the deployment of defensive artillery. These structures had guns at several levels, but usually lighter, lower-caliber weapons than those used on the walls. Heavier weapons would have created unbearable noise and smoke in the small rooms in which they were discharged. In several conventional medieval towers, the roof was removed and a gun platform install.

Later Renaissance

Near the close of the 15th century, Italian architects and engineers invented a new type of defensive trace, improving upon the bulwark design. In the "Italian trace" triangle-shaped bastions with thick, outward-sloping sides were pointed out from the main defensive wall, with their top at the same level as the wall. At Civitavecchia, a port near Rome used by the papal navy, the city walls were fortified with bastions in 1520—the first example of bastions completely circling a defensive wall. Bastions solved several problems of the bulwark system, especially with bastions joined to the wall and not placed a short distance away, where troops

could be cut off by enemy troops. The most important improvement was the elimination of the blind spot caused by round towers and bulwarks; gunners had a complete sweep of enemy soldiers in the ditches below. Development of the bastion design in Italy was a direct response to the 1494 invasion by the troops of Charles VIII and the superior artillery of France at that time, and to continued threats from the Turks. Bastion-dominated fortifications were constructed along the Mediterranean coast to create a line of defense against naval attacks. Several such fortifications were built in northern Europe, beginning with Antwerp in 1544. In some instances fortifications were not feasible, for reasons such as very hilly terrain or opposition from estate owners reluctant to lose property, and in some regions military threat was not extreme enough to warrant the effort of constructing new fortifications. In such cases, an existing fortress might be renovated and strengthened to create a citadel. Municipalities often opposed construction of citadels, which symbolized tyranny, because they were imposed on defeated cities by warlords. Citadels proved to be an effective means, however, for providing a protective enclosure during enemy attacks. By the mid-16th century, the expense of fortifications was exorbitant. Henry VIII, for example, was spending more than one-quarter of his entire income on such structures, and the kingdom of Naples was expending more than half.

MAJOR LEAGUES, BATTLES, SIEGES, AND PEACE TREATIES

Leagues

Each of the leagues discussed in the following sections was involved in conflicts concerning religious differences, either Catholic versus Protestant, one Protestant sect against another, or Christian versus Muslim.

League of Cambrai:

Formed in 1508 with the ostensible purpose of controlling the Turkish threat, the League of Cambrai consisted of the kings of France, England, Spain, and Bohemia/Hungary; the Holy Roman Emperor; the pope; the marquis of Mantua; and the duke of Ferrara. Their secret agenda, however, was to seize the mainland territory of Venice. Although they were successful in 1509 at the Battle of Agnadello, the league dissolved in 1510 because of conflict among its members. Within eight years, Venice regained most of its lost territory.

Catholic League (French Holy League):

Militant Catholics organized in France in 1576, led by the duke of Guise, with the aim of resisting Protestant advancement. In 1584 this group narrowed its focus to oppose Henry IV as the heir to the throne, and the duke was murdered.

Catholic League of Nuremberg:

This association of German Catholic princes was formed in 1538 in response to the Schmalkaldic League (discussed later).

Holy Leagues:

There were four associations known as the Holy League or simply "the League" between 1495 and 1571, in addition to the French Catholic League. The 1495 Holy League, or Holy League of Venice, consisted of Venice, Milan, the emperor, the pope, and the king of Spain, formed for the purpose of forcing Charles VIII out of Italy. The main Holy League, usually referred to without a date although it was formed in 1511, consisted of the kings of England and Spain, the pope, and the republic of Venice. The emperor allied himself with this group in 1512 after its hostile stance against France became clear. The 1538 Holy League—the pope, the emperor, and Venice—joined to fight the Turks and the Barbary pirates. The 1571 League of the pope, the king of Spain, and Venice was formed for the same purpose. Although not called a "Holy" League, the anti-imperial League of Cognac (1526) included the pope, along with the duke of Milan, the republic of Venice, and the kings of France and England.

Charles V responded to the threats of this League by sacking Rome in 1527.

Schmalkaldic League:

In 1531, several Protestant towns and states joined together under the leadership of Johann Friedrich I, elector of Saxony (1503–54), and Philip of Hesse (1504–67) to oppose Charles V and his Catholic troops.

Swabian League:

The Swabian League was a confederation of several cities in the southern part of present-day Germany created in 1488 to assure peace in their immediate territory. Gradually it was enlarged to include Bayreuth, Baden, and all of Bavaria. In 1534 the league was broken up as a result of disagreements stemming from the Protestant Reformation.

Battles and Sieges

1415—Battle of Agincourt:

During the Hundred Years' War, Henry V of England invaded France, and his army of some 10,000 men was repelled by the French. Then his soldiers were trapped as they attempted to retreat to Calais (English territory at the time). With only 5,000 archers and perhaps 1,000 other foot soldiers, Henry's strategy of deploying archers along both sides of a muddy gully yielded victory for the English. The 20,000 horsemen of the French cavalry, slowed by the terrain, were annihilated when they charged. The resulting Treaty of Troyes restored Normandy to the English, with other provisions (see later discussion).

1428—Siege of Orléans:

As the English were besieging the town of Orléans in 1429, Joan of Arc rallied French troops to repulse the enemy and conducted Charles VII to Reims for his coronation.

1450—Battle of Formigny:

Charles VII led French troops against the English at Formigny, putting Normandy under the French Crown.

1453—Siege of Constantinople:

Turkish forces assaulted Constantinople, which fell in 1453. Many Byzantine scholars escaped to Italy, taking manuscripts and knowledge of ancient and early Christian Greek authors.

1485—Siege of Ronda:

Spanish troops under Ferdinand and Isabella successfully besieged Muslim troops in Ronda (western Granada), where Spanish artillery was a decisive factor.

1503—Battle of Cerignola:

Gonzalo Fernández de Córdoba (1453–1515) led Holy League troops to defeat the French near this southern Italian town in the Neapolitan campaign. His success marked the first time that the arquebus had been instrumental in winning a military victory. Holy League troops simply dug trenches and waited until the French were within range.

1509—Battle of Agnadello (Battle of Giaradadda):

The Battle of Agnadello was fought on the border between the territories of Venice and Milan. Here the troops of the League of Cambrai, commanded by the condottiere Gian Giacomo Trivulzio (1441–1518), handed the Venetian army its worst loss in history. Charles, duke of Bourbon (1490–1527), played an important part in the victory.

1512—Battle of Ravenna:

Although the French were victorious in the Battle of Ravenna, both sides lost so many men that this was the bloodiest confrontation to date in the Wars of Italy.

1513—Battle of Novara:

At Novara, Swiss forces defending Milan defeated the French army led by Gian Giacomo Trivulzio.

1515—Battle of Marignano:

French troops and German Landsknechte commanded by Gian Giacomo Trivulzio defeated soldiers of the Swiss Confederation in a humiliating victory at Marignano (near Milan), leaving Milan open for French occupation. Artillery played a large part in the victory.

1522—Battle of Biocca:

At Biocca (near Milan) Ferdinando d'Avalos (1489–1525) led German and Spanish Imperial troops to defeat the French army.

1525—Battle of Pavia:

Imperial troops under Ferdinando d'Avalos and Charles, duke of Bourbon, attacked French troops laying siege to Pavia. They defeated the French and took Francis I as prisoner.

1526—Battle of Mohács:

Suleiman's Turkish army defeated Hungarian troops and killed their king. From Mohács the victorious army marched on Buda, and occupied the city in the name of the sultan.

1527—Sack of Rome:

Charles, duke of Bourbon (1490–1527), fought in the Italian Wars for Louis XII. Francis I appointed him constable of France, putting him in charge of the French military. After he served as governor of Milan, Charles became alienated from the king and defected to Charles V. He was killed in the 1527 attack on Rome, after which his soldiers rioted and sacked the city.

1535—Battle of Tunis:

Imperial land troops led by Alfonso d'Avalos and a naval force commanded by Andrea Doria, with Charles V personally at the head of his army, took Tunis from the Muslims. The caliph Mohammed VI was put in charge of the city as a vassal of Spain.

1529—Siege of Vienna:

Among the several sieges of Vienna, the most famous is that of 1529, when the city held off the Turkish army of Suleiman I. Because the sultan's troops were so far from Constantinople, communication became difficult and supply lines were strained. With the onset of winter and approach of the Imperial army Suleiman withdrew his troops.

1547—Battle of Mühlberg:

The battle of Mühlberg was the decisive victory of the Schmalkaldic War. Imperial soldiers and the army of Saxony defeated the Protestant army.

1553—Battle of Marciano:

The battle of Marciano is famous for the blatantly defensive tactics of both the Imperial army and the Sienese-French coalition. After a week-long stalemate, the French were running short of supplies and attempted to retreat. They lost at least one-third of their 12,000 soldiers in the resulting assault.

1557—Battle of Saint Quentin:

Spanish forces stationed in the Netherlands marched on Picardy in 1557 in retaliation for French attempts to recapture Naples. Although the soldiers fighting for Spain won a resounding victory and might have been able to take Paris, they refused to continue because they had not been paid.

1571—Battle of Lepanto:

Fought near the Gulf of Corinth, the naval battle of Lepanto was among the most famous events of the 16th century. Don Juan of Austria, commanding more than 200 ships of the Holy League, defeated the Turkish navy. This victory was seen as a triumph for Christianity.

1588—Spanish Armada:

Also known as the "Invincible" Armada, this Spanish naval attack on England never reached shore, partly because of wretched weather conditions. It is one of the most famous failures in Spanish military history. The Spanish fleet of 130 ships sailed from Lisbon, with the goal of picking up the army of the duke of Parma on the coast of Flanders and then invading England. With long-range cannon on more rapid ships, English captains such as Sir Francis Drake (1540 or 1543–96) and John Hawkins prevented the Armada from reaching Flanders. Skirmishes lasted for two weeks, at the end of which violent storms battered the Spanish vessels and scattered the fleet.

Peace Treaties and Settlements

1420—Treaty of Troyes:

Located southeast of Paris, Troyes was the seat of government between 1419 and 1425, during the Hundred Years' War between England and France. As of result of this treaty ending a stage of the conflict, Henry V of England married Catherine, daughter of Charles VI of France. Charles VI named Henry V as heir to the French Throne, ignoring the rightful heir, Charles VII.

1435—Treaty of Arras:

The Burgundian factions, led by Philip the Good, recognized Charles VII as king of France in the treaty.

1444—Treaty of Tours:

In the treaty of Tours the Hundred Years' War hostilities between England and France finally ended.

1454—Peace of Lodi:

Signed by Milan and Venice, the Peace of Lodi led to an important nonaggression pact by these two powers, along with Florence, the Papal States, and the kingdom of Naples.

1485—Battle of Bosworth:

The English civil war known as the Wars of the Roses ended at the Battle of Bosworth. Henry VII was recognized as king of England, thus securing the succession for the Tudors.

1494—Treaty of Tordesillas:

The treaty of Tordesillas, with papal sanction, partitioned the New World between Spain and Portugal, giving Portugal claim to Brazil.

1526—Treaty of Madrid:

Signed by Francis I and Charles V, the treaty allowed the French king to be released from prison in Spain. In his place his two young sons were sent to Spain as hostages.

1529—Treaty of Saragossa:

In a modification of the Treaty of Tordesillas, Portugal was given rights to the Moluccas (Spice Islands).

1529—Peace of Cambrai:

Also known as the "Ladies' Peace," the Peace of Cambrai was negotiated by Louise of Savoy, mother of Francis I, and Margaret of Austria, aunt of Charles V. In addition to territory exchange, the two sons of Francis I who had been held hostage for nearly three years in Spain were returned home, and the French king married Eleanor, Charles's sister.

1555—Peace of Augsburg:

The religious wars of the Protestant Reformation were concluded by this peace settlement, by which Catholicism and Lutheranism (though not Calvinism) were recognized as valid religions in Germany. (Chapter 2 discusses the Diet of Augsburg, which preceded the peace settlement, and the Wars of Religion in general.)

1559—Peace of Cateau-Cambrésis:

A set of treaties concluded the drawn-out Italian Wars that began in 1494. Savoy was returned to the duke of Savoy, Spanish claims to Italian possessions were recognized, Burgundy was returned to France, and Florence gained Siena. In addition, France respected the autonomy of Mary, queen of Scots, and Philip II of Spain married Elizabeth Valois, daughter of the French king.

1598—Peace of Vervins:

The treaty between Philip II and Henry IV reiterated the territorial distribution of the Peace of Cateau-Cambrésis agreed upon by Spain and France, and France regained land in Flanders. Spain turned over control of the Spanish Netherlands to Isabella, the king's daughter, and her future husband, Albrecht von Habsburg.

MAJOR FIGURES

Albrecht III Achilles of Brandenburg (1414–1486), Hohenzollern elector, fought with Imperial troops against the Hussites and later against the Poles. He established primogeniture in Brandenburg.

Alexander VI, pope (*Rodrigo de Borja y Doms*) (1431–1503), born in Valencia (Spain), studied law in Bologna. He became the most nepotic pope of the 15th century, installing his illegitimate children in positions of power. These included the territory of Naples, disputed by Spain and France, instigating Charles VIII's invasion of Italy.

Alfonso V, king of Aragon (*Alfonso I, king of Naples*) (1396–1458) invaded Corsica and Sicily, adding them to his Aragonese empire. After the war of succession for the kingdom of Naples, the city of Naples became the cultural center of his domains.

Álvarez de Toledo, Fernando, duke of Alba (1507–1582) was one of the most powerful military figures serving the Crown of Spain. He was commander in chief of Spanish forces in Italy under Charles V, and then viceroy of Naples under Philip II. In 1580 he led the Spanish troops that conquered Lisbon.

Anne of Brittany (1477–1514) was the daughter of François, duke of Brittany, whom she succeeded as duchess. By marriage she was twice the queen of France, and her daughter, Claude, married the future Francis I, placing Brittany under control of the Crown.

Attendolo, Micheletto (c. 1390–1451) was a victorious condottiere who fought for Naples, the Papal States, Florence, and Venice. He was instrumental in the Florentine victory at the Battle of Anghiari.

d'Avalos del Vasto, Alfonso (1502–1546), marquis of Pescara, fought with Imperial troops at the Battle of Pavia and led the land forces of Charles V at the Battle of Tunis. In 1538 he became Imperial governor of Milan.

d'Avalos, Ferdinando Francesco, marquis of Pescara (1489–1525), fought for Spain and Emperor Charles V. As Imperial lieutenant, he commanded the troops at the Battle of Pavia and took Francis I prisoner.

Bandello, Matteo (1485–1561), Italian diplomat and soldier, was also a writer. He lost everything he owned in the Spanish attack on Milan and ultimately moved to France.

Barbarossa (*Khayr ad-Dīn*) (c. 1465–1546), or "Red-beard," was admiral of the Turkish navy. Along with his brother, Horuk, Barbarossa harassed the fleets of every major Mediterranean power and conquered the north African coast. The fleet of Charles V was defeated several times by ships under Barbarossa's command. He also fought for Francis I, when the French king was briefly allied with the sultan.

Bloody Mary See MARY TUDOR, QUEEN OF ENGLAND.

Borgia, Cesare (1475–1507) was one of the four illegitimate children of Pope Alexandria VI. As papal legate he ingratiated himself with the king of France, Louis XII, who made him duke of Valentinois. Borgia led troops in campaigns to reclaim parts of the Papal States and was made *gonfalionere* of the church by his father.

Botero, Giovanni (1544–1617) was a Savoyard political philosopher whose writings advocated that Christian morality govern the life of the state. He opposed the political morality espoused by Machiavelli.

Bourdeille, Pierre de, seigneur de Brantôme (c. 1540–1614), was an aristocratic soldier who participated in the Wars of Religion. After an injury in 1584, he began to write biographies of his fellow soldiers (not published until 1665).

Braccio da Montone See FORTEBRACCIO, ANDREA.

Bussone da Carmagnola, Francesco (c. 1385–1432) was the most important condottiere of Filippo Visconti, duke of Milan, and defeated the Swiss army at Arbedo. His services were needed by both Milan and Venice, and Carmagnola vacillated between the two powers; he eventually was tricked and beheaded by the Venetians.

Caraccioli, Giovanni (1487–1550), condottiere, fought for the Republic of Florence and later became governor of Marseille and the Piedmont under the French Crown.

Castelnau, Michel de sieur de la Mauvis-Sière (c. 1520–1592), soldier and diplomat, fought in the Italian Wars. He was involved for many years in various negotiations with the English.

Charles V, Holy Roman Emperor (*Charles I, king of Spain*) (1500–1558), whose election as emperor made him a lifelong enemy of Francis I, who had competed for the honor. Charles V's reign was plagued by war with France, hostility from the Turks, the Protestant Reformation, and revolts in Spain. Although he was able to claim a famous victory at the Battle of Tunis, Christian forces were not able to hold the city.

Charles VII, king of France (1403–1461), with the help of Joan of Arc, was crowned in 1419. The first few years of his reign were spent in fighting the English and their Burgundian supporters. Then he created a regular army that he used to suppress the power of feudal lords within French territory. The duke of Burgundy remained hostile, and the dauphin, Louis XI, who feared his father, lived at the Burgundian court until he became king. Charles was married to Marie d'Anjou, of the house who claimed the kingdom of Naples.

Charles VIII, king of France (1470–1498), the only son of Louis XI, participated in the Italian Wars; he invaded Italy in 1494, conquered Naples in 1495, and claimed his Anjou inheritance. He was succeeded as king of France by his cousin, who became Louis XII.

Charles VIII, king of Sweden (1408/1409–1470), joined in a revolt against the ruling house of Denmark in 1436. The Estates elected him as king of Sweden in 1448.

Charles IX, king of France (1550–1574), allowed his mother, Catherine de' Medici, to rule as regent even after he became of age. She was partly responsible for the Saint Bartholomew's Day Massacre (see chapter 2) and Gaspard Coligny's murder.

Charles the Bold, duke of Burgundy (1433–1477), led the final threat from Burgundy to the monarchy of France. Married to Margaret of York, sister of the

English king, Charles enlisted the aid of England in his bids for the French Crown and the kingdom of Burgundy. Leading his troops against the forces of Lorraine and the Swiss Confederation, he was killed in battle.

Charles, duke of Bourbon (1490–1527), fought in the Italian Wars for Louis XII. Francis I appointed him constable of France, in charge of the French military. After he served as governor of Milan, Charles became alienated from the king and defected to Charles V. He was killed in the 1527 attack on Rome, after which his soldiers rioted and sacked the city.

Christian IV, king of Denmark (1577–1648), was crowned in 1598. He created a resplendent court at the turn of the 17th century that was especially famous for its Italian, Dutch, and English singers and musicians. In Renaissance military affairs, Christian improved fortifications in Denmark.

Christine de Pisan (c. 1364–c. 1430) was born in Venice, the daughter of an astrologer. Because her father was appointed as royal astrologer for Charles V, king of France, Christine was raised at the French court. She became a writer and translator. One of her works pertinent to military history was the French translation of *Epitoma rei militaris* (On military affairs) by Vegetius, updated with information about contemporary warfare.

Clement VIII, pope (*Ippolito Aldobrandini*) (1536–1605), began his diplomatic career as a papal legate. Among other achievements, he negotiated a settlement in Poland between the Habsburgs and Sigismund III Vasa. He recognized Henry IV as king of France and helped to engineer the Peace of Vervins.

Coligny, Gaspard de (1519–1572), admiral of France and commander in chief of the Huguenot army, served the Crown in the Italian Wars before he was captured. In prison he converted to Protestantism, alienating himself from the powerful queen mother, Catherine de' Medici. His death was one of the worst individual losses of the Saint Bartholomew's Day Massacre.

Colleoni, Bartolomeo (1400–1475), condottiere, served the Republic of Venice for most of his career. After the Peace of Lodi, he was appointed captain-general of Venice.

Commynes, Philippe de (c. 1446–c. 1511) was a Flemish historian and diplomat, who served as ambassador for Louis XI. He was also a soldier, who fought at the Battle of Fornovo.

Cortés, Hernán (1485–1547), Spanish conquistador, conquered the Aztec capital city of Tenochtitlán by besieging it for three months, including cutting off the water supply, in spring 1521. Charles V appointed him governor of New Spain. After rebuilding the capital, Cortés continued to explore and conquer parts of Mexico and Central America.

Cosimo I de' Medici, duke of Florence and grand duke of Tuscany (1519–1574), financed his wars of expansion by assassinating suspected enemies and seizing their property, mainly in Tuscany.

Devereux, Robert, earl of Essex (1566–1601), led naval forces that captured Cádiz in 1596 and was assigned to quell Tyrone's rebellion in Ireland. Failing in that effort, he returned to England and was later executed for treason.

Doria, Andrea (1466–1560) was a condottiere who became a naval commander, leading the ships of Charles V at the Battle of Tunis. He helped place his native Genoa under French control, hoping in vain for autonomy, and later established the Republic of Genoa with support from the emperor. Many of his naval encounters were with Turkish marauders and Barbary pirates.

Drake, Sir Francis (1540 or 1543–1596), who circumnavigated the world in 1577–80, fought for England against Spanish naval forces. He played an instrumental part in the defeat of the Spanish Armada.

Dudley, Robert, earl of Leicester (1532–1588), a favorite of Elizabeth I's, was general of her troops in the Netherlands. He also served as her privy counselor.

Elizabeth I, queen of England (1533–1603), had a relatively peaceful reign, with the exception of the Scottish disputes that resulted in the execution of Mary, queen of Scots, and of England's victory over the Spanish Armada.

d'Este, Alfonso I, duke of Ferrara (1486–1534), was an important military figure in the Italian Wars. Interested in artillery, he established a foundry for casting cannons. With the support of such firepower, Alfonso was appointed commander of papal troops by Julius II.

Farnese, Alessandro, duke of Parma (1545–1592), soldier and diplomat, was raised at the Netherlandish court of his mother, Margaret of Austria. He grew up with the future Charles V and Don Juan of Austria and served with the latter at the Battle of Lepanto. After conquering the southern Netherlands, Alessandro became involved with the Wars of Religion in France, fighting on the side of Spanish Catholics.

Ferdinand I, Holy Roman Emperor (1503–1564), was the younger brother of Charles V. Early in his career Ferdinand married a Hungarian princess and fought for supremacy in Hungary. His chief military encounters were against the Turks.

Ferdinand V, king of Spain [Castile and León] *(Ferdinand II, king of Aragon)* (1452–1516) married Isabella I in 1469 and consolidated non-Moorish Spain. He was also known as Ferdinand the Catholic. Their long reign saw the establishment of the Inquisition, Jews' expulsion from the territory, the conquest of Granada, and exploration in the New World.

Fernández de Córdoba, Gonzalo (1453–1515), Spanish soldier, was among the officers who received the surrender of the Moors at Granada in 1492. He distinguished himself driving the French out of Spanish possessions in Italy, earning the nickname "El Gran Capitán." The Swiss Square battle formation (discussed previously) was invented by Fernández de Córdoba.

Ferrante I, king of Naples (1423–1494), as an illegitimate son of Alfonso V spent much of his reign protecting his claim to the Crown. He died shortly before Charles VIII of France attacked the city of Naples.

Foix, Gaston de, duke of Nemours (1489–1512) and nephew of King Louis XII, commanded French troops fighting members of the Holy League during the Italian Wars. Although he conquered both the Spaniards and the Venetians, he was killed at the Battle of Ravenna.

Fortebraccio, Andrea *(Braccio da Montone)* (1368–1424), condottiere, served Pope John XXIII as captain-general and captured Perugia. His military specialty was the simultaneous use of multiple small units of soldiers reinforcing each other.

Francis I, king of France (1494–1547), was a lifelong enemy of Charles V's, partly because Francis had wanted to be named Holy Roman Emperor. Participating in the Italian Wars, Francis I won the Battle of Marignano to assure French dominance of Milan, but he lost the Battle of Pavia and was taken as prisoner to Spain. A low point of his reign was the bargaining of his freedom in exchange for his two young sons' being sent to Spain as hostages.

François, duke of Anjou (1554–1584), fourth son of Henry II, king of France, and Catherine de' Medici. He supported the Huguenots in the Wars of Religion. With the support of Elizabeth I, whom he almost married, "Monsieur" (as he was called) attempted to seize Antwerp but was driven back.

Frundsberg, Georg von (1473–1528) was an illustrious German soldier who fought in the Imperial army. He advised Maximilian I on military reforms and later commanded troops in the Swabian League. His son and grandson also served as Imperial soldiers.

Gattamelata, Il *(Erasmo da Narni)* (1370–1443), condottiere whose nickname means "Tabby Cat," began his career fighting for Florence. In 1434 he entered the service of Venice, leading troops against the forces of Milan and ultimately becoming captain-general.

Giorgio Martini, Francesco di (1439–1501) was a painter, sculptor, architect, and engineer. His writings on military engineering, well known by his contemporaries through manuscript copies, were important for the development of the bastion in fortification.

Giovanni della Banda Nere   See MEDICI, GIOVANNI DE'.

Giustiniani, Pompeo (1569–1616), condottiere, was nicknamed "Iron Arm" because he lost an arm in battle and used an artificial limb. He served Alessandro Farnese in the Netherlands and fought the Turks in Crete.

Gonzaga, Gianfrancesco I (1395–1444), condottiere, fought first for Venice and later for Milan, then vacillated for and against Venice. Formerly captain-general, he became marquis of Mantua in 1433.

Gonzaga, Gianfrancesco II, marquis of Mantua (1466–1519), was a soldier who served as captain-general of Venice. He was away from his court for long periods, fighting in turn for France, Florence, and Pope Julius II, then being imprisoned for a year by the Venetians. During the marquis's absences, his wife, Isabella d'Este (1474–1539), became an important patron of art.

Gonzaga, Ludovico II, marquis of Mantua (1412–1478), was a military commander who fought for both Venice and Milan. For the first decade of his marquisate, Ludovico was involved in war against Venice, which was finally settled by the Peace of Lodi.

Granvelle, Antoine Perrenot de (1517–1586), a Spanish minister of state in the Netherlands, was also a bishop. In this double role he negotiated peace settlements, royal weddings, and church councils. Granvelle eventually became a cardinal and viceroy of Naples, contributing to the strategic planning for the Battle of Lepanto. Near the end of his career, he returned to Spain and advised the king on the invasion of Portugal.

Gritti, Andrea, doge of Venice (1455–1538), was a military leader in the campaign against the League of Cambrai. His study of the defense system for Venice's mainland led to improvements in fortifications.

Guicciardini, Francesco (1483–1540), one of the most famous historians of the Renaissance, documented the Italian Wars of 1494–1534 in his *Storia d'Italia* (History of Italy, published after his death in 1561 and swiftly translated into six languages).

Gustavus Vasa, king of Sweden (1496–1560), founded the Vasa dynasty. He was involved in the movement to win Sweden's independence from Denmark. The Stockholm Bloodbath of 1520 led to a revolution, and Gustavus was elected in 1523. Under his reign, in 1544, the Swedish monarchy became hereditary rather than elected. He also established Lutheranism as the state religion.

Guzmán, Alonso Pérez de, duke of Medina-Sidonia (1550–1619), commanded the Spanish Armada.

Hawkwood, Sir John de (c. 1320–1394) was an English condottieri. After fighting for France, he and his troops spent 35 years in Italy serving various rulers. He ended his career in Florence, where a fresco in his honor was painted in the cathedral.

Helmschmied family   For more than a century, this family was famous as armor makers in Augsburg. In the 15th century the original family name Kolman was changed to Helmschmied (literally "helmet makers"). Much of their work, especially in etched parade armor, was for the Holy Roman Emperors. Lorenz Helmschmied (1445–1516), for example, produced a full set of armor for both Emperor Friedrich III and his horse.

Henry V, king of England (1387–1422), was the last English chivalric knight to wear the crown. His goals as king included reclaiming what he considered English territory in France and reuniting Christian Europe after the Great Schism. Henry V is most famous for the victory of Agincourt in 1415.

Henry VII, king of England (1457–1509), was crowned in 1485 after defeating Richard III at

Bosworth. He ended the civil war between the houses of York and Lancaster by marrying Elizabeth of York.

Henry VIII, king of England (1491–1547), waged his own religious war within England when he established the Church of England, nullifying the power of the papacy. Near the end of his reign, Henry instigated futile wars with France and Scotland.

Henry II, king of France (1519–1559), was mortally wounded in a tournament celebrating the Treaty of Cateau-Cambrésis. Although Henry was wearing full jousting armor, the tip of a wooden lance pierced the eye slit of his helmet and entered his brain.

Henry III, king of France (1551–1589), participated in the Wars of Religion. He was partly responsible for the Saint Bartholomew's Day Massacre. In his fight to quell the Huguenots, he allied himself with Henry of Navarre against Henry, duke of Guise, in the War of the Three Henrys. After the duke of Guise and Henry III were both assassinated, Henry of Navarre became King Henry IV.

Henry IV, king of France (1553–1610), was raised as a Protestant. After becoming king, he converted to Catholicism in 1593 to create peace in his troubled country, with the famous remark "Paris is well worth a mass."

Hus, Jan (c. 1372–1415) was a reformer in Bohemia who followed the principles of John Wycliffe. Hus criticized social hierarchies, spoke out against the ownership of private property, and had numerous followers. He was excommunicated and expelled from Prague. Attending the 1414 Council of Constance to appeal his excommunication, Hus was seized and burned at the stake. The Hussite Wars erupted after his murder.

Isabella I, queen of Spain [Castile and León] (1451–1504), married Ferdinand II of Aragon in 1469 and consolidated non-Moorish Spain. She was also known as Isabella the Catholic. Their long reign saw the establishment of the Inquisition, Jewish expulsion from the territory, the conquest of Granada, and exploration in the New World.

Ivan IV, first czar of Russia (*Ivan the Terrible*) (1530–1584), greatly expanded Russian territory but failed in his wars with Poland over the Baltic Sea. The sobriquet "Terrible" would be better translated as "Mighty."

Joan of Arc (*the Maid of Orléans*) (1412–1431), visionary military leader, roused the French to raise the siege of Orléans and led Charles VIII to his coronation in Rheims cathedral. Betrayed by the duke of Burgundy, she was sold to the English and burned at the stake.

Johann Friedrich I, elector of Saxony (1503–1554), was coleader of the Protestant Schmalkaldic League with Philip of Hesse. He was taken prisoner at the Battle of Mühlberg in 1547 and imprisoned until 1552.

John VIII Palaeologus, emperor of Byzantium (1390–1448), was involved in the Council of Florence decreeing the primacy of the papacy. John VIII attempted to organize a crusade against the Turks, but military efforts failed and his rule was restricted to the area in and near Constantinople.

John III, king of Sweden (1537–1592), fought against his brother, Eric, to become king in 1569. He was able to conclude peace with Denmark in 1570. A Catholic sympathizer, he installed his Catholic son, Sigismund, as king of Poland.

John the Fearless, duke of Burgundy (1371–1419), fought the Turks at the Battle of Nicopolis. In France he feuded with the Armagnacs and refused to lead his troops into the Battle of Agincourt, thus contributing to the English victory. He ordered the massacre of Armagnac family members in Paris in 1418. In the following year John was assassinated by a soldier of the king.

Juan of Austria (*Don Juan of Austria*) (1545–1578) was one of the most illustrious Spanish soldiers of his time. The illegitimate son of Charles V, he was recognized as a half brother of Philip II when the emperor died. His initial fame derived from commanding a squadron of galleys against Barbary pirates, shortly after which he drove rebellious Moriscos out of

Granada. Don Juan became governor-general of the Netherlands, where he defeated the rebels in 1578.

Julius II, pope *(Giuliano della Rovere)* (1443–1513), is best known in military history for donning full battle armor to lead the papal army against Perugia and Bologna. He expended an inordinate amount of effort, both in fighting and in negotiating, attempting to expand the Papal States.

Khayr ad-Dīn See BARBAROSSA.

La Noue, François de (1531–1591) was a French Huguenot soldier known as "Iron Arm" because of the prosthesis he wore after losing an arm in battle. His *Discours politiques et militaires* (Political and military treatise, 1587) was an important account of the Wars of Religion from the Protestant point of view.

Lasseran-Massencôme, Blaise de, seigneur de Monluc (1520–1577), was a French soldier who fought in the siege of Siena. After participating in the Wars of Religion, he became *maréchal* (Marshal) of France under Henry III.

Leo X, pope *(Giovanni de' Medici)* (1475–1521), was very deeply involved in the Italian Wars. At first opposing French claims to Naples and Milan, Leo X finally sued for peace, making certain that Florence went to the Medicis.

Leonardo da Vinci (1452–1519), brilliant artist and engineer, left notebooks containing designs for various military machines. None of these designs was known by his contemporaries.

Lorraine, François de, duke of Guise (1519–1563), fought in the Italian Wars. He was instrumental in seizing Naples and Calais and became a powerful figure in France. His troops instigated the Wars of Religion in 1562 by annihilating a congregation of Huguenots.

Lorraine, Henri de, duke of Guise (1550–1588), led the Catholic forces during the Wars of Religion. He was involved in the planning of the Saint Bartholomew's Day Massacre and the murder of Gaspar de Coligny.

Louis XI, king of France (1423–1483), alienated himself from the powerful Burgundian faction. With the help of the Swiss Confederation and allies in France, Louis XI managed to create a unified France by seizing Burgundy and other domains.

Louis XII, king of France (1462–1515), began his military career by attempting to seize power from the regent and spent three years in prison. He was embroiled in the Italian Wars for much of the remainder of his reign, with virtually no political gains as a result.

Louis de Bourbon, prince of Condé (d. 1569), served the Crown as a soldier and later became a leader of the Huguenots. He was shot and killed by the Catholic enemy upon surrendering after the Battle of Jarnac.

Louise of Savoy, duchess of Angoulême (1476–1531), was the mother of Francis I. During the years when he was on campaign in Italy, she virtually ruled France.

Machiavelli, Niccolò (1469–1527), most famous for his treatise on princely attributes, also wrote *Dell' arte della guerra* (On the art of war, 1519–20), a book that was read throughout much of western Europe. It was influenced by Valturio's *De re militari* (On military affairs).

Malespini, Celio (1531–c. 1609), condottiere, was a Venetian who served in the Spanish army, fighting in the Netherlands and Italy. He became a literary translator from Spanish to Italian and from French to Spanish.

Margaret of Austria, duchess of Savoy (1480–1530), was regent of the Netherlands from 1507 until her death. Her father was the emperor Maximilian I.

Margaret, duchess of Parma (1522–1586), was regent of the Netherlands from 1559 until her resignation in 1567, compelled by severe opposition to her instigation of the Inquisition. She was succeeded by her son, Alessandro Farnese.

Mary, queen of Scots (*Mary Stuart*) (1542–1587), was queen of Scotland and France. Her claim to the throne of England was supported by her Catholic allies. She was beheaded by order of Elizabeth I.

Mary Tudor, queen of England (*Mary I or Bloody Mary*) (1516–1558), ruled from 1553 to 1558. During her reign, she attempted to reinstate Catholicism as the official religion of England, and several Protestant martyrs were burned at the stake.

Matthias Corvinus (1443–1490), king of Hungary, spent much of his reign in military encounters, including struggles concerning the Crown of Bohemia and campaigns against the Turks in Bosnia. Matthias also engaged in a war with the emperor, taking Vienna in 1485, which then became a court center along with that of Buda.

Maurice, count of Nassau (1567–1625), was the military commander during the Revolt of the Netherlands. Studying treatises on warfare, he reorganized the army into small battalions, including specialists in artillery and supplies. Between 1588 and 1598, his troops drove the Spanish from the northern regions of the Netherlands.

Maximilian I, Holy Roman Emperor (1459–1519), commanded Imperial troops in France, Italy, and his eastern European territories. His French claims stemmed from his marriage to Mary of Burgundy, and he campaigned in vain against Louis XI to hold the province. Much of his participation in the Italian Wars was in opposition to the French. He managed to drive the Hungarians out of Vienna and to repulse the Turks at Villach. Among his military reforms was the establishment of the Landsknechte, foot soldiers fighting with long pikes who could be deployed with either artillery or cavalry.

Medici, Catherine de', queen of France (1519–1589), was a powerful figure during the reign of her sons. Although initially she attempted to keep peace by allowing concessions to Protestants, the Wars of Religion nevertheless erupted in 1562.

Medici, Giovanni de', (*Giovanni della Banda Nere*) (1498–1526), was a condottiere from Florence who fought for Pope Leo X and later for the king of France.

"Monsieur" See FRANÇOIS, DUKE OF ANJOU.

Montefeltro, Federigo II da, duke of Urbino (1422–1482), condottiere, fought for Milan, for Florence, and most notably for the king of Naples, leading a combined force from all three areas against the papal army. In 1474 the pope created him duke of Urbino, after which Federigo led the papal troops.

Moro, Il See SFORZA, LODOVICO.

Narni, Erasmo da See GATTAMELATA, IL.

Narváez, Pánfilo de (1470/80–1528), Spanish conquistador, served under Diego Velázquez. In Mexico he fought against Cortés, whom Velázquez was attempting to remove from command, and as a result lost an eye.

Navarro, Pedro (c. 1460–1528), Spanish military engineer, began his career by fighting in Africa. During the Italian Wars, he specialized in explosives, such as mines and charges to breach defensive walls. In 1515 he began service to Francis I as artillery commander.

Negroli family Some two dozen members of the Negroli family worked in the family armor-making business in Milan during the 16th century. They were most famous for their highly decorative embossed ceremonial armor. Filippo Negroli (fl. 1531–51) created the parade armor for Charles V.

Niccolò da Tolentino (*Niccolò Mauruzi della Stacciola*) (c. 1350–1435), condottiere, spent most of his career fighting for Florence against the forces of Milan. In 1431 he became commander in chief of the Florentine army.

O'Neill, Hugh, earl of Tyrone (c. 1540–1616), a rebel in Ireland, held off English troops for seven years with support from Catholics on the continent.

Paré, Ambroise (1510–1590) studied medicine in Paris. He began serving as an army surgeon in 1537, revolutionizing the treatment of gunshot wounds and introducing a safer method of amputation. Paré published *La méthode de traiter les plaies faites par arquebustes et autres bastions à feu* (Method of treating wounds made by muskets and other firearms) in 1545.

Philip II, king of Spain (1527–1598), was also king of Portugal after he invaded the country with troops led by the duke of Alba in 1580. During the first three years of his reign, 1556–59, he lived in Brussels while waging war against France. In 1559 he returned to Spain, expelling the *morisco* rebels. Although his ships won the Battle of Lepanto, Spain later lost ground to the Turks and was forced to award autonomy to the southern Netherlands.

Philip of Hesse (1504–1567), a German landgrave, was coleader of the Schmalkaldic League. A convert to Lutheranism, he sent his own troops to support the Huguenots in France and the Protestant rebels in the Netherlands.

Philip the Good, duke of Burgundy (1396–1467), joined forces with the English against the French Crown. In 1420 he reluctantly recognized Charles VIII as king. Much of the remainder of his rule was focused on the rebellious Netherlands. His triumph at the Battle of Gavere was at the cost of some 20,000 dead enemy soldiers.

Piccinino, Niccolò (1386–1444), condottiere, was a cavalryman who spent the most important years of his career in the service of Milan, fighting against the papal army, Florence, and Venice.

Porto, Luigi da (1485–1529), a soldier who became a historian, mainly fought for Venice as a cavalry officer. He wrote a sort of memoir documenting military affairs in the Venetian mainland between 1509 and 1524, *Lettere storiche* (Historical letters).

Raleigh, Sir Walter (1554–1618), best known as a courtier and explorer, was also a naval commander. He fought with Essex in the 1596 attack on Cadíz.

Requeséns y Zúñiga, Luis de (1528–1576), who became Spanish governor of the Netherlands, was in charge of suppressing the *moriscos* in Granada. His years as governor were full of conflict, partly because he refused to accommodate the Protestants.

Sampiero da Bastelica (*Sampiero Corso*) (1498–1567), condottiere, was a Corsican who fought for both Giovanni de' Medici and France. A leading figure on his native island, Sampiero caused several years of bloody conflict there, with Imperial and Genoese forces against Turkish troops supported by France.

Sebastian I, king of Portugal (1554–1578), crusaded against the Moors in north Africa. Obsessed with military affairs, he was killed in the second African expedition.

Sforza, Caterina, countess of Forlí (c. 1462–1509), is one of the few illustrious women in Italian military history. When her husband died, she occupied the fortress and put herself in command of her husband's troops. They held Forlí and Imola for nearly two years.

Sforza, Francesco I, duke of Milan (1401–1466), was also a condottiere, who fought both for and against Venice and the papacy. He expanded Milanese territory and worked with Cosimo de' Medici to conclude the Peace of Lodi.

Sforza, Lodovico, duke of Milan (1442–1508), began his participation in the Italian Wars by supporting Naples and Florence, but in 1493 he allied himself with Venice and the pope. After the French attacked Milan in 1500, Ludovico was imprisoned in France, where he later died.

Sickingen, Franz von (1481–1523) began his career as a German soldier serving in the Imperial army under Maximilian I. Then he became a mercenary who extorted large sums of money, enlarging his estates. Von Sickingen is most famous for leading his troops into Frankfurt during the Imperial election of 1519 and helping to elect Charles V, though he had accepted a bribe from Francis I to oppose Charles.

Sigismund, Holy Roman Emperor (*also king of Hungary and Bohemia*) (1368–1437), was not crowned emperor until 1433. The military history of his reign included a resounding defeat in his crusade against the Turks, his struggle to assert his authority in Hungary, and campaigns against the Hussites.

Sigismund I, king of Poland (1467–1548), was at war during most of his reign. He finally suppressed the Teutonic Knights in 1521, and he waged several campaigns against Ivan IV of Russia.

Sigismund III Vasa, king of Poland (1566–1632), instigated a war with Sweden over his claims to the throne. His troops occupied Moscow, asserting that his son should be Czar, and fought the Turks in Moldavia. Sigismund III also influenced the cultural history of Poland by moving the court from Krakow to Warsaw.

Suleiman (c. 1494–1566) was the Ottoman (Turkish) sultan for 46 years, during which he expanded the Turkish empire to its greatest territorial boundaries. Had he not been defeated in his effort to take Vienna in 1529, parts of western Europe might have fallen under Turkish rule.

Terrail, Pierre, siegneur de Bayard (c. 1473–1524), was a brilliant military tactician from Savoy who fought for three French kings during the Italian Wars. He was most famous for holding Mézieres (in the Ardennes) with 1,000 men against an Imperial siege of some 35,000 troops, thus preventing the invasion of France. Bayard, a model of chivalry, opposed the use of firearms.

Trivulzio, Gian Giacomo (1441–1518), a noble Milanese condottiere, fought for Louis XI in Brittany and then for the Sforza family in Italy. Later he returned to service for France, commanding troops of the League of Cambrai who defeated Venice at the battle of Agnadello. Trivulzio also led his soldiers to victory at the battle of Marignano.

Valturio, Roberto (1405–1475), Italian writer, specialized in warfare. He served at the court of Sigismondo Malatesta in Rimini as a diplomat and published an influential treatise, *De re militari* (On military subjects, 1472). This book, with its 82 illustrations of war machines, discussed weaponry, battle strategy, and other pertinent topics.

Velázquez de Cuéllar, Diego (1461/66–1524), Spanish conquistador, was leader of the troops invading Cuba in 1511. Three years later he was appointed governor of the island. He also assisted Cortés in the conquest of Mexico.

William of Orange, count of Nassau (1533–1584), allied as a young man with the Habsburgs, gradually became alienated from the Imperial house. He became a leader in the Revolt of the Netherlands, fighting Spanish troops, and was proclaimed a traitor by Philip II. He was assassinated by a Spanish loyalist.

READING

Major Wars

Burne 2002: Hundred Years War; Goodman 1981: Wars of the Roses; Hale 1986: effects of major conflicts; Kaeuper 1988: Anglo-French conflicts; Seward 1978: Hundred Years War; F. L. Taylor 1973: Italian Wars.

Armor and Traditional Weaponry

Blair 1958: (general survey); Domínguez Ortiz 1991: illustrations of armor, including details; Hall 1997: information on the effectiveness of armor against gunfire; Vale 1981: England, France, and Burgundy; Verbruggen 1977: armor in warfare.

Fired Projectiles

Hale 1986: the effect of firearms battle on formations; Hall 1997: extensive information on the manufacturing of gunpowder; Rice 1970, 10–18: guns and the balance of power.

Soldiering

Gouwens 1998: accounts of the sack of Rome; Hale 1986, proportions of cavalry to infantry in 12 battles between 1474 and 1610, p. 53; Hall 1997: weapons' effects on the daily life of soldiers; Mallett 1974: mercenaries; Martines 1988: Italy; Millar

1980: mercenaries; Murrin 1994, 79–102: literary depictions of sieges; 179–196: literary depictions of officers; Showalter 1993: command structure; Vale 1981: England, France, and Burgundy; Verbruggen 1977: (general history).

Military Medicine

Hale 1986, 120–121: hospitals; Lindemann 1999, 141–147, especially military hospitals; Siraisi 1990, 181–183: field surgeons.

Fortifications

Hale 1986, 206–209, 234–235: modification of existing structures; Hall 1997, 163: illustration of the Italian trace.

8

COMMERCE

Between 1400 and 1500, Europe experienced an economic revolution as the beginnings of capitalism developed alongside more archaic economic systems. Many aspects of life were intertwined to bring about this change, including new designs for ships that made long voyages for the purpose of trade an important part of European commercial enterprises. Large-scale manufacturing endeavors that thrived during this period involved mining, textiles, and building, the first of these dependent on slave labor in the Americas. Slaves were themselves treated as commercial entities, not only as objects to be bought and sold but also as producers and consumers. Businesses developed new markets during the Renaissance as a result of new products from colonial possessions, including exotic plants. The publishing of printed books, which began during the second half of the 15th century, was flourishing by 1600. This new venture, itself contributing to the European economy, disseminated information that improved various aspects of business. Books explained such practical topics as double-entry bookkeeping, the principles of crop rotation, and techniques to operate hydraulic pumps. Books also helped teach the basic skills of reading and numeracy; the relatively sophisticated economy of the Renaissance could not have functioned successfully without such knowledge.

Businesses that produce commodities for trade depend on standards of weight and measure, and the lack of universal standards was a problem during the Renaissance. There were hundreds of names and units with which to measure length, weight, and volume. Long before 1400, the uniform Roman system had been contaminated by local usage, with the result that Europe had no international standards. Moreover, the standards that did exist were poorly regulated. Attempts at regulation were haphazard and confused, as numerous officials were involved in setting and maintaining standards. Devices for recording and standardizing weight and measure were made of substances such as wood and iron, which were altered slightly by frequent usage and changes in the weather. To add to the confusion, different units of weight and measure often were based on various standards, even within the same country. In addition, a unit such as the foot, known by the same word in several languages, did not contain the same actual measure from one country to another. Linear units were usually longer on sea than on land. A French league, for example, was approximately one-third longer on the open sea. Measurements of area could be based on several factors, such as the amount of rent or annual income that the field could be expected to produce. Measurements of volume often were determined by the linear measurement of the rope or string needed to tie the items together. Finally the same unit often was referred to by two or more words; for example the English pint, was called a jug or stoup. Few countries had units of measure that were multiples of smaller units. England, however, did have such a system. For liquid volume, the quart contained two pints, the gallon equaled four quarts, the barrel 31.5 gallons, the hogshead 63, the butt (or pipe) 126, and the tun 252 gallons. The English mile was established at 5,280 feet, the furlong at 660, the fathom at six, the pace at five, the yard at three, the cubit at 18 inches, the span at nine, and the palm at three.

BANKING AND ACCOUNTING

Banking changed dramatically between 1400 and 1600. Pawnbrokers, who charged exorbitant rates of interest, had to compete with publicly owned banking institutions by the 16th century. While powerful merchant banks continued to function internationally during the Renaissance, especially in the use of bills of exchange, privately owned local deposit banks gradually closed as their clients turned to the public banks. In general, financial documentation began to be more professional as account books and journals supplemented the new system of double-entry bookkeeping.

Banking

Banking in the Renaissance began with a long recession during the second half of the 14th century, caused chiefly by the plague, defaulted loans, and severe fluctuations in the market. Several important banking houses in Italy became bankrupt, including that of the renowned Acciaiuoli family. With the growth of banks in Barcelona and Genoa during the early 15th century, along with the establishment of the Medici bank in Florence, finances became more stable. Toward the close of the 15th century, the German city of Augsburg flourished as the banking capital of northern Europe. Banks in Augsburg owned by the Fuggers, Weslers, and Höchstetters became known throughout the Mediterranean. Wealthy individuals functioned as bankers to kings and other rulers. Agostino Chigi (1465–1520), for example, served as papal banker.

Renaissance Europe had four types of money-lending institutions: pawnbrokers, merchant banks, local deposit banks, and public banks. The rate of interest at some pawnbrokers' shops was quite high, as much as 40 or even 60 percent. The majority of pawnbrokers during the early Renaissance were Christians, not Jews, in spite of the Catholic Church's prohibition against usury (lending money and charging interest). Many more pawnbrokers were Jewish by the late 15th century, and they were criticized for practicing usury. *Montes pietatis* (literally mountains of piety) operated in Italy by the Catholic Church functioned as special nonprofit banks. They lent relatively small amounts to private citizens in exchange for pawned property. Founded in 1461 by the Franciscan order, these banks were established so that people might avoid the "sin" of usury, especially the usury of Jewish sources of money. In 1515 the Fifth Lateran Council (see chapter 2) approved this system and branches were opened in France, Spain, Germany, and the Netherlands.

Merchant banks functioned as international organizations, issuing credit and invigorating the market. Activities of these banks, which were administered chiefly by the extended families of wealthy merchants, included insurance (especially for ships), financial speculation, and foreign exchange. Bills of exchange facilitated the operation of merchant banking. These bills involved money lent to the issuer of a bill of exchange, with the amount payable in the future in another currency at another bank. Although interest per se was not charged, a profit often was realized though differences in exchange rates. Thus the lender received

more money than was originally lent to the borrower. By the 16th century, lenders were endorsing their bills of exchange, transforming them into negotiable commodities, much like checks. In the Republic of Venice, however, the bearer of a bill of exchange could not transfer it to a third party and had to be physically present at the bank to complete the transaction. Besides earning a slight profit for the lender, bills of exchange permitted merchants and their associates to travel internationally with no need to transport heavy chests full of coins. The risk of theft by highway robbers was also greatly reduced. (See chapter 9 for more information about merchants and travel.)

Local private banks, as well as the larger public banks that eventually replaced them, functioned somewhat as today's banks do. Current accounts, or short-term accounts, did not earn any interest. Long-term accounts, similar to modern savings accounts, did bear interest over a period. Local deposit banks evidently began in Genoa during the Middle Ages, and Venice dominated the market by the 15th century. These banks were failing by the close of the century, partly because they were foolishly speculating with the deposits, significantly reducing the necessary reserve of funds. Public banks were monitored by public officials employed by the government, which operated these lending institutions. Different rules applied in different regions; some public banks were not allowed to make loans to private individuals. Money could, however, be deposited into savings accounts. During the 16th century, several public banks benefited from the tremendous influx of silver and gold from South America. The discovery of silver in central Europe simulated the growth of public banks in Germany as money was minted from the silver extracted in the mining operations.

MONEY

While bills of exchange were used in Renaissance banking, currency in the form of paper money did not yet exist. Medal coins manufactured under government control, the majority made from alloys of copper and silver, served as money. Because these coins were struck by hand with a hammer and die, the shapes often were irregular and the weight

largest coins were quite heavy; Spanish pieces of eight, for example, weighed 30 grams each. In 1400 several cities and countries had a gold coin of equal value, approximately 3.5 grams each in 24-karat quality: the Hungarian ducat, the Aragonese ducado, the French salut, the Venetian ducat, the Genoese genovino, and the Florentine florin. Such equivalences, however, were never a constant in Renaissance finance. Debasement of coinage presented a recurring problem, partially caused by the excessive expense of military campaigns, for which governments minted more and more money. Nevertheless, in spite of inflation, the larger gold coins were usually worth several hundred dollars each in today's money.

Accounting

Except in German domains, double-entry bookkeeping had become popular across western Europe by the late Renaissance. Probably originating in Tuscany in the late 13th century, this system was first used among merchants in Genoa. In its simplest format, double-entry bookkeeping consisted of two columns on a page, each with a heading of the same date. The left-hand column listed debits and the right-hand columns listed credits. Some merchants also kept a journal as well as an account ledger, for the purpose of cross-indexing in both. The procedures for double-entry bookkeeping were first discussed in print by the mathematician Luca Pacioli in his *Summa de arithmetica* (Summary of arithmetic, 1494). Besides helping to make businesses more profitable, double-entry bookkeeping, with its supporting documentation, helped merchants keep better track of inventories and other aspects of their enterprises that benefited from improved records.

MINING

Mining was a large-scale operation that required managers and workers with specialized experience. Central Europe had several mining centers, for silver,

8.1 Man Weighing Gold. *By Adriaen Isenbrandt, c. 1515–20.* (The Metropolitan Museum of Art, The Friedsam Collection, bequest of Michael Friedsam, 1931 [32.100.36])

could vary slightly. In Augsburg circa 1550, mass-produced coins cut from sheets of metal created new standards of precision for Renaissance money. Coins were produced in the mints, from metal supplied by merchants, bankers, and others involved in finance. Those supplying the metal received payment in coins; some of the money was paid in taxes to the government and some kept by the mint for operating expenses. Each type of metal was made into coins of varying weights, with the heaviest, of course, being the most valuable. Some of the

copper, and rock salt. Cornwall in England was known for its tin mines, and coal mining rose to importance in England during the 16th century. By the latter 16th century, the silver and gold mines of South America were sending significant amounts of metal to Spain. Exploitation of slave labor was especially severe in Peru and Mexico, where generations of slaves were worked to death in mining and smelting operations (see pages 218–219). Though men often died while working in mines in both the Old and New Worlds, the job was safer in the Renaissance than it had been previously because of new machinery. Giant water wheels as large as 30 feet in diameter were used to power winches and lift buckets filled with ore. Some of these wheels were not powered by water, but rather by two or more men who ran together inside the wheel (as hamsters run on a wheel in their cage). Mining shafts often were ventilated by mechanized processes, and more efficient designs for hydraulic pumps not only contributed to the safety of mining, but also expedited the digging.

During the course of the Renaissance the extraction of metallic ore was increasingly dependent on machines, such as hammering devices for crushing ore. More individuals had money to invest in mining operations, and more metals and alloys were needed for weaponry and armor for the wars that plagued Europe. This unprecedented combination of economic forces resulted in improvements in technology and specialized labor. Metallurgy became a scientific field, and treatises such as *De re metallica* (On metallurgy, 1556), by Georg Agricola, illustrated the subject in abundant detail. Manuals explaining how to test ores and minerals were published, contributing to the standardization of processes as well as vocabulary. These treatises also emphasized the role of machines and engineering in commercial production, enhancing the possibility of mechanized processes in other fields.

Investment in mining made the fortunes of several families in northern Europe. Jakob Fugger (1459–1525), for example, lent money to the archduke of the Tyrol in 1487 and received among types of security the controlling interest in the most lucrative silver mine of the Tyrol. Three years later the emperor Maximilian I (1459–1519) became head of the Tyrolean government and borrowed money from the Fuggers for military

expenses. As a result, Jakob negotiated even better terms on the income from his silver mine. With the emperor holding a monopoly on the minting of money, the Fugger family earned a concession of 50 percent of the proceeds of each silver coin (mark) produced. This amount was eight florins per coin, which was approximately enough money for a family of four to live modestly for about one month. Because trading in silver was prohibited in Austria and Hungary at this time, Jakob Fugger dominated the silver market. His initial investment of 20,000 ducats lent to the archduke constituted

8.2 *Hydraulic pump for mining operations. Woodcut in Georgius Agricola*, De re metallica (*On metallurgy, 1561*). (Photograph courtesy of Sotheby's Inc., © 2003)

the foundation of the Fugger's multimillion-dollar empire of the 16th century.

TEXTILES

The creation of textiles was part of the life of every household. This domestic production, of peasants' making their own cloth and other textile items, should be distinguished from the manufacture of textiles in workshops run by guilds (see page 216). Textiles manufactured for sale included woolen cloth, linen cloth, and silk woven in various weights and patterns, such as velvet and brocade. Producing wool involved five processes, namely, carding (combing), spinning, weaving, fulling, and dyeing. Florence was internationally famous for the quality and quantity of wool produced there during the 14th century; its silk luxury goods became an important commodity during the Renaissance.

Florence dominated the European supply of luxury fabric in the 15th century, including the furs and elaborately woven cloth produced for the papacy. Clients for Florentine cloth ranged from the courts of Burgundy to harems in Turkey. By offering tax relief to silk workers who relocated to Florence, the city guaranteed a large pool of skilled spinners and weavers. In addition, new types of silk cloth were developed, the most popular of which was "shot silk" in a taffeta weave with the warp and weft threads of different colors. The color of a gown designed from this fabric would change, depending on shifting light and shadow as the wearer moved. Such novelties enhanced the appeal of silk across Europe and beyond.

Woolen and silk cloth alone were expensive, and tailoring and embellishment such as embroidery added to their cost. Some embroidery threads consisted of spun gold or silver, making them costly indeed. In Florence, silk workers were paid much

8.3 Brocaded velvet, with silk and metallic thread, late 15th or early 16th century. (The Metropolitan Museum of Art, Rogers Fund, 1912 [12.49.8])

better than wool workers, an important reason why silk fabric could cost five to six times more than wool. Even though the manufacture of woolen cloth required 27 steps and that of silk only nine, the relatively low wages of wool workers by the 15th century resulted in a lower-priced product. In addition, the weaving of fine silk was quite time-consuming on the hand-powered looms of the Renaissance. A skilled weaver might take as long as three months to produce enough brocaded silk velvet for a sleeveless overgown. Cloth of gold, with gold or silver threads woven as an additional weft, was so costly that an outfit might have only the sleeves made of this luxury fabric. The fashion in Florence after about 1450 was detachable sleeves for fancy gowns, which allowed the wearer to display a variety of sumptuous fabrics with a single gown. The dyeing process also added to the cost of both silk and wool, especially since the deep red preferred by many people derived from a very expensive powder. The status of the cost may have been one reason why the aristocracy conspicuously wore such a color. That red was, in fact, created from the kermes louse, dried and ground into powder in the Far East and shipped to Florence.

Investing in luxury items such as silk was smart financial strategy in the expanding economy of mid-15th-century Europe. As is wool, refined from the fiber shaved from sheep, silk fibers are produced by an animal. Sericulture is the growing of mulberry trees on which silkworms can feed to produce their fibers. Naturally the manufacture of silk textiles was related to sericulture, and regions that cultivated their own silkworms usually made a better profit in silk manufacture because the raw fibers were not supplied by a third party. The relatively mild climate of Europe permitted the spread of sericulture, even in England.

In addition to textiles manufactured from raw materials found in Europe, cotton was a desirable trade good purchased by the European market. Cotton's role in the economic balance of trade was related to that of other commodities shipped from the Middle East. Cotton yarn and bales of cotton from Syria, for example, reached European cities via the port of Venice. Much of this fiber was woven into a popular utilitarian cloth called fustian, with a woof of cotton and a warp of flax (the fiber from which linen was made). (For more information on textiles, see chapter 12.)

AGRICULTURE

Grain was by far the most crucial agricultural commodity of the Renaissance, especially wheat and rice. Census takers did not count the number of people in a household, but rather the number of grain consumers (meaning that small children usually were not included). The main goal of agronomy was to learn how to improve the supply of grain, of all types. Renaissance agronomy began with the study of classical texts on the subject, and, of course, the ancient Roman sources pertained to the Mediterranean basin. In addition, because of the mild climate of most of western Europe, successful experiments in one region could help improve agricultural production in other areas. The two most significant changes were the elimination of fallowing (in which fields were left unused for a season or more) and cross plowing. With previously fallowed fields kept in production, three crops per year could be produced in warmer regions. An increase in the use of manure helped accomplish this innovation. Cross plowing, as opposed to plowing of parallel lines in ridges, produced perpendicular lines, which opened more of the earth to receive seeds. The forage crops grown during the crop rotation in this system provided more fodder, which could feed more animals during the winter. A greater supply of manure from the additional animals perpetuated this cycle of abundance. The chief new forage crop was alfalfa (an Arabic word), which supplied nitrogen, supplemented by clover. Although lost to most of Europe after antiquity, alfalfa was still grown in the Muslim dominions of Spain. Known as Spanish grass in Italy during the 16th century, alfalfa became a mainstay in the diet of farm animals.

Improved irrigation systems as well as new hydraulic machinery that could drain wet areas for cultivation made untended land available for Renaissance agriculture. In his *Obra de agricultura* (Book of agriculture, 1513), the horticulturist Gabriel Alonso de Herrera (born c. 1470) insisted that regular supplies of water were more important than fertilizer. Working in Granada, Herrera observed firsthand the sophisticated Muslim irrigation systems of southern Spain. Other improvements to European farming included new cultivators created in 16th-century botanical gardens and new plants from the Americas. Maize was grown in Spain before 1500, and western Europe was producing sweet potatoes during the 16th century. The white potato, however, was not consumed as food. Along with tobacco, it was grown for medicinal purposes. The tomato, considered inedible at this time, was cultivated as an ornamental plant.

The general statements in this section should be supplemented in further study by more detailed analysis of individual regions where the local terrain dictated agricultural techniques. The Italian Peninsula, for example, had (and has) three large agricultural regions, Lombardy in the north, Tuscany in the center, and the south. Lombardy is relatively flat with heavy soil, so fields could easily be irrigated and diverse crops grown for market. Dairy farming thrived, and cheeses from the region around Parma were famous during the 15th century. In Tuscany, with its hills, thinner soil, and sparse rainfall, grapes and olives did well. Peasants grew food for their own consumption, rotating three crops per year. Although sheep were cultivated there, the wool was not valued very highly. Most of the southern zone, with its poor soil, was divided into large estates, many of which produced lemons and oranges. The land was also used for grazing. Farms that did grow food products did so with only a two-crop rotation. The entire peninsula was beginning to feel the effects of deforestation by the 16th century as massive numbers of trees were removed for shipbuilding and fuel.

During this period the state became much more interested in measuring and managing rural land use, and regional officials gathered information on agricultural production. Cities were naturally linked with their rural neighbors because much of their food supply was local. Farms and larger estates also provided another important raw material to urban areas, namely, peasants, who did the menial tasks that kept roads passable, raw goods delivered, workshops clean, and so on. The rate of mortality among the lower classes in cities was very high: Only about half of these individuals lived past the age of 20. Living conditions of the urban poor were appalling by modern standards; urban people were continuously exposed to the filth of daily life (see chapter 12).

Wine, Beer, and Spirits

Wine and beer were the favorite beverages of the Renaissance. In general, the upper classes drank wine and the lower classes drank beer, and northern and eastern Europeans drank more beer than did southern Europeans. Freshly made beer and wine were preferred because the barrels in which they were stored did not preserve them very well. Each season the arrival of new wine was a cause for celebration as the first barrel was tapped. Although strong spirits were first consumed as beverages during the Renaissance, their manufacture and daily consumption were more widespread after 1600.

Wine

The upper classes as well as people who grew their own grapes drank wine on a daily basis. Viniculture was a good business in southern Europe, with vineyards operating commercially as far north as the 49th parallel. In France the mouth of the Loire River was the demarcation line for large-scale wine production. Wine made in Europe was not stored in bottles at this time, but in wooden barrels, or casks, and it was rather high in alcohol content. Wine did not age well, often turning to vinegar when being transported in hot weather. New wine was preferable, at times commanding prices as much as eight times higher than those for older wine. In general, both red and white wine were considered undrinkable after five or six years of storage in the cask.

The Azores and the islands of Madeira and the Canaries had flourishing wine markets; ships stopped in the Azores to take on fresh barrels of wine, and vineyards in Madeira and the Canaries sent wine via the water routes to England and the Americas. Although wines from Chile were already gaining a reputation in the 16th century, Europeans drank wine made chiefly in Europe. Because wine was such a necessity among the upper classes, gov-

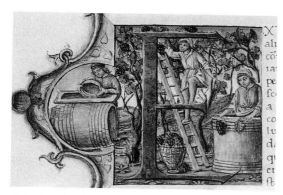

8.4 Historiated initial E depicting grape picking and wine making. Manuscript on vellum of Pliny's Natural History, *Italy, 15th century.* (Biblioteca Marciana, Venice Italy/Lauros / Giraudon / Bridgeman Art Library)

Spirits

Until the 16th century, alcoholic spirits made from distilled wine were used for medicinal purposes, often in monasteries that added spices and herbs to distilled wine. Brandy, the most common spirit, was thought to help protect against the plague, cure toothache, preserve one's youth, and confer other benefits, when consumed in moderation. Near the end of the 15th century, people began drinking alcoholic liquor in greater quantities, especially during public festivities. Within a decade town governments in France had seized upon brandy production as a new source of revenue from customs fees and taxes. Although documentation concerning the spread of spirits as a commercial venture is lacking, we do know that brandy was being shipped internationally by the late 16th century. Taking up the same space in the holds of ships as did casks of wine, brandy and other spirits turned a greater profit because they were more expensive.

ernments knew that they could easily tax wine merchants, providing a steady source of income to the municipalities that instigated such a tax. Many merchants set up their wine stalls outside town walls to avoid payment.

Beer

Beer was the standard beverage of the lower classes, especially in northern Europe, because wine usually became more expensive the farther it was transported from the source of supply. Members of the northern aristocracy were also fond of beer, the most famous example was the emperor Charles V (1500–1558), who was raised in Flanders. Created from brewed grain, such as barley, beer has additional ingredients to enhance the flavor. During the Renaissance brewers experimented with various additions, such as honey and bay leaves, for flavor, as possible preservatives, and for their potential medicinal effects. Although the brewing of beer sometimes was not legally permitted in powerful wine-growing regions, especially in France, the beverage was so popular that taverns in these regions imported barrels of beer. Peasants were great beer drinkers, sometimes imbibing more than a gallon each day (about two six-packs).

CRAFTS

Almost everything produced during the Renaissance was made individually by hand. The two exceptions were coins (see previous discussion) and printed texts—and the presses that created them were, of course, pulled by hand. The industrial age had not yet begun. Workshops functioned in a quasi-industrial fashion in the textile (see pages 212–213), mining (see pages 210–211), and building fields. Most crafted items were made by guild members, and a master craftsman (and they were always men) was in charge of each workshop. Although women did assist in the shops, they did so as the wife or daughter of the guild member.

Shipbuilding

The construction of ships, a branch of building, required special skills and tools, and the workshop had to be located near a body of water. Venice's Arsenal complex was one of the most famous shipbuilding yards of the Renaissance, employing several thousand workers. Among them were numerous women, who were employed to sew the sails. Interestingly, the Arsenal workshops were reorganized during the 16th century: The usual Renaissance workshop system of masters' training apprentices and journeymen was suppressed, and each worker was forced to perform one single task repeatedly. This model of labor increased productivity but was relatively rare in the building trade at this time. Frequent naval battles and the resultant loss of Venetian ships may have necessitated the new system. Shipbuilding workshops in northern Europe had artisans who could carve the decorative figureheads that began to be placed at the front of ships after the mid-16th century. Popular on medieval ships, the figurehead disappeared from galleons because of the design of these large vessels. Although the modern imagination usually thinks of a ship's figurehead as a mermaid or similar female figure, the most popular 16th-century figureheads were of animals or mythological deities such as Neptune.

Guilds

As European cities became important economic centers during the late Middle Ages, wealthy merchants and government officials were able to purchase not only expensive paintings, tapestries, and sculpture, but also beautifully made household items in leather, metal, wood, and other materials. These handicrafts—even the paintings were considered handicrafts in 1400—were created by artisans organized into guilds. In some cities each guild monopolized the production of one type of craft. In others larger guilds consisted of several groups of artisans, each group specializing in a particular craft. Joining a guild entailed working first as an apprentice (see chapter 11, on education), then as a journeyman, and finally as a master in one's own workshop. The number of masters was often limited, to prevent undue competition within the guild. Although women were not permitted to join guilds, masters usually had to be married because the wife was expected to assist in the shop. Guild members helped support the economic welfare of their city, providing aid to masters who

became too old to work, as well as to orphans and widows of masters. Guilds were also patrons of art. Several of the most impressive altarpieces were commissioned by guilds, which also paid for elaborate church funerals for their members. On feast days and during civil ceremonies, guild members banded together and paraded in uniform costume, similarly to members of confraternities (see chapter 2, on religion). In fact, guild members constituted many of the confraternities, extending their contributions to the city's social welfare beyond the immediate families of the guild itself. Thus some guilds became not only powerful commercial forces within the framework of European cities, but also notable political groups.

By the 16th century many guilds were producing goods via the "putting-out system," as wealthier masters invested in the handicrafts produced by the poorer households. Instead of one artisan's making an entire item in his workshop, the item might be passed from one workshop to the next, until all the steps of its production were complete. This system, somewhat like a mobile assembly line, could manufacture handicrafts much faster than the simple workshop system. The results, however, were less prestige and usually less income for the individual artisan.

PRINTING AND PUBLISHING

The first books printed in Europe were block books, with each page cut from a single block of wood. Occasionally these books were produced in two colors. Because the process of cutting letters into the wood was quite laborious, such books often had only a few pages. In the mid-15th century, the Mainz goldsmith Johannes Gutenberg (c. 1394/99–1468) discovered a method for making punches and casting type for letters that allowed him to print a book (the Gutenberg Bible) with movable type. The first such letters were in gothic script, copying the gothic style of lettering in manuscripts.

Two innovations of Renaissance publishing were the more readable italic script, modeled on humanistic cursive hands, and pocket editions, both developed by the Venetian printer and publisher Aldus Manutius (c. 1450–1515). Trained as a humanistic Greek scholar, he first offered Greek texts in large-format folio volumes, at expensive prices. Copies were still in stock a decade later. He then decided to market inexpensive textbooks of classical authors. Although the Aldine press was shut down twice by warfare (in 1506 and again in 1510–15), Aldus (as he is usually called) eventually produced books that most scholars could afford. Fluctuations in the profits of his business exemplify the experimental nature of publishing as a commercial enterprise during the first century of its existence. Other publishing houses, desiring a wider market, issued books in the vernacular languages, which, in turn, encouraged more works to be written in those tongues. During the 16th century, secular publications such as school texts, geographies, and literature were marketed along with the Bibles and devotional works that had become popular during the early decades of book publishing in Europe.

Printing

The first printed European work with a date in movable type is a papal indulgence of 1454 produced in Mainz. During the 1460s, German printers established workshops in Rome, Venice, and Basel (German territory at the time). Toward the end of the 1460s, a press was founded in Paris that printed texts for use in the university curriculum of the Sorbonne. By 1480, important print shops were functioning in Utrecht, Nuremberg, Cracow, and Budapest, and in several cities in England, France, Italy, the Netherlands, Portugal, and Spain. When studying incunables (books printed before 1501), determining the precise place of production can be difficult because many printers moved from city to city, taking their casting molds and matrices with them. Many early books did not have title pages, only the names of publishers or printers at the end, along with the date of publication. These early printers were imaginative and creative, capable of issuing books with Greek by 1465, music by 1473, and mathematics by 1482. Although most of the earliest printed books were in Latin, books in the vernacular languages became a major component of the European market by 1500.

Publishing as an Investment

Setting up a workshop for printing books was an expensive undertaking because of the tools and machinery required. The early printers were their own publishers, but by the 16th century, more and more printers were funded by other individuals, who assumed most of the costs as well as the financial risks. Many of the title pages of Renaissance books state at the bottom that the work was "printed by xxx for xxx." The name after the *for* is the publisher or bookseller of the book, who sometimes was responsible for paying for part of the equipment and supplies in the print shop and who often shared income from the print run with the printer. Local bankers were among the earliest investors in publishing ventures, from the 1480s. In Geneva, merchant bankers such as the Fuggers funded the publishing of Calvinist works. Many books were published under the auspices of an important patron, such as the pope, a monarch, or a wealthy cardinal. Aldus, for example, issued several titles with papal support.

Most publishing projects were meant to make a profit, but not necessarily immediately. Print runs were surprisingly large, suggesting that most publishers must have been fairly confident of their market. Whereas items printed for special occasions, such as memorial pamphlets, might have only 50 to 100 copies, an ordinary print run usually had between 1,000 and 1,250. Bibles and devotional tracts often had much larger printings, between 3,000 and 4,000. The first edition of the Bible translated into German by Martin Luther (1483–1546) was printed in 4,000 copies. Between jobs for printing books, the specialized workers in print shops were never idle during the workday. They produced numerous single-sheet (broadside) works, such as prayers and devotional woodcuts, as well as little ABC books for children and short collections of popular verse.

Printing Privileges

Because publishing entailed such an extraordinary investment of time and money, printers and publishers naturally wanted to protect their investment. Before publishing a specific text, the printer would request the "privilege" from governing authorities of having a monopoly on printing that text. These privileges normally extended for a significant length of time, between 10 and 20 years. They functioned in effect as copyrights, but for the printer, not the author or editor. Piracies abounded, however, especially when the jurisdiction of the authority issuing the privilege did not extend into the territory where the piracy occurred. Printers in Florence, for example, pirated Aldus's 1528 edition of the *Book of the Courtier* issued with a papal privilege. Much of the investment for a book could be lost if a pirated edition flooded the market.

Related Businesses

Book publishing required tremendous amounts of paper and ink, as well as of metal to cut type. Paper represented the lion's share of the cost, approximately two-thirds of production expenses. On average, most presses used 1,500 sheets of paper each day. With several thousand print shops in operation during the 16th century, the need for paper was extreme. To guarantee regular supplies of paper, some printers bypassed merchants and purchased their paper in volume directly from the paper mills. Printers had standing orders with paper makers, and some printers ordered massive amounts of paper several years in advance from the mills. The best solution for a few printers was to invest in their favorite paper mills, with an agreement that paper would be constantly supplied. Although the binding of books usually was not the responsibility of printers, who issued books with paper wrappers, the explosion of printing during the 16th century resulted in the growth of binderies. Bookbinders, in turn, stimulated the manufacturing of leather in Europe as well as the importing of leather. The book trade also helped expand the annual Frankfurt fair into an international event each spring (and continues to play an important part in that famous trade fair even today).

SLAVERY

People were enslaved in the ancient world as galley slaves, domestic workers, artisans, and other labor-

ers. During the Middle Ages, with the use of enserfed peasants, estate owners no longer needed to purchase slaves for fieldwork and other grueling tasks. Domestic slaves, however, continued to form part of the household of wealthy individuals. Many of these served as sexual partners for their owners. The Black Death of the 14th century that killed thousands of serfs precipitated an urgent need for groups of hard-working, inexpensive laborers. During the early 15th century, slaves from the Circassian mountains and other regions to the east were sold to individuals in Genoa and other coastal cities. This "white slave trade," both men and women, replicated the Muslim system operating in southern Spain and north Africa. Other cities, notably Venice, used young indentured servants sold to the captains of ships by their own parents along the Dalmatian coast and on the islands of the Adriatic Sea. Unlike slaves, indentured servants usually worked for their owners for a specific number of years and were freed at the end of their contract. Unlike the people enslaved as a result of the African slave trade that began in the mid-15th century, indentured servants were not legally defined as property.

With their navigational skills and proximity to the coast of Africa, the Portuguese ventured into northern Africa and conquered the town of Ceuta in 1415. From this base of operations, Portuguese merchant seamen slowly began trading with Africans, purchasing grain and textiles from the Moroccans. In 1434 the Portuguese expeditions passed Cape Bojador, and seamen began capturing Africans along the coast for the developing slave trade. Rather quickly, slaves became a valuable commodity. The city of Seville had one of the largest slave populations of western Europe, more than 7 percent of the total inhabitants in the mid-16th century. Many of the owners were artisans, who purchased slaves to work in their shop. English sea captains as well as the Portuguese participated in the slave trade, supplying workers to the Spanish colonies. (It was a Dutch sea captain who sold slaves to the English colony of Jamestown, Virginia, in 1620.) African slaves were considered the legal property of their owner and were treated as a commodity. Unlike grain, textiles, and similar trade goods, African slaves were not consumed and usually did not wear out for a long time. Moreover, they produced more slaves when given the chance to mate. For slave traders who failed to recognize Africans as human beings, slaves were a good investment. During the Renaissance, between 300,000 and 400,000 Africans were forced to toil as slaves, the majority in the Atlantic islands and the New World. (That number rose dramatically during the 17th century.) The relatively small number of African slaves in Europe were located mostly in Portugal, Spain, and Italy.

Slaves in Spanish America had a champion in Bartolomé de Las Casas (1474–1566), a priest who became a wealthy landowner in Cuba. Stunned by the cruel treatment of American Indians, he first attempted to free them from slavery by suggesting that each landowner who freed Native American slaves could have a dozen African slaves in return. A few years later, however, Las Casas spoke out against the very concept of human bondage, publishing several books voicing his concerns. Because of the economic dependence of American settlers on slavery, changing the system was a difficult task. During his trips to Spain, Las Casas finally persuaded those in power that the Indians, at least, should not be enslaved. This is the compromise for which he became famous. Although the new Laws of the Indies passed in 1543 prohibited using Indians as slaves, the legislation hardly improved the situation of most Native Americans. Instead of working as slaves, they worked equally hard in exchange for food and housing.

Sugarcane Plantations

Sugarcane plantations in the Atlantic islands, such as Madeira and the Canaries, were prototypical examples of the sort of large-scale slave labor used later in the Americas. The Portuguese in Brazil and Spaniards elsewhere in the New World rapidly exhausted sources of native labor. Partly because the Indian population had never been exposed to European diseases such as smallpox, they were wiped out by various sicknesses. In addition, as of 1543, the Spanish government prohibited the enslavement of Native Americans because they were considered as subjects of the Crown. Both of these factors caused colonialists to invest in African slaves, who cultivated the sugarcane and provided the backbreaking labor to operate sugar refineries. Producing sugar required

a tremendous amount of wood for the burners, and slaves had to chop down trees and cut them up for fuel. Plantation owners preferred African slaves, who were said to be able to do the work of four or more American Indians. It was virtually impossible for a black African slave to become free (be given manumission). Because of their skin color, slaves might escape but could not easily hide and were usually caught and punished severely, if not killed. In addition, the slave trade dislocated families so that a slave's relatives could not find their relative, even if they could afford the price of manumission.

Mining

Slaves consigned to the mines of Spanish America usually fared much worse than those on sugar plantations. Working conditions were horrific, even by Renaissance standards, with many hours spent in heat, dust, and semidarkness with inadequate oxygen. Silver mines at this time were tortuous chambers winding back and forth beneath the access pit, not straight mine shafts supported by wooden beams. Workers descended and ascended by ropes and ladders, carrying out the ore on their back, a very slow process. The key to commercial success in mining gold and silver was high productivity, and mining had no off-season. Unlike agricultural endeavors, mining could continue night and day, and it was exhausting work. Moreover, toxic chemicals such as mercury were utilized in the refinement process, and miners were exposed to poisonous gases in the tunnels. The mortality rates for slaves used in mining must have been quite high, but more slaves simply took the place of those who died. Labor was the most costly aspect of mining operations, but slaves were cheap compared with paid workers.

MAJOR FIGURES

Acciaiuoli family bank had its headquarters in Florence, with branches in Rome, Naples, and Athens. When the king of England defaulted on his loans in 1350, the business became bankrupt.

Agricola, Georg (1494–1555) was a German mineralogist who became burgomaster of Chemitz, in a major mining region. He wrote a treatise on mining and smelting, *De re metallica* (On metallurgy, 1556).

Barbarigo, Andrea (1399–1449) was a member of a family of merchants in Venice. His account books are an important resource on early Renaissance practices.

Biringuccio, Vannoccio (1480–1539) was a metallurgist and engineer who concluded his career as superintendent of the papal arsenal. His *Pirotechnia* of 1540 (Fireworks, in a more general sense than today's word) illustrated mining and smelting, the manufacture of glass and gunpowder, and other processes involving fire or extreme heat. This book was translated and went through several editions.

Bodin, Jean (1530–1596), philosopher and economist, wrote a detailed analysis of 16th-century inflation in France, *Discours sur les causes de l'extrème cherté qui est aujourd'hui en France* (Treatise on excessive inflation in contemporary France, 1574). The topics he discussed included wages, prices, and the supply of money.

Chigi, Agostino (1465–1520), of a wealthy family in Siena, founded a bank in Rome and helped financed the projects of several popes. He also held the concession of the alum mines in Tolfa.

Coeur, Jacques (1395–1456) was the son of a French merchant. Trading in textiles from Damascus, he became very wealthy and was appointed master of the mint and steward of the royal treasury. Coeur loaned the king of France money for his campaign in Normandy against the English.

Fugger family of Augsburg was the most prominent dynasty of bankers in Germany and one of the wealthiest mercantile families in western Europe. In addition to banking, their main commercial areas were textile manufacturing and distribution, mining, and the spice trade. Emperor Maximilian I depended on the Fuggers for loans, and they funded the election of Charles V. They were rewarded with the management of income from Spanish mining operations in both Spain and the Americas.

Gresham, Sir Thomas (1519–1579), English merchant, spent some 20 years in Antwerp as the financial adviser for Elizabeth I. He also administered her loans.

Grimaldi family were prominent bankers in Genoa. They became rulers of Monaco in 1458, a dynasty that continues to this day.

The Höchstetter family owned an important bank in Augsburg but became bankrupt when the head of the family failed in his attempt to corner the market on mercury in 1529.

Las Casas, Bartolomé de (1474–1566) was the first priest ordained in the New World. Opposing slavery, he was instrumental in persuading the Spanish government to pass new laws in 1543 prohibiting the use of Native Americans as slaves.

Manutius, Aldus (c.1450–1515) was a printer and publisher in Venice. He was the first to publish books in italic (cursive) script, and he published the first pocket-sized book (the octavo format), which made reading material more portable.

Medici family founded their bank in Florence and subsequently established branches elsewhere, notably in Antwerp. One of the wealthiest families in Italy, they used their money to install family members as popes, cardinals, and other church officials. The Medici bank became bankrupt in 1494 when Florence was captured by the king of France.

Oresme, Nicole (c. 1320–1382) was a French economist, whose treatise *De moneta* (On money) was first published in 1488 and had several Renaissance printings.

Pacioli, Luca (c. 1445–1517), a mathematician who worked at several courts in northern Italy, published the first explanation of double-entry bookkeeping in his *Summa de arithmetica, geometria, proporzioni et proportionalità* (Summary of arithmetic, geometry, and proportion, 1494).

Piccolomini family Sienese merchants, had a lucrative commercial network that extended from the port cities of Genoa and Venice into France and Germany. They also had significant investments in real estate.

Strozzi family and their bank were the main rivals of the Medici in Florence. They had an impressive mercantile empire.

Welser family founded a banking dynasty in Augsburg with branches throughout western Europe. They invested in trade from the Far East and had several mineral rights in the Americas as a result of loans to Charles V.

READING

Appuhn 2002: economic development; Berriman 1953: weights and measures; Braudel, *Perspective* 1992, pp. 1–174: (general survey); Brotton 2002: "A Global Renaissance," pp. 33–61, on trade between the Ottomans and Europe; Frick 2002: p. 97 table listing estimated annual earnings in Florence during the 15th century for 19 categories of employment, from lawyer to carpenter, in descending order; Kula 1986: weights and measures; Miskimin 1977: (general history).

Banking and Accounting

Center for Medieval and Renaissance Studies 1979: banking; De Roover 1966: Medici bank; Edwards 2000: accounting; Ehrenberg 1963: banking; Goldthwaite 1987: banking; Lane 1985: banking; Munro 1992: banking; Tenenti 1991: (character study).

Mining

Braudel, *Structures*, 1992; (general survey); Hatcher 1973: English tin; Tylecote 1992: metallurgy.

Textiles

Braudel, *Structures*, 1992; (general survey); Frick 2002: Florence; Molà 2000: Florentine silk.

Agriculture

Ambrosoli 1997: botanical studies; Appuhn 2002: economic development; Braudel, *Structures*, 1992: (general survey); Fusell 1972: classical Roman methods of farming.

Wine, Beer, and Spirits

Braudel, *Structures*, 1992 (general survey).

Crafts

Appuhn 2002: economic development; Braudel, *Wheels* 1992: markets; Frick 2002: Florence.

Publishing

Eisenstein 1983: social context of printing; Hindman 1991: social context of books; Hirsch 1974: literacy and the book market; Jardine 1998: "The Triumph of the Book," pp. 135–180: popularity of printed books.

Slavery

Knight 1993: Spain and Portugal; Marino 2002: economic impact; Panzer 1996: papal involvement; Phillips 1993: the Americas; Solow 1993; Atlantic basin.

9

EXPLORATION
AND TRAVEL

Outside the large cities, travel within Europe was not much different from travel during the later Middle Ages—dirty, slow, and often dangerous. The few improvements were along routes used for mail delivery, which by the 16th century was regulated by the state in some areas. Whether traveling by water or land, people during the Renaissance had a problem transporting their money. Because all money was in the form of coins, a pack animal was sometimes required to carry the heavy sacks or a cart or wagon was needed to transport a chest of coins. Such conveyances targeted travelers for highway robbers and other disreputable people. Most travelers had to stay in roadside inns, which were crowded and flea-ridden; pilgrims, however, sometimes were permitted to stay overnight in hospitals when there was enough room.

Ancient texts of geography, navigational knowledge and tools from Arabic sources, and maps drawn from firsthand observation all contributed to a new world picture for Renaissance Europeans. Between 1400 and 1600, the world seemed to double in size. This information did not, however, cause most Europeans to cease thinking of themselves as the most powerful people on the face of the Earth. Descriptive reports from geographers, explorers, and other travelers convinced the pope and other rulers that Catholic Europeans were morally and spiritually superior to the "heathens" in newly explored and conquered territory. Voyages of exploration had a twofold purpose, in that the conversion of the native population to Christianity was almost as important as foreign trade. This pious attitude did not hinder the development of the slave trade, which became an impetus for voyages to Africa.

With the modern world's comfortable and reliable means of transoceanic travel, it may be difficult to comprehend the extreme risk of voyaging into the open ocean during the Renaissance. Letters, logbooks, and literature of the 15th and 16th centuries refer to rocky promontories, mighty waves, ice storms, and destructive winds in metaphorical as well as literal descriptions. Exploring the world's oceans had captured the popular imagination. During the period covered by this book, Portugal and Spain dominated the voyages of exploration; France and England sent out only a few explorers. By the later 16th century Dutch and Flemish cartographers dominated the map market.

9.1 Illustrations of the "heathens" and "monstrous races" believed to inhabit foreign lands. Woodcut title page in John Mandeville's Libro de maravillas (Book of marvels, 1531). (Courtesy of The Hispanic Society of America)

GEOGRAPHY AND CARTOGRAPHY

Geography and cartography are complementary disciplines; cartography graphically depicts information about the Earth related through geographical study. Because of new Renaissance mathematical computation techniques, both fields advanced significantly between 1400 and 1600. Knowledge from ancient texts, as well as from medieval Arabic sources translated into Latin, contributed to the enhancement of research concerning the Earth's surface. Manuscript maps and Portolan charts (sailing charts) proliferated during the Renaissance. In addition, new techniques for engraving on copper plates led to the production of finely drawn maps that could be printed in multiple copies. During the mid-16th century, engraved maps were marketed by Italian map publishers, who occasionally sold small collections of maps in albums. The first album of maps describing the entire known world was published by a Flemish cartographer in 1570. World globes were created from engraved globe gores pasted onto a round plaster base. These gores contained a map of the world printed in a series of almond-shaped sections, wider across the equator and tapering to a point at the North and South Poles. When cut apart and trimmed along the edges, globe gores fit perfectly over a round form.

Descriptive geography and ornamental cartography presented information about physical and cultural aspects of foreign lands. Often exaggerated, the published reports of explorers and travelers gave Europeans their earliest knowledge of West African flora and fauna, customs of India, indigenous inhabitants of the New World, and the promise of gold and fertile land in the Americas.

Geography

Geography, or writing about the Earth, developed as a scientific discipline during the Renaissance. Unlike cosmography (see chapter 10), which related the Earth's relationship with the known universe, geography focused on divisions of the Earth itself. Chorography, a branch of geography (from the Greek word *choros*, place), consists of topographical and historical descriptions of districts or regions. During the Renaissance, this specialized field often included genealogical information. Geographic measurement benefited tremendously from advances in mathematics, and geographical mathematics was invigorated after 1410 by the translation into Latin of Ptolemy's (c. 100–c. 170) Greek treatise on geography. This field of mathematics was used to determine the location and size of parts of the Earth's surface, and pilots

and surveyors added information on the shapes of coastlines and the contours of rivers. Ptolemy's technique for describing the Earth's surface, including lines of latitude and longitude, created the foundation text for Renaissance geographical studies. (The actual positions of longitude could not be determined by Renaissance navigators because they needed an accurate portable clock. The longitude lines on maps and charts were largely ignored by those charting courses for ships.) The Greek author Strabo (c. 63 B.C.E.–c. 20 C.E.) provided the ancient model for descriptive geography. Renaissance authors wrote about the distinctive characteristics, political as well as physical, of Europe and of exotic locales.

Many texts of descriptive geography included ethnographic information. During this period, newly revealed geographic details about the Old World contributed to the development of national identities. In addition, detailed information on European colonies in the east and west, often couched in imperialist vocabulary, heightened the sense of superiority of Europeans in relation to other societies. As Europeans measured other parts of the Earth with mathematical geography, they assumed that they could control them. As Europeans learned about other places and cultures via descriptive geography, they decided that they *should* control them. A French adventurer wrote the following description of Brazilian natives in 1556: "Those who live upstream near the equator are evil and vicious; they eat human flesh. Those further from the equator, being lowland people, are more tractable. All the said savages, both upstream and down, go naked; their huts and houses are covered with leaves and bark" (Lestringant 1994, p. 134). Other reports of "barbarous" living conditions reached the eyes of European readers from Africa and from the Far East, prompting Christian Europe to attempt to convert the "heathens" while exploiting their natural resources.

Gomes Eanes de Zurara (1410/20–74), a Portuguese historian, used the government archives in Lisbon to write the first known account of tropical Africa by a European. Zurara's work, however, was not published during the Renaissance, although copies circulated in manuscript. Such reports were considered state secrets and not to be shared with foreigners. Firsthand geographic information from the voyages of Vasco da Gama (c. 1460–1524), Pedro Cabral (c. 1467–c. 1520), and other explorers nevertheless was translated into Italian and published in 1507 as *Paesi novamente retrovati* (Newly discovered lands). Although much of the country described was in the Americas, this very popular book also included reports on parts of the Orient. There were 14 16th-century editions of this text alone, plus many "adaptations" by others. The majority of European readers probably learned about foreign lands by reading this book.

The first significant description of part of America appeared in Pietro Martire d'Anghiera's (1457–1526) *De orbe novo* (On the New World, part 1, 1511). His conversations with explorers who sailed for Spain were the basis of much of the information in this book. The description of the island of Hispaniola, for example, began by stating that its shape is that of the leaf of a chestnut tree. After extolling the climate and fertility of the soil, the author described a valley with many rivers: "Out of the sands of them all there is found plenty of gold," with reports of nuggets of gold as large as a walnut, an orange, and even a child's head (Ross and McLaughlin 1968, pp. 148–149). A report from the first European exploration in the land called Virginia, published in 1589, mentioned that the natives were "handsome and goodly people" and that the "island [Roanoke] had many goodly woods, and full of deer, conies [rabbits], hares and fowl" and "the highest and reddest cedars of the world" (Scott 1976, p. 264). Reports such as these, in which the Americas were touted as a golden land, persuaded Europeans to leave their home and family to settle in "paradise." Because the natives were said not to be realizing the potential of the land and its abundance, Europeans presumed that they had the right to do so.

Cartography

The art and science of cartography depict geographical information in a graphic format. Renaissance cartography visually reinforced the divisions of the Earth described by geography. (For celestial cartography, see chapter 10). Engraved maps, which presented much greater detail than most woodcut maps, were issued in single sheets as well as in atlases. Many people could afford to buy single-sheet printed maps. During the 16th century, individual maps of France,

England, Spain, and other political entities contributed to the developing concept of nations within Europe, and maps of Europe emphasized the familiar heterogeneity of the continent, as opposed to unknown regions in Africa, Asia, and the Americas.

The Contarini world map of 1506, of which only one copy remains (in the British Museum), was the first printed map to display results of recent explorations. America is depicted but not labeled. A caption states (incorrectly, of course) that Columbus arrived on the coast of Asia to the west of Japan. The earliest printed map with the New World named *America* (after Amerigo Vespucci, 1454–1512) was a world map engraved in 1507. Created by the German cartographer Martin Waldseemüller (1470–1518), this rather large map represents South and North America as separate continents, the latter extremely narrow. (Today the unique extant example is in Wolfegg Castle, Württemberg.) A third early world map depicting America was made by Johannes Ruysch and inserted in copies of his *Cosmographiae introductio* (Introduction to cosmography, 1507–8). Amazingly accurate, Ruysch's map was drawn from firsthand observations during an expedition to the New World.

Printed maps of faraway lands often included exotic imagery in the cartouche, especially depictions of natives, and animals and plants decorated the body of the map. Decorative aspects of cartography were familiar to Renaissance navigators because they sometimes appeared on manuscript portolan charts. Many portolan charts were art objects, valued for their ornamentation as much as for their geographic information. Crafted in guilds by illuminators, and occasionally highlighted in gold, the best charts were made to order. The larger charts drawn on parchment required the entire skin of a small sheep. From extant contracts pertaining specifically to portolan charts, we know that a client paid more for extra compass roses, human figures, gold detailing, and other additional decoration.

During the 14th century, portolan chart production in the Iberian Peninsula and the kingdom of Naples was stimulated by royal mandates. Each ship had to carry at least two portolan charts of its sailing routes. Many of these charts were crafted by Majorcan chart makers, who were subjects of the king of Aragon. After the Portuguese king enticed a Majorcan

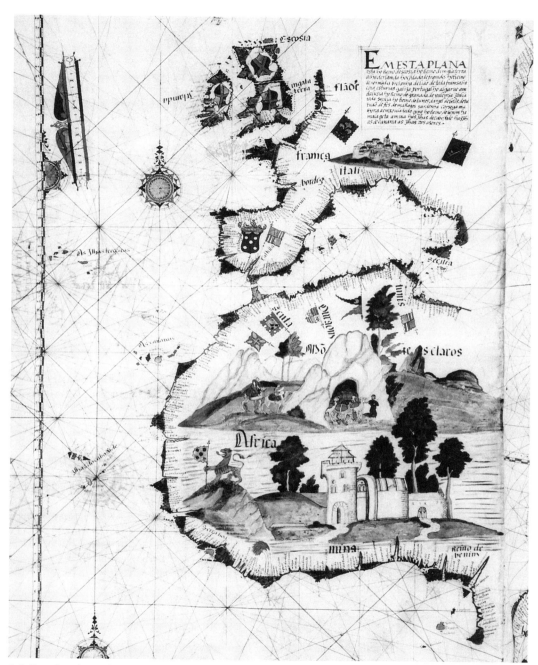

*9.2 Portolan chart of western Europe and northwestern Africa. By the Portuguese cartographer Luís Lazaro,
16th century.* (Academia das Ciencias de Lisboa, Lisbon, Portugal/Bridgeman Art Library)

cartographer to Portugal, Portuguese artists learned to make portolan charts. In addition to the geographic information learned from Majorcan chart making, the Portuguese cartographers incorporated "secret" reports from the overseas empires in Asia, Africa, and Brazil. By the 16th century, portolan charts made by the Portuguese were in demand in the major courts of Europe. These charts were not, however, readily available because navigational reports, as was descriptive geography from Portuguese sources, were secret state documents. If a Portuguese ship was attacked and the captain decided that his ship might be taken, his orders were to destroy the portolan charts. Several Portuguese chart makers were responsible for disseminating the secrets in their charts. They left Portugal and worked in the pilots' schools of other governments; one Portuguese cartographer became the chief pilot of the school in Seville. Their charts were esteemed by the captains and navigators of the voyages of exploration. Giovanni da Verrazano (1485–1528), for example, carried Portuguese portolan charts on his ships.

With Renaissance advances in mathematical cartography, the discrepancies in portraying sections of the curved surface of the Earth on a flat surface became glaringly obvious. The rhumb lines of portolan charts, radiating from central points known as wind roses, were used by navigators rather loosely. Although such directional lines following the major winds were adequate for coastal sailing, or for sailing short distances in open water, they did not conform to the Earth's curve and introduced serious errors in navigating. The Flemish cartographer Gerhard Mercator (1512–94) produced a world map with a revised system of projection in 1569. The Mercator projection, still used by mapmakers today, improved Renaissance cartography by curving the lines of latitude and the meridians (lines of longitude). By the latter 16th century, terrestrial globes (of the Earth's surface), particularly those with the Mercator projection, were used on ships and by merchants surveying the global market. They usually were displayed on carved wooden globe stands, with the globes themselves colored by hand to delineate political divisions. Many atlases featured hand-colored maps; those produced by the Flemish shop of Abraham Ortelius (1527–98) were especially desirable. In 1575 Ortelius was appointed cartographer to the king of Spain, the culmination of a remarkable career as an engraver, cartographer, and map dealer. He continued to publish numerous editions as well as three translations of his *Theatrum orbis terrarum* (Atlas of the Earth's globe), originally issued in 1570. Ortelius's workshop functioned as a map-coloring studio, where his daughter, Anne, was a talented watercolor artist.

Toward the end of the 16th century, Amsterdam emerged as a center for printed maps, globes, and navigational instruments, as the Blaeu family established a cartographic dynasty that endured for several decades. The founder was Willem Janzoon Blaeu (1571–1638), an astronomer who had studied with Tycho Brahe (1546–1601; see chapter 10). The large-scale world map that he published in 1605 included inset views of famous cities along the borders. Known as a planisphere because it presents the spherical Earth as two hemispheres on a flat surface, this style of world map was popularized by the Blaeu firm.

TRAVEL

In 1400 the world of most people was defined first by their local surroundings and then by their region or province. Except for peddlers, pilgrims, soldiers, and sailors, members of the lower classes did not usually travel because they could not leave their farm or workshop. For these people, the walk to a fair in a neighboring village was probably as far as they ever traveled from home. Moreover, most roads were no more than rocky pathways, dangerous in many areas because of bandits, and travel by sea was even riskier because of storms and pirates. The merchants, missionaries, diplomats, artists, students, and others who journeyed cross-country or across the oceans used horses, mules, carts, wagons, coaches, riverine vessels, coasting vessels, and seafaring carracks that could transport nearly 1,000 people. Some journeys, of course, were easier than others. Slaves stacked by the hundreds in the hold of ships surely experienced the worst of Renaissance travel; members of royal families transported in the elegant, padded carriages of the late 16th century traveled in comparative luxury. Europe was flooded with reports of new lands and new opportunities between 1493 and 1600, prompt-

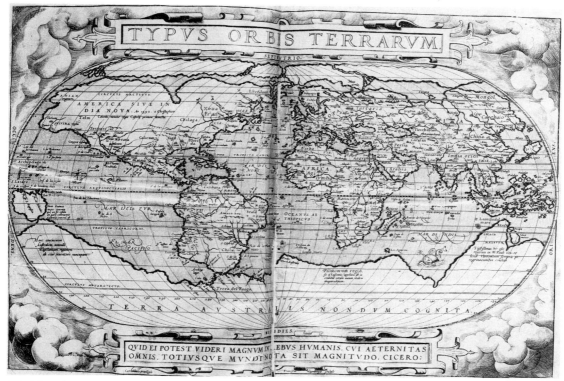

9.3 Map of the world. Engraving published in the 1574 Latin edition of Ortelius's atlas. Note the extraordinary size of Antarctica, covering the entire southern portion of the globe. (Photograph courtesy of Sotheby's, Inc., © 2003)

ing numerous individuals to depart from the relative safety of home with the knowledge that they probably would never return. By 1600 even those who stayed home were aware of a much larger world than that of the previous century. Travel literature and engravings of distant places put the world at their door.

Inland Waterways and Harbors

INLAND WATERWAYS

People and merchandise traveled inland via lakes, rivers, and canals. A journey by boat across a large lake could be relatively fast; travel via rivers and canals was notoriously slow. Rivers, of course, had currents, which could work for or against the traveler. Most merchandise transported on rivers or canals was pulled along on a barge by a horse walking on a pathway beside the water. Going downstream, a moderately loaded barge unhindered by other traffic might have taken no longer than 24 hours to travel across one-third of France; this speed would be possible under optimal weather conditions, with the river clear of debris and not at low water. A trip upstream on the same river could take a week or more. Whereas people usually traveled on single boats or barges, products such as grain and textiles often were transported in a line of barges grouped together, which moved slowly indeed. In addition, some rivers and canals had tolls, decreasing the speed of travel when several vessels lined up to pay the toll. There were few inland canals in Europe before the 17th century. Although Leonardo da Vinci (1452–1519) is thought to have designed several locks for the Milan canals in 1487, the use of locks for moving vessels from one level of water to another was largely unknown during the Renaissance. Canals were very practical, however, in flat areas such as the Netherlands. Barges hauled by a horse did not travel much faster than three miles per hour in canals. Even if vessels could have moved faster, their wash would have eroded the dirt banks of the canal. Very few inland canals were constructed with stone or brick walls. Finally, rivers and canals were not always dependable means of transportation because in very dry seasons they simply did not contain enough water.

HARBORS

Several European rivers were deep enough, and ships were small enough, that oceangoing vessels could dock in riverine harbors such as Antwerp on the Scheldt River. Even where the rivers flowing by such harbors were shallow, new designs for dredging machines usually kept the traffic flowing. Several harbors were constructed or renovated in Europe during the 15th and 16th centuries, notably the Tuscan port of Livorno. Located near Pisa, on the northwestern coast of the Italian Peninsula, the village of Livorno was selected by Cosimo I de' Medici (1519–74) to replace Pisa when the latter city's harbor began silting in at an alarming rate. Florentine artists and architects participated in an ambitious project to reclaim marshy land, construct a wharf, and dig a canal between Livorno and Pisa. The Florentine government encouraged settlers, including Jews, Moors, and Turks (not welcome in many areas of western Europe), successfully transforming the village of Livorno into a thriving port city by the end of the 16th century.

The largest inland harbor in western Europe, and one of the busiest, was Seville, located 55 miles from the Atlantic Ocean. Seville dominated shipping in the western Mediterranean, just as Venice led in the east. After the establishment of the Casa de Contratación (house of trade) in Seville in 1505, the city's harbor had a monopoly on trade with Spain's colonial possessions, including silver bullion. Impressive new buildings were erected for the pilots' school and other organizations that served Spanish navigation and trade. Travelers entering the teeming port of Seville during the 16th century must have felt that they were at the nexus of European wealth and power.

Coastal Navigation

Coastal navigation required charts, though most coasting vessels stayed within sight of land. Submerged rocks and shipwrecks, sandbars, treacherous currents, and estuaries were indicated in the better portolan charts, whose cartographic accuracy was impeccable. To aid sailors as they navigated, portolan charts also featured iconic depictions of port cities and prominent topographic elements, such as mountains and lighthouses. Several extant portolan charts have small holes around the edges, suggesting that these charts were either nailed to a table or wall or laced with cord and mounted on a frame. Pinpricks in the center of wind roses indicate that a measuring compass was centered in the middle of the winds and rotated in an arc to determine sailing directions. During the early Renaissance, ships from Genoa, Venice, Marseilles and Catalan ports dominated the Mediterranean, sailing mostly along the coasts with the aid of portolan charts, a magnetic compass, and an astrolabe, an instrument used by Islamic astronomers. During the 16th century, the most famous northern port for navigators was Dieppe, on the coast of France, whose cartographic school was renowned for its portolan charts. Besides coasting south to the mouth of the Mediterranean, sailors from Dieppe ventured to Africa and across the Atlantic. By the late 15th century, sailors realized that the magnetic compass did not take into account the magnetic declination of the Earth, and the azimuth compass was invented. This instrument contributed to the accuracy of navigation in general. With the astrolabe ("star taker"), sailors could fix their position within a specific latitude.

Navigating beyond the Coast

During the 15th century Portuguese captains navigating the African coast and the oceans beyond were faced with the problem of sailing without the North Star. This star was the point of reference for determining latitude in northern waters. In the school founded by Prince Henry the Navigator (1394–1460), geographers and astronomers worked on revising tables for the declination of the Sun, which moved to a different position relative to the horizon each day. Improved knowledge of the ecliptic (the Earth's solar orbit) gave navigators a better tool for sailing with confidence below the equator, and far out into the ocean. Although relatively few documents of the early Portuguese and Spanish voyages remain, the few that survive, especially the logbooks, record the procedures of navigating in the open ocean. One of the most famous is the daily logbook of da Gama's first voyage, compiled by a member of the expedition. By far the most valued navigational document of the Renaissance was (and is) the journal kept by Christopher Columbus (1451–1506) during the first voyage, which survived in a reliable 16th-century copy. Greatly abridged, the journal was published in 1493 in four cities, introducing European readers to Columbus's momentous "discovery."

By the late 15th century, commercial ships were outfitted with large square sails, necessary for moving heavy cargo through rough seas. It was impossible to sail such ships close to the wind to change directions easily. The smaller caravels used for many of the voyages of exploration had lateen (triangular) primary sails that could be augmented by one or more square sails. The Renaissance innovation of combining triangular and square sails resulted in the construction of ships that could respond with more flexibility to the unpredictable conditions of ocean travel. With lateen sails navigators could slowly move within 10 degrees of the wind, or tack against it in a zigzag course. Although manipulating lateen sails was rather time-consuming, the ultimate gain in speed surpassed the capabilities of square-rigged ships. Once the wind direction was set with the lateen sails, a ship with both types of sails could hoist the square-rigged sails and quickly follow its course.

From the latter 16th century, several reports from English navigators were published by Richard Hakluyt (c. 1552–1616). Among other topics, these document the particular hazards of sailing into northern waters. The expedition of Martin Frobisher (1535–94), for example, experienced an ice storm in 1576 in their attempt to locate a Northwest Passage to the Orient. Great slabs of sharp ice were pushed against the ships, threatening to crash through timber three inches thick: "(The sailors) strengthened the sides of their ships with junks of cable, beds, masts, planks, and such like, which

being hanged overboard . . . might better defend them from the outrageous sway and strokes of the said ice. . . . For some, even without board upon the ice, and some within board upon the sides of their ships, having poles, pikes, pieces of timber, and oars in their hands, stood almost day and night without any rest, bearing off the force, and breaking the sway of the ice with such incredible pain and peril, that it was wonderful to behold" (Scott 1976, p. 248). Such accounts, eagerly read by the public, heroicized explorers and encouraged young adventure seekers to join future expeditions.

Traveling by Land

People traveled overland for many purposes, including commerce, diplomacy, pilgrimages, postal services, education, spa treatment, and warfare (see chapter 7, Warfare). Merchandise was moved by a variety of means, including carts, pack animals, and large wagons. Merchants often transported goods in caravans of several pack animals or wheeled conveyances. Caravans of several travelers provided some security against bandits, and extra pack animals could carry provisions for the merchants and their animals. Just as today's automobiles require fuel, animals transporting people and commodities had to be fed. The roadside inns charged exorbitant prices, knowing that they had a captive market. Moreover, eating and sleeping in an inn were not pleasant experiences, because three or more strangers had to share each bed, which often was infested with fleas. Inns also attracted unsavory characters, notably mercenary soldiers looking for a victim, and prostitutes.

The vast majority of travelers by land journeyed on foot, especially those on religious pilgrimages. As these travelers passed local shrines, they could acquire souvenirs such as metallic pilgrim badges that were fastened to hats and clothing. Rome, Jerusalem, Santiago da Compostela, and Canterbury were the preferred destinations, where merchants hawked pilgrim badges as well as statuettes, candles, and other devotional objects. By the 16th century printed views of the cathedrals and schematic maps of the pilgrimage routes were available. Pilgrimages were ambitious undertakings, often requiring several weeks of travel. Walking purposefully from

Mainz to Venice, for example, required 15 to 20 days, a distance of 370 miles. Traveling by both land and sea, a pilgrim could leisurely make the journey from Germany to Jerusalem in three months.

Walking was usually as fast as traveling by coach or wagon because the roadways outside cities and towns were in terrible condition, not much better than they were during the Middle Ages. Wheels became stuck in ruts or mired in mud, with the draft horses or mules struggling along in adverse conditions. In dry seasons, passengers in wagons were subjected to clouds of dust churned up by the horses. Mounted on the axles of wooden wheels, even private coaches with padded seats were quite uncomfortable, bouncing and shifting with every rut and curve in the road. More comfortable were the newer coaches suspended from thick leather straps or litters (sedan chairs) suspended on wooden poles with one horse in front and another behind. Horseback riding was the fastest mode of travel. In some regions travelers could rent horses at stations along the roadway, changing horses as pony express riders did in the Old West. Couriers on horseback were the speediest travelers in Renaissance Europe. Changing to a fresh horse every 12 miles or so, an experienced courier could cover as many as 50 miles per day. By the latter 15th century, both France and Spain had postal service using couriers. During the 16th century the postal systems of the Holy See and of the Habsburg empire were models of efficient courier service.

TRAVEL LITERATURE

Renaissance pilgrims were guided by informational publications that described and depicted not only the main roads, but also scenic or inspirational side trips. These books and pamphlets were quite popular. In France, for example, approximately 8 percent of all books printed in the 16th century were guidebooks for pilgrims. One of the earliest books printed in English was *Informacion for Pylgrymes unto the Holy Londe* (1498), because Jerusalem was an important destination. Letters sent from foreign missionaries provided descriptive accounts of distant locales that could be savored by those unable or unwilling to travel, just as the itineraries marketed to students attending foreign universities could also be enjoyed by their family and friends at home. Several practical road guides were published during the 16th century, a few claiming to describe all the roads of the world. Travel as a metaphor for one's life became quite popular during the Renaissance, probably as a result of the heightened interest in actual travel, in Europe as well as abroad.

EXPLORATION

Until the Renaissance voyages of exploration, the world was defined with Europe at its center. Although politically this assumption still pertained in 1600, geographically it had been proven false. In 1400, the average educated European possessed knowledge of geography that extended from Scandinavia across to the British Isles, down the western coast of Europe to the north coast of Africa, across and up to the eastern shore of the Black Sea, and back along the Danube River into eastern Europe. Although sea captains knew of the existence of present-day Iceland, Greenland, and various islands, their size and exact locations on the globe were a mystery to most people. Europe's information about sub-Saharan Africa, south Asia, and the Far East was obtained from the few travelers who had journeyed there and written about their experiences, whose observations were often exaggerated or distorted. Manuscript maps, however, did show Africa with its entire coastline, along with descriptive captions concerning gold-producing areas in West Africa.

At the beginning of the Renaissance, not even scholars of mathematics could measure the Earth's circumference (although they did know that it was roughly spherical), and the equator of the Earth was thought to be so hot and fiery that no human being could survive in that zone. Through explorations funded by the Portuguese in Africa and the East, and by the Spanish, French, and English in the Americas, the world was enlarged in Europe's imagination by 1600. The possibility of expanding commercial ventures far beyond Europe, and of converting countless thousands to Christianity, prompted governments as well as individuals to commit themselves to further exploration. Of all the voyages of exploration undertaken between 1400 and 1600, the most impressive

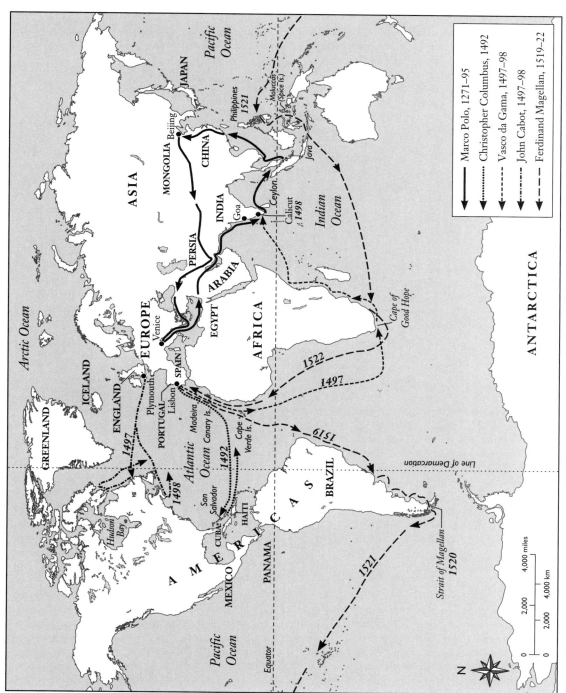

Map 4. *Major Voyages of Exploration*

→	Marco Polo, 1271–95
→	Christopher Columbus, 1492
→	Vasco da Gama, 1497–98
→	John Cabot, 1497–98
→	Ferdinand Magellan, 1519–22

was the circumnavigation of the globe (1519–22) begun by Ferdinand Magellan (1480–1521), a Portuguese who sailed for the king of Spain. Grossly underestimating the size of the Pacific Ocean (which he named), Magellan nevertheless led his five ships around the southern tip of South America, reached the Philippines, and claimed them for Spain. Although he was killed in a battle with natives and his associate Juan Sebastián del Cano (1476–1526) finally reached Spain with only one ship (the *Victoria*), Magellan's voyage was pivotal. Not only did the expedition determine the vastness of the Pacific, it also helped define Portuguese and Spanish territory for future trade and colonization (see later discussion).

Africa

In 1479 the rulers of Spain and Portugal agreed that Spanish ships would not trade in the Portuguese Atlantic islands or in West Africa, and Spain (Castile and León) acquired rights to the Canary Islands along with other concessions. Portuguese incursions into Africa were mainly commercial ventures, but Portugal's king, John II (1455–95), did send Pêro da Covilhã (fl. 1487, d. 1525) to search for Ethiopia and its legendary Christian king, Prester John. Covilhã first traveled by land and sea to Calicut (India) and sent back a report to the king about the lucrative spice trade. He reached Ethiopia in 1490 and was forced to remain there until his death. A Portuguese priest who visited him wrote *Verdadera informaçam das terras do Preste João* (True account of the lands of Prester John, 1540). Some attempts were made to introduce Christianity to West Africa, and the king of the Congo converted to Christianity. For other African rulers in that region, Christianity was only a curiosity.

In 1483, Diogo Cão (fl. 1482–86) set out from Portugal to explore the west coast of Africa. The first European to navigate the Congo River, he captured Africans, whom he took home to sell as slaves. Returning to the Congo in 1486, Cão made an arrangement with the local ruler to supply him with more slaves, usually African prisoners of war. Thus a Christian king in West Africa benefited economically from the black slave trade. With Portugal's flourishing African trade in pepper and gold, and with the new commercial venture of slavery, John II decided to send an expedition that might determine

the southern extent of Africa for future trading posts as well as locate a possible route by sea from Africa to India and the Far East.

To the East

Bartolomeu Dias (fl. 1478, d. 1500) sailed with Diogo Cão and was familiar with the winds along the west coast of Africa. Dias was in charge of the royal storage facility in the fortified African trading post of São Jorge da Mina in Guinea. He also may have been a privateer who operated in Genoese waters in the 1470s. His experience of the African coast and navigational expertise caused John II to assign Dias as captain of three caravels that sailed out of Lisbon's harbor in 1487 toward Africa. During the journey Dias had difficulty pushing toward the south because the prevailing winds along the southwestern coast of Africa blow toward the northwest. Passing into uncharted waters and fighting the wind, Dias made the decision to turn into the open sea, where he traveled for nearly two weeks. When the air began to feel cooler, he turned his ships back toward the east and discovered that he had sailed past the Cape of Good Hope. When Dias returned in triumph to Lisbon, Columbus was in the city and must have known about his success.

After Columbus completed his second voyage (see later discussion), the king of Portugal commissioned the most ambitious expedition yet, from Lisbon to India. Under the assumption that Columbus had reached the Far East, Portugal needed to explore the possibility of navigating around the tip of Africa and through the Indian Ocean to establish control of the spice trade. In 1497 Vasco da Gama (c. 1468–1524) was commissioned to lead the first expedition destined for India via the Cape of Good Hope. Instead of hugging the coast of Africa, almost impossible because of the prevailing winds, da Gama set out from the Cape Verde Islands toward the open ocean. In a daring feat of navigation, he sailed for 93 days on the open ocean to reach the southern coast of Africa. This extent of time spent at sea was a record for any European vessel, at least for any that returned to tell the story. To put da Gama's achievement (or possibly his great good luck) in perspective, we should note that the 1492 voyage of Columbus took only 36 days. After rounding the tip of Africa, da Gama reached

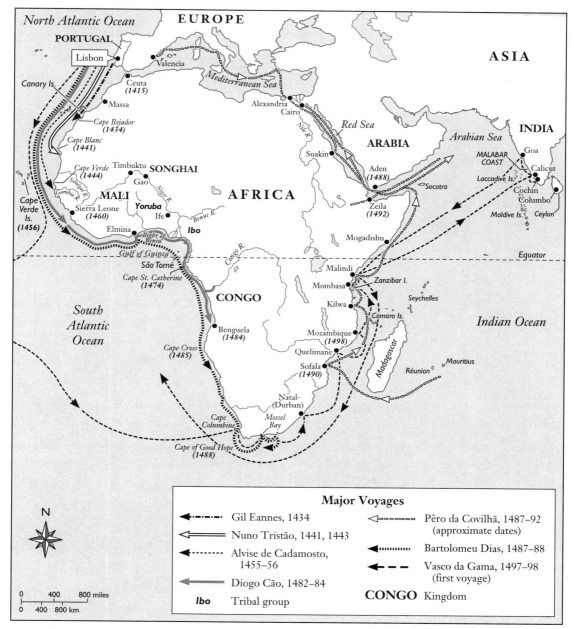

Map 5. *Portuguese Voyages to 1498*

waters into which no European had ever navigated. Fighting the Agulhas current, he finally arrived at Mozambique, where his Arabic interpreter hired local pilots to help him navigate to Malindi. There, another pilot, Ahmed ibn Majid, was hired to sail the rest of the way to Calicut (Kozhikode). This teeming

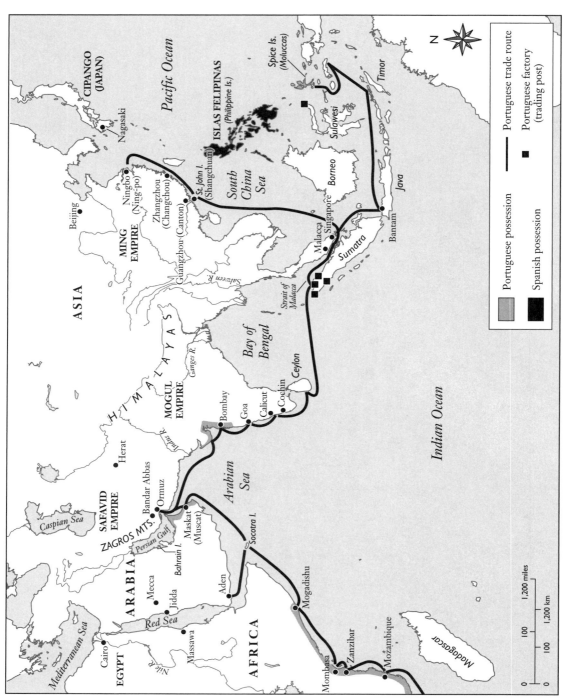

Map 6. Asia and the Indian Ocean, 16th century

port was the most important commercial center for the East–West market. Although da Gama lost half his ships and more than half of his sailors to scurvy (deficiency of vitamin C), he returned to Lisbon with a shipment of pepper and cinnamon. More important, he now knew how to reach India by sailing south. The king of Portugal quickly launched another fleet of ships, under the command of Pedro Álvars Cabral (c. 1467–c. 1520). Following da Gama's instructions, Cabral attempted to sweep toward the tip of Africa by using prevailing winds. Instead his ships were blown much farther out into the Atlantic and Cabral sighted the coast of present-day Brazil. Ordering one ship to return to Lisbon to report this unknown land in the west, Cabral continued on to India with the fleet. Rather accidentally, Cabral discovered that during the summer (monsoon season) the prevailing winds in the Indian Ocean could assist navigators voyaging from Africa to India. Thus da Gama's two-year trip was accomplished by Cabral in 17 months. (Unfortunately, very little is known about the first decade of Portuguese exploration in Brazil. Many of Portugal's historic documents from this period were destroyed in Lisbon in the horrific earthquake and tidal wave of 1755.)

The voyages of Columbus spurred the Portuguese to compete with the Crown of Spain diplomatically as well as nautically. After Columbus returned to Spain from his 1492 voyage (discussed later), announcing that he had sailed to the Orient, the monarchs of both Spain and Portugal claimed territory in the fabled Indies. They approached the pope and asked him to divide the world between them. Earlier in the 15th century, Portugal had been granted the rights to the Indies, mainly because this geographic area was assumed to be located near the coast of Africa. Columbus's 1492 voyage and his subsequent claims prompted Spain to request partial rights to the East Indies and its trade commodities, especially spices and textiles (silk and fine cotton). In 1494, the papal Treaty of Tordesillas established the line of demarcation near the longitudinal 50th degree west of Greenwich, England, granting Brazil to Portugal. The treaty was modified in 1529 by the Treaty of Saragossa (Zaragoza), in which Portugal paid Spain for rights to the Moluccas, or Spice Islands. Portugal never contested Spain for the Philippines, located within the Portuguese zone.

(None of the other governments of Europe honored these treaties as competition for the spice trade increased during the 16th century and especially the 17th century.)

The Moluccas should not be confused with Malacca, a major port in East Asia not far from Singapore. Malacca was an important intermediate city for the Portuguese, approximately halfway between India and China, and India and the Moluccas. Having captured the Indian port of Goa in 1510, Portuguese forces sailed for Malacca the following year. Led by Afonso de Albuquerque (c. 1453–1515), admiral of the fleet, they drove out the Muslims and assumed control of the city for more than a century. Albuquerque sent an embassy to Rome, where the pope publicly celebrated this Christian victory over the "infidels," as the Portuguese ambassador and his entourage paraded exotic animals and wealth from the Orient. The Portuguese traded with both China and Japan and founded the colony of Macao in

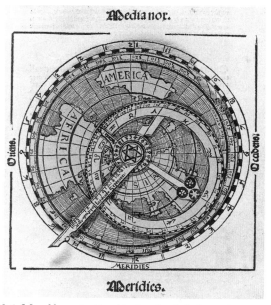

9.4 Movable navigational tool used to help determine a ship's position in the open sea. Woodcut device in the 1524 edition of Petrus Apianus's Cosmographia *(Cosmography), 1524. (The device is called a volvelle and can be turned.)* (Photograph courtesy of Sotheby's, Inc., © 2003)

1557. Reports of European travelers to Asia published in the 16th century corrected and clarified geographical knowledge of that far-off region of the globe, and new maps published toward the end of the century began to demystify the Far East for educated Europeans.

To the West

Several of the captains who led Renaissance voyages of exploration from Europe to the west, from Columbus to Sir Humphrey Gilbert (c. 1539–83), were looking for a shorter route to Japan, China, and the East Indies. For nearly 20 years before his 1492 voyage, Columbus had corresponded with scholars about geographical and cartographic questions. He concluded that the Asian landmass was much larger than it actually is, an error that would have located Japan much closer to Europe. Columbus began discussing his ideas for a western voyage to the Far East in 1485, attempting to persuade the Spanish Crown to finance his expedition. Meanwhile, his brother approached the king of France as well as the king of England, who declined. Finally Queen Isabella I (1451–1504) decided to support the endeavor. In 1492 Columbus thought that he had reached islands near the Orient. Instead, his first sighting was of present-day Watling's Island in the Bahamas, where the flagship, *Santa María*, along with the *Pinta* and *Niña* stayed for three days. Before Columbus reached Hispaniola (the island where present-day Haiti and Dominican Republic are located), the captain of the *Pinta* sailed away and the ship was missing for a time. After claiming Hispaniola for Spain and exploring the island, Columbus set sail to return across the Atlantic. Almost immediately the *Santa María* was smashed on a reef, and the *Niña* returned to harbor. Columbus had no choice but to leave some of his men as settlers, ordering them to construct a small fort with timbers from the wrecked ship. Thirty-nine settlers remained on Hispaniola as Columbus captained the *Niña* toward Spain. His ship met the *Pinta* along the way back, but that ship's captain abandoned Columbus once again to return to Spain before him. Queen Isabella refused to grant him an audience, and Columbus was credited with the success of the expedition. After

he described the infinite riches of the islands and exhibited the Native Americans whom he had transported to the court in Barcelona, Columbus was given an impressive command of 17 ships and some 1,500 men. His passengers included craftsmen, government officials, a surgeon, and other potential settlers lured by tales of the fortunes to be made in Spain's new dominion.

Landing at Hispaniola, Columbus founded another settlement (Isabela) because the first group of settlers had been killed by local inhabitants. After exploring the coasts of Cuba and Jamaica for five months, Columbus returned to Isabela to discover hostile natives and sickness among the settlers. When he returned to Spain, his brother moved the Isabela settlers along the coast to the location of Santo Domingo, thus founding the oldest European town in the New World. Once again Columbus, who had taken back solid evidence of gold and other riches, was hailed as a conquering hero in Spain. During his third voyage (if not during the second—the point is disputed), Columbus reached the American mainland in 1498. He sailed into the Gulf of Paria, claiming Venezuela for Spain, along with the pearl fisheries in the gulf. Arriving at Santo Domingo, Columbus found the settlement close to mutiny and learned that these conditions had been reported to the Spanish authorities. Columbus and his two brothers supposedly governing the settlement were placed in chains and taken to Spain. Isabella, nevertheless, had him released and put in charge of a fourth voyage. Off the coast of Honduras, he came upon a canoe in which the natives had copper vessels and other indications of a relatively advanced civilization (Mayan and Aztec). Instead of exploring the land from which they had sailed (Yucatán), Columbus persevered in his attempt to find a strait through which he could reach the Orient. This was his final voyage of exploration, which ended with his being shipwrecked and marooned for a year before returning to Spain.

As soon as letters from Columbus about his first voyage were published, the kings of England and France became interested in exploring the new lands. Early 16th-century reports increasingly persuaded Europeans that the territory was indeed not the Orient, but a New World, which came to be called America. While Spaniards certainly dominated the

QVI RATE VELIVOLA OCCIDVOS PENETRAVIT AD IDOS
PRIMVS ET AMERICAM NOBILITAVIT HVMVM

CHRISTOPHORVS COLVMBVS LIGVR, INDIARV PRIM'INVEⁱⁱᵗ A'1492

ASTRORVM CONSVLT, ET IPSO NOBILIS AVSV
CHRISTOPHOR' TALI FRONTE COLVMB'ERAT

9.5 Portrait of Christopher Columbus. Engraving in Jean-Jacques Boissard, Icones . . . virorum illustrium
(Portraits of famous men, 1597–99). (Photograph courtesy of Sotheby's, Inc.,© 2003)

California coast, the Caribbean, Mexico, Central America, South America, and southeastern North America, both France and England had settlements in North America. England first explored the new lands to the west in an official way when John Cabot (a citizen of Venice) sailed from Bristol in 1497, across the Atlantic, and along some part of the northeastern seaboard. On his second voyage, Cabot may have traveled as far south along the coastline as Cape Hatteras, North Carolina. Although he founded no settlements, Cabot was credited with informing the English about the Grand Banks off Newfoundland. This section of the Atlantic became a very productive fishing ground for Renaissance mariners. The first English settlement was established in 1585 by Sir Walter Raleigh (1554–1618), on Roanoke Island (off the coast of present-day North Carolina). The colony failed, however, and the survivors were taken home by Sir Francis Drake (1540 or 1543–96) in one of his privateering ships that had been menacing the Spanish. A second group of settlers on the same island became known as the "lost colony" because all traces of them disappeared.

In 1523 Giovanni Verrazano (a Florentine) sailed under the flag of France to search for a sea passage to the Orient. Landing on the North Carolina coast, he turned north and became the first European to explore the harbor of present-day New York City. The French king's determination to locate a Northwest Passage by sea to the Orient resulted in the French exploration of what would become Canada. Financed by the French Crown, Jacques Cartier set out from Saint Malo in 1534 and explored the Gaspé Peninsula and surrounding coastal regions. Returning to France with reports about three Indian kingdoms in the north that might be comparable to the rich kingdoms of Mexico, Cartier was outfitted by the king for another voyage. With captured natives to guide him, Cartier traveled nearly 1,000 miles up the Saint Lawrence River, to the site of present-day Montreal. Though a climb up Montreal's mountain showed Cartier that land stretched as far as he could see, he remained hopeful and returned home with more captives and stories of potential wealth. During his final voyage of 1541 Cartier founded the colony of Cap Rouge (near present-day Quebec City), but the previously friendly natives withdrew their support when their relatives taken as "guests"

did not return home, and the colonists suffered from the frigid winter. The colony ended in 1543 when the settlers sailed back to France.

Summary of Major Explorations and Conquests

1434	Gil Eannes reaches Cape Bojador on the coast of West Africa.
1484	Diogo Cão sails into the estuary of the Congo River.
1488	Bartolomeu Dias voyages beyond the Cape of Good Hope.
1492	Christopher Columbus sails to the Caribbean islands.
1497	John Cabot reaches North America.
1497–98	Vasco da Gama sails around the tip of Africa to reach India.
1500	Pedro Cabral sights the coast of Brazil.
1511	Portuguese troops capture the city of Malacca.
1513	Vasco Núñez de Balboa sees the Pacific Ocean.
1513	Juan Ponce de León explores the Florida coast.
1519–22	Ferdinand Magellan sets out to circumnavigate the globe and dies along the way; the voyage is completed by Sebastian del Cano.
1519–38	Hernán Cortés explores and conquers Mexico.
1523	Giovanni da Verrazano sails from France, along the eastern North American seaboard, and into present-day New York harbor.
1534–35	Jacques Cartier enters the Gulf of Saint Lawrence.
1539–41	Hernando de Soto explores the present-day southeastern United States.
1540	Hernando de Alarcón reaches California.
1540–42	Vázquez de Coronado travels through the present-day southeastern and south central United States.
1576–78	Martin Frobisher attempts to find a Northwest Passage.
1577–80	Sir Francis Drake circumnavigates the globe.

1583	Sir Humphrey Gilbert reaches Newfoundland.
1585	Sir Walter Raleigh and associates establish the first English colony in America on Roanoke Island.
1596	Willem Barents explores the Arctic.

Major Figures

Alarcón, Hernando de (c. 1500–c. 1542) commanded the Spanish expedition to California in 1540. Exploring the Baja coast, he determined that Baja was not an island, as had been assumed, but rather a peninsula.

Albuquerque, Afonso de (c. 1453–1515) was a Portuguese admiral who became the second viceroy of India, significantly enlarging the eastern empire.

Apianus, Petrus (1501–1552), astronomer and mathematician, taught mathematics at Ingolstadt. His *Cosmographia* (Cosmography) of 1520 applied information from Renaissance exploration to update Ptolemy's ancient work on geography.

Azurara, Gomes Eanes de.   See ZURARA, GOMES EANES DE.

Balboa   See NÚÑEZ DE BALBOA, VASCO.

Barbaro, Giosofat (1413–1494) was a merchant in Venice whose business took him to Russia and the Caucasus for 15 years. Subsequently he was appointed as the ambassador of the Venetian republic to Persia, where he remained for four years. Barbaro thus combined two classes of Renaissance travelers, the businessman and the diplomat.

Barents, Willem (1550–1597), Dutch navigator, explored the Arctic region during the 1590s.

Barros, João de (1496–1570) led an expedition to northern Brazil in 1539. After returning to Portugal, he wrote about the Portuguese conquest of Asia.

Behaim, Martin (c. 1436–1507), German geographer, resided at the Portuguese court during the reign of John II. Behaim sailed with Diogo Cão on his second African expedition. In 1492 he made the first known terrestrial globe (today in the German National Museum in Nuremberg, Behaim's native city).

Blaeu, Willem Janszoon (1571–1638) was a Dutch cartographer and publisher of maps who had studied astronomy with the Danish astronomer Tycho Brahe. Blaeu's publishing house issued globes as well as atlases, and in 1605 he published a famous large-scale world map.

Bry, Théodore de (1528–1598), Flemish engraver, founded a printing workshop in Frankfurt specializing in travel books and related material. He published Las Casas's 1552 account of atrocities against New World natives. De Bry and his sons provided Europeans with visual documentation of Renaissance exploration and colonialization.

Cabeza de Vaca, Álvar Núñez (c. 1500–c. 1564) was one of the few surviving victims of an exploratory voyage to Florida and wandered across the present-day southern United States for some nine years. His account of this experience was published in 1537. Cabeza de Vaca became governor of Río de la Plata and Paraguay.

Cabot, John (*Giovanni Caboto*) (c. 1450–c. 1498), an Italian in the service of England, made two Atlantic crossings, sailing from England. His son, Sebastian, continued his explorations of the North Atlantic after 1498.

Cabot, Sebastian (1476–1557), son of John Cabot, explored the northeastern shores of the present-day United States in attempts to discover a Northwest Passage to the Far East.

Cabral, Pedro Álvars (c. 1467–c. 1520), Portuguese explorer, landed on the coast of Brazil in 1500 after setting sail for India via Africa. He claimed the country for Portugal and then journeyed on to India.

Cadamosto, Alvise de (1432–1488), Venetian navigator, explored the western coast of Africa in the service of Portugal. His account of his voyages was published in 1507.

Cano, Juan Sebastián del (1475–1526), who captained one of Magellan's five ships, assumed command after Magellan was killed. When he finally arrived in Seville with only his ship, he was hailed as the first to sail around the world.

Cão, Diogo (fl. 1482–1486) was a Portuguese explorer and the first European to navigate the Congo River; he returned home with a cargo of African slaves.

Cartier, Jacques (1491–1557) made three voyages searching for a Northwest Passage to the Far East. He claimed Canada for France and took back several Native Americans.

Cavendish, Thomas (1560–1592), sea captain and explorer, became the second Englishman to circumnavigate the globe.

Champlain, Samuel (1567–1635) explored the Caribbean, indicating that a canal could be dug across the isthmus of Panama. Later he set up a trading post at Mont Royal (present-day Montreal) and became governor of New France (Canada).

Chancellor, Richard (d. 1556) explored the Arctic region, traveling overland from the White Sea to make trading contacts with the Russians.

Colón, Diego (1478/79–1526), son of Christopher Columbus, inherited his father's titles and became governor of Hispaniola.

Columbus, Christopher (1451–1506), born in Genoa, explored the Caribbean islands, insisting that they were part of the Far East. He died without realizing that in 1492 he had reached a region of the world unknown to Europeans.

Contarini, Ambrogio (1429–after 1496) was a Venetian traveler who joined Giosofat Barbaro in Persia.

Conti, Niccolò de (c. 1395–1469) left Venice in 1419 and journeyed for 25 years in the Middle East, India, and Java.

Coronado   See VÁZQUEZ DE CORONADO, FRANCISCO.

Corte Real family of explorers were the father, João, who sailed to Newfoundland circa 1472, and his sons, Gaspar (c. 1450–1501) and Miguel (c. 1450–1502). The latter son may have explored the area that is now Massachusetts.

Cortés de Albacar, Martin (c. 1510–1582) wrote *El arte de navigar* (The Art of navigating, 1551), which included information about magnetic declination.

Coryate, Thomas (c. 1577–1617) walked through much of western Europe and published an account of his journey in 1611. The following year he traveled to India by land, a journey of four years.

Cosa, Juan de la (d. 1510), Columbus's cartographer on the second voyage to the Caribbean, made subsequent voyages to the New World. In 1500 he published a map of the world, the first to include the Americas.

Covilhã, Pêro da (fl. 1487, d. 1525) was charged by the king of Portugal with discovering the source of cinnamon as well as a land route to Ethiopia. Covilhã sailed to India, and sent back information to Portugal with recommendations concerning the best ocean route for Vasco da Gama; he then in 1490 traveled to Ethiopia. Although honored by the king, he was placed under house arrest for the remainder of his life.

Cunha, Tristão da (c. 1460–1540) explored the South Atlantic and the east coast of Africa, and later joined Afonso de Albuquerque on an expedition. He presented souvenirs of the Indies to Pope Leo X in 1513.

Davis, John (1550–1605) sailed in search of a Northwest Passage. He also invented the backstaff, a device by which the observer faces away from the

Sun and measures its altitude from its shadow, thus calculating latitude.

Dias, Bartolomeu (fl. 1478, d. 1500) was the first European to sail past the Cape of Good Hope (southern tip of Africa). He also sailed as far as the Azores with da Gama and to Brazil with Cabral.

Díaz del Castillo, Bernal (1492–c. 1581) sailed to Central America in 1514 and eventually settled in Guatemala. His account of the conquest of Mexico published in 1632 became quite popular.

Díaz de Solís, Juan (1470–1516) explored the Atlantic coast south of North America and succeeded Amerigo Vespucci as royal chief pilot.

Drake, Sir Francis (1540 or 1543–1596), privateer, was instrumental in the defeat of the Spanish Armada. In 1577–80 he circumnavigated the globe.

Elcano, Juan Sebastián del See CANO, JUAN SEBASTIÁN DEL.

Esquivel, Juan de (fl. 1494–1519) sailed on Columbus's second voyage. He later conquered Jamaica, where his brutal treatment of the natives was infamous.

Federmann, Nikolaus (c. 1501–1542), an agent of the Welser bank in Augsburg, explored Venezuela and later the Orinoco basin. His account of his experiences was published in 1557.

Fenton, Edward (d. 1603) sailed with Frobisher in his attempts to discover a Northwest Passage.

Fernandes, Álvaro (fl. 1440s) explored the western coast of Africa, the first European to sail past Cape Verde.

Fernández, Juan (c. 1536–c. 1604) explored the western coast of South America, determining that the voyage from Peru to Chile could be shortened by sailing far from shore and taking advantage of the currents.

Fernándes de Quirós, Pedro (1570–1615) was a Portuguese navigator who sailed for Spain (at a time when Spain ruled Portugal). He spent most of his career in search of the southern continent, Australia.

Frobisher, Sir Martin (1535–1594) attempted to discover a Northwest Passage. Frobisher Bay, off Baffin Island, bears his name.

Gama, Vasco da (c. 1460–1524) made two major voyages from Portugal to India, the first the subject of *The Lusiads* by Camões. During the second voyage, he bombarded Calicut in retaliation for the murder of men left there by Cabral.

Garay, Juan de (1528–1583) helped colonize Argentina. He enslaved the native population, several of whom later assassinated him.

Gemma Frisius, Reinerus (1508–1555) made globes and maps. His treatise *De principiis astronomiae et cosmographiae* (Principles of astronomy and cartography, 1530) suggested that longitude could be determined using a clock. Although impractical for the 16th century, this idea was later proved correct when portable clocks became much more accurate.

Gilbert, Sir Humphrey (c. 1539–1583) reached Newfoundland in 1583, exploring a route for the Northwest Passage. He also published a treatise on the passage that prompted others to make the attempt to find it.

Gomes, Diogo (fl. 1440, d. 1482) explored the western coast of Africa and wrote about African's geography and people.

Gosnold, Bartholomew (d. 1607) sailed along the eastern coast of North America, trading with Native Americans. He also helped colonize Jamestown, where he died.

Grijalba, Juan de (c. 1480–1527) participated in the 1511 Spanish expedition that conquered Cuba. He traveled along the eastern coast of Mexico and established contact with the Aztec.

Hakluyt, Richard (c. 1552–1616) compiled first-hand accounts of English exploration, first published in 1589 in his *Principal Navigations, Voyages, Traffics and Discoveries of the English Nations.*

Harriot, Thomas (c. 1560–1621) was Raleigh's tutor in mathematics. He sailed with him as his surveyor on the Virginia expedition and published *A Brief and True Report of the New-Found Land of Virginia* in 1588.

Hawkins, Sir John (1532–1595) was a sea captain and slave trader.

Heemskerk, Jacob van (1567–1607) accompanied Barents on two voyages of exploration; he later commanded his own ship and died after a naval battle against Spanish forces.

Henry the Navigator (*Infante Dom Henrique*) (1394–1460) was the fifth son of King John I. He directed numerous voyages of African exploration from Sagres, his residence at the southern tip of Portugal, aided by a fine collection of navigational and astronomical instruments.

Hernández de Córdoba, Francisco (d. 1517) (not to be confused with the conquistador of the same name). He was part of the expedition that conquered Cuba, went on to the Yucatan, and became the first European to have contact with the Maya. He was hunting for people to enslave.

Hirschvogel, Augustin (1503–1553) was an etcher, potter, and cartographer known for his etchings of maps and landscapes.

Hondius, Jodocus (*Josse de Hondt*) (1563–1611), cartographic engraver, had shops in both London and Amsterdam. He bought Mercator's engraved plates and in 1606 issued an atlas, which included 37 new plates. This publication became a bestseller.

Hudson, Henry (d. 1611) worked as an explorer for the Muscovy Company. He also sailed up the Hudson River and into Chesapeake Bay on behalf of the Dutch.

Lancaster, Sir James (c. 1555–1618) was in charge of the first expedition sent by the East India Company.

Las Casas, Bartolomé de (1474–1566), the first priest ordained in the New World, dedicated his life to abolishing slavery and improving conditions for Native Americans. He wrote several publications on the topics that were published during his lifetime.

Le Clerc, François (*Jambe de Bois* or *Peg Leg*) (d. 1563) was a Huguenot pirate in the service of France, attacking the Spanish in the Caribbean.

Leo Africanus (c. 1495–c. 1550) was a Moor from Granada who journeyed across north Africa and to the Near East. He wrote an account of his travels that appeared in translation during the 16th century.

Linschoten, Jan Huyghen van (1563–1611) spent several years in India, then was shipwrecked for two years in the Azores. The account of his Indian experiences was first published in 1595.

Magellan, Ferdinand (1480–1521) first sailed with Almeida to India, where he stayed for seven years. In 1519 under the flag of Spain he set out with five ships to find a western sea route to the Spice Islands. The Straits of Magellan at the southern tip of South America are named after him. He was killed in an engagement against native warriors on an island in the Philippines.

Martire d'Anghiera, Pietro (1457–1526), an Italian humanist and soldier, served at the Spanish court as a teacher. Appointed as an administrator of Spanish colonies in the Americas, he met many explorers, including Columbus. Martire d'Anghiera's *De orbe novo* (On the New World, 1511–30) contained the first major published account of the Americas. The work was translated into English in 1555.

Mauro, Fra (d. 1459) was a monk in Venice who was commissioned by the king of Portugal to paint a huge circular world map (75 inches in diameter) using information from contemporary exploration. After completing the map for his commission, Fra Mauro painted a copy, which is now displayed in the Biblioteca Marciana in Venice.

Mercator, Gerard (1512–1594), cartographer and cosmographer, began his career assisting Gemma

Frisius. He made maps for globes as well as flat maps, creating the Mercator projection in which lines of latitude and longitude cross at right angles. This projection is still used on globes today.

Münster, Sebastian (1489–1552) was professor of mathematics at the University of Basel. A cosmographer and Hebrew scholar, he published his major cosmological treatise in 1544.

Narváez, Pánfilo de (1470/80–1528) was part of the expedition that conquered Cuba. Then he was sent to Mexico, where he lost an eye in a violent encounter with Cortés. In 1528 Narváez led a large company into Florida, where many of his men died.

Niño, Pedro Alonso (1468–c. 1505) explored the western coast of Africa with Portuguese explorers, then accompanied Columbus on his third voyage.

Nunes, Pedro (1492–1577) was professor of mathematics at the University of Coimbra; he was appointed royal cosmographer in 1529. Among his publications is *De arte atque ratione navigandi* (On the art and method of navigating, 1546), which includes information on scientific instruments used aboard ships.

Núñez de Balboa, Vasco (1475–1519) was one of the many conquistadores from the remote western region of Spain known as Estremadura. After escaping from Hispaniola, where he became bankrupt, Balboa (as he is usually called in English) explored the isthmus of Panama and led the first company of Europeans who saw the Pacific Ocean. In Panama he founded a colony, today known as Antigua, and became the first governor of the new province. He was arrested by his replacement, who had him beheaded.

Ojeda, Alonso de (1465–1515) sailed with Columbus on his second voyage. Exploring the Caribbean coast of South America, he named Venezuela. Ojeda was appointed governor of Colombia's coastal region on the Caribbean.

Ortelius, Abraham (1527–1598), engraver and cartographer, became royal cartographer for Philip II in 1575. The world atlas that he published in 1570 went through 25 editions before 1600.

Pereira, Duarte Pacheco (c. 1460–1533) explored the western coast of Africa and sailed to Brazil with Cabral. After spending some time in India, Pereira was appointed governor of El Mina in West Africa. He published a geographic treatise that included information on Africa.

Pigafetta, Antonio (fl. 1491–c. 1526), an Italian sailor, was among the 18 men who survived the Magellan circumnavigation. He wrote an account of the voyage that was first published in 1524 or 1525.

Pinto, Fernão Mendes (c. 1510–1583) journeyed for 21 years through Ethiopia and on to the Far East. His published account of this adventure is quite exaggerated.

Pinzón brothers were Martín Alonso (c. 1440–1493) and Vicente Yáñez (fl. 1492–1509), both captains, and Francisco, pilot for Martín. On Columbus's first voyage he himself commanded the *Santa Maria*, Martín the *Pinta*, and Vicente the *Niña*. In 1499 Vicente led an expedition exploring Brazil, where he landed three months before Cabral.

Pizarro brothers were Francisco (1476–1541), conqueror of Peru, and his younger half brothers, Fernando (fl. 1530–60) and Gonzalo (1511/13–48), both of whom assisted him. They all ended badly, with Francisco assassinated, Gonzalo executed, and Fernando spending the last two decades of his life in prison.

Ponce de León, Juan (c. 1460–1521) was present during the conquest of Hispaniola and became governor of Boriquien (present-day Puerto Rico). In 1513 he landed on the coast of Florida and named the site Saint Augustine. Although he founded a colony on the west coast of Florida, its location is unknown.

Prester John (*Prester from presbyter*), who apparently did not actually exist, was thought to rule a

Christian kingdom somewhere in the East. By the 14th century this land was identified as Ethiopia.

Raleigh, Sir Walter (1554–1618) explored the coast of Virginia and founded a colony, Roanoke, whose inhabitants disappeared. He introduced tobacco and potatoes into England.

Ramusio, Giovanni Battista (1485–1557) compiled firsthand accounts of travelers, translating several of them, which he published between 1550 and 1559.

Ribault, Jean (1520–1565) was a French Huguenot in charge of founding a colony for refugees in the southeast region of North America. Although the colony failed, his *True and Last Discovery of Florida* (in English) was published in 1563. On another voyage to North America Ribault was captured by Spaniards and executed as a heretic.

Ruysch, Johannes (d. 1533), German geographer, sailed on an expedition to the North American coast. His world map depicting the Americas was printed in 1507 or 1508 and inserted in copies of his *Cosmographiae introductio* (Introduction to cosmography, 1507–08).

Sarmiento de Gamboa, Pedro (1532–1592), historian and navigator, traveled in Peru and wrote *Historica Indica* (Indian history, in manuscript, 1570–72), describing violence and injustice against the Inca. The work was not published until 1906.

Saxton, Christopher (c. 1542–1611) surveyed and mapped the counties of England and Wales. The result, published in 1579, was the first provincial atlas.

Schouten, Willem Corneliszoon (fl. 1590–1619) was a captain in the Dutch East India Company who sailed around the southern tip of South America to reach the Spice Islands. He named that cape Horn after Hoorn, his hometown.

Soto, Hernando de (c. 1500–1542) was part of the force that conquered Guatemala in 1519. After leading troops to assist Pizarro in Peru, Soto was one of the first Europeans to enter the Inca capital of Cuzco. Later he spent three years exploring the present-day southeastern United States, reaching the region just west of the Mississippi River.

Speed, John (c. 1552–1629) was a cartographer who published *The Theatre of the Empire of Great Britain* in 1611.

Toscanelli, Paolo dal Pozzo (1397–1482) was a Florentine mathematician who determined that a ship might sail westward to reach Asia, but he measured the Earth as somewhat smaller than it actually is. Columbus had access to this information, which may have encouraged his plans to travel west to reach the East.

Tristão, Nuno (d. 1446) several times explored the western coast of Africa in the service of Henry the Navigator. He was killed by Africans whom he was attempting to capture for the slave trade.

Varthema, Lodovico de (c. 1470–1517) was an Italian traveler who immersed himself in the Middle East for several years, then went on to India. His *Itinerario* (Itinerary) describing these experiences was published in 1510.

Vázquez de Ayllón, Lucas (c. 1473–1526) became an administrator and businessman in Hispaniola. He established a colony (location unknown) on the Atlantic coast of North America, where African slaves were part of the population. When the colony failed, many of the slaves escaped into the wilderness.

Vázquez de Coronado, Francisco (c. 1510–1554) was an explorer who became governor of New Galicia. Coronado (as he is usually called in English) led two ambitious expeditions searching for riches, including the quest for the mythical city of "Quivira," which took him as far as present-day Kansas. Written accounts of these adventures include descriptions of bison and of the Grand Canyon.

Verrazano, Giovanni da (1485–1528) sailed for France to search for a Northwest Passage. He explored the eastern coast of North America, the first European to visit what is now New York City. In 1528 he led another expedition into the Lesser Antilles, where he was killed by the Carib people.

Vespucci, Amerigo (1454–1512), for whom America was named, began his career as a shipping agent for a Medici firm in Seville. His various voyages to the Americas have been questioned, as well as his possible service for the king of Portugal. Rather than an intrepid explorer, he may have been an adroit publicist. Vespucci was granted Spanish citizenship for his alleged accomplishments and was appointed principal navigator for the Casa de Contratación (house of trade) in Seville. (This building now houses Spain's Archive of the Indies.)

Villegaignon, Nicolas Durand de (1510–1571) established a Protestant colony for France in Brazil; it was attacked and ultimately destroyed by the Portuguese.

Waghenaer, Lucas Janszoon (c. 1534–1605), cartographer, published *Spieghel der Zeevaerdt* (Mariner's mirror) in 1588.

Waldseemüller, Martin (1470–1518) was a German cartographer who included a world map showing the Americas in his *Cosmographiae introductio* (Introduction to cosmography, 1508).

Wright, Edward (1558–1615), English mathematician, worked on errors in navigation after a voyage to the Azores. He lectured on this topic to members of the East India Company.

Zurara, Gomes Eanes de (1410/20–74), historian and descriptive geographer, wrote the earliest extant report on the Portuguese in West Africa, *Crónica do descobrimeno e conquista de Guiné* (Chronicle of the discovery and conquest of Guinea).

READING

Geography and Cartography

Buisseret 1992: political applications; Cormack 1997: England; Gambi 1997: Vatican map gallery; Lestringant 1994: cartography; Mundy 1996: Americas; Penrose 1967: "The Geographical Literature of the Renaissance," pp. 274–326: (bibliographic information); Randles 2000: nautical astronomy; Sider 2000: portolan charts; Woodward 1991: cartography and concepts of space.

Travel

Allen 1972: postal service; Braudel *Wheels*, 1992: (general survey); Febvre 1977: "The Renaissance Merchant," pp. 91–121: (character study); Gardiner 1994: ships; Lay 1992: roadways; Massing 1991: exotic images; Penrose 1967: "Some Free-Lance Travelers of the Early Renaissance," pp. 21–32: individual journeys.

Exploration

Albuquerque 1991: Portugal; Chiappelli 1976: Americas; Dutra 1995: Brazil; Elliott 1970: Americas; Hale 1968:(general history); Jackson 2001: ethnography; Manchester 1993: "One Man Alone," pp. 223–296; Magellan; Morison 1974: Americas; Ptak 1995: China; Sauer 1971: North America; Thornton 1992: Africa; Thornton 1995: West Africa; Todorov 1991: cross-cultural contact; Verlinden 1995: Portugal.

10

SCIENCE
AND MEDICINE

Advancements in science and medicine affected every aspect of Renaissance life. Although many fields of scientific investigation, such as physics and chemistry, did not yet exist as such, the 15th and 16th centuries witnessed extraordinary developments in astronomy, mathematics, optics, botany, and anatomy. Ancient Greek scientific texts preserved through Arabic sources and edited by medieval scholars were studied throughout the Renaissance, then compared with newly discovered Greek texts. Renaissance editors of the ancient treatises thus drew upon several resources for new scholarly treatments. Individuals studying scientific topics began to combine medieval methods with more advanced ideas. Allopathic and homeopathic medical remedies might involve the application of new instruments and techniques, especially toward the end of the 16th century. New mathematical knowledge, for example, in triangulation, led to better scientific instruments for surveying and navigation. Both the reduction compass and the proportional compass were invented during this era, and the magnetic compass benefited from William Gilbert's (1544–1603) work on magnetism.

The Renaissance study of natural history comprised many areas of science, including botany and geology. The general study of nature as a whole was called both natural philosophy and natural science (*scientia* is the word for knowledge in Latin). Deriving chiefly from the works of Aristotle, natural philosophy was split into two schools, one more theoretical and the other more practical. Medicine and anatomy, for example, fell into the latter group. Some of the arguments and conflicts among Renaissance scholars involved in the study of natural philosophy were caused by advocacy of "book learning" versus experience in the field. The best scientific minds of the Renaissance used both.

Astronomical discoveries of the Renaissance were momentous in that the Earth was no longer the center of the universe by the early 17th century. This repositioning of the world itself rocked the foundations of all scientific thought. Nicolas Copernicus (1473–1543) disproved the Ptolemaic geocentric (Earth-centered) universe. He did not permit his book *De revolutionibus orbium calestium* (On the revolutions of the heavenly orbs) to be published until shortly before his death, because such an opinion

was potentially heretical; in fact, the Catholic Church strongly discouraged any teaching of the Copernican system. Medieval cosmology, the study of the world in relation to the heavens, had to be rewritten by the end of the 16th century. The genius who did so was Galileo Galilei (1564–1642), whose major contributions are beyond the scope of the present book. We should note that his famous experiment of dropping objects from the leaning campanile of Pisa may never have happened; by 1609, however, he knew that the speed of a falling body varies according to the time of its fall, not the distance. Johannes Kepler (1571–1630), as did Galileo, did most of his important astronomical work after 1600. Earlier he was influenced by the work of Copernicus and studied with Tycho Brahe (1546–1601) in Prague. Kepler's *Mysterium cosmographicum* (Cosmographic mystery, 1596) supported Copernicus's heliocentric system. He also correctly defined gravity as a force of mutual attraction among celestial bodies.

ASTRONOMY AND ASTROLOGY

Renaissance astronomy during the 15th century and early 16th century was based on the geocentric universe, even though a few imaginative theologians believed in a much less rigid cosmos of infinite possibilities. Copernicus was the first astronomer to publish a scientific description of the heliocentric universe. Without supporting the Copernican system, Tycho Brahe made further advances by disproving the assumption that the cosmos was enclosed by a fixed, crystalline sphere. Brahe also developed a geoheliocentric system, in which the Earth remained fixed at the center of the cosmos, with the planets orbiting the Sun, which in turn orbited the Earth. Geocentrism prevailed into the early 17th century in this guise.

Astrology remained very popular during the Renaissance, when printed horoscopes and prognostications enhanced its popular appeal. Astrologers were consulted for numerous reasons, and those with compatible horoscopes were encouraged to join in various undertakings, from commercial ventures to marriage. Commanders in chief often based the precise day and hour to launch an attack on astrological predictions, and almanacs followed the Moon and stars to advise farmers on propitious dates for planting and harvesting. In spite of, and perhaps because of, the greater knowledge of the cosmos developed between 1400 and 1600, astrology was taken as seriously as the actual science of astronomy.

Astronomy

Long before 16th-century astronomers began to suggest changes in the concept of the universe, theologians such as Nicholas Cusanus (1401–64) described an endless, infinite universe consisting of many inhabited worlds. Cusanus also believed that the Earth rotates and is not immovable. The radical Dominican friar Giordano Bruno (1548–1600) went so far as to teach that the Sun was only a star among many such stars, in multiple solar systems expanding into the universe. His belief in innumerable planets similar to the Earth revolving around many Suns was one of the heretical notions for which Bruno was burned at the stake. Counter-Reformation policies and the power of the Inquisition threatened astronomical progress for more than a century.

The science of astronomy, assiduously studied by ancient Greeks, treats the location, movement, and size of heavenly bodies as physical facts. Astrology (see later discussion) studies the possible influence of celestial bodies on earthly events. A Renaissance astronomer might predict the precise date of a planetary conjunction; an astrologer would interpret what the conjunction might mean for a specific individual or town. Astronomy had its origins in ancient cosmology; medieval cosmographic illustrations to Ptolemy's *Almagest* and other works showed an immovable Earth at the center of the universe. The days, years, and seasons of our world were explained as movements of the Sun, stars, and planets. Because Copernicus based his discoveries of the heliocentric (Sun-centered) universe on arguments against the Ptolemaic system, *Epitome in Almagestum Ptolemaei*

(Summary of the Almagest of Ptolemy), published in 1496, was an important starting point. That work was partially edited by Georg von Peurbach (1423–61), whose own research on planetary movement was printed several times during the 16th century. The *Epitome* was completed by Peurbach's disciple Regiomontanus (1436–76).

Copernicus began formulating his theories more than two decades before they were published. Anomalies in planetary movements and other celestial events persuaded the astronomer that something was wrong with the current understanding of the cosmos. When he positioned the Sun at the center of our planetary system, several of the inconsistencies and errors were removed. This correction, in Copernicus's opinion, restored celestial harmony: "We find, therefore, under this orderly arrangement, a wonderful symmetry in the universe, and a definite harmony in the motion and magnitude of the orbs, of a kind it is not possible to obtain any other way" (Ross and McLaughlin 1968, p. 596). By defining the heliocentric system, Copernicus described the Earth as a planet that rotated daily on its axis and revolved around the Sun each year. His drive for perfect harmony, however, held him to the concept of concentric spheres, with circular orbits for the planets. Elliptical orbits would be revealed in Kepler's reforms of the Copernican system in the early 17th century.

Kepler was a student of the brilliant Danish astronomer Tycho Brahe (1546–1601), who built an observatory on an island given to him by the king of Denmark, designing his own instruments. Remarkably, Renaissance astronomers accomplished their discoveries without the aid of a telescope, which was not invented until the 17th century.

Astrology

Astrology was one of the most important components of magic; the person who produced magical effects was called a magus. During the Renaissance natural (or white) magic was considered beneficial, especially when it involved medical procedures, as opposed to the demonic (or black) magic of witches and other practitioners. These occult studies often hinged on astrology because the stars and planets

were conceived of as superior intelligences that could be invoked for various purposes. Moreover, each heavenly body was thought to possess specific properties, and objects such as plants and stones were thought to have an affinity with these properties. All the senses were involved in certain incantations; sounds and smells were employed as objects, arranged in patterns and sequence. Astrology, then, was used not only to predict the future, but also to affect it. The great Neoplatonic scholar Marsilio Ficino (1433–99) developed a new theory of supernatural forms, with mystical wisdom released from the mind itself. Pico della Mirandola (1463–94) supported the idea of Christian Cabala in which positive heavenly forces could be summoned by numerical combinations, Hebrew letters, and other tools to combat the negative influence of demonic power. In these and most other Renaissance perceptions of astrological forces, human beings are a microcosm reflecting and communing with the macrocosm of the universe.

Astrology informed the decisions of many of Europe's rulers, just as some of today's political leaders have depended on astrological advice. John Dee (1527–1608), royal astrologer at the English court, advocated an eclectic approach. His predictions combined knowledge of navigation and weather with the inspiration derived from dreams. Astronomers were not exempt from the fascination of astrological influence. Regiomontanus, for example, hoped for support from the king of Hungary because of their compatible horoscopes: "The ascendant of my nativity is no more than 12 degrees away from the ascendant of his; given his birth, he will offer me the offices of friendship. Similarly, the moon in his nativity is in the position of Jupiter in my nativity" (Grafton 2001, p. 114). Numerous prognostications concerning royal marriages, treaties, travel, and even diet were pronounced by astronomers after studious deliberation, for which they were very well paid. Girolamo Cardano (1501–76), who wrote several treatises on astrology

and medicine, helped to promote astrology as a rigorous intellectual system. Astrology may be seen as quasi-scientific in its taxonomic structure and reliance on cause and effect.

CHEMISTRY

Renaissance chemistry was studied in the context of alchemy, a discipline concerned with much more than just converting base metals into gold and silver. The main applications of chemistry during this period were medical (see later discussion), metallurgical, military, and artisanal. Vannoccio Biringuccio (1480–c. 1539), for example, investigated the properties of gunpowder, smelting processes, and the effect of alcohol and acids in distillation. Artisanal applications of chemistry included improvements in glassmaking and textile dyeing. For the latter, the preparation of alum as a mordant to fix the dye became a major chemical industry during the 15th century.

Early chemists, influenced by the philosopher and physician Paracelsus (1493–1541), worked from the three principles of salt, sulfur, and mercury. These were the organizing elements of experimentation, in the sense of inherent qualities of matter. Stability was represented by salt, liquidity and fusibility by mercury, and combustion by sulfur. During any specific experiment, several salts, sulfurs, and mercuries might be applied or combined. As for air, Paracelsus referred to it as "chaos," a term that was corrupted into "gas" during the 17th century. Raised in a mining town, Paracelsus was familiar with the chemistry of metallurgy as well as of alchemical treatises, from which he incorporated processes into his research. The main purpose of his own work, however, focused on chemical applications for medicine, or iatrochemistry (see later discussion).

Andreas Libavius (c. 1540–1616) trained as a historian, applied the discerning eye of a student

---

10.1 (opposite) Illustration of an armillary sphere. Woodcut in the first edition of Johannes Regiomontanus's summary of the Almagest of Ptolemy, 1496. The horizontal bands of the sphere indicate the Earth's zones. (Photograph courtesy of Sotheby's, Inc., © 2003)

of history to his criticisms of contemporary alchemists and their methods. Although Libavius called himself an alchemist and thought that transmutation of metals was possible, he either discovered several new substances or was the first to publish about them. Among his discoveries was ammonium sulfate, and he found a new process for producing sulfuric acid. Libavius's major work on chemistry, entitled *Alchemia*, first appeared in 1597. The second edition, published in 1606, featured many illustrations of furnaces and glass containers, along with instructions for organizing a chemical laboratory.

MATHEMATICS

Renaissance mathematicians did not have some of the basic tools for solving problems, notably proper logarithmic tables, analytic geometry, and differential calculus. Nevertheless major progress was made in algebra and geometry. Before the 14th century, algebraic problems were expressed mostly in narrative language, as in a literary text. Most numbers and expressions were written out, hindering visualization of the problem. Then during the early 14th century European mathematicians began to learn the Hindu-Arabic method for writing out their problems in a sort of shorthand, which included the symbolic letters of today's algebra. The familiar notations used in algebra were a Renaissance invention. In mathematics in general, the Arabic base 10 system of arithmetic was adapted by Europeans during this time. Advancements in geometry were important for art, as human proportions were better represented and linear perspective was applied to painting (see chapter 3). The new geometric knowledge also contributed to improvements in surveying, navigation, and cartography (see chapter 9). Trigonometry began to be understood, and multiple-angle formulas were used for the trigonometric functions. The combination of rediscovered ancient Greek sources and increasingly sophisticated commercial problems requiring computation created new opportunities for mathematicians to experiment and learn.

Algebra

Arithmetic, with geometry, astronomy, and music, was part of the quadrivium, the upper level of university studies during the Middle Ages. These four areas composed the mathematical sciences (see chapter 11, Education); geometry was studied in relation to astronomy, and arithmetic in conjunction with theoretical aspects of music. Arithmetic was purely a computational tool involving real numbers, not a science of numbers in general. Mathematics as an abstract science began to develop during the Renaissance, with 16th-century publications leading the way for some of the major discoveries of the 17th-century scientific revolution.

Methods for solving cubic equations (equations in which the largest sum of exponents of variables is 3) were not fully successful in Europe until the 16th century. The first important Renaissance book on mathematics, by Luca Pacioli (c. 1445–c. 1514) 1494, stated that it is impossible to solve cubic equations algebraically. A teacher of mathematics in Verona, Niccolò Tartaglia (c. 1499–1557), determined how to solve such equations using algebra. He became famous in Italian learned circles because of this knowledge. Girolamo Cardano persuaded Tartaglia to reveal his secret, promising not to share it with anyone. Instead, Cardano published it in his *Ars magna* (The great art, 1545), probably the best known book about algebra for Renaissance readers. Tartaglia was furious and rightly attempted to take credit for the work, but his method is known today as Cardano's solution.

When Cardano published *The Great Art*, mathematicians were not yet accustomed to using abbreviations and symbols in algebraic publications. Cardano wrote out the solution, with actual numbers instead of symbols serving as his model. During the second half of the 16th century, mathematical notation became more symbolic and abstract. Robert Recorde (c. 1510–58), for example, wrote *The Whetstone of Wit* (1557), the first mathematical book to use the equal (=) sign. German mathematicians were the first to use the square-root sign ($\sqrt{}$) while their Italian contemporaries were still using the letter *R*. Sixteenth-century mathematicians dealt with some of the more abstruse qualities of algebra; Pedro Nunes, for example, already in 1532 was writing about

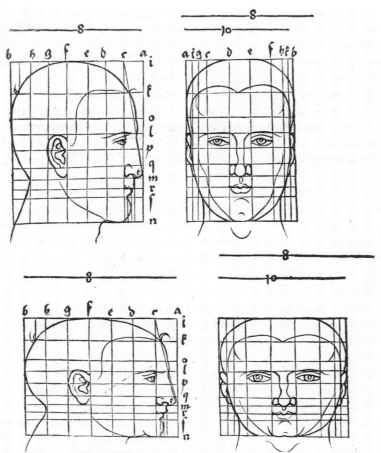

 S ist im cubo noch weyter zu verendern (dardurch das haubt anderst gestalt wirdt) einer solchen meynung/wie hernach folgt/also das der cubus auff dem obersten plano oder eb⸗ nen auff allen seyten gleych erweytert werde/vnd als vil er oben auß geleynt wirdet das er vnden auff dem vndern plano als vil vnd gleych eyngezogen werd.

  Darnach thut man disem widersins/So nun der cubus durch die zweyerley weg ver⸗ kert ist/das erst mal oben weyt vnden eng/vnd widerumb oben eng vnden weyt/als dann zeuch ich die gestrackten linien des erst beschrybnen haubts wider durch den weler veren⸗ dert darein mit sambt den gestalt linien des angesicht/So werden die zweyerley sort der angesicht/das erst haubt wirdt oben groß vnden kleyn/aber das ander haubt wirdt oben klein vnd vnden groß/Solichs mag man durch den gantzen leyb brauchen.

  Vnd eben wie die verkerung im cubo oben vnd vnden gebracht würdet/Also brauchet man das im cubo hinden vnd forn/dañ so der cubus forn auff seim blano erweytert wirdt er hinden in seinem blano so vil eyngezogenn/Des gleychen so man dem widersins thut

10.2 *Geometrical studies of the human face. Woodcut in the first edition of Albrecht Dürer's book on human proportions, 1528. This book included the earliest printed descriptions of spatial geometry; Dürer himself checked the proofs shortly before his death.* (Photograph courtesy of Sotheby's Inc., © 2003)

square roots and quadratic equations. His *Libro de algebra en arithmetica y geometria* (Book of algebra in arithmetic and geometry) was published much later, in 1567.

The French humanistic scholar François Viète (1540–1603) contributed in several ways to the development of algebra. His mathematical publications were the first to put equations in a separate area of the text block, making them visually accessible and highlighting their importance. Viète made an attempt to create trigonometrical tables in his *Canon mathematicus* (Mathematical canon) of 1572 but subsequently discovered numerous errors in the work and had most of the copies destroyed. His status among mathematicians was established in 1593 when he won an algebraic contest, solving an equation of the 45th degree. Viète also published the first infinite series in algebraic literature, to express π. Simon Stevin (1548–1620) taught mathematics at the University of Leiden. He was unusual among the famous Renaissance mathematicians in that he was an accountant and applied his knowledge of numbers to financial problems. As superintendent of the financial administration of the Netherlands, Stevin published a useful table for determining compound interest. He contributed to the theory of equations by explaining that signs could be attached to individual numbers, and he popularized the use of decimal fractions, which elegantly simplified commercial transactions.

Geometry

Discoveries in Renaissance geometry were most significant for architecture, art, optics, cartography, navigation (see the Mercator projection in chapter 9), and surveying. In 1400, the basic text for geometry in universities were the first few books of Euclid's *Elements*. Pertaining mostly to triangles and circles, Euclid's text had been used in schools since antiquity. Other Greek texts on geometry, however, had been lost. Renaissance humanists produced new editions of these works as they were discovered, often adding lengthy commentaries. An important Greek text on conics was published in Latin in 1566, and the works of Archimedes appeared in print in 1588. Meanwhile, in the abacus schools (see chapter 11) where

technical subjects were taught, solid geometry was beginning to be developed. The three-dimensional technique required for surveying also applied to architecture and painting, and Luca Pacioli and Daniele Barbaro (1513–70) contributed significant publications. Pacioli taught mathematics throughout much of northern Italy, discussing his ideas with colleagues in several cities. Leonardo de Vinci (1452–1519), who was interested in geometry, illustrated Pacioli's 1509 publication on proportion. Barbaro's profusely illustrated *La practica della perspettiva* (The practice of perspective, 1568, 1569) included information on polyhedra. More important, he expounded the intellectual value of studying such shapes, because "by the secret intelligence of their forms we ascend to the highest speculations concerning the nature of things" (Kemp 1990, p. 76).

No one studied forms more closely than artists. Several 15th-century artists contributed to the development of linear perspective (see chapter 3), notably Leon Battista Alberti (1404–72) and Filippo Brunelleschi (1377–1446). Although not published during the Renaissance, *De prospettiva pingendi* (On perspective in painting) by the painter Piero della Francesca (c. 1420–92) circulated in manuscript copies after circa 1474. Written from a practical point of view, this treatise explained through geometric diagrams the techniques for drawing three-dimensional objects in a two-dimensional space. Commencing with Euclidean principles, Piero described additional proportional relationships, paying particular attention to the sides and diagonals of geometric shapes. Albrecht Dürer published *Underweysung der Messung* (Treatise on measurement, in four sections) in 1525. Because he was famous as an artist, and because this was the first printed treatise in German on geometry, the book was quite popular. Besides illustrating theoretical points, Dürer applied geometric polyhedra to several artisanal topics, such as typography. The first section of the book, on lines, illustrates how to create sections of cones; the second treats both the theory and the applications of polygons; the third discusses the attributes of solid forms; the fourth pertains to polyhedra. This last book shows solids in two-dimensional shapes, flattened out as templates.

The problem of expressing three-dimensional shapes on a two-dimensional surface also concerned navigators and cartographers (see chapter 9). The Mercator projection, though useful, was not to scale, and shapes of the continents were somewhat distorted. Mercator's system, based on the concept of cylindrical projection, allowed mariners to set their course in a straight line, but measurement of distance was problematic. After gaining practical experience in navigation, the English mathematician Edward Wright (1558–1615) used trigonometry to calculate latitudinal distances. His 1599 treatise, *Certain Errors in Navigation Detected and Corrected*, interpreted and improved Mercator's system.

OPTICS

Renaissance optical studies benefited from advances in geometry, from tables of refraction measuring starlight to geometric diagrams explaining retinal images. Although the properties of vision itself became better understood between 1400 and 1600, Renaissance eyeglasses were only concave lenses. Invented during the late 13th century, eyeglasses were rare even in the 14th century. Evidence in art suggests that they had become something of a status symbol by the 16th century. The eyes, of course, were understood as the pathway of all visual knowledge. Renaissance scholars and artists realized that the eye was a receptor for images rather than a projector. The learned Frenchman Petrus Ramus (1515–72) collaborated with Friedrich Risner (d. 1580) to publish a work in 1572 that included scholarly editions of two important texts on optics. Entitled *Opticae thesaurus* (Thesaurus of optics), this publication influenced the study of optics for the next few decades. The work presented the work of Alhazen, a medieval Arabic scholar who had studied ancient Greek scientific treatises to create his own theory of vision, as well as the conclusions of Witelo, a student of Roger Bacon's, written circa 1270. Not published until 1611, the work of a Benedictine monk, Francesco Maurolico (1494–1575) on optics would have been important if others had known about it. Maurolico explained the camera obscura in geometric terms, quantified the light reflected from mirrors of various shapes, and discussed refraction in the eye.

Anatomical discoveries included significant changes in assumptions about the eye and vision. Dissecting eyeballs, Leonardo realized that the external image received on the retina was inverted. He thus was able to compare the eye to the camera obscura, experimenting with variations in the pupil's diameter. Although Renaissance researchers did not quite comprehend how the eye acts as a lens, they did locate the lens, which they called the crystalline humor. Experiments by Kepler, working on optics pertaining to astronomy, further distinguished various functions of vision. Giambattista Della Porta (c. 1535–1615) was a Neapolitan who studied what he called "natural magic." The second edition of his book with this title, *Magia naturalis*, discussed his experiments with refraction of light. This topic very much appealed to Della Porta, who subsequently wrote a book focusing on refraction, *De refractione* (1593). His research with concave and convex lenses, and with the pupil of the eye, contributed to studies concerning distance vision and the invention of the telescope in the early 17th century.

BOTANY AND DRUGS

The study of plants in the Renaissance focused on their medicinal properties and on proper identification of plants described by ancient writers as well as of unknown plants introduced to Europe by travelers and explorers. Medicinal lore and basic information about each plant were published in herbals, books consulted by all levels of society. Humanistic editions of classical texts concerning botany included works by Aristotle, Theophrastus, Galen, Pliny, and, above all, Dioscorides. Renaissance botanists also learned about numerous other plants through Arabic sources. During the 16th century, many hundreds of plants were added to the classical list, many of them illustrated from nature in life-sized woodcuts. By 1600 botanists had described approximately 5,400 more plants than the 600 known to Dioscorides. Each plant was assumed to have medicinal properties, regardless of whether

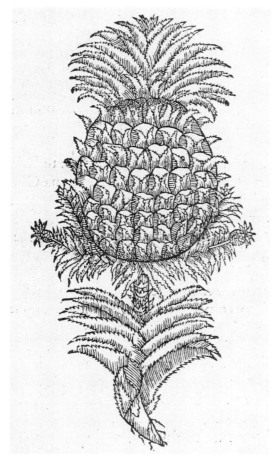

10.3 Illustration of a pineapple. Woodcut in the first edition of Tractado de las drogas, y medicinas de las Indias, con sus plantas *(Treatise on drugs and medicines of the Indies, with its plants, 1578) by Cristóbal de Acosta and García de Orta. Many exotic plants were studied for their potential medicinal uses.* (Photograph courtesy of Sotheby's, Inc., © 2003)

these were fully understood. Botanical gardens were established in several cities to enable researchers to study living plants in a controlled environment. The first successful examples were planted in northern Italy during the 1540s and 1550s. Herbs were also

studied in herbaria, collections of pressed plants, of which the earliest known example dates from 1532.

Botany

Botany truly developed as a science during the 15th and 16th centuries, as scholars and researchers faced the task of identifying and describing new plants from the Americas and Asia. In addition, many European plants had different names in various sources. The same plant could have different names in Greek, Arabic, Latin, and the vernacular languages. Further confusion was caused by the fact that some authors simply transliterated Greek and Arabic into similar sounds in Latin or the vernacular, and others translated the meaning of the plant name. As a result, the same plant might have several names, or, even worse, different plants might have the same name or very similar names. Every Renaissance botanist had to deal with these taxonomic difficulties. Andrea Cesalpino (1519–1603), papal physician, recommended in 1583 that plants be described according to their purposes. In this Aristotelian system, roses would be grouped with roses, fruit trees with fruit trees, and so on. Other botanists of the time followed other organizational principles, such as pharmacological purposes, edibility, or morphological characteristics.

Ancient botanical information not accessible during the Middle Ages was made available to scholars by 15th-century humanists. Ermolao Barbaro the Younger (1454–93), for example, spent several years working on his most famous work, *Castigationes Pliniae* (Emendations of Pliny, 1493). He made thousands of improvements in Pliny's text of natural history, determining that Pliny himself had misdescribed some plants. The definitive edition of *De materia medica* (Medical materials, 1544) of Dioscorides was that of the physician Pierandrea Mattioli (1500 or 1501–77). He included in this publication several European plants as well as exotic plants sent to him by friends traveling in foreign lands. Beautifully illustrated, this book was extensively reprinted during the 16th century. The works of several botanists were published by Christophe Plantin (c. 1520–89) or by his son-in-law, Jan Moretus (1543–1610). Plantin operated the largest printing house in northern Europe, with shops in Antwerp and Leiden, running as many as 22 presses. (His Antwerp shop is now the Musée Plantin-Moretus, still set up as a 16th-century print establishment.) The herbals and other botanical books issued by this firm contained woodcuts by artists and engravers who worked directly for Plantin. The remarkable quality of these illustrations helped to popularize the study of botany. Carolus Clusius (1526–1609) worked for Plantin, translating Dutch, French, Portuguese, and Spanish botanical treatises. Such translations also contributed to furthering the knowledge of botany.

10.4 Botanical illustration and analytical text. Hieronymus Bock, Kreutterbuch *(Herbal, 1595).* (Photograph courtesy of Sotheby's Inc., © 2003)

Drugs

Medication was the most prevalent method of treating illnesses during the Renaissance. The main alternative was phlebotomy (bloodletting, discussed later), with its inherent dangers. Most medicinal remedies of the Renaissance were known in the Middle Ages, if not in the ancient world. Tea made from willow bark, for example, was used to reduce fever. (We now know that willow bark contains salicylates, the main component of aspirin.) Plant products from colonies in the Far East and the Americas significantly improved Renaissance pharmacology. One of the more beneficial drugs was ipecacuanha, which could loosen chest congestion. Even chocolate, coffee, and tobacco were first recommended for their medicinal properties. Although Europeans were also curious about exotic animals such as the armadillo, they were serious in their study of exotic plants because of their potential pharmacological value.

Drugs were usually dispensed by apothecaries, who learned their trade in the guild system. In many cities apothecaries competed with physicians, offering medical advice along with their products. During the 16th century, several cities, such as Amsterdam, passed ordinances prohibiting apothecaries from selling medication without the written order of a physician. Outwardly conforming to local legislation, most apothecaries evidently continued to advise "patients," some of whom simply wanted the distilled alcoholic concoctions sold at apothecary shops. Apothecaries were, in fact, as well trained in pharmacopoeia as many physicians. They experimented with different combinations of medication and learned, as best they could, to substitute ingredients for items in ancient recipes that were no longer available.

Leonhard Fuchs (1501–66), chair of the medical faculty at the University of Tübingen, wrote the best medical herbal of the first half of the 16th century. His *De historia stirpium* (History of plants, 1542) established a new standard of excellence in botanical publications. The woodcut illustrations were particularly important as great care was taken in their execution. One of the works translated by Carolus Clusius was the 1563 Portuguese account of the drugs of India by Garcia de Orta (c. 1500–c. 1568), a physician who lived in Goa. His entry on cinnamon typifies the clarity of his work. Stating that cinnamon is both a spice and a drug, the author explained that, because of linguistic corruption, it had two names in Malaysia. He described both the tree and its bark in great detail. Modern scholars have suggested that the Renaissance impulse to measure and quantify such commodities in colonial territory was one way of gaining control over unfamiliar, unknown lands and people.

Many researchers studying medicinal plants worked closer to home. Ulisse Aldrovandi (1522–1605), professor of natural history at the University of Bologna, investigated plants in the herbarium that he founded there, which can be visited today. (For more information on drugs, see chapter 12.)

ANATOMY AND MEDICINE

Anatomical writings in the Western world began with the Greek physician Galen, who dissected monkeys because they were the animals most closely resembling human beings. During the Middle Ages students in the renowned medical school at Salerno (southern Italy) dissected pigs. Until the 13th century, the dissection of human beings was largely prohibited. Thus medieval attempts to understand the structure of the human body had a zoological context; bodies of different mammals were seen to have similar organs and the same basic skeletal frame. When human dissections were performed in the early Renaissance, the bodies were often those of condemned criminals. Both males and females were dissected, and a pregnant woman was dissected in Bologna during the 16th century. In some instances, the medical professor would sit in an elevated chair behind the dissecting table, reading from Galen or another ancient authority while an assistant performed the cutting and sawing. Other professors, such as Andreas Vesalius (1514–64), did the dissecting themselves. Physical anomalies were often overlooked because the purpose of the dissection was to illustrate information

in the text of Galen. During the course of the Renaissance, anatomists increasingly paid more attention to the body itself. Leonardo da Vinci, who obtained cadavers from a hospital in Florence, was one of the first anatomists to learn about the body directly from its physical evidence, letting the body teach him. His drawings of organs and of nude figures indicate the wisdom of such an approach. Leonardo's work, however, was not published during the Renaissance. Vesalius, who lectured on anatomy at the University of Padua, influenced the course of Renaissance anatomy with his *De humani corporis fabrica* (On the structure of the human body, 1543). (For information on anatomy and Renaissance art, see chapter 3.)

Renaissance medical practitioners were divided between physicians and surgeons. Unlike surgeons of today, who command a very high salary and have the respect of their community, surgeons in the early Renaissance were on the social level of barbers and butchers. This attitude changed by 1600, when barber-surgeons performed only minor procedures and professional surgeons were respected for their skill. Physicians hardly examined the body of their patients, using other means to make diagnoses, such as inspection of urine and fecal matter. These men studied at universities and usually had a medical degree. They prescribed drugs and advised patients about general health practices. Surgeons, on the other hand, learned their trade in the field as apprentices and had no university accreditation of their capabilities. Surgery was greatly feared by most people because there was no effective anesthetic. In addition, surgeons were associated with the negative connotations of failed childbirth. After a midwife had exhausted every effort to deliver a baby lodged in the birth canal, a surgeon would have to be called in to dismember and extract the stillborn baby to save the mother's life. (Forceps were not routinely used in live births until the 17th century.) Surgeons, in general, had to deal with patients in tremendous pain, bleeding excessively and highly susceptible to infection and amputation. Through his publications and reputation, the French military surgeon Ambroise Paré (1510–90) raised the status of surgeons among his contemporaries. (For more information on medicine, including hospitals, see chapters 7 and 12.)

Anatomy

Human dissection in the Renaissance apparently began in Bologna, with autopsies done in response to legal questions. From performing autopsies, it was a short step to dissecting human cadavers for purposes of instruction. By 1400 the medical faculties in both Bologna and Padua were teaching anatomy through dissection, and university statutes required at least one dissection each year. These had to be done during the winter months, and the work usually was accomplished quickly, before the organs began to decay. Executions of criminals were sometimes scheduled at the convenience of professors of anatomy. Until the 16th century dissections simply showed students the location and physiological characteristics of body parts. Anatomists did not understand bodily functions beyond what was taught in the Galenic corpus, which consisted of Galen's texts as well as later commentaries. Medieval lore pertaining to certain body parts also prevailed into the Renaissance, such as the idea that the uterus has seven sections. The "warmer" sections on the right were thought to conceive males; the "colder" ones on the left, females; and the central section, hermaphrodites.

The basic presumption of 16th-century anatomy, that observation of nature could produce results superior to those of traditional authorities, assured its success. Galen openly admitted that his own work on human anatomy had been hindered by being limited to study of the anatomy of monkeys. Researchers such as Vesalius spent their career correcting Galen and adding information to his basic account of the human body. Vesalius may have been the first professor of anatomy to perform his own dissections on the human body in a university setting. Vesalius followed in the Greek physician's footsteps, performing human dissections in the same order on the body as Galen used for monkeys, commencing with the bones and ending with the brain. He did not hesitate to correct Galenic misconceptions that had persisted for centuries, such as the assumption that the liver has five lobes whereas it actually has none. His *De humani corpus fabrica* (Structure of the human body), published in a folio edition, had numerous full-page illustrations that enhanced the educational value of the book.

Drawn under Vesalius's supervision, the illustrations were done by a pupil of Titian's (c. 1489–1576). In addition to his own masterwork, Vesalius contributed to editions of Galen's texts, notably the book on dissecting arteries and veins.

Building on Vesalius's discoveries, and often attempting to compete with him, other anatomists focused on specific parts of the body. Comparative anatomy appealed to both Gabriele Falloppio (c. 1523–62) and the papal physician Bartolomeo Eustachio (c. 1520–1574). Falloppio, for whom the fallopian tubes are named, taught anatomy at the famous medical school in the University of Padua. His *Observationes anatomice* (Anatomical observations, 1561), which included new information about the female reproductive organs, emphasized the functions of various body parts. Eustachio, for whom the eustachian tubes in the ear are named, was the first to publish a correct description of the adrenal glands. Falloppio's most famous pupil was William Harvey (1578–1657), whose discoveries concerning circulation of the blood belong to the 17th century. During the 16th century, however, Harvey's predecessors at Padua performed dissections on living animals (vivisection). They learned how blood from the pulmonary artery enters the lungs to take on air before being pumped by the heart throughout the body. This discovery was one of the first steps toward the knowledge that the same blood, continuously refreshed, flowed in a circular manner and was controlled by valves (or "little doors" as they were called).

Medicine

Throughout the Renaissance medical diagnosis was grounded in the belief that the human body comprises four humors: black bile, yellow bile, phlegm, and blood, associated with the four primal qualities of cold, dry, wet, and hot, and with the four elements of earth, air, water, and fire. Each person was thought to have some of all four humors, with one humor dominating the others and thus forming the individual's body type and personality. Allopathic medicine treated an illness with the "other" (the meaning of allopathic). A person who had an excess of heat, for example, a sanguine type, would be

10.5 Example of a patient in full-body traction. New medical knowledge gained by the study of ancient Greek texts and of practical anatomy led to innovative treatments such as that depicted here. The patient probably suffered an injury to the back. Woodcut in Guido Guidi, Chirurgia *(Surgery, 1544).* (Photograph courtesy of Sotheby's, Inc., © 2003)

ized that pain or discomfort in one part of the body could be caused by problems in another part. Redistributing or repairing the humors was thought to be one possible cure.

Renaissance physicians were university men, and most of them were scholars for whom ancient medical texts of Hippocrates and Galen were as important as new works published by their colleagues. Paracelsus stood outside this model, vehemently criticizing Galenic medicine. Even though many of his ideas about medicine were bizarre, even for the time, he may have foreseen why vaccinations are effective. Paracelsus suggested that a mild case of a disease might prevent a more serious case of the same malady. He also recommended homeopathic treatment, in which the plant from which a medication was derived had a similarity, visual or otherwise, to the organ or other body part being treated. His major contribution to medicine were chemical remedies, especially compounds of salts, minerals, and metals. The principles of effervescence and fermentation used in iatrochemistry were later applied to basic human physiological functions. Iatrochemistry was used to treat the new disease called syphilis. Introduced to Europe from the Americas, syphilis became the scourge of the 16th century. The ailment was treated chiefly by mercury, which slowly poisoned the patient and rotted the bones. Fortunately for Europe, the virulent strain that killed thousands during the 16th century evolved into a less deadly form of the disease. Girolamo Fracastoro (1478–1553), a Veronese physician, wrote a famous Latin poem entitled *Syphilis, sive morbus Gallicus* (Syphilis, or the French sickness, 1530), in which he discussed several possible treatments, as well as the gruesome symptoms.

Barber-surgeons could perform minor procedures, such as bloodletting with leeches or cupping. The latter procedure involved heating the inside of a glass cup and quickly sliding it over the skin, usually on the back. The slight vacuum would then break minor capillaries. Phlebotomy was sometimes done by barber-surgeons, even though cutting into a vein was supposed to be the job of an actual surgeon. A basic knowledge of anatomy was necessary to prevent cutting into an artery and risking the patient's bleeding to death, or into a nerve and causing partial paralysis. Veins in the arms were normally used for

treated with a medication having the property of cold. Special diets, not very different from today's diets according to blood type, were recommended for each predominant humor. Each new drug discovered in the Americas or Asia was adapted to the humoral system, which prevailed into the 17th century. Humors were conceptualized as actual physical components of the body, which could be damaged or putrefied and become life threatening. Although their logic was fallible, Renaissance physicians real-

bloodletting, unless the specific condition called for release of bad humors from another part of the body. Physicians argued about whether blood should be released from the side of the body that had a problem, or from the opposite side to draw the illness away from its location. Physicians also debated the amount of blood to release; some argued for small amounts over time and others advised a gush of blood until the patient fainted. Phlebotomy was practiced as holistic medicine; the procedure was planned around the patient's diet, routine, humors, and specific illness, with attention paid to the season of the year and phases of the Moon. In spite of advances in anatomy and general medical knowledge, such treatments continued well past the Renaissance.

Considering the simple knives, razors, and lancets available to Renaissance surgeons, they accomplished amazing feats of healing. Surgeons knew how to couch cataracts (displacing the lens into the vitreous part of the eye), remove kidney stones, diagnose and excise malignant breast cancer, and even perform trepanation (rarely undertaken). Although many Renaissance procedures had been known since ancient times, surgical knowledge during the later 15th and 16th centuries benefited from the severe wounds resulting from firearms used in warfare. Ambroise Paré (1510–90), a field surgeon in the French army, improved the treatment of infection by dealing with gunshot wounds. He also made significant advances in the procedures for amputation, previously a major cause of death because of bleeding and shock (see chapter 7). Paré published several surgical manuals, including *Deux livres de chirurgie* (Two books of surgery, 1572), which explained his method of turning a breech baby in the womb. In recognition of his expertise, he was appointed surgeon to the king of France, Henry II (1519–59). During a jousting tournament, the tip of a wooden lance pierced the king's temple and lodged in his brain. Although both Paré and Vesalius were at his bedside and treated him, not even their best efforts could save him.

MIDWIFERY

Pregnancy was not considered an illness, though many women died in childbirth or occasionally afterward as a result of infection. (Childbed fever was not a serious problem until much later, when more children were born in hospitals and with the aid of unsterilized instruments.) Though physicians treated gynecological problems, they were not obstetricians. Not until the 18th century did male surgeons routinely attend normal births. In the Renaissance babies were delivered at home by midwives, older women in the community who usually had learned their skills from women in their family. Midwives did not have professional organizations or apprenticeships in guilds, and for most of them midwifery supplied only part of their income, because many were married to artisans or farmers.

The midwife was called as soon as a woman began labor. Examining the patient with her hand in the birth canal, the midwife would determine the dilation of the cervix by using her fingers. If birth seemed likely to occur within a few hours, she would stay with the patient, encouraging her and helping to keep her in good spirits. During this time the patient's entire family was likely to be in the room with her. A positive mental attitude and family support were considered important for a successful birth. Midwives knew how to straighten twisted limbs in the birth canal during delivery, and some midwives knew how to turn a breech baby in the uterus. After delivery the midwife tied the umbilical cord, helped the mother deliver the placenta, and cleaned and inspected the baby. She also knew how to dress vaginal abrasions and stitch tears. The midwife advised a mother who was giving birth to her first child about breast-feeding. Although midwives were not permitted to administer drugs to women during or after childbirth, many had their own recipes for soothing potions and aids for sleeping.

MAJOR FIGURES

Acosta, José de (1539–1600), Spanish Jesuit serving as a missionary in Peru, wrote a catechism in Indian dialects and an influential work on the flora and fauna of the New World, *Historia natural y moral de las Indias* (Natural and moral history of the Indies, 1590).

Aldrovandi, Ulisse (1522–1605) held the chair of natural history at the University of Bologna and established a botanical garden in the city. His treatise on drugs published in 1574 was partially based on research involving plants in the garden.

Apianus, Petrus (1501–1552) was professor of mathematics at Ingolstadt. His *Cosmographia* of 1520 included information based on Renaissance voyages of exploration. He also published on astronomical topics.

Argyropoulos, Johannes (c. 1415–1487), a teacher of Greek and medicine from Constantinople, translated works of Aristotle, including *Physics*, into Latin.

Bacon, Francis (1561–1626) studied at Cambridge and became an advocate of the inductive method, studying the book of nature. His *Advancement of Learning* (1605) contributed to the scientific revolution of the 17th century.

Barbaro, Daniele (1513–1570), Venetian humanist and diplomat, translated Vitruvius's classical Latin text on architecture into Italian. Using the work of Piero della Francesca, Barbaro wrote an influential book on perspective that also discussed polyhedra, *La practica della perspettiva* (The practice of perspective, 1568, 1569).

Barbaro the Younger, Ermolao (*Almoro di Zaccaria*) (1454–1493), Venetian humanist and diplomat, published editions of and commentaries on classical Greek authors. His most famous work is *Castigationes Pliniae* (Emendations of Pliny, 1493), with thousands of corrections and additions, especially pertaining to botany.

Bauhin, Gaspard (1560–1624), the son of French parents, was born in Basel, where he later held the chairs of both Greek and botany at the university. Bauhin's botanical publications codified thousands of native plants.

Bayer, Johann (1572–1625) was an astronomer who invented the system of using letters from the Greek alphabet to indicate the brightness of stars in each constellation.

Benedetti, Giovanni Battista (1530–1590), mathematician, specialized in geometry. In 1574 he published an important treatise on sundials.

Benzi, Ugo (1376–1439), physician, wrote a treatise in Italian (first printed in 1481) concerning good health.

Biandrata, Giorgio (c. 1515–1588) was a physician who specialized in female disorders, serving as physician to the dowager queen of Poland and then to women in the royal family at the court of Transylvania. He was also known for his Unitarian beliefs.

Biringuccio, Vannoccio (1480–c. 1539) was a chemist who studied combustibles, distillation, and metallurgy. His *De la pirotechnia* (On fireworks) was published in 1540.

Bombelli, Rafael (1526–1572) spent most of his life working as an engineer. He was also a brilliant mathematician, whose *L'algebra* of 1572 discussed the square roots of negative quantities (imaginary numbers).

Brahe, Tycho (1546–1601), one of the most illustrious astronomers of the Renaissance, was given the island of Hveen in 1574 by the kind of Denmark. He founded his observatory, Uraniborg, there and designed the instruments himself. Later he became imperial mathematician at the court of Rudolf II in Prague.

Brunfels, Otto (c. 1489–1534) was a botanist who wrote an important Renaissance herbal, published in 1530–36 with illustrations drawn from life.

Cardano, Girolamo (1501–1576) worked as a physician and mathematician, making significant improvements in the study of algebra. He also wrote several treatises on astrology and medicine.

Cesalpino, Andrea (1519–1603) was a physician and director of the botanical garden in Pisa. Late in life he moved to Rome, where he served as papal physician.

Clavius, Christoph (1537–1612) was a Jesuit astronomer who supported the calendar reforms of

Pope Gregory XIII. In the early 17th century he approved the work of Galileo but did not agree with the heliocentric cosmos. He also wrote mathematical school texts.

Clusius, Carolus (1526–1609) one of the most famous botanists of the 16th century, was invited by Maximilian I to create a medicinal garden in Vienna. He also established the botanical garden in Leiden. Clusius collected plants throughout Europe and was sent specimens from Turkey, and he did pioneering research on tulips.

Copernicus, Nicolas (1473–1543) was a physician in Poland who studied astronomy, abandoning the Ptolemaic theory of the universe with the Earth at its center. Copernicus determined that the universe is heliocentric, but he understood that this theory could be considered heretical. His treatise *De revolutionibus orbium calestium* (On the revolutions of the heavenly orbs) was not published until shortly before he died.

Danti, Egnazio (1536–1586), mathematician, contributed to the 1582 reform of the calendar. He was also a geographer, appointed papal cosmographer for Gregory XIII.

Dee, John (1527–1608) was astrologer to Mary I and lectured on astrology and navigation at the court of Elizabeth I. He also experimented in the occult sciences in Poland and Bohemia.

Della Porta, Giambattista (c. 1535–1615) was born in Naples. Influenced by Neoplatonism, he studied unexplained natural phenomena, including refraction. His book on the topic, *De refractione*, was published in 1593. In 1560, Della Porta founded the earliest Renaissance scientific academy, the Academia Secretorum Naturae (Academy of the secrets of nature).

Digges, Leonard (c. 1515–c. 1559) wrote practical manuals on geometry and surveying. Thomas Digges was his son.

Digges, Thomas (c. 1546–1595), eldest son of Leonard Digges, was educated by John Dee. He edited work by his father and published his own writings concerning geometrical solids.

Dodoens, Junius Rembert (1517–1585), Flemish physician, published an important herbal influenced by the work of Leonhard Fuchs.

Dürer, Albrecht (1471–1528) was an engraver and painter who in 1525 published the first book in German on geometry, *Underweysung der Messung* (Treatise on measurement).

Estienne, Charles (1504–1564) published a treatise on anatomy. For 10 years he was also a printer in Paris.

Eustachio, Bartolomeo (1520–1574), papal physician, was author of *Opuscula anatomica* (Anatomical treatise, 1564). This work described the adrenal glands for the first time and included information on kidneys and ears. The eustachian tube and eustachian valve are named after him.

Fabrici, Girolamo (1537–1619), who studied with Fallopio, became professor of anatomy at the University of Padua. Fabrici did pioneering work in the study of embryos and of the venous system.

Falloppio, Gabriele (c. 1523–1562) preceded Fabrici as professor of anatomy at Padua, supervising the dissections for which his department was famous. Important reports on his anatomical research concerning the female reproductive and sexual organs are contained in his *Observationes anatomice* (Anatomical observations, 1561). The fallopian tubes are named after him.

Fernel, Jean François (1497–1558) was physician to Diane de Poitiers and her lover, Henry II, king of France. His medical textbook of 1554, reprinted numerous times, was the first publication to use *psychology* as a medical term.

Ferrari, Lodovico (1522–1565), Cardano's assistant known for his expertise in algebra, became professor of mathematics at the University of Bologna.

Fracastoro, Girolamo (1478–1553) was a physician and writer in Verona. His most famous work is a Neo-Latin poem entitled *Syphilis, sive morbus Gallicus* (Syphilis, or the French sickness, 1530), in which he described symptoms and proposed cures.

Fuchs, Leonhard (1501–1566) was chair of the medical faculty at the University of Tübingen. He published an influential treatise on medicinal plants in 1542 that included descriptions of North American species. The flowering plant fuchsia is named after him.

Galilei, Galileo (1564–1642), known simply as Galileo, was the most famous astronomer of the first half of the 17th century. Although most of his work is beyond the chronological limits of the present book, he is mentioned here because his ideas about the universe were influenced by the heliocentric concept of Copernicus.

Gerard, John (1545–1612) was a physician who had an extensive knowledge of herbs. His herbal published in 1597 became a classic in the field.

Gesner, Conrad (1516–1565) spent the years of his retirement in Zurich doing research in botany and zoology and publishing prolifically. His five-volume zoological survey was among his most important contributions.

Gilbert, William (1544–1603), physician to Elizabeth I during the final years of her reign, published his influential work on magnetism in 1600.

Kepler, Johannes (1571–1630), as did Galileo, did most of his important astronomical work after 1600. Earlier he was influenced by the work of Copernicus and studied with Brahe in Prague. Kepler's *Mysterium cosmographicum* (Cosmographic mystery, 1596) supported Copernicus's heliocentric system.

Libavius, Andreas (c. 1540–1616), a follower of Paracelsus's, published his own *Alchemia* (Alchemy) in 1597. Although grounded in medieval alchemy, the book presented chemical research in an organized, methodical manner and encouraged further experimentation.

Lobelius, Matthias (1538–1616), French botanist, published an herbal in 1571 in which plants were organized according to their leaves. Also a skilled herbalist, Lobelius was one of the physicians of William of Orange, count of Nassau (1533–84). He ended his career as royal gardener at the English court.

Lopez, Rodrigo (d. 1594) was a Jewish physician who left Spain in 1559 to settle in England. While serving as chief physician to Elizabeth I, he was found guilty of treason and hanged, unleashing a wave of anti-Semitism.

Mattioli, Pierandrea (1500 or 1501–1577) worked as a physician in Italy and Prague. In 1544 he published an annotated edition of the herbal of the ancient Greek author Dioscorides. This publication became a classic text and was reprinted several times.

Müller, Johannes See REGIOMONTANUS.

Nunes, Pedro (1492–1577), Portuguese mathematician, became royal cosmographer in 1529. His published works include an edition of Ptolemy, a navigational treatise, and a book on mathematics, *Libro de algebra en arithmetica y geometria* (Book of algebra in arithmetic and geometry) (1567).

Orta, Garcia de (c. 1500–c. 1568) was a physician who immigrated to the Portuguese court at Goa, and published his work on the drugs of India in 1563.

Pacioli, Luca (c. 1445–c. 1514) taught mathematics throughout much of northern Italy. Leonardo de Vinci illustrated his 1509 publication on proportion. Pacioli's major work on arithmetic and geometry was published in 1494, *Summa de arithmetica, geometrica, proportioni et proportionalita* (On arithmetic, geometry, proportions, and proportionality).

Paracelsus (1493–1541), an idiosyncratic physician who dabbled in alchemy, may have been the first to suggest that a disease might be cured by inducing a mild case of it. He thus foresaw the principle of vaccination.

Paré, Ambroise (1510–1590) first worked as a field surgeon in the French army and later practiced general surgical medicine. He published pioneering books on gunshot wounds, amputations, fractures, and obstetrics. His final work, *Deux livres de chirurgie*

(Two books of surgery, 1572) explained his method of turning a baby in the womb.

Peurbach, Georg von (1423–1461), Austrian astronomer, wrote an important elementary treatise on planetary movement, first printed in the 1480s and reprinted several times during the 16th century.

Piero della Francesca (c. 1420–1492) was a painter interested in theoretical aspects of his art. Around 1474 he wrote *De prospectiva pingendi* (On perspective in painting), a geometric treatise that was read in manuscript copies.

Ramus, Petrus (1515–1572) worked with Friedrich Risner to publish *Opticae thesaurus* (Thesaurus of optics, 1572).

Recorde, Robert (c. 1510–1558) was a Welsh mathematician who published several books, including *The Whestone of Wit* (1557), the first algebra book to be printed in English and the first mathematical publication to use the equal (=) sign. Recorde also practiced medicine and for two years was surveyor of mines for Ireland.

Regiomontanus (*Johannes Müller*) (1436–1476) studied astronomy under Peurbach at the University of Vienna and became his colleague. He later established an observatory in Nuremberg and was asked by Pope Sixtus IV to help reform the calendar. He died, however, at the age of 40. Peurbach published several of the mathematical treatises of Regiomontanus.

Reinhold, Erasmus (1511–1553) was a German astronomer instrumental, along with George Rheticus, in Copernicus's publishing of his *De revolutionibus* (On [planetary] revolutions) positing the heliocentric universe. Reinhold then made his own astronomical tables in 1551, using the theories of Copernicus.

Rheticus, Georg (1514–1576), along with Erasmus Reinhold, persuaded Copernicus to publish *De revolutionibus* (On [planetary] revolutions) before his death in 1543. For nine years Rheticus was professor of mathematics at Leipzig.

Risner, Friedrich (d. 1580) collaborated with Petrus Ramus to publish *Opticae thesaurus* (Thesaurus of optics, 1572).

Robin, Jean (1550–1629) was a botanist in Paris asked by the University of Paris in 1597 to design a botanical garden, today's Jardin des Plantes.

Rondelet, Guillaume (1507–1566), marine zoologist, taught medicine in Montpelier after traveling around Italy and studying specimens. He published two important works on ichthyology, with many illustrations.

Sacrobosco, Johannes de (fl. c. 1250) was a medieval writer whose *De sphaera* (On the sphere) became a popular astronomical textbook during the Renaissance.

Stevin, Simon (1548–1620), Flemish mathematician, worked as an engineer for Maurice of Nassau and taught at Leiden. His many publications discussed music, astronomy, navigation, and hydrostatics, and he formulated the concept of fluid pressure. His mathematical work *De Thiende* (The tenth), published in 1585, was translated into French the same year, making the text more accessible.

Tartaglia, Niccolò (c. 1499–1557) taught mathematics in Verona and discovered a method to solve cubic equations, which he explained to Cardano, who subsequently published this information. A bitter controversy developed, during which the two men engaged in a famous problem-solving contest.

Vesalius, Andreas (1514–1564) began his career by lecturing on anatomy in Paris. Between 1537 and 1543, he dissected the cadavers of criminals who had been executed and publishing the results of his investigations in *De humani corporis fabrica* (On the structure of the human body, 1543). Subsequently Vesalius served as court physician to Charles V and then Philip II.

Viète, François (1540–1603) was a French mathematician who contributed to the study of algebra. Most importantly, he treated the equations as equivalent to their explanatory text, setting them off visually in his publications. Most other writers had incorporated elements of the equations into the text.

Vigo, Giovanni da (1450–1525) was papal surgeon for Julius II. He published two practical manuals of surgery.

Wilhelm IV, landgrave of Hesse (1532–1592), established an observatory at Kassel to study the fixed stars. His work contributed to that of Brahe.

Wright, Edward (1558–1615), mathematician, recognized the difficulties of applying Mercator's projection to actual navigation during a voyage to the Azores. Wright's 1599 treatise, *Certain Errors in Navigation Detected and Corrected*, interpreted Mercator's system for pilots.

Zaccaria, Almoro di See BARBARO THE YOUNGER, ERMOLAO.

Zacuto, Abraham (c. 1450–c. 1515) began his career as a mathematician in Salamanca, then immigrated to Portugal in 1492 when Spain expelled its Jewish residents. There he advised Vasco da Gama but was expelled from Portugal in 1497. Columbus carried copies of Zacuto's astronomical tables aboard his ships.

READING

Gilbert 1960: scientific method; Hawkes 1981: instruments; Michel 1967: instruments; Turner 1987: instruments.

Astronomy and Astrology

Biagioli 1993: Galileo; Gingerich 1975: Copernicus; Grafton 2001: astrology; Pedersen 1993: early physics; Rosen 1971: Copernicus; Westman 1975: Copernicus.

Chemistry

Debus 1977: Paracelsus; Sarton 1958: chemistry, pp. 104–115; Shumaker 1972: occult sciences.

Mathematics

Field 1997: art and mathematics; Hay 1988: printing mathematics; Rose 1975: Italian humanists; Sarton 1958: "Mathematics and Astronomy," pp. 23–76; Struik 1986: (general survey).

Optics

Kemp 1990: art and optics; Kubovy 1986: perspective; Lindberg 1976: vision; Veltman 1986: Leonardo da Vinci.

Botany and Drugs

Greene 1983: (important landmarks); Morton 1981: (general history of botany); Reeds 1991: botany in the universities; Riddle 1997; gynecological drugs; Sarton 1958: "Natural History," pp. 128–171.

Anatomy and Medicine

Cipolla 1976: public health; Goodrick-Clarke 1990: Paracelsus; Lind 1975: anatomy before Vesalius; Loudon 1997: medicine (many illustrations); Lyons 1978: medicine (illustrations); Sarton 1958; "Anatomy and Medicine," pp. 172–218: (general history); Sawday 1995: dissection; Wear 1985; medicine in the 16th century.

11

EDUCATION

Renaissance humanism was the single greatest innovation in education during the 15th and 16th century. The second important current in education was the Protestant Reformation, which resulted in the founding of Protestant universities. Until the 15th century, medieval grammar schools, conducted in Latin, had functioned relatively unchanged for hundreds of years, using a combination of basic Roman texts combined with primers and the Psalter or other devotional texts. These schools taught the elementary skills of literacy. Medieval European universities awarded the doctoral degree in the disciplines of theology, medicine, and law, a system that continued into the Renaissance, but improved by humanistic texts in these fields and an emphasis on classical rhetoric. The lower degree awarded was master of arts; the seven liberal arts were the trivium of humanities (rhetoric, logic, and grammar) and the quadrivium of mathematical sciences (arithmetic, geometry, astronomy, and music). By 1500 approximately 100 universities were in existence across western Europe, one-third more than in 1400. Education, particularly of young men, flowered during this time. Greek studies were enhanced by scholars' traveling in Europe, mainly in Italy, and then fleeing to Italy from Constantinople after the city was captured by the Turks in 1453. In addition, the printing press made more texts available to a broad spectrum of students. These books included not only humanistic works, but also practical handbooks teaching commercial skills, such as accounting.

HUMANISTIC EDUCATION

Long before the Renaissance of the 15th and 16th centuries, western Europe had other periods of classical rebirth. Knowledge of Greek and Roman learning never completely died out, but was kept alive in monasteries where texts of the classical era were studied and copied. After Charlemagne was crowned emperor in A.D. 800, he began to revive Roman literature, law, and art across western Europe. This effort at revival included copying of numerous ancient manuscripts in an elegant, rounded script (Carolingian minuscule) that later would be used by 15th-century humanists. They assumed that this manner of writing was adopted from ancient Rome, so the new texts were "reborn" in form as well as in content. Being much easier to read than the tight, spiky Gothic text of the Middle Ages, the rounded humanistic script facilitated reading. Because the new learning originated in Italy, we shall focus on that region in this subchapter, then discuss the spread of humanistic education (*studia humanitatis*) to other parts of western Europe.

The rise of education based on humanistic texts helped to define the very meaning of the Renaissance as a period of rebirth. Lost texts of the classics, in both Greek and Latin, rose as the proverbial phoenix did from the ashes of antiquity. It is important to remember that during the early Renaissance Latin was the preferred language for writing among the upper class. The newly edited texts of classical Latin provided new models of style and eloquence. Discoveries of works long thought to have been lost caused unprecedented excitement in learned circles. Along with the rediscovered texts was a revival of the urbane, polite society of republican Rome, as well as an affinity for the grandeur of imperial Rome. Italians assimilated these aspects of the classics most completely, to the extent that in England members of the upper class were often ridiculed for putting on "Italian" airs. Humanistic education generated not only new modes of thinking, but also new behavior and attitudes. Analogies were drawn between the state of learning in Renaissance Italy and that in ancient Rome, as Leonardo Bruni (1370–1444) explained in his *Le vite di Dante e di Petrarca* (The Lives of Dante and Petrarch, 1436): "The Latin language was most flourishing and reached its greatest perfection at the time of Cicero. . . . One can say that letters and the study of the Latin language went hand in hand with the state of the Roman republic" (Brown 1997, pp. 95–96).

Greek learning, secondary to that in Latin, was a more rarified course of study. Nevertheless those who did pursue this more difficult subject were able to shed light on the Greek basis of Roman culture. This aspect of ancient history became part of the humanistic curriculum. On the whole, advanced humanistic education took place in private schools or academies.

11.1 Classroom scene. Woodcut in a French edition of the Romance of the Rose *by Guillaume Lorris and Jean de Meung, 1531.* (Photograph courtesy of Sotheby's, Inc., © 2003)

Many grammar schools, however, quickly adapted precepts of the elementary humanistic curriculum. The Commune of Lucca, for example, ordered its teachers in 1499 to include in their daily lessons the following: grammar, a historian, an orator or epistles, a poet, and basic Greek. This program of study was renewed at least three times between 1499 and 1574. Whereas the newly founded universities were immediately receptive to the new classical curriculum, most of the medieval institutions resisted the intrusion of humanism until well into the 16th century.

Pedagogical Treatises

The pedagogical treatises of a classical Greek author, assumed by humanists to be Plutarch, and of the classical Roman author Quintilian helped to prompt the new philosophy of education in early 15th-century Italy. The Greek text *On Educating Children* was translated into Latin by Guarino Guarini (1374–1460) in 1411 as *De pueris educandis*. In 1417 at the Saint Gall monastery, Poggio Bracciolini (1380–1459) discovered Quintilian's *Institutio oratoria* (On the education of an orator). Both texts were disseminated in manuscript copies, teaching educators and upper-class parents alike that children would benefit from what we now call positive reinforcement. The curriculum was to be appropriate for various levels of age and ability, and broader, with recreational activities balancing more serious study. Quintilian's work became a Renaissance bestseller: More than 100 editions were published. This was also one of the basic texts for rhetorical training, which became an important element of humanistic education.

In addition to Quintilian's work and the pseudo-Plutarchan Greek text, four treatises originating in the 15th century were seminal guides for humanistic educators. Their authors were Piero Paolo Vergerio the Elder (1370–1444), Leonardo Bruni, Aeneas Silvius Piccolomini (1405–64, who became Pope Pius II in 1458), and Battista Guarini (b. 1434). Vergerio and Bruni studied Greek in Florence near the close of the 14th century with Manuel Chrysoloras (c. 1350–1415), a diplomat and friend of Emperor Manuel II's. Chrysoloras helped to found humanistic Greek studies in Italy, and he taught Greek in Constantinople to Guarino Guarini and other foreigners residing in the city. Leonardo Bruni began his career in Rome, working for the papal secretariat between 1410 and 1415. Returning to Florence, he eventually became chancellor in 1427 and used that position to promote humanism and other aspects of Renaissance culture. Bruni was famous as a translator, including of major works by Plato and Aristotle. Piccolomini was given a humanistic education in Siena and Florence; one of his teachers was Francesco Filelfo (1398–1481; see later discussion). He became involved in papal politics and worked as a diplomat for Emperor Friedrich III, at the same time writing humanistic essays such as the treatise discussed in this section. Guarini, the son of Guarino Guarini, was educated at his famous school in Ferrara (discussed later). Battista Guarini's educational treatise describes the curriculum of his father's school.

Pier Paolo Vergerio's treatise, completed circa 1403, was entitled *De ingenuis moribus et liberalibus adulescentiae studiis liber* (On the character and studies appropriate for a free-born adolescent). Written for a young nobleman, this treatise emphasized that the virtuous, educated man must excel in both physical prowess (bearing of arms) and intellectual endeavors. One of Vergerio's most important pedagogical points was that the curriculum must be adapted to the strengths and weaknesses of the student. Among the physical activities to be learned and practiced were wrestling, boxing, throwing of the javelin, shooting of arrows, rolling of rocks, breaking of horses, and swimming. Relaxation, however, with caution, was also necessary: "Dancing to music and group dances with women might seem to be pleasures unworthy of a man. Yet there might be certain profit in them, since they exercise the body and bring dexterity to the limbs, if they did not make young men lustful and vain, corrupting good behavior" (Kallendorf 2002, p. 87). For the study of texts Vergerio insisted that students must memorize as much as possible: "In this regard we should know that memory apart from intellect is not worth much, but intellect without memory is worth almost nothing, at least as far as learning disciplines is concerned. Yet such a mind can have value in matters of action, since it is possible to write down things that have been done or must be done to compensate for poor memory. Nevertheless, in the case of book-learning, whatever we do not have by heart or cannot easily recall we seem not to know at all" (Kallendorf 2002, p. 57).

Leonardo Bruni's *De studiis et litteris liber* (On the study of literature, c. 1424) was the only one of these treatises dedicated to a woman, Battista Malatesta of Montefeltro. Although he cautioned her that oratory was not fitting for women, who would not be expected to speak in public, Bruni otherwise outlined a comprehensive program of classical reading and study: "In sum, then, the excellence of which I speak comes only from a wide and various knowledge. It is necessary to read and comprehend a great deal, and to bestow great pains on the philosophers, the poets, the orators and historians and all the other writers. For thus comes that full and sufficient knowledge we need to appear eloquent, well-rounded, refined, and widely cultivated. Needed too is a well-developed and respectable literary skill of our own. For the two together reinforce each other and are mutually beneficial" (Kallendorf 2002, p. 123). Finally, Bruni recommended that her humanistic education be undertaken with the assumption that moral philosophy and religion are paramount, and indeed that the classical authors must be subservient to those two superior subjects. Authors whose works might encourage vices of any sort were to be avoided.

Aeneas Silvius Piccolomini wrote *De liberorem educatione* (On the education of boys, 1450) for Ladislaus V (1440–57), king of Hungary, Austria, and Bohemia, born a few months after his father had died. Ladislaus's mother, Elizabeth, was the daughter of Emperor Sigismund. Had he lived beyond the age of 17, the young king could have become a powerful figure in European political affairs and in spreading of humanistic education to northern Europe at an early date. This lengthy treatise was written at the request of Ladislaus's teacher. Piccolomini instructed the boy-king to focus on his religious education, then on a curriculum balancing physical exercise and training with study of the classical authors. At the beginning of his text, the author praises Ladislaus's noble lineage; he then explains that Ladislaus must be deserving of such ancestors: "You are succeeding to men of noble rank: take care that you become likewise their heir in virtue. Nobility clothed in holy morals is deserving of praise. Nothing vicious is noble. For who would call a man noble who is unworthy of his family and distinguished only by a famous name?" (Kallendorf 2002, p. 129). The entire purpose of the treatise was to help make Ladislaus a better king, learning enough in each subject but not so much as to distract him from the overall goal: "You should know what the duty of an orator is, and you should learn how properly to discover, arrange, embellish, memorize, and deliver the parts of an oration. But since our desire is that you be a perfect king more than a good orator, we do not require of you the eloquence of a Cicero or a Demosthenes" (Kallendorf 2002, p. 245). This concept of moderation in education would become a general principle during the Renaissance, except in schools run by the Jesuits and other strict orders.

Battista Guarini's *De ordine docendi et studendi* (On a curriculum of teaching and learning) was written in 1459. This treatise documented the program of learning instituted by his father, Guarino, at the court of Ferrara, which influenced much of the humanistic teaching in western Europe as his students established schools of their own. Because Guarino was the first Italian to place as much emphasis on the Greek part of the curriculum as on the Latin, his son's treatise is an important record of pedagogical methodology. Many words in Greek are explained, including their context, and grammar is highlighted as a major component of humanistic learning. He recommended orderly, regular work habits: "Students should not engage in indiscriminate reading of miscellaneous books. They should establish fixed hours for particular readings. This is the single most useful practice for achieving a range of reading and for finishing tasks" (Kallendorf 2002, p. 301).

Italy and the Italian City-States

One of the first humanistic teachers was Gasparino Barzizza (c. 1360–1431), who edited recently discovered texts of Cicero. Between 1387 and 1392 he had studied with the noted professor of rhetoric Giovanni Trevisi da Cremona at the University of Pavia. Barzizza lectured at the universities of Padua, Pavia, and Bologna. Between 1407 and 1421 he also taught students in Padua who boarded in his home, sometimes as many as 20 at once. Barzizza wanted to reform the medieval system of *ars dictaminis* (learning to write prose letters) by using the new epistolary texts, especially of Cicero. Although his teaching methods remained medieval, Barzizza's enthusiasm for humanistic texts spread throughout much of Italy via his students.

After returning from Constantinople (see previous discussion), Guarino Guarini established humanistic schools in Florence and Venice. In 1418 he married a wealthy woman from Verona and moved with her back to her native city. His independent school founded there in 1419 was recognized the following year by the Commune of Verona, which gave him a five-year appointment at a generous salary of 150 gold ducats. This teaching contract awarded in 1420 was an important step in Latin education for the Renaissance. Ten years later Guarino was called to Ferrara, honored by an appointment as the tutor of Leonello d'Este (1407–50), who would later become lord (*signore*) of Ferrara in 1441. In 1442 Guarini was appointed as a professor at the University of Ferrara.

Vittorino da Feltre (1378–1446) established his famous Casa Giocosa (House of Games or Merry House) at the court of Mantua. By its very name his school indicated that Vittorino incorporated recreational activities into his pedagogical precepts. Having learned Greek from Guarino Guarini in Venice, Vittorino taught in Padua and then established a school in Venice in 1423. That same year he accepted the invitation of Gianfrancesco Gonzaga

(1395–1444), a condottiere (see chapter 7, on warfare) who governed Mantua and founded his humanistic school in the city. Selected poor children attended the Casa Giocosa alongside the Gonzaga children, including a few girls and children as young as four years old. There was no fee for the lessons. All students were trained to read, speak, and write in both Greek and Latin. The "games" referred to by the name of his school included physical exercise such as that mentioned earlier. More advanced students learned moral philosophy, especially that of the Stoics, and all the students were attentive to their religious duties of attending mass and confession. Other teachers were hired to teach the mathematical sciences, including astronomy.

By the 1430s students of Barzizza, Guarini, and Vittorino were opening schools of their own, taking over leadership of their cities, and, in several instances, marrying each other. Marguerita Gonzaga, a student of Vittorino's, married Leonello d'Este in 1435. Such marriages ensured that the humanistic legacy would be continued with their own children and those of others at court. Because the majority of students instructed by the first humanistic teachers were members of the powerful governing class, the new system of education rapidly began to replace that of the medieval curriculum.

Francesco Filelfo (1398–1481) is an example of the second generation of humanistic scholars. He studied with Barzizza between 1416 and 1417, then in 1420 went to Constantinople as secretary to the Venetian legation. There he studied Greek and married a Greek woman. Returning to Italy in 1427, Filelfo took with him some 40 manuscripts of ancient Greek texts that he labored to translate so that students would be able to read them in Latin. He was one of numerous students of early humanistic teachers who helped to change western Europe's philosophy of education.

France

Although small towns and villages in France were hardly aware of humanistic education, the new curriculum was welcomed at the court of Francis I and by the urban elite. The exciting new studies promulgated by the Italian governing class were viewed as a means to revivify France and pay homage to the king. Some French teachers, however, were wary of a program that emphasized Latin, which they found Italianate. Texts in French thus remained part of the program of study. Many municipal and several university grammar schools called colleges (*collèges*) that followed the humanistic curriculum were established by the 1530s. In Paris some of the university colleges incorporated the study of classical authors as the basis for the curricula of liberal arts and theology. The humanist and jurist Guillaume Budé (1467–1540) was one of the driving forces in French humanistic education. Appointed as the first royal librarian (see chapter 5), Budé also was in charge of the study groups that later evolved into the Collège de France. A serious Hellenist, he translated Plutarch, and his classical philology provided texts useful for students, such as *Commentarii linguae Graecae* (Commentaries on the Greek language, 1529). Budé also improved the study of Roman law by advocating close textual analysis and the study of legal history through humanistic sources.

A few of the cathedral schools also accepted the humanistic educational program, for example, at Carpentras, under the auspices of Cardinal Jacopo Sadoleto (1477–1547). Educated as a humanist, Sadoleto had been a papal secretary writing perfectly Ciceronian letters and copying them in the preferred humanistic script (chancery cursive, or *cancelleresca corsivo*). Assigned by the pope in 1542 to negotiate a truce between the king of France and Emperor Charles V (1500–1556), Sadoleto spent must of his time in France on this futile mission. Sadoleto wrote a pedagogical treatise entitled *De pueris recte instituendis* (On the education of boys), using classical authors. The cathedral school at Carpentras benefited from his expertise and interest. By the latter 16th century, however, religious conflicts and a lack of well-trained teachers caused the quality of teaching to deteriorate in many of the schools across France. Counter-Reformation dogma increasingly emphasized religious education and French chauvinism rejected the Latin culture of classical Rome. Jesuit private schools (for boys only, of course) applied a highly disciplined classical curriculum; however, their main emphasis was on religious history and spiritual doctrine.

Spain, Portugal, and the Spanish Kingdom of Aragon, Naples, and Sicily

The Jesuit system of secondary education had infiltrated both Portugal and Spain by the latter 16th century; nearly 120 Jesuit colleges in Spain by 1600 had graduated some 10,000 boys each year. There evidently has been no extensive study concerning the curricula of public schooling in either country during the Renaissance published, and we cannot assume that humanistic education reached small towns whose citizens had no strong connections to the court. Before the Jesuits virtually took over secondary education, however, the courts of both Spain and Portugal responded positively to humanistic educators during the 15th and early 16th centuries. The universities in Spain boasted several noted teachers of Greek and even of Hebrew, trained as students by humanists in Italy. The greatest of these was Antonio Lebrija (1442–1522), who returned from Italy in 1473 to teach at the University of Salamanca and then at the University of Alcalá de Henares. His Spanish-Latin dictionary was used in the Spanish school system, and his compendium of classical rhetoric became part of the humanistic curriculum.

During the 15th century the Spanish court in Naples ruled by Alfonso V (1396–1458), king of Aragon from 1416 to 1458 (partially in dispute; see chapter 1), was an important humanistic center. Selected as his capital city in 1443, Naples hosted humanists, artists, and architects, such as Francesco Filelfo. Alfonso V founded a Greek school in Messina as well as a university in Catania (Sicily), and he expanded the University of Naples. The king's devotion to the classical authors, for example, that he carried copies of works by Julius Caesar and Livy on military expeditions, was legendary. Some of the universities in Italy had separate humanistic college for students from other countries, notably the College of San Clemente at the University of Bologna, attended by many Spanish students. Others studied at the university in Rome or Florence, learning about classical authors through Italian humanistic programs. Isabella I (Isabella the Catholic, 1451–1504), queen of Castile and Aragon, was the first Spanish monarch to establish humanistic education at the court. She hired the noted humanist Pietro Martire d'Anghiera (1457–1526) to organize a school for the sons of nobility (which a few noble girls attended). Martire d'Anghiera was famous as both a teacher and a soldier, as a participant in the expulsion of the Moors and Jews from Granada in 1492. Doubtless this experience doubly qualified him to train the future leaders of Iberia.

From the Portuguese court, students often attended the university in Paris because of ties between the courts of France and Portugal. By the beginning of the 16th century King Manuel I (1469–1521) had introduced humanism to his court. In 1496 he married a daughter of Isabella I, and after her death he married her sister, Maria, both of whom had been raised at the humanistic court of Spain. The king hired the Portuguese scholar Arias Barbosa to establish a school at the Portuguese court. Barbosa, who had studied Greek in Italy under Angelo Poliziano (1454–94, a renowned Hellenist and poet, had distinguished himself as a professor of Greek for 20 years at the University of Salamanca. The Portuguese humanist-poet García de Resende (c. 1470–1536), who had studied in Spain under Antonio Lebrija, served as Manuel I's private secretary.

Germany and the Netherlands

In the late 14th century a religious group called Brethren of the Common Life was founded in Germany, its members the chief supporters of *devotio moderna* (modern devotion; see chapter 2). Although the Brethren of the Common Life had died out by the 17th century, during the 15th and 16th centuries their emphasis on private pietism contributed significantly to the improvement of education. The more learned a person could be, the more completely that person's understanding might be developed. Many famous humanists were trained in schools founded by the Brethren, including Desiderius Erasmus (c. 1466–1536), arguably the most important humanistic scholar of the Renaissance (see England and Scotland, pages 276–277). In general, humanistic curricula in northern Europe had a religious undercurrent, and biblical studies were a core component of the program. Philipp Melanchthon (1497–1560) was one of the leading theologians of the Protestant Reformation (see chapter 2). A professor of Greek who corrected Luther's German translation of the New Testament, Melanchthon was a reforming educator. He had a humanistic school in his own home, and his Latin curriculum combining biblical passages with the Latin classics was adopted throughout Germany.

During the Renaissance Strasbourg, today in eastern France, was part of Germany. In 1538 the reformer Johannes Sturm (1507–89) moved to Strasbourg and founded a gymnasium (public secondary school) that would become a model of the humanistic curriculum. At times it had as many as 500 students. Sturm had been educated by the Brethren of the Common Life and at the humanistic University of Louvain. Before moving to Strasbourg, he had lived among humanists in Paris, teaching the literature of the classics. His program at the Strasbourg gymnasium, of which he was rector, included the dramatic presentation of classical plays. This pedagogical tool, also utilized by Jesuit schools in other parts of western Europe, became more prevalent in education by the close of the 16th century. Sturm's curriculum consisted of eight divisions of students (like today's grades) with strict standards for advancement. His school had an outstanding faculty, many of whom published grammars and textbooks. These publications were disseminated throughout Europe by German publishers.

Juan Luís Vives (1492–1540) was a humanistic scholar from Valencia who had studied in Paris. He taught privately in Bruges and then Louvain and returned to Bruges after spending five years teaching and advising the queen in England. Humanism in public schools in the Netherlands was promoted as a result of Vives's treatise *De disciplinis libri xx* (Twenty books on education, 1531). He advocated teaching in the vernacular, as well as in Latin and Greek; associative learning; and pious devotion to one's education. His other pedagogical works included *Linguae latinae exercitatio* (Exercises in the Latin language, 1539, dialogues for beginning students). As a result of the influence of Vives and his contemporaries, the Netherlands instituted a rigorous, comprehensive humanistic educational system that remains influential even today.

England and Scotland

Christ Church, Canterbury, had the first humanistic school in England, led by the prior William Sellyng (d. 1494), a Benedictine monk, from 1472 until his death. Sellyng had studied Greek in Italy and taken home manuscripts of Homer and Euripides. He was known as a Latin orator, applying the rhetorical principles of ancient writers, and oratory was featured in his curriculum. The most famous Renaissance humanistic school was that of Saint Paul's in London, refounded by John Colet (c. 1466–1519) with his family inheritance. Dean of the school from 1505 to 1519, he appointed the Greek scholar William Lyly (c. 1468–1522) as the first headmaster. Colet and Lyly were friends of Sir Thomas More (1478–1535), who instructed his own daughters in the classics, and of Erasmus, who was teaching in England between 1509 and 1514; while residing there he wrote *De ratione studii* (On the method of study, 1511), which argued for early fluency in Latin and copious reading in addition to memorization of grammar. Sir Thomas Elyot (c. 1490–1546) in his *Book Named the Governor* (1531) explained how humanistic education benefited the state and provided better service to the monarch. The fact that he published this treatise in English contributed to its popularity.

The school for children at the royal court provided the most progressively humanistic education in the country. From 1526 to 1528 Juan Luís Vives lived at court, serving as councilor to Queen Catherine of Aragon and contributing to the humanistic ambience of her court. Roger Ascham (1515–68), author of *The Scholemaster* (1570), tutored the royal children with humanistic methods (see later discussion). The 1548–52 notebooks of the boy-king Edward VI (1537–53) document his classical education under the head tutelage of Sir John Cheke (1514–57), one of the most outstanding Greek scholars of his generation. The first book printed in England in Greek type was his edition of the sermons of Saint John Chrysostom in 1543. His program of studies for the young king was developed from that taught to the undergraduates at Saint John's College, Cambridge, which combined a study of historical authors with Latin essays and Greek orations, moral philosophy, mathematical sciences, geography, music (he played the lute), and Protestant doctrine.

Schools in Scotland had humanistic teachers by the mid-16th century, but no consistent curriculum as each teacher created an individual program of study for a specific school. The humanist-poet George Buchanan (1506–82) instituted a curriculum of classical studies at Saint Andrews that may have been implemented elsewhere in Scotland. Buchanan obliquely influenced the growth of humanism in the British Isles by tutoring the son of Mary, queen of Scots (1542–87), who would become James I, king of England (1566–1625, James VI of Scotland). Near the end of the 16th century, the prestigious grammar school in Edinburgh incorporated Buchanan's humanistic program into its curriculum.

UNIVERSITY EDUCATION

During the early Renaissance universities maintained the medieval educational model of reading and disputation (debating) of existing texts. The canon was expanded by the addition of humanistic material, as the basic pedagogical model was slowly altered in some universities by a new emphasis on classical stylistics and oratory. During the Renaissance, experimental science was not part of a university education, which focused on the seven liberal arts and professional studies. The increased number of students during the Renaissance led to the founding of new universities. Those founded during the 15th century included universities in Leipzig, Trier, Basel, Mainz, Copenhagen, Uppsala, Poitiers, Nantes, Bourges, Saint Andrews, and Glasgow; 16th-century institutions were established in the Spanish cities of Alcalá, Seville, Valencia, and Granada, among others.

Study of the Liberal Arts

For educational purposes the seven liberal arts were divided into the three-part trivium of grammar, rhetoric, and logic (or dialectic) and the four-part quadrivium of arithmetic, astronomy, geometry, and music (mainly theoretical). Many students reached the university with some preparation in grammar, which they had learned earlier along with reading and writing. Grammar, with rhetoric and logic, was taught to students entering the university. These basic skills of expression and argumentation were necessary for advancing to the quadrivium of mathematical science. Arithmetic was learned in conjunction with theoretical problems of music, and geometry was necessary to the understanding of astronomy. For geometry the text was the *Elements* of the Greek author Euclid, chiefly the first few chapters concerning triangles. Arithmetic was taught from an expanded version of Euclid's later chapters, with special emphasis on determining ratios such as those in musical intervals.

Professional Training

THEOLOGY

Until the Protestant Reformation training in theology meant the Christian theology of the Catholic Church. Theology, literally "the study of gods," in western Europe referred to the one god, the Christian God. In the theology of Saint Augustine (354–430) God is a distant, omniscient power, and this church father dominated much of religious thought during the Renaissance. Entire faculties of universities worked on his texts, and an 11-volume opus was published in Antwerp in 1577. Saint Augustine's concepts of predestination and grace were two of the subjects debated in schools of theology. The theological works of Saint Thomas Aquinas (d. 1274) were promoted by members of his order, the Dominicans (literally dogs of God). Saint Thomas's God was more anthropomorphic than that of Saint Augustine; by the time of the Renaissance God was visualized as a wise old man. Thomism, as his theology was called, served to formulate many decrees at the Council of Trent (1545–63, several separate meetings). Theological studies included the subjects of the seven sacraments, the Holy Trinity, biblical traditions, prayer, purgatory, and the place of miracles in church history. Most humanists criticized the cerebral, dialectical method of theological dispute, in which all conclusions were based on predetermined authority. Humanists, on the other hand, advocated the rhetorical approach to teaching and debate, which could move the emotions of listeners if effective. Desiderius Erasmus was quite outspoken against the Scholastic disputations by which theology was being taught. In his *Moriae encomium* (Praise of folly 1511), Erasmus strongly criticized the labyrinthine expostulations of theologians, complaining that not even the apostles could follow such arguments.

MEDICINE

Around 1328 Emperor Frederick II established a university in Padua, which became the most famous medical school of the Renaissance. Its students included several of the individuals discussed in chapter 10, Science and Medicine. Some universities had a separate school of medicine; in others the medical faculty shared a facility with liberal arts. Medical schools graduated physicians, who supposedly understood the nature of illnesses and the theoretical basis of treatments and were thus prepared to treat internal ailments. Although surgeons did not attend the university, but were trained in an apprenticeship system of hands-on experience, famous surgeons could become professors of medicine. Midwives, of course, received no formal training and developed expertise through instruction by other midwives, often their mother or aunt. The university schooling of physicians during the Renaissance directly benefited from humanistic study of the ancient Greek medical texts of Galen and Hippocrates. Galen's works had nearly 600 printings in the 16th century, which generated a multitude of textbooks for medical students. Not only the texts themselves provided instruction; so also did the humanistic criticism of certain points of anatomy. Dissections of human cadavers, mostly of criminals condemned to death, were of paramount importance in the training of young physicians. This pedagogical tool had been introduced in European medical schools during the 14th century. Andreas Vesalius (1514–64), a Flemish physician trained in Paris, entered the faculty of the Padua school of medicine in 1537. His extensively illustrated anatomical handbook *De humani corporis fabrica* (On the structure of the human body, 1543) revolutionized the study of anatomy.

LAW

As urban societies spread throughout western Europe during the 11th and 12th centuries and trade increased during the Crusades, the secular worlds of commerce and politics demanded new systems of legal and political administration. Culture in general became more secular, though religion continued to play a major role in daily life. The 12th century, in fact, experienced a "renaissance" in classical studies that many scholars consider more significant than that of the 15th and 16th centuries. The study of canon (ecclesiastical) law was revived along with a new focus on Roman (civil) law. During the Middle Ages legal scholars at the University of Bologna studied the sources for both canon and civil law, preparing glosses (commentaries). They debated questions that involved current legal affairs as well as textual problems. Law students were expected to do research on the questions at hand and participate in the debates. Gradually jurists in towns across Italy wrote books of statutes codifying the law, a system that came to be called common law in England. In addition, some courts and towns created statute books of their own local laws; law students in the Renaissance had to consider these additional laws in their deliberations. Training in the law was complicated because areas of western Europe operated under different rules of law. Unlike medical training, which was relatively universal because physical maladies had common treatments, legal training necessitated a knowledge of regional interpretations and local precedents.

The system of legal education that developed during the Middle Ages continued to be used into the Renaissance, becoming more complicated as more laws were recorded in writing. Universities that had not previously included legal training in the curriculum established law schools, and chairs in law were funded by monarchs such as Henry VIII (1491–1547). Law students had to learn how to document legal procedures and contracts, which required the skill of a notary. Scribes who wrote letters and other simple texts were not qualified for legal writing. Notaries became an important asset for law schools and formed their own guilds. Several Italian humanists, including Petrarch (1304–74), Salutati, and Leon Battista Alberti (1404–72), were trained in law and members of such a guild. They first learned to interpret classical texts through the standard sources of Roman law.

Protestant Universities

The first Protestant university was founded in Marburg in 1527, under the aegis of Philip the Magnanimous (1504–67), landgrave of Hesse. His motive was purely political as he had converted to Lutheranism in 1524 to assemble a league of Protestant leaders against the Habsburg empire. The university in Marburg served as encouragement for the founding of other Protestant universities in Germany and elsewhere. By the late 16th century, there were several Protestant universities in the Netherlands, and Trinity College had been established in Dublin. Protestantism itself was partly based on a skeptical attitude toward contemporary religious authority, and thus toward the inherent truth of the Catholic religion. Protestant universities taught that personal reading and interpretation of the Bible and related texts in their original languages, unmediated by priests or the pope, would reveal religious truth. By the mid-16th century, Protestant scholars were debating points of theology on the basis of differing philological conclusions about the texts at hand. In addition points of canon law were set aside or called into question. Students could see that metaphysical truth was questionable, and that insight introduced philosophical questions about the nature of truth itself. This critical and inquisitive attitude, already awakened in some of the humanists who were editing classical texts, may have contributed to the development of experimental science during the 17th century.

EDUCATION IN THE VERNACULAR LANGUAGES

The word *vernacular* derived from the Latin word *vernaculus* (native), which in turn derived from *verna* (a slave born in the master's house). During the Renaissance, as discussed in chapter 5, Latin was the universal language of the educated class in western Europe. These were men—women were not accepted—who attended universities to become physicians, lawyers, and theologians, as well as priests who perfected their Latin at the seminary. This class of educated men advised rulers, governed cities and provinces, and became professors themselves. Most of the population of western Europe, involved in the world of business that sustained the economy, did not belong to this class. Although the Latin of lawyers was often required for business transactions, business people and artisans did not need to know the language themselves. The Protestant Reformation, teaching that Christians should be able to read sacred texts in their own language, supported education in the vernacular.

Primary Education in the Vernacular

Primary education in the vernacular languages took place in classes for younger, nonuniversity students. There were several different types of environments for learning the basic skills of literacy—being able to read simple texts, write school exercises, and count—and not all were formal classrooms. Many children were taught at home by hired tutors or family members. By the early 16th century, printed grammars and primers for learning how to read were being used throughout much of western Europe, and these could easily be used in the home. The printed book allowed both learning and reading to become private, self-directed endeavors, especially for those destined to become merchants or otherwise involved in the everyday world of commerce. In Germany, England, France, and Spain many more books were published in the vernacular languages than in Latin, providing an abundance of reading material for those unable or unwilling to read Latin. These books included Protestant religious handbooks appropriate for young men and women. Aldus Manutius (c. 1450–1515), Venetian printer and publisher, was the first to produce "pocket books" in a format small enough to be easily portable. His books pertained almost exclusively to the classics, but publishers of vernacular language books, including primers and grammars, soon followed his example. Only those students destined for the university or an ecclesiastical career needed the formal guidance of an instructor, and these individuals attended Latin grammar schools rather than learning the basics of reading and writing in vernacular schools, at home, or, as did some apprentices, on the job.

Secondary Curriculum and Method of Learning

Before the invention of printing, pupils listened to a teacher and took notes by hand, just as students do today. Unlike in today's schools, students could not verify their information via the Internet or books readily available in the school library. There was no standard textbook in any of their subjects. Thus pupils learned to listen well if they wanted to excel in their studies. Whereas humanistic education mainly used classical texts, education in the vernacular focused on whatever texts the teacher decided to use or parents could provide. There were no systems of accreditation and no guidelines for the curriculum. Basically the vernacular texts read by the parents of children were those taught by their teachers. Medieval chivalric romances were popular, as well as catechisms, books about the saints, and other texts meant to encourage virtuous behavior. Although these topics may sound boring today, in an age without comic books, television, or cinema, the colorful adventures of saints spurning temptation would have held the attention of young students. Teachers also included devotional and spiritual training as part of the day-to-day vernacular classroom activity. The most widely read text in Italy was *Fior di virtù* (Flower of virtue), which was first printed circa 1471 and had an astonishing 56 printings before 1501. Some of these editions were illustrated with woodcuts, which could only have increased the book's appeal to schoolchildren. These basic texts had rather simple vocabulary and grammar. They could be read easily by students who had made their way through a primer in the vernacular tongue, especially if parents helped them at home. Parents (including fathers) were encouraged to take part in their children's instruction. Sir Thomas Elyot in *The Book Named the Governor* (1531) wrote: "It shall be no reproach to a nobleman to instruct his own children . . . considering that the Emperor Octavius Augustus disdained not to read the

works of Cicero and Virgil to his children and nephews" (Brown 1997, p. 103).

Study of Practical Mathematics

Mathematics in humanistic schools and at the university had a theoretical focus that did not serve any practical purpose in the world of Renaissance commerce. Students planning to enter the business world needed another sort of mathematics, which would teach them how to determine the cost of merchandise, deal with the varying standards of weights and measures, measure for surveying, and handle similar problems of daily business. In practical mathematics each problem was reasoned through on its own, sometimes with educated

11.2 Allegory of Arithmetic. *Woodcut by Gregor Reisch in the* Margarita philosophica *(Philosophical Pearl, 1504).* (Bibliothèque de la Faculté de Médecine, Paris, France/Archives Charmet/Bridgeman Art Library)

guesses to test possible conclusions. The basic textbook for this study was *Liber abbaci* (Book of abaci, early 13th century). Although the title was derived from the abacus used for calculations by sliding counters along rods, the reasoning process called *abbaco* in Italian was accomplished on paper. The book's author was the medieval mathematician Leonardo Fibonacci (c. 1170–after 1240), or Leonardo of Pisa. A businessman who studied Arabic and visited Arab regions, Fibonacci was instrumental in popularizing the Hindu-Arabic systems of numerals in western Europe. These replaced the Roman numerals and made computation much simpler. *Abbaco* loosely translates as "accounting," the single most important skill of any Renaissance merchant. Textbooks for teaching *abbaco* often included woodcut illustrations, such as pictorial tables for reckoning on the fingers while computing long division and multiplication. The fingers on the left hand were bent and straightened in various combinations while the right hand noted the answers on a piece of paper. The final stage of learning in *abbaco* mathematics was algebra, including the solving of cubic equations.

11.3 Carpenter's apprentice cutting wood. This 15th-century French woodcut illustrates one of the menial tasks assigned to apprentices. (Bibliothèque des Arts Décoratifs, Paris, France/Archives Charmet/Bridgeman Art Library)

APPRENTICESHIP

Apprenticing, which derives from the Latin word *apprendere* (to learn), was the system by which young men learned a trade. Many of today's young people learn how to be a tradesperson, such as an electrician or plumber, by apprenticeship. In spite of the number of universities in Europe by 1500, the majority of people did not attend them; rather they learned to work with their hands or in a commercial activity such as banking. Some of the greatest artists of the period never attended a university, absorbing their knowledge of color, line, form, and materials from master painters, sculptors, and builders. The apprenticeship system was rigorous, and today students might be shocked at the young age of novice apprentices (usually between 12 and 14 years of age) and the strict working conditions under which they labored for several years (occasionally as long as 12 years).

Apprenticeship in General

Apprenticeship contracts and working conditions were regulated by guilds, whose members desired to uphold standards of quality in the commodities they produced. There were statutes pertaining to the number of apprentices that a master could train concurrently and the length of time that apprentices should serve. It was forbidden for apprentices to sell their work outside the workshop or to change masters. If these two rules were broken, there could be legal and financial repercussions for the apprentice's parent or guardian who had signed the contract. The oath of an apprentice was strict, as exemplified by part of the oath sworn in 1504 in England by an apprentice to the Mercers' (Merchants') Company: "Ye shall hold steadfastly, secretly and for counsel all and every the lawful ordinances, whatsoever they be, to the Craft or occupation of the Mercery belonging, and . . . ye shall observe, hold and keep, and not to break, discover, open or show any of them to any person, but unto such as unto the fellowship of the Mercery is here according to this oath sworn" (Scott 1976, p. 130). Their clothing was equally severe—a simple, flat cap over short hair and coarsely woven coats.

When an apprenticeship was completed, the individual usually set out on a Wanderjahr (year of traveling around), which often extended to several years in different locations. The English word *journeyman* literally expresses this idea. Unlike in today's "gap year" in which students travel as tourists or work as volunteers for humanitarian causes, the journeyman worked for different masters, learning special techniques or processes from each one. He (and it was always a "he") was paid for this work; many journeymen saved income from the Wanderjahr to return home and establish their workshop as master. Then they, too, could train apprentices, thus supporting the apprenticeship system in which they had learned their trade. The Wanderjahr was significant in the dissemination of new techniques and processes; the Wanderjahr for artists was especially important in the development of Renaissance art. New types of imagery as well as new techniques and processes were taken home by traveling apprentices.

Apprenticeship of Artists

We know quite a bit about the apprenticeship of artists and artisans during the Renaissance, partly because extensive research concerning this subject has been done. There are also several contemporary documents written by the artists themselves. In *Il libro dell'arte* (Art handbook, c. 1400), for example, Cennino Cennini (c. 1370–c. 1440) included information about his apprenticeship with Agnolo Gaddi (d. 1396), son of the famous Taddeo Gaddi (see chapter 3), in this first treatise of the Renaissance on painting. Although none of Cennini's paintings has survived, this treatise alone makes him an important figure in Renaissance art history. Above all else his apprenticeship focused on drawing, beginning with copying and tracing the paintings and drawings of others. Exercises in drawing continued throughout

the years of his study with Gaddi. The methodology was imitative, as the apprentice learned from good models. Cennini spent 12 years studying with Gaddi, the first half of his apprenticeship occupied with technical skills such as mixing pigments, and the second half focused on the application of paint to panels and walls. Other apprentices in Tuscany learning to be painters probably followed a similar program.

EDUCATION OF GIRLS AND WOMEN

As are most Western societies, the Renaissance societies of western Europe were patriarchal. As scholars have recently noted, the Renaissance was not a rebirth for women. Until well into the 17th century, the place of girls and women was in the home or convent. The education of young women usually was accomplished within a spiritual context, and often inside a convent, much as it was during the Middle Ages. Although a few schools specifically founded for girls of noble families were established during the 16th century, spiritual enrichment and moral training remained the chief goals of the educational process. A famous example of such a school was the Jesuit institution founded in Milan in 1557 by Ludovica Torelli (1500–1569), daughter of the duke of Guastella. As might be expected, young women potentially destined to be the companions of rulers were trained in court etiquette and languages. Members of royalty, such as princesses, often shared lessons with their brothers, benefiting from excellent tutors. The examples of powerful women in northern Italy during the 15th century, and across much of Europe during the 16th, suggest that some upper-class women were educated in subjects of history, statecraft, and other knowledge useful for the ruling class. Although Ludovico Dolce (1508–68) in his *Dialogo della institutione delle donne* (Dialogue on the instruction of ladies, 1545) recommended that women not learn as much as men, he encouraged women destined to rule to study the entire humanistic curriculum.

Childhood Education

Children were considered a blank slate, hardly human at all until they reached one year of age. The mother had the task of instilling moral precepts into her children. Although the Renaissance learned from classical authors, such as Quintilian, that both parents should set an example of virtue for their children, mothers were responsible for teaching young children. In turn, this meant that girls realized early in life that they would bear this responsibility if they became mothers. Needlework, spinning, simple weaving, and sometimes lacemaking were part of the childhood education of girls, who would later provide the cloth

11.4 Saint Anne reading to the Virgin. Netherlandish oak sculpture, first quarter of the 16th century. Saint Anne's reading to her daughter was a popular model for childhood education. (Photograph courtesy of Sotheby's, Inc., © 2003)

and textiles for their own home. Upper-class girls were expected to master the art of embroidery, one of the signs of a cultivated woman. Mary Stuart (1542–87), for example, created exquisitely embroidered pillow covers while imprisoned by Queen Elizabeth I (1533–1603). By the 14th century girls were being taught to read and write, especially in the vernacular, as long as the subjects were virtuous or spiritual. Although many parents liked for their young daughters to learn to sing and play an instrument, some pedagogical theorists taught that such "vanities" should not detract from other lessons. The social class of a girl determined the extent of her basic education; upper-class girls even learned some arithmetic, girls of lower status learned only to read and write, and poor girls learned only to read well enough to comprehend their book of prayers, if that. Only a small percentage (probably less than 10 percent) of teachers were women. They instructed primary school pupils, both girls and boys, in the vernacular.

Humanistic Education for Young Women

Humanistic education for young women usually occurred within the supportive environment of court culture, beginning in northern Italy during the 15th century. The main exception was the educational program for young women taught by members of the various religious orders, such as the Ursulines during the latter 16th century. In their schools, chiefly in northern Europe and Venice, the students learned Latin, geography, and composition, in addition to the usual spiritual training. Learned women of ancient Greece and Rome were presented as role models in the humanistic education of upper-class young women. The basic text for this information was Giovanni Boccaccio's (1313–75) *De claribus mulieribus* (On famous women, c. 1362). For the first time in western Europe, biographies of famous women of classical times were gathered into one work. It has rightly been pointed out that the virtuous models presented by Boccaccio, along with the harsh punishments of women who misbehaved, emphasized the "proper" roles for women during the Renaissance. Nevertheless this text and others like it helped to open the door to study of the classics for young women because they read them in Latin. In addition young women learned in school that a woman could achieve recognition outside her home and family for notable achievements; Isis, "Queen of Egypt," for example, was credited with inventing an alphabet and a written language. But at the same time female students were encouraged to admire the great women of history acclaimed as weavers and spinners of cloth.

We should note that young women enrolled in humanistic schools who did not plan to become nuns were expected to learn the domestic skills necessary to run a household, and all young women were taught that their spiritual and religious training took priority. Young men, on the other hand, could focus almost exclusively on their studies of the classics. The few pedagogical treatises that included advice about schooling for girls, even those that supported secondary education for young women, cautioned that there were limits to what they should (and could) learn. Advanced oratory was considered inappropriate and unnecessary, as was higher training in mathematics. The Spanish humanist Juan Luís Vives wrote the most comprehensive Renaissance treatise specifically about female education, *De institutione feminae christianae* (On the instruction of a Christian woman, 1523). Published in Spanish in 1528 and in English in 1540, this influential book had dozens of editions during the Renaissance. Although its curriculum advocated the reading (in Latin) of Cicero, Plato, and Seneca, in addition to biblical texts and church fathers, Vives insinuated that young women should learn to be silent, chaste, and obedient. They were not trained in rhetoric and oratory, which might teach them to speak their mind, or logic, which might teach them how to argue. Above all young women were advised not to neglect their family in favor of their studies. In spite of all these obstacles, the Renaissance produced some outstanding learned women, as the following examples demonstrate. In most instances, however, such women had little influence on the education of other women.

Examples of Learned Women

Christine de Pisan (c. 1364–c. 1430) was the well-educated daughter of an Italian serving as royal astrologer at the French court. Widowed at a young age with small children to support, Christine became a writer. She wrote wittily in Latin as well as French and obviously knew the works of classical authors. Because of her fame as a poet, Christine de Pisan's treatise *Livre de la cité des dames* (Book of the city of ladies, c. 1405) was well known among her contemporaries. In it she argued that girls might learn more readily than boys if given the opportunity, and she continued to support female abilities in the literary Debate of the Rose against several male opponents. She countered derogatory remarks about women made in the medieval *Roman de la rose* (Romance of the rose). Although Christine's writings were popular among the nobility, with dedication copies in manuscript presented to the queen and other members of the nobility, her prehumanistic feminism had little effect on the education of girls. Scholasticism was firmly entrenched in 15th-century French domains.

The courts of northern Italy, on the other hand, were experiencing the effects of humanistic education by the early 15th century. During the Renaissance the greatest number of learned women were found in the courts of Mantua, Urbino, Modena, Ferrara, and Verona, where bright young women learned Greek, delivered orations in Latin, and corresponded in Latin with noted male humanists. Although most of them evidently abandoned their studies upon marrying, a few continued their studies by teaching their children or by refusing to marry at all. At the court of Mantua, Cecilia Gonzaga (1425–1451) was reading ancient Greek at the age of seven with Vittorino da Feltre at the Casa Giocosa (see earlier discussion), and she could write Greek compositions by the time she was 10. In Ferrara, Olympia Morata (1526–55) learned both Greek and Latin, writing poems and dialogues in these languages. Isotta Nogarola (1418–66), at the court of Verona, was fluent in Latin and spoke at learned conferences. She had received a humanistic education in Latin from a pupil of Guarino Guarini's. During her 20s Isotta took up the study of theology, in addition to her program of studying the classics. She became famous among her contemporaries for shutting herself up in solitude in her family's house, to be able to focus on her studies. Isotta's readings turned to dialectic and philosophy, evoking praise from fellow humanists, but she was cautioned to remain a virgin so that she would maintain her scholarly focus. Women involved with daily life and the demands of the body were not considered fit to pursue the pleasures of the mind.

By the late 15th century young noblewomen in other parts of western Europe had tutors in classical Latin and Greek. Most of these educated women entered convents, and some of them continued their studies there. One of the best examples in Germany was Caritas Pirckheimer (b. 1467), sister of the scholar and translator Willibald Pirckheimer (1470–1530) in Nuremberg, who gave his daughters a humanistic education. Caritas Pirckheimer was considered almost an equal among German humanists. When she was appointed abbess of her convent, however, her superiors instructed her that she would no longer be permitted to write in Latin, and she complied. Having escaped a patriarchal family life, she was trapped within the patriarchal church. In France the king's elder sister, Marguerite de Navarre (1492–1549), was the first well-known female humanist. A patron of the arts and learning, she was a writer herself. Her collection of stories titled *Heptameron* (not published until after her death in 1558), loosely modeled on Boccaccio's tales in *Decameron*, had much to say about a woman's place in society.

The Spanish humanistic tradition reached the Tudor court of England through none other than Vives, hired by Catherine of Aragon (1485–1536) as tutor for the young Mary Tudor. The first wife of Henry VIII, Catherine was a scholar herself and daughter of Queen Isabella I, who had learned Latin as an adult. Mary Tudor, who potentially could have ruled England, was taught to read and write both Greek and Latin, as was her younger half sister, Elizabeth. The English humanist Roger Ascham was hired by Henry VIII to tutor Elizabeth, who eventually became Elizabeth I. Ascham's pedagogical treatise *The Scholemaster* (first published in 1570) outlined the proper humanistic education for a young man, and that was the approximate curriculum that he established for Elizabeth during the two years he was her tutor. She read classical Greek authors in the morning, then Latin authors along with church fathers and the New Testament in the afternoon. Unfortunately for young women in England who wished to study the classics during and after Elizabeth's reign, the antipapal sentiments in England prevented any serious study of Latin. The humanistic studies that sometimes had been allowed in convents were no longer possible because Henry VIII had closed them earlier in the century.

MAJOR FIGURES

Ascham, Roger (1515–1568), who wrote *The Scholemaster, or Plain and Perfect Way of Teaching Children the Latin Tongue* (1570), was Latin secretary for Mary I (Mary Tudor, 1516–58) and served as a tutor for both Elizabeth I and Edward VI. He also wrote a handbook on archery, *Toxophilus* (1545), which served as a model of the dialogue format.

Barbosa, Arias established a humanistic school at the Portuguese court during the reign of Manuel I, teaching the royal children Alfonso and Enrique. He had studied Greek in Italy under Angelo Poliziano and was a professor of Greek for 20 years at the University of Salamanca.

Barzizza, Gasparino (c. 1360–1431) founded an institute for classical Latin in Padua in the early 15th century. Between 1407 and 1421 he taught students in Padua, who boarded in his home. Barzizza's lifelong goal was to edit classical texts and restore them to their original purity. His letters in Latin became stylistic models for other humanists.

Bracciolini, Poggio (1380–1459) served in the papal scriptorium for many years; he returned to Florence and became chancellor in 1453. Poggio advocated the teaching of Latin as a living language, versus the strictly Ciceronian style of Lorenzo Valla (1407–57), with whom he had a famous feud over Latin (see chapter 5). Humanism flourished in Florence during his term as chancellor.

Bruni, Leonardo (1370–1444) returned to Florence in 1415 after working for the papal secretariat. He became chancellor of Florence in 1427, championing humanistic studies from this position of power. Bruni translated several ancient Greek authors into Latin and wrote an important history of the Florentine people modeled on classical historiography.

Buchanan, George (1506–1582) was a Scottish humanist and philosopher. He taught at universities in France and Portugal and returned to Scotland in 1561 as a Protestant. Buchanan was the principal of Saint Leonard's College, Saint Andrews, and was tutor to the future James I, whom he taught that the people are the source of all political power.

Budé, Guillaume (1467–1540), humanistic jurist, was King Louis XII's (1462–1515) ambassador to Pope Leo X (1475–1521) and later Francis I's royal librarian at Fontainebleau. He was a renowned classical philologist, publishing on Roman law, weights and measures, and the Greek language.

Colet, John (c. 1466–1519) was an instrumental reformer of the curriculum in England, instituting humanistic studies at Saint Paul's School. Along with William Lyly, Colet wrote a Latin grammar that was widely used in England. His educational philosophy was published in *On the Basis of Study* (1511).

Christine de Pisan (c. 1364–c. 1430) was born in Venice, the daughter of an astrologer. Because her father was appointed as royal astrologer for Charles V, king of France, Christine was raised at the French court. She became a poet, championing the cause of women in prehumanistic France and advocating equal educational opportunities for young women.

Elyot, Sir Thomas (c. 1490–1546) wrote the *Book Named the Governor* (1531), explaining how humanistic education benefits the state. Sir Thomas translated several treatises concerning statecraft and served the English Crown as a diplomat.

Erasmus, Desiderius (c. 1466–1536) was born in Rotterdam of humble origins. Trained as a humanist, Erasmus advocated reform within the Catholic Church. His philological work included editing texts for publishers such as Aldus Manutius, and he taught in several countries. In England he lectured at Cambridge, where he became friends with Colet and More. His pedagogical writings and international correspondence were extremely influential on humanistic education.

Guarini, Battista (b. 1434) (not to be confused with the 16th-century Italian playwright of the same name) was the son of Guarino Guarini, whose teaching methods are documented in Battista's *De ordine docendi et studendi* (On a curriculum of teaching and learning), written in 1459.

Guarini, Guarino *(Guarino da Verona)* (1374–1460) lived in Constantinople from 1403 to 1408, studying Greek and collecting manuscripts. After teaching in Venice, Florence, Padua, and Verona, Guarini was chosen to establish a humanistic school at the court of Ferrara. There he remained for 30 years, perfecting his famous curriculum in classical literature. He was the father of Battista Guarini.

Lebrija, Antonio *(also Antonio Nebrija)* (1442–1522) studied at the universities of Salamanca and Bologna. Most of his career was spent teaching the classics at the University of Alcalá de Henares, where he became Spain's most illustrious humanistic scholar. In addition to his publications on ancient texts, Lebrija wrote the first grammar of Castilian Spanish (1492). He also was a member of the committee that produced the Complutensian Polyglot Bible (see chapter 2).

Martire d'Anghiera, Pietro (1457–1526), Italian humanist and soldier, moved to Spain and taught at the court of Queen Isabella I. He established a humanistic school where the royal children and sons of the nobility were instructed. Because Martire d'Anghiera became involved in administering Spain's colonial empire, he was familiar with the explorers in service to the Crown of Spain. His *De orbe novo* (On the New World, 1511) was the first extensive documentation of Spanish exploration.

More, Sir Thomas (1478–1535) supported humanistic education, including that of his daughters. He became lord chancellor for Henry VIII in 1529 but was executed in 1535 because he spoke out against the new religious regime and the king's attacks on Catholic institutions.

Marguerite de Navarre *(also Marguerite d'Angoulême)* (1492–1549), queen of Navarre, was the sister of Francis I. A patron of learning and the arts, she wrote religious poetry as well as the stories of her *Heptameron* (1558) exploring relations between the sexes and women's place in society.

Nebrija, Antonio   See LEBRIJA, ANTONIO.

Melanchthon, Philipp (1497–1560) was Luther's friend and is buried beside him in Wittenberg. A noted Greek scholar, Melanchthon was involved in the major religious polemics of his day. His Latin curriculum combining biblical passages with the Latin classics was adopted throughout Germany.

Piccolomini, Aeneas Silvius (1405–1464) was elected as Pope Pius II in 1458. Educated as a humanist, he appointed humanistic scholars to posts in his administration. Although much of his reign was occupied with attempts to lead another Crusade against the Turks, Pius II helped to found the University of Basel in 1459 and supported humanistic schools.

Salutati, Coluccio (1331–1406) served as chancellor of Florence for three decades, attracting humanistic scholars such as Manuel Chrysoloras to the city. Salutati wrote poetry and works of moral philosophy based on classical sources, as well as letters in classical style. It was partly due to the efforts of Salutati that Florence became a mecca for Renaissance humanism in the early 15th century.

Sellyng, William (d. 1494) studied in Italy and journeyed there several times on diplomatic missions for the king of England. His monastery of Christ Church, Canterbury, was among the earliest study centers for classical Greek literature in England. Sellyng had returned from his travels with copies of Greek manuscripts that could be used as texts.

Sturm, Johannes (1507–1589), a Protestant convert, founded an important humanistic gymnasium in Strasbourg (then part of Germany). His writings include a biography of Beatus Rhenanus (1485–1547), a German printer of humanistic texts and friend of Erasmus.

Vergerio the Elder, Piero Paolo (1370–1444), trained as a humanist, served in the administrations of two popes between 1406 and 1409. From 1418 until his death Vergerio worked for the imperial court. His treatise *De ingenuis moribus et liberalibus adulescentiae studiis liber* (On the character and studies appropriate for a free-born adolescent) was the first comprehensive Renaissance work on the humanistic curriculum.

Vesalius, Andreas (1514–1564) served as personal physician to both Emperor Charles V and Philip II, king of Spain (1527–98), having achieved international fame for his anatomical masterpiece, *De humani corporis fabrica* (On the structure of the human body, 1543). Although much of his work depended on the classical writings of Galen, advancements in dissection and medical illustration helped Vesalius's book become a standard of medical education.

Vittorino (Rambaldoni) da Feltre (1373/78–1446/47) learned Greek from Guarino Guarini and later opened a school in Venice. Selected to educate the children of nobility at the court of Mantua, Vittorino moved there and established his Casa Giocosa. This was the first school in Italy to teach Greek; its notable instructors included Theodore Gaza (c. 1415–75/76) and George of Trebizond (1396–1472/73).

Vives, Juan Luis (1492–1540) studied in Valencia and Paris; he finally settled in Bruges after residing for a while at the English court. His pedagogical works include a handbook of dialogues for learning Latin and the influential *De institutione feminae christianae* (On the instruction of a Christian woman, 1523).

READING

Huppert 1984: education in France.

Humanistic Education

Grafton 1986: general survey; Grendler 1989: Italy; Kallendorf 2002: translations of Renaissance pedagogical treatises; Kekewich 2000: impact of humanism; Nauert 2000; cultural contexts.

University Education

Carlsmith 2002: Jesuits; Koen Goudriaan 2004: Netherlands; Ruggiero 2002: medicine; Rummel 1998: theology; Schwinges 2000: Germany.

Education in the Vernacular Languages

Grendler 1989, 273–329: Italy; Pardoe 2000: Germany.

Education of Girls and Women

Adelman 1999: Jewish women; Donawerth 1998: conversation; Grendler 1989, 87–102: Italy; King 1991; Italy; Michalove 1999: aristocratic women; Stevenson 1998: humanism; Watson 1972: Vives.

12

DAILY LIFE

The conditions of daily life in the Renaissance depended on gender, class, geographic location, precise period, and other factors, such as a person's religion. Previous chapters of this book have touched upon several aspects of daily life, especially those concerning education, religion, travel, and warfare. The present chapter explores what it might have been like to live a secular, moderate, Christian life during the Renaissance, and what experiences and events directly affected the majority of individuals living outside convents and monasteries. In 1400 Europe had two main social classes, the nobility and the peasants or workers, and some peasants and workers were exposed to upper-class life because they worked as servants or artisans in houses of the wealthy. By 1600 the inflated cash economy had fragmented this relatively simple social structure into a multiclass society, which still included the upper and lower classes, in addition to a new middle class and a desperately poor lower class. A city might have as many as 8 percent of its people supported by charity, and approximately 20 percent of the general population occasionally needed assistance simply to survive. These people lived on the margin of subsistence and could be thrown into abject poverty with the slightest downward shift in their financial circumstances.

Urban life, of course, differed from rural life. Only 5 percent of Europe's population lived permanently in a city of significant size (more than 100,000), and only 25 percent lived in a city at all. The larger the city, the more complex it tended to be. Although major cities had more wealthy citizens paying taxes that supported the infrastructure, larger cities had more problems with sanitation and other issues pertaining to public health. Much of the information in the present book focuses on cities, but the majority of individuals lived in rural areas, in villages or small towns. Most people were born, married, and died in or near the same place; attended the same country church; and regulated their life by church bells and hours of sunshine. Daily life in either town or country was odoriferous, and that atmosphere probably would be the first thing we would notice if transported back to Renaissance times. The farm animals and hay-strewn dirt floors of rural living would have been an assault to modern sensibilities; the sewage and garbage flow-

12.1 *Legal tribunal with the prince adjudicating. Woodcut title page from a 1507 treatise on Salic law (the law of the Salian Franks), which governed several aspects of personal life in northern Europe. Most notably, daughters were not permitted to inherit land.* (Photograph courtesy of Sotheby's, Inc., © 2003)

ing down city passageways would have been worse. People everywhere had a strong odor because bathing was infrequent, to say the least, and outer garments were rarely laundered. Babies also were pungent because their swaddling clothes usually were changed only a few times each day, except in wealthy households.

Men in all classes were considered superior to women, who remained girls (referred to as virgins and expected to remain so) until their betrothal or wedding. All children were raised by the mother until about age seven, at which point boys would be handed over to tutors or taken to live with influential uncles or other relatives. Girls remained at home unless they were placed in a convent, helping their parents in the field or shop or with household chores. Girls learned the skills of managing a house, especially the crafts pertaining to textiles. Renaissance inventions, such as the treadle for spinning wheels, helped make these tasks a little easier than they had been in past centuries. In most parts of Europe mothers and daughters did not venture away from their home except to shop, attend church, or visit nearby relatives. Whereas boys were free to roam the streets after a certain age, girls were never seen in public alone. Because their greatest value was as a virgin bride, their honor and the honor of their father had to be protected. Girls who stayed at home and never married were never regarded as fully adult. Gender-based differences were also reflected in the legal system, as discussed later.

TIME AND THE CALENDAR

The installation of town clocks, timepieces carried in the pocket, and arguments concerning the calendar made time a palpable force by the 16th century. For city dwellers removed from the rhythm of farm life, the workday was arbitrarily divided into hours, or o'clocks. Unlike the canonical hours that sounded for prayers approximately every three hours, clock hours divided the days and nights into smaller, yet arbitrary segments. The calendar was out of sync with the equinoxes, and Easter fell earlier each century. Reform of the calendar undertaken in the 1570s resulted in an adjustment of the date for Easter, but also in political conflict that continued for many years.

Time

The perception of daily time was changing during the Renaissance, especially in urban centers, where public clocks struck on the hour. Whereas church bells might toll for some or all of the canonical hours throughout each day, a clock striking each hour must have created a greater awareness of time's passing as it broke the day into smaller units. Early Renaissance clocks struck each of the 24 hours in succession, but people found counting so many bongs difficult. For this reason the 24-hour day was divided into two equal parts, so that a clock did not strike more than 12 times. Medieval clocks were cumbersome, weight-driven mechanisms, which had to remain upright and stationary. During the 15th century spring-driven clocks were invented, facilitating the production of smaller, portable clocks for the home. In the early 16th century the pocket watch appeared, enabling an individual to know the time at all times. These first pocket watches were called Nuremberg eggs, from the city of their manufacture and their oval shape. Although not very accurate, they must have prompted their owners to look at them several times each day and to show them to other people. The early pocket watches were relatively expensive, but people also had pocket sundials as well as a short stick called a hand dial. Held by the thumb over the palm of the hand and pointed toward the North Pole, the stick cast a shadow on the outstretched hand that allowed a person to determine the approximate time. The point for 12 noon was located at the outer edge of the palm, one o'clock at the base of the pinkie finger, and so on. (The term *o'clock* simply means "of clock," or a time shown on a clock face.)

Time functioned on an annual schedule, much as it does today, signified by the seasons and by religious celebrations and observances. The seasons revolved around planting and harvest, which were especially busy times of the year. Each city, town, and village had religious celebrations on the important dates of the Christian calendar, notably Easter and Christmas. Every local area also had its patron saint's day, one of the grandest celebrations of the year. In locations dominated by Protestants, however, the saint's day was no longer observed. Renaissance time comprised all these events, as most people lived life in a cycle of predictable, familiar activities, with the week punctuated by Sunday church service.

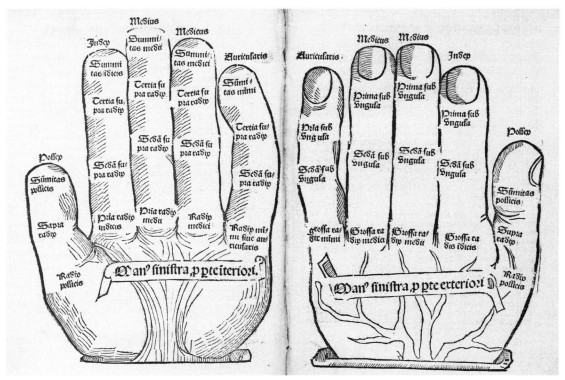

12.2 System for counting by one's fingers. Woodcut in a book by Anianus on computing, 1490/91. Time, measurement, and money could all be tallied by mnemonic systems using the fingers and hands. (Photograph courtesy of Sotheby's, Inc., © 2003)

The Calendar

In 1400 the European calendar was based on the Roman calendar established by Julius Caesar. Known as the Julian calendar, this system assumed that one year has exactly 365 1/4 days, whereas the Earth's path around the Sun is actually slightly shorter. Leap year was added every four years to this calendar, to account for the quarter-day. Because the Julian year was 11 minutes and 42 seconds more than the actual year, this extra time became quite noticeable by the 14th century, especially in relation to the placement of Easter in the Christian liturgy. Whereas most Catholic feasts are on fixed dates, Easter is a movable feast, depending on the lunar calendar. Easter is celebrated after the full Moon that follows the vernal

(spring) equinox. Although the equinox was fixed on March 21, the actual equinox was occurring 10 days earlier. Easter and all its attendant outdoor celebrations were slowly moving toward winter, and particularly for northern Europeans something had to be done. In the early 1560s the Council of Trent proclaimed that the pope should reform the calendar.

Pope Gregory XIII (1502–85) convened a commission for this purpose that lasted nearly a decade. Its members made several changes, for both long-term and immediate correction. Three leap years were to be removed in 400 years, and any leap year divisible by 100 (such as 1900) would instead be a normal year, whereas any leap year divisible by 400 (such as 2000) would still be a leap year. Then 10 days were removed from the calendar to make the actual equinox fall on March 21. In 1582 the calendar went from October 4 to October 15, a decision not welcomed in part of Europe, and certainly not in Protestant countries because the pope was in charge of the reform. Most Catholic areas had adopted the Gregorian calendar by 1583; many other areas had not. In fact some countries began using the Gregorian system only in the early 20th century. England not only refused to comply until 1752, but also kept March 25 as the beginning of the new year until the same date. Several other countries and cities, such as Florence, had observed New Year on March 25 until 1582. (That is the reason why some dates prior to 1582 are now expressed as two years, e.g., 1526/27. The pertinent event occurred between January 1 and March 24 of what is not the Gregorian year of 1527, but was 1526 at the time. For England, of course, this anomaly pertains for dates until 1752.)

FAMILY LIFE

A family consisted of a married couple and their children, occasionally with other immediate relatives. Wives stayed at home and husbands worked, and children who were older often helped in the shop or fields. Because people married to have children, sex and procreation were important topics about which numerous manuals were written in the 15th century. With the advent of printing, these pamphlets spread throughout Europe. Those intended for the use of priests instructing betrothed couples were rather general; others were quite specific concerning sexual positions and activities. Although the husband had legal control over his wife, she could complain to the priest if he wanted to engage in "inappropriate" activities, meaning any

12.3 Venetian lacquered wood chest, c. 1580. Islamic influence can be seen in the lacquerwork and arabesque ornament. (Photograph courtesy of Sotheby's Inc., © 2003)

sexual act that could not result in pregnancy. Although women often had as many as 10 or 15 children, only two or three might survive to adulthood.

Couples enjoyed domestic pastimes, such as games and music, and small children played with pets, rolled hoops, and participated in ball games and similar activities involving simple, handmade toys such as stuffed dolls and hobbyhorses. Older children helped with the work or focused on their studies (see chapter 11, Education). Except for the upper classes, houses were quite small, often no more than two rooms with a low ceiling, and a family of four usually slept in one large bed. In winter houses in northern Europe were chilly, dark, and dank. Fireplaces were used for most domestic cooking and heating, meaning that the house could be smoky whenever the weather was warm and humid unless it had a metal stove. In summer houses in southern Europe were stifling in the daytime heat, so that meals and many other household activities occurred outside. A small loom, for example, might be set up on a terrace. Families regulated their life according to sunlight, rising with the Sun and going to bed not long after sunset. The day usually began and ended with the family's kneeling in prayer. Outside cities people were relatively self-sufficient, making almost everything they needed. Until the consumer society of the latter 16th century, most families had simple needs: a couple of outfits and pair of shoes each; some kitchen utensils; a bed, chamberpot, table, bench, and chest, lamps; and tools for the farm or workshop.

Marriage

Renaissance writers compared the proper relationship between wife and husband to that of a magistrate carrying out the orders of a higher official, in a social relationship reflecting the political hierarchy of the state. Men were in charge of families and could beat, starve, or otherwise abuse their wife as well as their children. This is not to say that most husbands did so, but that the legal system allowed such behavior. Church authorities were the only recourse for an abused wife. A priest could shame an abusive or adulterous husband in cases in which the state would do nothing. Although being sinful was not necessarily illegal, such behavior could be condemned by the congregation and community. Households usually consisted of a nuclear family having a few surviving children, especially in urban centers. Rural families with estates of any size might have a more extended network of relatives to help run the farm. Because the normal life expectancy was approximately 40 years, relatively few grandparents lived for any length of time in the houses of their sons or daughters. People married relatively late, considering how quickly they died. Most couples in a first marriage were fairly close in age, the wife usually younger. Young women of 14 or 15 sometimes married much older men, however, partly as a result of the plagues of the 14th century, when the population balance was destroyed. In most Renaissance societies, such a May/December couple was viewed as inappropriate and would have been subjected to a raucous charivari (see later discussion) on the first night of their marriage.

WIDOWHOOD

Widows who functioned as the head of a household were the only secular women considered to be adults, and they held an ambiguous position in society. On the one hand they commanded respect because of their station; on the other hand they sometimes were the subject of suspicion because they had been sexually active. Widows outnumbered widowers by far because women were somewhat younger than their husband. Young widows almost always remarried, but older widows, especially those at the cusp of childbearing years, often did not. Their widowhood was the first time in their life when they experienced independence, and those with money had no need to remarry. In some regions a widow had to forfeit a percentage of her husband's estate if she remarried. Children were the property of their father but not of their mother in most countries on the Continent. A widow was not necessarily allowed to keep her children if powerful male relatives of her husband intervened. The marriage contracts of some couples specifically named the wife as guardian of any children and of the estate to protect the woman's rights should her husband predecease her. Poverty-stricken widows were cared for by family members or by charitable organizations.

BETROTHALS

Except for young women whose family lived in poverty, brides were expected to bring a dowry to the marriage. In most cases, the dowry signified all the property that a woman might expect as an inheritance from her father's estate. Her husband managed the money or property and actually owned it, but the bride was usually entitled to have the dowry returned if the marriage was annulled. Betrothal was a solemn vow, as binding as the marriage vow. Announced in public, often at the door of a church and in the presence of a priest, the betrothal could be broken only if both parties agreed. Betrothed couples occasionally had sexual intercourse, which legally bound them as if they were already officially married. Because of the confusion between the betrothal ceremony and the wedding, formal betrothals were discouraged during the 16th century. Subsequently the actual wedding ceremony began to assume more significance. Marriage was (and is) a sacrament in the Catholic Church, but between two individuals rather than between an individual and a priest. According to the Council of Trent a marriage was valid if vows were spoken before a priest and witnesses. Parental consent (i.e., from the fathers) was not required for Catholics, but most Protestant sects did require permission.

SEXUAL ADVICE AND ACTIVITY

Advice concerning sexual activity abounded during the Renaissance, some of it from ancient Greek sources. This advice was meant for married couples because only they were supposed to be having sexual intercourse. An impressive percentage of these texts pertained to fertility and conception, and much of the information was quite specific, such as the advice to tie a string around the left testicle in order to conceive a male child. Although married partners were not expected to exult in sexual activity—such sentiment would have been "lustful"—the satisfaction of sexual urges was assumed to be part of a married couple's obligation to each other. Some writers, such as the Florentine preacher Girolamo Savonarola (1452–98), agreed with the ancient Greek physician Galen that the wife had to reach orgasm in order to conceive. (Rape was never supposed to result in

pregnancy. A raped women who conceived was assumed to have enjoyed the act and had no means of punishing her attacker.)

Moderation was the keyword, as newlyweds were cautioned to drink sweet wine and chicken soup, rest more, and save their strength. Sperm was thought to be more potent if a man abstained from sexual activity for a time. Older men who wished to impregnate their wife were advised to use the 40 days of Lent to store sperm and enhance its power. Abstention was required not only during Lent, but also on Sundays, religious feast days, and three days before and after receiving Holy Communion. Men were requested by priests to respect the wishes of a wife who wanted to take Communion, even if she chose to do so several times a year. Abstention was also suggested during pregnancy, breast-feeding, and menstruation. Some people had a very interesting sex life: The prohibitions against having intercourse in public or in church must have been enacted because such behavior had been observed.

Adultery was a very serious offense, at all levels of society. Offenders were sometimes forced to sit in church, wrapped in a white sheet or wearing other signs of shame. An adulterous woman might have her head shaved or her clothing torn. Members of guilds who were married, especially in northern Europe, were subject to expulsion if they were known to have committed adultery. Dishonoring the marriage vows was said to dishonor the guild, but having one less member in a guild also reduced the competition for available work. In addition a man would usually be expelled from the guild if his wife committed adultery and he continued to cohabit with her. In general the adultery of a wife was viewed as a much more serious offense than a husband's philandering. If a husband caught his wife in the act and killed her, usually he would not be punished.

Children

The role of a married woman was to have babies, and women desired to have many babies because only a few of them normally would live to adulthood (see page 294). Some women were pregnant most of their adult life. Poorer women nursed their own babies; however, most babies had wet nurses selected

12.4 Two Children Teasing a Cat. *Annibale Carracci, between the later 16th century and 1609.* (The Metropolitan Museum of Art, purchase, Gwynne Andrews Fund, and bequests of Collis P. Huntington and Ogden Mills, by exchange, 1994 [1994.142])

by the father, who evaluated the nurse's health and character. Wet nurses were paid for their services under the terms of a contract signed by the father. Many wet nurses lactated for years because healthy women usually continue to do so when a child is suckling. Some wet nurses had babies of their own; others had older children or a baby who had recently died. Wives who did not breast-feed their own infants were more likely to conceive again sooner. Renaissance physicians did not understand why but assumed that the uterus was connected to the breasts and that menstrual blood was transformed into milk after a baby was delivered.

Toddlers did not normally roam freely around the house or yard. They were kept in wooden walk-ers that functioned as today's walkers do; they had four or five wheels around a bottom rim and a nar-rower top rim with a seat into which the child was placed. Toddlers were also connected to their nurse, mother, or a stationary object by means of a long strap or rope. Small children had to be kept away from the fireplace, which contained not only burning wood but also boiling liquids and hot grease. Outside they had to be kept away from garbage, bodies of water, the well, and unpre-dictable roving dogs and other animals. Boys of about seven no longer stayed all day with their mother because they had to learn to be men. This was the age at which children were considered capable of reason. Some older boys had tutors at home, others attended a grammar or abacus school near home (see chapter 11), and others left home to be raised at court or at the home of a well-placed relative. Around the age of 14 boys became young men who could enter an apprenticeship, become sailors, join the army, begin studying for the priesthood, or simply work at menial labor. In very poor families children aged nine or even younger were sent to work as servants in wealthy houses, chiefly because their parents could no longer afford to feed them. In spite of entering the adult world so early, between the ages of eight and 14, most boys and girls did not experience puberty until the age of 15 or even later.

ORPHANS

Orphans whose parents had been married and were deceased enjoyed a special status in Renaissance society, as opposed to foundlings (abandoned children), generally referred to as bastards. During the 15th century both classes of parentless children were usually cared for by the same hospitals operating as care centers. Some of these institutions had a horizontal wheel beside an interior wall that could be rotated from outside the wall and positioned in front of an opening. The foundling was placed on the wheel, which was then turned again to take the infant into the hospital anonymously. Some community leaders complained that providing institutions for unwanted children encouraged immorality, but others argued that the rather undesirable alternative was infanticide. Foundlings who survived to become older children were often able to make their way in the world, working as laborers or servants and occasionally even being adopted by childless couples. By the 16th century separate foundations were being established for orphans, endowed with money for education, clothing, and other provisions. One unfortunate result was even greater discrimination against foundlings.

Housing

Housing, like clothing, visually distinguished the upper classes from the middle class and both from the lower class. Extremely poor people subsisted in

shantytowns, hovels made of earth and hay. Peasants had a house built of wood or of earth with a thatched roof and a floor of packed dirt or tiles. Their windows were simply rectangular holes covered with shutters. The ground floor of most houses was covered in flowers and herbs in the summer and hay in winter, most likely to mask odors. Many town houses for the middle class were constructed entirely of wood, or of the wood and stucco combination known as Tudor style, with a slate or tile roof. Because of their narrow street frontage, these houses usually had only two or three small rooms on each floor, connected by a spiral staircase that required less space than a stairway. Where stone was more plentiful than wood, stones formed both the inner and outer walls, with the roof made of thatch or tiles. Bricks were used in areas where clay was

12.5 Fifteenth-century merchant's home, Dinan, France. The shop was on the ground floor with living quarters above. (Courtesy of Sandra Sider)

of wooden shutters, for ventilation and better security at street level. Renaissance craftsmen did not have the technology to produce large, flat single panes of glass. Indoor plumbing did not exist in Europe until the 17th century, although some experiments were made with flush toilets before 1600.

Games and Sports

GAMES

Middle- and upper-class couples of the 15th century favored the game of chess, which had entered Europe via Arabic players in Spain. Originally the game had a vizier and not a queen accompanying the king. During the reign of Isabella I (1451–1504) the queen replaced the vizier. Also, instead of being moved only diagonally as the vizier was, the queen could be moved in any direction. Modern scholars have suggested that the appearance and power of the queen on the European chessboard may have reflected the power of Queen Isabella. By the late 16th century chess was more often played by males as the pace of the game became much faster. Although queens such as Catherine de' Medici (1519–80) and Elizabeth I (1533–1603) were devoted chess players, women in the domestic environment were subject to numerous interruptions. They either had to tend to children and cooking or supervise servants doing those tasks. The courtly, leisurely game of chess played by women during the Renaissance became too fast paced and professionalized for them to enjoy it.

Many people played card games, and some very beautiful hand-colored cards are extant from this period, probably commissioned by avid players. By the time of the Counter-Reformation, card playing had fallen into disrepute because preachers and priests warned that this pastime encouraged the vice of gambling. Nevertheless soldiers on campaign, sailors at sea, and innumerable couples housebound during the winter continued to play. Other games of chance involved dice, coins, and dominos. Children probably had board games, which were simple to make. There were also musical games, as well as music played to accompany singing.

12.6 Iron door knocker, Spain, 16th century. (Courtesy of The Hispanic Society of America, R128)

plentiful and became more popular in towns toward the end of the 16th century. Although wooden houses were somewhat less expensive, they presented a serious fire hazard in crowded urban centers. (See chapter 4 for information about villas and other housing for the upper classes.) Windows could have several designs, depending on climate and the homeowner's budget. One ingenious solution was to build a large window in which the upper half consisted of stationary leaded glass, for light, and the bottom half

SPORTS

Many outdoor games would qualify as sports since they required active physical participation. Church groups played ball games, community members challenged each other to races, and, on a grander scale, tournaments enacted the chivalric competitions of the Middle Ages. Women and girls usually were spectators at outdoor events unless dancing, as in maypole celebrations, was involved. Renaissance humanists taught the ancient Greek ideal of the benefits of physical exercise for young men, in a balanced regimen of wrestling, running, hunting, swimming, and other activities. Although the classes might mingle in sporting activities, peasants were not expected to best noblemen. Among the upper classes tennis became very popular during the 16th century. Golf was revived in Scotland, its homeland, and a version of soccer was played in England. Animal sports such as bearbaiting drew huge crowds, even though the violent nature of these events was criticized by religious leaders.

CEREMONIES, FESTIVITIES, AND OTHER PUBLIC EVENTS

The premier festivity in most areas of Europe was carnival, with its preceding weeks of indulgence in rich food, alcoholic beverages, sexual activity, and hectic street theater. Although of religious derivation, carnival was celebrated in a very secular manner. Observance of saints' days, civic processions, weddings, and triumphal entries also drew communities together. Entertainment for such events included pantomimes, public declamations, recitations of poetry, singing, and participatory dancing. Artists made drawings of many royal festivities, and tapestries were sometimes woven to commemorate these events. Visitors to palaces and chateaux were reminded of the festive occasion whenever they viewed these large-scale scenes.

Carnival

As part of the Christian calendar, carnival took place immediately before the beginning of Lent, with its 40 days of fasting and abstaining from bodily pleasures. The carnival season could start several weeks before the actual day of carnival itself, which in Italy meant the Thursday before Ash Wednesday (first day of Lent) and the Tuesday before Ash Wednesday in other parts of Europe. The French expression for this day, *mardi gras* (Fat Tuesday), is the way carnival is often referred to in English. The word *carnival* means taking away meat; Christians were not permitted to consume meat during Lent. Meat became symbolic of carnival, with giant, phallic sausages paraded through the streets and floats advertising the butchers' guild. The carnival season was a time for butchering hogs and gorging on various meat products, such as sausages and roasts. For those who could afford the ingredients, rich desserts were also part of carnival meals. In private festivities the world was topsy-turvy, with servants dressed in finery and masters pretending to be servants, waiting on them at table. Cross-dressing contributed to the confused world of carnival, and ordinary people acted out impromptu street theater, usually in a comical or satirical mode. In Protestant Europe carnival floats often made fun of the pope or of local preachers. With the consumption of alcoholic beverages that accompanied public celebration, crowds could become rowdy. Sporting activities were a bit more violent than usual, and riots could ensure. Masks and disguises added to the festival nature of carnival; Venice was (and is) particularly famous for its artistic masks and costumes. Masked couples flirted and danced, heightening the sexual charge of carnival. Sexuality was enhanced, and more babies were conceived during this season than at any other time of the year. (Although Christians in the far north of Europe, such as in England, celebrated carnival, their major outdoor festivals occurred during the spring and summer.)

Civic Processions and Public Gatherings

Civic processions that took place on a regular basis consisted of two major types, the ritualistic celebration of local saints and parades by civic organizations. Patron saints were thought to protect the localities in which they were revered, functioning as intermediaries between citizens of the town and the Virgin. Many paintings were commissioned of the *sacra conversatione* (sacred conversation) depicting Mary and the infant Jesus with these intercessionary saints. When a saint's day was observed, the citizens were often required to participate; it was part of their civic duty. These processions were especially elaborate in southern Europe. Most towns had one or more relics of their patron saint, and parading relics through the streets, from the church and back again, propitiated the saint and honored the saint's name. Alternately, the procession might begin from a city gate and proceed around town, finally arriving at the church containing the relic. The parades and processions of civic organizations derived from the model of saints' processions, with a rigid hierarchy of position of each official in the group as it paraded. The organizations that participated included militias, guilds, and confraternities. These events were quite colorful as each group displayed banners or flags and uniform costumes. Members of the public observing the festivities also enjoyed allegorical *tableaux vivants* (living pictures) in which costumed actors staged static scenes without speaking, moving pantomimes in which they also were silent, and declamatory scenes in which the actors spoke their lines. The content of these presentations could be quite political and propagandistic; even mythological scenes sometimes had veiled references to current events.

Two of the most lavish civic processions in northern Europe were the London mayoral inauguration of the latter 16th century and the Ommeganggen (guild processions) of Antwerp. During the Renaissance, London's mayor was always a guild member, and his guild was responsible for the festivities. In a competitive spirit each guild tried to surpass the efforts of previous ceremonies, with boats, chariots, floats, stationary stages, and ephemeral works of art, drama, and poetry commissioned for the occasion. Each guild in Antwerp owned a large wagon or chariot used for the Ommegangen. This procession was linked to the August 15 Assumption of the Virgin and always took place on the following Sunday. The themes of the floats could be religious or secular, often relat-

ing to some aspect of travel, trade, or commerce. Because Antwerp was an important artistic center, the statues, paintings, and music in this procession often were of professional quality.

FEAST OF FOOLS

The Feast of Fools, or Feast of Asses, was a jubilant winter celebration in which misrule reigned. Taking place not long after Christmas, this festival consisted of mock mass pronounced in church, with a young man pretending to be a bishop or other high church official. A donkey might be taken into the sanctuary, and everyone, including the priest, brayed during parts of the liturgy. This sort of irreverent hilarity was strongly discouraged by the Counter-Reformation and eventually died out, at least within the church building itself.

EXECUTIONS AND CORPORAL PUNISHMENT

Although the number of public executions declined toward the end of the 16th century, many thousands of city dwellers witnessed hangings, burnings, and the mutilation of human beings. These severe punishments were usually reserved for murderers and violent thieves, but in some areas, notably Florence, personal "crimes" such as sodomy were punishable by hanging. Punishment occasionally entailed desecration of the criminal's corpse. A hanged person's body could be left to rot and be picked on by carrion birds, or "drawn and quartered," a punishment in which the body was spread out and split into four pieces. Very rarely was a living person executed in this fashion or burned at the stake. The Renaissance was a violent era, and people, especially children, who witnessed such public events must have been affected by the spectacle.

Triumphal Entries and State Funerals

Monarchs and other royalty officially visiting a city or town would usually be given an extravagant welcome, in the form of a sumptuous banquet and reception, preceded by a public procession known

12.7 *Tomb monument for the duchess of Albuquerque, 16th century. Nineteenth-century drawing by Arthur Byne.*
(Courtesy of The Hispanic Society of America, A313)

as a triumphal entry. These entries derived from the processions of emperors and other leaders in Rome when they returned as conquering heroes. The common element of such events was the triumphal arch, a two- or three-story temporary structure made of wood and gesso, painted in a classicizing style with emblematic texts, coats of armor, allegorical scenes, and portrait medallions. Other ephemeral architectural structures, such as platforms and stages, were placed along the processional route for actors and musicians. The procession usually began at a city gate, where civic leaders greeted the person honored. The celebration ended at the cathedral, where the bishop or another church official led the crowd in a devotional prayer. Along the way the entertainment might include mechanical giants or animals, such as the automaton of a lion created by Leonardo for the 1507 entry of the French king into Milan. Tapestries and banners floated from windows and balconies, contributing to the festive atmosphere, and fireworks lit up the night sky. Tapestries, in fact, provided decoration for numerous public events because they were somewhat portable. Funerals for monarchs, including the funeral procession, could be as elaborate as triumphal entries. Proxy funerals were held in several cities for emperors, kings, and queens, with temporary catafalques equaling the grandeur of triumphal arches.

Triumphal entries and civic processions were major events, when work stopped so that people might participate in and applaud them. For many peasants and other lower-class workers, the decorations for these processions and parades were the only reflections of the classical influences on upper-class Renaissance culture to which they were exposed. People living in rural areas never experienced this panoply of imagery while it was taking place, but they did have opportunities to see it reproduced. Andrea Mantegna (1430/31–1506), for example, documented Roman triumphal entries in several drawings that were later issued as engravings. Although most people could not afford the printed and engraved festivity books describing these public events, many could afford a single print to nail to the wall or pass among friends. Such prints served as powerful reminders of the lofty status of Renaissance monarchy.

Weddings

Wedding ceremonies differed, depending on religious persuasion and social status, but usually involved a wedding ring, the clasping of hands, and the father's giving away of the bride. Except among Protestant couples, wedding celebrations consisted of processions through the streets, during which the bride wore a beautiful dress. Music was an important component of such events, including outdoor dancing and singing if the weather was good. In some societies, the bride was led through town on horseback. The main purposes of weddings among the upper classes were to celebrate the bride and display the wealth and social status of the groom. The bride's father contributed her dowry and trousseau to the marriage; the groom provided a rich countertrousseau, including jewels. Although the velvet or brocaded overgown might be borrowed or rented, the other finery became part of the marriage property, meaning that it was owned by the husband. Royal wedding festivities were among the grandest of all public celebrations during this period. Actors portraying cupids and nymphs participated in ballets and mock battles, "love boats" sailed on artificial lakes, mythological couples celebrated the married state, and other thematically appropriate performances entertained the newlyweds, their guests, and onlookers.

Charivari

Charivari, or shivaree, derives from the ancient Greek for "heavy head," or headache. A charivari was a very noisy event, when young men banged on pots and pans and shouted as loudly as possible. Acted out as a sort of folk justice, the charivari focused on people who had stepped outside the normal bounds of their community, such as adulterers, husband beaters, couples who did not have children, and newlywed couples who had a significant difference in their ages. The victims might be chased through town, dunked in water, or otherwise ridiculed publicly. Unpopular mayors and tax collectors could find themselves led across town, facing backward on a donkey. Charivari functioned as an escape valve for community conflict and could become dangerous if the behavior escalated into violence.

CLOTHING AND COSTUME

Because of sumptuary laws, class differences were emphasized by a person's attire. Members of the lower classes, for example, were not permitted to wear certain furs or silk. Excellent documentation of Renaissance clothing, from Europe and elsewhere, is available in archival records as well as books and other visual sources. Fashion trends between 1400 and 1600 included the lowering of women's necklines and the shortening of men's pants, and prominent codpieces appeared during the 16th century. Members of the upper classes luxuriated in fine silk, woven as velvet and brocade, and in jewelry consisting of pearls, precious metals, and gemstones.

Sumptuary Laws

Laws regulating consumption and conspicuous display dated from as early as the 12th century. Although such rules originated with the Catholic Church, by the 15th century they were issued as civil legislation. Fines for no-observance were thus paid to local authorities. The rules concerning the wearing of fur exemplify the class-structured aspects of these rules. Only royalty could wear ermine, and workers could wear only fur of low value, such as cat, fox, and rabbit. Women's necklines were a particular focus of sumptuary law, especially when lowered necklines were used to show off gold necklaces and pendants of precious jewels. A Renaissance version of fashion police would stop offending women in the street and issue a fine. In some parts of Europe the tailor who made the dress might also be fined. In 15th-century Florence the tailor was fined twice as much as the women who wore an illegal garment.

Clothing

Our knowledge of Renaissance clothing is more complete than that of many other aspects of daily life because of documentation in guild records, notarial inventories, and visual sources such as paintings, prints, and tapestries. Extant tapestries are a particularly good source for costume study because of their large scale, which allows details of ornamentation to be seen. Especially during the 16th century, several artists made ethnographic drawings of clothing and costume, and costume manuals were published as well as other books that had costume illustrations. Some of these compared European clothing to that of other regions, such as the Americas and Africa, and a few included comments about the occupations or activities of those depicted. Renaissance interest in foreign costume probably was related to the fascination with new

12.8 Portrait of Sebastian Brant in a brocaded garment and fur hat. Woodcut in Nicholas Reusner, Icones sive imagines virorum . . . illustrium *(Icons or images of famous men, 1587). Brant, a prominent jurist, was author of* The Ship of Fools. (Photograph courtesy of Sotheby's, Inc., © 2003)

geographical and topographical publications. The 1572 *Civitates orbis terrarum* (Cities of the world), for example, included figures of men and women in the foregrounds of city views, wearing the costumes of various classes.

Clothing for the lower classes was simple and drab, made of unbleached linen or rather coarse wool, depending on the climate. The colors were usually dull, mostly black, gray, or brown because dyes were relatively expensive. Men wore knee-length pants and jackets with buttons; women wore long skirts, aprons, and tight bodices. Silk and velvet were prohibited to the lower classes in many parts of Europe. Details of sleeve length, collars, tucks, pleats, darts, and modest ornamental detail varied across Europe, but the outfits were similar. Women knitted and crocheted the family's hats and scarves, and men usually wore wide-brimmed hats. The upper classes dictated fashion, and the middle class copied details of elite style as budgetary limitations and sumptuary laws would permit. The clothing of middle-class Protestants, especially of Calvinists, was usually plain and severe. Iconoclastic tendencies extended to the exclusion of bright colors and shiny decoration.

Men's upper-class fashion was as ornate as that of women, and both spent a long time dressing. Mens' jackets tended to have a broader silhouette during the 16th century, the shoulders stuffed with straw and other padding. Many garments, for both sexes, were held together by "points," lace or ribbons used to tie parts of the piece of clothing together. The assistance of a servant was required because the wearer could not reach all the ties. The chief fabrics were wool and linen, but of a much finer weave than that worn by the lower classes and often dyed in brilliant hues. Red was a popular color, especially in Italy. As the Habsburg court gained power during the 16th century, the rich black woolens and velvets of Spanish fashion made their way across Europe. In general Italian styles dominated the 15th century, Spanish and German the 16th century. The puffed, slashed men's garments of the latter 16th century originated in Germany and Switzerland, as did the prominent codpieces sported by upper-class gentlemen. Men's shirts and jackets during that period extended just to the thighs, and the legs were covered by tight-fitting hose. Although women's dresses remained long throughout the Renaissance, their necklines fluctuated tremendously, with the breasts partially exposed at several courts. By the end of the 16th century necklines had crept up again, to be adorned by the ruff in England and the north. Luxury fabrics made of silk were quite extravagant, and some silks were woven in two colors of thread so that a garment would seem to change colors as the wearer moved or the light shifted. Brocade weaves were very much desired for their swirling patterns, and some brocade had armorial motifs. Aristocratic clothing might also have ornate embroidery along with encrustations of pearls and other jewels. Mention should also be made of underwear, which most people wore by the 15th century. Upper-class women were donning corsets in the Renaissance, some of them very snug and tightened by a key.

Jewelry and Other Accessories

Men wore rings, ropelike necklaces of gold or silver, and jewels or medallions in their hat. Toward the close of the 16th century hats for many upper-class men were rather flat, decorated with a jaunty feather. Women again began wearing earrings, which had not been favored during the Middle Ages and early Renaissance, around 1525. Women also wore rings and bracelets, and even lower-class women had a betrothal or wedding ring. (People did not wear both an engagement and a wedding ring, as people in some societies do today.) Long strings of pearls were very desirable for the necklaces of wealthy women, as were pendant necklaces displaying stones in a silver or gold setting. For special occasions women would have pearls, jewels, ribbons, and flowers tied and woven into their hair. Jewels also bedecked shoes and even fans. During the early Renaissance smooth cabochon stones were preferred, then faceted stones became popular by the 16th century. Goldsmiths also created small, perforated spheres with hollow centers to be worn as pomanders, with cloves or other spices enclosed. Several stones, such as sapphires, were thought to have medicinal value and were designed in settings that would allow the stone to have contact with the skin.

FOOD AND COOKING

Public events involving food and drink had to conform to laws that dictated which food and how much of it could be served to people in different social classes. Special occasions, such as weddings, were regulated by local officials to limit the amounts spent on comestibles. Dining was crude, by modern standards, with everyone digging into common dishes without the aid of serving utensils. Fine manners in dining did not evolve until the 17th century, and even then they could be considered pretentious. Members of the upper classes consumed more meat; the lower classes had more grain and vegetables in their diet. Everyone ate relatively large quantities of bread, except the very poor.

Food

Sumptuary laws pertained to food and drink as well as to clothing and jewelry; in 16th-century Scotland, for example, members of the nobility might consume eight or more plates (courses) during a meal, but members of the middle class were not allowed to have more than three. In various parts of Europe the amount of money that could be spent on wedding banquets and other celebratory dining was strictly regulated, partly to prevent families from bankrupting themselves by the financial burden of organizing a public event. Meals consumed in one's private home were not regulated, and Europeans, especially the wealthy, consumed an enormous quantity of meat compared with most of the rest of the world at that time. They might have three or four different kinds of meat in one meal, sometimes prepared one inside another. Small birds with heavy sauces accompanied other types of meat. Europeans in general were fortunate in their climate and terrain, in which herds of animals could easily be maintained. In the south freshwater fish was an important part of the diet because eating of meat was forbidden on Friday. In the north more saltwater fish was consumed, especially herring and cod.

Eggs and cheese were eaten throughout Europe; more butter and lard were used in the north and more olive oil in the south. Because butter was made from animals, it was forbidden during the 40 days of Lent, when everyone was supposed to cook with oil. From our modern point of view, the lower classes had a more healthful diet because they could not afford to eat much meat, fatty food, or sweet dessert. A typical meal for them might be dark bread, such as rye; beans or peas; and cheese or salted fish, washed down with beer, cider, or red wine. Few people drank water by itself, although water was used to dilute heavy wine. The lower classes had many more vegetables in their diet, and poorer people consumed large quantities of grain, in soup and porridge. The very poor often had only a few pieces of bread most days. Most larger households produced their own beverages, brewing beer and ale as well as pressing cider in the north and making wine in the south. The medieval drink mead, consisting of fermented honey, was still enjoyed during the Renaissance. (See chapter 8, on commerce, for more information concerning alcoholic beverages.)

Cooking and Serving

Most people did not have ovens. Bread was cooked communally in a shared bread oven or made by a baker. Covered iron pots on short legs served as roasting pots, placed near the fire. (Today these are called Dutch ovens.) Meat was also grilled or fried, but the most ubiquitous method of cooking was by stewing in iron pots. Porridge was also cooked in such a pot. Large hooks for holding pots with a handle extended into fireplaces, usually pivoting over the fire and back into the room. Toasting and grilling irons clamped bread, fish, vegetables, or meat inside a flat cage for holding it over the fire. Wealthier homes with larger fireplaces had a horizontal rod onto which meat or fowl could be inserted for rotisserie cooking. Salt was a staple of Renaissance cuisine, along with native herbs such as mustard, parsley, basil, and thyme. Although Europeans were quite fond of exotic spices, such as pepper, and sugar, only the upper classes could afford to cook with them on a regular basis.

During the 15th century food was often served in the medieval fashion, from a trencher in the middle of the table. For the lower class, the trencher might be a long wooden bowl or even a large loaf of bread, with the top sliced off for serving and stew or beans ladled

12.9 Kitchen still life. Pieter Aertsen, between 1557 and 1575. (Photograph courtesy of Sotheby's Inc., © 2003)

on the top. Pieces of bread were used to scoop and sop up the food, with scant attention to table manners as we know them; most people ate with their fingers. The trenchers in upper-class homes might be metal instead of wood but the manner of eating was very similar. The idea of each diner's having an individual plate did not take hold until the mid-16th century, and the fork was not introduced until about the same time. Southern Europeans popularized the use of ceramic tableware, which was being used across Europe by the late 16th century. Even relatively poor households could afford a brightly painted pitcher or platter.

DISEASE, ILLNESS, AND DEATH

During the early Renaissance most hospitals were not like our modern institutions. They could func-tion as hospices, providing comfort and minor medical care for those who were weak and dying, and as temporary shelters for pilgrims, widows, abused wives, and orphans. By the 16th century in Italy some hospitals included healing the seriously ill among their mission, and several rather large institutions were established for that purpose. A few hospitals, for example in Bologna, began training doctors on site. The more ambitious institutions had pharmacists and surgeons available when needed. Thus the Renaissance saw the beginning of the professionalization of hospital services.

At least 20 and as many as 40 percent of all babies, regardless of class, died within the first 12 months of life. For this reason many babies were baptized immediately after birth. Half of those who survived infancy died before they reached the age of 10. Although some scholars have stated that parents resigned themselves to the deaths of infants and did not become emotionally attached to children until they reached the age of two, there is much firsthand evidence to contradict such an assumption. Fathers wrote letters to friends expressing their grief at the death of a small son, and mothers rejoiced in their babies. Beatrice d'Este (1475–97) wrote to her sister, Isabella d'Este (1474–1539), about her infant son, "I often wish that you could be here to see him, as I am quite sure that you would never be able to stop petting and kissing him" (Durant 1953, p. 587). Babies and small children slept in a cradle that was often suspended from the ceiling to prevent mice and bugs from crawling up the legs and to keep the child away from the cold floor. These cradles sometimes were draped with netting to guard against insects. Unfortunately most cradles were placed near the fireplace for warmth, and occasionally their blankets and netting caught on fire. Toddlers who slept in the bed with their parents or older siblings were sometimes accidentally smothered, or "overlaid" in Renaissance legal terminology. Another hazard that could kill an infant but not necessarily an older child was tainted drinking water; that is one reason why water was not a popular beverage during this period.

Most common illnesses were treated with home remedies, and girls were trained by their mother to be fairly competent nurses. Aloe juice, for example, was used as a purgative and as a dressing to soothe burns. The flower, stalk, and root of lilies of the valley were known to help prevent apoplexy, and indeed this flower has some of the properties of the digitalis taken today as heart medication. Many other herbs and flowers were used against head lice, chest congestion, mild forms of influenza, internal parasites, toothache, and similar conditions. The Renaissance had nothing with which to battle the major diseases that attacked thousands, including dysentery, diphtheria, ergotism, tuberculosis, smallpox, syphilis, a sickness that may have been typhus fever, and, of course, plague. Both smallpox and plague were known to spread rapidly, even though the precise mechanism of their epidemic nature was not clearly understood. Civil authorities attempted to control their virulence by quarantining households and even neighborhoods. If anyone in a family contracted plague or smallpox, the entire family could be boarded up inside the house for several weeks. By the late 16th century Europe had many times more people living in dire poverty than in 1400. Hunger, then, was almost a disease and people did starve to death. Those who managed to cling to life were much more susceptible to illness and disease because of their weakened physical state.

Treatises were written on "the good death" and on preparation for the inevitability of dying. Woodcuts of skeletons leading the Dance of Death were popular in northern Europe. These publications constituted the genre known as *ars moriendi* (the art of dying). Based on ancient philosophical ideas, the Stoical attitude toward one's death was said to facilitate access to purgatory. Mourning was to be subdued because, for Christians, death was considered the pathway to eternal life. A proper death included disposition of one's worldly goods through a legally binding testament and setting aside of money for funeral masses that might speed one's way to purgatory. Catholic funerals could be lavish; Protestant funerals were usually rather somber and plain. All funerals involving burial of the corpse took place as soon as possible after death because embalming was not done. In northern Europe there were visual reminders of death's triumph. Tomb sculpture often depicted skeletal imagery. Because most people did not live beyond the age of 40, death and the dying were a constant presence, simply a fact of life.

12.10 *Allegory of avarice, with skeleton. Jacopo Ligozzi, between the latter 16th century and 1626.* (The Metropolitan Museum of Art, gift of Eric Seller and Darcy Bradbury, and Edward A. and Karen S. W. Friedman, 1991 [1991.443])

READING

Clark 1976: urban life; Cowan 1998: urban life.

Time and the Calendar

Gregorian Reform of the Calendar 1983; Philip 1921: calendar history; Richards 2000: cultural contexts.

Family Life

Ariès 1989: private life; Bell 1999: sex; Cavallo 1999: widows; Cunningham 1995: children; Gelis 1991: childbirth and other topics; Harrington 1995: marriage; Houlbrooke 1984: England; Howell 1998: marriage; Jordan 1986: feminism; King 1991: women; Klapisch-Zuber 1985: women and ritual in Italy; Moulton 2002: sex, crime; Ozment 1983: Reformation families; Pullan 1989: orphans; Weinstein 2004: marriage in Italy; Wiesner 1986: cloth production; Yalom 2004: chess, women.

Ceremonies, Festivities, and Other Public Events

Bergeron 2003: England; Bryant 1986: Paris; Burke 1978: popular culture; Cunningham 1965: England (dancing); Davis 1975: social contexts; Mitchell 1981: Italy; Muir 1981: Venice; Saslow 1996: Medici wedding; Strong 1984: festivals and art; Yates 1975: France (evidence in tapestries).

Clothing and Costume

Davenport 1970: (costume survey); Frick 2002: Florence; Hackenbroch 1979: jewelry; Jordan 1999: Oriental fans; Laver 1951: (fashion survey); Victoria and Albert Museum 1980: jewelry; Weiditz 1994: Germany (facsimile of costume book).

Food and Cooking

Braudel *Wheels* 1992: markets; Freeman 1943: herbs; Henisch 1976: feasts and fasting; Jeanneret 1991: banquets; Mintz 1985: sugar; Revel 1982: cultural contexts; Riley 1993: recipes.

Disease, Illness, and Death

Brockliss 1997: France; Cipolla 1976: public health; Cohn 1992: Italy; Freeman 1943: medicinal herbs; Gittings 1984: England (burial); Herlihy 2001: Black Death; Lindemann 2002: cures; Marland 1993: midwifery; Strocchia 1992: Florence (death rituals).

13

CONCLUSION: LEGACY OF THE RENAISSANCE

SCHOLARSHIP

Any discussion of the legacy of the Renaissance should consider the major historians and critics who interpreted the Renaissance for their contemporaries. Every historical period is filtered through the lens of later writers, who have conscious or subconscious agendas of their own. Those writers most influential in Western culture before the 20th century were Giorgio Vasari (see chapters 3 and 4), Jules Michelet (1798–1874), Jakob Burckhardt (1818–97), John Ruskin (1819–1900), John Addington Symonds (1840–93), and Walter Pater (1839–94). The 20th-century writers who have significantly directed our vision of the Renaissance included three specialists in art history, Bernard Berenson (1865–1959), Aby Warburg (1866–1929), and Erwin Panofsky (1892–1968), along with the historians Johan Huizinga (1872–1945), Hans Baron (1900–1988), Eugenio Garin (b. 1909), and Paul Oskar Kristeller (1905–99).

Jules Michelet was one of the most eminent French historians of the 19th century. His work, however, was grounded in the romantic ideal of humanity's close relationship with nature. Michelet's treatment of the Renaissance disallowed the enduring force of Catholicism and church politics, emphasizing instead a new age of individualism inspired by pagan antiquity. Jakob Burckhardt's historical approach attempted to understand past epochs not through actual documents, but through reading of literary works and other publications to capture the spirit of the times. As did Michelet, he focused on what he believed was a new attitude of individualism, oversimplifying perceived differences between the Renaissance and preceding centuries. Nevertheless, Burckhardt's unified myth concerning the development of human nature stimulated many scholars to turn to the Renaissance as a field of study. John Ruskin, who loved Venice, wrote mainly about architecture and art. Judging Renaissance art with a 19th-century critical eye, he faulted most 16th-century works as too analytical and mathematical, preferring what he described as the more natural styles of the latter 15th century. As many critics did, Ruskin judged the creative work of earlier times not by the standards of their contemporaries, but by his own aesthetic rules. John Addington Symonds's multivolume publications interpreted the ideas of Burckhardt for English readers, expanding on his concept of the individual. As did Burckhardt, he failed to see the continuing importance of organized religion for Renaissance culture, in both its negative and its positive manifestations. The work of Walter Pater has been a major influence on many other scholars, especially his impressionistic yet uncannily effective discussions of the Renaissance artistic mentality. Although much of his criticism makes grand assumptions about an artist's personality from the person's works, that point of view has provided rich territory for later research.

Bernard Berenson's own legacy included his Villa I Tatti near Florence, bequeathed to Harvard University as a center for studying the Italian Renaissance. Berenson trained himself in connoisseurship, identifying artists and their schools chiefly by morphological characteristics (shapes of details such as ears and eyes in artworks). He always focused on the art objects themselves, not the culture in which they were produced. Berenson's publications helped to popularize the art of the Renaissance, which he considered a golden age of creativity. Unlike Berenson, Aby Warburg was a cultural historian. Part of his personal legacy is his library, the Warburg Institute in London. Warburg's iconographic research reached across scholarly disciplines, foreshadowing the multidisciplinarity prevalent in today's Renaissance scholarship. His research into the pagan deities of antiquity informed not only his own publications but also those of his students. Erwin Panofsky, a Jewish student of Warburg's, escaped to the United States in 1934. Subsequently most of his publications, in English, were very influential on art history as a new scholarly field in his adopted country. Panofsky taught iconography, the "what" of Renaissance art, as well as iconology, the "why," interpreting the art object in its cultural context.

Johan Huizinga criticized the emphasis placed on the individual by Burckhardt and his followers. He viewed the Renaissance not as a golden age, but rather as a turbulent transitional period between the Middle Ages and modern times. Huizinga probably would have agreed with today's scholars who have replaced the term *Renaissance* with *Early Modern* to describe the epoch. Hans Baron fled from Nazi persecution to the United States in 1938. As were those of Panofsky, his major works were published in English, giving his ideas a much larger initial audience than if they had been published in German. Baron viewed 15th-century humanism as more politically and socially engaged than earlier movements, teaching that Renaissance civic humanism contained the seeds of modern republicanism. His close study of the political works of Machiavelli revealed nascent republican tendencies in this 16th-century writer. Eugenio Garin, a professor of the history of philosophy, investigated philosophical aspects of Renaissance humanism. *Philosophy* itself means "love of wisdom," and Garin's publications presented several sources of wisdom and learning important for Renaissance humanists. Paul Oskar Kristeller also escaped from Germany to the United States, where he joined the faculty of Columbia University in 1939. He may have published more on Renaissance topics than any other American scholar during the 20th century. His massive bibliography and fortunate longevity reinforced the hegemony of Italy. Kristeller emphasized the significance of humanism in Renaissance education, and he dedicated part of his career to unearthing the manuscripts that were available to scholars during the 15th and 16th centuries.

INFLUENCES OF THE RENAISSANCE

The Renaissance model of humanistic education persisted in the Western world until the mid-20th century, with an emphasis on languages and philology, and with lessons taught in Latin until the 19th century. Many of the classical texts used in classrooms had been discovered and edited by Renaissance humanists. The admiration of classical Roman republicanism promulgated by the Renaissance was emulated in both Europe and the United States during the 18th century. Both the French and American Revolutions were conceived by individuals inspired by the republican models of Renaissance Venice and Florence. In a few European countries, notably Poland, the modern nation was formed in the 19th century, inspired by its own Renaissance model.

As the new republics of the late 18th and early 19th centuries began erecting noteworthy buildings, the most pervasive architectural models were buildings by Palladio. Thomas Jefferson, for example, owned a copy of Palladio's work on architecture and designed his Virginia home, Monticello, after the Villa Rotonda of Palladio. In both England and the United States Palladio was popular for his association with the Republic of Venice as much as for his architectural expertise. Among bankers and other wealthy merchants of the 19th and early 20th centuries, the semiclassical styles of Renaissance palaces became popular. Their association with the Medici and other powerful financial figures of the Renaissance gave them an aura of authority and permanence.

The scientific revolution of the 17th century originated with Renaissance humanists who questioned the authority of classical texts. New editions and translations of Greek mathematicians turned the attention of scholars to this field, and advances in algebra and geometry culminated in scientific discoveries a century later. The study of medicine during the 17th and 18th centuries was rooted in anatomical publications of the 16th century. Clinical medicine also had its beginnings in the Renaissance as students observed their teachers in the hospital environment. More than anything else, the Copernican universe, displacing the Earth as the center of the cosmos, taught that even the most basic assumptions of science should be examined and perhaps modified.

All the arts have benefited from Renaissance contributions. Lyrics and music were first performed in a unified manner during this time; the madrigal is a perfect example. Opera has often retold Renaissance history, and Verdi's *Don Carlo* (1867) is a notorious example of creative manipulation of historical facts. The foundations of modern literary theory can be attributed to Renaissance scholars who argued about the purpose of literature. Ideas about literary genres discussed during the Renaissance helped later critics formulate their own theoretical stance. Realistic figural sculpture, reborn during the Renaissance, remains the basis of many monumental forms commissioned today. Painters have followed Renaissance models for creating the illusion of three dimensions in a two-dimensional picture plane. The principles of Renaissance perspective are still taught in drawing classes. Techniques of printmaking developed during the Renaissance have persisted through the centuries. Today's printmakers working in intaglio use the same tools and techniques as their predecessors. Iconographically the Renaissance probably has influenced more artists than any other epoch. Even today the photographer Cindy Sherman, for example, has presented herself in the manner of Renaissance portraits. Whether parodying artists of the Renaissance or nodding to their talents, visual artists continue to be inspired by their work.

In popular culture the Renaissance lives on, though often distorted and exaggerated. The plays of Shakespeare have been, by far, the most pervasive cultural artifacts of the Renaissance in modern theater and cinema. There have been some two dozen films of his plays and more than a dozen based on his plays, from Akira Kurosawa's *Ran* (*King Lear*) in 1985 to a modern-day version of *Hamlet*. More than three dozen films have dealt with the historical period of the Renaissance, almost all focusing on the excesses of the time—greed, sex, cruelty, and violence. Several of these films present the biographies of famous artists and rulers, confirming modern assumptions that Renaissance figures were larger than life. The life they were larger than, however, is our own. The Renaissance had its own standards of behavior and levels of expectations. If we are to understand anything at all about this period of Western history, we must approach it on its own terms.

GLOSSARY

abatis French term for defensive fortification consisting of rows of tree branches or of small trees sharpened at one end, pointing toward the enemy, with the branches sometimes fastened together with wire or rope

all'antica Italian term meaning "in the antique (Roman) style"

altarpiece a painted or carved representation of the Crucifixion or other Christian subjects, which may be in one piece or in several sections hinged together, placed on, behind, or above an altar in a church or chapel

anamorphosis distorted image that must be viewed obliquely or with a curved mirror

Annunciation announcement by the angel Gabriel to the Virgin Mary that she is pregnant with the Christ child

Apocalypse book of revelation in the Bible, full of symbolic imagery prophesizing the cataclysmic destruction of the forces of evil

arcade several arches on columns or piers in a series

arcuated having arches in any form

arquebus heavy yet portable matchlock gun usually fired from a support

artillery weaponry used for firing projectiles (used here for pieces that could not be transported by an individual soldier)

azimuth compass navigational compass that accounts for the magnetic declination of the Earth (*azimuth* is from the plural of an Arabic word that means "the way")

ballade French medieval poetic form set to music, usually rhyming AAB, very popular during the 15th century

barrel vault "tunnel" vault, in half-cylindrical form

bas relief French term meaning "low relief" for sculpture projecting from its background in low profile

basse danse French and Italian music in a simple series of long notes, the basis for improvising music for a graceful courtly dance

bastion (or bastion trace) projecting area of a fortified building, angling out from the main walls and usually wider at the base than at the top

billhook or bill   long rod with a hook-shaped blade

blank verse   unrhymed iambic pentameter verse, important in English poetry

block book   pictorial book printed from wood-blocks during the 15th century, mostly in Germany and the Netherlands

blunderbuss   See MUSKET

bombard   type of cannon for hurling stones

boulevard   See BULWARK

bulwark   solid defensive wall, usually consisting of earth, timber, and stone in a U-shaped formation

burin   tool for cutting an engraving, with an oblique sharp point

caltrop   defensive device consisting of sharp spikes or nails pointing out in at least four directions from a central block, camouflaged or thrown out on the ground and designed to halt foot soldiers or horses (derived from the Old English word for "star thistle")

cameo   engraved gem carved to produce a design above the surface, in relief; see also INTAGLIO

cantus   (Latin for "song") general word for melody, also the part for the upper voice in polyphony

cantus firmus   (Latin for "fixed song") the melody (often plainchant or plainsong) that provides the basis for polyphony

capital   top of a column, often with sculpted detail

cartoon   image drawn on paper in full size, for transferring to a design for painting, tapestry, fresco, mosaic, and other media.

cartouche   ornamental design with edges consisting of scrolled shapes, often used as a label or a frame for a coat of arms

cavalry   division of an army mounted on horseback

centric point   See PERSPECTIVE

chanson   general word for a lyric poem, also for polyphonic song (French for "song")

cheval-de-frise   French term for a defensive device consisting of a thick wooden frame, log, or barrel embedded with numerous spikes, often used to fill a breach in a wall (plural *chevaux-de-frise*)

chiaroscuro   Italian term meaning "bright-dark" first used in the 17th century to describe engravings with emphatic shading

chivalric romance   work in prose or verse emphasizing the fine manners and high ideals of medieval courtly society (from French *chevalier*, knight)

clerestory   part of a roof rising above the lower section, usually with windows

coat of arms   heraldic design, often with a crest at the top, identifying an individual, corporate body, or institution

coffers   recessed panels decorating a ceiling

column   vertical support, usually cylindrical in form

comedy   amusing dramatic work with a happy ending

compass rose   a circular design drawn around the converging rhumb lines in a Portolan chart, naming the wind directions; compass roses became quite colorful and elaborate during the 16th century

condottiere   Italian term for leader of a band of mercenary soldiers, consisting of at least a troop of armored cavalry (plural *condottieri*)

contrapposto   Italian term meaning "opposite," used for the upright human figure in classicizing sculpture, with one leg slightly forward and (usually) the opposite arm extended or bent

copla Spanish poetic form, usually rhyming ABCB

cornice section of the entablature that extends out from the roofline

crossbow short bow mounted perpendicular to its base, with tension on the bow produced by winding a windlass; the bow is horizontal to the ground when an arrow is released

Crucifixion depiction of Christ hanging from the cross, present in every Catholic Renaissance household

damascene to decorate metalwork with inlaid designs of precious metals (from Damascus), also the work itself

Dance of Death representation of a dance that includes the dead, usually skeletal figures, with the living

Deposition act of removing Christ from the cross

device See *IMPRESA*

diptych altarpiece or other painting consisting of two hinged panels

drypoint technique of scratching on a copper plate with a sharp needle, sometimes to sketch the main design and sometimes to enhance it; the resulting lines are slightly soft

earthwork field fortification, such as an embankment, consisting of earth moved into position

eclogue short poem, often on a pastoral subject in dialogue form (from the Greek word for "to choose," meaning a choice poem)

elegy lament, usually on death, in verse form

emblem hybrid literary and pictorial format invented in the early 16th century, consisting of a motto, picture, and poem or short prose passage

emboss to decorate in raised relief on a flat or rounded surface

embossed metal manipulated to produce an image or pattern in relief

enfilade fire gunfire shot along the enemy line from a flanking position

engraving (intaglio) printmaking process of cutting designs with a burin into metal or wood, with the ink from these designs printed onto paper or vellum by the pressure of rollers

entablature upper section of a classical façade consisting of the architrave (base), frieze (midsection, with ornamentation or inscription), and cornice (top)

epic narrative poem, usually quite long, celebrating a heroic character (either historical or fictional)

epigram short, often witty poem on a single subject

Epiphany viewing of the newborn Christ child in Bethlehem by the three Magi (wise men) (January 6)

epitaph tomb inscription or brief statement commemorating the deceased (e.g., "sleeps with the angels")

etch to decorate a surface by using a chemical agent such as an acid to eat into the material along an inscribed design

Eucharist celebration of the mass in which worshipers partake of the host (holy wafer) and sometimes of the wine symbolizing Christ's blood

euphuism use of antithesis (contrasting of ideas) to an extreme degree (taken from Lyly's prose romance *Euphues* of 1578)

faience Italian majolica, known as faience in most other parts of Europe because it was manufactured in Faenza

farce   humorous satirical drama with improbable turns of plot, often with burlesque or gross components

fire lance   primitive flame thrower

firearm   weapon used for firing projectiles (used here for pieces that could be transported by an individual soldier, such as an arquebus or musket)

fletch   an arrow (from French *flèche*)

flintlock   mechanism with a flint in the hammer of a gun, so that a spark can be struck to light the charge

fresco   Italian term meaning "fresh," for the process of applying pigments dissolved in water to freshly plastered walls; see also *SECCO*

friar   member of a mendicant order

gabion   large wicker basket filled with earth as a barrier against gunfire from soldiers on the ground or in a trench

galliard   triple-meter lively dance music, very popular in late 16th-century England

gauffering   technique for decorating the gilt edges of bound books and manuscripts with a heated tool to create dots, flowers, and other simple motifs

genre painting   subjects and scenes from everyday life (first used in the 18th century as a term to describe art)

gesso   gypsum paste for casts and decorative details in furniture, also thinned out to spread on the surface as a ground for panel paintings

gonfalone   Italian for "military banner"

gonfaloniere   head of an administrative district in Italian territory (in Florence, also used for the head of the political council)

graffito   Italian term (plural *graffiti*) for a design created by scratching on a surface, especially scratching through one layer of paint to produce a design in another color painted beneath it

grisaille   French term meaning "grayish" to denote painting in monochrome

grotesque   fantastic motifs in wall decoration from ancient Rome, discovered during the Renaissance in grottoes (thus "grotesque" and not *grotesque* in the modern sense of horrible)

guild   group of people with a common interest, usually producing items for sale, and with an organized membership structure (from an Old English word for "payment")

gunpowder   explosive mixture of sulfur, charcoal, and potassium nitrate ground together

halberd   pike and battle ax mounted on a shaft approximately six feet long

harquebus   See ARQUEBUS

heraldry   the act of tracing genealogies, also devising and recording coats of arms

Huguenot   French Calvinist (the word *Huguenot* was derived from a German word meaning "confederate")

Hussite   follower of the reformer Jan Hus

iconoclasm   the destruction of icons or images in general, notably the Protestant destruction of Catholic imagery

impresa [plural *imprese*]   Italian term for a symbolic image accompanied by a motto (*device* in English)

incunable   book printed in Europe before 1501 (from the Latin for "cradle," i.e. cradle of printing)

infantry   foot soldier

intaglio   engraved gem carved to produce a design below the surface; see also CAMEO, ENGRAVING

intarsia mosaic work in wood (from Italian *tarsia*); see also MARQUETRY

intermedio originating near the end of the 15th century, a dramatic musical interlude performed between the acts of plays

Lamentation act of mourning over Christ's body after the Deposition

Landsknechte German term meaning "men of the plain," usually denoting the German Imperial army (infantrymen) of the 16th century

lantern crown of a dome, often open to allow light and air to enter

Last Supper supper of Christ and his disciples on the night he was betrayed by Judas; see also EUCHARIST

loggia arcade open on one or both sides

Lollard follower of the reformer John Wycliffe

longbow handheld wooden bow that is vertical to the ground when an arrow is released

lunette a semicircular shape (from Latin *luna*, "Moon")

madrigal secular nonstrophic verse in a refined musical setting, beginning in the 16th century (the late medieval madrigal was another genre)

Magnificat sacred music for the biblical text of Luke 1: 46–55 celebrating the Virgin

majolica ceramics with a glaze containing tin; see also FAIENCE

Mannerism term describing the exaggerated, witty forms in some Italian Renaissance art after c. 1520

mantlet shelter, usually on wheels, that protected troops who were attacking a besieged structure

marquetry decorative work consisting of small pieces of wood, mother-of-pearl, ivory, and other materials, inserted into a wood veneer; see also INTARSIA

mass musical settings that originated in the seventh century, celebrating the Eucharist; by the 16th century, most music for the mass was polyphonic; there were special types of music for mass, such as the Requiem Mass for the dead.

matchlock match that burns slowly to ignite the charge in the breech of a musket

mercenary soldier paid to serve in a foreign army

militia citizens organized and available for military service

miniature (1) a painted ("illuminated") picture in a manuscript, from the Latin *miniare* (to illuminate); (2) a portrait painted in small format, usually a bust portrait or head

monk male member of a religious order residing in a monastery

monstrance vessel in which the host (holy wafer) is displayed (from Latin *monstrare*, "to show")

Morisco Moor living in Spain

mosaic small pieces of colored glass, ceramic, marble, or stone embedded in stucco or cement to create pictorial or geometric designs

motet very general musical term during the Middle Ages; an important genre of polyphonic composition

musket portable shoulder gun loaded via the muzzle

Nativity birth of the Christ child (Christmas, December 25)

novel narrative work of prose fiction, with a complex, lengthy plot

novella prose fiction of intermediate length (shorter than a novel)

nun female member of a religious order residing in a convent (as of the mid-16th century)

octava rima Italian verse form in eight-line stanzas rhyming ABABABCC

ode poem on a serious subject written in complex, formal verse (during the Renaissance, often used to commemorate a state event such as a coronation or funeral)

order system for describing columns, based on their capitals and proportions: Tuscan, Doric, Ionic, Corinthian, and Composite

ordnance See ARTILLERY

palisades defensive fence of sharpened stakes

parchment skin of a sheep or goat prepared without tanning for printing or painting; see also VELLUM

parody to imitate the style of another author, usually for comic purposes

Passion events immediately preceding and following the Crucifixion, with specific symbols pertaining to each event

pastoral poetic or dramatic work set in the countryside, usually involving shepherds and shepherdesses

pavan double-meter stately dance music

pediment triangle formed by two sloping cornices and a horizontal base, often found in temple façades

pendentive transitional masonry supporting a dome over a square base

Pentateuch See TORAH

Pentecost event when the apostles of Christ received the Holy Spirit, usually in the form of a dove (Whitsunday, the seventh Sunday after Easter)

perspective artistic technique to create the illusion of three dimensions in a two-dimensional space, using the idea of the vanishing point by which parallel lines converge in the distance (the Renaissance term for this is *centric point*)

Petrarchism imitation of the literary work of Francesco Petrarch, usually his poetry

piazza Italian word for a city square

picaresque novel prose fiction relating outlandish adventures in first-person narrative (from Spanish *pícaro*, "roguish")

pier usually a massive vertical support, square in shape; also can be used for the mass between other vertical elements (e.g., windows)

pike heavy spear with a long shaft

pilaster flattened columnar shape slightly projecting from the wall (usually rectangular)

platitude a trite remark, usually rather dull and sometimes annoying (e.g., "I know how you feel")

Pléiade group of seven French poets, named after the Pléiade poets of ancient Alexandria (who in turn were named after the seven stars known as the Pleiades, the seven daughters of Atlas in mythology)

polyptych altarpiece or other painting consisting of more than three panels

portico roofed colonnade at the entrance to a building

portolan text of navigational instructions for sailing along a coastline

portolan chart a type of map, usually on parchment, that charts the coastline and has rhumb lines radiating from central points; also called a rutter (because it shows the route) in northern Europe; see also COMPASS ROSE, WIND ROSE

predella Italian term for small images (usually) along the bottom of altarpieces, often depicting events from the life of a saint, the Virgin, or Christ

prie-dieu French term ("pray to God," plural *prie-dieux*) for a kneeling desk with support for a prayer book, used in private devotion

putto Latin term for "boy" (plural *putti*), depicted as a nude young boy with wings and usually associated with Eros (Cupid), the god of love

regulars members of the clergy who also took vows of poverty and obedience, often living away from the world in cloistered communities (from Latin *regula*, "rule," namely, the rules of their order)

reliquary an object, often costly and ornate, in which a holy relic is kept

Resurrection rising of Christ from his tomb

rhumb lines straight lines on a Portolan chart radiating out from central points, used as sailing directions; see also COMPASS ROSE, WIND ROSE

rifled gun with spiral grooves cut inside the bore of the barrel

romance See CHIVALRIC ROMANCE

rondeau song with a refrain, from the idea of "ronde" (round) as the refrain came back around at the end of each verse; the dominant form of song in western Europe during the 15th century

rustication masonry chiseled with rough texture

rutter See PORTOLAN CHART

sacra converzatione Italian for "sacred conversation"; a painting in which the Virgin and Christ Child are depicted with a saint or saints

satire work in any genre ridiculing or scorning vices and human weaknesses, often using irony or sarcasm

secco Italian term meaning "dry," for the process of applying pigments dissolved in water to dry plaster; see also FRESCO

serpentine swivel gun

sfumato Italian term, meaning "smoked," used to describe the subtle transition of dark colors not defined by lines

siege tower tower on wheels for storming the walls of a tall structure

siglo de oro "Golden Age" in Spanish, pertaining to literature and art of the High Renaissance in Spain

smoothbore gun with a smooth, unrifled bore

sonnet 14-line poem in iambic pentameter (iambic hexameter in France), often with a turn of thought after the octave or after three quatrains when there is a closing couplet (from the Italian word *sonetto*, little song)

tempera pigment tempered with another medium, usually egg yolk, used in a thinly layered process by which luminosity is achieved by allowing the white ground to show through

terra-cotta Italian for "baked earth," denoting unglazed red ceramics, chiefly bricks and tiles; also used as the name for a color resembling that of the ceramics

terza rima Italian verse form in three-line stanzas rhyming ABA BCB, and so on (e.g., Dante's *Divine Comedy* was written in *terza rima*)

Torah first five books of the Old Testament, the Pentateuch or books of Moses, written on a leather or parchment scroll

trace ground plan of a fortification

tragedy   drama in which the protagonist battles a more powerful force, resulting in a piteous or terrifying conclusion

tragicomedy   dramatic work mingling comedy and tragedy, using both "high" and "low" characters

trebuchet   siege engine that either catapulted missiles of various types, including cows and prisoners, or was used to batter a defensive wall with stones

triptych   altarpiece or other painting consisting of three panels, sometimes hinged

trompe l'oeil   French term meaning "it fools the eye": fictive three-dimensional architecture and objects in two-dimensional painting or intarsia (mosaic work in wood)

trou de loup   French term (wolf hole) for a camouflaged round pit with inwardly sloping sides, dug a little deeper than a person's height, with a sharp stake embedded in the earth at the bottom

vellum   fine skin of a lamb, kid, or calf prepared without tanning for printing or painting; uterine vellum was made from the skin of stillborn or newly born animals; see also PARCHMENT

villancico   Spanish popular verse set to music, beginning in the 15th century; madrigals influenced poly-phonic additions during the 16th century, and content became more spiritual toward the end of the century

virelai   French medieval poetic form set to music, usually rhyming ABBAA, popular during the 15th century

volley fire   simultaneous discharge of a group of missiles (such as arrows)

Wagenburg   German for "wagon fortress" (literally, wagon mountain), a defensive strategy first implemented by the Hussites in the 15th century, consisting of several carts chained together in a circle or half-circle, a few possibly upended, with 15 to 20 soldiers in the center using firearms and crossbows (the same concept as "circling the wagons" in the American West); also a single large cart having several small cannons

wheel lock   mechanism in a muzzle-loading gun in which sparks are struck by a wheel to light the charge

wind rose   the points on portolan charts where rhumb lines converge; see also COMPASS ROSE

woodcut relief   printmaking process of cutting into a wood block with a burin, leaving a design in the uncut areas, with the ink from these designs printed onto paper or vellum by the pressure of rollers

CHRONOLOGICAL CHART

1400	Death of Geoffrey Chaucer
1401	Lorenzo Ghiberti wins the competition to create bronze panels for the baptistry doors in Florence
1407	Founding of first public bank, in Genoa
1414–1418	Council of Constance
1415	Jan Hus is burned at the stake
1415	Battle of Agincourt
1417	End of the Great Schism in the papacy
1420	Treaty of Troyes
1428	Siege of Orléans
1430–1432	Donatello creates his bronze statue of David
1431	Joan of Arc burned at the stake
1431–1449	Council of Basel
c. 1432	*Ghent Altarpiece* completed
1434	Gil Eannes reaches Cape Bojador on the coast of West Africa
1435	Filippo Brunelleschi completes the dome of Florence Cathedral
1435	Leon Battista Alberti writes his treatise on painting
1436	Treaty of Arras
1438	Habsburgs establish control of the Holy Roman Empire
1438	Pisanello casts first portrait medal of the Renaissance
1438–1445	Council of Florence (Council of Ferrara-Florence)
1444	Treaty of Tours
1450	Battle of Formigny
c. 1450	Renovations of Tempio Malatestiano completed
1450s	Successful application of movable type for printing
1453	Turkish army conquers Constantinople
1454	Peace of Lodi
1455–1460	Piero della Francesca paints his fresco *Legend of the True Cross*
1469	Union of Spain through the marriage of Isabella and Ferdinand
1484	Diogo Cão sails into the estuary of the Congo River
1485	Battle of Bosworth
1485	Siege of Ronda
1488	Bartolomeu Dias voyages beyond the Cape of Good Hope
1490	First printed edition in Latin of the works of Galen
1492	Muslims defeated in Granada by Spanish troops
1492	Expulsion of Jews from Spanish territory
1492	Christopher Columbus sails to the Caribbean islands
1494	French troops invade Italy
1494	Savonarola hanged and his body burned at the stake

1494	Treaty of Tordesillas
1497	John Cabot reaches North America
1497–1498	Vasco da Gama sails around the tip of Africa to reach India
1498	Albrecht Dürer issues his prints *Apocalypse*
1500	Pedro Cabral sights the coast of Brazil
1503	Battle of Cerignola
c. 1505	Invention of the pocket watch
1509	Battle of Agnadello (Battle of Giaradadda)
1511	Portuguese troops capture the city of Malacca
1512	Battle of Ravenna
1512–1517	Council of Lateran V
1513	Battle of Novara
1513	Juan Ponce de León explores the Florida coast
1513	Nuñez de Balboa sees the Pacific Ocean
1513	Niccolò Machiavelli writes *The Prince*
1515	Battle of Marignano
1517	Martin Luther posts his Ninety-five Theses on the church door in Wittenberg
1519–1522	Ferdinand Magellan sets out to circumnavigate the globe, dies along the way; Sebastian del Cano completes the voyage
1519–1538	Hernán Cortés explores and conquers Mexico
1521	Siege of Tenochtitlán
1522	Battle of Biocca
1523	Giovanni da Verrazano sails from France, along the eastern North American seaboard, and into present-day New York harbor
1525	Battle of Pavia
1526	Battle of Mohács
1526	Treaty of Madrid
1527	Imperial troops sack Rome
1528	Baldassare Castiglioni writes *The Book of the Courtier*
1529	Peace of Cambrai
1529	Siege of Vienna
1529	Treaty of Saragossa

1532	François Rabelais begins publication of his satirical novel
1534	Henry VIII proclaims his supremacy and confiscates Catholic Church property
1534	Society of Jesus founded by Ignatius of Loyola
1534–1535	Jacques Cartier enters the Gulf of Saint Lawrence
1535	Battle of Tunis
1539–1541	Hernando de Soto explores the present-day southeastern United States
1540	Fernando de Alarcón reaches California
1540–1542	Vázquez de Coronado travels through the present-day southeastern and south-central United States
1541	Jean Calvin establishes the Protestant Reformation in Geneva
1543	Andreas Vesalius publishes his first anatomical treatise
1543	Nicholas Copernicus publishes his heliocentric theory of the universe
1545–1563	Council of Trent (with several long breaks)
1547	Battle of Mühlberg
1550	Giorgio Vasari publishes his *Lives of the Artists*
1553	Battle of Marciano
1555	Peace of Augsburg
1556	Georg Agricola publishes his *On Metallurgy*
1557	Battle of Saint Quentin
1559	Peace of Cateau-Cambrésis
1567	Villa Rotonda begun by Andreas Palladio in Vicenza
1569	Mercator's projection in cartography first published
1571	Battle of Lepanto
1576–1578	Martin Frobisher attempts to find a Northwest Passage
1577–1580	Sir Francis Drake circumnavigates the globe
1580	Spain begins rule of Portugal
1582	Gregorian reform of the calendar
1583	Sir Humphrey Gilbert reaches Newfoundland

1585	Sir Walter Raleigh and associates establish the first English colony in America on Roanoke Island	1588	Failure of Spanish Armada in attack on England
1588	Michel de Montaigne writes his *Essays*	1594–1597	Willem Barents explores the Arctic
		1598	Peace of Vervins
		1616	Death of William Shakespeare

MUSEUMS AND OTHER COLLECTIONS

Austria, Vienna: Kunsthistorisches Museum
Belgium, Antwerp: Musée Plantin-Moretus
Canada, Montréal: Museum of Fine Arts
Canada, Toronto: National Gallery
England, Leeds: Royal Armouries Museum
England, London: British Library
England, London: British Museum
England, London: National Gallery
England, London: National Maritime Museum
England, London: Victoria and Albert Museum
England, London: The Wallace Collection
England, Oxford: Ashmolean Museum of Art
 and Archaeology
England, Oxford: Museum of the History
 of Science
England, Oxford: The Sackler Library
France, Chantilly: Musée Condé
France, Lyon: Musée des Tissus et des Arts
 Décoratifs
France, Paris: Bibliothèque Nationale
France, Paris: Musée du Louvre
Germany, Berlin: Gemäldegalerie, Staatliche
 Museen
Germany, Dresden: Rüstkammer, Staatliche
 Kunstsammlungen
Germany, Hamburg: Kunsthalle
Germany, Mainz: Gutenberg Museum
Germany, Munich: Alte Pinakothek
Germany, Nürnberg: Germanisches
 Nationalmuseum

Italy, Faenza: Museo Internazionale
 delle Ceramiche
Italy, Florence: Galleria degli Uffizi
Italy, Florence: Galleria dell'Accademia
Italy, Florence: Istituto e Museo di Storia
 della Scienza
Italy, Florence: Museo Nazionale del Bargello
Italy, Milan: Biblioteca-Pinacoteca Ambrosiana
Italy, Milan: Pinacoteca di Brera
Italy, Rome: Museo Nazionale degli Strumenti
 Musicali
Italy, Vatican City: Musei Vaticani
Italy, Venice: Galleria dell'Accademia
Netherlands, Amsterdam: Rijksmuseum
Netherlands, Amsterdam: Scheepvaartmuseum
Netherlands, Leiden: Museum Boerhaave
Netherlands, Rotterdam: Museum
 Boijmans-van Beuningen
Portugal, Lisbon: Biblioteca Nacional
Portugal, Lisbon: Museu da Música
Portugal, Lisbon: Museu Nacional do Azulejo
Russia, Moscow: Glinka State Museum of Musical
 Culture
Russia, St. Petersburg: Hermitage Museum
Scotland, Edinburgh: National Gallery
Spain, Barcelona: Museu Maritim
Spain, Madrid: Biblioteca Nacional
Spain, Madrid: Museo Nacional del Prado
Spain, Madrid: Museo Thyssen-Bornemisza
Switzerland, Geneva: Musée Ariana

United States, Boston: Museum of Fine Arts

United States, Chicago: Art Institute of Chicago

United States, Los Angeles: J. Paul Getty Museum

United States, Los Angeles: Los Angeles County Museum of Art

United States, New York City: Metropolitan Museum of Art

United States, New York City: The Morgan Library

United States, New York City: The Frick Collection

United States, Pasadena: Norton Simon Museum

United States, Philadelphia: Philadelphia Museum of Art

United States, Washington, D.C.: Folger Shakespeare Library

United States, Washington, D.C.: National Gallery of Art

BIBLIOGRAPHY

BASIC REFERENCE WORKS

The Cambridge Modern History. Vol. 1, *The Renaissance.* New York: Macmillan, 1902.

Campbell, Gordon, ed. *The Oxford Dictionary of the Renaissance.* Oxford: Oxford University Press, 2003.

Durant, Will. *The Renaissance: A History of Civilization in Italy from 1304–1576 A.D. The Story of Civilization: Part V.* New York: Simon & Schuster, 1953.

Fletcher, Stella. *The Longman Companion to Renaissance Europe, 1390–1530.* New York: Longman, 1999.

Grendler, Paul, ed. *Encyclopedia of the Renaissance.* 6 vols. New York: Scribner in association with the Renaissance Society of America, 1999.

Hale, John Rigby, ed. *A Concise Encyclopedia of the Italian Renaissance.* New York and Toronto: Oxford University Press, 1981.

Hillerbrand, Hans J., ed. *The Oxford Encyclopedia of the Reformation.* 4 vols. New York and Oxford: Oxford University Press, 1996.

Ross, James Bruce, and Mary Martin McLaughlin, eds. *The Portable Renaissance Reader.* New York: Viking Press, 1968.

Rundle, David. *The Hutchinson Encyclopedia of the Renaissance.* Boulder, Colo.: Westview Press, 1999.

Whitlock, Keith. *The Renaissance in Europe: A Reader.* New Haven, Conn.: Yale University Press, 2000.

REFERENCES FOR THE READINGS

Ackerman, James. *The Architecture of Michelangelo.* Harmondsworth: Penguin Books, 1971.

Adams, Kenneth, Ciaran Cosgrove, and James Whiston, eds. *Spanish Theatre: Studies in Honour of Victor F. Dixon.* Woodbridge, Suffolk, U.K.: Tamesis, 2001.

Adelman, Howard. "The Literacy of Jewish Women in Early Modern Italy." In Barbara J. Whitehead, ed. *Women's Education in Early Modern Europe: A History, 1500–1800.* New York: Garland, 1999, pp. 133–158.

Agrippa, Henricus Cornelius. *The Nobility and Preeminence of the Female Sex.* Edited and translated by Albert Rabil, Jr. Chicago: University of Chicago Press, 1996.

Alberti, Leon Baptista. *On Painting.* Translated by John R. Spencer. New Haven, Conn., and London: Yale University Press, 1966.

———. *On the Art of Building in Ten Books.* Translated by Joseph Rykwert, Neil Leach and Robert Tavernor. Cambridge, Mass.: MIT Press, 1997.

Albuquerque, Luís. "Portuguese Navigation: Its Historical Development." In Jay Levenson, ed. *Circa 1492: Art in the Age of Exploration.* Washington, D.C.: National Gallery of Art, 1991, pp. 35–39.

Alden, Dauril. *The Making of an Enterprise: The Society of Jesus in Portugal, Its Empire, and Beyond, 1540–1750.* Stanford, Calif.: Stanford University Press, 1996.

Allen, E. John B. *Post and Courier Service in the Diplomacy of Early Modern Europe.* The Hague: Nijhoff, 1972.

Ambrosoli, Mauro. *The Wild and the Sown: Botany and Agriculture in Western Europe.* Translated by Mary McCann Salvatorelli. Cambridge: Cambridge University Press, 1997.

Amico, Leonard N. *Bernard Palissy: In Search of Earthly Paradise.* Paris and New York: Flammarion, 1996.

Amos, N. Scott, Andrew Pettegree, and Henk van Nierop, eds. *The Education of a Christian Society: Humanism and the Reformation in Britain and the Netherlands.* Aldershot, Hants, U.K.: Ashgate, 1999.

Amussen, Susan D., and Adele Seeff, eds. *Attending to Early Modern Women.* Newark: University of Delaware, 1998.

Appleby, John C., and Paul Dalton, eds. *Government, Religion and Society in Northern England 1000–1700.* Stroud, U.K.: Alan Sutton, 1997.

Appuhn, Karl. "Tools for the Development of the European Economy." In Guido Ruggiero, ed. *A Companion to the Worlds of the Renaissance.* Oxford: Blackwell, 2002, pp. 259–278.

Aretino, Pietro. *The Letters of Pietro Aretino.* Edited and translated by Thomas Caldecott Chubb. N.p.: Archon Books, 1967.

Ariès, Philippe, and Georges Duby. *A History of Private Life.* Vol. 3. Edited by Roger Chartier and translated by Arthur Goldhammer. Cambridge, Mass., and London: Belknap, 1989.

Armour, Rollin S. *Islam, Christianity, and the West: A Troubled History.* Maryknoll, N.Y.: Orbis Books, 2002.

Arnold, Thomas F. "Violence and Warfare in the Renaissance World." In Guido Ruggiero, ed. *A Companion to the Worlds of the Renaissance.* Oxford: Blackwell, 2002.

Aylmer, Gerald, and John Tiller, eds. *Hereford Cathedral: A History.* London: Hambledon Press, 2000.

Babelon, Jean. "Mannerism in Northern Europe and the School of Fontainebleau." In René Huyghe, ed. *Larousse Encyclopedia of Renaissance and Baroque Art.* Middlesex, U.K.: Hamlyn House, 1968, pp. 203–215.

Bainton, Roland H. *The Reformation of the Sixteenth Century.* Boston: Beacon Press, 1956.

Balázs, György. *The Magyars: The Birth of a European Nation.* Budapest: Corvina, 1989.

Baldwin, Charles Sears. *Renaissance Literary Theory and Practice: Classicism in the Rhetoric and Poetic of Italy, France, and England, 1400–1600.* Gloucester, U.K.: P. Smith, 1959.

Barasch, Moshe. *Light and Color in the Italian Renaissance Theory of Art.* New York: New York University Press, 1978.

Barkan, Leonard. *Unearthing the Past: Archaeology and Aesthetics in the Making of Renaissance Culture.* New Haven, Conn., and London: Yale University Press, 1999.

Barker, Nicolas. "A Contemporary Panegyrist of the Invention of Printing: The Author of the *Grammatica Rhythmica.*" In Martin Davis, ed. *Incunabula: Studies in Fifteenth-Century Printed Books Presented to Lotte Hellinga.* London: British Library, 1999, pp. 187–214.

Barolsky, Paul. "Naturalism and the Visionary Art of the Early Renaissance." In Andrew Ladis, ed. *Franciscanism, the Papacy, and Art in the Age of Giotto.* New York: Garland, 1998, pp. 317–324.

Baron, Hans. *The Crisis of the Early Italian Renaissance: Civic Humanism and Republican Liberty in an Age of Classicism and Tyranny.* 2 vols. Princeton, N.J.: Princeton University Press, 1955.

Barraclough, Geoffrey. *The Origins of Modern Germany.* New York: Norton, 1984.

Baskins, Cristelle Louise. *Cassone Painting, Humanism, and Gender in Early Modern Italy.* Cambridge and New York: Cambridge University Press, 1998.

Baumgartner, Frederic J. *France in the Sixteenth Century.* Basingstoke, U.K.: Macmillan Press, 1995.

Baxandall, Michael. *Painting and Experience in Fifteenth Century Italy.* Oxford: Clarendon Press, 1972.

Bayne, Diane Valeri. "The Instruction of a Christian Woman: Richard Hyrde and the Thomas More Circle," *Moreana* 12 (February 1975): 5–15.

Becker, Marvin. *Civility and Society in Western Europe, 1300–1600.* Bloomington: Indiana University Press, 1988.

Beckingham, Charles Fraser. *Between Islam and Christendom: Travelers, Facts, and Legends in the Middle Ages and the Renaissance.* London: Variorum Reprints, 1983.

Bell, Rudolph M. *How to Do It: Guide to Good Living for Renaissance Italians.* Chicago and London: University of Chicago Press, 1999.

Belloc, Hilaire. *Characters of the Reformation.* Rockford, Illinois: Tan Books, 1992.

Berenson, Bernard. *The Italian Painters of the Renaissance.* London: Phaidon, 1952.

Bergeron, David M. *English Civic Pageantry, 1558–1642.* Tempe: Arizona Center for Medieval and Renaissance Studies, 2003.

Bergsma, Wiebe. "The Intellectual and Cultural Context of the Reformation in the Northern Netherlands." In N. Scott Amos, Andrew Pettegree, and Henk van Nierop, eds. *The Education of a Christian Society: Humanism and the Reformation in Britain and the Netherlands.* Aldershot, U.K.: Ashgate, 1999, pp. 243–261.

Berriman, A. E. *Historical Metrology.* London: Dent, 1953.

Biagioli, Mario. *Galileo, Courtier: The Practice of Science in the Culture of Absolutism.* Chicago and London: University of Chicago Press, 1993.

Binns, J. W., ed. and trans. *Latin Treatises on Poetry from Renaissance England.* Signal Mountain Tenn.: Published for the Library of Renaissance Humanism by Summertown, 1999.

Birnbaum, Marianna D. *Humanists in a Shattered World: Croatian and Hungarian Latinity in the Sixteenth Century.* Columbus, Ohio: Slavica, 1985.

Black, Christopher. *Italian Confraternities in the Sixteenth Century.* Cambridge and New York: Cambridge University Press, 1989.

Blair, Claude. *European Armour, circa 1066 to circa 1700.* London: Batsford, 1958.

Blanks, David R. *Images of the Others: Europe and the Muslim World before 1700.* Cairo: American University in Cairo Press, 1997.

Blunt, Anthony. *Art and Architecture in France 1500–1700.* London: Viking Penguin, 1991.

————. *Artistic Theory in Italy 1450–1600.* London: Oxford University Press, 1973.

Boccaccio, Giovanni. *Famous Women [De mulieribus claribus].* Edited and translated by Virginia Brown. Cambridge, Mass.: Harvard University Press, 2001.

Bohanan, Donna. *Crown and Nobility in Early Modern France.* Houndmills, U.K., and New York: Palgrave, 2001.

Böker, Hans J., and Peter M. Daly, eds. *The Emblem and Architecture.* Turnhout, Belgium: Brepols, 1999.

Bonfil, Roberto. *Rabbis and Jewish Communities in Renaissance Italy.* Oxford: Oxford University Press, 1990.

Bosher, J. F. "Government and Private Interests in New France." In A. J. R. Russell-Wood, ed. *Government and Governance of European Empires, 1415–1800.* Aldershot, U.K.: Ashgate, 2000, pp. 519–532.

Bowen, Barbara C. *Humour and Humanism in the Renaissance.* Aldershot, U.K.: Ashgate, 2004.

Braudel, Fernand. *The Perspective of the World: Civilization and Capitalism, 15th–18th century.* Vol. 3. Translated by Siân Reynolds. Berkeley and Los Angeles: University of California Press, 1992.

————. *The Structure of Everyday Life: Civilization and Capitalism, 15th–18th century.* Vol. 1. Translated by Siân Reynolds. Berkeley and Los Angeles: University of California Press, 1992.

————. *The Wheels of Commerce: Civilization and Capitalism, 15th–18th century.* Vol. 2. Translated by Siân Reynolds. Berkeley and Los Angeles: University of California Press, 1992.

Brockliss, Laurence, and Colin Jones. *The Medical World of Early Modern France.* Oxford and New York: Oxford University Press, 1997.

Brotton, Jerry. *The Renaissance Bazaar: From the Silk Road to Michelangelo.* Oxford and New York: Oxford University Press, 2002.

Brown, Alison, ed. *Language and Images in Renaissance Italy.* Oxford: Clarendon Press, 1995.

Brown, Alison. *The Renaissance.* New York and London: Longman, 1997.

Brown, David. *Virtue and Beauty: Leonardo's Ginevra de' Benci and Renaissance Portraits of Women.* Washington, D.C.: National Gallery of Art, 2001.

Brown, Howard M., and Louise K. Stein. *Music in the Renaissance.* Upper Saddle River, N.J.: Prentice-Hall, 1999.

Brown, Jonathan. "Spain in the Age of Exploration: Crossroads of Artistic Cultures." In Jay Levenson, ed. *Circa 1492: Art in the Age of Exploration.* Washington, D.C.: National Gallery of Art, 1991, pp. 41–49.

Brown, Michelle. *Understanding Illuminated Manuscripts: A Guide to Technical Terms.* Malibu, Calif.: Getty Museum, 1994.

Brown, Patricia Fortini. "*Renovatio or Concilatio?* How Renaissances Happened in Venice," In Alison Brown, ed. *Language and Images in Renaissance Italy.* Oxford: Clarendon Press, 1995, pp. 127–154.

———. *Venice and Antiquity: The Venetian Sense of the Past.* New Haven, Conn., and London: Yale University Press, 1996.

Brucker, Gene. *The Civic World of Early Renaissance Florence.* Princeton, N.J.: Princeton University Press, 1977.

Bryant, Lawrence M. *The King and the City in the Parisian Royal Entry Ceremony: Politics, Ritual, and Art in the Renaissance.* Geneva: Librairie Droz, 1986.

Bryce, Judith. "Performing for Strangers: Women, Dance and Music in Quattrocento Florence," *Renaissance Quarterly* 54, no. 4.1 (2001): 1074–1107.

Buisseret, David, ed. *Monarchs, Ministers, and Maps: The Emergence of Cartography as a Tool of Government in Early Modern Europe.* Chicago and London: The Newberry Library, 1992.

Burckhardt, Jacob. *The Civilization of the Renaissance in Italy.* New York: Harper, 1958.

Burgess, Clive. "Mapping the Soundscape: Church Music in English Towns," *Early Music History* 19 (2000): 1–46.

Burke, Peter. *The European Renaissance.* Oxford: Blackwell, 1998.

———. *Popular Culture in Early Modern Europe.* New York: New York University Press, 1978.

Burne, Alfred Higgins. *The Hundred Years' War.* London: Penguin, 2002.

Burnett, Charles, and Anna Contadini, eds. *Islam and the Italian Renaissance.* London: The Warburg Institute, 1999.

Burns, James Henderson. *The True Law of Kingship: Concepts of Monarchy in Early Modern Scotland.* Oxford: Clarendon Press, 1996.

Campbell, Lorne. *Renaissance Portraiture: European Portrait-Painting in the 14th, 15th and 16th Centuries.* New Haven, Conn., and London: Yale University Press, 1990.

Campbell, Thomas, et al. *Tapestry in the Renaissance: Art and Magnificence.* New York: Metropolitan Museum of Art, 2002.

Cantor, Norman. *In the Wake of the Plague: The Black Death and the World It Made.* New York: Perennial, 2002.

Cardini, Franco. *Europe and Islam.* Translated by Caroline Beamish. Oxford: Blackwell, 2001.

Carlsmith, Christopher. "Struggling toward Success: Jesuit Education in Italy, 1540–1600," *History of Education Quarterly* 42, no. 2 (2002): 215–246.

Carsten, F. L. *Princes and Parliaments in Germany, from the Fifteenth to the Eighteenth Century.* Oxford: Clarendon Press, 1959.

Cavallo, Sandra, and Lyndan Warner, eds. *Widowhood in Medieval and Early Modern Europe.* New York: Longman, 1999.

Cellini, Benvenuto. *The Autobiography of Benvenuto Cellini.* Translated by George Bull. Harmondsworth, U.K.: Penguin Books, 1976.

Cennini, Cennino. *The Craftsman's Handbook.* Translated by Daniel V. Thompson, Jr. New York: Dover, 1954.

Center for Medieval and Renaissance Studies, University of California, Los Angeles. *The Dawn of Modern Banking.* New Haven, Conn.: Yale University Press, 1979.

Cereta, Laura. *Collected Letters of a Renaissance Feminist.* Edited and translated by Diana Robin. Chicago: University of Chicago Press, 1997.

Chapuis, Julian et al. *Tilman Riemenschneider: Master Sculptor of the Late Middle Ages.* Washington, D.C.: National Gallery of Art, 1999.

Chiappelli, Fred, ed. *First Images of America: The Impact of the New World on the Old.* 2 vols. Berkeley and Los Angeles: University of California Press, 1976.

Cipolla, Carlo. *Public Health and the Medical Profession in the Renaissance.* Cambridge and New York: Cambridge University Press, 1976.

Claridge, Amanda. *Rome: An Oxford Archaeological Guide.* Oxford: Oxford University Press, 1998.

Clark, Peter, ed. *The Early Modern Town.* New York: Longman, 1976.

Cohn, Samuel K., Jr. *The Cult of Remembrance and the Black Death: Six Renaissance Cities in Central Italy.* Baltimore and London: The Johns Hopkins University Press, 1992.

Cormack, Lesley B. *Charting an Empire: Geography at the English Universities, 1580–1620.* Chicago: University of Chicago Press, 1997.

Corteguera, Luis R. *For the Common Good: Popular Politics in Barcelona, 1580–1640.* Ithaca, N.Y.: Cornell University Press, 2002.

Courtenay, William J., ed. *Universities and Schooling in Medieval Society.* Leiden: Brill, 2000.

Cowan, Alexander. *Urban Europe, 1500–1700.* London and New York: Arnold, 1998.

Cox, Virginia. *The Renaissance Dialogue: A Literary Dialogue in Its Social and Political Contexts, Castiglione to Galileo.* Cambridge and New York: Cambridge University Press, 1992.

Crowder, C. M. D. *Unity, Heresy, and Reform: 1378–1460.* New York: St. Martin's Press, 1977.

Cunningham, Hugh. *Children and Childhood in Western Society since 1500.* New York: Longman, 1995.

Cunningham, James P. *Dancing in the Inns of Court.* London: Jordan, 1965.

Cuttler, Charles. *Northern Painting from Pucelle to Brueghel.* Fort Worth, Tex.: Holt, Rinehart & Winston, 1991.

D'Amico, Jack. *The Moor in English Renaissance Drama.* Tampa: University of South Florida Press, 1991.

———. *Renaissance Humanism in Papal Rome: Humanists and Churchmen on the Eve of the Reformation.* Baltimore and London: The Johns Hopkins University Press, 1991.

Darby, Graham, ed. *The Origins and Development of the Dutch Revolt.* London and New York: Routledge, 2001.

Darling, Linda T. "The Renaissance and the Middle East." In Guido Ruggiero, ed. *A Companion to the Worlds of the Renaissance.* Oxford: Blackwell, 2002, pp. 55–69.

Davenport, Millia. *The Book of Costume.* New York: Crown Publishers, 1970.

Davids, Karel, and Jan Lucassen, eds. *A Miracle Mirrored: The Dutch Republic in European Perspective.* Cambridge and New York: Cambridge University Press, 1995.

Davis, Martin, ed. *Incunabula: Studies in Fifteenth-Century Printed Books Presented to Lotte Hellinga.* London: British Library, 1999.

Davis, Natalie Zemon. *Society and Culture in Early Modern France.* Stanford, Calif.: Stanford University Press, 1975.

Debus, Allen G. *The Chemical Philosophy: Paracelsian Science and Medicine in the Sixteenth and Seventeenth Centuries.* New York: Science History Publications, 1977.

Decker, Heinrich. *The Renaissance in Italy: Architecture, Sculpture, Frescoes.* New York: Viking Press, 1969.

DeMolen, Richard L., ed. *Religious Orders of the Catholic Reformation.* New York: Fordham University Press, 1994.

De Roover, Raymond. *The Rise and Decline of the Medici Bank.* New York: W. W. Norton, 1966.

Diefendorf, Barbara B. *Beneath the Cross: Catholics and Huguenots in Sixteenth-Century Paris.* New York and Oxford: Oxford University Press, 1991.

Domínguez Ortiz, Antonio et al. *Resplendence of the Spanish Monarchy: Renaissance Tapestries and Armor from the Patrimonio Nacional.* New York: Metropolitan Museum of Art, 1991.

Donaldson, Gordon. *All the Queen's Men: Power and Politics in Mary Stewart's Scotland.* London: Batsford, 1983.

Donawerth, Jane. "Changing Our Originary Stories: Renaissance Women on Education, and Conversation as a Model for our Classrooms." In Susan D. Amussen and Adele Seeff, eds. *Attending to Early Modern Women.* Newark: University of Delaware, 1998, pp. 263–277.

Donnelly, John P., ed. *Confraternities and Catholic Reform in Italy, France, and Spain.* Kirksville, Mo.: Thomas Jefferson University Press, 1999.

Doyle, Daniel R. "The Sinews of Habsburg Governance in the Sixteenth Century: Mary of Hungary and Political Patronage," *Sixteenth Century Journal* 31, no. 2 (2000): 349–360.

Dutra, Francis A. "The Discovery of Brazil and Its Immediate Aftermath." In George D. Winius, ed. *Portugal, the Pathfinder.* Madison, Wis.: Hispanic Seminary of Medieval Studies, 1995, 145–168.

Edington, Carol. *Court and Culture in Renaissance Scotland: Sir David Lindsay of the Mount.* Amherst: University of Massachusetts Press, 1994.

Edwards, John Richard, ed. *A History of Financial Accounting.* London and New York: Routledge, 2000.

Ehrenberg, Richard. *Capital and Finance in the Age of the Renaissance: A Study of the Fuggers and Their Connections.* New York: A. M. Kelley, 1963.

Eisenstein, Elizabeth. *The Printing Revolution in Early Modern Europe.* Cambridge and New York: Cambridge University Press, 1983.

Elliott, John Huxtable. *Imperial Spain, 1469–1716*. London: Penguin, 2002.

———. *The Old World and the New, 1492–1650*. Cambridge: Cambridge University Press, 1970.

———. *Spain and Its World*. New Haven, Conn. and London: Yale University Press, 1989.

Elmer, Peter, ed. *The Renaissance in Europe*. New Haven, Conn., and London: Yale University Press, 2000.

Elsky, Martin. *Authorizing Words: Speech, Writing, and Print in the English Renaissance*. Ithaca, N.Y.: Cornell University Press, 1989.

Etty, Claire. "A Tudor Solution to the 'Problem of the North'? Government and the Marches toward Scotland," *Northern History* 39, no. 2 (2002): 209–226.

Eyck, Frank. *Religion and Politics in German History: From the Beginnings to the French Revolution*. New York: St. Martin's Press, 1998.

Fallows, David. "Polyphonic Song." In Tess Knighton and David Fallows, eds. *Companion to Medieval and Renaissance Music*. Oxford and New York: Oxford University Press, 2003, pp. 123–126.

Febvre, Lucien. *Life in Renaissance France*. Translated by Marian Rothstein. Cambridge, Mass., and London: Harvard University Press, 1977.

Ferguson, Margaret W., Maureen Quilligan, and Nancy J. Vickers, eds. *Rewriting the Renaissance: The Discourses of Sexual Difference in Early Modern Europe*. Chicago and London: University of Chicago Press, 1986.

Ferguson, Wallace. *The Renaissance in Historical Thought: Five Centuries of Interpretation*. Boston: Houghton Mifflin, 1948.

Fernández Collado, Angel. "The Mozarabic Chant Books of Cisneros," *Sacred Music* 128, no. 4 (2001): 14–18.

Field, Judith Veronica. *The Invention of Infinity: Mathematics and Art in the Renaissance*. Oxford and New York: Oxford University Press, 1997.

Finlay, Robert. *Politics in Renaissance Venice*. New Brunswick, N.J.: Rutgers University Press, 1980.

Fleming, Peter, Anthony Gross, and J. R. Lander, eds. *Regionalism and Revision: The Crown and Its Provinces in England*. London: Hambledon, 1998.

Foster, Verna A. *The Name and Nature of Tragicomedy*. Aldershot, U.K.: Ashgate, 2004.

Fowler, Alastair. *Renaissance Realism: Narrative Images in Literature and Art*. Oxford and New York: Oxford University Press, 2003.

Fowler, Elizabeth, and Roland Greene, eds. *The Project of Prose in Early Modern Europe and the New World*. Cambridge and New York: Cambridge University Press, 1997.

Franklin, David. *Painting in Renaissance Florence 1500–1550*. New Haven, Conn., and London: Yale University Press, 2001.

Freedman, Luba. *The Revival of the Olympian Gods in Renaissance Art*. Cambridge: Cambridge University Press, 2003.

Freeman, Margaret B. *Herbs for the Medieval Household for Cooking, Healing, and Divers Uses*. New York: The Metropolitan Museum of Art, 1943.

Frick, Carole Collier. *Dressing Renaissance Florence: Families, Fortunes, and Fine Clothing*. Baltimore and London: The Johns Hopkins University Press, 2002.

Friedrich, Karin. *The Other Prussia: Royal Prussia, Poland, and Liberty, 1569–1772*. Cambridge and New York: Cambridge University Press, 2000.

Frigo, Daniela, ed. *Politics and Diplomacy in Early Modern Italy: The Structure of Diplomatic Practice, 1450–1800*. Translated by Adrian Belton. Cambridge and New York: Cambridge University Press, 2000.

Frojmovic, Eva, ed. *Imagining the Self, Imagining the Other: Visual Representation and Jewish–Christian Dynamics in the Middle Ages and Early Modern Period*. Leiden: Brill, 2002.

Fubini, Riccardo. "Diplomacy and Government in the Italian City-States of the Fifteenth Century (Florence and Venice)." In Daniela Frigo, ed. *Politics and Diplomacy in Early Modern Italy: The Structure of Diplomatic Practice, 1450–1800*. Translated by Adrian Belton. Cambridge and New York: Cambridge University Press, 2000, pp. 25–48.

Fuchs, Barbara. *Mimesis and Empire: The New World, Islam, and European Identities*. Cambridge and New York: Cambridge University Press, 2001.

Fuller, Mary C. "English Turks and Resistant Travelers: Conversion to Islam and Homosocial Courtship." In Ivo Kamps and Jyotsna G. Singh, eds. *Travel Knowledge: European "Discoveries" in* the Early Modern Period. New York: Palgrave, 2001, pp. 66–73.

Fumerton, Patricia, and Simon Hunt, eds. *Renaissance Culture and the Everyday*. Philadelphia: University of Pennsylvania Press, 1999.

Fusell, G. E. *The Classical Tradition in West European Farming*. Newton Abbot: David and Charles, 1972.

Gaimster, David, and Paul Stamper, eds. *The Age of Transition: The Archaeology of English Culture 1400–1600*. Oxford: Oxbow Books, 1997.

Gambi, Lucio. *The Gallery of Maps in the Vatican*. Translated by Paul Tucker. New York: George Braziller, 1997.

Gardiner, Robert, ed. *Cogs, Caravels, and Galleons: The Sailing Ship, 1000–1650*. London and Annapolis, Md.: Conway Maritime Press, 1994.

Garin, Eugenio, ed. *Renaissance Characters*. Translated by Lydia G. Cochrane. Chicago and London: University of Chicago Press, 1991.

Gelderen, Martin van. *The Political Thought of the Dutch Revolt, 1555–1590*. Cambridge and New York: Cambridge University Press, 1992.

Gelderen, Martin van, and Quentin Skinner, eds. *Republicanism: A Shared European Heritage*. Vol. 1, *Republicanism and Constitutionism in Early Modern Europe*. Cambridge: Cambridge University Press, 2002.

Gelis, Jacques. *The History of Childbirth: Fertility, Pregnancy, and Birth in Early Modern Europe*. Cambridge: Polity Press, 1991.

Gentrup, William F., ed. *Reinventing the Middle Ages and the Renaissance*. Turnhout, Belgium: Brepols, 1998.

Giedion, Sigfried. *Space, Time and Architecture*. Cambridge, Mass.: Harvard University Press, 1967, pp. 1–100.

Gilbert, Felix. *Machiavelli and Guicciardini: Politics and History in Sixteenth-Century Florence*. Princeton, N.J.: Princeton University Press, 1965.

Gilbert, Neal Ward. *Renaissance Concepts of Method*. New York: Columbia University Press, 1960.

Gilmore, Myron. *Humanists and Jurists: Six Studies in the Renaissance*. Cambridge, Mass.: Belknap Press of Harvard University Press, 1963.

———. *The World of Italian Humanism*. New York: Harper & Row, 1962.

Gingerich, Owen, ed. *The Nature of Scientific Discovery: A Symposium Commemorating the 500th Anniversary of the Birth of Nicholas Copernicus*. Washington, D.C.: Smithsonian Institution Press, 1975.

Gitlitz, David M. *Secrecy and Deceit: The Religion of the Crypto-Jews*. Philadelphia: Jewish Publication Society, 1996.

Gittings, Clare. *Death, Burial, and the Individual in Early Modern England*. London: Croon Helm, 1984.

Goldschneider, Ludwig. *Unknown Renaissance Portraits: Medals of Famous Men and Women of the XV and XVI Centuries*. London: Phaidon Press, 1952.

Goldthwaite, Richard. "The Medici Bank and the World of Florentine Capitalism," *Past and Present* 14 (1987): 3–31.

Gombrich, Ernst. *New Light on Old Masters: Studies in the Art of the Renaissance*. Vol. 4. Chicago: University of Chicago Press, 1986.

Goodare, Julian. *State and Society in Early Modern Scotland*. Oxford: Oxford University Press, 1999.

Goodman, Anthony. *The Wars of the Roses*. New York: Dorset, 1981.

Goodrick-Clarke, Nicholas. *Paracelsus: Essential Readings*. Wellingborough, Northamptonshire: Crucible, 1990.

Goudriaan, Koen, Jaap van Moolenbroek, and Ad Tervoort, eds. *Education and Learning in the Netherlands, 1400–1600*. Leiden: Brill, 2004.

Gouwens, Kenneth. *Remembering the Renaissance: Humanist Narratives of the Sack of Rome*. Leiden: Brill, 1998.

Grafton, Anthony. *Cardano's Cosmos*. Cambridge and London: Harvard University Press, 2001.

———. "The Vatican and Its Library." In Anthony Grafton, ed. *Rome Reborn: The Vatican Library and Renaissance Culture*. Washington, D.C.: Library of Congress, 1993, pp. 3–46.

Grafton, Anthony, ed. *Rome Reborn: The Vatican Library and Renaissance Culture*. Washington, D.C.: Library of Congress, 1993.

Grafton, Anthony, and Lisa Jardine. *From Humanism to the Humanities: Education and the Liberal Arts in Fifteenth- and Sixteenth-Century Europe*. Cambridge, Mass.: Harvard University Press, 1986.

Greenblatt, Stephen. *Marvelous Possessions: The Wonder of the New World*. Chicago: University of Chicago Press, 1992.

———. *Renaissance Self-Fashioning, from More to Shakespeare.* Chicago: University of Chicago Press, 1980.

Greene, Edward Lee. *Landmarks of Botanical History.* 2 vols. Edited by Frank N. Egerton. Stanford, Calif.: Stanford University Press, 1983.

Gregorian Reform of the Calendar. Rome: Pontifica Academia Scientiarum, 1983.

Grendler, Paul F. *Schooling in Renaissance Italy: Literacy and Learning, 1300–1600.* Baltimore and London: Johns Hopkins University Press, 1991.

———. "The University of Bologna, the City, and the Papacy," *Renaissance Studies* 13, no. 4 (1999): 475–485.

Griffiths, Gordon. *Representative Government in Western Europe in the Sixteenth Century.* Oxford: Clarendon Press, 1968.

Gschwend, Annemarie Jordan. "In the Shadow of Philip II, El Rey Lusitano: Archduke Albert of Austria as Viceroy of Portugal (1583–1593)." In Werner Thomas and Luc Duerloo, eds. *Albert and Isabella, 1598–1621.* Turnhout, Belgium: Brepols, 1998, pp. 39–46.

Gundersheimer, Werner L., ed. *French Humanism 1470–1600.* London: Macmillan, 1969.

Haar, James. "Value Judgments in Music of the Renaissance." In Tess Knighton and David Fallows, eds. *Companion to Medieval and Renaissance Music.* Oxford and New York: Oxford University Press, 2003, pp. 15–22.

Hackenbroch, Yvonne. *Renaissance Jewelry.* London, Sotheby Parke Bernet: 1979.

Haggh, Barbara, ed. *Essays on Music in Honor of Herbert Kellman.* Paris: Minerve, 2001.

Haines, John, and Randall Rosenfeld, eds. *Music and Medieval Manuscripts: Paleography and Performance.* Aldershot, U.K.: Ashgate, 2004.

Hale, John Rigby. *Renaissance Europe: Individual and Society.* Berkeley and Los Angeles: University of California Press, 1971.

———. *Renaissance Exploration.* New York: British Broadcast Corporation, 1968.

———. *War and Society in Renaissance Europe, 1450–1620.* Baltimore: Johns Hopkins University Press, 1986.

Hall, Bert S. *Weapons and Warfare in Renaissance Europe.* Baltimore: Johns Hopkins University Press, 1997.

Hallman, Barbara McClung. *Italian Cardinals, Reform, and the Church as Property, 1492–1563.* Berkeley: University of California Press, 1985.

Hampton, Timothy. *Literature and Nation in the Sixteenth Century: Inventing Renaissance France.* Ithaca, N.Y.: Cornell University Press, 2001.

Hankins, James. "The Popes and Humanism." In Anthony Grafton, ed. *Rome Reborn: The Vatican Library and Renaissance Culture.* Washington, D.C.: Library of Congress, 1993, pp. 47–85.

Hannay, Margaret, ed. *Silent but for the Word: Tudor Women as Patrons, Translators, and Writers of Religious Works.* Kent, Ohio: Kent State University Press, 1985.

Harper, John. "Music and Liturgy, 1300–1600." In Gerald Aylmer and John Tiller, eds. *Hereford Cathedral: A History.* London: Hambledon Press, 2000, pp. 375–397.

Harrington, Joel. *Reordering Marriage and Society in Reformation Germany.* Cambridge and New York: Cambridge University Press, 1995.

Hatcher, John. *English Tin Production and Trade before 1550.* Oxford: Clarendon Press, 1973.

Hawkes, Nigel. *Early Scientific Instruments.* New York: Abbeville Press, 1981.

Hay, Cynthia, ed. *Mathematics from Manuscript to Print, 1300–1600.* Oxford and New York: Oxford University Press, 1988.

Hay, Denys. *The Church in Italy in the Fifteenth Century.* Cambridge and New York: Cambridge University Press, 1977.

Hayum, Andrée. *The Isenheim Altarpiece: God's Medicine and the Painter's Vision.* Princeton, N.J.: Princeton University Press, 1989.

Henisch, Bridget Ann. *Fast and Feast.* University Park: Pennsylvania State University Press, 1976.

Henze, Catherine A. "Women's Use of Music to Motivate Erotic Desire in the Drama of Beaumont and Fletcher," *The Journal of Musicological Research* 20, no. 2 (2001): 97–134.

Herlihy, David. *The Black Death and the Transformation of the West.* Edited and with an introduction by Samuel K. Cohn, Jr. Cambridge, Mass., and London: Harvard University Press, 2001.

Herman, Peter C., ed. *Opening the Borders: Inclusivity in Early Modern Studies: Essays in Honor of James V. Mirollo.* Newark: University of Delaware Press, 1999.

Heydenreich, Ludwig H. *Architecture in Italy 1400–1500*. Revised by Paul Davies. New Haven, Conn.: and London: Yale University Press, 1996.

Hillgarth, J. N. *Spain and the Mediterranean in the Later Middle Ages*. Aldershot, U.K.: Ashgate, 2003.

Hindman, Sandra, ed. *Printing the Written Word: The Social History of Books, circa 1450–1520*. Ithaca, N.Y.: Cornell University Press, 1991.

Hirsch, Rudolf. *Printing, Selling, and Reading 1450–1550*. Wiesbaden, Ger.: Harrassowitz, 1974.

Holt, Elizabeth Gilmore, ed. *A Documentary History of Art*. Vol. 1. Princeton, N.J.: Princeton University Press, 1981.

Holt, Mack P. *The French Wars of Religion, 1562–1629*. Cambridge and New York: Cambridge University Press, 1995.

Holyoake, Sydney John. *An Introduction to French Sixteenth-Century Poetic Texts*. Manchester: Manchester University Press, 1973.

Hood, William. "Creating Memory." In Alison Brown, ed. *Language and Images in Renaissance Italy*. Oxford: Clarendon Press, 1995, pp. 157–169.

Houlbrooke, Ralph A. *The English Family 1450–1700*. London and New York: Longman, 1984.

Housley, Norman. *Crusading Warfare in Medieval and Renaissance Europe*. Aldershot, U.K.: Ashgate, 2001.

Howard, Maurice. "Civic Buildings and Courtier Houses: New Techniques and Materials for Architectural Ornament." In David Gaimster and Paul Stamper, eds. *The Age of Transition: The Archaeology of English Culture 1400–1600*. Oxford: Oxbow Books, 1997, pp. 105–114.

Howell, Martha. *The Marriage Exchange: Property, Social Place, and Gender in Cities of the Low Countries, 1300–1550*. Chicago: University of Chicago Press, 1998.

Hunter, George Leland. *Tapestries, Their Origin, History, and Renaissance*. New York: John Lane, 1912.

Huppert, George. *Public Schools in Renaissance France*. Urbana: University of Illinois Press, 1984.

Huyghe, René, ed. *Larousse Encyclopedia of Renaissance and Baroque Art*. Middlesex, U.K.: Hamlyn House, 1968.

Jackson, Peter. "Christians, Barbarians and Monsters: The European Discovery of the World beyond Islam." In Janet L. Nelson, ed. *The Medieval World*. London and New York: Routledge, 2001.

Jardine, Lisa. *Worldly Goods: A New History of the Renaissance*. New York: Norton, 1998.

Jeanneret, Michel. *A Feast of Words: Banquets and Table Talk in the Renaissance*. Translated by Jeremy Whiteley and Emma Hughes. Chicago: University of Chicago Press, 1991.

Johnson, Charles. *Religion and Politics: The Renaissance Print in Social Context*. Richmond, Virginia: Marsh Art Gallery, 1999.

Jordan, Annemarie. "Exotic Renaissance Accessories: Japanese, Indian and Sinhalese Fans at the Courts of Portugal and Spain," *Apollo* new series, 150, alt. no. 453 (1999): 25–35.

Jordan, Constance. "Feminism and the Humanists: The Case for Sir Thomas Elyot's *Defense of Good Women*." In Margaret W. Ferguson et al., eds. *Rewriting the Renaissance: The Discourses of Sexual Difference in Early Modern Europe*. Chicago and London: University of Chicago Press, 1986, pp. 242–258.

———. *Renaissance Feminism: Literary Texts and Political Models*. Ithaca, N.Y.: Cornell University Press, 1990.

Jourdain, Margaret. *English Decoration and Furniture of the Early Renaissance (1500–1650)*. London: Batsford, 1924.

Kaeuper, Richard W. *War, Justice, and Public Order: England and France in the Later Middle Ages*. Oxford: Clarendon Press, 1988.

Kallendorf, Craig W. *Humanist Educational Treatises*. Cambridge, Mass., and London: Harvard University Press, 2002.

Kamps, Ivo, and Jyotsna G. Singh, eds. *Travel Knowledge: European "Discoveries" in the Early Modern Period*. New York: Palgrave, 2001.

Kavaler, Ethan Matt. "Renaissance Gothic in the Netherlands: The Uses of Ornament," *The Art Bulletin* 82, no. 2 (2000): 226–251.

Kekewich, Lucille, ed. *The Renaissance in Europe: A Cultural Enquiry: The Impact of Humanism*. New Haven, Conn., and London: Yale University Press, 2000.

Kelley, Donald R. *The Beginning of Ideology: Consciousness and Society in the French Reformation*.

Cambridge and New York: Cambridge University Press, 1981.

Kemp, Martin. *The Science of Art: Optical Themes in Western Art from Brunelleschi to Seurat*. New Haven, Conn., and London: Yale University Press, 1990.

Kempers, Brian. *Painting, Power, and Patronage: The Rise of the Professional Artist in the Italian Renaissance*. Translated by Beverley Jackson. London and New York: Penguin Press, 1992.

King, Margaret L. *Venetian Humanism in an Age of Patrician Dominance*. Princeton, N.J.: Princeton University Press, 1986.

———. *Women of the Renaissance*. Chicago and London: University of Chicago Press, 1991.

Kinney, Arthur F. *The Cambridge Companion to English Literature 1500–1600*. Cambridge: Cambridge University Press, 2000.

Klapisch-Zuber, Christiane. *Women, Family, and Ritual in Renaissance Italy*. Translated by Lydia Cochrane. Chicago: University of Chicago Press, 1985.

Kloczowski, Jerry. *A History of Polish Christianity*. Cambridge and New York: Cambridge University Press, 2000.

Knecht, Robert J. "Francis I and Charles V: The Image of the Enemy." In *(Re)constructing the Past = Het verleden als instrument = Le passé recomposé: Proceedings of the Colloquium on History and Legitimisation Organised by the Charles V 2000 Committee: 24–27 February 1999, Brussels, Belgium*. Brussels: Colloquium on History and Legitimisation, 1999, pp. 47–65.

Knight, Franklin W. "Slavery and Lagging Capitalism in the Spanish and Portuguese American Empires, 1492– 1713." In Barbara L. Solow, ed. *Slavery and the Rise of the Atlantic System*. Cambridge: Cambridge University Press and the W. E. B. Dubois Institute for Afro-American Research, 1993, pp. 62–74.

Knighton, Tess, and David Fallows, eds. *Companion to Medieval and Renaissance Music*. Oxford and New York: Oxford University Press, 2003.

Koenigsberger, H. G. *Estates and Revolutions: Essays in Early Modern European History*. Ithaca, N.Y.: Cornell University Press, 1971.

Kristeller, Paul Oskar. *Renaissance Thought: The Classic, Scholastic, and Humanist Strains*. New York: Harper & Brothers, 1961.

Kubovy, Michael. *The Psychology of Perspective and Renaissance Art*. Cambridge and New York: Cambridge University Press, 1986.

Kula, Witold. *Measures and Men*. Translated by Richard Szreter. Princeton, N.J.: Princeton University Press, 1986.

Labalme, Patricia, ed. *Beyond Their Sex: Learned Women of the European Past*. New York: New York University Press, 1980.

Ladis, Andrew, ed. *Franciscanism, the Papacy, and Art in the Age of Giotto*. New York: Garland, 1998.

Landau, David, and Peter Parshall. *The Renaissance Print: 1470–1550*. New Haven, Conn.: Yale University Press, 1994.

Lane, Frederic C., and Reinhold Mueller. *Money and Banking in Medieval and Renaissance Venice: Coins and Moneys of Account*. Baltimore: Johns Hopkins University Press, 1985.

Langmuir, Gavin. *History, Religion, and Antisemitism*. Berkeley: University of California Press, 1990.

Laver, James. *Costume of the Western World: Fashion of the Renaissance in England, France, Spain and Holland*. New York: Harper & Brothers, 1951.

Lay, Maxwell G. *Ways of the World: A History of the World's Roads and of the Vehicles That Used Them*. New Brunswick, N.J.: Rutgers University Press, 1992.

Leach, Lois Elaine Triller. *Renaissance Instruments*. Welland, Canada: Welland County Roman Catholic Separate School Board, 1973.

León, Vicki. *Outrageous Women of the Renaissance*. New York: John Wiley & Sons, 1999.

———. *Uppity Women of the Renaissance*. Berkeley: Conari Press, 1999.

Le Roy Ladurie, Emmanuel. *The Royal French State, 1460–1610*. Translated by Juliet Vale. Oxford: Blackwell, 1994.

Lestringant, Frank. *Mapping the Renaissance World*. Translated by David Fausett. Berkeley and Los Angeles: University of California Press, 1994.

Le Sylvain. *The Orator, handling a Hundred several Discourses, in Forme of Declamations*. London: Adam Islip, 1596.

Levenson, Jay A., ed. *Circa 1492: Art in the Age of Exploration*. Washington, D.C.: National Gallery of Art, 1991.

Lewis, C. S. *English Literature in the Sixteenth Century Excluding Drama*. Oxford and New York: Oxford University Press, 1954.

Lillie, Amanda. "The Humanist Villa Revisited." In Alison Brown, ed. *Language and Images in Renaissance Italy*. Oxford: Clarendon Press, 1995, pp. 193–215.

Lind, Levi Robert. *Studies in Pre-Vesalian Anatomy*. Philadelphia: American Philosophical Society, 1975.

Lindberg, David C. *Theories of Vision from Al-Kindi to Kepler*. Chicago and London: University of Chicago Press, 1976.

Lindemann, Mary. *Medicine and Society in Early Modern Europe*. Cambridge: Cambridge University Press, 1999.

———. "Plague, Disease, and Hunger." In Guido Ruggiero, ed. *A Companion to the Worlds of the Renaissance*. Oxford: Blackwell, 2002, pp. 427–443.

Lockwood, Lewis Henry. *Music in Renaissance Ferrara 1400–1505: The Creation of a Musical Center in the Fifteenth Century*. Oxford: Clarendon Press, 1984.

Loudon, Irvine, ed. *Western Medicine: An Illustrated History*. Oxford: Oxford University Press, 1997.

Lowe, Kate, ed. *Cultural Links between Portugal and Italy in the Renaissance*. Oxford: Oxford University Press, 2000.

Lübbeke, Isolde. *Early German Painting, 1350–1550*. Translated by Margaret Thomas Will. Stuttgart: Klett-Cotta, 1991.

Lubkin, Gregory. *A Renaissance Court: Milan under Galeazzo Maria Sforza*. Berkeley: University of California Press, 1994.

Lyons, Albert et al. *Medicine: An Illustrated History*. New York: H. N. Abrams, 1978.

Mack, Peter, ed. *Renaissance Rhetoric*. New York: St. Martin's Press, 1994.

Macy, Laura W. "Women's History and Early Music." In Tess Knighton and David Fallows, eds. *Companion to Medieval and Renaissance Music*. Oxford and New York: Oxford University Press, 2003, pp. 93–98.

Mallett, M. E. *Mercenaries and Their Masters: Warfare in Renaissance Italy*. Totowa, N.J.: Rowman, 1974.

Manchester, William. *A World Lit Only by Fire: The Medieval Mind and the Renaissance, Portrait of an Age*. Boston: Little, Brown, 1993.

Marino, John A. "Economic Encounters and the First Stages of a World Economy." In Guido Ruggiero, ed. *A Companion to the Worlds of the Renaissance*. Oxford: Blackwell, 2002, pp. 279–295.

Marland, Hilary, ed. *The Art of Midwifery: Early Modern Midwives in Europe*. London and New York: Routledge, 1993.

Martín González, J. J. "Sculpture in Castile." In Jay Levenson, ed. *Circa 1492: Art in the Age of Exploration*. Washington, D.C.: National Gallery of Art, 1991, pp. 51–54.

Martines, Lauro. *Power and Imagination: City-States in Renaissance Italy*. Baltimore: The Johns Hopkins University Press, 1988.

Mason, Roger A. *Kingship and the Commonweal: Political Thought in Renaissance and Reformation Scotland*. East Lothian, U.K.: Tuckwell Press, 1998.

Massing, Jean Michel. "The Quest for the Exotic: Albrecht Dürer in the Netherlands." In Jay Levenson, ed. *Circa 1492: Art in the Age of Exploration*. Washington, D.C.: National Gallery of Art, 1991, pp. 115–119.

Mastnak, Tomáz. *Crusading Peace: Christendom, the Muslim World, and Western Political Order*. Berkeley: University of California Press, 2002.

Mateer, David, ed. *The Renaissance in Europe: A Cultural Enquiry. Courts, Patrons, and Poets*. New Haven, Conn., and London: Yale University Press, 2000.

McDonald, William L. *The Pantheon: Design, Meaning, and Progeny*. Cambridge, Mass.: Harvard University Press, 2002.

McGinness, Frederick J. *Right Thinking and Sacred Oratory in Counter-Reformation Rome*. Princeton, N.J.: Princeton University Press, 1995.

McGrattan, Alexander. "Italian Wind Instruments at the Scottish Royal Court during the 16th Century," *Early Music* 29, no. 4 (2001): 534–551.

McIver, Katherine A. *Art and Music in the Early Modern Period: Essays in Honor of Franca Trinchieri Camiz*. Aldershot, U.K.: Ashgate, 2002.

McKendrick, Malveena. *Theatre in Spain 1490–1700*. Cambridge: Cambridge University Press, 1992.

Meiss, Millard. *French Painting in the Time of Jean de Berry. The Limbourgs and Their Contemporaries*. New York: Braziller, 1974.

———. *The Great Age of Fresco.* New York: George Braziller, 1970.

Meyers, Charles, and Norma Simms, eds. *Troubled Souls: Conversos, Crypto-Jews, and Other Confused Jewish Intellectuals from the Fourteenth through the Eighteenth Century.* Hamilton, New Zealand: Outrigger, 2001.

Michalove, Sharon D. "Equal Opportunity? The Education of Aristocratic Women 1450–1550." In Barbara J. Whitehead, ed. *Women's Education in Early Modern Europe: A History, 1500–1800.* New York: Garland, 1999, pp. 47–74.

Michel, Henri. *Scientific Instruments in Art and History.* Translated by R. E. W. Maddison and Francis R. Maddison. New York: Viking, 1967.

Millar, Gilbert J. *Tudor Mercenaries and Auxiliaries, 1485–1547.* Charlottesville: University Press of Virginia, 1980.

Miller, Gregory. "Luther on the Turks and Islam," *Lutheran Quarterly* 14, no. 1 (2000): 79–97.

Milward, Peter, ed. *The Mutual Encounter of East and West, 1492–1992.* Tokyo: The Renaissance Institute, Sophia University, 1992.

Minchilli, Elizabeth Helman. *Deruta: A Tradition of Italian Ceramics.* San Francisco: Chronicle Books, 1998.

Mintz, Sidney W. *Sweetness and Power: The Place of Sugar in Modern History.* New York and London: Sifton, 1985.

Miskimin, Harry A. *The Economy of Later Renaissance Europe, 1460–1600.* Cambridge and New York: Cambridge University Press, 1977.

Mitchell, Bonner. *The Majesty of the State: Triumphal Progresses of Foreign Sovereigns in Renaissance Italy (1494–1600).* Princeton, N.J.: Princeton University Press, 1981.

Molà, Luca. *The Silk Industry of Renaissance Florence.* Baltimore: Johns Hopkins University Press, 2000.

Montaigne, Michel de. *The Autobiography of Michel de Montaigne.* Translated by Marvin Lowenthal. Jaffrey, N.H.: David R. Godine, 1999.

Montagu, Jeremy. *The World of Medieval and Renaissance Musical Instruments.* Woodstock, New York: Overlook Press, 1976.

Morgan-Russell, Simon. "St. Thomas More's Utopia and the Description of Britain," *Cahiers élisabéthains* 61 (2002): 1–11.

Morison, Samuel Eliot. *The European Discovery of America: The Southern Voyages, A.D. 1492–1616.* New York: Oxford University Press, 1974.

Morton, Alan G. *History of Botanical Science.* London and New York: Academic Press, 1981.

Moulton, Ian Frederick. "The Illicit World of the Renaissance." In Guido Ruggiero, ed. *A Companion to the Worlds of the Renaissance.* Oxford: Blackwell, 2002, pp. 491–505.

Muir, Edward. *Civic Ritual in Renaissance Venice.* Princeton, N.J.: Princeton University Press, 1981.

Mulcahy, Rosemarie. *The Decoration of the Royal Basilica of El Escorial.* Cambridge: Cambridge University Press, 1994.

Mulgan, Catherine. *Renaissance Monarchies, 1469–1558.* Cambridge: Cambridge University Press, 1998.

Mulsow, Martin, and Richard H. Popkin. *Secret Conversions to Judaism in Early Modern Europe.* Leiden: Brill, 2004.

Mundy, Barbara E. *The Mapping of New Spain: Indigenous Cartography and the Maps of the Relaciones Geográficas.* Chicago: University of Chicago Press, 1996.

Munro, John H. A. *Bullion Flows and Monetary Policies in England and the Low Countries, 1350–1500.* Aldershot, U.K., and Brookfield, Vt.: Variorum, 1992.

Munrow, David. *Instruments of the Middle Ages and Renaissance.* London: Oxford University Press Music Department, 1980.

Murray, Peter, and Linda Murray. *Art of the Renaissance.* New York: Thames & Hudson, 1985.

Murrin, Michael. *History and Warfare in Renaissance Epic.* Chicago and London: University of Chicago Press, 1994.

Nauert, Charles G., Jr. *Humanism and the Culture of Renaissance Europe.* Cambridge: Cambridge University Press, 2000.

Navarrete, Ignacio. "Francisco Sà de Miranda, Garcilaso de la Vega, and the Transfer of Italian Poetic Forms to Portugal and Spain," *Viator* 31 (2000): 291–309.

Nelson, Bernadette. "Ritual and Ceremony in the Spanish Royal Chapel," *Early Music History* 19 (2000): 105–200.

Nelson, Janet L., ed. *The Medieval World.* London and New York: Routledge, 2001.

Nichols, Fred J., ed. and trans. *An Anthology of Neo-Latin Poetry*. New Haven, Conn.: Yale University Press, 1979.

Nogarola, Isotta. *Complete Writings: Letterbooks, Dialogue on Adam and Eve, Orations*. Edited and translated by Margaret L. King and Diana Robin. Chicago: University of Chicago Press, 2004.

Noone, Michael. "A Manuscript Case-Study." In Tess Knighton and David Fallows, eds. *Companion to Medieval and Renaissance Music*. Oxford and New York: Oxford University Press, 2003, pp. 239–246.

Oakley, Francis. *The Western Church in the Later Middle Ages*. Ithaca, N.Y.: Cornell University Press, 1979.

Oberman, Heiko Augustinus. *The Impact of the Reformation*. Grand Rapids, Mich.: W. B. Eerdman, 1994.

Oettinger, Rebecca Wagner. *Music as Propaganda in the German Reformation*. Aldershot, U.K.: Ashgate, 2001.

———. *The Roots of Antisemitism in the Age of the Renaissance and Reformation*. Translated by James I. Porter. Philadelphia: Fortress Press, 1984.

O'Malley, John W. *Praise and Blame in Rome: Rhetoric, Doctrine, and Reform in the Sacred Orators of the Papal Court, c. 1450–1521*. Durham, N.C.: Duke University Press, 1979.

Ormrod, Mark. *The Black Death in England*. Stamford, Conn.: Paul Watkins, 1996.

Ozment, Steven. *When Fathers Ruled: Family Life in Reformation Europe*. Cambridge, Mass.: Harvard University Press, 1983.

Paganelli, Sergio. *Musical Instruments from the Renaissance to the 19th Century*. London: Cassell, 1988.

Panofsky, Erwin. *Early Netherlandish Painting: Its Origin and Character*. 2 vols. Cambridge, Mass.: Harvard University Press, 1953.

———. *Renaissance and Renascences in Western Art*. New York: Harper & Row, 1972.

Panzer, Joel S. *The Popes and Slavery*. New York: Alba House, 1996.

Pardoe, Elizabeth Lewis. "Education, Economics, and Othodoxy: Lutheran Schools in Württemberg, 1555–1617," *Archiv für Reformationsgeschichte* 91 (2000): 285–315.

Partner, Peter. *The Lands of St. Peter: The Papal State in the Middle Ages and the Early Renaissance*. Berkeley: University of California Press, 1972.

———. *The Pope's Men: The Papal Service in the Renaissance*. Oxford and New York: Oxford University Press, 1990.

Payne, Alina. *The Architectural Treatise in the Italian Renaissance*. Cambridge and New York: Cambridge University Press, 1999.

Pedersen, Olaf. *Early Physics and Astronomy*. Cambridge and New York: Cambridge University Press, 1993.

Pelikan, Jaroslav, Valerie R. Hotchkiss, and David Price. *The Reformation of the Bible/The Bible of the Reformation*. New Haven, Conn.: Yale University Press, 1996.

Penrose, Boies. *Travel and Discovery in the Renaissance, 1420–1620*. Cambridge, Mass.: Harvard University Press, 1967.

Perrone, Sean. "Clerical Opposition in Habsburg Castile," *European Historical Quarterly* 31, no. 3 (2001): 325–352.

Peters, Edward. *Inquisition*. New York: Free Press, 1988.

Peters, Gretchen. "Urban Minstrels in Late Medieval Southern France: Opportunities, Status and Professional Relationships," *Early Music History* 19 (2000): 201–235.

Pevsner, Nikolaus. *A History of Building Types*. Princeton, N.J.: Princeton University Press, 1976.

Philip, A. *The Calendar, Its History, Structure and Improvements*. Cambridge: Cambridge University Press, 1921.

Phillips, William D., Jr. "The Old World Background of Slavery in the Americas." In Barbara L. Solow, ed. *Slavery and the Rise of the Atlantic System*. Cambridge: Cambridge University Press and the W. E. B. Du Bois Institute for African and African American Research, 1993, pp. 43–61.

Pointer, Richard W. "The Sounds of Worship: Nahua Music Making and Colonial Catholicism in Sixteenth-Century Mexico," *Fides et Historia* 34, no. 2 (2002): 25–44.

Polk, Keith. "Instrumental Music in Brussels in the Early 16th Century," *Revue Belge de Musicologie* 55 (2001): 91–101.

Pollard, A. J. "The Characteristics of the Fifteenth-Century North." In John C. Appleby and Paul Dalton, eds. *Government, Religion and Society in Northern England 1000–1700.* Stroud, U.K.: Alan Sutton, 1997, pp. 131– 143.

Pope-Hennessy, John. *Italian Renaissance Sculpture.* San Francisco: Chronicle Books, 1996.

Preminger, Alex, ed. *Princeton Encyclopedia of Poetry and Poetics.* Princeton, N.J.: Princeton University Press, 1965.

Prodi, Paolo. *The Papal Prince: One Body and Two Souls: The Papal Monarchy in Early Modern Europe.* Translated by Susan Haskins. Cambridge: Cambridge University Press, 1987.

Ptak, Roderich. "Early Sino-Portuguese Contacts to the Foundation of Macao." In George D. Winius, ed. *Portugal, the Pathfinder.* Madison, Wis.: Hispanic Seminary of Medieval Studies, 1995, pp. 269–289.

Pullan, Brian. *Orphans and Foundlings in Early Modern Europe.* Reading: University of Reading, 1989.

Quint, David. *Origin and Originality in Renaissance Literature: Versions of the Source.* New Haven, Conn.: Yale University Press, 1983.

Rabb, Theodore K. *Renaissance Lives: Portraits of an Age.* New York: Basic Books, 2000.

Rabil, Albert, Jr., ed. *Renaissance Humanism: Foundations, Forms, and Legacy.* 3 vols. Philadelphia: University of Pennsylvania Press, 1988.

Racaut, Luc. *Hatred in Print: Catholic Propaganda and Protestant Identity during the French Wars of Religion.* Aldershot, U.K.: Ashgate, 2002.

Rae, Thomas I. *The Administration of the Scottish Frontier, 1513–1603.* Edinburgh: Edinburgh University Press, 1966.

Raggio, Olga. *The Liberal Arts Studiolo from the Ducal Palace at Gubbio.* New York: Metropolitan Museum of Art, 1996.

Raitt, Jill, Bernard McGinn, and John Meyerdorff, eds. *Christian Spirituality: High Middle Ages and Renaissance.* New York: Crossroad, 1987.

Randles, W. G. L. *Geography, Cartography and Nautical Science in the Renaissance.* Aldershot, U.K.: Ashgate, 2000.

Rebhorn, Wayne A., ed. and trans. *Renaissance Debates on Rhetoric.* Ithaca, N.Y., and London: Cornell University Press, 2000 (including 25 texts by Renaissance authors).

(Re)constructing the Past = Het verleden als instrument = Le passé recomposé; Proceedings of the Colloquium on History and Legitimisation Organised by the Charles V 2000 Committee: 24–27 February 1999, Brussels, Belgium. Brussels: Colloquium on History and Legitimisation, 1999.

Reeds, Karen Meier. *Botany in Medieval and Renaissance Universities.* New York: Garland, 1991.

Reinharz, Jehuda, and Daniel Swetschinski, eds. *Mystics, Philosophers, and Politicians: Essays in Jewish Intellectual History in Honor of Alexander Altmann.* Durham, N.C.: Duke University Press, 1982.

The Renaissance in Europe: An Anthology. Edited by Peter Elmer, Nick Webb, and Roberta Wood. New Haven, Conn., and London: Yale University Press, 2000.

Revel, Jean-François. *Culture and Cuisine.* Translated by Helen R. Lane. Garden City, N.Y.: Doubleday, 1982.

Rhodes, Neil, ed. *English Renaissance Prose: History, Language, and Politics.* Tempe, Ariz.: Medieval & Renaissance Texts & Studies, 1997.

Rice, Eugene F., Jr., and Anthony Grafton. *The Foundations of Early Modern Europe 1460–1559.* New York and London: W. W. Norton, 1970.

Richards, E. G. *Mapping Time: The Calendar and Its History.* Oxford and New York: Oxford University Press, 2000.

Richardson, Glenn. *Renaissance Monarchy: The Reigns of Henry VIII, Francis I and Charles V.* London and New York: Arnold and Oxford University Press, 2002.

Riddle, John M. *Contraception and Abortion from the Ancient World to the Renaissance.* Cambridge, Mass., and London: Harvard University Press, 1994.

———. *Eve's Herbs: A History of Contraception and Abortion in the West.* Cambridge, Mass., and London: Harvard University Press, 1998.

Riley, Gillian. *Renaissance Recipes.* San Francisco: Pomegranate Artbooks, 1993.

Robinson, Marsha. *Writing the Reformation: Actes and Monuments and the Jacobean History Play.* Aldershot, U.K.: Ashgate, 2002.

Rodrigues, Dalila. "Italian Influence on Portuguese Painting in the First Half of the Sixteenth Century." In Kate Lowe, ed. *Cultural Links between Portugal and Italy in the Renaissance*. Oxford: Oxford University Press, 2000, pp. 109–123.

Rose, Paul Lawrence. *The Italian Renaissance of Mathematics: Studies on Humanists and Mathematicians from Petrarch to Galileo*. Geneva: Droz, 1975.

Rosen, Edward, ed. and trans. *Three Copernican Treatises*. New York: Octagon Books, 1971.

Ross, James Bruce, and Mary Martin McLaughlin, eds. *The Portable Renaissance Reader*. New York: Viking Press, 1968.

Roth, Cecil. *The Jews in the Renaissance*. Philadelphia: The Jewish Publication Society of America, 1984.

Rouse, A. L. *The Elizabethan Renaissance: The Cultural Achievement*. New York: Charles Scribner's Sons, 1972.

———. *The Elizabethan Renaissance: The Life of the Society*. New York: Charles Scribner's Sons, 1971.

Rowland, Ingrid. *The Culture of the High Renaissance: Ancients and Moderns in Sixteenth-Century Rome*. Cambridge: Cambridge University Press, 2000.

Rubenstein, Nicolai. *The Government of Florence under the Medici (1434–1494)*. Oxford and New York: Oxford University Press, 1997.

Ruderman, David B. *Essential Papers on Jewish Culture in Renaissance and Baroque Italy*. New York: New York University Press, 1992.

———. *The World of a Renaissance Jew*. Cincinnati: Hebrew Union College Press, 1981.

Ruggiero, Guido, ed. *A Companion to the Worlds of the Renaissance*. Oxford: Blackwell, 2002.

Ruiter, David. *Shakespeare's Festive History: Feasting, Festivity, Fasting and Lent in the Second Henriad*. Aldershot, U.K.: Ashgate, 2003.

Rummel, Erika. *The Humanist–Scholastic Debate in the Renaissance and Reformation*. Cambridge, Mass., and London: Harvard University Press, 1998.

Russell-Wood, A. J. R., ed. *Government and Governance of European Empires, 1415–1800*. Aldershot, U.K.: Ashgate, 2000.

Sagerman, Robert. "A Kabbalistic Reading of the Sistine Chapel Ceiling," *Acta ad Archaeologiam et Artium historiam Pertentia* 16 (2002): 91–177.

Sarton, George. *Six Wings: Men of Science in the Renaissance*. London: The Bodley Head, 1958.

Saslow, James M. *The Medici Wedding of 1589: Florentine Festival as "Theatrum Mundi."* New Haven, Conn.: Yale University Press, 1996.

Sauer, Carl O. *Sixteenth Century North America: The Land and the People as Seen by the Europeans*. Berkeley and Los Angeles: University of California Press, 1971.

Sawday, Jonathan. *The Body Emblazoned: Dissection and the Human Body in Renaissance Culture*. London: Routledge, 1995.

Schmitt, Charles B. *Aristotle and the Renaissance*. Cambridge, Mass.: Harvard University Press, 1983.

Schwinges, Rainer C. "On Recruitment in German Universities from the Fourteenth to Sixteenth Centuries." In William J. Courtenay, ed. *Universities and Schooling in Medieval Society*. Leiden: Brill, 2000, pp. 32–48.

Scott, A. F. *Every One a Witness: The Tudor Age, Commentaries of an Era*. New York: Thomas Y. Crowell, 1976.

Serlio, Sebastiano. *The Five Books of Architecture: An Unabridged Reprint of the English Edition of 1611*. New York: Dover, 1982.

Seward, Desmond. *The Hundred Years War*. New York: Atheneum, 1978.

Shepherd, Simon, ed. *The Women's Sharp Revenge: Five Women Pamphleteers from the Renaissance*. New York: St. Martin's Press, 1985.

Showalter, Dennis F. "Caste, Skill, and Training: The Evolution of Cohesion in European Armies from the Middle Ages to the Sixteenth Century," *The Journal of Military History* 57 (July 1993): 407–430.

Shumaker, Wayne. *The Occult Sciences in the Renaissance: A Study in Intellectual Patterns*. Berkeley: University of California Press, 1972.

Sider, Sandra. "Manneristic Style in Portuguese and Italian Compass Roses on Manuscript Portolan Charts." In Kate Lowe, ed. *Cultural Links between Portugal and Italy in the Renaissance*. Oxford: Oxford University Press, 2000, pp. 125–138.

Signorotto, Gianvittorio, and Maria Anto Visceglia, eds. *Court and Politics in Papal Rome, 1492–1700*. Cambridge and New York: Cambridge University Press, 2002.

Silver, Isidore. *Ronsard and the Hellenic Renaissance in France. Vol. 2, Ronsard and the Grecian Lyre, Part 1. (Travaux d'Humanisme et Renaissance, no. CLXXXII.)* Geneva: Librairie Droz, 1981.

Siraisi, Nancy. "Life Sciences and Medicine in the Renaissance World." In Anthony Grafton, ed. *Rome Reborn: The Vatican Library and Renaissance Culture.* Washington, D.C.: Library of Congress, 1993, pp. 169–197.

———. *Medieval and Early Renaissance Medicine: An Introduction to Knowledge and Practice.* Chicago and London: University of Chicago Press, 1990.

Smith, Hopkinson. "Plucked Instruments: Silver Tones of a Golden Age." In Tess Knighton and David Fallows, eds. *Companion to Medieval and Renaissance Music.* Oxford and New York: Oxford University Press, 2003, pp. 135–137.

Snyder, James C. *Northern Renaissance Art: Painting, Sculpture, the Graphic Arts from 1350 to 1575.* New York: Abrams, 1985.

Solow, Barbara L., ed. *Slavery and the Rise of the Atlantic System.* Cambridge: Cambridge University Press and the W. E. B. Du Bois Institute for African and African American Research, 1993.

Sparrow, John. *Visible Words: A Study of Inscriptions in and as Books and Works of Art.* Cambridge: Cambridge University Press, 1969.

Stadtwald, Kurt. *Roman Popes and German Patriots: Antipapalism in the Politics of the German Humanist Movement.* Geneva: Droz, 1996.

Staikos, Konstantinos. *The Great Libraries: From Antiquity to the Renaissance (3000 B.C. to A.D. 1600).* New Castle, Del., and London: Oak Knoll Press and the British Library, 2000.

Stefoff, Rebecca. *The Young Oxford Companion to Maps and Mapmaking.* New York and Oxford: Oxford University Press, 1995.

Stephenson, Barbara. *The Power and Patronage of Marguerite de Navarre.* Aldershot, U.K.: Ashgate, 2004.

Stevenson, Jane. "Women and Classical Education in the Early Modern Period." In Yun Les Too and Niall Livingstone, eds. *Pedagogy and Power: Rhetorics of Classical Learning.* Cambridge and New York: Cambridge University Press, 1998, pp. 83–109.

Stock, Jan van der. *Printing Images in Antwerp: The Introduction of Printmaking in a City.* Translated by Beverley Jackson. Rotterdam: Sound & Vision Interactive, 1998.

Strocchia, Sharon T. *Death and Ritual in Renaissance Florence.* Baltimore: Johns Hopkins University Press, 1992.

Strong, Roy. *Art and Power: Renaissance Festivals, 1450–1650.* Berkeley: University of California Press, 1984.

Struik, Dirk Jan, ed. *A Source Book in Mathematics, 1200–1800.* Princeton, N.J.: Princeton University Press, 1986.

Strunk, Oliver, ed. *Source Readings in Music History: The Renaissance.* New York: Norton, 1965.

Sullivan, Robert G. *Justice and the Social Context of Early Middle High German Literature.* New York: Routledge, 2001.

Swerdlow, N. M. "The Recovery of the Exact Sciences of Antiquity." In Anthony Grafton, ed. *Rome Reborn: The Vatican Library and Renaissance Culture.* Washington, D.C.: Library of Congress, 1993, pp. 125–168.

Taunton, Nina. *1590s Drama and Militarism: Portrayals of War in Marlowe, Chapman and Shakespeare's Henry V.* Aldershot, U.K.: Ashgate, 2001.

Taylor, F. L. *The Art of War in Italy, 1484–1529.* Westport, Conn.: Greenwood, 1973.

Taylor, James H. M., and Lesley Smith, ed. *Women and the Book: Assessing the Visual Evidence.* London and Toronto: The British Library and University of Toronto Press, 1997.

Tedeschi, John. *The Prosecution of Heresy: Collected Studies on the Inquisition in Early Modern Italy.* Binghamton, New York: Medieval & Renaissance Texts & Studies, 1991.

Tenenti, Alberto, "The Merchant and the Banker." In Eugenio Garin, ed. *Renaissance Characters.* Translated by Lydia G. Cochrane. Chicago and London: University of Chicago Press, 1991, pp. 154–179.

Thomas, Werner, and Luc Duerloo, eds. *Albert and Isabella, 1598–1621.* Turnhout, Belgium: Brepols, 1998.

Thornton, John Kelly. *Africa and Africans in the Making of the Atlantic World, 1400–1680.* Cambridge and New York: Cambridge University Press, 1992.

———. "Early Portuguese Expansion in West Africa: Its Nature and Consequences." In George

D. Winius, ed. *Portugal, the Pathfinder.* Madison, Wis.: Hispanic Seminary of Medieval Studies, 1995, pp. 121–132.

Tilmans, Karin. "Republican Citizenship and Civic Humanism in the Burgundian-Habsburg Netherlands." In Martin van Gelderen and Quentin Skinner, eds. *Republicanism: A Shared European Heritage.* Vol. 1, *Republicanism and Constitutionism in Early Modern Europe.* Cambridge: Cambridge University Press, 2002, pp. 107–125.

Todorov, Tzvetan. "Voyagers and Natives." In Eugenio Garin, ed. *Renaissance Characters.* Translated by Lydia G. Cochrane. Chicago and London: University of Chicago Press, 1991, pp. 250–273.

Too, Yun Lee, and Niall Livingstone, eds. *Pedagogy and Power: Rhetorics of Classical Learning.* Cambridge and New York: Cambridge University Press, 1998.

Trachtenberg, Marvin, and Isabelle Hyman. *Architecture from Prehistory to Postmodernity.* New York: Harry N. Abrams, 2002, pp. 212–325.

Trapp, J. B., ed. *Manuscripts in the Fifty Years after the Invention of Printing: Some Papers Read at a Colloquium at The Warburg Institute on 12–13 March 1982.* London: The Warburg Institute, 1983.

Turner, Anthony. *Early Scientific Instruments: Europe, 1400–1800.* London: Published for Sotheby's Publications by Philip Wilson Publishers, 1987.

Turner, James Grantham. "Literature." In Guido Ruggiero, ed. *A Companion to the Worlds of the Renaissance.* Oxford: Blackwell, 2002, pp. 366–383.

Turner, Jane, ed. *Encyclopedia of Italian Renaissance and Mannerist Art.* 2 vols. London: Macmillan Reference, 2000.

Tylecote, R. F. *A History of Metallurgy.* London: Institute of Materials, 1992.

Unghváry. A. Sándor. *The Hungarian Protestant Reformation in the Sixteenth Century under the Ottoman Impact.* Lewiston, N.Y.: E. Mellen Press, 1989.

Vale, Malcolm. *War and Chivalry: Warfare and Aristocratic Culture in England, France, and Burgundy at the End of the Middle Ages.* Athens: University of Georgia Press, 1981.

Vasari, Giorgio. *The Lives of the Artists.* Translated with an introduction and notes by Julia Conway Bondanella and Peter Bondanella. Oxford and New York: Oxford University Press, 1998.

Vecellio, Cesare. *Vecellio's Renaissance Costume Book.* New York: Dover, 1977 (facsimile).

Veltman, Kim H. *Studies on Leonardo da Vinci I: Linear Perspective and the Visual Dimensions of Science and Art.* Munich: Deutscher Kunstverlag, 1986.

Verbruggen, J. F. *The Art of Warfare in Western Europe during the Middle Ages.* Antwerp: North Holland, 1977.

Verlinden, Charles. "Economic Fluctuations and Government Policy in the Netherlands in the Late XVIth Century," *The Journal of European Economic History* 10, no. 1 (1981): 201–206.

———. "European Participation in the Portuguese Discovery Era." In George D. Winius, ed. *Portugal, the Pathfinder.* Madison, Wis.: Hispanic Seminary of Medieval Studies, 1995, pp. 71–80.

Victoria and Albert Museum. *Princely Magnificence: Court Jewels of the Renaissance, 1500–1630.* London: Debrett's Peerage in association with the Victoria and Albert Museum, 1980.

Vives, Juan Luis. *The Education of a Christian Woman.* Edited and translated by Charles Fantazzi. Chicago: University of Chicago Press, 2000.

Von Barghahn, Barbara. *Age of Gold, Age of Iron: Renaissance Spain and Symbols of Monarchy.* Lanham, Md.: University Press of America, 1985.

Waite, Gary K. *Reformers on Stage: Popular Drama and Religious Propaganda in the Low Countries of Charles V, 1515–1556.* Toronto: University of Toronto Press, 2000.

Warnke, Martin. *The Court Artist: On the Ancestry of the Modern Artist.* Cambridge: Cambridge University Press, 1993.

Watson, Foster, ed. *Vives and the Renascence Education of Women.* New York: Kelly, 1972.

Wear, Andrew, Roger Kenneth French, and Iain M. Lonie, eds. *The Medical Renaissance of the Sixteenth Century.* Cambridge and New York: Cambridge University Press, 1985.

Weber, Wolfgang. "'What a Good Ruler Should Not Do': Theoretical Limits of Royal Power in European Theories of Absolutism, 1500–1700," *Sixteenth Century Journal* 26, no. 4 (1995): 897–915.

Weiditz, Christopher. *Authentic Everyday Dress of the Renaissance: All 154 Plates from the "Trachtenbuch."* New York: Dover, 1994.

Weinberg, Bernard. *A History of Literary Criticism in the Italian Renaissance.* 2 vols. Chicago: University of Chicago Press, 1961.

Weinstein, Donald. *Savonarola and Florence: Prophecy and Patriotism in the Renaissance.* Princeton, N.J.: Princeton University Press, 1970.

Weinstein, Roni. *Marriage Rituals Italian Style: A Historical Anthropological Perspective on Early Modern Italian Jews.* Leiden: Brill, 2004.

Weiss, Roberto. *The Renaissance Discovery of Classical Antiquity.* Oxford: Basil Blackwell, 1969.

Weisser, Michael. *Crime and Punishment in Early Modern Europe, 1350–1850.* Hassocks, U.K.: Harvester Press, 1979.

Welch, Evelyn. *Art in Renaissance Italy 1350–1500.* Oxford: Oxford University Press, 2000.

Wells-Cole, Anthony. *Art and Decoration in Elizabethan and Jacobean England: The Influence of Continental Prints, 1558–1625.* New Haven, Conn.: Paul Mellon Centre for Studies in British Art by the Yale University Press, 1997.

Westman, Robert S. *The Copernican Achievement.* Berkeley and Los Angeles: University of California Press, 1975.

Whinnom, Keith. *Medieval and Renaissance Spanish Literature: Selected Essays.* Edited by Alan Deyermond, W. F. Hunter, and Joseph T. Snow. Exeter: University of Exeter, 1994.

Whitehead, Barbara J., ed. *Women's Education in Early Modern Europe: A History, 1500–1800.* New York: Garland, 1999.

Wiesner, Merry E. *Gender, Church, and State in Early Modern Germany.* London and New York: Longman, 1998.

———. "Spinsters and Seamstresses: Women in Cloth and Clothing Production." In Margaret W. Ferguson et al., eds. *Rewriting the Renaissance: The Discourses of Sexual Difference in Early Modern Europe.* Chicago and London: University of Chicago Press, 1986, pp. 191–205.

Willett, Laura, trans. *Poetry and Language in 16th-Century France: Du Bellay, Ronsard, Sébillet.* Toronto: Centre for Reformation and Renaissance Studies, 2004.

Winius, George D., ed. *Portugal, the Pathfinder.* Madison, Wis.: Hispanic Seminary of Medieval Studies, 1995.

Winn, Mary Beth. "Antoine Vérard's Presentation Manuscripts and Printed Books." In J. B. Trapp, ed. *Manuscripts in the Fifty Years after the Invention of Printing: Some Papers Read at a Colloquium at The Warburg Institute on 12–13 March 1982.* London: The Warburg Institute, 1983, pp. 66–74.

Wittkower, Rudolf. *Architectural Principles in the Age of Humanism.* New York and London: W. W. Norton, 1971.

Woods-Marsden, Joanna. "'Ritratto al naturale': Questions of Realism and Idealism in Early Renaissance Portraits," *Art Journal* 46, no. 3 (fall 1987): 209–216.

Woodward, David. "Maps and the Rationalization of Geographic Space." In Jay Levenson, ed. *Circa 1492: Art in the Age of Exploration.* Washington, D.C.: National Gallery of Art, 1991, pp. 83–87.

———. *Maps as Prints in the Italian Renaissance: Makers, Distributors and Consumers.* London: British Library, 1996.

Wright, George Thaddeus. *Hearing the Measures: Shakespearean and Other Inflections.* Madison: University of Wisconsin Press, 2001.

Wright, Georgia Summers. "The Reinvention of the Portrait Likeness in the Fourteenth Century," *Gesta* 39, no. 2 (2000): 117–134.

Yalom, Marilyn. *Birth of the Chess Queen: A History.* New York: HarperCollins, 2004.

Yates, Frances A. *The Valois Tapestries.* London: Routledge & Kegan Paul, 1975.

Zigrosser, Carl. *Six Centuries of Fine Prints.* New York: Garden City Publishing, 1939.

INDEX

Boldface page numbers indicate major treatment of a subject. *Italic* page locators indicate illustrations. Page numbers with suffix *m* denote a map; suffix *c* denotes a chronology; and suffix *g* denotes a glossary.

INDEX